**The Composition of Everyday Life:
A Guide to Writing, Third Edition**

John Mauk • John Metz

Publisher: Lyn Uhl

Development Editor: Stephanie
Pelkowski Carpenter

Assistant Editors: Lindsey Veautour
and Amy Haines

Editorial Assistant: Kyley Caldwell

Media Editor: Amy Gibbons

Executive Marketing Manager:
Mandee Eckersley

Marketing Manager: Jennifer Zourdos

Senior Marketing Communications
Manager: Stacey Purviance

Production Manager: Samantha Ross

Senior Content Project Manager:
Lauren Wheelock

Senior Art Director: Cate Rickard Barr

Senior Print Buyer: Betsy Donaghey

Rights Acquisition Account
Manager–Text: Mardell Glinski
Schultz

Text Researcher: Paula Sutherland

Production Service: Laura Horowitz,
Hearthside Publishing Services

Interior Design and Composition:
Greg Johnson, Art Directions

Permissions Account Manager,
Images: Don Schlotman

Photo Researcher: PrePress PMG

Cover Designer: Cabbage Design
Company

Cover Image: Bonsai tree silhouette
© stockxpert by Jupiter images

For product information and technology assistance, contact us at
Cengage Learning Academic Resource Center, 1-800-423-0563

For permission to use material from this text or product,
submit all requests online at **www.cengage.com/permissions**
Further permissions questions can be e-mailed to
permissionrequest@cengage.com

Library of Congress Control Number: 2008939833

ISBN-13: 978-1-4282-1157-5

ISBN-10: 1-4282-1157-8

Wadsworth
25 Thomson Place
Boston, MA 02210
USA

Cengage Learning products are represented in Canada by Nelson Education, Ltd.

For your course and learning solutions, visit **www.cengage.com.**

Purchase any of our products at your local college store or at our preferred online
store **www.ichapters.com.**

Printed in Canada
1 2 3 4 5 6 7 12 11 10 09

THIRD EDITION

THE composition OF everyday life

A GUIDE TO WRITING

JOHN MAUK
Northwestern Michigan College

JOHN METZ
Umpqua Community College

WADSWORTH
CENGAGE Learning™

Australia • Brazil • Japan • Korea • Mexico • Singapore • Spain • United Kingdom • Unit

BRIEF CONTENTS

CONTENTS

Chapter 7 Making Arguments   208

Chapter 8 Responding to Arguments   258

Chapter 9 Evaluating   296

Chapter 10 Searching for Causes   332

Chapter 15 Rhetorical Handbook   652

Using CEL as a Thematic Reader

Here we suggest how readings from different chapters might be grouped together thematically. As you explore a particular subject (Education and Learning, for example), you might focus on a particular rhetorical aim (such as evaluating or proposing a solution). Or you might explore a subject area without a particular aim in mind, eventually discovering not only a writing topic but also the rhetorical aim into which it falls.

Education and Learning

Are students customers? What is the practical value of studying great works of literature? Is school too easy? The essays listed below explore the complexity of education and learning. Through reading, writing, and discussion, you might explore and come to think differently about education and its role in people's lives. You might discover an important point about education by exploring a memory, a relationship, an observation, a concept, and so on.

"The Grapes of Mrs. Rath," *Steve Mockensturm* (2)
"Have It Your Way," *Simon Benlow* (5)
"What Is Education?" *Petra Pepellashi* (5)
"Why a Great Books Education Is the Most Practical!" *David Crabtree* (7)
"Floppy Disk Fallacies," *Elizabeth Bohnhorst* (7)
"What Orwell Didn't Know," *George Lakoff* (8)
"Entitlement Education," *Daniel Bruno* (8)
"Reality Check," *Alison Hester* (8)
"Goodbye Cruel Word," *Steven Poole* (9)
"How to Say Nothing in 500 Words," *Paul Roberts* (11)
"Attending to the Word," *Deirdre Mahoney* (11)
"Not Homeschooling? What's Your Excuse?" *Tricia Smith Vaughan* (14)
"A *Beat* Education," *Leonard Kress* (14)
"What the Honey Meant," *Cindy Bosley* (14)
"Why We No Longer Use the 'H' Word," *Dan Wilkins* (14)
"When Bright Girls Decide That Math Is a 'Waste of Time,'" *Susan Jacoby* (14)
"Television: Destroying Childhood," *Rose Bachtel* (14)
"Group Minds," *Doris Lessing* (14)

Justice and Equality

A quick survey of the readings about justice and equality suggests a range of areas: Native American rights, body type, legal drugs, the mentally and physically challenged, wildlife, and so on. These readings can help you identify and explain a relationship, analyze a concept (such as "justice" or "equality"), respond to an argument, identify a cause, propose a solution, and so on. What is justice, and how might exploring the concept of justice in today's world be of value? What revelatory idea about justice and equality might you discover and share with others?

"What Is Education?" *Petra Pepellashi* (5)
"Cruelty, Civility, and Other Weighty Matters," *Ann Marie Paulin* (7)
"What Orwell Didn't Know," *George Lakoff* (8)
"Star Trek," *Jaren Provo* (8)
"Why Doesn't GM Sell Crack?" *Michael Moore* (12)
"An Apology to Future Generations," *Simon Benlow* (12)
"A More Perfect Union," *Barack Obama* (14)
"Not Homeschooling? What's Your Excuse?" *Tricia Smith Vaughan* (14)
"Why We No Longer Use the 'H' Word," *Dan Wilkins* (14)
"Crimes Against Humanity," *Ward Churchill* (14)
"Beware of Drug Sales," *Therese Cherry* (14)
"Is Hunting Ethical?" *Ann F. Causey* (14)

Environment and Animals

These readings, which offer different ways of looking at the environment and animals, encourage you to explore ideas beyond your initial thoughts and beyond conventional beliefs. What is your relationship to the land? To the air? To the animals? How might you think differently about that relationship? And what might be the consequence of your new way of thinking?

"Americans and the Land," *John Steinbeck* (3)
"Living Like Weasels," *Annie Dillard* (4)
"The Front Porch," *Chester McCovey* (4)
"An Apology to Future Generations," *Simon Benlow* (12)
"Planting a Tree," *Edward Abbey* (14)
"Gombe," *Jane Goodall* (14)
"Is Hunting Ethical?" *Ann F. Causey* (14)
"Technology, Movement, and Sound," *Ed Bell* (14)
"Farming and the Global Economy," *Wendell Berry* (14)

Consumerism and Economy

Several readings in this book encourage you to think about yourself as a consumer. What and how do you consume? And what, if anything, do you produce by consuming? As with other subjects in CEL, you might spend an entire semester exploring this area, or you might explore it for just one assignment. It could be of great value to spend an entire semester exploring just one question: What does it mean to be a consumer?

"The Front Porch," *Chester McCovey* (4)
"Have It Your Way," *Simon Benlow* (5)
"What Is Education?" *Petra Pepellashi* (5)
"Rise of the Image Culture: Re-Imagining the American Dream," *Elizabeth Thoman* (6)
"The Mighty Image," *Cameron Johnson* (6)

America

These readings deal with America and being American. They allow you to explore the relationship between yourself and your country. (International students may find this subject to be especially interesting as they bring a unique perspective to the topic.) To what degree do the two—individual and country—influence each other? You can make observations, evaluate, identify causes, propose solutions, and so on. And, you can explore how America communicates with and influences you.

Self

Readings in this book encourage you to explore your own life in a way you have perhaps not done before. These readings about self go beyond mere expressive writing. They encourage you to connect with others, even though—or perhaps *especially when*—you are looking inward at yourself. You can explore how these readings, your own writing, and focused discussion with others helps you to see differently—to learn something about yourself and connect it to the world around you.

Others (Community)

Can we look at ourselves without looking at our community? Both subjects (self and others) explore relationships between the individual and his or her surroundings. What is community? How is community created? These readings will help you to explore what we commonly call *community,* to consider how it works, and to examine your place in it. An entire writing course might be an exploration of one very important question: What is the relationship between community and communication?

Language and Culture

What is the relationship between language and culture? For example, how does the way that a group of people communicates affect their shared values, beliefs, customs, attitudes, and practices—and vice versa? (How, for example, does what a group values about education influence the way that group uses, and thinks about, language?) These readings and others will help you step back and explore the relationship between words, ideas, and actions. Through exploration of this subject, you might discover that your college writing class is something more than you had originally imagined it to be.

Gender and Identity

What does it mean to be male or female? How does gender affect our identities? What influence can we have on issues of gender and identity? This group of readings can be used in combination with other reading groups—from America or pop culture, for example. Instead of exploring just gender and identity, you might narrow your focus to readings that relate to gender and identity *and* pop culture.

Parents and Family

What role do our parents play in our lives? Such a question might be explored endlessly with interesting results for both writer and reader. You might spend an entire semester exploring issues about parents and family. Such a simple subject area can prove to be far more complicated—and interesting—than you first imagined. What might be the value of thinking analytically and finding public resonance regarding the subject of parents and family?

Popular Culture

What is the relationship between the individual and his or her popular culture? In what ways are we products of our own pop culture? From beauty pageants to theme parks, these readings allow you to consider the world that surrounds you from a fresh perspective. You can explore the *why* of your own behavior, considering how you and others are influenced by pressures of which you are both very aware and barely aware.

Technology

We cannot overlook technology. How does it influence the way we live? Through reading, writing, and discussion, you can explore beyond your initial thoughts and perceptions to consider the complex relationship in today's world between the individual and technology—or between one individual and another *because of technology*. What idea about technology might you discover and share with others, helping them to think or act differently?

Note to Instructors

Like most college writing instructors, we see English composition as the most vital component of an academic career. Without a transformative composition experience, many college students will struggle, fumble, or worse. And beyond the college classroom, we see writing instruction as intimately connected to students' everyday lives. We believe that composition courses are not only preparation for more academic work but also a genuine study of one's own rhetorical situations. More specifically, we assume that student writing should do two things:

1. It should emerge from the discursive entanglements of students' everyday lives. Student writing is often stiffened by the popular-but-distant topics of the day: gun control, abortion, cloning, cell phone use, and so on. Of course, for some students, these topics intersect with everyday life, but for the vast majority, they are glorified encyclopedic pre-formulations. They offer no possibility for new connections, no possibility for radical re-thinking, no hope for discovery, and no exigence whatsoever. They are dead. Therefore, we hope to offer a pedagogy that genuinely guides students into the tensions, cracks, and un-seen notches of their own lives. Perhaps, then, they will see that this whole enterprise is worthy of the immense intellectual energy it requires.

2. It should prompt students to think more adeptly, to invent a better way of knowing. We believe the only reason to write an essay is to generate a better way of thinking about a topic. In professional academic work, essays are not written to prove grammatical prowess or syntactic proficiency, but to share an important new insight, to contribute to an ongoing conversation, to reveal an otherwise hidden position or viewpoint. In the composition course, it should be no different. And it's been our experience that classroom engagement increases dramatically when students understand this rhetorical mission.

Over the editions of this book, we've been asked: why such focus on invention? What led us to place invention at the center of the pedagogy? Initially, this focus came from understanding our own students—from witnessing how they struggle, succeed, and fail. We asked ourselves some basic questions: What do we value but fail to teach explicitly? What do other writing instructors value and assess? What are the gaps between proficient high school writing and proficient college writing? What we discovered was a type of hidden curriculum. Instructors want revelation, discovery, depth, rigor, intellectual richness. But such qualities are not taught explicitly and consistently at the high school level. Students entering college often lack the discursive tools for generating the richness and complexity that college composition instructors hope to see. Our conclusion: students need specific guidance in developing that complexity.

As we looked closely and consistently at our students, we noticed that successful writers tend to:

- Start thinking about their topics and their own responses early on
- Turn ideas and positions around—investigating intellectual possibilities
- Re-think based on the values, assumptions, and claims of others
- Address and even envelop opposing ideas

In short, successful writers invent. They do what the classical rhetoricians taught: use language to explore what's possible.

Contrarily, unsuccessful writers skip invention. Their relationship with language is at best tentative . . . at worst, antagonistic. And they often carry some counterproductive notions about thinking and writing: ideas emerge fully formed from an individual's head; good writers do not struggle or re-think; the only way to develop an idea is by adding facts; an essay is good if it's properly arranged and grammatically correct. Such assumptions work against writers—even more than their unfamiliarity with grammatical conventions or other "basics." Before they even begin a course or an assignment, these quiet notions stymie many students' foray into an intensive writerly experience.

With *The Composition of Everyday Life*, we hope to vitalize students' assumptions about writing, and to dramatize a simple but crucial point: language is not merely a conduit for expression but a tool for developing ideas. We hope that students imagine writing as an act of public exploration, a process of inventing and sharing what can be thought, what can be said, what can be known. This book, then, is grounded in and driven by a set of principles that we've deemed *invention pedagogy*. It emerges not only from our understanding of students but also from the pre-Socratic Greek sophists—those folks who invented rhetoric (and the practice of democracy). The broader goal is to get students using language in public writing to develop increasingly sophisticated ideas. More specific goals are tied up in the sections of each chapter:

Point of Contact sections encourage students to slow down and notice the nuances of life around them while considering possibilities for writing topics. The questions pull students away from stiff and distant topics and toward the real entanglements of their own lives.

Analysis sections help students develop meaning and significance while prompting them to explore their topics with questions and dialogic activities.

Public Resonance sections draw attention to the rhetorical situation—to the assumptions, values, and beliefs of others. Writers are prompted to explore what others believe and how the particular writing project can influence common belief.

Thesis sections in each invention chapter help students to hone their ideas to a fine edge. Each section contains prompts, sample thesis statements, common thesis problems, and an Evolution of a Thesis chart, which illustrates the gradual development of an idea.

Rhetorical Tools sections explain the support strategies that are most applicable and appropriate to the writing situation. The sections teach students that all rhetorical tools (such as narration, argumentative appeals, allusions, and so on) can be applied according to the writer's particular needs.

Vitality sections explain and illustrate particular strategies for pruning, weeding, trimming, and vitalizing the writing. With this section, students can see that deliberate and repeatable strategies can make sentences more intense and lively. (We hoped to diffuse the mystery and fog created by "awk" and other such codes.)

Delivery sections contain questions about the consequences of students' writing. Students are prompted to see the relationship between their work and the world around them. The Delivery sections also invite students to go "Beyond the Essay"—to take their ideas from the chapter and re-cast them in some other format: a poster, a cartoon, and so on.

As they work through the sections, students may feel their ideas getting more complex, even unwieldy. That's okay. In fact, if we are doing our jobs well, our students' thinking will likely get messier. But if we walk through the entire intellectual journey (i.e. assignment) with them, students may see their ideas re-gain focus. They may see assignments as intellectual pathways.

As all writers know, good ideas require intellectual grappling, occasional cognitive slippage, and plenty of revision. We think students at this particular point in history, in these particular economic and cultural times, must learn how to grapple and re-think. We cannot assume that such critical and nuanced skills will seep into student consciousness—that some lucky students will "pick up on" the most crucial discursive moves. If writing instructors value rigorous (*inventive, rich, deep, intensive, analytical, critical*) thinking, and if we reward it with a grade, then we owe students the tools for making it happen. We cannot simply provide interesting samples and expect them to extract the epistemology. If we value invention, we must teach students how to explore, how to unpack their initial thoughts, and how to persist beyond the commonplaces.

A quick glance at the economy, labor relationships, world politics, and demographic shifts portends a new kind of literacy: People will need intellectual agility; they will have to think around topics, beyond themselves, beyond their initial assumptions, to simply get along in a fast-changing cultural landscape. Having an opinion and writing it neatly in five coherent paragraphs will be its own kind of illiteracy. Those who can only say what they think will get left behind. Those who can invent new intellectual postures for themselves and others will thrive.

New to This Edition

- New Chapter 1, "Inventing Ideas." In previous editions, the "Note to Students" (preface) gave general information about the invention/writing processes—in a sense, how to use the sections and chapters of the book to develop increasingly sophisticated projects. In the third edition, this information will be a full first chapter—to provide a more substantial springboard into college-level thinking and writing.

- Consistent invention workshops. Because students benefit from focused public discussion about their own thinking, Invention Workshops are now included in each chapter.

- More focus on Invention. In previous editions, the readings (or sample essays) in the chapters took up as much space as invention sections; chapters were half readings, half invention. CEL 3/e features three sample essays and moves more quickly to the invention process.

- Three Sample Essays Per Chapter: Each chapter now features a carefully selected triad: a professional writer, a student writer, and a commissioned writer. While students are comforted at seeing another student's approach to the chapter, the student essays illustrate only one approach. So we asked writers, many of them composition instructors themselves, to work through the chapter invention sections and to develop a project of their own that takes into account the audience (students and instructors of college composition) and illustrates "what's possible" in each particular situation. The result is a compelling range of essay projects that illustrate key moves and increase the continuum of possibility.

- Clean design. The new edition retains the visual liveliness of previous editions, but helps students focus more easily on the key ideas and activities in each chapter.

- The updated edition of *The Composition of Everyday Life,* 3/e, will include completely revised MLA guidelines based on the publication of the 2009 MLA Handbook for Writers of Research Papers, 7/e. Accordingly, all MLA-style student papers in this book will also be updated to reflect the new style guide changes.

Instructor Resources

The Composition of Everyday Life: A Guide to Writing, Custom Version

An additional chapter, "Exploring the Arts," is available in a custom version of *The Composition of Everyday Life*. Examining the ways in which art is connected to how and what people think, this chapter includes literary and other artistic selections, along with essays responding to them.

The Composition of Everyday Life: A Guide to Writing, Brief Third Edition

A brief edition of *The Composition of Everyday Life* includes fourteen chapters, omitting the handbook.

The Composition of Everyday Life: A Guide to Writing, Concise Third Edition

The concise version of *The Composition of Everyday Life* includes thirteen chapters, omitting the handbook and anthology.

Instructor's Manual and Survival Guide for Teachers

John Mauk and John Metz have revised the instructor's manual alongside the third edition of *The Composition of Everyday Life*, updating its numerous resources to help you prepare for class. Teaching tips, syllabus planning, and lesson organization are all included.

Companion Website for The Composition of Everyday Life: A Guide to Writing, Third Edition

In addition to a great selection of password-protected instructor resources, the free book companion website contains many interactive resources for students, including model student papers, links to other useful websites, and animated tutorials on researching, revising, grammar usage, and more.

English21 for Composition

The largest compilation of online resources ever organized for composition and literature courses, **English21** is a complete online support system that weaves robust, self-paced instruction with interactive assignments. Easily assignable **English 21** engages students as they become better-prepared and successful writers. **English21** supports students through every step of the writing process, from assignment to final draft. **English21** includes carefully crafted multimedia assignments; a collection of essays that amounts to a full-sized thematic reader; a full interactive handbook including hundreds of animations, exercises, and activities; a complete research guide with animated tutorials and a link to Gale's InfoTrac® database; and a rich multimedia library with hand-selected images, audio clips, video clips, stories, poems and plays. Access to **Personal Tutor**, an easy-access online environment with one-on-one tutoring and on-demand assignment help from experienced tutors, is included with English21. To learn more, visit www.cengage.com/english21.

English21 Plus for Composition

Access to **English21 Plus** is available for a nominal fee when packaged with new copies of the text. **English21 Plus** includes all of the features mentioned above plus access to Wadsworth's **InSite for Writing and Research™. InSite** features an electronic peer review system, an originality checker, a rich assignment library, and electronic grade marking. To learn more, visit www.cengage.com/english21.

Infotrac® College Edition with InfoMarks™

ISBN-10: 0534558534 | ISBN-13: 9780534558536

InfoTrac® College Edition, an online research and learning center, offers over 20 million full-text articles from nearly 6,000 scholarly and popular periodicals. The articles cover a broad spectrum of disciplines and topics—ideal for every type of researcher.

Wadsworth's InSite for Writing and Research™

ISBN-10: 1413009190 | ISBN-13: 9781413009194

TITLE: Wadsworth's InSite for Writing and Research™

This online writing and research tool includes electronic peer review, an originality checker, an assignment library, help with common grammar and writing errors, and access to InfoTrac® College Edition. Portfolio management gives you the ability to grade papers, run originality reports, and offer feedback in an easy-to-use online course management system. Using InSite's peer review feature, students can easily review and respond to their classmates' work. Other features include fully integrated discussion boards, streamlined assignment creation, and more. Visit www.cengage.com/insite to view a demonstration.

Turnitin®

ISBN-10: 1413030181 | ISBN-13: 9781413030181

This proven online plagiarism-prevention software promotes fairness in the classroom by helping students learn to correctly cite sources and allowing instructors to check for originality before reading and grading papers. Visit www.cengage.com/turnitin to view a demonstration.

CengageNOW™ for Writing

ISBN-10: 1413032451 (2-Semester Printed Access Card) | ISBN-13: 9781428231061
ISBN-10: 1413032168 (2-Semester Instant Access Code) | ISBN-13: 9781413032161

This powerful and assignable online teaching and learning system contains diagnostic quizzing and multimedia tutorials that work with students to build personalized study strategies and help them master the basic concepts of writing. It features reliable solutions for delivering your course content and assignments, along with time-saving ways to grade and provide feedback. CengageNOW provides one-click-away results: the most common reporting tasks that instructors perform everyday are always just one click away while working in the CengageNOW gradebook. For students, CengageNOW provides a diagnostic self-assessment and Personalized Study Plan that enables them to focus on what they need to learn and guides them in selecting activities that best match their learning styles. Access to **Personal Tutor**, an easy-access online environment with one-on-one tutoring and on-demand assignment help from experienced tutors, is included with CengageNOW for Writing. Visit www.cengage. com/now to view a demonstration. To package access to CengageNOW for Writing with every new copy of this text, contact your Wadsworth representative.

Merriam-Webster's Collegiate® Dictionary, 11/e (Casebound)

ISBN-10: 0877798095 | ISBN-13: 9780877798095
Available only when packaged with a Wadsworth text, the new 11/e of American's best-selling hardcover dictionary merges print, CD-ROM, and Internet-based formats to deliver unprecedented accessibility and flexibility at one affordable price.

The Merriam-Webster Dictionary (Paperbound)

ISBN: 087779930X | ISBN-13: 9780877799306
Available only when packaged with a Wadsworth text, this high-quality, economical language reference covers the core vocabulary of everyday life with over 70,000 definitions.

Dictionary/Thesaurus (Paperbound)

ISBN: 0877798516 | ISBN-13: 9780877798514
Available only when packaged with a Wadsworth text, this dictionary and thesaurus is two essential language references in one handy volume. Included are nearly 60,000 alphabetical dictionary entries integrated with more than 13,000 thesaurus entries including extensive synonym lists, as well as abundant example phrases that provide clear and concise word guidance.

Acknowledgments

A textbook is a big invention workshop, and we have been fortunate to have extremely savvy collaborators throughout the invention and revision processes. We offer our humble gratitude: to our development editor, Stephanie Pelkowski Carpenter, for her powerhouse clarity, nuanced decision-making, and persistent wisdom; to Lyn Uhl for reinforcing the company's commitment to our work; to Lindsey Veautour for expertly managing a range of things on the inside; to Greg Johnson for again lending his skill and agility to the book's landscape; to Lauren Wheelock for kicking production into gear; to Janet McCartney for, again, checking the soundness and accuracy of every assertion; to Steve Mockensturm at Madhouse for consistently jumping to our aid; to Laura Horowitz for administering the final and chaotic phases; to the marketing crew at Cengage, particularly Jennifer Zourdos and Mandee Eckersley, who deal with our sensitivities and hopes; and as always, to the intensive sales folks throughout the country who give arms and legs to our books.

Thanks also to our students and colleagues who graciously stumble along with us in our efforts to transcend what is and to invent what could be. Thanks to our families and friends for enduring yet another project—who have stopped saying, "I thought you were done."

Any textbook project requires hearty professionals who give up their time and energy to help steer the pedagogy in valuable directions. We relied heavily on the insights of our reviewers and were often humbled at their prowess. We are indebted to the following teachers, theorists, rhetoricians, and scholars:

Susan Achziger, *Community College of Aurora*
Belinda Adams, *Navarro College*
Sonja Andrus, *Collin College*
Larry Beason, *University of South Alabama*
Goretti Benca, *SUNY New Paltz*
Russell Bodi, *Owens State Community College*
Robert Bonds, *New England Institute of Art*
Jim Bosinger, *University of Toledo*
Ron Brooks, *Oklahoma State University*
Jon Brooks, *Okaloosa-Walton College*
Harryette Brown, *Eastfield College*
Thomas Barthel, *Herkimer County Community College*
Patricia Buck, *East Tennessee State University*
Jolene Buehrer, *Bowling Green State University-Firelands*
Walter Cannon, *Central College*
Peter Caster, *University of South Carolina Upstate*
Carole Chapman, *Ivy Tech Community College of Indiana*
Colin Charlton, *University of Texas-Pan American*
Kirk Colvin, *American River College*
Lucinda Coombs, *Central Maine Community College*
Sheilah Craft, *University of Indianapolis*

Bryan Davis, *Georgia Southwestern State University*
Martha Dede, *California State University, Long Beach*
Dominique Dieffenbach, *Florida Community College at Jacksonville*
Mariellen Dietz, *Wartburg College*
Lori Doddy, *Texas Woman's University*
Steve Edgehouse, *Bowling Green State University*
Dianne Fallon, *York County Community College*
Daniel Fitzstephens, *University of Colorado*
Saundra Foderick, *Argosy University Twin Cities and Online*
Erwin Ford, *Albany State University*
Luisa Forrest, *El Centro College*
Anne Marie Fowler, *Keiser University*
Todd Fox, *California State University, Long Beach*
Linda Fricker, *North Dakota State University*
Jackie Garfat, *Dakota High School*
Sharon George, *College of Charleston*
Patricia Golder, *Victor Valley College*
Nate Gordon, *Kishwaukee College*
Rebecca Gorman, *Metropolitan State College of Denver*
Jack Grier, *Wilkes University*
Susan Grimland, *Collin County Community College*
Eduard C. Hanganu, *University of Southern Indiana*
Robin Hanson, *Minnesota State Community and Technical College*
Betty Hart, *The University of Southern Indiana*
Valerie Hockert, *TESC, Axia*
William Hutchings, *University of Alabama at Birmingham*
Tammy Jabin, *Chemeketa Community College*
Lowell Jaeger, *Flathead Valley Community College*
Hershman John, *Phoenix College*
Darlene Johnston, *Ohio Northern University*
Darlene Johnston, *Ohio Northern University*
Peggy Jolly, *University of Alabama at Birmingham*
Peggy Karsten, *Ridgewater College*
Mark Kessler, *Washington State Community College*
Elizabeth Kleinfeld, *Red Rocks Community College*
David Konitzer, *Art Institute of Tampa*
Elizabeth Kuipers, *Georgia Southwestern State University*
Jane Lasarenko, *Slippery Rock University of Pennsylvania*
Jeanette Lugo, *Valdosta State University*
Criostoir MacSuibhne, *SUNY Canton*
Mercedes Martinez, *Global Language Institute*
Sean Mathews, *Adirondack Community College*
Diane Matza, *Utica College*
Sheila McAvey, *Becker College*
Jim McKeown, *McLennan Community College*
Pat McQueeney, *Johnson County Community College*

Neil Michaels, *Saginaw Valley State University*
Mutiara Mohamad, *Fairleigh Dickinson University*
Missy-Marie Montgomery, *Springfield College*
Cleatta Morris, *Louisiana State University in Shreveport*
Mary Ellen Muesing, *UNC Charlotte*
Beverly Neiderman, *Kent State University*
Pam Nichols, *Alma High School*
Julie Nichols, *Okaloosa-Walton College*
Deborah Noonan, *University of South Florida*
James Pangborn, *SUNY at Oswego*
Carolyn Perry, *Westminster College*
Robert Petersen, *Middle Tennessee State University*
Mary Peterson, *Avon Unit Community Schools*
Andrew Preslar, *Lamar State College-Orange*
Arthur Rankin, *Louisiana State University at Alexandria*
Robin Reid, *Texas A&M University-Commerce*
Diane Reuszer, *Northeastern Junior College*
Andrey Reznikov, *Black Hills State University*
Katherine Riegel, *SUNY Potsdam*
Rebekah Rios-Harris, *Cedar Valley College*
Danielle Saad, *Alvernia College*
Linda Sacks, *Monmouth University*
Michael Schanhals, *North Muskegon High School*
Lisette Schillig, *Lock Haven University of Pennsylvania*
Summer Serpas, *Orange Coast College*
Elizabeth Shannon, *West Allegheny*
Beverly Slavens, *Arkadelphia High School*
Jeff Tate, *Northern Oklahoma College*
Luke Tesdal, *University of Texas Arlington*
Donna Townsend, *Baker College of Clinton Township*
Rita Treutel, *University of Alabama at Birmingham*
John Wegner, *Angelo State University*
Vernetta Williams, *Southwest Florida College*
Robert Wilson, *Cedar Crest College*
Carmen Wong, *John Tyler Community College*
Elizabeth Wurz, *Columbus State University*

INVENTING IDEAS

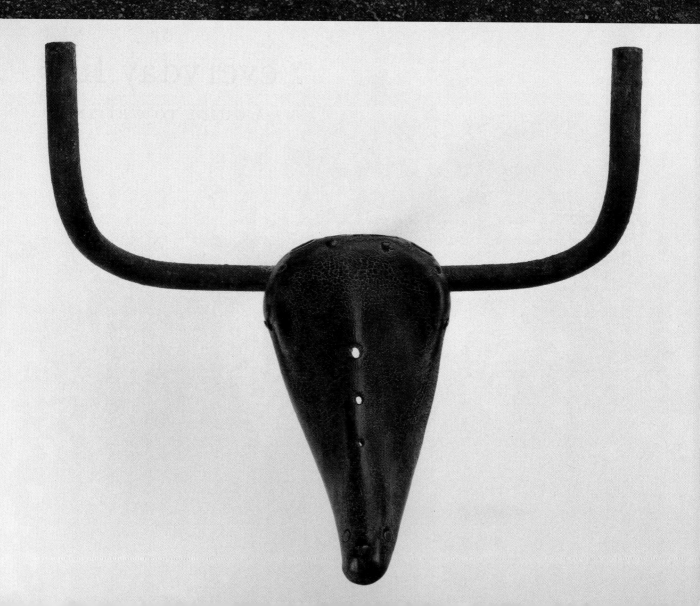

Chapter Contents

CHAPTER 1

Writing is not simply a one-way flow of information from the brain to the hand. Quite the opposite . . .

Thousands of students across the country are required to take introductory college writing courses. These courses are nearly universal requirements, and it seems reasonable to ask: Why? What's the purpose of these courses, and more specifically, what's the purpose of writing? How does writing well relate to engineering, nursing, photography, business management, or aviation? Why do business and governmental leaders throughout the country want all students to take more, not less, writing? If students will not be writing essays in their jobs, why should they write essays in college?

When asked such questions, people tend to respond that writing is important for two reasons: because it helps to *express* thoughts and *communicate* ideas. However, they often forget a third point. Beyond expression and communication, there is another, perhaps far more powerful, reason: Writing is an invention tool. It helps us to generate new ideas and add dimension to the ideas we already have. Writing is not merely the performance or expression of something we know or believe. It's also an *act of inventing, developing, and re-inventing what can be known.*

Writing is not simply a one-way flow of information from the brain to the hand. Quite the opposite—it actually produces new thoughts, changes everyday life, and develops the individual consciousness of the writer, the reader(s), and the people who interact with them both. These are the reasons that writing is nearly a universal requirement. And it is not simply because our culture needs better communicators, but because we will always need better ideas and better ways of thinking about the situations we face every day.

Have you ever asked yourself where ideas come from? Do they pop out of thin air? Do they come from divine beings whispering in our ears? Do they come from lab experiments? From chemical reactions in beakers and test tubes? From someone's heart? Another organ? Most scholars who wrestle with such questions believe that ideas come from language, that people build, refine, pull apart, and rebuild ideas with words. And while we can use words silently in our heads, the act of writing dramatizes and amps up the whole idea-making process. In other words, writing is like an idea calculator. It allows us to put ideas "out there" on a page or a screen and then process them—adding, subtracting, multiplying, and dividing. Writing allows us to put an idea into a formula, add exponents, radicalize. It allows us to keep several abstractions floating around at once, to link thoughts, to collapse them, to evaluate them, and even to cancel them out. Granted, some people can do these operations to some degree just by using language inside their heads. But the act of writing greatly increases almost everyone's ability to process ideas.

At the individual level, inside one's own head, writing is the act of developing a better relationship with ideas. (That's an important relationship!) When we develop a point in writing, we can get distance from it and see it in front of us. Like a painter, a writer cannot simply hold his or her ideas in the mind. They must be drawn out (in language). Then the writer can add color, shading, sky, ground, background—or even redraw from a different perspective.

At a social level, writing can be an invitation, a convergence of many minds. In fact, in academia, writing is seen as a tool for creating social and institutional momentum: for directing people's energies, for guiding policies, for urging on new and better enterprises. Writing changes the way people act, spend, vote, teach, think, and even hope—which means this is all pretty serious and heavy business.

ASKING QUESTIONS

One of the most powerful ways to invent ideas is to ask questions. For instance, let's explore a basic or common concept such as *freedom*. We might ask, What is it? First, we might write out some initial thoughts:

What is freedom?

Freedom is the ability to do whatever one wants. It's the feeling we get when we know that we can do whatever we want.

But can we go further? What else can be known or thought about freedom? Let's apply more questions:

What particular behaviors are associated with freedom?

Politically speaking, voting, protesting, speaking one's mind, worshipping whatever or whomever one desires—or not worshipping at all. Personally, free people do what they want whenever they want. They make their own choices: what they want to buy or drive or eat, how they want to spend their time, where they want to go, what they want to read, whom they want to love or marry.

What responsibilities come with freedom?

Maybe none. If people are free, they do what they want and let others clean up the mess or worry about the consequences. That sounds somehow wrong or bad, but that's what true freedom is. There's no impending rule that says one must do something or think something. Put this way, freedom—true freedom—might be pretty messy. People would get away with murder. Literally.

What hidden role does it play in people's lives?

Most people are always trying to get free—from work, duty, homework, etc. They want to be "done" with the things other people assign to them. They want Saturday afternoon—when no one is saying, "Be here and do this." And politically (again), people throughout the world are dying for it. They stand in front of tanks, blow up government buildings, or pack their families into a wagon and march for hundreds of miles so they can experience freedom. So those are the obvious ways freedom works. But "a hidden role"? Is freedom hidden? Do we hide it from ourselves? Why would we do that? Don't we want it? I think most Americans spend their time in some kind of duty—work, school, both. When they're not working under someone else's guidelines, they look to fill up the freedom-time. They schedule it. I wonder if people know what to do with freedom . . . with time not gobbled up by duty. Skateboard? Listen to music? Read? Watch TV? Is that what freedom is? What about retirement? Isn't that supposed to be total freedom? If so, why do people get lonely? Why do senior citizens want something to do? Why do they volunteer? (They're always the ones at voting booths, libraries, bake sales, etc.) Maybe people want to be given things to do. Maybe they want to be a part of something. Beyond having the right to speak, marry, vote, work, and travel at will, people want to feel commissioned—to be of some good use. And in some way, that's the opposite of freedom. People yearn for freedom, but suffer when they experience it in the extreme.

The three questions, which are part of a core set of questions called *Invention Questions* you'll find throughout this book, help to launch some thinking. They help the writer to uncover layers of a seemingly simple concept. The writer comes to recognize a potentially negative quality to freedom—that unmitigated freedom could be ugly. After the third question, the writer gets past the obvious, taken-for-granted layer and digs up some truly interesting ideas.

> **Obvious Layer:** freedom is about escaping duty.
>
> **Deeper Layer:** escaping all duty comes with a price.

This intellectual process is invention. Asking questions and writing responses makes writers go from an obvious idea (*freedom is doing whatever one wants*) to something less obvious (*freedom is the sometimes spiritually hollow lack of duty*). And in academic writing, readers are hoping for something less obvious. The goal isn't to state what most people, or even some people, already think. Rather, it is to bring hidden layers to the top.

This is no easy task. The process requires a certain degree of endurance—a willingness and ability to continue thinking through intellectual walls and past "answers." In other words, inventive writers do not imagine having answers stored up inside their heads. Instead, they imagine the questions as highways, roads, alleys, and hidden trails. Offering a quick answer to an Invention question is like stopping at the first rest area, and never leaving, when starting out on a cross-country trip.

ACTIVITY

With a small group, take a concept (such as education, individuality, authority, crime, or art) and try to dig up something new—some hidden layer or less obvious quality, something that others in your class may not imagine. Use the following questions:

- What is it?
- What particular behaviors are associated with it?
- What responsibilities come with it?
- What hidden role does it play in people's lives?

$$\text{Invention} = \text{Idea}^3$$

RE-INVENTING EDUCATION

Some may ask, *Why go through all this work? Why not just write a draft of the first idea that comes to our heads? Why twist and turn the ideas and potentially get confused?* These are fair questions. The answers again may lie in the broader goals of higher education and of writing courses. In the twentieth century, public education in the United States emphasized getting things in the right order. It was the age of factory thinking. Education adopted the industrial model of cranking out products (students) who fit a mold, who all knew the same kinds of things about the same topics. In writing classrooms, students wrote essays to demonstrate their mastery of a format. They mimicked the correct order of ideas. They were given formulas for making things look right: *Put your thesis, no matter what it is, at the end of the first paragraph; make sure your paragraphs are five to seven sentences long;* and so on. But such thinking, such assignments, such assumptions about good work are fading into history.

The world is changing at an exponential pace. Much of the information that you learn this year will be outdated, or completely irrelevant, in two to three years. Most of you will change careers, not simply jobs, several times throughout your lives. Many of you will have jobs that do not exist today in industries or services that are not even imagined. You will deal with problems that have no label yet. In this shifting professional life, workers, leaders, employees, and employers who can invent new ways to think, new ways to reach people, new ways to serve and connect people will thrive. Those who cannot will fall behind. More than any other time in human history, new ideas will matter. Because so many people will grasp for the same resources, good thinkers will be in high demand in every profession. And in this environment, the "correct" placement of your thesis is not as important as the development of a good idea.

Imagine that you're an employer. Your company is about to go global. In fact, in an indirect way, you're already global because similar companies from India, China, Canada, and Germany are putting offices in your state. Two essays walk into a job interview. (That's right. The candidates are essays—and they can walk.) You carefully review the candidates:

Essay A

- Gives three reasons why X is bad. (You've heard all three reasons many times before because the topic has been debated publicly for years.)
- The thesis is worded clearly at the end of the first paragraph.
- Includes a few statistics from an online encyclopedia.
- Grammar is okay, and sentences are consistently about the same length.
- Has a title: Three Reasons Why X Is Bad.

Essay B

- Offers a new perspective about an unusual topic.
- Addresses unstated assumptions of potential readers.
- Engages potentially opposing claims (fears and doubts about this new perspective).
- Explains a hidden complexity in the topic, something that people may otherwise ignore.
- Develops a careful line of reasoning.
- Grammar is okay, and sentence length varies to dramatize the thinking involved in each point.

Now, considering your company's situation, which essay would you rather hire? Which one will help contribute something in the shifting and complex global economy? Which one will add vitality?

If it's not clear already, we believe that the students who can invent ideas, who can develop an inventive intellectual posture, will thrive in their academic and professional lives. Those who can recalculate old formulas and feel comfortable writing their way to new ideas will fare far better than those who can only master conventional formats. But we must also admit that invention is difficult work. In fact, the act of writing is an intellectual struggle to shape thoughts and make connections that seem, at first, totally impossible. Good writers do not look for the easy topics; they understand that valuable ideas are not those that simply fall out of their brains and onto the page. And in the most difficult moments, they remember that difficulty is an essential part of the process. Because the human brain is not a *linear* machine (it does not necessarily produce thoughts that go from left to right and then down a page), writers understand that their ideas have to be formed and re-formed. And in that long, and sometimes exhausting, process, they turn frustration to inquiry. They hope to find valuable insights in moments of uncertainty.

And we should also note that invention—all the intellectual practices that work to develop increasingly focused insights—does not belong only to academic and professional life. It is, or can be, a vital practice in everyday life. After all, our domestic and social affairs often (maybe on an hourly basis!) call for good thinking, not just intellectual habit. An inventive thinker learns to ask productive questions and open possibilities, not simply for a composition assignment but for life's inevitabilities:

- How can I calm my mother-in-law's anger about my religious views?
- Why does my roommate think I'm against her?
- How do we get out of this constant battle with the neighbor's teenage kids?
- Which candidate will really change the economy for the better?

What we call *invention* was not created for school work, for essay assignments, or even for business. It was conceived 2,400 years ago by the ancient Greeks as a tool for analyzing and debating everyday issues. Invention was the first part of a bigger practice called *rhetoric*—the study or art of persuasion.

The Greeks had the radical notion that common people, not holy or military leaders, could think for themselves and even make policies best suited for their own affairs. In other words, the Greeks invented the thing we now call democracy! And when they started to solve problems and debate issues publicly, some people realized that successful thinkers and speakers employed certain moves; they weren't just the loudest talkers or the most charming personalities. It didn't take them long to realize that good thinking was about inventing new insights, not simply rephrasing a common opinion in fancy words. Good thinkers could ask hard questions. They could use language to show complexity and possibility. It was soon obvious to the Greeks that everyday life in a democracy requires good thinking—inventive thinking.

Colin Dixon/Arcaid/CORBIS

The Parthenon in Athens, Greece.

CONSIDERING THE ESSAY

Why do all of these introductory college courses assign essays? What's so important about an essay? After all, most people will not spend their post-college lives writing in essay format. So there must be something besides the format that people in higher education find valuable.

If the goals of college writing were only expression and communication, instructors could assign all kinds of texts, from posters to letters, that are much better at announcing opinions than the traditional academic essay. But college writing courses go far beyond the act of announcing an idea. These courses focus on the processes of refining and developing ideas—on inventing new ways to think about familiar issues. And to those ends, the essay still serves well. Perhaps more than any other kind of text, the essay is an open invitation for readers to think differently, even if only for a limited period of time. Every academic essay, no matter what the topic, says to readers, "Come into this space for the time being, and let us work through an idea. In fact, let us think differently about X." The essay is fundamentally different than other texts:

Posters and fliers <u>announce</u> ideas to readers.

Letters <u>share</u> ideas with a specific readership.

Reports <u>communicate</u> previously compiled information.

Memos <u>communicate</u> the status of some situation or bit of news.

Essays <u>work through</u> the complexity of a new or developing idea.

Of course, the distinctions are not quite this clean. Letters can work through complexity, and memos can share ideas and communicate information. And the goals of announcing and communicating are often reached through much thought and invention. But the driving force of an academic essay is somewhat different than that of other texts. Its goal is to help both writers and readers walk carefully through complexity.

But what about electronic texts? Technology has generated a range of new texts and new ways of dealing with ideas. Blogs, chat rooms, MOOs, and wikis, to name a few, have blended traditional types of writing to accommodate various communicative needs and desires of the information age. Blogs, for instance, borrow a great deal from the essay tradition, and, like the essay, they vary tremendously in their degree of formality and complexity. (Some blogs are unfocused political rants, some are daily personal expressions, and some are sophisticated examinations of current issues.)

Also, consider the significant role of the essay in academic life. The essay has become the most common tool in most fields for publicly working through new ideas. When engineers, philosophers, nurses, physicians, and scholars in all disciplines develop something helpful, some new way of practicing their trade, they do not simply announce it to their peers in an ad or memo. (A quick announcement is not likely to change how people think; it will not uproot common disciplinary practices or alter the flow of daily life.) Instead, they explain the new idea in a professional essay and publish it in a scholarly journal (*Journal of the American Medical Association, Social Psychology Quarterly, Rhetoric Review, Critical Care Nursing Quarterly*, and so on). These essays carefully walk readers through a new concept. They show the assumptions, previously held beliefs, conventional wisdom, and the writer's new contribution to the field. The essay is a tool for intellectual climate change.

In college classes, most instructors hope for the same: They hope that students will make some new contribution to conventional wisdom. They hope that essays will do more than announce a common opinion (that guns are dangerous, that abortion kills babies, that marijuana could solve a host of physical ailments if only Congress would awaken from the medicinal dark ages), and instead help readers to see those topics, or any topic, in a slightly different light. They hope your essay will help you and your peers to think differently. And they probably hope that your essay will change their own thinking for the better. (Believe it or not, most college instructors are waiting to be influenced by the essays they assign!)

This may be different than what you've been taught. Unfortunately, standardized tests and proficiency exams suggest that essays are proving grounds, places where students show they can properly perform good textual manners by arranging thoughts in the right order and punctuating correctly. While grammatical and stylistic conventions are important because they help with communication, they are not the sole features of an academic essay. As you will see by samples and readings in this book, an essay must, first and foremost, invite readers to think differently about a topic.

ACTIVITY

Find an academic journal article that corresponds to your major or a major that you've considered. Most college or university libraries have databases with long lists of academic journals. You might find them under *Periodicals* or *Journals*. Read the introduction to one of the essays. How does the essay relate to or speak to common practice or wisdom in the field?

College writing courses are not about *having* ideas but *refining* them.

GETTING BEYOND THE WEASEL:
Reading for Intellectual Agility and Rhetoric

If your situation is like that of nearly every other college student, instructors will ask you to read essays that have little or no obvious connection to your life. You may be interested in football, and your college English instructor may assign an essay about the punk movement in Europe or vineyards in Washington. Why? Why should urban students read about agricultural practice, weasels, or deer? Why should rural students read about the streets of Chicago, the Manhattan subway, the opera? Why should twenty-year-olds read about the role of the World War II generation in government? Is it because the instructors want students to get specific information on those topics? Probably not. In fact, reading assignments in college English courses are often connected to a larger academic goal: to broaden students' perspective.

As readers, most people ask themselves questions. Two questions seem to arise consistently:

Do I like this essay?

Can I relate to this information?

But those questions can limit readers. In fact, if they're the *only* questions available, they put the reader at a big disadvantage by limiting what he or she can learn. Most instructors want students to think about topics from different angles, and to realize the huge range of experience that supports life outside of their own sphere. In other words, instructors hope that students gain some *intellectual agility*—the ability to move from position to position without tremendous difficulty, to imagine a realm of experience and perspective beyond their own biases and reflexes.

If readers have some other questions in mind, some other reasons to continue (besides liking something or relating to it), they might discover something and gain intellectual agility. Imagine, for instance, how the following questions might take a reader somewhere more valuable than the two preceding questions:

How does this essay prompt me to think?

What new idea does it offer?

What new connections does it make?

Why am I resisting the point? Why do I agree with the point?

Where is this essay taking me? How far will it go?

With such questions swirling in their heads, good readers are more apt to push onward through foreign ideas, to examine new assumptions, to carry away something significant.

Good readers do more than read. They read and monitor their own thinking as they move through the text, and they allow themselves to go further than their personal likes or ability to relate. They tolerate (maybe even bask in) intellectual discomfort. They accept ideas and assumptions that might seem foreign, weird, abstract, or unnecessarily edgy.

So the purpose of reading in college goes far beyond the two most common questions readers may ask themselves. In an academic setting, we do not read merely to relate or associate with the information. We read to rethink issues, to discover positions we had not previously imagined, to revise common perceptions. And to fulfill such goals, we must expect to work through ideas, even struggle at times. Most importantly, we must expect to be surprised, to have our comfortable, tidy mental rooms messed up occasionally. Reading in academia means being intellectually adventurous and expecting something new or radically different.

In the world beyond college, employers are not looking for people who are deeply self-interested, those who can only be excited about their own interests, who can only think well about their favorite topics. They want people who can think well beyond their favorite talking points, who can shift perspectives and see an issue from another point of view. And shifting perspectives takes practice. It's not easy. One powerful way to warm up the intellectual muscles—to stretch how our minds work—is to read about people, places, and perspectives that are foreign to our experiences.

Another goal of reading assignments involves the *rhetorical* layer: Behind the obvious content of an essay, there lurks a complex set of *rhetorical tools*—strategies that persuade the reader to accept the writer's ideas. Even though an essay may be about pollution, cats, childhood obesity, or any other topic, it has another dimension, a rhetorical dimension. You might think of this as the machinery of the essay, the stuff that makes it go. And most often, that rhetorical dimension is the reason instructors assign particular essays. It's not the "information" that instructors want students to focus on, but the way information is dealt with (analyzed, revised, dramatized, even radicalized). For example, in Chapter 4, Annie Dillard's essay "Living Like Weasels" focuses on her surprise encounter with a weasel. The essay is widely read in college classes but not because instructors love small rodents, or even because people who teach writing love nature. So it must have some other appeal. It must be up to something other than celebrating the mighty weasel. And that something must be important to college writing—and to higher education. What is that something?

The answer lies in Dillard's rhetorical prowess: her ability to persuade readers to think differently, to

Jeff Venuga/CORBIS

yank readers' attention away from the mundane aspects of everyday life and conventional ways of thinking:

> I would like to learn, or remember, how to live. I come to Hollins Pond not so much to learn how to live as, frankly, to forget about it. That is, I don't think I can learn from a wild animal how to live in particular—shall I suck warm blood, hold my tail high, walk with my footprints precisely over the prints of my hands?—but I might learn something of mindlessness, something of the purity of living in the physical senses and the dignity of living without bias or motive.

It wouldn't matter if the essay were about weasels, house flies, or moths; what's important are her strategies for nudging readers to think—to re-see themselves, their lives, their biases and prejudices. So when you do get to the Dillard essay, don't be fooled. *It ain't about the weasel.*

Activity

When we see only the obvious content (or information) of the essay and miss the rhetorical dimension, we miss the most transferrable and usable part. It is like going for a drive and seeing only the windshield of your car; like seeing a movie and remembering only the names of the actors; like walking through a town and seeing only the street signs. To illustrate your understanding of this point, generate another analogy and share it with the class. *When we see only the obvious content of the essay and miss the rhetorical dimension, it's like _____.*

APPLYING RHETORIC TO YOUR OWN WRITING

The rhetorical dimension of an essay is the layer of strategies that prompt readers to accept its ideas. When we read an essay, we get not only the information but also the set of intellectual moves and rhetorical strategies the writer employs. We can learn from and use these strategies in our own writing. In the following passage, Annie Dillard gives a brief anecdote, or story, and then poses a set of questions:

> And once . . . a man shot an eagle out of the sky. He examined the eagle and found the dry skull of a weasel fixed by the jaws to his throat. The supposition is that the eagle had pounced on the weasel and the weasel swiveled and bit as instinct taught him, tooth to neck, and nearly won. I would like to have seen that eagle from the air a few weeks or months before he was shot: was the whole weasel still attached to his feathered throat, a fur pendant? Or did the eagle eat what he could reach, gutting the living weasel with his talons before his breast, bending his beak, cleaning the beautiful airborne bones?

The anecdote here is powerful and specific. We see riveting detail—a weasel's skull embedded in an eagle's throat. We see an intense re-creation of life and death. And the follow-up questions keep the anecdote alive. In this sense, Dillard does not simply give an anecdote and then move on; instead, she uses the brief story to springboard into new ideas. The follow-up questions suggest a point about the weasel (its persistence even at the moment of death) and reveal her own ability to wonder. If we take away the specific information about the eagle and the weasel, what do we have left? As writers, we might carry away some powerful moves from this brief passage:

- An anecdote works if the details are riveting.
- Grotesque details can be highly persuasive, even "beautiful."

- We can project a possible reality by asking questions.
- We can extend an anecdote by imagining what happened. We can ask questions and prompt the reader to wonder.
- As writers, we're allowed to wonder ourselves.

In another essay from Chapter 4: Observing, Chester McCovey contrasts the past and the present. Like Dillard, he does not simply say that something happened. He imagines how it happened and what it means:

> My grandparents' garages were small, just enough for one car and a few tools—not much of a garage for today's homeowner. In those days the garage kept a car and a small lawnmower, some rakes, and so on. The garage today must keep much more. One can see, then, how the exchange occurred. Like an old-fashioned trade in baseball, gone is the home team's beloved front porch, replaced by a big, new garage. Of course the trade is much more interesting than that. And a look at how it occurred enlightens us a little about the world in which we live. More importantly, it tells us not so much about how life is now but about how it came to be. And, I would argue, it shows us the way in which things will continue to change.

After making the simple contrast between the past and present, McCovey offers an analogy (a comparison to trading in baseball). And then he suggests some hidden complexity—some "interesting" dynamics going on behind the shift from porch to garage. (He later deals with these dynamics in the essay.) For both Dillard and McCovey, meaning lies beyond the facts of the case. The writer must probe behind the physical things that occur.

In his essay, "Americans and the Land," John Steinbeck describes how early Americans ravaged the continent, and he laments that modern Americans carry on those early traditions. In the following passage, he notes how carefully scientists work to avoid polluting outer space:

> Since the river-polluters and the air-poisoners are not criminal or even bad people, we must presume that they are heirs to the early conviction that sky and water are unowned and that they are limitless. In the light of our practices here at home it is very interesting to me to read of the care taken with the carriers of our probes into space, to make utterly sure that they are free of pollution of any kind. We would not think of doing to the moon what we do every day to our own dear country.

Steinbeck reveals the absurdity of common practice—a standard yet critical move for writers. His point is not simply "don't pollute," a common sentiment. Instead, he shows the blindness and hypocrisy of polluting one's own country. He references one behavior (being careful not to pollute the moon, where no one lives) and juxtaposes it to a common behavior (openly poisoning our land, where all humans live). From this passage, we might carry away a single powerful question: What act do we allow or even defend in one situation that we forbid in another?

Good reading leads to good writing. If we keep our radar on and look at the content and the rhetorical dimension of essays, we are more apt to see the moves, questions, and strategies that can be used for any topic.

Activity

Read the following passage from S. I. Hayakawa's essay, "What It Means to Be Creative." Behind the information (about creativity, new ideas, railroads), what is Hayakawa *doing*? What kinds of rhetorical moves does he make? How might a writer use those moves for another topic?

> Another characteristic of the creative person is that he is able to entertain and play with ideas that the average person may regard as silly, mistaken, or downright dangerous. All new ideas sound foolish at first, because they are new. (In the early days of the railroad, it was argued that speeds of twenty-five mph or over were impractical because people's brains would burst.) A person who is afraid of being laughed at or disapproved of for having "foolish" or "unsound" ideas will have the satisfaction of having everyone agree with him, but he will never be creative, because creativity means being willing to take a chance—to go out on a limb.

Good reading leads to good writing.

HOW TO USE *The Composition of Everyday Life*

As is probably clear, this book is about discovering and developing ideas through reading, inventing, and writing. Each of the main chapters (2–12) begins with three sample essays that illustrate key rhetorical moves. The Invention sections follow the sample essays and constitute the majority of each chapter.

Sample Essays

The essays in this book were written for fellow scientists, philosophers, economists, business leaders, politicians, family members, students, and public citizens. They show the real writing that gets done in the public sphere—how professionals in all walks of life talk to their colleagues and to the public. Despite their individual discipline or career field, the writers all seek to communicate a point that involves and impacts the world around them.

Each chapter features a professional writer (someone whose writing was published prior to this textbook), a commissioned writer (a writer or teacher who used the chapter to develop an essay), and a student writer (a first-year college student who used an earlier version of the textbook to create a successful project). Each type of writer (professional, commissioned, student) brings something unique to the chapter and shows a set of qualities that you might adopt in your own projects. And while some of the writing techniques and personal styles differ, some qualities are constant: valuable insights, well-supported ideas, and engaging voices.

To help you reach beyond the obvious content of each essay and get at the rhetorical dimension, each reading is followed by Writing Strategies and Exploring Ideas questions. Also, each chapter features an *annotated* essay (an essay with comments and analysis in the margins). These annotations show a reader stopping at certain places, noticing particular claims and strategies, and speaking back to ideas.

Writing Topics

The Composition of Everyday Life offers several possibilities for inventing and developing writing topics. You can (1) read the essays in a designated chapter and then use the Ideas for Writing after one or more of the essays; (2) use the Point of Contact section, which will help generate topics from everyday life; or (3) read several content-related essays, according to the thematic table of contents in the frontmatter of the book, and then develop topics that emerge from the readings. For all three options, the Invention section of each chapter can be used to develop writing projects.

As you consider your own writing projects, imagine that topics are not pre-packaged issues--as though writers simply choose something they like and start drafting. Instead, imagine topics as ideas that emerge slowly--as complex trains of thought that get built through an invention process. If you imagine topics as something to develop, rather than something to choose, your intellectual experience and your writing will likely be more intense.

Invention

"Invention is the mother of necessities."
–Marshall McLuhan

As we explain at the beginning of this chapter, invention is the process of discovering some new idea and developing that idea through focused exploration. It is often associated with one particular activity: coming up with an idea to write about. However, invention is a complex activity that extends far beyond the initial topic idea. It involves committing to an idea, exploring it in depth, and discovering its worth.

When writers take the time to explore topics, they discover something worth sharing, something that is not already floating around in everyone's minds. In short, invention makes all the difference between powerful, engaging writing that introduces new ideas and dull, lifeless writing that offers nothing but a writer's attempt to fulfill an assignment.

Because invention is the most difficult but most rewarding part of academic writing, this book devotes several sections per chapter to it. The following sections appear in each chapter and are designed to help you through the invention process:

- **Point of Contact** will help you discover a topic from everyday life.
- **Analysis** will launch you beyond initial thoughts and help you explore the topic.
- **Public Resonance** will help you extend the topic outward, to make the topic relevant to a community of readers.
- **Thesis** will help you focus your thinking and develop a revelatory point.
- **Rhetorical Tools** will help you support your point with a variety of common strategies.

The questions in each section are not meant to be answered directly in a final essay. But answering them at various points in your writing process will help you discover ideas and develop the most important layer to your project—the ideas worthy of sharing.

Invention Workshops

Throughout the Invention sections in the chapters, you will see Invention Workshops—prompts to enlist the help of others in the development of your projects. Rather than answer the Invention questions alone, you can gather in a small group and take turns explaining your topic to others. The whole group then can explore your topic with you by focusing on a single question or set of questions.

Invention Workshops can be the most powerful element in a composition course. If all parties are invested in the struggle to focus and vitalize ideas, the process can dramatically improve the thinking and writing for each project. But be warned! If approached uncritically or lackadaisically, workshops can decrease energy and deflate ideas. For example, in the first four workshops transcribed below, the ideas get derailed. One of the participants shuts down the thinking or diffuses it somehow. But in the fifth workshop, the participants take Linda's topic to a compelling place. By following the ideas put forward, they build to a new insight:

Workshop 1
LINDA: What is the significance of a tattoo?
MARCUS: The significance is just whatever people think it is.

Workshop 2
LINDA: What is the significance of a tattoo?
DIANA: Well, it depends on the actual tattoo, doesn't it? A flower has a different significance than a skull.
LINDA: Maybe. But why do people get any tattoos?
DIANA: They just want to. Everybody has their own reasons.

Workshop 3
LINDA: What is the significance of a tattoo?
JACK: What do you mean?
LINDA: What do tattoos mean, what's the meaning behind inscribing ink permanently onto the skin?
JACK: My cousin has this huge tattoo on his back.

Workshop 4

LINDA: What is the significance of a tattoo?

MARCUS: What do you mean, "significance"?

LINDA: You know, what's the fundamental meaning of a tattoo? What's the *meaning* behind inscribing ink permanently onto the skin?

DIANA: I think it's gross, myself. I mean, don't get me wrong, people can do whatever they want with their own bodies, but it's really disgusting to me.

Workshop 5

LINDA: What is the significance of a tattoo?

MARCUS: What do you mean, "significance"?

LINDA: You know, what's the fundamental meaning of a tattoo? What's the *meaning* behind inscribing ink permanently onto the skin?

DIANA: Well, when people get a tattoo, they're doing something permanent to themselves—or at least they assume they are.

MARCUS: They're making a statement of some kind.

DIANA: A statement that has permanence.

JACK: Yeah, that's gotta mean something. People must want to have something about themselves, on themselves, that is not going to go away. It must feel . . . sorta . . . important, ritualistic, big, you know . . .

LINDA: So, people long for permanence. That's interesting. And a tattoo is a little (maybe tiny) way of establishing that . . . on their own bodies.

MARCUS: It's also something that is totally personal. I mean, you can have a tattoo of anything and it's all your own.

DIANA: Yeah, that's why people get tattoos of their loved ones' names.

JACK: My brother has a tattoo of his old girlfriend's name.

DIANA: Yeah, my dad has a tattoo of some kind that doesn't really mean anything and he won't even tell us what it's from. He got it when he was a teenager.

LINDA: OK. But what do those examples show? Tattoos are still there, but their lives go on.

MARCUS: Well, life is change. You can't escape change.

LINDA: And tattoos are a way of resisting change? A way of marking the present on one's body—storing it, keeping it with you.

MARCUS: Right! That's the significance.

Activity

1. What rhetorical decisions derail the first four discussions?

2. What rhetorical decisions propel the discussion in #5?

3. Conduct your own invention workshop on the significance of tattoos. What other insight can you develop about the significance of tattoos?

Revealing complexity is at the heart of college writing.

Point of Contact

The Point of Contact section, the first part of the Invention section in each chapter, invites the writer to slow down, to stop, to notice common and not-so-common aspects of life. The *point of contact* refers to the intersection of the writer's perspective and the world. It is where the writer's vision collides with issues, events, situations, behaviors, and people. The idea in this section is that writing begins with a discovery—a realization about something that might otherwise go unnoticed. Therefore, writers have to be ready; their radar has to be on.

As you go through the Point of Contact sections, you will notice lists of questions that are designed to generate possibilities for writing topics. Think of the questions as exploration tools; they raise possible points of interest for writing. However, the lists are by no means exhaustive; they are simply examples of what can be asked. Follow up (in peer groups or alone) to generate more questions. (And if you are outside of an academic setting, it is certainly fair play to borrow a family member or friend to help with the invention process.)

Analysis

We are all familiar with analysis. We participate in it constantly. We see auto mechanics analyze our cars to discover the cause of the knocking sound. We see our doctors analyze conditions to understand why we feel sick. Basically put, such analysis is a process of discovering *why* and/or *how* something occurs. But analysis also involves discovering meaning. Writers are not content to simply see a person or situation or object. They explore the *significance*; that is, they imagine what ideas a thing might suggest. For instance, a writer sees an empty storefront in a strip mall and imagines that it suggests corporate irresponsibility or a declining economic system or even the end of an era when businesses lasted for several years before leaving a community. In other words, the storefront has potential meaning when analyzed (and often that analysis, as we will make clear in the next section, can make a topic relevant to a broader community).

Analysis leads to the complexities of issues, and revealing those complexities, rather than avoiding them, is at the heart of college writing. The Invention questions in each Analysis section are designed to help you reveal the complexities of your topic. (See the questions and responses about *freedom* on page 6.) As in all the Invention sections, the goal of the questions is to help generate some idea that is distinct, surprising . . . even weird.

Public Resonance

Perhaps the most important feature of writing is that it matters to a reader. This may sound obvious, but topics are not necessarily intrinsically relevant to people's lives. They need to be *made* relevant. They need to be expressed in a way that involves readers. Consider capital punishment: It is not, in itself, a relevant topic to the average college student, or even the average American citizen. Most people have not had a personal experience with the death penalty, but many people still have much to say about it. Why? The answer is rather simple: Capital punishment has been *made* relevant. Human rights activists, civil liberties groups, and religious groups have spoken or written the relevance of capital punishment into being. They have made the life of a death row inmate in Texas relevant to a suburban schoolteacher in Minnesota or a biology major at UCLA.

Good writers can make an issue resonate with their readers' feelings, thoughts, and situations. They can make personal situations resonate. They can transform a bad day at the office into an important efficiency issue for all workers. Or they can make a seemingly distant event, like the destruction of rainforests or the death of a prison inmate, real and immediate. They make a connection between two things: (1) what they see, know, do, believe, and feel; and (2) how that matters to other people. It may not matter to every other person, but generally it *resonates* with the public. It speaks to and engages the members of a community who, like the writer, are able to look beyond themselves (beyond the "me") and into the public arena (the "we").

The assumption behind public resonance is that we are deeply connected to others in our communities, and even beyond those communities. Our very identities are bound to a complex system of relationships that extend into all different realms of social life. We are tied by economic, social, institutional, political, familial, religious, and even physiological connections. We share laws, fears, dreams, and hopes. And when writers tap into those connections, when they make topics part of that large social network, they achieve public resonance.

Finally, consider the Public Resonance sections as Analysis. In these sections, we're not simply analyzing the topic; we're analyzing how people tend to think about the topic.

Analysis: Focus on the topic itself.

Public Resonance: Focus on how people think.

Writers cannot simply consider their topic. They must consider the values, assumptions, beliefs, and opinions that people have about the topic. Only then can they understand what to emphasize, what to minimize, what to insist upon, what to dramatize. Generally, writers can do this even without extensive research. By asking key questions, however, they can discover a great deal about the social realm. The following questions (taken from Chapter 5: Analyzing Concepts) might help us to discover some important layers to freedom:

Is the concept generally agreed upon?

Not really. People in the U.S. talk about freedom, but there are many disputes about it. Should people have the freedom to burn the flag, marry the person they love, get an abortion, have a machine gun or two around the house, stockpile hand grenades, or hold the majority of a company's stock and be the CEO at the same time? The answers to such questions are wrapped up with one's political beliefs.

What is the possible connection between the topic and some public concern?

People are deeply concerned not simply about their own freedom but other people's freedom. In the 2004 election, millions of people voted to make sure that other people didn't have the freedom to marry whom they want. In this sense, personal freedom is a kind of misnomer. It's not personal at all. An individual's freedom in the U.S. depends entirely on what everyone else thinks! I'm only free as far as others allow me to be.

Here, we're beginning to explore how complex freedom gets when it's analyzed against a backdrop of human affairs. This is the spirit of the Public Resonance sections throughout this book. The goal is to seek out the most resonant layers of the topic—the most powerful way the topic embeds itself into the deep structure of public life. This is no easy task. Often, the most resonant layer is the most hidden. For example, we can easily discover how freedom comes up in everyday life in songs, anthems, public documents, but it's more difficult to discover how freedom works in public thinking, beneath those songs and anthems.

Activity

Public resonance is about extending a topic outward—pulling it into social, political, cultural layers beyond the individual writer and reader. Consider one of the following topics: your pet, college loans, *American Idol*.

- Is the concept generally agreed upon?
- What is the possible connection between the topic and some public concern?

Try to discover how the topic wraps around the deep structure of public life—how it clings to some quiet values, ways of thinking, ways of believing.

Thesis

A thesis statement is more than a one-sentence summary of an essay. It represents an essay's most pointed and dense idea, the one that gives everything else in the essay purpose. Whether the essay project is observing, arguing, or problem solving, thesis statements focus writer and reader on some new insight.

Throughout the chapters, we make a distinction between flat and revelatory thesis statements—between statements that announce an obvious opinion and those that provoke a new way of thinking. Revelatory statements contribute something; they prompt readers to imagine topics differently; they pose alternative notions, reveal hidden sides.

Flat Statements: obvious, plain
Revelatory Statements: provocative, insightful, contributive

For example, the first statement below is flat, a simple announcement of common thinking. But the follow-up sentences dig up something new. The last three statements are ripe for a powerful essay on an otherwise typical topic:

Cell phones can make people behave rudely.

Cell phones enable teenagers to perform their social lives for others.

Cell phones reinforce the quiet notion that everyone is starring in his or her own reality show.

Cell phone calls crowd out time for the most important dialogue in life—the one in our own heads.

Creating revelatory statements is not magic. In fact, the process is driven by language. When writers replace words with other words in a sentence, they replace patterns for thinking. The revelatory statements about cell phones were created by trading out the main verb in the original sentence. The writer removed *can make* and started dropping in other verbs: *enable, reinforce, crowd out*. These verbs actually made the writer think differently: What acts or attitudes do cell phones enable? What ideas, behaviors, assumptions do cell phones reinforce? What voices do cell phones crowd out?

Thesis statements do not emerge out of thin air. They come from an intensive evolution in which writers develop ideas with hard questions, focused dialogue, and reflective writing. Therefore, each chapter of *The Composition of Everyday Life* includes a Thesis section with prompts, sample thesis statements, and common thesis problems. Each section also shows the Evolution of a Thesis, the gradual development of one writer's idea. (The section comes after the Analysis and Public Resonance sections to allow writers the opportunity to think through and around their topics, to imagine a range of possible positions and perspectives, before committing to a particular statement.)

Revelatory thesis statements show the writer and reader how to re-see the topic. They reveal something new, which is the goal of college writing.

Activity

Developing focused and revelatory thesis statements requires agile thinking. Writers first have to generate a statement and then work to narrow and shape it. In a group, take on the following flat statements. Replace the verbs to generate new ways of thinking, and then craft revelatory statements for each topic.

- Religion is the reason for many disputes in American politics.
- Advertising in popular culture makes women feel bad about their bodies.
- Television takes up too much time in children's lives.

Rhetorical Tools

As we mentioned, a *rhetorical tool* is a persuasion technique, a strategy for making people believe or accept an idea. Throughout the book, we will often refer to writers' rhetorical strategies—the techniques they use to convey their ideas and attempt to convince others to accept their positions. Good writers use good rhetorical tools. They come in many different forms:

Narration is the act of storytelling. Stories are often used to persuade people, to help them appreciate the value of an idea.

Description involves giving specific details to the reader. Sensory details (sounds, smells, sights, tastes, touches) prompt a reader to experience a topic and so accept the ideas that the writer offers.

Illustration is the graphic depiction of an idea. While illustration certainly suggests pictures and charts, it can also be accomplished with words.

Allusions are references to some bit of public knowledge such as a historical event, a news event, a popular culture icon, or a literary text.

Scenarios are hypothetical situations.

Testimony is an eyewitness account of a particular scene or situation.

The operating assumption is that these tools can be used for any topic, that writers can apply them according to their specific needs. For example, allusions function for a huge number of writing situations. Imagine that we're developing an analytical essay about freedom. We might refer to various moments in history: the Revolutionary War, the Emancipation Proclamation, women's suffrage, Woodstock, the Patriot Act, civil unions, and so on. These are well-known situations that writers can reference as a way to make meaning about the idea of freedom.

The Rhetorical Tools section in each chapter explains the strategies that are most applicable and appropriate to that writing situation. However, no strategy is exclusive to any particular kind of writing. (The tools depend on the task at hand—the purpose, the audience, the topic.) The strategies introduced throughout the book can be used for unlimited writing situations. In Chapter 7: Making Arguments, the rhetorical tools become a bit more complicated. They involve *appeals, counterarguments,* and *concessions.* As you will see, the latter chapters of the book (from Chapter 7 on) all involve argumentative rhetorical tools; however, those introduced earlier in the book (such as narration, allusion, and so on) can also apply to argumentative writing. As you move through the book, think of your collection of rhetorical tools growing.

"If school sucks, it's because all the invention has been removed, and students do little else besides practice and perform."

—Justin James

Organizational Strategies

Writers must decide when and where they will use different rhetorical tools. Whether narrating an event, describing a scene, offering evidence, or making an allusion, writers can arrange rhetorical tools in an unlimited number of ways. If a writer has succeeded, a completed text should read like a coherent journey: The reader begins with some sense of direction (a good introduction), passes through various locations and over different terrain (separate paragraphs), which are all connected with road signs (transitions). And finally, having traveled an intellectual route, the reader should feel as though he or she has arrived somewhere unique and valuable (a good conclusion).

The Organizational Strategies sections suggest various possible ways ideas might be arranged. They present common (and sometimes less-common) options for shaping essays, ordering points, and connecting ideas.

Writer's Voice

When we talk, we project a character or mood, not only by choosing certain words but also by changing the sound, pitch, and pace of our voices. (Some people talk with dramatic ups and downs; others blab at us in a single-note dirge.) Also, when we talk, we have the added tool of physical gestures. We can swing our hands around wildly, bow our heads, or open our eyes very wide at different moments of a sentence, simply to project an attitude. As writers, we have just as many strategies at our disposal. We may not be able to use our hands and eyes to gesture to the reader, but we have plenty of *writerly* strategies.

Every writer, for each writing event, creates a voice—the character that is projected by the language and style of the essay. Writers use a vast array of techniques to create voices. Sometimes those voices are very sober and formal. Other voices are comedic, even hilarious. This does not mean that the topic itself is funny; it means that the writer's presentation of ideas is humorous. Some of the best writers can make a potentially dull topic feel quirky, or a light topic have depth and profound significance. Of course, most writers fall somewhere in the middle between serious and comic, between utterly stiff and totally untamed.

You will create a voice . . . whether you know it or not.

Ultimately, you will create a voice, whether you know it or not. By simply writing a sentence, you create a voice in some small way. And since a writerly voice will emerge from your essays, it's certainly better to be crafty; otherwise, your voice might very well come off as . . . well . . . boring.

The Writer's Voice section in each chapter will help you to shape an appropriate voice or to explore different voices. While it is valuable to develop a personal voice (a style that feels unique or somehow genuinely more *you*), it is more valuable to experiment with voices. Because we often have to write in various different contexts, for various different audiences, and on various different occasions, we need to be flexible, able to fit into audiences' conventions and expectations. (A radically informal, knee-slappin' voice would not go over well in a formal report to a government agency, nor would an overly somber voice be appropriate for a public invitation to a community event.) Learning how to stylize voice according to the audience and situation is one of the most valuable skills for a writer.

Vitality

Vitalized writing is lively. It yanks on readers' awareness. Vitality sometimes calls for winding sentence patterns that bring the reader through important intellectual curves and into nuanced, layered thoughts. And it sometimes calls for brief statements—short pops to the brain. The important principle is that sentences are the only interaction between a reader and writer. If the sentences are full of empty phrases, stiffened by repetitious patterns, or slowed by jumbled clauses, the reading experience will be lifeless.

Creating vitality in writing requires close attention to sentence patterns as well as a commitment to shaping and reshaping the language. To that end, each chapter in *The Composition of Everyday Life* includes a section that explains and illustrates particular vitality strategies. Like rhetorical tools, vitality strategies are not exclusive to any one chapter or writing situation. They can be applied across the board, according to the writer's discretion.

Revision and Peer Review

Revision is about reapproaching ideas. As academic writers work, they constantly rethink their original ideas. To some degree, revision is fused into every act of the writing process. Writers are constantly asking questions: "Is this the best way to do this? Is there a better way to engage my reader?" Writers also benefit from a *holistic* rereading of their work: a process that involves first stepping away from the text for a period of time, and then re-examining everything (the main ideas, the supporting points, the organization, and even the voice). This probably sounds intimidating—rethinking everything after a significant amount of work has already gone into a draft. But revision is where a writer can make a text function as a whole by making important connections and adding necessary detail. Often, it is only through revision that a text comes to life. And then, after a holistic, or global, rereading of the text, writers go on to editing, making smaller, sentence-level changes.

Each chapter provides a variety of revision prompts. They appear throughout the Invention sections and invite you to stop, refocus on the ideas you've created, to investigate the value and complexity of those ideas, with the hope that everything can be more intense, more focused, more engaging. Each chapter also includes a Peer Review section so that writers can share their projects with others and receive focused and helpful feedback.

Delivery

One look at history tells us that writing changes the world. It provokes people to think differently and ultimately to act differently. Consider, for example, the Declaration of Independence: Thomas Jefferson's declaration helped a group of diverse colonies imagine themselves as a unified people against a tyrannical king. Or consider Mary Wollstonecraft's *Vindication of the Rights of Women,* which prompted increasingly public debate about the role of women in everyday life. And beyond these momentous historical texts, everyday writing, the kind that gets done in offices and homes and schools, also changes the world. Memos about office meetings or new policies directly impact people's behaviors. Letters (or e-mails) to friends and relatives can profoundly influence their behaviors and their attitudes. Advertising changes how we think about ourselves and the world around us: The constant presence of particular words and slogans eventually prompts us to think (even desire!) in certain ways. And we all use written instructions to get us through complicated tasks (like hooking up the video game console to the television).

But on a deeper level, beyond hooking up an Xbox, academia depends on the notion that writing affects how people think. The academic community works on the assumption that writing can motivate people to reconsider ideas or even consider something totally novel. The practice of writing, then, is deeply connected to the act of influencing thought.

At the end of each chapter in *The Composition of Everyday Life,* the Delivery section contains questions about the consequences of your writing. The goal is to see the relationship between your work (your thinking, your typing, your revising) and the world that surrounds you. The Delivery sections also invite you to go "Beyond the Essay"—to take your ideas from the chapter and recast them in some other format: a poster, a cartoon, and so on. The Delivery sections explore various possibilities for interacting with the world.

A Final Note

As you work through the chapters, remember that writing is not merely a tool for expressing opinions; rather, it is a tool for making new ideas, and for adding new dimensions to old ideas. Our purpose in writing is not merely to express what we think, but to shape what can be known. We are hoping to explore intellectual possibilities. In this light, the college essay can be seen as a record of intellectual exploration—a writer's attempt and invitation to figure out something new.

Our purpose: To explore and shape what can be known.

INVENTING IDEAS ASSIGNMENT

Remember that invention is the engine behind good writing. Picture yourself as a creator of ideas rather than a writer of essays. Work through the following activities:

1. Choose one of the following topics: college writing assignments, high school sports programs, public art in the United States, the status of hip-hop music, teacher salaries, ghosts, leash laws, UFOs, your local coffee shop.

2. Use the following **Invention questions** as springboards for thinking about your topic. Write out your responses. Like the passages about freedom (pages 6 and 20), try to seek new dimensions to the idea.

3. After working through the questions, review your invention work. Where did you reveal something? In other words, which statements or passages pose alternative notions or reveal hidden sides? Describe those statements or passages, and explain why you think they are the most revelatory.

Invention Questions

- Specifically, how does it influence or change people's lives?
- What particular emotions, behaviors, or ideas are associated with it?
- What hidden role does it play in everyday life?
- Are there complexities to the concept that people overlook?
- Is the concept generally agreed upon?
- Why is it important that people have an appropriate understanding of this concept?

You are an idea creator rather than an essay writer.

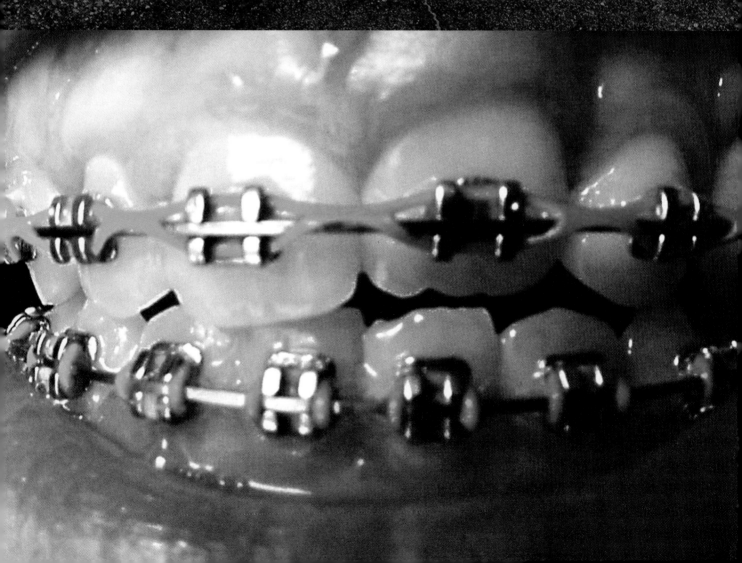

Chapter Contents

CHAPTER 2

"Those who fail to learn the lessons of history are doomed to repeat them."

—George Santayana

You have probably heard this famous statement—perhaps when someone in a history class asked plaintively, "Why do we have to learn this stuff?" Santayana's point, of course, is that the past is filled with situations that teach us about ourselves, and that ignoring the past results in blindness to the present and future. While Santayana's statement is most often applied to a collective history (e.g., American or world history), it also suggests something for the individual. In the same way that countries learn from their pasts, individuals come to new insights because of their own experiences. Obviously, we learn basic *dos* and *don'ts* from experience (not to ride a bike over the icy patch in the driveway, not to talk during math class, not to indulge too much the night before an exam). But our pasts are filled with more opportunity for insight beyond simple I'll-never-do-that-again situations. A vast array of moments lurks in the past, moments that may mean far more than what we have always assumed.

Writers looking into their pasts attempt to learn something new, to understand the importance of some moment, or to understand the significance of a situation. They are retrieving an event or situation, uncovering a moment, and examining it from their present perspective. The hope is that the writer will see more about the situation than he or she possibly could have seen in the past. Imagine an adult writer looking back at a childhood baseball game: As a child, he fretted over striking out in the last inning. But as an adult, he can see how important that moment of failure was to his life, to his intellectual and spiritual growth. The present (adult) writer is able to see this because the elapsed time has allowed him emotional and intellectual distance.

In academia, writers often look to their own pasts for insight:

- In a sociology course, students recall their childhood communities; they pay close attention to the institutions (churches and schools) they attended and include their memories in a theory about institutional affiliation.

- A psychology professor prompts students to recall their early experiences with nonparental authority (such as teachers, extended family, and baby-sitters) and form a theory of authority based on those experiences.

- In a Western Civilization course, students recall their early experiences with organized religion. They include their experiences in their collective examination of religious principles.

Memories do not, in themselves, teach us anything. We must create the lesson. We must look back at the past with a certain perspective: one of curiosity and possibility. Although we have lived through the past, we must entirely rediscover it if we are to learn.

This chapter will help you rediscover a specific situation or event from your past, explore it in depth, develop a particular point about it, and communicate your ideas in writing. The following essays will provide insight to various writing strategies. After you read the essays, you can find a topic in one of two ways:

1. Go to the Point of Contact section to find a topic from your everyday life. **or**
2. Choose one of the Ideas for Writing that follow the essays.

After you find a topic, go to the **Analysis** section to begin developing your ideas.

The Grapes of Mrs. Rath

Steve Mockensturm

We are often invited to think about the past as something that is behind us—something to forget about, something that can no longer influence who we are, how we think, what we value. But Steve Mockensturm, an artist, musician, and graphic designer, reminds us that the past looms all around us. The places we drive by, swing into, and rarely notice have absorbed the past and offer it back to us constantly. The buildings where we learned and lived have been defined by our own lives and the social events that swirl around them. And, more importantly for Mockensturm, these places have worked their way into our lives, into our understanding of ourselves and the world we inhabit.

I wonder if Mrs. Hulda Rath ever realized how much she affected my life. Probably not. It's funny how a teacher gets stuck in your head and you find yourself referencing that for the rest of your life.

Mrs. Rath taught English at DeVilbiss High School in 1975—my junior year. I say taught, but she didn't really teach. Didn't even talk that much, just gave us a lot of stories to read. She said they were classic, important books, but I'd never heard of any of them: *Animal Farm, Lord of the Flies, 1984, The Crucible, Cry the Beloved Country.*

DeVilbiss was a rough and rowdy school (inner city, a thousand kids, half black, half white) with a lot of distractions. During the '40s and '50s it was THE high school to attend, very academic, but by the mid-'70s it was starting to run down, perhaps stigmatized by a few race riots in '68.

Mrs. Rath had an ability to recognize the kids that actually wanted to read and learn and, often times, would send a few of us down to the library where it was quiet and we could have some sanctuary from the usual classroom shenanigans. Looking back, I realize how amazing and grand this school library was. It was bigger than the local public branch and very church-like with its vaulted ceiling and tall windows. Everything was made of wood—the chairs, the tables, the shelves, the big librarian's station in the middle—and it was always full of light, the windows exposed to the south and west. Three sets of large mahogany doors would clang and creak, echoing down the hall, up around the stairwell, and into our classroom.

5   It was in this environment that I was introduced to the work of John Steinbeck. Two of the books assigned were *The Grapes of Wrath* and *Of Mice and Men.* I was smitten with these masterpieces and savored Steinbeck's work like a rich meal. Reading these stories in the great, holy library of my young life is one of the happiest memories I have. These were stories about my country and my people. Flawed yet beautiful people in tough situations in an imperfect land. I was discovering America. I suddenly wanted to read everything Steinbeck had ever written.

"Sometimes I'll stand in the doorway and picture the room as it was back in '75, gazing around, putting old friends in their seats."

I checked out *Tortilla Flat* and *The Wayward Bus* from the library and asked Mrs. Rath what else he wrote and where I could get it. She loaned me her copy of "In Dubious Battle." Soon, I wanted to own all of Steinbeck's books. I scoured the bookstores to complete the collection, a collection that has traveled with me for 25 years.

The city sadly closed down DeVilbiss High School a few years after I graduated. It was too big and too expensive to maintain. Thankfully, they never tore it down and trimmed only a few trees from the large oak grove lining the front walkway. For years it sat empty, the massive entrance looking out on Upton Avenue with no expression.

Then, a few years ago, some parts of it reopened for special programs and the industrial skills center was transformed into a technology academy. My children were enrolled in the Horizons program at the old school. From time to time, during open house, I'll wander the halls and conjure up old voices. Many areas of the building are unsafe; the library is almost unrecognizable. It's a massive storage room now, crap piled to the ceiling, desks and shelves torn out and not a book in sight.

The girls have Russian language lessons in Mrs. Rath's old room at the top of the stairwell. Sometimes I'll stand in the doorway and picture the room as it was back in '75, gazing around, putting old friends in their seats. Whenever I'm reading Steinbeck, my memory goes back to this classroom, the library, and Mrs. Hulda Rath's quiet ways and I get the urge to plop down and read *Cannery Row*.

Writing Strategies

1. Describe Mockensturm's voice as a writer. That is, how does he come across to the reader? Refer to three specific passages to support your description.

2. If workshopping Mockensturm's essay, how would you answer the following questions: What do you like most about the essay? What suggestion do you have for the writer?

3. What would you say is Mockensturm's main idea? How does he convey it to the reader?

4. Identify the most effective uses of narration (storytelling) and description in Mockensturm's essay, and explain why they work.

Exploring Ideas

1. In groups, discuss how Mockensturm sees high school English differently from the way you see it. (Some may see it the same as he does.) What values, beliefs, or assumptions underlie the different ways people view high school English?

2. Visit your old school, an old playground, a park, or some other place from your past, and write down any memories that come to mind. What experience there influenced your identity—or still influences you today?

3. Consider the people from your past. Explain how their behaviors (even the very subtle ones) influenced your outlook on life.

Ideas for Writing

1. What high school experience do you view differently— for example, as more valuable or less valuable—than most of your peers do?

2. What individual influenced you growing up and may not realize it?

If responding to one of these ideas, go to the Analysis section of this chapter to begin developing ideas for your essay.

How I Lost the Junior Miss Pageant

Cindy Bosley

Most people have never participated in a beauty pageant. But nearly everyone has experienced the angst associated with the quiet pageantry of everyday life—the constant pressure to perform well in public, to look the part of a happy, stable, well-to-do member of society. Cindy Bosley, a teacher and published poet, is brave enough to share her early attempts at dealing with this pressure. On one hand, this essay is an examination of beauty pageants and the awkward system of values and beliefs that surround them; on the other, it is an intimate look at a mother/daughter relationship that is defined by the social goings-on of a small city in the middle of America.

Every evening of the annual broadcast of the Miss America Pageant, I, from the age of seven or so, carefully laid out an elaborate chart so that I might also participate as an independent judge of the most important beauty contest in the world. From my viewing seat on a green striped couch in my parents' smoky living room where the carpet, a collage of white, brown, and black mixed-shag, contrasted so loudly with the cheap 70s furnishings that it threatened my attention to the television set, I sat with popcorn and soda, pen in hand, thrilled at the oncoming parade of the most beautiful women in the world.

In the hours before the show began, I'd carefully written out in ink, sometimes over and over, names of all 50 states, Washington, D.C., and Puerto Rico along the *y* axis of my paper. And my categories of evaluation of the contestants ribbed themselves along the *x* axis— beauty, poise, swimsuit, evening gown—plus categories of my own—hair, likability, teeth. Over the years, an increasingly complex system of points and penalties evolved: an extra point for being tan, a loss of points for sucking up, more points for breasts, more points for unpainted nails, fewer points for big noses, fewer points for skinny lips, an extra point for smartness, subtraction of a point for playing the piano. Who wants to hear a sonata? Dance for me, bounce your bootie.

My mother had secret hopes. Finally divorced for the second time from the same man, my father, she sat with me and gave her own running commentary about who was cute, who smiled too much, who would find a handsome husband. My mother, having always been a little to a lot overweight, excelled at swimming, and she told me much later that she chose swimming because she didn't feel fat in the water. Her sister was the cheerleader, but she was a swimmer, too heavy for a short skirt of her own, she said. My mother's secret was that she wanted the winner to be her daughter. Sitting with me on the couch at 137 North Willard Street, she already knew I wasn't tall enough or pretty enough in the way of models and movie stars to ever stand a chance, but her real fear, which I only became aware of as an older teen, was that I would always be too chubby and too backward and too different and too poor, for which she blamed herself, to win a beauty pageant. Still, there were always those surprises of the contests—Miss Utah? She was no good! Why did she win? What were those judges thinking! It should have been Miss Alabama, anyone can see that. Who would have guessed Miss Utah, with that mole on her shoulder?

After my mother's never-subtle hints that if I'd just lose 20 pounds boys would like me and I might even win a beauty contest, it was my friend Bridget who wanted us to enter the Ottumwa (pronounced Uh-TUM-wuh) Junior Miss Pageant together. I secretly believed that I stood a better chance than Bridget did, though she had the right name and the right body, though she wore the right clothes and was more magazine-beautiful than I. I had *some* hope for the contest: I had *some* talents and a kind of baby-cute innocence complete with blond hair and blue eyes that I was sure the judges would find "charming and fresh." Yeah, okay, so I was already engaged to be married—so what—I was still on my way to college, and Bridget was not. And Judy was funny but had a flat face. Marcy was smart but had no breasts or hips. Carol was pretty but totally uncoordinated and her knees came together when she jumped. Desirea had enviable boobs, almost as nice as mine and probably firmer, but her chin did weird things when she smiled and her eyes were brown.

5 We practiced, all of us together, several times a week with a lithe woman—somebody's mom with good hair

and body—getting us into form for the stage. This was the era of *Flashdance,* so we all wore our own leg warmers and torn sweatclothes and fancy headband scarves. If you were one of the north-side girls (that meant your daddy was a businessman or doctor), you had gotten your leg warmers from Marshall Fields in Chicago. If you were Bridget, your dad worked at John Deere like mine but was in management and not out in the factory threading bolts on a greasy, noisy machine, so you got your leg warmers from the mall in Des Moines. If you were me, with a factory dad who didn't even live in the same house, you got your leg warmers from Kmart down the road because Target was all the way across town and too expensive, and Wal-Mart hadn't yet been born as far as we knew. The fancy mom-lady made sure everyone had a brochure about her charm school (this is small-town Iowa, mind you, so anyone operating a charm school and modeling agency in this town was kidding themselves. But making lots of money.).

So 14 of us, nervous, jealous, ears ringing with Mirror-Mirror-on-the-Wall, met daily for two weeks prior to the pageant to go over our choreographed group fitness routine to be performed, not in swimsuits, but in short-shorts and white T-shirts, Hooters-style (also not invented yet as far as we knew), and to discuss such techniques as Vaseline along the teeth and gum lines to promote smooth smiles, lest our lips dry out and get stuck in a grin during discussions with the judges of the agonies of world hunger. We were each responsible for our own talent routines and props, and each one of us had to provide a 5×7 black-and-white photo for the spread in the town paper.

The photographs were a problem. My father did not believe in such things for girls as shoes, clothes, haircuts, college, or photographs for Junior Miss, and so there was no way he was going to give a penny for a pageant-worthy dress or a professional photographer's 10-minutes-plus-proofs. I believe my mother even humiliated herself enough to ask. This was hard for her, since he'd admitted before leaving to a five-year affair with a woman who looked surprisingly like my mother but heavier. So Mom and I tried some Polaroid headshots against the side of the house, but me dressed up in my prettiest sailor blouse couldn't counteract the hospital green of the aluminum siding. We moved up

to our only other option, which was my mother's flash camera with Instamatic film, and still nothing suitable (I could have agreed on one of the Polaroid shots, but my mother knew it would knock me out of the contest for sure even before the night itself).

I don't know who she borrowed the money from or what she did to get the favor, but my mother had me down at Lee's Photography the very next afternoon, and he took one shot and offered us the one proof. Abracadabra, there was my face among all the other faces as a contestant in the Uh-TUM-wuh Junior Miss Pageant. From the layout in the paper, it looked to me, and to my flushed mother, as though I had as good a shot as any.

The contest night went quickly: my foot, couched, pinched, and Band-Aided uncomfortably in a neighbor's hand-me-down high heels, slipped (hear the auditorium's quick and loud intake of breath in horror!) as I walked forward to say my name with a strong, vibrant hello just like I'd been coached by the fancy-mom; my dress was last year's prom dress, which earned me no cool points with my peers but didn't lose me any either since I had none to subtract; I managed not to land on my bottom (as I had in every practice before the contest) in my gymnastics routine, self-choreographed with my own robot-style moves to the synthesizer-heavy tune "Electricity," by a band that was popular in Sacramento, California, in that year, 1985, but not yet in my hometown. (The cassette tape had been given to me by my Hispanic, juvenile delinquent, just-released-from-young-boy-prison-in-California ex-boyfriend Jim.)

10   My exercise routine went off very well in front of the crowd, and I don't think anyone could even tell that my shorts were soaking wet from having been dropped by me into the toilet just an hour before as I arranged my items for quick-change. My mother and fiancé were actually sitting together, their mutual hatred of each other squeezed like a child between them. I'd even kept myself from leaving my mother behind when, backstage after the contest as I hugged and cried in joy for the co-winners and out of desperate relief that it was over now, my mother, beside herself with embarrassment for me and disappointment for herself, and misunderstanding my tears, hissed loudly enough for the benefit of everyone, "STOP your crying, they'll think you're not a nice LOSER!"

So I had done it: I had been a contestant in the Junior Miss Pageant and my mother had the snapshots to prove it.

I'd lost the contest because I didn't yet know how to tell people what they wanted to hear. The small girl that boys secretly liked but wouldn't date doesn't win Miss America. The girl hiding in her room reading and writing poetry doesn't win Miss America. The girl playing violin despite her mother's anxiousness that other people will think she's weird doesn't win Miss America. The girl on Willard Street doesn't ever win Miss America.

But the truth is that I'd lost the contest when I told the judges, when they asked, that my most personal concern was my mother's loneliness, and if I could change anything at all, I would give her something—a man, God, anything to free her from that loneliness.

Clearly, I lacked the save-the-whales-and-rainforest civic-mindedness required not only of Miss America, but of Junior Miss America, too. Even, although one wouldn't think it, in Ottumwa, Iowa, where my mother would go on to work in a bathtub factory, and then a glue factory, and then an electrical connectors factory (the factory worker's version of upward mobility), and finally, a watch factory where they shipped and received not just watches but cocaine in our town that at that time had more FBI agents in it than railroad engineers. And even in this town where my sister would go to work the kill floor of the pork plant where, for fun, the workers shot inspection dye at each other and threatened each other's throats with hack-knives. And even in this town where my cousin, age 13, would bring a bomb to seventh grade for show-and-tell, and get caught and evacuated, and be given community service to do because the public-school-as-terrorist-ground phenomena hadn't yet been born. And even in this town where if you want to go to college, you better know someone who knows how to get you there because otherwise it's too far away and too much money and too much trouble and way, way, way beyond your own intellect and sense of self to do it alone. How scary (get married). How wasteful (get married). How expensive (get married). How strange (get married). How pretentious (get married). How escapist (get married).

15   If your parents are crazy and poor, and if you can't win the Junior Miss Pageant, and if it's the kind of town where you stay or they don't ever want you coming back, you get married, you move to Texas where your husband sells drugs, you hide away from the world until your self grows enough to break you out, and then you leave and you pray for your mother's loneliness and you spend your life learning to come to terms with your own, and you are smart and willful and strong, and you don't ever have to draw another chart before the pageant begins.

My mother told me later that she was just sure I would have won the Junior Miss contest if I hadn't made that awful mistake in my gymnastics routine (I don't know what mistake she was talking about—it was the least flawed part of the evening), but I knew the truth about why I'd lost, and I knew I'd lost even before the contest or the practices began. I'd lost this contest at birth, probably, to be born to my father who had a date that night, and to my mother who believed some girls—girls like me, and girls like her—had to try very hard to catch and keep a boy's attention. I'd lost the contest in borrowed shoes and an out-of-date dress. I'd lost the contest with the engagement ring on my seventeen-year-old finger. I'd lost the contest with wet shorts and too funky music. I'd lost the contest with a bargain photograph and Kmart leg warmers. I'd lost the contest with an orange Honda Express moped parked between the other girls' cars. I'd lost the contest in a falling-down green house. I'd lost the contest in the grease on my father's hands and hair and the taste of grease in his lunchbox leftovers. I'd lost the contest in my growingly cynical evaluation of Miss America as I'd gotten older—"chubby thighs touching, minus five points," "big hair, minus three points," "too small nipples, minus two," "flabby arms, minus five," and subtract and subtract and subtract. It's a contest no one should want to win. Our mothers should not have such dreams for us. Our mothers should not have such loneliness.

Writing Strategies

1. Bosley provides details throughout her essay. Which ones work best for you? Select several details and compare them to the ones your classmates selected. Attempt to explain why certain details made the essay more engaging to you.

2. What is the public resonance of Bosley's essay? That is, how does it matter to others? How does it matter to someone who doesn't care about pageants?

3. If workshopping Bosley's essay, how would you complete the following statements: What I like most about your essay is _____. The main suggestion I have about your essay is _____.

4. Bosley's title suggests that she will tell us how she lost the Junior Miss Pageant. Does she deliver? What is the point of her essay? How did she lose the pageant?

Exploring Ideas

1. Interview several classmates to find out how they view beauty pageants (or interview several people outside of class to find out their views). Record their responses, and then explain in writing what viewpoints seemed to be the most common, most unusual, most interesting, most thought-provoking.

2. How does Bosley's point about beauty pageants speak to larger (more general) issues, such as competition, class, tradition, media, and so on?

3. With others or alone, explore the past, identifying experiences that speak to the angst associated with the quiet pageantry of everyday life—the constant pressure to perform well in public, to look the part of a happy, stable, well-to-do member of society. What experiences of your own provide an intimate look at some relationship that is defined by social goings-on?

4. Do research to learn more about the history of the Miss America Pageant—its origins, its popularity, and how it has changed over the years. How has the pageant tried to stay in step with cultural trends? Why has the pageant, and American culture, changed?

5. Consider your responses to #4 above. How have other American traditions, besides the Miss America Pageant, changed with the culture?

Ideas for Writing

1. Discover the significance of an experience or activity you participated in with disappointing results. Perhaps it was sitting on the bench for an entire season in a sport, running for student council and not winning, pursuing a certain girl or boy without luck, or something else altogether.

2. Recall an experience or activity at which you exceeded your own expectations. What, now, is the significance of that experience to you?

If responding to one of these ideas, go to the Analysis section of this chapter to begin developing ideas for your essay.

The Thrill of Victory . . .
The Agony of Parents

Jennifer Schwind-Pawlak

In the margins of this essay, a reader's comments point to key ideas and writing strategies.

We often get caught up in the moment. As children—and as adults—we first react to situations one way, and then later make better sense of what happened. Jennifer Schwind-Pawlak, who wrote the following essay for a college writing course, explores one of these moments from her past. As you read the essay, notice how Schwind-Pawlak uses her own particular experience to tap into a more universal one. From a new perspective, allowed for by the distance of time, she finds the positive value of what appeared back then to be a negative experience. In this essay, she stands back and talks about the experience, engaging the reader with key details, a mature writer's voice, and an important lesson.

Writing Strategies

Exploring Ideas

Parents—one word that can strike many emotions in children when said aloud. Some children will smile and think about how silly their dad looked when he put carrot sticks up his nose that very morning, while others will cringe when they think about how their mother picked them up from school last week wearing orange polyester pants and a green shirt, oblivious to the hard work that some fellow went through to create the color wheel. My own emotional state of mind seemed to run the gamut throughout childhood. I chose to blame my parents for all of the traumatic events that unfolded but took pride in my obvious independence during the successes. One of the most heinous crimes that my parents committed was "the soccer foul." If I could have ejected them from the game of life at that point, I would have.

Ironically, I was not particularly fond of soccer. Being the youngest of four children, I often chose to run around the field with friends while my brothers and sisters performed feats of soccer, the likes of which had only been seen during the World Cup. I would happily contort my fingers into chubby pretzels while singing "The Itsy Bitsy Spider" as the game's events were recounted on the drives home. Still, whether by guilt or by the need to belong, I joined the team when I became of age.

The team that I played on was designed to turn the young and awkward into the swans of the soccer field. My father (a one-time soccer coach) explained several times that this was the time that I would learn the rules and workings of the game and that I shouldn't

Introduces general subject matter leading up to the main idea: Parent/child dynamics.

Develops essay through narration and description.

The relationship between parents and children. Parents commit "fouls" or "crimes."

expect much more than that. Since it was a child's league, learning and the team experience were the focuses. Winning was a pleasant bonus but should not be achieved at the cost of the main objectives. This litany was taken and stored somewhere in the recesses of my brain. For me, however, the main objective was looking cool while running down the field chasing a spotted ball. Everything else seemed secondary.

Due to the family history, I attended every Tuesday and Thursday practice and managed to make each a social occasion while going through the motions of the game. I succeeded in understanding the game and, though not the most skilled of players, began to enjoy the half game of playing time that was required by the league for each player. Though I was far from a star player, I felt that my contribution mattered to the overall outcomes of the games, all of which had been lost to this point.

5   Sunday, the morning of the fifth game of the season, came with no warning. I got up, went to church with the family, then came home to suit up for the game. Upon arrival at the field, I was greeted by the coach and went to take my place along the sidelines with the rest of my team. There was a buzz of excitement that left me with the feeling that I would get when my brother would poke me with his fingertip after dragging his stocking feet across the carpet. The team that we were playing had a record identical to ours. We could win this game. I didn't care what the parents said. Winning would be a blast.

The coach kept me on the sidelines the entire first half of the game, which my pre-adolescent mind attributed to my obviously increasing skill at the game. He was saving his trump card, me, for the last half of the game. I knew this was rare, but I was sure that his reason was to bedazzle the crowd and the other team with my pure firepower on the field. The other players, except one other girl, continued to cycle in and out of the game. While I was excited because we were winning the game, I was concerned that the coach had forgotten about me. I inched, ever so slowly, toward him and started mindless conversation to let him know that I was there. He spoke to me, so I knew that he could not have forgotten about me. As the game was winding down, I was sure that he must have decided to put me in for the last play of the game.

The game ended.

I was horrified to realize that I had not played one moment of the first win of the season. After all of that practice and the ugly uniform, I was deemed such a poor player that I was not even good enough to play one moment of that game. How would I ever live this down at school? How would I face all of my classmates

---

Margin notes (left):

Details are carefully selected: Father's explanation becomes key later in the essay.

Sums up practice and games thus far.

Sets up the fifth game. Excitement, suspense is building.

Description of the fifth game.

Three-word paragraph has dramatic effect.

Margin notes (right):

We have all participated in these childhood activities that were supposed to teach us lessons, about sportsmanship, teamwork, etc.

Her relationship with soccer seems to be developing, changing.

We all—most of us—have not gotten to play at some point: Common experience?

She is "horrified" not to play.

on Monday? My stomach began to churn, the way that it does when you are going down the first hill of any great roller coaster. I looked to my parents for support, which only added to the horror of that day.

Joann (the name I call my mother when she does something embarrassing) was screaming at the coach. In a voice so screeching that it rivaled fingernails on a blackboard, she told him that he was a disgraceful coach and that he should be ashamed of himself. She continued to point out the error of his ways by reminding him that I had not played at all in the game. How could she do this to me? My mother had managed to enlighten the few people that hadn't noticed on their own that I had not played at all. What was she thinking? She might as well have rented billboard space saying, "So what if Jeni sucks at soccer? The coach wouldn't let her play." My only thought was, "I don't want to go to school tomorrow!"

10   Looking back, I realize that it wasn't so bad the next day at school. I walked out to recess and talked about how nuts my mother was and everyone seemed to agree, sympathize, and get on with the important task of freeze tag. At that moment I wasn't sure that I would ever be able to forgive my mother for what happened that day, but, as far as I can recall, I began loving her again within the week. I am sure that she either cooked my favorite dinner, told a corny joke, or told me how much she loved me to make that lump of anger fade away.

I never went to soccer again. As a matter of fact, I never played another organized sport again. Maybe it was the fear of rejection. Maybe it was the uncertainty of my talent. Maybe I was just too busy with other things. I never really felt the urge to compete on that level after that day.

The relationship that I have with my parents has changed very much throughout the years. The polyester pants don't bother me anymore, but the carrot sticks still make me laugh. While their "soccer foul" embarrassed and angered me at the time, I understand and appreciate it now. My mother was angry *FOR* me. She was hurt *FOR* me. Through the pages of time, I can look back and see that, more often than not, I embarrassed her. She never stopped feeling for me, loving me, or protecting me. I have grown enough to realize that, though I often pointed out my parents' fouls, they scored countless goals that I didn't even notice.

Marginal notes (left):

Description of "the foul."

Reflects on her experience: What "looking back" means.

She wonders. What might be the reason she never played another organized sport again? What impact might this experience have had?

Finds meaning through reflection.

Marginal notes (right):

She is "horrified" and looks to her mother for help. Turns out, her mother is "horrified" too, and reacts in a way that makes things worse. What does she learn about her mother, parents, and relationships from her mother's reaction—and from her reaction to it?

She sees the experience differently now. Sometimes—many times—we see differently when something's happening than we do later on.

One consequence is that she quit soccer, sports. She's not sure why? Complexity.

She sees the experience differently now. Parents and children embarrass each other sometimes. This is part of the relationship. In this situation, though, her mother was angry/hurt FOR her.

Writing Strategies

1. Describe Schwind-Pawlak's opening strategy. Does it work for you? Do you want to read on? How else might Schwind-Pawlak have begun her essay?

2. Why does Schwind-Pawlak tell us that her father "explained several times that this was the time that [she] would learn the rules and workings of the game and that [she] shouldn't expect much more than that" (¶ 3)? Why does she place this information in her third paragraph? Where else might she have placed this information, and how would that placement affect her essay?

3. Describe the tone of this essay. Is it funny, serious, pensive, silly? Describe it with your own one-word description and then refer to three sentences that support your decision.

4. Explain the effect of Schwind-Pawlak's one-sentence paragraph: "The game ended." (¶ 7)

5. Schwind-Pawlak writes, "My mother was angry FOR me. She was hurt FOR me." (¶ 12) Why do you think she decides to both underline and all-cap the word "for"?

Exploring Ideas

1. Describe a particular childhood experience that you view differently now that you are older. You might, like Schwind-Pawlak, remember an experience involving a parent and yourself in a public setting.

   - How do you view the experience differently now?

   - Why are you able to view the experience differently now?

   - How might your new way of viewing the experience help you to view present or future experiences differently?

2. In groups, discuss a film or novel in which one of the characters comes to learn a valuable lesson from a childhood or other past experience.

3. Read Cindy Bosley's essay "How I Lost the Junior Miss Pageant" (earlier in this chapter) and compare Bosley's experience to Schwind-Pawlak's. Specifically, how do the two essays explore the angst and pressure involved in being a member of society?

Ideas for Writing

1. What is the significance of a big game or event from your past?

2. What emotional or intellectual experience has prevented you from ever doing something again? How has the experience influenced your later decisions?

If responding to one of these ideas, go to the Analysis section of this chapter to begin developing ideas for your essay.

Julie Elliott/StockXchng

Outside Reading

Find a written text about a memory, and print it out or make a photocopy. In journals or magazines, these texts are often called *memoirs.* You might find a memoir in a general readership publication (such as *Time, Newsweek, Reader's Digest,* or the *New York Times*). Some publications feature writers who tell their own stories. Enthusiast magazines (about specific hobbies and travel) often feature personal memoirs as well. (Check the table of contents for story titles with the first-person pronouns *I* or *my*.) To conduct an electronic search of journals and magazines, go to your library's periodical database or to InfoTrac College Edition (http://infotrac.cengage.com). In your library's database, perform a keyword search, or go to the main search box for InfoTrac College Edition and click on "keywords." Enter word combinations that interest you, such as *memoir and Jewish and women, memoir and Japan and war, memoir and soccer, memoir and punk rock.* (When performing keyword searches, avoid using the phrases or articles *a, an, the;* instead, use nouns separated by *and*.) The search results will yield lists of journal and magazine articles.

You can also search the Internet. Try the search engine Altavista.com. Like most Internet search engines, Altavista.com combines words using *and*. In the search box, try various combinations, such as those above.

The purpose of this assignment is to broaden the range of possibilities; that is, to help you discover more strategies for writing about the past. As you are probably discovering, this kind of writing varies widely in organization, voice, and even length. As you read through this chapter and begin your own writing, keep the memoir you have discovered close by and notice the elements and strategies the writer uses. Depending on your instructor's suggestions, do one or more of the following:

1. Notice how the writer applies various strategies from this chapter. On the hard copy or photocopy:
   - Highlight the thesis (or main idea about the memory) if it is stated. If the thesis is implied, write it in your own words.
   - Highlight the most descriptive or detailed passage(s).
   - Highlight any passages that suggest a connection between the writer's memory and the reader's (your) life. In the margin, write "public resonance."

2. Analyze the strategies employed by the writer. The following questions may be helpful:
   - How does the writer's approach differ from the readings in this chapter?
   - How does the writer connect his or her own experience to potential readers?
   - Who is the audience for this text?
   - How does the audience impact the kinds of things said in the memoir?

3. Write at least three "Writing Strategies" questions for the text you found.

4. Write at least three "Exploring Ideas" questions for the text you found.

5. Write two "Ideas for Writing" questions, such as the ones following the essays in this book, for the text you found.

INVENTION

"I'm digging in the dirt / To find the places
I got hurt / To open up the places I got hurt."

—"Digging in the Dirt," Peter Gabriel

Invention is not simply about finding a topic. It also involves exploring and analyzing that topic, examining your thoughts, and developing points. For a remembering essay, the process will be self-reflective. It will begin with a personal exploration, but the broader goal is to discover something that others can share. The following three sections are designed to help you through invention: specifically, to discover a particular topic, situation, or event from your past (in Point of Contact), to develop points about the topic (in Analysis), and to make it relevant to a community of readers (in Public Resonance). The Invention questions in each section are not meant to be answered directly in your final written assignment. But using them to explore ideas will help you begin writing and keep intensive ideas flowing.

THESIS

Like any essay, one that is based on a personal experience should have a main point or *thesis*. And that point should reveal something to the writer and reader. It may be tempting to offer an overly broad statement about life, but more valuable statements will narrow in on a particular quality, situation, relationship, or layer of everyday life. The first broad statement in each set can be developed into more revelatory possibilities:

1. People are deeply influenced by their friends.
   - Friends develop our sense of ambition—what we want for ourselves.
   - Friends create the intellectual terrain of our past and present.
   - Friends mirror our own worldviews back to us.

2. Family is all that matters.
   - Our early struggles with brothers and sisters create the limitations we place on ourselves later in life.
   - As we grow into adulthood, our siblings keep alive the memory of our childhood selves.
   - Fathers create a sense of place, a sense of location that looms throughout our lives, even when we are spinning far out of control.

3. Teenage years are wild.
   - During adolescence, the world makes sense, even though that sense is a complete illusion.
   - A fourteen-year-old boy can barely contain all the energy coursing through his veins. He spends most of his time struggling to tame instincts that he cannot even name.
   - Before leaving our formative years, we might glimpse the best and worst habits we have acquired from our families . . . if we are lucky.

So how does someone go from a broad, flat statement to a revelatory idea? Intensive analysis! More intensive analysis always (not sometimes, but *always!*) leads to more intensive and focused statements. But when writers have difficulty expressing an intensive single statement, they can re-tool the specific words—the key verbs and nouns. Notice how the more intensive and revelatory statements often avoid linking verbs (*is, am, are, was, were,* and so on). Instead, they rely on active verbs (*develop, create, mirror, keep, glimpse*) to pull the reader's mind through ideas. So changing the verb in a sentence can actually prompt the writer to think differently, in more intensive ways.

Activity

With a small group of peers, create a broad, flat sentence, something that offers very little new insight. Then, from that sentence, develop three or more intense, focused, and insightful statements. In these more insightful statements, try to reveal something that normally goes ignored or that rarely gets considered. To create more insightful statements:

1. replace broad nouns with more specific nouns;
2. replace linking verbs with active verbs. Use adventurous or unusual verbs . . . and see where your mind goes.

creates an image in the reader's mind because of the shared knowledge about the Hooters uniform. Later, when Bosley refers to "the save-the-whales-and-rainforest civic-minded-ness required not only of Miss America, but of Junior Miss America, too," she quickly communicates an idea that without the allusion would take much longer to explain. Because the allusion is public knowledge, the writer connects with the reader because the reader feels that she, too, is *in on it*.

In considering your essay, ask yourself: Does my situation relate to any historical situations, figures, or events? Any popular culture figures or fictional characters?

Activity

With a small group of peers, discuss what is communicated by Bosley's allusion to *Flashdance* (¶ 5), Mirror-Mirror-on-the-Wall (¶ 6), Kmart leg warmers (¶ 16).

Dialogue

Dialogue is discussion between two or more people. Portraying dialogue in an essay can make an event or memory more real and engaging to the reader. Dialogue is most valuable when it is used to emphasize a main point in an essay, rather than simply to convey events. Conveying general events is better left to narration. But dialogue is useful when a particular exchange of words shows something significant.

Formatting for dialogue involves several steps:

- Use quotation marks before and after the actual spoken words.
- Put end punctuation (such as a period) inside the end quotation marks.
- Indent when a new speaker begins.

Integrating a speaker's words can be accomplished in several ways:

- Use a comma between the quotation and the speaking verb (*explained, asked, said, yelled, proclaimed,* etc.).

  Louisa asked, "What are we going to do now?"

- Use a colon before the speaker's words. In this case, the narrator usually forecasts the ideas or mood of the speaker in the sentence preceding the colon.

  I was clearly agitated by her accusation: "What the heck are you talking about?"

- Work the speaker's words directly into the grammar of your sentence.

  But Louisa was convinced that our decision would "hurt us either way."

See all of these rules operating in the following exchange:

"Come on in," Mr. Smith said.

"Hey, something smells great," I said as I walked into his lamp-lit living room. The small terrier looked up out of its lazy place on the sofa as Mr. Smith reached to get his wallet.

"Yep, I've been cookin' my chili again. It's Max's favorite." He gestured at the complacent blurry-eyed dog. "So, is the price of papers still the same?"

"Well, as far as I know, it's still $4.25 for the month." And then without considering the consequences, I asked the wrong question: "How have you been, Mr. Smith?" It took him 45 minutes to explain his "return to normal" after a long spell of stomach flu.

In this example, notice how attributive phrases (such as *he said*), which give ownership to the spoken words, are absent after the second indentation. Generally, after the dialogue pattern is established and the reader can easily tell who is speaking at each indentation, attributive phrases are unnecessary.

If you are considering dialogue for your essay, ask yourself: *How does the dialogue help to show something in support of the main idea?*

ORGANIZATIONAL STRATEGIES

What Details Should I Include?

Sometimes when we tell stories (especially our own), they take over, and we wander through irrelevant details. If this happens, you might consider two primary strategies: (1) leave out irrelevant details that distract the reader, and (2) emphasize those details that help illustrate your main idea. For instance, Schwind-Pawlak is selectively specific as she details her youth soccer experience. In her second paragraph, she provides a few precise details to illustrate that playing soccer was not important to her: "I often chose to run around the field with friends while my brothers and sisters performed feats of soccer, the likes of which had only been seen during the World Cup. I would happily contort my fingers into chubby pretzels while singing 'The Itsy Bitsy Spider' as the game's events were recounted on the drives home."

Next, Schwind-Pawlak shares important information her father told her about youth soccer:

> My father (a one-time soccer coach) explained several times that this was the time that I would learn the rules and workings of the game and that I shouldn't expect much more than that. Since it was a child's league, learning and the team experience were the focuses. Winning was a pleasant bonus but should not be achieved at the cost of the main objectives.

Her father probably told her many things about playing soccer, but she draws attention to this particular message because it is important to what happens later, when her mother reacts in a way that contradicts her father's talk.

In the following paragraph, Schwind-Pawlak summarizes the early part of the season. She made practice "a social occasion while going through the motions of the game"; she "began to enjoy the half game of playing time that was required by the league for each player"; and all the games "had been lost to this point." Sharing particulars about her socializing, about plays she made (or didn't make), and

detailing how each game had been lost could bog down the essay and distract the reader from the main point. As the fifth game of the season arrives (¶ 5), she slows down and focuses on more of the details.

As in Schwind-Pawlak's essay, details should add up to the main point. That is, as readers work through the text, gathering details along the way, they should be led to the main idea; they should, in fact, experience the deep complexity of living in a particular moment. And without those details, the reader will merely experience being told something about a distant time and place. As you consider your own narrative, think of the details that can help illustrate your point. If the moment is important, do not hold any detail back. If you were sitting in an alley, for instance, explain the color of the empty bottles and the smell of the damp brick. If you were standing in a classroom at the end of a day, explain the placement of the desks and the dying fern by the window. If you were swimming in a pond, explain how the weeds waved back and forth from the impact of your movements. But only focus on such particulars when they help get your reader closer to the main idea.

Ask yourself: What details from the past will help the reader to fully understand my point?

How Should I Begin?

As with any essay, introduction strategies are limitless. One strategy is to begin in the past, taking the readers back in time from the first sentence:

> Every evening of the annual broadcast of the Miss America Pageant, I, from the age of seven or so, carefully laid out an elaborate chart so that I might also participate as an independent judge of the most important beauty contest in the world. (Bosley)

Bosley begins narrating and waits to characterize or give meaning to the events until later in her essay. Still another option is to make a general statement about the subject, and then begin narrating events. Notice Schwind-Pawlak's strategy:

> Parents—one word that can strike many emotions in children when said aloud. Some children will smile and think about how silly their dad looked when he put carrot sticks up his nose that very morning, while others will cringe when they think about how their mother picked them up from school last week wearing orange polyester pants and a green shirt, oblivious to the hard work that some fellow went through to create the color wheel. My own emotional state of mind seemed to run the gamut throughout childhood. I chose to blame my parents for all of the traumatic events that unfolded but took pride in my obvious independence during the successes. One of the most heinous crimes that my parents committed was "the soccer foul." If I could have ejected them from the game of life at that point, I would have.

She begins with a statement that has public resonance; that is, she makes a point that readers can immediately share, and then integrates her own particular experience.

Activity

After writing an introduction for your essay, share it with two classmates (either in class or by e-mail). Each classmate should write an alternative introduction, using an entirely different strategy. Do the same for each classmate. After each writer has seen the others' alternatives to his or her introduction, discuss the strategies and decide if they might inspire changes.

How Should I Conclude?

Perhaps the most popular strategy for concluding a remembering essay is to explain the significance and/or public resonance in the last paragraph. Bosley ends her essay by explaining the importance of her memory, even suggesting that others can share the personal significance:

> It's a contest no one should want to win. Our mothers should not have such dreams for us. Our mothers should not have such loneliness.

Schwind-Pawlak explains the significance of her memory in her conclusion:

> The relationship that I have with my parents has changed very much throughout the years. The polyester pants don't bother me anymore, but the carrot sticks still make me laugh. While their "soccer foul" embarrassed and angered me at the time, I understand and appreciate it now. My mother was angry *FOR* me. She was hurt *FOR* me. Through the pages of time, I can look back and see that, more often than not, I embarrassed her. She never stopped feeling for me, loving me, or protecting me. I have grown enough to realize that, though I often pointed out my parent's fouls, they scored countless goals that I didn't even notice.

Activity

Share your conclusion with two classmates. How does each conclusion explain the significance and/or public resonance of the essay? How might the significance or public resonance be made more clear?

WRITER'S VOICE

A writer's voice characterizes the ideas in a text. It creates the mood in which the reader will approach the ideas. Imagine walking into a party and the host greets you at the door: "Hey! Look what the cat dragged in!" Her interaction would prompt you to assume that the party is fairly informal and festive. But the host could also greet you more soberly: "Hello. Please come in. May I take your coat?" In this case, her voice would lend formality to the affair. In other words, the host creates a particular mood for the incoming guests. Likewise, a writer creates the mood in which readers will enter the text. And this can be accomplished in a variety of ways.

Using Figurative Language

Figurative language is non-literal. It goes beyond words' basic definitions and uses them to suggest imaginative connections between ideas. Consider the following four strategies:

Metaphor A comparison of one thing to another in which one thing is made to share the characteristics of another: Her home was a sanctuary, where we felt healed spiritually and psychologically.

Simile A comparison of two seemingly unrelated things using *like* or *as:* Life is like a box of chocolates.

Similes and metaphors help create voice. For example, Forrest Gump's simile, above, fits with his uncomplicated and easygoing character. A box of chocolates is a simple, pleasant surprise, and so it equates with his character. (It certainly would not be fitting for Gump to say, "Life is like a raging volcanic explosion bursting forth from the fires of the earth.")

Jennifer Schwind-Pawlak's metaphors help create her voice:

At that moment I wasn't sure that I would ever be able to forgive my mother for what happened that day, but, as far as I can recall, I began loving her again within the week. I am sure that she either cooked my

favorite dinner, told a corny joke, or told me how much she loved me to make that lump of anger fade away.

Her anger is "a lump," not a mountain or a raging river. The smaller, more manageable, lump fits the mood of a child. We get the sense from her language that she is effectively over her childhood emotions.

Understatement A claim that is deliberately less forceful or dramatic than reality: Hurricanes tend to create a little wind.

Hyperbole A deliberate exaggeration: I'm so hungry, I could eat a horse.

These strategies lend a certain layer of informality to writing. That is, writers who are attempting to lay low, to remain seemingly invisible, or to write formally usually refrain from hyperbole and understatement.

Choosing Details

The details one chooses help create voice. Both Bosley and Schwind-Pawlak focus on their mothers, but they give different details. While Schwind-Pawlak's details are comedic and light, Bosley's details are serious. The details alone make the reader experience the memories and the writers differently:

Schwind-Pawlak:
Some children will smile and think about how silly their dad looked when he put carrot sticks up his nose that very morning, while others will cringe when they think about how their mother picked them up from school last week wearing orange polyester pants and a green shirt, oblivious to the hard work that some fellow went through to create the color wheel.

Bosley:

My mother had secret hopes. Finally divorced for the second time from the same man, my father, she sat with me and gave her own running commentary about who was cute, who smiled too much, who would find a handsome husband. My mother, having always been a little to a lot overweight, excelled at swimming, and she told me much later that she chose swimming because she didn't feel fat in the water. Her sister was the cheerleader, but she was a swimmer, too heavy for a short skirt of her own, she said.

In your own writing, how do you want to appear to the reader: darkly reflective, comfortable, learned, free-spirited? Your decision will influence what details you mention and what moments you emphasize. The details will affect how the reader understands you (as a writer) and the ideas you communicate. (This is a powerful lesson about writing: It not only conveys ideas but also shapes how people feel about those ideas.)

Using Sentence Length

Sentence structure is perhaps the most powerful, yet most invisible, tool a writer has for creating voice. Sentence length, specifically, can create a wide variety of different effects, depending on the context (or material surrounding the sentence). Long, winding sentences, which travel in and out of various ideas before returning the reader to the original path, can create a self-reflective and sophisticated voice, one that considers complexities. Short sentences can create a determined voice. Notice the difference between the following:

Childhood was a gas.

Childhood was a raucous journey of twists and turns in which each moment was its own forever and every day a monument.

While the metaphors help create distinct voices, the sentence length also helps characterize the writers.

Although sentence length alone does not automatically create voice, it figures into the process. Notice, again, Bosley's passage to the left and how the sentence length tugs and pulls at the reader. The first sentence is short—and because of the content, it is almost a whisper. The second, longer sentence takes the reader further into the idea. Both sentences, working together, create the sensation of a living person telling a story. The movement, the back and forth between long and short sentences, helps conjure the sense of a real human telling a real story. And the content of those sentences helps communicate the feelings and emotional complexities of that human.

A writer's voice characterizes the idea in a text. It creates the mood in which the reader will approach the ideas.

VITALITY

Vitality is life. Writing that has vitality keeps readers' minds awake and moving. Vitalized writing does not draw attention to itself with overly elaborate structures, but it does move the reader into and through ideas. When readers encounter vitalized writing, they may not know exactly what's happening, but they find themselves easily gliding along—almost disappearing into the text.

There are many strategies for sentence vitality, but applying even the three listed below can make a dramatic difference between flat, exhausted sentences and intensive, lively writing.

Combine Sentences

Sentences cue the reader. A period says, "Stop." A new sentence says, "Go." This stopping and starting helps create life. (Readers, like all humans, are drawn to pulsating movement.) But too many starts and stops keep readers from settling into ideas, so writers should combine sentences to keep readers gliding along.

Sentences can be combined with *coordination* (adding together clauses of equal importance):

> My father did not believe in such things for girls as shoes, clothes, haircuts, college, or photographs for Junior Miss, **and** so there was no way he was going to give a penny for a pageant-worthy dress or a professional photographer's 10-minutes-plus-proofs.

> I was starving for adult conversation, **but** with family and friends scattered across the country, I didn't feel like I could call back the troops.

> Mrs. Rath had an ability to recognize the kids that actually wanted to read and learn and, often times, would send a few of us down to the library where it was quiet **and** we could have some sanctuary from the usual classroom shenanigans.

The highlighted conjunctions in these sentences show where the writers joined ideas together. Information before and after the conjunctions is equal; the grammar cues the reader to give them equal intellectual weight.

Sentences also can be combined with *subordination* (making an idea less important than the main part of a sentence). Subordination involves tucking some ideas into others, creating the critical overlapping quality of good writing:

> For years it sat empty, the massive entrance looking out on Upton Avenue with no expression.

> As hoped for and expected, a figure appeared out of nowhere.

> Almost half a day later, around midnight, the train crunched into Chicago, where I hopped off, exhausted and exhilarated.

These examples of subordination show a variety of possibilities. Each sentence has a main clause (underlined), and other parts attached to it. Notice how the third sentence above, from Leonard Kress's "A Beat Education," would read differently if the ideas were separated into full sentences:

> Almost half a day later, around midnight, the train crunched into Chicago. I hopped off, and I felt exhausted and exhilarated.

Although the difference is small, this version creates more stops and starts for the reader. Those shorter separated ideas sometimes are valuable, but good writers subordinate less important information. Hopping off the train is necessary information for Kress's narrative, but it is not something readers need at the front of their minds. Kress thus subordinates the fact to other details.

Repeat Structures

Although readers need a variety of patterns, a constant change in length and structure, vitalized writing sometimes repeats key phrases or clauses. It is the writerly equivalent of pounding on a podium, driving a set of ideas at the audience:

> I never went to soccer again. As a matter of fact, I never played another organized sport again. Maybe it was the fear of rejection. Maybe it was the uncertainty of my talent. Maybe I was just too busy with other things.

> I'd lost the contest because I didn't yet know how to tell people what they wanted to hear. The small girl that boys secretly liked but wouldn't date doesn't win Miss America. The girl hiding in her room reading and writing poetry doesn't win Miss America. The girl playing the violin despite her mother's anxiousness that other people will think she's weird doesn't win Miss America. The girl on Willard Street doesn't ever win Miss America.

The repeating patterns here create a cyclical feel, making the reader return to the same feeling established at the start of each passage.

Intensify Verbs

Readers like intense verbs, those that create specific images of movement. It is easy to use weaker verbs, such as *is, was, are, were,* and so on. But such verbs do little to propel the reader's mind through ideas. In the following passages, the first from Leonard Kress and the others from essays in this chapter, notice the verb use:

> I couldn't open the can of beans I'd brought along, and the slices of bread I'd <u>stuffed</u> into my rucksack <u>fell</u> onto the floor and <u>coated</u> themselves in rust-flecked grease. The freight did, however, <u>grant</u> me a spectacular view of the setting sun as it <u>ambled</u> ever so slowly along the banks of Lake Michigan.

> I would happily <u>contort</u> my fingers into chubby pretzels while singing "The Itsy Bitsy Spider" as the game's events <u>were recounted</u> on the drives home.

> I <u>checked out</u> *Tortilla Flat* and *The Wayward Bus* from the library and <u>asked</u> Mrs. Rath what else he <u>wrote</u> and where I <u>could get</u> it. She <u>loaned</u> me her copy of "In Dubious Battle." Soon, I <u>wanted</u> to own all of Steinbeck's books. I <u>scoured</u> the bookstores to complete the collection, a collection that <u>has traveled</u> with me for 25 years.

The verbs in these sentences do more than point out the action of the world. They portray that action—a necessary quality of vital writing.

Vital writing does not merely describe action. It portrays the movement of the world.

PEER REVIEW

Your instructor may arrange for someone else to read your essay and for you to read someone else's. Or it may be up to you to arrange this on your own. Any interested person can provide helpful feedback, but working with a conscientious classmate may be especially helpful—to both of you. Peer review can be done in various ways. Your instructor may provide specific guidelines and, of course, you are always free to try different approaches outside the classroom. Some general advice, however, can be given to ensure that you work efficiently and get positive results.

The writer should

- Provide the reader with a readable copy of the rough draft.
- Help to focus the reader by asking questions about several major concerns you have. Write down your questions, wording them carefully.

The reader should

- Carefully read the draft at least twice, and then respond in writing (not just verbally) to the writer's main concerns.
- Be specific. In addition to saying what you think, say why you think it.
- Be encouraging *and* honest. Providing only praise will not help the writer, yet phrasing your comments in too negative terms might be discouraging.

1. Write down your overall impression of the essay.
2. Write down a summary of the writer's main points. (For example, instead of saying, "I understood what you were saying," say, "I think you were saying. . . ." Then, if the writer was not trying to say that at all, he or she knows that in this case the point was not successfully communicated.)
3. Write down specific responses to the writer's questions about the essay.
4. Write down any major concerns that you feel the writer should have raised but didn't.

The writer should

- Not defend your essay, but instead view it as a work in progress.
- Listen carefully, ask questions only to clarify what the reviewer means, take notes on *all* verbal comments for later reference, and thank the reader for his or her help.
- Later, carefully consider all comments and make only the changes that you consider to be appropriate.

You might do peer review face to face, discussing the papers as you go; or you might read and write comments without any verbal discussion between writer and reader. You might even do peer review over the Internet. If you are pressed for time, or if you have difficulty staying focused on the work at hand, exchanging written comments without discussion can be an efficient peer review strategy.

Peer Review Truisms

- **The process can make writers think differently about their own work.** Humans are great modelers. We model our behavior after others, and we make all kinds of subtle changes to our thinking when we read others' work. As modelers, peer reviewers can discover new approaches to an assignment, new writerly moves, new patterns of thinking, or new strategies for creating an engaging voice. (Reviewers can also discover qualities that they want to avoid in their own writing. They might discover some sentence or organization patterns and try to avoid them!)

- **Even the most inexperienced writer can offer valuable comments.** Some people believe that they have little to offer: "I'm not the teacher!" they'll announce. However, peer review is not about pointing out wrongs and rights. It's about reading closely and responding as a thoughtful human in a shared situation. If you can read and focus your attention, you can be a valuable reviewer. In fact, fellow students may even have more to offer one another because they're in a similar situation—faced with a similar task, experiencing the same pressures, at the same moment, in the same place.

- **Chat is the great enemy of good analysis.** Some instructors may set up sessions so that writers can converse about their drafts. Such sessions can be valuable and engaging—even intense and animated. But the danger is that they can devolve into chat sessions about the topics (or something else!). While chatting about one's topic is helpful (and can be worked into a class), a focused and intensive peer review session has its own kind of value.

- **Peer review can be the most valuable component of a writing class.** Writing in college is a social occasion. An academic essay (or any writing assignment) is an intersection of writers, instructors, and students. Peer review brings that to life. It makes the interaction of thinkers real and dramatic. When reviewers take the process seriously, it increases the value of the experience.

- **All writers need help.** Even the best of the best writers rely on the insights and assistance of others. Name a great writer from the past or the present (Steinbeck? Tolkien? Morrison? Dillard?). Each used the ideas and thoughts of others to help shape their projects and even their sentences.

- **Done carelessly, peer review can be a terrible thing.** If peer reviewers read drafts quickly and only point to small, surface-level issues, they waste their partners' time. It is a similar waste if they read for "agreement" and "disagreement"—simply looking for passages they agree or disagree with—and then announce their approval or disapproval of certain points.

After you exchange drafts with another writer, use the following questions to guide your review:

1. How does the essay prompt you to think differently? (For instance, do you see something with more complexity, more beauty, more ugliness, or more intensity than you did before reading? Explain, specifically, what the essay helps you to see differently. If you have a difficult time answering this question, perhaps the essay has not yet gone far enough.)

2. Point to any clichés (or statements that you've heard many times) that the writer can rethink.

3. Which details best illustrate the main idea? (Which details make you picture something specific and reinforce the main idea?)

4. Which details could be added to illustrate the main idea? (What particular behaviors or events could be further dramatized with details?) For instance, the essay probably has a focused moment—a specific event that holds intense meaning. Could that moment use more detail?

5. Which details do not seem related to the thesis of the essay? Why not?

6. How could the writer create more public resonance? (Refer to the Public Resonance section of this chapter.)

7. Are the paragraphs *coherent*? Or do you get the sense that a paragraph is merely wandering through the past, giving details that seem to hold more meaning for the writer than for the point of the essay?

8. How could the writer begin the essay with more intensity? (For instance, if the writer begins with a broad statement about children, such as *Children are curious creatures,* the writer could instead begin with his or her narrative or with a more surprising and focused statement.)

9. Describe the writer's voice. Is it consistent and appropriate? Could the writer use details or metaphors that are more fitting (more comedic or sobering)? What about sentence length? Where do you feel the voice flatten out (get boring!) because of overly consistent sentence length?

10. Focus on sentence vitality. Point to sentences that could be rewritten to create more vitality. Use the following to help guide your attention:

    - Where can the writer combine sentences with coordination?

    - Where can the writer combine with subordination?

    - Help the writer intensify the action with more sensory verbs.

    - Help the writer avoid common grammatical errors: comma splices, sentence fragments, or pronoun/antecedent agreement.

DELIVERY

Any act of writing is an act of creation. And the act of creation, say many philosophers, is the greatest act of humanity, the single act that announces to the world that an individual exists . . . here, in this place, in this time. An academic essay is no different. It is a record of intellectual life within a particular culture.

Consider Cindy Bosley's essay. While it recounts the details of a beauty pageant in Ottumwa, it also chronicles the nature of working-class life in the Great Plains during the late 20th century. It shows what people at the time valued, how they imagined themselves, how they treated others in their community, how they yearned to be different, how they celebrated what they might be. Beyond the narrow focus of Bosley's essay, in the margins of the narrative, we learn about a type of desperation running through the town. Behind the pageantry of civil life is a bigger, less made-up human drama, involving cocaine, factory work, isolation, distinct social classes, and the desperate attempts at concealing it all. This is the hidden, quiet, unperformed life that surrounds Bosley's memory.

Consider other essays in the chapter:

- What does Staples' essay reveal about the relationship between individual existence and public space?
- Based on Schwind-Pawlak's essay, what are children supposed to believe about themselves?

Now that you have spent many hours generating an essay, crafting your ideas for a particular audience, what does your essay say about you—as an individual human being living in a particular society within the giant wash of history? How is your essay an artifact of its time? What does it reveal about American life in the late 20th/early 21st century? Look beyond the essay's main idea, at the particulars layered throughout the essay.

Beyond the Essay

An *autobiography* is an account of a person's life, told by that person. A *biography* is an account of a person's life told by someone else. While we generally think of biographies as written works, films or television shows can also be *biographical*. For example, each weekend the television series "Biography" on A&E gives an account of a series of events making up a person's life. Films, too, such as *Ali* or *Ray,* tell a person's life story by relating a series of events.

Biographies and autobiographies are like remembering essays in that they do not merely report what happened. Instead, they present certain events in a particular light so as to tell a story or make a point. For example, two different biographies of Muhammad Ali might present him quite differently. One might show him as a great American hero by focusing on his role as an activist or humanitarian. The other might show him as a great heavyweight boxer, focusing on his career as a fighter. Both biographies could be accurate and interesting, yet very different. The selection and arrangement of details would present two different Alis.

- Consider one biography or autobiography you have read. How did it make a particular point by presenting certain events or details of a person's life?
- Consider one biographical or autobiographical television show or movie you have seen. How did it make a particular point by presenting certain events or details of a person's life?

Any act of writing is an act of creation.

EXPLAINING RELATIONSHIPS

Chapter Contents

CHAPTER 3

"The human beings depended on the aid and charity of the animals. Only through interdependence could the human beings survive. Families belonged to clans, and it was by the clan that the human being joined with the animal and plant world. Life on the high arid plateau became viable when the human beings were able to imagine themselves as sisters and brothers to the badger, antelope, clay, yucca, and sun. Not until they could find a viable relationship to the terrain, the landscape they found themselves in, could they emerge."

—Leslie Marmon Silko

In the above passage, from "Landscape, History, and the Pueblo Imagination," Silko explains the conceptual and physical relationship between the pueblo Native Americans and their surrounding landscape. It was a subtle and complex relationship, one that went far beyond harvesting crops and extracting resources. The land, for the Pueblo people, helped them to know who they were; it helped them to have a particular identity and culture. Silko's explanation sheds light on this particular relationship.

Explaining relationships is common daily work: People on city councils explore the relationship between neighborhoods to help their cities better understand ethnic diversity; corporate executives constantly try to understand the relationship between their own companies and their competitors; and certainly, everyone is aware of the ongoing attempts by political leaders to explain the relationships between countries or regions. In a shrinking world in which people of vastly different value systems attempt to coexist, explaining relationships is more than an exercise—it is an act of survival. It might even be argued that the greatest philosophical and scientific discoveries have involved the discovery of relationships—between, for example, atomic elements, religious practices, geological events, historical figures, or heavenly bodies.

In all academic disciplines, people work to understand and communicate the nature of relationships:

- In a computer technology course, students study the relationship between an individual computer and a network of computers, or between a group of users and the Internet.

- In an anthropology course, students explore the relationship between a particular waterway and the ruins of a past civilization.

- In a biology course, students and faculty work to see the relationship between two forms of bacteria.

- In an interior design course, students examine the relationship between a large interior office space and a front entrance to a particular building.

This chapter explores relationships—between places, things, events, people, even ideas. The goal here is to investigate, to seek out some of the hidden dynamics of relationships, to discover the nature of a relationship, or to discover a relationship where one is not necessarily seen.

This chapter will help you discover a topic (a particular relationship), explore that relationship in depth, and explain the nature of the relationship in writing. The following essays will provide valuable insight and necessary strategies for exploring relationships. After reading the essays, you can begin looking for a particular relationship in one of two ways:

1. Go to the Point of Contact section to find a relationship from everyday life. **or**

2. Choose one of the Ideas for Writing that follow the essays.

After finding a topic, go to the Analysis section to begin developing the evaluation.

Americans and the Land

John Steinbeck

In John Steinbeck's novels, such as *The Grapes of Wrath* and *Of Mice and Men,* the setting is a vital element of the stories. Steinbeck often draws attention to the ways in which the land influences people's lives. In this essay, from *America and Americans,* Steinbeck focuses on the American settlers' impact on the land. Notice that the land, here, is not something to simply live *on* or even *from.* Instead, it is something to live *with*—or, in the case of many early Americans, to live *against.* As with so many of his novels and stories, this essay invites readers to see the relationship that people cultivate with the world around them.

I have often wondered at the savagery and thoughtlessness with which our early settlers approached this rich continent. They came at it as though it were an enemy, which of course it was. They burned the forests and changed the rainfall; they swept the buffalo from the plains, blasted the streams, set fire to the grass, and ran a reckless scythe through the virgin and noble timber. Perhaps they felt that it was limitless and could never be exhausted and that a man could move on to new wonders endlessly. Certainly there are many examples to the contrary, but to a large extent the early people pillaged the country as though they hated it, as though they held it temporarily and might be driven off at any time.

This tendency toward irresponsibility persists in very many of us today; our rivers are poisoned by reckless dumping of sewage and toxic industrial wastes, the air of our cities is filthy and dangerous to breathe from the belching of uncontrolled products from combustion of coal, coke, oil, and gasoline. Our towns are girdled with wreckage and the debris of our toys—our automobiles and our packaged pleasures. Through uninhibited spraying against one enemy we have destroyed the natural balances our survival requires. All these evils can and must be overcome if America and Americans are to survive; but many of us still conduct ourselves as our ancestors did, stealing from the future for our clear and present profit.

Since the river-polluters and the air-poisoners are not criminal or even bad people, we must presume that they are heirs to the early conviction that sky and water are unowned and that they are limitless. In the light of our practices here at home it is very interesting to me to read of the care taken with the carriers of our probes into space, to make utterly sure that they are free of pollution of any kind. We would not think of doing to the moon what we do every day to our own dear country.

When the first settlers came to America and dug in on the coast, they huddled in defending villages hemmed in by the sea on one side and by endless forests on the other, by Red Indians and, most frightening, the mystery of an unknown land extending nobody knew how far. And for a time very few cared or dared to find out. Our first Americans organized themselves and lived in a state of military alertness; every community built its blockhouse for defense. By law the men went armed and were required to keep their weapons ready and available. Many of them wore armor, made here or imported; on the East Coast, they wore the cuirass and helmet, and the Spaniards on the West Coast wore both steel armor and heavy leather to turn arrows.

5   On the East Coast, and particularly in New England, the colonists farmed meager lands close to their communities and to safety. Every man was permanently on duty for the defense of his family and his village; even the hunting parties went into the forest in force, rather like raiders than hunters, and their subsequent quarrels with the Indians, resulting in forays and even massacres, remind us that the danger was very real. A man took his gun along when he worked the land, and the women stayed close to their thick-walled houses and listened day and night for the signal of alarm. The towns they settled were permanent, and most of them exist today with their records of Indian raids, of slaughter, of scalpings, and of punitive counter-raids. The military leader of the community became the chief authority in time of trouble, and it was a long time before danger receded and the mystery could be explored.

After a time, however, brave and forest-wise men drifted westward to hunt, to trap, and eventually to bargain for the furs which were the first precious negotiable wealth America produced for trade and export. Then trading posts were set up as centers of collection and the exploring men moved up and down the rivers and crossed the mountains, made friends for mutual profit with the Indians, learned the wilderness techniques, so that these explorer-traders soon dressed, ate, and generally acted like the indigenous people around them. Suspicion lasted a long time, and was fed by clashes sometimes amounting to full-fledged warfare; but by now these Americans attacked and defended as the Indians did.

For a goodly time the Americans were travelers, moving about the country collecting its valuables, but with little idea of permanence; their roots and their hearts were in the towns and the growing cities along the eastern edge. The few who stayed, who lived among the Indians, adopted their customs and some took Indian wives and were regarded as strange and somehow treasonable creatures. As for their half-breed children, while the tribe sometimes adopted them they were unacceptable as equals in the eastern settlements.

Then the trickle of immigrants became a stream, and the population began to move westward—not to grab and leave but to settle and live, they thought. The newcomers were of peasant stock, and they had their roots in a Europe where they had been landless, for the possession of land was the requirement and the proof of a higher social class than they had known. In America they found beautiful and boundless land for the taking—and they took it.

It is little wonder that they went land-mad, because there was so much of it. They cut and burned the forests to make room for crops; they abandoned their knowledge of kindness to the land in order to maintain its usefulness. When they had cropped out a piece they moved on, raping the country like invaders. The topsoil, held by roots and freshened by leaf-fall, was left helpless to the spring freshets, stripped and eroded with the naked bones of clay and rock exposed. The destruction of the forests changed the rainfall, for the searching clouds could find no green and beckoning woods to draw them on and milk them. The merciless nineteenth century was like a hostile expedition for loot that seemed limitless. Uncountable buffalo were killed, stripped of their hides, and left to rot, a reservoir of permanent food supply eliminated. More than that, the land of the Great Plains was robbed of the manure of the herds. Then the plows went in and ripped off the protection of the buffalo grass and opened the help-less soil to quick water and slow drought and the mischievous winds that roamed through the Great Central Plains. There has always been more than enough desert in America; the new settlers, like overindulged children, created even more.

10   The railroads brought new hordes of land-crazy people, and the new Americans moved like locusts across the continent until the western sea put a boundary to their movements. Coal and copper and gold drew them on; they savaged the land, gold-dredged the rivers to skeletons of pebbles and debris. An aroused and fearful government made laws for the distribution of public lands—a quarter section, one hundred and sixty acres, per person—and a claim had to be proved and improved; but there were ways of getting around this, and legally. My own grandfather proved out a quarter section for himself, one for his wife, one for each of his children, and, I suspect, acreage for children he hoped and expected to have. Marginal lands, of course, suitable only for grazing, went in larger pieces. One of the largest land-holding families in California took its richest holdings by a trick: By law a man could take up all the swamp or water-covered land he wanted. The founder of this great holding mounted a scow on wheels and drove his horses over thousands of acres of the best bottomland, then reported that he had explored it in a boat, which was true, and confirmed his title. I need not mention his name; his descendants will remember.

Another joker with a name still remembered in the West worked out a scheme copied many times in after years. Proving a quarter section required a year of residence and some kind of improvement—a fence, a shack—but once the land was proved the owner was free to sell it. This particular princely character went to the stews and skid rows of the towns and found a small army of hopeless alcoholics who lived for whisky and nothing else. He put these men on land he wanted to own, grubstaked them and kept them in cheap liquor until the acreage was proved, then went through the motions of buying it from his protégés and moved them and their one-room shacks on sled runners on to new quarter sections. Bums of strong constitution might prove out five or six homesteads for this acquisitive hero before they died of drunkenness.

It was full late when we began to realize that the continent did not stretch out to infinity; that there were limits to the indignities to which we could subject it. Engines and heavy mechanical equipment were allowing us to ravage it even more effectively than we had with fire, dynamite, and gang plows. Conservation came to us slowly, and much of it hasn't arrived yet. Having killed the whales and wiped out the sea otters and most of the beavers, the market hunters went to work on game birds; ducks and quail were decimated, and the passenger pigeon eliminated. In my youth I remember seeing a market hunter's gun, a three-gauge shotgun bolted to a frame and loaded to the muzzle with shingle nails. Aimed at a lake and the trigger pulled with a string, it slaughtered every living thing on the lake. The Pacific Coast pilchards were once the raw material for a great and continuing industry. We hunted them with aircraft far at sea until they were gone and the canneries had to be closed. In some of the valleys of the West, where the climate makes several crops a year available, which the water supply will not justify, wells were driven deeper and deeper for irrigation, so that in one great valley a million acre feet more of water was taken out than rain and melting snow could replace, and the water table went down and a few more years may give us a new desert.

The great redwood forests of the western mountains early attracted attention. These ancient trees, which once grew everywhere, now exist only where the last Ice Age did not wipe them out. And they were found to have value. The Sempervirens and the Gigantea, the two remaining species, make soft, straight-grained timber. They are easy to split into planks, shakes, fenceposts, and railroad ties, and they have a unique virtue: they resist decay, both wet and dry rot, and an inherent acid in them repels termites. The loggers went through the great groves like a barrage, toppling the trees—some of which were two thousand years old—and leaving no maidens, no seedlings or saplings on the denuded hills.

Quite a few years ago when I was living in my little town on the coast of California a stranger came in and bought a small valley where the Sempervirens redwoods grew, some of them three hundred feet high. We used to walk among these trees, and the light colored as though the great glass of the Cathedral at Chartres had strained and sanctified the sunlight. The emotion we felt in this grove was one of awe and humility and joy; and then one day it was gone, slaughtered, and the sad wreckage of boughs and broken saplings left like nonsensical spoilage of the battle-ruined countryside. And I remember that after our rage there was sadness, and when we passed the man who had done this we looked away, because we were ashamed for him.

15   From early times we were impressed and awed by the fantastic accidents of nature, like the Grand Canyon and Yosemite and Yellowstone Park. The Indians had revered them as holy places, visited by the gods, and all of us came to have somewhat the same feeling about them. Thus we set aside many areas of astonishment as publicly owned parks; and though this may to a certain extent have been because there was no other way to use them, as the feelings of preciousness of the things we had been destroying grew in Americans, more and more areas were set aside as national and state parks, to be looked at but not injured. Many people loved and were in awe of the redwoods; societies and individuals bought groves of these wonderful trees and presented them to the state for preservation.

No longer do we Americans want to destroy wantonly, but our new-found sources of power—to take the burden of work from our shoulders, to warm us, and cool us, and give us light, to transport us quickly, and to make the things we use and wear and eat—these power sources spew pollution on our country, so that the rivers and streams are becoming poisonous and lifeless. The birds die for the lack of food; a noxious cloud hangs over our cities that burns our lungs and reddens our eyes. Our ability to conserve has not grown with our power to create, but this slow and sullen poisoning is no longer ignored or justified. Almost daily, the pressure of outrage among Americans grows. We are no longer content to destroy our beloved country. We are slow to learn; but we learn. When a super-highway was proposed in California which would trample the redwood trees in its path, an outcry arose all over the land, so strident and fierce that the plan was put aside. And we no longer believe that a man, by owning a piece of America, is free to outrage it.

But we are an exuberant people, careless and destructive as active children. We make strong and potent tools and then have to use them to prove that they exist. Under the pressure of war we finally made the atom bomb, and for reasons which seemed justifiable at the time we dropped it on two Japanese cities—and I think we finally frightened ourselves. In such things, one must consult himself because there is no other point of reference. I did not know about the bomb, and certainly I had nothing to do with its use, but I am horrified and ashamed; and nearly everyone I know feels the same thing. And those who loudly and angrily justify Hiroshima and Nagasaki—why, they must be the most ashamed of all.

Writing Strategies

1. Evaluate Steinbeck's opening paragraph. How does it function? Does it state or imply the main idea? How does it establish Steinbeck's voice? Does it invite the reader into the essay? If so, how?

2. Throughout the essay, Steinbeck describes detailed situations (anecdotes) that illustrate his point. Which of these are the most effective?

3. In paragraph 10, Steinbeck describes the people that the railroad brought west as "land-crazy" and says they moved "like locusts." Identify other expressions he uses to describe the people. Which expressions are especially effective?

4. Describe Steinbeck's voice. Is his essay inviting to the reader, or does it put the reader off? Support your response with specific references to the text.

5. Describe Steinbeck's conclusion. Where does he end up—that is, where does he ultimately take the reader? Is his conclusion effective or not?

Exploring Ideas

1. What does Steinbeck say about Americans and the land? What is he trying to accomplish in this essay?

2. What does your response to the reading tell you about the way that you view "the land" or "the environment"?

3. What is your relationship with the land? What everyday actions of your own have a positive impact on the land? What everyday actions of your own have a negative impact on the land?

4. Observe the way land is used in your community. Take field notes. Then organize the information you have collected into two categories: observations that support what Steinbeck says, and observations that refute what he says.

Ideas for Writing

1. What is the relationship between Americans and the land today?

2. Describe your relationship with your immediate surroundings (your house, bedroom, apartment, dorm, etc.). How is it typical (or not typical) of your broader attitude concerning the relationship of humans to the land?

3. Discuss your observations (Exploring Ideas #4) with others, looking for ways that you might participate in Steinbeck's discussion of Americans and the land. How might you contribute to this discussion? What idea, for example, could use further explanation or clarification?

If responding to one of these ideas, go to the Analysis section of this chapter to begin developing ideas for your essay.

Mugged

Jim Crockett

Jim Crockett, a Spanish instructor, songwriter, farmer, and carpenter, has been drinking coffee for 48 years. As with millions of other Americans, coffee is fused to his everyday life. In this essay, Crockett focuses on a particular part of his relationship with coffee. But the essay goes far beyond his personal rituals and habits. It reveals something about the "small behaviors we cling to," and the size and scope of those seemingly simplistic habits that create meaning and familiarity.

I have been mugged. Not accosted as I walk to my parked truck across a dark lot; not waylaid by thugs in the night. But mugged, nevertheless. I have been mugged by insinuation, by the insertion into my life of a cylindrical drinking vessel: one that holds coffee. I have been mugged by a to-go cup.

The relationship, or mugging, that has developed with my coffee mug is one-sided and is, because a mug's needs are simple, an easy relationship to maintain. Oh, I rinse and wipe it out every morning, and occasionally wash it with detergent, but these are minimal maintenance requirements, ones easily met. So why, if all this object does is simply hold coffee, would I consider our relationship worthy of the time and effort spent in its exploration and explication? Why would I seek depth of meaning in a seemingly superficial attachment to such a mundane object? Maybe the very mundanity of the object, the very quotidian nature of the relationship, deepens the attachment, suggests that the relationship goes symbolically deeper, symptomatically deeper, than I think.

In exchange for its minimal upkeep, my coffee mug gives back much more than it takes. Its secure lid keeps my mustache drip-free and, therefore, my books, shirts, and papers clean. My mug is insulated so it delivers hot, delicious, organically shade-grown, fair trade coffee for a couple of hours at a time, and in so doing, helps me directly support the small coffee growers and their cooperatives around the world. It is also an environmentally friendly mug. When I buy a cup of coffee, I only buy coffee: the paper cup and insulating sleeve, both little bits of tree, remain in the store. I remain weaned from dependence upon the earth- and human-pillaging multinational coffee cartel.

Wrought in stainless steel and plastic, this bit of industrial-designer paraphernalia (it holds my drug of choice) is every cup holder's dream. Its shape, curvaceous, tapered, slim-waisted and a bit heavier on top, is designed to fit cup holders in most vehicles, while being a natural-feeling extension of the human hand; or, in my case, a necessary adjunct to, a logical appurtenance thereof. My coffee cup is in my hand a lot.

5   In fact, when it is not in my hand, when I misplace it momentarily, or when, like the other day, I leave it on the bumper of my truck and see a flash in the rearview mirror as my mug goes airborne into the filthy slush of the winter street, I feel a twinge of separation anxiety. When I stop traffic to rescue it from the gutter after a close call with a Chevy Suburban, impatient and angry faces glare through wiper-slapped windshields to remind me that the small choices we make, the small behaviors we cling to, affect the way in which we are perceived in the world.

I worry, at times, when students and colleagues ask how much coffee I drink, or say they've never seen me without my coffee mug, that my attachment to my little friend is symptomatic of some neurosis or other, or that it indicates an obsessive/compulsive disorder. I don't, however, worry for long. Because, even though my mug is always nearby, whether on the lectern or table in front of the classroom, in the cup holder on the dashboard of my truck, on the desk where I am writing this essay, or just dangling from my hand, all it really signifies is an addiction to caffeine and the need, because I am human, for some small and securing daily grounding ritual. In an *econoculture* so far removed from its agrarian and wilderness roots, from its time-worn rituals of life, my coffee mug provides a needed, however tiny, bit of continuity in my daily doings, a small tie to place and home.

Writing Strategies

1. How does the connotation of *mugged* impact your reading of the essay? How does the idea add to Crockett's point about his own relationship with coffee?

2. Although this essay focuses primarily on Crockett's personal relationship, how does it make broader, more public, points? What particular passages or sentences pull the reader beyond Crockett's personal situation?

3. Describe Crockett's voice. How does word choice impact the "sound" of his voice?

4. In his conclusion, Crockett characterizes the society around him as an *econoculture*. What idea is he creating with that term? How does it resonate with other passages or points in this essay?

5. What is Crockett's most compelling rhetorical move?

Exploring Ideas

1. Crockett claims that humans need "some small and securing daily grounding ritual." What is a grounding ritual? Do you think it is, indeed, a fundamental human need?

2. Some sociologists, psychologists, and writers claim that the small moments in everyday life tell us the most about human behavior. Does this seem like a fair claim? In considering your own life, your own habits, is it true?

3. Why do people "cling" to their own habits?

4. Some historians have noted that the arrival of coffee and tea in medieval Europe could have been primary catalysts of the Renaissance. Caffeine, they say, woke up Europe. To what extent does caffeine impact our present culture—or your own ability to participate in the *econoculture*?

Ideas for Writing

1. What is the most consistent daily ritual in your life? What does it reveal about your identity?

2. What common ritual do you share with millions of others?

3. Crockett says, "Maybe the very mundanity of the object, the very quotidian nature of the relationship, deepens the attachment, suggests that the relationship goes symbolically deeper, symptomatically deeper, than I think." What mundane object is symbolically, symptomatically fused to your identity?

If responding to one of these ideas, go to the Analysis section of this chapter to begin developing ideas for your essay.

Political Adaptation

Daniel P. Doezema

Daniel Doezema wrote this essay for his first-semester composition course. One of the options on the assignment asked students to explore a three-way relationship. Doezema chose to examine the dynamics among his girlfriend's father, himself, and politics. In this sense, Doezema reminds us that interpersonal relationships are often far more complex than we think: They are not merely about the two people involved. Often, another entity—in this case, politics—sits in the room and animates what is said, what is not said. As Doezema explains, relationships like this are a kind of "dance."

Writing Strategies

Mention of the war creates immediate public resonance.

Immediately, we're introduced to the participants in this relationship—and even the political/spatial relations.

The paragraph shifts for each new speaker.

The television has its own paragraph—as though it's a speaker, a participant, which it is.

It's a normal summer day, deep blue sky with two clouds carelessly floating by, very hot and humid. Outside I can hear crickets and cars passing by in the distance. The noise outside is muffled by the constant drone of fans in every window, trying in vain to relieve the stress of the day. The television is talking in the front room of the house, dominating any conversation to be had. Talk of Iraq, still no weapons of mass destruction, and more violence in the country.

I sit uncomfortably, my arms and legs stuck to the leather couch as I change positions. I can hear my girlfriend, Amanda, walking across the floor upstairs, getting ready to go into town. A few feet to my right is her father, Larry, who's sitting on a chair watching the television while occasionally looking through a newspaper that had been hastily refolded and left out from the day before. His face shows no signs of surprise or frustration, but rather, he seems calm and unfazed by the recent developments.

I start to talk in a frustrated tone, "This is ridiculous. We're stuck there because Bush lied to us!"

Larry's attention immediately shifts from the television to me. I can tell my anger has struck a chord with Larry by the annoyed expression starting to form across his face. He pauses for a few long seconds before finally leaning in to talk. "Bush acted on the information he was given and, besides, Saddam was a bad guy. He tortured people. We did the right thing by going in there," he says in a firm defensive tone.

5   The television's voice seems silent now—the humidity replaced by growing tension and anger.

I fire back, "There was much more intelligence stating there were no weapons, and he chose to ignore it. There are a million 'bad guys' in this world that we actually know 100% have nukes. . . ."

Exploring Ideas

This is a normal situation. Nothing spectacular—something that we all might experience.

Is it coincidence that Larry's to "the right" of Daniel? (This is, after all, about political adaptation.)

They're both repeating the mantras and commonplaces of their political positions.

Now, we get to the main point about this relationship.

Nice dramatic strategy: The initial outdoor noises come back into play after Amanda pulls the two out of their brief duel.

The entire conversation is dramatized—to illustrate the thesis of the essay.

The most explicit move to create public resonance: He connects the specific situation to broader social tension.

Some good analysis here, where the writer reveals some important complexity that drives the relationship.

"We'll go after them too!" he quickly remarks. The conversation starts to turn into something else, not an argument, something more personal. The mutual respect for one another is momentarily lost, seemingly dashed away by the intense winds of disagreement in political viewpoints and opinions.

Amanda can hear the yelling and tries to diffuse the conversation. "What are you boys yelling about," she says from upstairs in a half-joking way. It hits both of us at that moment. We realize that our disagreement is stirring up emotions of unease and strain in the others around us. The room is silent. The sounds of the fans and television start to move toward the foreground, the long arching shrill of a cicada can be heard from outside.

With Larry's attention redirected by Amanda, he slowly leans back into the chair, letting out a muffled sigh. Looking away toward the window, he says in low and uncaring tone, "Whatever, it was the right thing to do."

10   I pause for a moment while trying to collect myself, trying to suppress the feelings of anger and frustration. Slowly I stand up and start walking toward the front door. Underneath my breath I slowly tell Larry, "Yeah, whatever."

The country as a whole seems to be at this point, unable to hold a reasonable discussion on political views without a heated argument. Families and friends become polarized on issues. Middle ground rapidly erodes away. Emotionally charged arguments take place across the nation that only serve to isolate Americans from one another. An atmosphere has taken hold in which we either support the party or become an enemy of the party, and in both cases, we're considered *un-American*. A team mentality replaces reason. Being on the winning side means being right without question or cause.

The relationship between Larry and me has suffered in some ways because of our political views. Our different backgrounds may have lead to these views. I was raised in a city setting for all of my life. Rarely did I ever venture out into the rural areas around Traverse City, MI; for the most part I was sheltered. My parents are both moderates and always taught me to ask questions of authority, regardless of political party or affiliation. Larry, however, was raised in a very rural setting in Acme, MI. He's been hunting since he was a child, and has been a truck driver for over 25 years. We are from different generations. He was born in 1952 and I was born in 1983, a 31-year difference. These aspects of our lives give Larry and me very little common ground or experiences we can share.

What's more personal than an argument? He's pointing to a destructive kind of interaction— something that they *could* fall into.

They try to reinforce their points, sliding in one last jab.

Doezema acknowledges the very tension that he enacts. (Are others willing to do this? Are they able?)

How much does generation and geography impact political positioning?

An important transition—
from difference to com-
monality.

Despite all of our differences, which would normally drive most people apart, we have managed to maintain a fully functioning and meaningful relationship. We've found our common ground built around family, and it's the most powerful tie in our relationship, what allows it to persevere. Still, it can be difficult to judge when to let things go or when a comment may have crossed a line. We both feel strongly about our views and can't help but get vocal about them occasionally. We are careful not to let political issues consume us. Extra effort is put forth by both of us in trying to skirt around potentially explosive topics. At times, our relationship allows us the flexibility to express our own views, to disagree, and even argue. Other times, it is best to let the differences in our political views fade and be forgotten, so that we can enjoy activities that bring us together, like a backyard bonfire or a canoe run down the Platte River.

Our relationship emphasizes how political differences don't have to dictate the functionality of a relationship. In the end, Larry and I may never agree on the political issues, but we know the people in our lives get us past the disagreements or hostilities.

They are "careful," but it seems not too careful at times. (Amanda's presence may have saved them earlier.)

Fair enough. But what if there is no Amanda between political positions? (What then?)

The country as a whole seems to be at this point, unable to hold a reasonable discussion on political views without a heated argument.

Writing Strategies

1. How does the introduction function in this essay? Why do the physical details of the setting matter?

2. Narratives are often told in past tense, but Doezema's essay begins in present tense. How does the verb tense figure into the overall point of the essay?

3. How does Doezema create public resonance? What particular passages seem most important?

4. In describing his exchange with Larry, Doezema says, "The conversation starts to turn into something else, not an argument, something more personal." How would you describe this move? Rhetorically, what's Doezema doing here? What does he want us to think?

5. Doezema's thesis seems to come in the conclusion. How does this placement work? Why is it a logical or illogical place for the main idea?

Exploring Ideas

1. Why are people like Doezema and Larry so passionate about the Iraq war? (Why has the Iraq war divided so many people in the United States?)

2. Some experts on etiquette advise not to bring up politics or religion in "polite company." Why? What is so offensive or dangerous or impolite about these topics?

3. Teachers throughout the country have explained that their students get angry, hostile, or indignant when the Iraq war comes up in class. Therefore, they avoid the topic if possible—even when teaching argument. What advice might Doezema offer?

4. To what extent are politicians to blame for people's inability to talk constructively about differing political opinions? How do our paid public servants benefit from, help to calm, or help to promote angry political rhetoric?

Ideas for Writing

1. How does a particular political issue influence a relationship in your life?

2. How does a particular political party platform figure into your intimate friendships, marriage, or dating decisions?

If responding to one of these ideas, go to the Analysis section of this chapter to begin developing ideas for your essay.

Outside Reading

Find a written text that explains or points out an unusual relationship. Go to a library database or search engine and experiment by typing in combinations of words (joined by *and*). To conduct an electronic search through journals and magazines, go to your library's periodical database or to InfoTrac College Edition (http://infotrac.cengage.com). For your library database, perform a keyword search, or for Info-Trac College Edition, go to the main search box and click on "keywords." In the search box, enter word combinations, such as *water and politics, lakes and engineering, nursing and chemistry.* (When performing keyword searches, avoid using phrases or articles *(a, an, the);* instead, use nouns separated by *and.*) The search results will yield lists of journal and magazine articles. The same strategy can be used with an Internet search. Try Google.com and enter various word combinations. Once you find an interesting text, print it out.

The purpose of this assignment is to explore a broad spectrum of possible relationships and to discover more about explanatory writing. You may discover relationships you never imagined, and will probably witness a variety of writing strategies. As you read through this chapter, keep the document you have discovered close by and notice the elements and strategies the writer uses. Depending on your instructor's suggestions, do one or more of the following:

1. Notice how the writer applies various strategies from this chapter. On the hard copy:
   - Highlight the thesis (main point about the relationship) if it is stated. If the thesis is implied, write it in your own words.
   - Identify the major rhetorical tools (narrative, description, allusion).
   - Identify any passages that show public resonance (in which the writer makes the relationship a public issue or concern).

2. Analyze the strategies employed by the writer. The following questions may be helpful:
   - How is the writer's voice different from the essays in this chapter?
   - How does the writer support or illustrate his or her thesis?
   - Who is the audience for this text?
   - How does the audience impact the kinds of things said in the text?

3. Write at least three "Writing Strategies" questions for the text you found.

4. Write at least three "Exploring Ideas" questions for the text you found.

5. Write two "Ideas for Writing," such as the ones following the essays in this book, for the text you found.

INVENTION

Invention is the activity of discovering ideas, developing points, and thinking through a topic. For academic writers, it is a necessary activity, one that leads to vital and valuable ideas. In this chapter, the process will involve focusing on a particular relationship and exploring its possible meaning. The following sections are designed to help you through the invention process: specifically, to discover a topic (in Point of Contact), to develop particular points about the topic (in Analysis), to make it relevant to a community of readers (in Public Resonance), to develop a focus (in Thesis), and to generate support (in Rhetorical Tools). The Invention questions in each section are not meant to be answered directly in your final written assignment. Rather, they are meant to help you develop increasingly intense ideas for your project.

POINT OF CONTACT

When you hear the word *relationship,* you may imagine an intimate personal bond between significant others, family members, or friends. But consider the relationships that are less obvious, those that surround or define us but remain hidden by the patterns of everyday life. Imagine the intense, but also subtle, relationships that define life as we know it: between an old man and his backyard, among people in a large corporate office, between a lake and a local economy, between pigeons and people in a park. When we examine such relationships, we are apt to discover some hidden workings and ideas—which is often the purpose of writing in academia.

As you explore possible topics, ask yourself: "What is the nature of this relationship?" Don't be discouraged if nothing falls from the sky and says, "Hey! I'm a great topic!" That rarely happens. Use these suggestions and questions to find and develop a topic:

- **Visit a Public Place**
  —How do the people interact or depend on each other?
  —How do the people relate to their surroundings? To objects? To buildings? To nature?
  —How do the objects (buildings, tools, products, shops) relate?
  —How do people or objects influence each other?

No topic is inherently interesting. The process of developing the topic will make it interesting.

- **Examine a Job Site**
  —How do workers relate to their tools or equipment?
  —How must the people relate to each other? (How must they influence or depend on each other?)
  —How do workers relate to their environment?
  —How do workers relate to the public?

- **Examine Everyday Civic Bonds** Between a customer and a sales clerk, a customer and a mail carrier, the public and a city police force, a politician and her constituents, or an artist and the public.

- **Imagine Human/Object Relationships** Between a person and a computer, a person and a musical instrument, a person and a car; or between two objects, such as a college course and a textbook, a book and a computer, an old car and a new one, a road and a house.

- **Examine Relationships in Your Academic Major**
  —Between the professionals in your field of study and the public (such as nurses and their patients, or business marketing professionals and potential consumers).
  —Between two things in your field of study. Students of criminal justice, for instance, can explore how one case (or one kind of case) relates to another; environmental scientists can explore the relationship between waterways and surrounding land or between trees and animal life.
  —Between your field of study and another field. Most academic disciplines and professional fields define themselves in conjunction with other fields. For instance, biology explores its relationship with ethics, computer technologies involve visual or graphic design, and political science involves religious studies.

ANALYSIS

Analysis is the process of inspecting how or why something works, but analysis also involves discovering connections and meaning. In this chapter, analysis involves investigating all the possible ways two entities relate to each other. It means going beyond the obvious relationship and exploring the hidden or abstract connections.

Invention Questions

Use the following questions to explore deep layers of the relationship that you will explain in your essay:

- Is the relationship difficult? Why?
- What keeps it going?
- How does the presence of one entity (person or thing) influence the other? In what hidden or indirect ways do they influence one another?
- What would occur to one if the other were gone?

If you examine an intimate personal relationship, try to go beyond the initial common thoughts ("it is supportive"; "it is difficult"; "it has ups and downs"; "it is loving") and find some hidden complexity.

Use the following to explore the complexities of a human relationship:

- In what ways do I communicate with this person?
- To what degree do I share in his or her personal crises?
- Do I ever feel obligated to do, think, or say something for this person?
- Why am I in this relationship?
- What kinds of disagreements arise in the relationship? Do they become sources of debate and tension, or do they fade away?

As you work through these Invention questions, use them to develop ideas. For example, Jim Crockett's invention writing (excerpted below) helped him to discover the insights he shares in his essay. In his responses to the Invention questions, we can see how important concepts emerge and lay the groundwork for his essay:

In what hidden or indirect ways do they influence one another?

At the outset, I'm really wondering why I need to use the same mug every day and not one of the many on the shelf that perform the same function, i.e., keep my mustache dry and drip-free while keeping coffee hot. Maybe it's because I received this mug for my birthday a few years back—received it from good friends. Maybe it's the functional good looks of the stainless steel and plastic—industrialized design good looks. Maybe it's because I have a need to carry a security object (Linus's blanket). What if I have an obsessive/compulsive disorder? What if? Does it really matter? Do I really care? Is this really a big deal? Maybe not, but it's probably worth looking into—probably worth unraveling the thread of the warm blanket (warm sweater?) of my relationship with my coffee mug.

Here, Crockett explores various layers. He raises some questions that later evolve into the essay, and he makes two important discoveries: That any possible psychological "disorder" is less important than some basic human need, and he also connects his mug with security.

In his invention work, Daniel Doezema begins digging into the tension lurking in a human relationship. Notice that Doezema does not merely explain why the other person in the relationship is "wrong." Instead, he takes a more fruitful and challenging route—explaining how the tension began, how it evolved, and how it persists:

Is the relationship difficult? Why?

At first, no, it wasn't. I think it really only started to get "tense" when the U.S. invaded Iraq. From that point on our common ground on politics went downhill. You have to be careful whenever you mention anything about politics or any social aspect of society that will conflict with his point of view, that being a Republican point of view.

Short comments of your opinion or views on a matter can ignite a firestorm of disagreement, shouting, and anger.

It's to the point where you can no longer discuss it any more, it will inevitably turn into a shouting match, almost no critical thinking will be involved, because it seems there is a "team" mentality that somehow trumps all the wrongs and idiocies of the current administration. I'm not part of any team, but somehow I will get labeled as one in these conversations, treated like an enemy of his point of view, and that's what it becomes, a battle of sides, black and white. We become polarized to a ridiculous degree, so much so that we lose sight of all the things that should really be concerning us and affecting us in politics.

Now imagine a different topic and writer. In the following, Marcus uses the Invention questions to explore the relationship between a police department and the surrounding community. Notice how Marcus's response to the last question (Why am I in this relationship?) takes him further into his own thinking. Although the question seems unrelated to his topic, it actually prompts him to see an essential point: *People can be in a relationship without consciously thinking about it.*

Is the relationship difficult?

Yes. My father is a police officer, and he is constantly stressed about the work. Patrolling in some neighborhoods is hard work—and dangerous. And even though many officers face dangerous situations, they are expected by people in the community to be totally passive. It's nearly impossible work.

What keeps it going?

People stay in the job for obvious reasons: They need money, they have the training, they get some satisfaction out of the job (most of them still assume that they are "protecting and serving"). But the real question is: What keeps the tension going? And that's a mixture of things: On one side, economic problems in the city create bad neighborhoods where people are desperate. On the other side, every time the news reports anything involving the police, it's going to be bad, so people learn to associate police cars and uniforms with negative feelings.

Why am I in this relationship?

Technically, I'm not in it. Or maybe I am. I am "the community." But I guess most people probably don't think they are in the relationship until they see the flashing lights behind them. That's also part of the reason that the tension keeps going. People in the community don't see themselves as part of the relationship—maybe they don't even see a relationship.

In this chapter, analysis involves investigating all the possible ways two entities relate to each other. It means going beyond the obvious relationship and exploring the hidden or abstract connections.

Thinking Further

How do writers identify potentially interesting ideas? Of all the ideas swimming around, how do they decide which to pursue and which to ignore? You might consider two key strategies:

1. **Capitalize on uncertainty.** If you are uncertain how to answer a question, or you can answer it several different ways, explore further. (The uncertainty is a sign of complexity!) For example, Marcus writes, "Technically, I'm not in it. Or maybe I am." As Marcus reviews his notes, he should focus on this indefinite answer.

2. **Look for fresh or foreign ideas.** Occasionally you might see a topic differently than most other people. Because writers are looking for a new perspective, such realizations are vital. For example, when Marcus writes "the tension keeps going" because "people in the community don't see themselves as part of the relationship," he has discovered an important idea worth pursuing further.

If writers discover some uncertainty or fresh perspective, they can then ask even more questions to pursue their thinking. For example, Marcus might explore further by asking the following questions:

"Technically, I'm not in it. Or maybe I am."

- Am I in the relationship or not? What is the nature of the relationship?
- Can I ever get out of the relationship? What would happen if I did?
- How does the relationship influence me in hidden ways? How does it influence law enforcement?

"That's also part of the reason that the tension keeps going. People in the community don't see themselves as part of the relationship—maybe they don't even see a relationship."

- Why don't people in the community see the relationship? How is their not seeing helpful or harmful?
- Who does see the relationship? How do people who see the relationship act differently?
- If more people saw the relationship, would it be less difficult? Would people be influenced differently?

Invention Workshop

Meet with at least one other writer and use one of the Invention questions (on page 82) to initiate a focused discussion on your topic. Briefly explain your topic to the other writer(s), and then ask one of the Invention questions. Try to stay focused on that question until you've reached some new insight about the relationship.

Go beyond what you have always assumed and what most people overlook about the nature of the relationship. Look into the deep connections of present and past; look at the consequences of actions; consider the effects of attitudes. And remember two key strategies: 1) Capitalize on uncertainty. 2) Look for fresh or foreign ideas.

PUBLIC RESONANCE

Remember that you are not writing entirely for yourself. You are writing to explain something for others. The particular relationship you are explaining may be specific and narrow (perhaps between two people), but it may suggest something beyond the particular—something that is relevant or important to your readers.

As you consider your own topic, ask the following questions:

- Does the relationship reveal something about people's strengths or weaknesses?
- Why is it important that people see the meaning of the relationship?
- Is there something unusual or usual about this relationship?
- Does this relationship show how difficult, easy, or valuable human relationships can be?
- Does this relationship show how rewarding or valuable a particular kind of relationship can be?

Exploring public resonance can be hard work. But the process takes writers somewhere important, even vital: to new insights. In his project, Jim Crockett discovers the bigger significance of a relationship—that his simple mug is not merely a personal habit but a representation of human habit, a basic need. He also considers how the specific relationship functions within the broader sphere of relations between humans and their economy, humans and their home, and humans and their past:

> **Why is it important that people see the meaning of the relationship?**
>
> We all need daily ritual in our lives in an increasingly alien world—a culture, econoculture removed from the time-worn agrarian rituals, from the ties to place and home. How much coffee do you drink anyway? The cup/mug is natural—a natural extension of the human hand, a necessary adjunct to, a logical appurtenance thereof. Small choices—these small behaviors we cling to—affect the way in which we are perceived in the world.

Likewise, Daniel Doezema uses the Invention questions to see the broader significance of his relationship:

> **Does this relationship show how difficult, easy, or valuable human relationships can be?**
>
> I feel it shows how difficult *and* easy a relationship can be with your partner's parents. Many people have dealt with some form of tension, frustration, or even hate with an in-law or their partner's parents. These people all find their own ways to deal with their disagreements among each other. Some choose compromise, others avoidance of issues, and some just decide to cut themselves off completely.
>
> But people can have disagreements and still co-exist and be able to relax around each other. It just takes some common ground or a shared relationship important to both people for them to be able to maintain a positive relationship even if there are deep and passionate disagreements. Some may call this a type of false relationship, and this is true on some level. But out of this, people can grow a better relationship than that of a nonexistent relationship that can stress or hurt the others around you. Having a balance in a relationship that is both difficult and easy is always there in some form. We all have to find our own ways of getting to some gray area in between the black and white polarization of ideas and opinions.

Research

Discuss your topic with a friend or family member. Ask about his or her take on the topic: "Have you ever thought about the relationship between _____ and _____?" Record the responses, which may show common thinking about your topic.

You can also explore your topic in secondary sources. To find out what else has been said about your topic, do an Internet or online database search. For specific guidance, see Research & Writing, pages 442–527.

THESIS

As you focus your topic, you will also be narrowing in on a thesis statement or main idea. Like many writers, you may write your way to a thesis, or you may try to focus the idea before drafting. Either way, you need to have a single statement that not only gives focus to your topic but also gives your particular insight on that topic. Your project might do one of the following:

- **Explain the significant qualities of a particular kind of relationship.**
  —Human/dog relationships rely on so little understanding and effort from humans and so much work, agility, and determination from the dog.
  —Rock stars and their fans both rely on a sense of urgency and exclusivity.

- **Explain what is sometimes hidden in a particular kind of relationship.**
  —Beneath the obvious authority issues between teachers and students, there exists a mutual kind of awe in which each marvels at the will of the other.
  —Home owners often forget the powerful underground struggle between plumbing and trees—until they see stems and leaves swimming in the toilet.

- **Explain the difficulties or problems of being a child, friend, parent, or significant other.**
  —Our children's birthdays are a tangle of joy and unutterable sadness that comes with knowing how time will eventually do its work and create absence.
  —College friends are surrogate families, which means they always fall short in some quiet way.

- **Explain how a particular relationship (say, with a pet) is much like something else (say, an accidental fall down a mountainside).**
  —Presidential candidates and their potential supporters are both authors of fiction, each conjuring visions of what the other will certainly do.
  —If the surrounding neighborhood is a family, the 7-11 is like a bad in-law that has slowly been accepted.

- **Explain how a particular relationship reveals something important about a subject.**
  —The river's color beyond the city shows how water willingly carries the by-products of human endeavor.
  —The association between gun and police officer speaks of our culture's assumption about power.

Regardless of your approach, avoid the fog. Steer clear of unfocused generalizations. A narrower and more particular thesis will create a more intensive experience for both writer and reader. Notice the difference among the following:

General	Specific	More Specific
Students	Third-grade girls	The attitudes of third-grade girls
Employees	Retail sales associates	Retail sales associates' energy
Campus	The new buildings	The look of the new buildings

The more specific subjects help readers (and writers!) focus on more specific insights. They help readers and writers tune in to intricacies and intimacies. (They actually help sharpen consciousness!) In considering the focus of your project, examine the nouns you use. Can they be more specific?

If nouns (or subjects in sentences) help create focus, then verbs can help create *revelation*. A revelatory thesis statement shows something new—a commonly overlooked layer, connection, or idea. Notice the following statements:

- The attitudes of third-grade girls <u>depend</u> upon the number of close friends.
- Retail sales associates' energy <u>relies</u> on the number and nature of customers.
- The flat, corporate look of the new buildings on campus <u>competes</u> with the traditional stone giants and illustrates the clash between the old academic tradition and the new corporate designs on education.

In these statements, the verbs *(depend, relies, competes)* are active and intensive. They help show how two things or groups of people relate.

Evolution of a Thesis

Writers should allow their initial ideas to become increasingly more focused and revelatory. Notice how a broad statement can become more intense and sophisticated as it becomes more focused:

- Runners develop an intense relationship with the road.

  Here, "intense relationship" can be defined or narrowed. It's potentially interesting, but we need to see the intensity.

- Runners share space with humans and machines.

  The writer can keep thinking about that space—what happens in that shared space?

- Runners must confront the overwhelming presence of both cars and car culture when they take to the road.

  The writer has helped us to see a kind of difficulty or tension in the relationship. We're examining not only the physical presence of cars, but some set of assumptions or attitudes related to cars.

Revision

A key part of writing is developing an intellectual rearview mirror: a habit of looking back and redirecting your course. Apply the following questions:

- In my thesis, what nouns could be narrower, more specific?
- In my thesis, what verbs could be intensified to reveal more about the relationship?
- How does the statement offer something beyond a commonsense or simplistic assumption? How is it revelatory?

Other writers can help you with this process. Try exchanging your initial ideas with others and using the above questions for peer evaluation.

Do yourself and your reader a favor: Avoid the fog!

RHETORICAL TOOLS

The next step is to develop and support ideas. Remember that a potential reader already knows about relationships in general. (He or she is certainly mired in several.) But in your essay you have the opportunity to shed light, to go beyond ordinary thinking, and to reveal something that most people do not necessarily consider.

Using Narration

Narration, or storytelling, is appropriate for many kinds of writing. It is not simply relegated to remembering events. You might consider beginning your essay with a brief retelling of a situation regarding the relationship, or using a brief account to illustrate something about the relationship. (For example, Daniel Doezema and Jim Crockett both use narration at important points.) If you decide to use narration, make good choices:

1. Start the narrative at an appropriate place. That is, limit your story to include only relevant parts of the situation.

2. Focus on only the relevant details of the events.

3. Use consistent verb tense. (In most cases, past or present tense can work in retelling a story. However, you must be consistent throughout the narrative.)

4. At some point, make sure to explain the significance or relevance of the narrative to the reader.

5. Refer to Chapter 2 for other valuable narrative strategies.

An essay is an invitation to discover a new way of thinking.

Using Description

Readers like details. The more detailed the images, the more intensely the reader will experience them. In this essay, you might decide to describe the people involved in the relationship—their particular postures, facial expressions, and gestures. Or you might need to detail more abstract qualities—their imaginations, their appetites, their pride, their esteem, their effect on strangers. In the following, a writer is describing the relationship between a coffee shop and the students who frequent the place. The first passage is broad, undetailed:

> The coffee shop makes them feel more academic. It is more than a location to do homework and drink caffeine. It is a place where students totally surround themselves in college work.

These are valuable statements, but they remain abstract, general, and ultimately unhelpful to the reader. But the ideas come to life more with details:

> The coffee shop is more than a location for doing homework. It is like a satellite campus where students and professors alike work, talk, reflect. On any given day, several tables will be pushed together while a group of students work together on a project, their papers and notebooks scattered between coffee cups and half-eaten bagels. Invariably, a professor, graduate student, or staff member from the college will sit in one of the corner tables reading a newspaper. Several students will be perched on the windowsill, their backs against the outside world as they read through textbook chapters.

You might need to describe a particular situation in detail. In that case, narration and description will work together. For instance, Steinbeck includes several situations or anecdotes in his essay that dramatize the relationship between American settlers and the land:

> Another joker with a name still remembered in the West worked out a scheme copied many times in after years. Proving a quarter section required a year of residence and some kind of improvement—a fence, a shack—but once the land was proved the owner was

free to sell it. This particular princely character went to the stews and skid rows of the towns and found a small army of hopeless alcoholics who lived for whisky and nothing else. He put these men on land he wanted to own, grubstaked them and kept them in cheap liquor until the acreage was proved, then went through the motions of buying it from his protégés and moved them and their one-room shacks on sled runners on to new quarter sections. Bums of strong constitution might prove out five or six homesteads for this acquisitive hero before they died of drunkenness.

Using Figurative Language

Any explanatory essay can benefit from figurative language, which is language that goes beyond words' basic definitions and uses them to suggest imaginative connections between ideas. Figurative language does more than just make interesting comparisons. It also reveals a new dimension to the topic; it helps writers and their readers to see the topic in a new light.

Metaphor: A metaphor is a comparison in which one thing is made to share the characteristics of another. In his essay, Jim Crockett slides in a subtle metaphor that graphically describes most consumers' relationship with big coffee corporations:

> When I buy a cup of coffee, I only buy coffee: the paper cup and insulating sleeve, both little bits of tree, remain in the store. <u>I remain weaned from dependence</u> upon the earth- and human-pillaging multinational coffee cartel.

Simile: A simile is a comparison that uses *like* or *as*. John Steinbeck's similes help to characterize the nature of the relationship between American settlers and the land:

> I have often wondered at the savagery and thoughtlessness with which our early settlers approached this rich continent. They came at it <u>as though it were an enemy</u>, which of course it was.

> There has always been more than enough desert in America; the new settlers, <u>like overindulged children</u>, created even more.

As you consider your own topic, apply the following questions:

- What brief story will help the reader to see my point about the relationship?
- What vivid details will help demonstrate the precise nature of the relationship?
- Can I compare the relationship (or the entities in the relationship) to an animal? A thing? A place? A person? What new dimension would this comparison reveal?

Revision

As with all academic essays, the supporting material should lead the reader to a focused main idea—hopefully, to the idea the writer intends. You might think of the essay as an elegant equation:

Rhetorical Tools (narration + description + figurative language + other variables) = Thesis

Consider your supporting material. What information does not lead the reader toward the thesis? What elements might have to be deleted from this equation? What information would better lead the reader to your thesis?

ORGANIZATIONAL STRATEGIES

How Should I Begin?

If a good introduction comes to mind, by all means, write it down. But if one doesn't, don't worry. Go ahead and write the essay without an introduction. Once you have a draft (without the introduction), you'll have a better idea what you are introducing; thus, the introduction should be easier to write.

As we will suggest throughout this book, the possibilities for introductions are boundless. For this particular essay, you might:

- Begin with a general statement about the relationship. Steinbeck begins with a general statement about American settlers and the land:

  I have often wondered at the savagery and thoughtlessness with which our early settlers approached this rich continent. They came at it as though it were an enemy, which of course it was. They burned the forests and changed the rainfall; they swept the buffalo from the plains, blasted the streams, set fire to the grass, and ran a reckless scythe through the virgin and noble timber.

- Begin with a brief story or anecdote about the relationship. Doezma begins his essay with an anecdote that develops the main idea. (But also notice that the story eventually gives way to some analysis, some explanation of the meaning in the events.)

- Begin with a typical belief or stereotype about the relationship, and then turn to your particular insight. Imagine a writer focusing on the relationship between the police and the surrounding community:

  Most people assume they have no relationship with their local police departments. Other than an emergency situation, most are even reluctant to acknowledge police officers. They often treat them as uniformed specters lurking on the roads of their towns. But the police of any community are deeply connected to the everyday patterns of life. They are serving their communities and participating in daily routines at all levels.

- Begin with a fictional account, or scenario, of a relationship. Imagine the same topic about police and communities beginning differently:

  Imagine a community in which the police only appeared for emergencies, in which people had to make a 911 call simply to get a police car to visit the area. Imagine the streets of a crowded city without the occasional police cruiser. Imagine the downtown stores without the presence of a city officer.

Where Should My Thesis or Main Point Go?

Remember that a thesis can be either explicitly stated or *implied* (suggested by the content but not stated in the essay). Of course, even if a thesis is implied, the author needs to know the main idea. A thesis for this essay might go:

- At the very beginning—the first sentence of the first paragraph
- At the end of the first paragraph
- In the conclusion
- After a brief account that illustrates the main idea

When Should I Change Paragraphs?

Remember that paragraphs are tools for focusing and refocusing your readers' attention. Paragraph breaks stop readers and signal them to refocus their attention. Particularly for this essay, you might change paragraphs:

- When beginning a scenario or narrative
- When offering a memory
- When changing scenes or time in the middle of a longer narrative
- When offering a detailed allusion

How Should I Make Transitions?

You might think of paragraph transitions in two ways. Sometimes making paragraph transitions is as easy as choosing the right information to come next—that is, as choosing the most appropriate information to begin the paragraph. In these cases, the content of the paragraphs works to bridge the gap between them. (See Steinbeck ¶ 7–9. The content of each paragraph follows logically from the preceding paragraph. Steinbeck uses a time sequence to move from one point to the next, so explicit transitions are unnecessary.) Often, however, the writer needs to create a phrase, sentence, or sentences at the beginning of the new paragraph so that the relationship between the old and the new is clear. This sentence or phrase helps to bridge the gap between points. In the following, Jim Crockett provides a very small, but important, bridge between two paragraphs. The small phrase "in fact" carries the reader from an idea to a closer examination of that idea:

> My coffee cup is in my hand a lot.
>
> In fact, when it is not in my hand, when I misplace it momentarily, or when, like the other day, I leave it on the bumper of my truck and see a flash in the rearview mirror as my mug goes airborne into the filthy slush of the winter street, I feel a twinge of separation anxiety.

As you consider transitions, do not be deterred. If you cannot see the relationship between paragraphs as you are drafting, continue onward. (Don't get held up trying to imagine one perfectly crafted phrase!) Writers often come back through their drafts and fill in the cracks—adding transitional phrases, sentences, or entire paragraphs. After they have developed all the nuances of their thinking, they can then ask questions: How do the paragraphs relate? Are they contrary? Is one an extension of the other? Is the second paragraph more particular than the first? Or is the second more broad?

How Should I Conclude?

As with introductions, the possibilities for conclusions are limitless. Short explanatory essays (such as those under 1,000 words) usually do not need to summarize main points. Instead, writers often use conclusions to suggest the significance of the ideas expressed in the body of the essay. For this essay, you might consider concluding with:

- The overall statement on, and particular meaning of, the relationship (the thesis).

- An allusion that best illustrates your points about the relationship. An allusion can be a powerful conclusion strategy because it projects the point of the essay onto some other subject or idea. It extends the essay's reach outward. Notice Steinbeck's use of a historical allusion:

  > But we are an exuberant people, careless and destructive as active children. We make strong and potent tools and then have to use them to prove that they exist. Under the pressure of war we finally made the atom bomb, and for reasons which seemed justifiable at the time we dropped it on two Japanese cities—and I think we finally frightened ourselves. In such things, one must consult himself because there is no other point of reference. I did not know about the bomb, and certainly I had nothing to do with its use, but I am horrified and ashamed; and nearly everyone I know feels the same thing. And those who loudly and angrily justify Hiroshima and Nagasaki—why, they must be the most ashamed of all.

- A return to an introductory image or scene that reveals something significant about that image. This strategy is often called "framing." Having gone through the complexities of the essay, the readers now know something special and different about the opening image. Returning to it does not merely recap the point but helps the readers understand just how far they've gone. They understand a new poignancy, a new sticking point, about the topic.

WRITER'S VOICE

Some writers create very serious, sober voices. They offer claims with the utmost formality. Sentences may be consistent in length and structure. Slang words and contractions are often absent, as in this passage from John Steinbeck's essay:

> This tendency toward irresponsibility persists in very many of us today; our rivers are poisoned by reckless dumping of sewage and toxic industrial wastes, the air of our cities is filthy and dangerous to breathe from the belching of uncontrolled products from combustion of coal, coke, oil, and gasoline.

Other writers create more relaxed or even humorous voices; they offer asides (in parenthetical statements) and fun metaphors. Their allusions also might be informal. For example, in an essay about his relationship with his dog, David Hawes alludes to the Beatles:

> I realize this is an odd paraphrase of the Beatles, but it certainly seems fitting: I have a dog, or should I say, my dog has me? Often it seems unclear which of us is in charge in this arrangement.

As you write, decide how you want to come off to the reader, how you want to posture yourself. The following strategies can be used for various kinds of voices, whether formal, comedic, or somewhere in between. These strategies help make any voice more engaging.

Writerly Whispers
(Ways to Draw Readers in Closer)

- Parenthetical statements can offer gentle asides, as in Jennifer Schwind-Pawlak's essay in Chapter 2:

  > Joann (the name I call my mother when she does something embarrassing) was screaming at the coach. In a voice so screeching that it rivaled fingernails on a blackboard, she told him that he was a disgraceful coach and that he should be ashamed of himself.

  Or in Jim Crockett's essay:

  > Wrought in stainless steel and plastic, this bit of industrial-designer paraphernalia (it holds my drug of choice) is every cup holder's dream.

- Longer sentences with long phrases can create a sense of delicacy and can bring the reader into the subtleties of a thought. In Jim Crockett's concluding paragraph, the intricacy of his long sentences brings the reader into the quiet complexities of the relationship:

  > Because, even though my mug is always nearby, whether on the lectern or table in front of the classroom, in the cup holder on the dashboard of my truck, on the desk where I am writing this essay, or just dangling from my hand, all it really signifies is an addiction to caffeine and the need, because I am human, for some small and securing daily grounding ritual.

As you write, decide how you want to come off to the reader, how you want to posture yourself.

Writerly Yells
(Ways to Give Emphasis)

- Interrupting the natural flow of a sentence with a phrase or clause can draw attention to an idea. This does not mean that the writer is angry or shouting at the reader; rather, it allows the writer to guide the reader's attention to particular ideas. This is often done, as in Daniel Doezema's essay, with appositive phrases, set off by commas—or even dashes:

  > An atmosphere has taken hold in which we either support the party or become an enemy of the party, and in both cases, we're considered *un-American.*

- Repeating words, phrases, or clauses can highlight an idea. John Steinbeck repeats *us* to highlight the collective nature of the issue:

  > No longer do we Americans want to destroy wantonly, but our new-found sources of power—to take the burden of work from our shoulders, to warm us, and cool us, and give us light, to transport us quickly, and to make the things we use and wear and eat—these power sources spew pollution on our country, so that the rivers and streams are becoming poisonous and lifeless.

- Very short, even one-sentence, paragraphs can highlight an important point. or create a stark jolting feeling between ideas. Doezema uses this strategy effectively:

  > The television's voice seems silent now—the humidity replaced by growing tension and anger.

- Short sentences can work many ways. Paradoxically, they can work as whispers or as yells, depending on the content and the context. They sometimes create emphasis because of their placement after longer sentences or after questions, such as in David Hawes's essay:

  > Do I spoil him? Of course I do. Isn't that the whole point of having a dog?

- Exclamation points . . . of course!

Writerly Pace
(Ways to Control Speed and Time)

- Having more details slows down time for the reader. Like in a film, time slows down when a writer (or producer) focuses in on many particular details. Steinbeck uses details throughout his essay to focus on particular moments in history:

  > Quite a few years ago when I was living in my little town on the coast of California a stranger came in and bought a small valley where the Sempervirens redwoods grew, some of them three hundred feet high. We used to walk among these trees, and the light colored as though the great glass of the Cathedral at Chartres had strained and sanctified the sunlight. The emotion we felt in this grove was one of awe and humility and joy; and then one day it was gone, slaughtered, and the sad wreckage of boughs and broken saplings left like nonsensical spoilage of the battle-ruined countryside.

- Having fewer details speeds up time for the reader. The fewer details a reader gets, the more quickly he or she moves through the events or thoughts in a text. Certainly, it is important to decide which ideas you want the reader to slow down for—and which ideas you want the reader to move quickly through.

Daniel Doezema begins his essay with very detailed narrative in which time moves slowly but he ends with more general points which omit detail:

> Despite all of our differences, which would normally drive most people apart, we have managed to maintain a fully functioning and meaningful relationship. We've found our common ground built around family, and it's the most powerful tie in our relationship, what allows it to persevere. Still, it can be difficult to judge when to let things go or when a comment may have crossed a line.

VITALITY

The delete key is perhaps the most underused key in college writing (and college textbooks!). Deleting anything often seems like a burden, like working against our own goals as writers. But good writers face their own sentences and willingly cast away clauses and phrases that dull the ideas, slow down the reader, and lessen the intensity.

Avoid *Be* Verbs When Possible

Be verbs are also called linking verbs: *is, am, are, was, were, being, been,* etc. They link the subject of a sentence to a quality or other noun.

> The kittens are cute.
> The government is out of control.
> Sentences are cues for the reader.

Although such verbs are often necessary and valuable, they are often overused—hanging around in a sentence that would benefit from a more active verb. Notice the small, but important, change to the final example sentence above. We can make the verb active—and shorten the sentence:

> Sentences cue the reader.

This may not mean much for one sentence, but changing *be* verbs to active verbs throughout an essay can have dramatic effects. For instance, in the following passage, John Steinbeck's verbs pull the reader through the ideas:

> The great redwood forests of the western mountains early attracted attention. These ancient trees, which once grew everywhere, now exist only where the last Ice Age did not wipe them out. And they were found to have value. The Sempervirens and the Gigantea, the two remaining species, make soft, straight-grained timber. They are easy to split into planks, shakes, fenceposts, and railroad ties, and they have a unique virtue: they resist decay, both wet and dry rot, and an inherent acid in them repels termites. The loggers went through the great groves like a barrage, toppling the trees—some of which were two thousand years old—and leaving no maidens, no seedlings or saplings on the denuded hills.

Activity

1. Rewrite Steinbeck's passage using *be* verbs instead of active verbs. For instance, replace *decay* with *are resistant to decay*. How do these changes impact the nature of the passage?

2. Examine a paragraph from your current draft. Rewrite the paragraph by simply changing any *be* verbs (*is, am, are, was, were,* and so on) to more active verbs. How do those changes impact the nature of the passage?

Turn Clauses to Phrases

Clauses (elements that include both a subject and verb) can often be shortened to phrases so that sentences become more concise and concentrated. The following two sentences represent a common opportunity for collapsing a clause into a phrase, thereby combining the sentences. The second sentence, from Daniel Doezema's essay, avoids the unnecessary "it is":

> The country as a whole seems to be at this point. It is unable to hold a reasonable discussion on political views without a heated argument.

> The country as a whole seems to be at this point, unable to hold a reasonable discussion on political views without a heated argument.

The same goes for the following sentence. Notice how the second version, from John Steinbeck's essay, trims the clause into a phrase:

> When a super-highway was proposed in California which would trample the redwood trees in its path, an outcry arose all over the land that was so strident and fierce that the plan was put aside. And we no longer believe that a man, because he owns a piece of America, is free to outrage it.

When a super-highway was proposed in California which would trample the redwood trees in its path, an outcry arose all over the land, so strident and fierce that the plan was put aside. And we no longer believe that a man, by owning a piece of America, is free to outrage it.

Although these differences are slight, the phrases increase the sentences' vitality. And if the strategy is spread out over several pages of text, the essay reads more smoothly, more intensively. (Often, when students are concerned about "the flow" of their essays, this is exactly the type of strategy that could be applied. It is one of many tools for creating a more sophisticated sounding text.)

Turn Phrases to Words

The same principle can be applied to phrases; they can often be boiled down into single words. Consider the following two sentences. The second, also from Steinbeck's essay, boils down a common phrase to a more succinct word:

> Almost every day, the pressure of outrage among Americans grows.

> Almost daily, the pressure of outrage among Americans grows.

Although the differences are slight, such small transformations can build up throughout an essay, creating the difference between slower, droopier writing and intensive, vitalized writing. The process also makes writers search for thicker, more concentrated words—as in the following:

> The decision was not very smart.

> The decision was illogical.

> Back in the day, people did not assume that all communication should be instantaneous.

> Historically, people have not assumed that all communication should be instantaneous.

Are Sentence Fragments Legal?

You may have seen well-known writers break important sentence rules. You may have thought: "Why can they do that when I cannot?" Is it a special privilege? Do the laws vary from state to state, school to school? Not exactly. Many writers intentionally massage the conventions—and their readers allow it, even revel in it. For example, you may have seen fragments, often called *stylistic fragments,* that create an informal voice. Jim Crockett's introduction includes a stylistic fragment:

> I have been mugged. Not accosted as I walk to my parked truck across a dark lot; not waylaid by thugs in the night. But mugged, nevertheless.

The fragment does something significant, and many would say helpful, to the movement of the passage. If this seems like an attractive move, ask your instructor his or her thoughts about the strategy. Is it in or out of bounds? Is it valued? Under what circumstances?

PEER REVIEW

Exchange drafts with at least one other writer. Before passing your draft to others, underline the thesis, or write it on the top of your essay. This way, reviewers will get traction as they read.

As a reviewer, use the following questions to guide your response.

1. Point out any phrases in the thesis that could be more specific. (See the Thesis section for more guidance.)

2. Where can the writer do more analysis and reveal more about the relationship? (Point to passages that seem most obvious to you.) As you read, look for claims that anyone could immediately offer without intensive analysis. Beside these passages, write: "More analysis?" If you can suggest an interesting idea, explain it on the back of the writer's draft.

3. Help the writer illustrate his or her claims with details. As you read, look for broad characterizations. If you see phrases such as "influence one another" or "depend on one another," ask yourself: Could this be more specific? Can we *really* see the influence or dependence? In the margin, write "more details" where the writer could more intensely show the points.

4. Offer some figurative language to help characterize the relationship. After you have read the entire draft, offer your own metaphor or simile about the relationship. Give your suggestion on the back of the draft. Make sure it is something that fits the writer's voice—something that he or she could use.

5. Are the paragraphs coherent? Do you ever get the sense that a paragraph is wandering—giving you details that seem unrelated to one another or unrelated to the point of the essay? In the margin, write: "check paragraph coherence."

6. Help the writer kick-start the essay. The writer might begin with a broad statement about the relationship—or about something even broader. But the most focused statement possible often makes for a better introduction. Suggest a surprisingly focused opening statement.

7. Consider the writer's voice. Where could the writer employ a whisper (see page 92) or a yell (see page 93) to better engage the reader?

8. Point to particular sentences and phrases that could gain vitality and intensity. Use the following questions:

   - Where can the writer change *be* verbs to active verbs?

   - Look for clauses (especially those that begin with *which are, which is, that are, that is,* etc.). Suggest a strategy for boiling down the clause to a phrase.

   - Look for phrases (especially prepositional phrases that begin with *about* or *of*). Suggest a strategy for boiling down the phrase to a word.

   - Consider vitality strategies from the previous chapter:
     —Combine sentences
     —Repeat structures
     —Intensify verbs
     —Help the writer avoid common grammatical errors: comma splices, sentence fragments, or pronoun/antecedent agreement.

Avoid telling writers what they already know. Offer new ideas about their work.

Questions for Research

If the writer used outside sources,

- Where must he or she include in-text citations? (See pages 484–485.)

- Are quotations blended smoothly into the argument and punctuated correctly? (See pages 475–478.)

- Where could more direct textual cues or transitions help the reader? (See pages 479–481.)

- Is the Works Cited page formatted properly? (See pages 486–497.)

DELIVERY

Throughout the country, colleges and universities require one, two, even three semesters of college writing for every academic major. In those courses, most students write personal essays. But once they enter their job fields, many students may never be asked to write a formal essay again. Apparently, the academic world (and the business, governmental, and civic organizations that evaluate, fund, and support it) puts a great deal of stock in a student's ability to write essays. There must be something about an essay, besides the form, that offers something to writers and readers. What is it?

- What do you think the academic community values about the essay and the essay-writing process?

- Why are essay-writing classes required?

- Consider each of the essays in this chapter. What value does each have within this broader academic tradition?

- What about your own essay? How is your essay a complement to this entire belief system? How does your essay give hope to all the interests involved?

Beyond the Essay

The ideas generated in writing courses do not belong exclusively to essays. Those ideas can take many forms or extend to various media. Find an image that relates to your essay. If you can't find one, or if you prefer, create an original image: a drawing, painting, photograph, sculpture, and so on.

1. After you have found or created an image, explain how the image reveals something about the nature of the relationship. How does it, for instance, reveal some complexity in the relationship between dogs and people, between alcohol and people, between prescription drugs and people, between people and the land they inhabit?

2. Present the image to others in your class. Explain how the image reinforces ideas in your essay. Also explain how the image and essay differ: What complexities does the image suggest beyond your essay? What does your essay reveal that the image conceals? Does your essay go further than the image? How?

OBSERVING

Chapter Contents

CHAPTER 4

Living Like Weasels

Annie Dillard

It is easy to imagine weasels as nothing more than wild animals and to see them as entirely divorced from human affairs. After all, we are civilized. Weasels live in holes and eat mice. But in this essay, Annie Dillard, a Pulitzer Prize winning author, invites us to rethink weasels and our own everyday lives. She insists that something can be learned behind the stare of a simple animal, something essential about life's purpose. After a brief encounter with a weasel, Dillard goes beyond the first glimpse and creates important meaning for herself and others. "Living Like Weasels" first appeared in Dillard's book *Teaching a Stone to Talk* (1982).

A weasel is wild. Who knows what he thinks? He sleeps in his underground den, his tail draped over his nose. Sometimes he lives in his den for two days without leaving. Outside, he stalks rabbits, mice, muskrats, and birds, killing more bodies than he can eat warm, and often dragging the carcasses home. Obedient to instinct, he bites his prey at the neck, either splitting the jugular vein at the throat or crunching the brain at the base of the skull, and he does not let go. One naturalist refused to kill a weasel who was socketed into his hand deeply as a rattlesnake. The man could in no way pry the tiny weasel off, and he had to walk half a mile to water, the weasel dangling from his palm, and soak him off like a stubborn label.

And once, says Ernest Thompson Seton—once, a man shot an eagle out of the sky. He examined the eagle and found the dry skull of a weasel fixed by the jaws to his throat. The supposition is that the eagle had pounced on the weasel and the weasel swiveled and bit as instinct taught him, tooth to neck, and nearly won. I would like to have seen that eagle from the air a few weeks or months before he was shot: was the whole weasel still attached to his feathered throat, a fur pendant? Or did the eagle eat what he could reach, gutting the living weasel with his talons before his breast, bending his beak, cleaning the beautiful airborne bones?

I have been reading about weasels because I saw one last week. I startled a weasel who startled me, and we exchanged a long glance.

Twenty minutes from my house, through the woods by the quarry and across the highway, is Hollins Pond, a remarkable piece of shallowness, where I like to go at sunset and sit on a tree trunk. Hollins Pond is also called Murray's Pond; it covers two acres of bottomland near Tinker Creek with six inches of water and six thousand lily pads. In winter, brown-and-white steers stand in the middle of it, merely dampening their hooves; from the distant shore they look like miracle itself, complete with miracle's nonchalance. Now, in summer, the steers are gone. The water lilies have blossomed and spread to a green horizontal plane that is terra firma to plodding blackbirds, and tremulous ceiling to black leeches, crayfish, and carp.

5   This is, mind you, suburbia. It is a five-minute walk in three directions to rows of houses, though none is visible here. There's a 55 mph highway at one end of the pond, and a nesting pair of wood ducks at the other. Under every bush is a muskrat hole or a beer can. The far end is an alternating series of fields and woods, fields and woods, threaded everywhere with motorcycle tracks—in whose bare clay wild turtles lay eggs.

So. I had crossed the highway, stepped over two low barbed-wire fences, and traced the motorcycle path in all gratitude through the wild rose and poison ivy of the pond's shoreline up into high grassy fields. Then I cut down through the woods to the mossy fallen tree where I sit. This tree is excellent. It makes a dry, upholstered bench at the upper, marshy end of the pond, a plush jetty raised from the thorny shore between a shallow blue body of water and a deep blue body of sky.

The sun had just set. I was relaxed on the tree trunk, ensconced in the lap of lichen, watching the lily pads at my feet tremble and part dreamily over the thrusting path of a carp. A yellow bird appeared to my right and flew behind me. It caught my eye; I swiveled around— and the next instant, inexplicably, I was looking down at a weasel, who was looking up at me.

Weasel! I'd never seen one wild before. He was ten inches long, thin as a curve, a muscled ribbon, brown as fruitwood, soft-furred, alert. His face was fierce, small and pointed as a lizard's; he would have made a good arrowhead. There was just a dot of chin, maybe two brown hairs' worth, and then the pure white fur began that spread down his underside. He had two black eyes I didn't see, any more than you see a window.

The weasel was stunned into stillness as he was emerging from beneath an enormous shaggy wild rose bush four feet away. I was stunned into stillness twisted backward on the tree trunk. Our eyes locked, and someone threw away the key.

10   Our look was as if two lovers, or deadly enemies, met unexpectedly on an overgrown path when each had been thinking of something else: a clearing blow to the gut. It was also a bright blow to the brain, or a sudden beating of brains, with all the charge and intimate grate of rubbed balloons. It emptied our lungs. It felled the forest, moved the fields, and drained the pond; the world dismantled and tumbled into that black hole of eyes. If you and I looked at each other that way, our skulls would split and drop to our shoulders. But we don't. We keep our skulls. So.

"If you and I looked at each other that way, our skulls would split and drop to our shoulders."

He disappeared. This was only last week, and already I don't remember what shattered the enchantment. I think I blinked, I think I retrieved my brain from the weasel's brain, and tried to memorize what I was seeing, and the weasel felt the yank of separation, the careening splashdown into real life and the urgent current of instinct. He vanished under the wild rose. I waited motionless, my mind suddenly full of data and my spirit with pleadings, but he didn't return.

Please do not tell me about "approach-avoidance conflicts." I tell you I've been in that weasel's brain for sixty seconds, and he was in mine. Brains are private places, muttering through unique and secret tapes—but the weasel and I both plugged into another tape simultaneously, for a sweet and shocking time. Can I help it if it was a blank?

What goes on in his brain the rest of the time? What does a weasel think about? He won't say. His journal is tracks in clay, a spray of feathers, mouse blood and bone: uncollected, unconnected, loose-leaf, and blown.

I would like to learn, or remember, how to live. I come to Hollins Pond not so much to learn how to live as, frankly, to forget about it. That is, I don't think I can learn from a wild animal how to live in particular—shall I suck warm blood, hold my tail high, walk with my footprints precisely over the prints of my hands?—but I might learn something of mindlessness, something of the purity of living in the physical senses and the dignity of living without bias or motive. The weasel lives in necessity and we live in choice, hating necessity and dying at the last ignobly in its talons. I would like to live as I should, as the weasel lives as he should. And I suspect that for me the way is like the weasel's: open to time and death painlessly, noticing everything, remembering nothing, choosing the given with a fierce and pointed will.

15   I missed my chance. I should have gone for the throat. I should have lunged for that streak of white under the weasel's chin and held on, held on through mud and into the wild rose, held on for a dearer life. We could live under the wild rose wild as weasels, mute and uncomprehending. I could very calmly go wild. I could live two days in the den, curled, leaning on mouse fur, sniffing bird bones, blinking, licking, breathing musk, my hair tangled in the roots of grasses. Down is a good place to go, where the mind is single. Down is out, out of your ever-loving mind and back to your careless senses. I remember muteness as a prolonged and giddy fast, where every moment is a feast of utterance received. Time and events are merely poured, unremarked, and ingested directly, like blood pulsed into my gut through a jugular vein. Could two live that way? Could two live under the wild rose, and explore by the pond, so that the smooth mind of each is as everywhere present to the other, and as received and as unchallenged, as falling snow?

We could, you know. We can live any way we want. People take vows of poverty, chastity, and obedience—even of silence—by choice. The thing is to stalk your calling in a certain skilled and supple way, to locate the most tender and live spot and plug into that pulse. This is yielding, not fighting. A weasel doesn't "attack" anything; a weasel lives as he's meant to, yielding at every moment to the perfect freedom of single necessity.

I think it would be well, and proper, and obedient, and pure, to grasp your one necessity and not let it go, to dangle from it limp wherever it takes you. Then even death, where you're going no matter how you live, cannot you part. Seize it and let it seize you up aloft even, till your eyes burn out and drop; let your musky flesh fall off in shreds, and let your very bones unhinge and scatter, loosened over fields, over fields and woods, lightly, thoughtless, from any height at all, from as high as eagles.

Writing Strategies

1. What might Dillard be trying to achieve with her introduction? Does she achieve it? Does her introduction make you want to read on? Why or why not?

2. How did you react when Dillard addressed you directly in paragraph 8? ("He had two black eyes I didn't see, any more than you see a window.") Were you startled? Did you know what she meant? When you write, do you sometimes speak more directly to the reader than at other times? Provide a few examples of how the writing situation influences how directly you speak to the reader.

3. Dillard describes the weasel's face as "fierce." Is this a good description? What are the characteristics of a fierce-looking face? Did her description, or word choice, help you get a better mental image of a weasel? How else might she have described the weasel?

4. What point is Dillard making in her concluding paragraph? How might she have stated her main point in a less poetic essay?

Exploring Ideas

1. What is Dillard trying to accomplish in this essay?

2. What change does Dillard's essay call for? How does she ask the reader to think or live differently?

3. Dillard's experience with the weasel affected her strongly, prompting her to explore her thoughts on how she lives. What similar personal experiences have prompted you to think differently about how you, and others, live?

4. Interview others, asking them what small experiences made them think differently about their lives. Ask them to describe the experience and how it influenced their thinking.

5. Discuss your interview responses from #4 above with classmates. Which responses were most common? Which were most unusual? Which would make for the most interesting essay and why?

Ideas for Writing

1. What person, place, or thing can you describe as a way of making an interesting point?

2. Have you interacted with an animal in the way Dillard has, or in some other thought-provoking way?

If responding to one of these ideas, go to the Analysis section of this chapter to begin developing ideas for your essay.

Ultimately, this essay is not about weasels. What is it about?

The Front Porch

Chester McCovey

Chester McCovey's observing essay illustrates how one can use an observation as a point of contact and then, through analysis, explore why the observation matters. McCovey makes a simple observation: That people don't sit out on their front porches like they did when he was a kid. Then he explores and determines that the loss of the front porch equals a loss of community. Through analysis, he goes from a specific observation (about garages and porches) to a general insight (about a loss of community).

Writing Strategies

The essay begins with a personal observation and connects with the reader.

States the main observation: porch replaced by garage.

The writer uses personal details to develop the observation.

The essay moves toward analysis. Why did this happen, and what does it mean?

If you walk through my neighborhood, you won't see many porches, at least not the kind people sit on in the evenings. Those days are gone where I live, and likely where you live, too.

The front porch has been replaced—by the two-car garage. Both sets of my grandparents, who lived in the same small town, had big front porches, and summer visits often meant sitting on the porch, talking, and watching cars and people out walking. After a while someone might have suggested getting some ice cream. The adult conversation was often dull, sometimes painfully so for a child, but sometimes it was interesting. The everyday people a child sees in church or at the Little League field in a small town have a few years behind them, and what person who has lived a little doesn't have a story to tell—or a story to be told about them? Sometimes those stories would come out and bring to life a previously uninteresting Frank or Gretchen. Small towns are full of life's everyday dramas. A child hears and figures out many things on a place like a front porch on a thing like a warm summer night.

My grandparents' garages were small, just enough for one car and a few tools—not much of a garage for today's homeowner. In those days the garage kept a car and a small lawnmower, some rakes, and so on. The garage today must keep much more. One can see, then, how the exchange occurred. Like an old-fashioned trade in baseball, gone is the home team's beloved front porch, replaced by a big, new garage. Of course the trade is much more interesting than that. And a look at how it occurred enlightens us a little about the world in which we live. More importantly, it tells us not so much about how life is now but about how it came to be. And, I would argue, it shows us the way in which things will continue to change.

Back then, our own garage held two cars, a riding lawnmower, a push mower, bicycles, and lots of tools. We had a front porch and

Exploring Ideas

The front porch was a place where people used to talk (pass the time, shoot the breeze).

The shift from porch to garage tells us about the world in which we live, how it came to be and how it will continue to change.

sat on it, but mostly just when we had company. Our house, then, represents the transition between two generations: my grandparents' generation that traveled less, received only three television stations (*sans* remote control), and didn't have air conditioning and my own generation that is more likely to be on the go (driving from one place to another) or sitting inside, on the computer or watching TV.

5   The front porch fell victim to its two natural enemies: the internal-combustion engine (automobiles) and electricity (air conditioning, lights, and TV). Now, instead of gathering on our front porch as our grandparents did, we are either gone somewhere thanks to our transportation or we are at home but indoors.

> how life must have splashed
> out of the cup
> on warm summer nights
> before the cool air
> of electricity
> urged us all to relax
> in the fluttering glow
> of color tv

We have traded sitting on the front porch for sitting in traffic, or to be more positive about it, for sitting in our automobile as we speed along to some very important place to be. The shift from porch to garage is beautifully simple. It goes like this: I need a place to park my transportation machine (car, truck, SUV) and I don't need a large, outdoor room for sitting. The reasoning (the reality of the situation) is just as simple: There's not as much action on the sidewalk as there once was (the neighbors are indoors or driving somewhere) and I don't need to sit outdoors to stay cool on muggy nights (the air conditioning indoors takes care of that). So, a need or desire—to stay cool, to be entertained, to keep up with what's going on—is replaced not by a different need or desire but instead by a new way of meeting it.

> Need or Desire—To Stay Cool
> Previously met by evening breeze; now
> met by air conditioning
>
> Need or Desire—To Be Entertained
> Previously met by conversation with
> neighbors; now met by TV, computer,
> shopping at the mall, conversation with
> friends who we drive to see
>
> Need or Desire—To Keep Up with What's

The writer's own childhood house illustrates the transition from porch to garage.

Main Ideas: What happened to the front porch and why: automobile and electricity. What happened because of that: we are either gone or indoors.

Explanation: How/why the shift occurred.

Because of automobiles and electricity, we spend more time driving alone or watching TV than we do talking with our friends and neighbors. Is this a problem? A loss of community?

Going On
Previously met by discussion with
neighbors and friends; now met through
national media (TV and Internet)

I am not saying there are no front porches. Obviously there are. And I am not saying everyone has a two-car garage instead. In my neighborhood, small garages not connected to the house still reign. But obviously, their days are numbered. The new houses sometimes look as much like a house attached to a garage as a garage attached to a house. Today's garage often dominates the house.

To avoid oversimplifying, the writer qualifies the point and concedes that there are still front porches, but that their days are numbered.

Finally, the careful reader is insisting that I deal with the backyard patio deck. What about *it*? When we do sit outdoors, we choose to do it out back, away from the rest of the world. This is interesting. We need a break, I would suggest, from the hustle and bustle of daily life, so we retreat to our own backyard to be left alone with our families. But that hustle and bustle is mostly the hustle and bustle of traffic, radio, television, and a few quick transactions with total strangers. Of course another reason for opting to relax in the backyard is that, as previously mentioned, there just isn't that much going on out front these days. (If there were, I wonder if we would sit on the front porch and watch it . . . *and* contribute to it.) I am arguing that we lose something very basic—very fundamental—when we lose the front porch culture.

Anticipates a potential concern of the reader: What about the back deck?

The back deck takes us out back, away from community.

On Sunday drives through the country, I see big new houses with big new porches. As Americans we can have it all—the house with the big front porch *and* the big garage. But I never (I am tempted to qualify this statement and say "almost never" or "rarely" but I have been thinking about it and I do mean "never")—I never see anyone out sitting on those porches. I am not prepared here to argue that we are a civilization in deep trouble because of this, though it does seem to me appropriate that we should lament, at least a little, the loss of the front porch.

Main point: We lose something very basic—very fundamental—when we lose the front porch culture. Leaves the reader to consider the cost of this change.

Sunday drives in the country bring to mind an earlier time, when people hung out on the front porch talking with neighbors.

Ironically, McCovey is driving around.

Imagine: Being entertained by sitting on a porch and talking.

Concludes by asking the reader to imagine.

Where do people talk like they used to on a front porch: the kitchen table, the student lounge, Facebook, Twitter?

Writing Strategies

1. Why might McCovey address his reader directly in his first paragraph? Is this strategy effective? What effect does it have on you?

2. McCovey uses the first-person "I" in his essay, referring to his grandparents' houses, his own childhood house, and the houses in his neighborhood today. How might his essay be different had he avoided using "I"? Would it be better? Worse? No different?

3. McCovey deals in his third-to-last paragraph with the backyard deck. Why? Is this an essential part of his essay? What else might he have dealt with?

4. Identify McCovey's use of one metaphor or simile (comparing two unlike things: *The clerk was a bear* [metaphor]; *The clerk was like a bear* [simile]). Think of a metaphor or simile of your own that might work well in this essay.

5. Imagine that you are helping McCovey revise his essay and he is not happy with his conclusion. What suggestions would you make?

Exploring Ideas

1. Based on this essay, what does McCovey value? To what degree do you value the same thing?

2. In your own words, summarize McCovey's main idea. Then share your summary with several classmates who have also read the essay. Discuss your understanding of McCovey's main idea, and then reread his essay and revise your summary as necessary.

3. To further explore this issue, share your summary (via e-mail or in person) with people of various age groups, asking them to respond to McCovey's ideas. Describe how their views are similar to or different from McCovey's.

Ideas for Writing

1. Besides the move from *porch* to garage, what other change has taken place? How has that change impacted everyday life?

2. Observe some difference in a way of living, whether it be the result of time (your grandparents and you, for example) or location (southern Californians and Midwesterners). Do not be afraid to generalize, as long as you do it thoughtfully and are mindful of exceptions.

If responding to one of these ideas, go to the Analysis section of this chapter to begin developing ideas for your essay.

Corpse Colloquy

Justin Scott

Justin Scott, a Biology major at Western Michigan University, uses the Invention questions in this chapter to look beneath the surface and find new meaning in a familiar place, the graveyard. "Corpse Colloquy" is an example of how an observation essay goes beyond mere description. Through careful observation and analysis, Scott helps the reader see cemeteries differently, as "the key to a more exposed and fulfilling life."

The cemetery nestles within the confines of the city. "Oakwood," the sign announces. One can hardly help but wonder if the name is meant to reference the now-sparse trees, or if perhaps it refers to the dense forest of tombstones laden with a 6-foot-shallow bone root system. One must battle traffic and stoplights to gain entrance rather than multi-headed dogs and demanding ferry captains. The other thing that separates this still world of the dead from the busy world of the living is the winter skeleton of a hedge.

One thing is immediately obvious in this cemetery: Those laden with the gifts of life often choose to utilize them in death, and those less fortunate make do with what they must. Class warfare spills into the afterworld: Business owner is segregated from bricklayer, clergy is separated from atheist. There are large domineering crypts bearing the surnames of the wealthy dead inside, branch-scraping obelisks with ornate script, tombs carefully sculpted to resemble tree stumps, small temples dedicated to their dead in ancient Greek style, and, inevitably, the sunken, flat, and nondescript markers of the poor or humble. Some of the dead have even had exclusive gated communities constructed; large, elegant gravestones are surrounded with walls of iron or marble to keep the pauper corpses at a proper distance. The military and various secret societies have also their own niches; war memories, ranks carved into stones, and Mason symbols can be found throughout the cemetery, often placed more prominently than the name of the dead or when they were alive. Did people value their association with a group more than their own identity?

Toward the center of the field is an open plot with a marker denoting a common grave. Here lie the forgotten. Time will not remember their names any more readily than they were remembered while alive, for here are the mentally ill, the locked away and the vagrants. One large marker bids us to forget identity entirely.

Religion separates the dead as surely as the living. While in the living world the borders are less physically concrete, here signs announce the religious preference of those buried underneath. A walking tour reveals that here lie the Catholics, there the Jews, and over yonder are sundry reformists. Crosses, six-pointed stars and IHS[1] are distributed freely.

5   Neatly shorn trees line the carefully built roads. Were they interred there to keep the bony remains underneath from warring over wealth and religion as they would in life? Were it not for the snow, one would surely find grass cared for with the precision of a golf course and symmetrically trimmed bushes. The roads inside are paved but do not bear names; only the dead have that privilege here.

Modern society has a calculated and placated feel to it. Most things are carefully contrived in order to generate the most profit, and we are medicated to be placid and unfeeling; in the end, we are dedicated consumers in all things. Our deaths are as sterile and distant from us as the cemeteries in which our remains rest forever; manicured nails and laws make way for manicured plots of land and stones and preservation via formaldehyde. We supposedly live in *post-ironic* times. "Irony is dead," some would say. But irony is alive and well and can unmistakably be found among the dead in cemeteries worldwide.

It is said that only two things are certain in life: death and taxes. The cemetery, despite pomp, segregation, and sundry other shows for the living, does not belie that old aphorism. Everyone resting in that place, under or above earth, Catholic, Protestant, or Jew, poor or rich, remembered or forgotten, has succumbed to the scythe. Everyone dies. Yet in the frenzied pace of modern life this truth is lost, and we as ever fall into the patterns of exclusivity, neglect, bigotry, and *schadenfreude*.

[1] An abbreviation for the name of Jesus in Greek letters.

More time should be spent learning the dead. Their testament is spoken to us from within the maelstrom of coffins and gravestones. Their ghosts bade us not to be concerned with materialism, creed, or race; through them and the past they represent is the key to a more exposed and fulfilling life. *Graveyards are the doppelganger of the living world.* Seeing and recognizing the shadow-self of the graveyard allows us to enrich our lives and live beyond the lessons it presents. The cemetery, above all, tells us of acceptance and judgment: to embrace the former and neglect the latter. Life is finite, precious, and far too short to waste on arrogant trappings already so thoroughly explored by those entombed under earth.

Dona eis requiem sepiternam.[2]

[2] Angus Dei: "Grant them eternal rest."

Used by permission of the authors.

Writing Strategies

1. In Scott's essay, what does a cemetery reveal about life?

2. What details are most effective in helping the reader understand and accept Scott's main point?

3. Describe Scott's writer's voice. Refer to three sentences to support your description.

4. What other paragraph in the essay could Scott have used as the opening paragraph? Why would or wouldn't that paragraph be an effective new beginning?

5. How is Scott's essay a call to action?

Exploring Ideas

1. What does Scott value? How might his essay connect with a reader because he or she values the same thing?

2. How is the way you see a cemetery different from the way Scott sees one? Go beyond the casual glance. What else might a cemetery symbolize or reveal?

3. Talk to several people to find out their views on cemeteries. Do they visit cemeteries often? What word would they use to describe a cemetery: *peaceful, spiritual, creepy*? Why do people view cemeteries differently?

4. Research the modern cemetery. When did cemeteries become park-like, and why?

Ideas for Writing

1. Visit a few cemeteries, and carefully observe how they are set up and maintained. What is valued, and why? Try to reveal something new about cemeteries and life; help the reader see things differently.

2. Walk across campus with a few classmates or friends, drawing each others' attention to details people usually overlook. Take notes and make connections between various overlooked details. What new idea can you share about college, your college campus, education, life?

If responding to one of these ideas, go to the Analysis section of this chapter to begin developing ideas for your essay.

What, beyond cemeteries, is this essay ultimately about?

ANALYSIS

Details do not have their own meaning. It is up to people to *make* meaning from details. As we analyze, we move from observation notes to focused ideas, from a collection of potentially unrelated details to a set of particular points. Analysis prompts us to see patterns, connections, and paths within the particulars.

Invention Questions

The following questions can help you to make meaning out of your observation notes, and to look at the subject as something more than its physical characteristics:

- What is unique about the subject?

- What is ordinary about this subject? (How are its qualities common to other places, people, or animals?) What does that quality show?

- Is this subject symbolic of something? (Does it stand for some idea or ideal?)

- Does the subject seem different after the observation (more complicated, less intimidating, more human, less human, more predictable, and so on)?

- What does the subject "say" about life (about human interaction, social behavior, institutions, nature, and so on) in this place and time?

Attempt to gain insight beyond the simple glance, beyond the drive-by appearance of things.

While focusing on and gathering details may be a challenging aspect of observation, analyzing those details poses a difficulty of its own. Because a list of details offers so many options and no obvious path for making meaning, the process can be uncertain and confusing. However, it can be an intensive and valuable process. Imagine a student, Linda, who observed people at her place of work, a small factory. Her observation notes include long lists of details about the environment, the lighting, the physical actions of the workers, their interaction with the machines and with each other. But as she begins to analyze, using one of the Invention questions, she finds connections in those details. Notice how she goes beyond her first simplistic answer to a more complex idea:

> **What does the subject "say" about life (about human interaction, social behavior, institutions, nature, and so on) in this place and time?**
>
> At first, I thought that my coworkers were just miserable people at a job. They work at their individual stations, occasionally interact to communicate something about a machine part or materials, and then go to breaks—or home. But outside of that, I couldn't see anything important. But the more I looked over my notes, I realized something was going on in those small and infrequent interactions between people. While they might seem miserable and disconnected at times (maybe even most of the time), they all offer some support to one another: a small glance, a shared roll of the eyes when the supervisor inspects one person's work, the way Rob, the oldest in the shop, actually runs over to someone who needs help with something, the extra cup of coffee Bob got Maria because she didn't have time during break. All these things mean something—the underground, almost secretive, strategies to keep each other afloat in their shared situation. After I realized this, I went back over all my notes, and remembered things I had not written down. The days are actually filled with these little gestures; they happen at all times: at breaks, on the way into the shop in the morning, while the machines are operating.

Linda could then go on to develop this point in her writing. In fact, the idea may even develop into a thesis statement. This would mean that many other details (about physical structure, about the machines themselves) might be abandoned, unless they have some significance for worker interaction. In this way, Linda's observation goes from a list of seemingly unrelated details to a focused idea.

Activity

Observe the activities in your classroom. Consider actions and behaviors among work groups, among demographic groups, before the instructor arrives, or as the class ends. As a class or in a group, discuss the possible meaning or significance of particular events, behaviors, or interactions.

In Chester McCovey's invention notes, he explores the possible meaning of the garage—not simply what it does for people (store their cars) but how it works in their lives, how it says something about the way people live.

Is this subject symbolic of something? (Does it stand for some idea or ideal?)

It is, perhaps. These big garages are obviously a necessity for today's homeowner. I mean, most of these homes are not within walking distance of where the owner works. Many, I suspect, can only be afforded if both husband and wife work—two cars! Now, fill the garage up with all the other machinery you need to maintain the yard. The garage quite simply says "go," "drive," "automobile," "transportation." I am at home, but not for long. No doubt the cars have air conditioning, as does the house. One need never be hot (or cold). The garage has replaced the porch. You pull into the garage and go inside and stay inside the house. Then get in the air-conditioned space bubble car when you want to leave. Of course there is recreation, but recreation is getting away from life and not a part of it. Let's take a break in our day and burn some calories, not let's burn some calories in the natural course of our day. The garage symbolizes driving, moving, loss of neighborhood, community, wealth, poverty . . .

Thinking Further

Reread McCovey's invention writing. Notice that he explores possibilities and ultimately decides that the garage symbolizes six ideas: "driving, moving, loss of neighborhood, community, wealth, poverty." This list is an indication that McCovey is not yet done thinking about the symbolism of the garage.

Activity A For practice, pick up where McCovey's invention writing leaves off, taking his thinking even further. Consider the following questions:

- Which of the six ideas, if any, can be eliminated from the list, and why?
- What other items might be added, and why?
- How can the big garage symbolize both wealth and poverty?

For help, explore ideas further through discussion with classmates or with others outside of class.

Activity B Now consider your own invention writing, as you considered McCovey's above. For help, explore ideas further through discussion with classmates or with others outside of class.

- What new way of thinking (what insight, what revelation) did you discover?
- How might you explore the complexities of that idea further? For example:

   —How might that thinking be wrong?

   —How might that thinking be more complex than you presently imagine?

   —What apparent contradictions or inconsistencies must be explained?

PUBLIC RESONANCE

Writers do more than focus on a subject: They also make the subject resonate with the lives of others. When we read Annie Dillard, for instance, she prompts us to consider our connection to the natural world and the essence of our own lives. When we read Chester McCovey, we consider how the world around us is changing, and the effects those changes have on our lives.

The following questions will help broaden your subject's perspective and make it resonate with a potential audience:

- Why is this subject important to people? (Why is its uniqueness important?)
- Why should your peers know about this subject?
- What do people normally experience, understand, or assume about the subject?
- Does the presence or action of this subject teach people something—about themselves, about life, about work, about happiness, about materialism, about sincerity, about identity, about relationships, about the past, about the future, about death?

Notice how Chester McCovey explores the breadth of his subject—how the question helps him to see the broad implications of porches and garages. Also notice how the initial question leads McCovey to more questions:

> **Does the presence or action of this subject teach people something—about themselves, about life, about work, about happiness, about materialism, about sincerity, about identity, about relationships, about the past, about the future, about death?**
>
> What we see is a loss of community. The big garage shows us we're leaving our own neighborhood a lot. The fact that the garage is connected to the living space shows us that we go from our living area directly, by

pushing a button that opens the door, into the street and to another community far enough away that we drive to it. We don't interact with our neighbors (we might not even know their names). We drive past them with our windows rolled up. We maybe don't even smell or feel our neighborhood (I guess that's an exaggeration, but there's something there). Remember, we're not talking about all houses. We're talking about the ones built today. Is loss of neighborhood a loss to the people who live in those neighborhoods? Does big garage/no front porch mean loss of neighborliness? Yes, these relationships—or ones like them—can exist outside one's own neighborhood. But what is the effect of this? What is a neighbor anymore?

Some subjects seem to have public resonance automatically. The initial steps of analysis involve making connections to broader cultural trends. For instance, McCovey's focus on porches is a public trend. Some subjects, perhaps most, need to be *made* relevant to the audience, and it is up to a writer or speaker to make the connection.

For example, the stare of a weasel, one might think, has nothing whatsoever to do with the life of humans (or, specifically, the life of Annie Dillard's readers), but she makes a connection. She prompts the readers to compare their own ordered and calculated lives to the pure moment-by-moment life of the weasel. As Dillard shows, even the most personal observations can have public resonance; even the stare between one woman and one weasel can be connected to the lives of others:

> We could, you know. We can live any way we want. People take vows of poverty, chastity, and obedience—even of silence—by choice. The thing is to stalk your calling in a certain skilled and supple way, to locate the most tender and live spot and plug into that pulse. This is yielding, not fighting. A weasel doesn't "attack" anything; a weasel lives as he's meant to, yielding at every moment to the perfect freedom of single necessity.

Invention Workshop

Public Resonance: Remember that an essay does not simply relay information. Rather, it invites readers (and the writer) to re-see something, to think differently, and to discover something new in a familiar world. For example, if you think a writing topic (a place, a person, an animal, your major) is boring, then you have an opportunity to analyze and unpack the familiar boredom, finding something new worth sharing with others (something new *that matters*—that you can make matter—to others). Instead of allowing a dull topic to stop one's thinking, a good observer uses analysis to make the topic interesting.

Form a group with one or two other writers. Each writer should explain his or her observation to the others and read his or her initial responses to the Invention questions on page 118. Then, the others should address the following:

1. Help the writer go further by applying the strategy McCovey uses in his invention writing on page 118. That is, try to discover what the subject shows about the way people live, about the way people see the world around them.

2. Return to the Invention questions in this section and collectively offer responses for the writer's subject.

Make certain to spend equal time on each writer's observations. The goal is to develop new insights for each project. After the workshop session, each writer should return to the Invention questions on page 118 and write down how his or her thinking developed for each question. What new insights emerged?

Analysis: We do not mean to suggest that analysis and public resonance are always distinctly separate steps in thinking. Exploring the public resonance of a subject involves analysis, and responding to the Analysis prompts may lead to ideas about public resonance.

After exploring the public resonance of your topic with others and writing down any new insights, return to the Analysis questions on page 116. Respond in writing to these questions again, now that you have focused on the public resonance of the subject. See what else you can find. As you write, think about how you can reapproach the questions from a new, more-informed perspective. For example, how might you see something else unique about the subject now? Or, does the subject now seem less unique, or unique in some less obvious way?

1. What new insights emerged from your second round with the Analysis questions?

2. What new questions emerged? In groups or alone, explore these new questions through research and writing.

Writers do more than focus on a subject: They also make the subject resonate with the lives of others.

THESIS

The thesis of an essay offers a writer's specific insight on the subject. Remember that a thesis can be *explicit* (stated directly) or *implied* (unstated but suggested by the details). Either way, a writer benefits from having a single focused statement to guide the process. For this project, the main idea should reveal a new insight about a subject. The more narrow the insight, the more focused and intensive the writing will be. Although it is easy to offer a first-glance statement, try to narrow in on a particular quality. Notice how the following bulleted statements offer broad and even predictable ideas. But the purple statements reveal something unique and specific:

- The people at the local tavern keep to themselves.

  In the dark, smoky quiet of Timothy's Pub, the regulars face straight ahead but share intimate crises in their quick coded exchanges.

- The neighborhood is a quiet place.

  The disappearing porches in the neighborhood signal a shift to a more disconnected, isolating, but technologically advanced time.

- The Fun Factory has a spirit of competition.

  Once the games begin at The Fun Factory, the players shift radically: from unfocused adolescent "dorks" to focused competitive intellectuals.

Notice how the more specific theses focus on more particular subjects:

> people vs. regulars
> neighborhood vs. disappearing porches
> Fun Factory vs. players

The sentences bring the reader up close. (We can even imagine a television camera literally zooming in to the more particular subjects.) Also, the purple sentences have stronger verbs:

> *keep* vs. *face/share*
> *is* vs. *signal*
> *has* vs. *shift*

The stronger verbs do more than create action in the sentences. They actually enrich the content—making the nouns work harder. As a result, the sentences push the reader's (and writer's) consciousness through the sentence with more energy.

Activity

In small groups, present your thesis statements. (If possible, write the statements on a board.) The group should analyze each statement and try to create more focus. Apply the following:

1. For each noun, suggest a more specific word.

2. Suggest stronger verbs.

For this project the main idea should reveal a new insight about the subject. The more narrow the insight, the more focused and intensive the writing will be.

Evolution of a Thesis

Imagine a writer is observing students at a community college. She notices many things about the students: their clothes, their ages, and so on. But she decides to focus on a particular point: *The students at Beach Community College spend their time coming and going primarily alone.* Such a statement offers a particular idea about the college students. The essay, then, would focus on the solitary nature of the students. The point might grow and develop layers throughout the invention process:

Point of Contact:

- The majority of the students coming in and out of the buildings are alone; they do not talk together or in groups. If people are talking, they are talking on cell phones.

Analysis:

- Although I have always associated college with social life, the students at Beach Community College show that college is often a solitary experience.

Public Resonance:

- When most people talk about college, they inevitably bring up campus life: the parties, the Greek system, the study groups, etc. They think of all the movies and stories about those crazy college years, but the reality may be fundamentally different for many students.

Working Thesis:

- Despite the popular notions of social life on college campuses, the students at Beach Community College show that higher education can be a solitary experience.

Use the Invention questions on pages 116 and 118 to help develop the thesis of your essay. Or you might examine your notes and find one common idea or thread of details, which can lead to a general statement about the subject.

Revision

Develop a chart like the one below that shows the evolution of your thesis from Point of Contact through Working Thesis. Try to represent the way your thesis gains focus and depth. You might refer to your field notes and specific Invention questions that help generate and focus your ideas. Then ask yourself: *What words or phrases are too broad? Can I make the subject more specific? Can I strengthen the verbs?*

Point of Contact:

_____

_____

_____

Analysis:

_____

_____

_____

Public Resonance:

_____

_____

_____

Working Thesis:

_____

_____

_____

RHETORICAL TOOLS

An observing essay seeks to show a reader something new about a particular subject and to lead a reader to an insightful conclusion about that subject. That insight, the writer's particular understanding about the subject, is the value for the reader—the thing he or she will carry away from the essay. So an observing essay goes far beyond offering details; it offers a unique awareness about a subject and its significance, an awareness that the writer has gained through careful study and examination.

Using Details

Remember that the details of the essay should lead the reader to the same conclusion that the writer makes. Refer to your notes from the Point of Contact section and find all the specific details to support your main point. Your essay should be generated *only* from the details that help to show that point. Unrelated details may be left behind. For example, consider Annie Dillard's observation of a weasel. Her main point focuses on the weasel's "purity of living." She gives us details and images that communicate that idea. You can imagine many other details (such as where the weasel went after the encounter or general information about weasel life), but such information would not support her main idea. The essay includes details that show the contrast between Dillard's life of motive and the weasel's life of purity.

Using Narrative

Many writers choose to narrate the events of an observation—to explain the events leading up to a particular moment of discovery. Such narration can help to place the observation in time and help to situate the reader. Dillard uses narration particularly well at the beginning of her essay. She takes the reader through several paragraphs that lead up to the moment of her encounter with the weasel. Here, Dillard uses narration to narrow her focus from a broader view of the natural surroundings to a particular animal:

> The sun had just set. I was relaxed on the tree trunk, ensconced in the lap of lichen, watching the lily pads at my feet tremble and part dreamily over the thrusting path of a carp. A yellow bird appeared to my right and flew behind me. It caught my eye; I swiveled around— and the next instant, inexplicably, I was looking down at a weasel, who was looking up at me.

The narration creates a powerful contrast between the nonchalant, relaxed feeling of the surroundings and the weasel's intense stare.

If you are considering using narration in your writing, ask yourself the following questions:

- Would narrating the events leading up to the observation help engage the reader?
- Would narrating part of the observation help to engage the reader?

Caution: Using narrative can make an observation less formal. Instructors in some disciplines may want you to avoid narration.

Using Allusions

Allusions are references to bits of public knowledge, things, events, or people outside of the main subject being observed. Writers use allusions to help illustrate a point or create a feeling. For instance, McCovey alludes to baseball when discussing the front porch:

> One can see, then, how the exchange occurred. Like an old-fashioned trade in baseball, gone is the home team's beloved front porch, replaced by a big, new garage.

McCovey's allusion calls the reader back to an earlier time when people sat outside on front porches and talked to neighbors passing by. The allusion to baseball helps to create the feeling of which McCovey speaks in his conclusion: "I am not prepared here to argue that we are a civilization in deep trouble because of this, though it does seem to me appropriate that we should lament, at least a little, the loss of the front porch." Some (not all) readers will immediately identify with the feeling the allusion conjures, of a time in baseball before free agency when many players began and ended their careers with the same team, when fans became more attached to their hometown players and were more likely to lament their departure, when life was simpler, the pace slower, and baseball was the national pastime.

McCovey's allusion to the old-fashioned trade in baseball illustrates both the value of and the concern with using allusions. Some readers won't pick up on the baseball allusion. McCovey decides to use it anyway, understanding this. The allusion adds texture and depth of meaning for some readers, but McCovey does not allow the overall meaning of his essay to be lost on a reader who doesn't understand the allusion. (A reader would not say: I didn't understand his main idea because I don't know what an old-fashioned trade in baseball is.)

The following questions will help you develop allusions for your own writing:

- Does my subject relate to any political event or situation?
- Does my subject relate to any social or cultural event or situation?
- Does my subject relate to any person or event in history? In literature? In popular culture (movies, television, music)?

Using Simile and Metaphor

Similes and metaphors are comparisons that point out or create similarities between two or more seemingly different things. (A simile uses "like" or "as.") Writers use them to help create pictures for readers, to make points more engaging and intense. Notice how Dillard compares meeting a weasel to meeting a lover or deadly enemy:

> Our look was as if two lovers, or deadly enemies met unexpectedly on an overgrown path when each had been thinking of something else: a clearing blow to the gut. It was also a bright blow to the brain, or a sudden beating of brains, with all the charge and intimate grate of rubbed balloons. It emptied our lungs. It felled the forest, moved the fields, and drained the pond; the world dismantled and tumbled into that black hole of eyes. If you and I looked at each other that way, our skulls would split and drop to our shoulders. But we don't. We keep our skulls. So.

As you consider your own writing, remember that figurative language such as similes and metaphors should be used to direct the reader's perception toward your main ideas. Such figurative language should be used sparingly.

The following questions will help you develop similes and metaphors for your own writing:

- Can I compare my subject to an animal? A thing? A place? A person?
- What purpose would this comparison serve?

Activity

Find other similes or metaphors in the chapter readings and explain how they help extend the writer's thinking or support the writer's points.

ORGANIZATIONAL STRATEGIES

How Should I Deal with Public Resonance?

The questions relating to public resonance might simply help the writer develop a sense of mission. However, writers sometimes choose to make a direct appeal to the audience; that is, they invite the reader directly into the issue at hand. Annie Dillard's essay invites the reader with a question. After describing her experience, she asks,"Could two live that way? Could two live under the wild rose, and explore by the pond, so that the smooth mind of each is as everywhere present to the other, and as received and as unchallenged, as falling snow?" Her answer includes the audience:

> We could, you know. We can live any way we want. People take vows of poverty, chastity, and obedience—even of silence—by choice. The thing is to stalk your calling in a certain skilled and supple way, to locate the most tender and live spot and plug into that pulse. This is yielding, not fighting. A weasel doesn't "attack" anything; a weasel lives as he's meant to, yielding at every moment to the perfect freedom of single necessity.

Chester McCovey extends his observation to the reader's situation. This is an explicit strategy to make the subject relate to the reader:

> If you walk through my neighborhood, you won't see many porches, at least not the kind people sit on in the evenings. Those days are gone where I live, and likely where you live, too.

As his essay develops, McCovey makes his observation a public concern, and by the concluding paragraph, suggests something about the nature of American public life:

> On Sunday drives through the country, I see big new houses with big new porches. As Americans we can have it all—the house with the big front porch *and* the big garage. But I never (I am tempted to qualify this statement and say "almost never" or "rarely" but I have been thinking about it and I do mean

"never")—I never see anyone out sitting on those porches. I am not prepared here to argue that we are as a civilization in deep trouble because of this, though it does seem to me appropriate that we should lament, at least a little, the loss of the front porch.

After describing the cemetery throughout his essay, Justin Scott makes sure the reader knows what his carefully selected details should mean to the reader:

> More time should be spent learning the dead. Their testament is spoken to us from within the malestrom of coffins and gravestones. Their ghosts bade us not to be concerned with materialism, creed, or race; through them and the past they represent is the key to a more exposed and fulfilling life. *Graveyards are the doppelganger of the living world.* Seeing and recognizing the shadow-self of the graveyard allows us to enrich our lives and live beyond the lessons it presents. The cemetery, above all, tells us of acceptance and judgment: to embrace the former and neglect the latter. Life is finite, precious, and far too short to waste on arrogant trappings already so thoroughly explored by those entombed under earth.

How Should I Arrange Details?

Of course, arrangement depends upon the subject to some degree, but writers make deliberate choices about the placement of details. You might decide on a *chronological* strategy (presenting details through time), as Dillard uses. This strategy depends on narrative. But notice that Dillard's essay does not depend entirely on narrative. She begins with general reflections and a related account about weasels before offering a brief narrative. After the narrative, she explains the meaning and significance of her observation. The narrative is only a strategy to relay the details of her observation.

But chronological organization does not work for all topics. Chester McCovey's essay illustrates another set of strategies for arranging details. Like Dillard, McCovey devotes much of his essay to the significance or meaning of his observation. But where Dillard gives a narrative of her observation, McCovey shrinks the observation into a short introductory paragraph. (In other words, we do not witness McCovey encountering porches the way we witness Dillard encountering the weasel.) Because McCovey's point involves history (front porches are no longer central to our way of life), he moves to the past in the second paragraph. His essay, then, is arranged to illustrate the difference between the past and the present.

When Should I Change Paragraphs?

You might think of paragraph changes as camera shifts. That is, if you have a subject that allows spatial arrangement, change paragraphs whenever you want to create a new field of vision—whenever you want the reader to "see" a new thing or imagine a new scene. For example, Annie Dillard uses paragraph breaks to shift focus: from a tree to a whole span of the scene and then to a weasel. (Notice, also, the extra space that Dillard inserts before the paragraph about the weasel. Some writers do this occasionally to create a more emphatic break in the action.)

> Then I cut down through the woods to the mossy fallen tree where I sit. This tree is excellent. It makes a dry, upholstered bench at the upper, marshy end of the pond, a plush jetty raised from the thorny shore between a shallow blue body of water and a deep blue body of sky.
>
> The sun had just set. I was relaxed on the tree trunk, ensconced in the lap of lichen, watching the lily pads at my feet tremble and part dreamily over the thrusting path of a carp. A yellow bird appeared to my right and flew behind me. It caught my eye; I swiveled around—and the next instant, inexplicably, I was looking down at a weasel, who was looking up at me.
>
> Weasel! I'd never seen one wild before. He was ten inches long, thin as a curve, a muscled ribbon, brown as fruitwood, soft-furred, alert.

Invention Workshop

Justin Scott uses paragraph changes in "Corpse Colloquy" to move the reader through the cemetery and through the points he makes about it. Below is the first sentence of each paragraph in Scott's essay. In groups, discuss the camera shift that takes place in each paragraph:

1. What is the focus of each paragraph?
2. How does the paragraph's focus support Scott's main idea?
3. How does the opening sentence of the paragraph help shift the reader's focus?

- The cemetery nestles within the confines of the city.
- One thing is immediately obvious in this cemetery: Those laden with the gifts of life often choose to utilize them in death, and those less fortunate make do with what they must.
- Toward the center of the field is an open plot with a marker denoting a common grave.
- Religion separates the dead as surely as the living.
- Neatly shorn trees line the carefully built roads.
- Modern society has a calculated and placated feel to it.
- It is said that only two things are certain in life: death and taxes.
- More time should be spent learning the dead.

Change paragraphs when you want to create a new field of vision.

WRITER'S VOICE

The Present "I"

Some writers choose to make themselves visible in the text. They refer to themselves and their interactions with the subject. McCovey includes himself in his observations and refers to his own presence in the scenes or situations. But he does not simply inject the "I" without good cause. McCovey's presence helps to show the lack of front porches in a particular area, but his personal history (recollections of his grandparents) helps to make a point about changes that have occurred in American society. His use of the personal and of the present "I" gives support to his more general claims.

The present "I" can also be used to illustrate important human responses to a situation. The actual encounter between Dillard and the weasel is vital to the point of her essay. The stare between them provides insight into the weasel's life, and into Dillard's connection to such a life. Without the "I," the natural world (the world of the weasel) would seem more disconnected to the reader.

Activity

Select a paragraph from either Dillard's or McCovey's essay that uses the "I." Without using the "I," rewrite that paragraph. Try to convey the information without attention to the writer. Then discuss how the change might influence how the essay is read.

The Invisible "I"

In observation, the writer is sometimes invisible. That is, the writerly "I" never appears; instead, the text focuses entirely on the subject. Justin Scott remains invisible in his observation, yet his essay still projects a particular voice:

> One thing is immediately obvious in this cemetery: Those laden with the gifts of life often choose to utilize them in death, and those less fortunate make do with what they must. Class warfare spills into

the afterworld: Business owner is segregated from bricklayer, clergy is separated from atheist. There are large domineering crypts bearing the surnames of the wealthy dead inside, branch-scraping obelisks with ornate script, tombs carefully sculpted to resemble tree stumps, small temples dedicated to their dead in ancient Greek style, and inevitably, the sunken, flat, and nondescript markers of the poor or humble. . . .

Scott's passage illustrates how a writer's voice can be projected not through "I," but through careful word choice and sentence structure. (See how this passage is used later to discuss voice, vitality, and sentence length.)

You might ask your instructor if he or she finds the writerly "I" valuable, but every writer should also ask some basic questions:

- Should I put myself in the observation?
- If "I" am in the observation, what purpose does it serve?

Level of Formality

Formality is the adherence to an established convention. A formal text is one that closely follows expectations and avoids slipping out of conventional language and organizational patterns. A business memo, for instance, has certain conventions or guidelines, and memo writers rarely deviate from them. This is because of *context*, the situation in which they are written and received. (Readers of memos in professional situations do not expect to follow a writer outside of the conventions.) Scientific reports also have specific conventions, depending on the discipline. The scientist follows the discipline's conventions so that the writing does not interfere with the ideas being communicated. A text that strictly follows conventions is usually considered formal, while a text that deviates is considered informal.

Because essays are used in a number of situations and academic disciplines, the conventions vary, and so does the expected level of formality. Generally, writing that draws no attention to the writer's presence or writing style is considered more formal, while writing that draws attention to the writer's presence and style is considered less formal. (Of course, this is a general rule, and it does not apply to all writing situations.)

In her essay, Dillard illustrates a variety of informal strategies. For instance, she makes explicit her own reflective state of mind. Here, Dillard constructs an elaborate metaphor and speaks directly to the reader (usually a more informal strategy). She draws attention to herself and her particular style with unconventional sentence structure. (Notice the one-word sentence, "So."):

> If you and I looked at each other that way, our skulls would split and drop to our shoulders. But we don't. We keep our skulls. So.

Much of Dillard's essay, in fact, is a study in breaking conventions of formality:

> I would like to learn, or remember, how to live. I come to Hollins Pond not so much to learn how to live as, frankly, to forget about it. That is, I don't think I can learn from a wild animal how to live in particular—shall I suck warm blood, hold my tail high, walk with my footprints precisely over the prints of my hands?—but I might learn something of mindlessness, something of the purity of living in the physical senses and the dignity of living without bias or motive.

In showing us the details of a weasel's life, Dillard goes beyond simply informing us. She does not say, "Weasels live in the purity of physical senses. They suck their prey's warm blood." Instead, she imagines herself in that purity ("Shall I suck warm blood?") and puts herself in the center of those details. Her sentence structure, which varies from very short,

one-word sentences to long, multi-layered musings, draws further attention to the writer's presence. In other words, as we read Dillard, we experience her particular style, her writerly strategies and intimate thoughts, as part of the essay. "Annie Dillard" is not simply a name inscribed at the top of the page. It is an identity competing for our attention and sharing her meditations on the essence of life.

Activity

Try to rewrite any paragraph in Dillard's essay using a very formal style that does not draw attention to the presence of the writer or the sentence structure. How does the level of formality affect the meaning?

As you consider your own writing, ask yourself:

- Should I break some academic conventions? What might be the consequences?
- Should I appear formal? Why? What good will it do?
- Should I put myself in the observation?
- Will my presence help communicate the main idea or distract the reader from experiencing the subject?

VITALITY

Sentences are the writer's only connection to readers. Engaging sentences lead to engaged readers. Flat, safe, unvaried sentences lead to disinterested readers. In short, sentence structure can make all the difference. Consider the following strategies:

Experiment with Length

If writers aren't careful, they can slip into monotone, in which every sentence has generally the same number of words, the same number of clauses, and the same types of phrases. Just as good speakers vary the sound of their voices, good writers vary the length of sentences. Notice how Scott varies sentence length in the following passage:

> One thing is immediately obvious in this cemetery: those laden with the gifts of life often choose to utilize them in death, and those less fortunate make do with what they must. Class warfare spills into the afterworld: business owner is segregated from bricklayer, clergy are separated from atheist. There are large overbearing crypts bearing the surnames of the wealthy dead inside, branch-scraping obelisks with ornate script, tombs carefully sculpted to resemble tree stumps, small temples dedicated to their dead in ancient Greek style, and inevitably the sunken, flat and nondescript markers of the poor or humble.

In his first two sentences, Scott uses a colon to connect an explanation to the preceding sentence part, an independent clause. The colons help to break up the ideas for the reader and create a rhythm and voice. By following these shorter sentences with a longer one that expresses the different ways people are segregated in a cemetery, Scott helps give the reader a sense that many ways exist. While Scott's final sentence is lengthy, because it is grammatically correct the reader will not become lost in the ideas.

Likewise, Cindy Bosley's stylistic sentence (from Chapter 2) is correct:

> So 14 of us, nervous, jealous, ears ringing with Mirror-Mirror-on-the-Wall, met daily for two weeks prior to the pageant to go over our choreographed group fitness routine to be performed, not in swimsuits, but in short-shorts and white T-shirts, Hooters-style (also not invented yet as far as we knew), and to discuss such techniques as Vaseline along the teeth and gum lines to promote smooth smiles, lest our lips dry out and get stuck in a grin during discussions with the judges of the agonies of world hunger.

Such extreme moves are perilous, adventurous, and powerful. They take control of the reader's mind and demand a commitment.

> ## Just as good speakers vary the sound of their voices, good writers vary the length of sentences.

Experiment with Brevity

Short sentences keep readers alert and moving—but only when they are interspersed with longer sentences. Short sentences can also help dramatize thought, as in this passage from McCovey:

> I am not saying there are no front porches. Obviously there are. And I am not saying everyone has a two-car garage instead. In my neighborhood, small garages not connected to the house still reign.

Or notice the nuances that Dillard brings out with her short/long/short pattern:

> I missed my chance. I should have gone for the throat. I should have lunged for that streak of white under the weasel's chin and held on, held on through mud and into the wild rose, held on for a dearer life. We could live under the wild rose wild as weasels, mute and uncomprehending. I could very calmly go wild.

In another passage, Dillard goes further with brevity—even breaking the rules of sentence construction:

> It felled the forest, moved the fields, and drained the pond; the world dismantled and tumbled into that black hole of eyes. If you and I looked at each other that way, our skulls would split and drop to our shoulders. But we don't. We keep our skulls. So.

For information on stylistic fragments, see the Vitality section of Chapter 12.

Change Out Vague Nouns

Vague nouns refer to nothing in particular: *people, society, things, everyone,* and so on. It is often tempting to rely on vague nouns to float ideas past readers. But vague nouns have at least two negative effects: (1) They keep the reader from focusing, and (2) they signal that the writer has not committed to a statement. Notice the difference between these two passages:

> Animals are wild. They do wild things that we humans cannot imagine.

> A weasel is wild. Who knows what he thinks? He sleeps in his underground den, his tail draped over his nose.

The first sentence starts with a vague noun: *animals.* (That means all animals, everywhere!) And because the subject of the first sentence is so vague, the second sentence (equally vague) seems okay. The vague nouns lull the writer and reader into a relaxed state—in which broad, ill-defined statements seem fine. But Dillard demands more of her nouns, more of herself, and more of her readers. She starts with a more specific noun—a sharper focus. From there, she maintains that focus—and as readers, we follow her into a weasel's den!

Frankly, vague nouns plague college writing (and instructors everywhere dislike them). While they are not inherently evil (sometimes writers need to use words such as *things* and *people*), they generally make for vague statements.

Invention Workshop

With one or two peers, inject more vitality into your writing. Point to particular sentences and phrases that could be more intense.

1. **Help the writer experiment with length and brevity.** Take one paragraph and rewrite its sentences. Combine some sentences, weaving together several interconnected ideas. Shorten other sentences so that the passage tugs and pulls, varying long and short sentences for a dramatic effect.

2. **Change out vague nouns.** Underline vague nouns (such as *people, society, things,* etc.) and suggest more specific words.

3. Consider vitality strategies from other chapters:
   —Change *be* verbs to active verbs.
   —Change clauses to phrases.
   —Change phrases to words.
   —Combine sentences.
   —Repeat structures.
   —Intensify verbs.

After you workshop for vitality, reflect on the changes you made. Making your writing more vital should make your thinking more vital. How did your thinking change or develop because of more vital writing?

Vital sentences demand the reader's commitment.

PEER REVIEW

Exchange drafts with at least one other writer. Before passing your draft to others, underline the thesis, or write it above your essay. This way, reviewers will get traction as they read.

As a reviewer, use the following questions to guide your response.

1. Point out any words or phrases in the thesis that could be more specific. (See the Thesis section for more guidance.)

2. Where can the writer do more analysis and reveal more about the subject in the observation? (Point to passages that seem most obvious to you. As you read, look for claims that anyone could immediately offer without intensive analysis. Beside these passages, write: "More analysis?" If you can suggest an interesting idea, explain it on the back of the writer's draft.)

3. Help the writer to illustrate his or her claims with details. As you read, look for broad characterizations—those that anyone could imagine without a close observation. Ask yourself: Could this be more specific? Can we *really* see the particular nuances of the subject? In the margin, write "more details" where the writer could more intensely show the points.

4. Offer some figurative language to help characterize the subject. After you have read the entire draft, offer your own metaphor or simile about the subject. Give your suggestion on the back of the draft. Make sure it is something that fits the writer's voice, something that he or she could use.

5. If the writer uses narrative, does it help support the main idea of the observation? How? (If you have difficulty explaining how it supports the main point, perhaps the writer should rethink its use in the essay!)

6. Are the paragraphs coherent? Do you ever get the sense that a paragraph is wandering—giving you details that seem unrelated to one another or unrelated to the point of the essay? If so, write in the margin: "check paragraph coherence."

7. The most focused statement possible often makes for a better introduction. Suggest a surprisingly focused opening statement. (The writer might decide to use it.)

8. Consider the writer's voice.
   - If the writer is present (using "I"), is this necessary? Explain how the presence of the writer helps make the point of the observation.
   - If the writer is invisible (no "I"), how is that beneficial?
   - Where could the writer be more informal (breaking some conventions) or more formal?

9. Help the reader avoid common grammatical errors: comma splices, sentence fragments, or pronoun/antecedent agreement.

10. Write down the specific subject of the observation: *weasels, porches, cemeteries,* for example. Then complete the following statement.

Ultimately, this essay is not about [the specific subject: *weasels,* for example].

It is about _____.

Peer Review Truisms

- The process can make writers think differently about their own work.

- Even the most inexperienced writer can offer valuable comments.

- Chat is the great enemy of good analysis.

- Peer review can be the most valuable component of a writing class.

- All writers need help.

- Done carelessly, peer review can be a terrible thing.

For more explanation, see Chapter 2, pages 60–61.

DELIVERY

What we value dictates how we see. What we believe in controls the conclusions we make about the world. For example, someone looking at a car lot full of shiny SUVs might see ridiculous and costly waste, while someone else might see opportunity and signs of success.

Person A

- Values moderation, health, conserving resources, family comfort.
- Believes that people should tread carefully upon the Earth.
- Believes most people are victims of materialist propaganda.
- Hopes for a future with cleaner air, better health, less poverty, and less international strife.
- Sees a lot full of SUVs as a shiny, attractive waste of resources, a nicely structured delusion about the present and the future.

Person B

- Values financial success, health, nice neighborhoods, family comfort.
- Believes that people should reap the benefits of their hard work, that human desire is good for the economy, that material things support the pursuit of happiness.
- Believes most people do not work hard enough for what they want.
- Hopes for a future of more economic stability, upward mobility, and less international strife.
- Sees a lot full of SUVs as a sign of America's economic success and people's individual hopes for a more stable and secure life.

Now that you have written an observing essay—and have come to your own conclusions—answer the following questions:

- What values lie beneath my conclusions?
- What beliefs (about people, the past, the present, the future, comfort, animals, cities, etc.) lie beneath my conclusions?
- What hopes for myself, for the future, for all people might have influenced the way I see the subject of the observation?
- More than anything else, what value or belief controlled the way I saw the subject?

Beyond the Essay: An Illustration

Sophisticated ideas can be embodied in various kinds of texts, not just essays. Many writers like to draw their ideas, illustrating them with images and symbols. In this rendering, Chester McCovey illustrates the main distinctions between the porch of the past and the garage of the present:

Consider your own observation. What is the main idea? What new insight do you offer? What important notion do you reveal? What hidden meaning do you dig up and share with readers? How can you illustrate those ideas?

Front Porch

• Sunlight
• Cool Breeze
• Visiting with Neighbors
• Simplicity
• Community

Big Garage

• Electricity
• Air Conditioning
• Sitting in Traffic
• High-Tech Machines

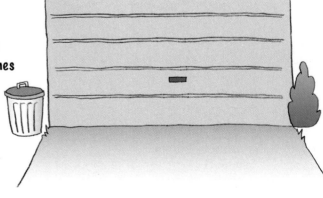

ANALYZING CONCEPTS

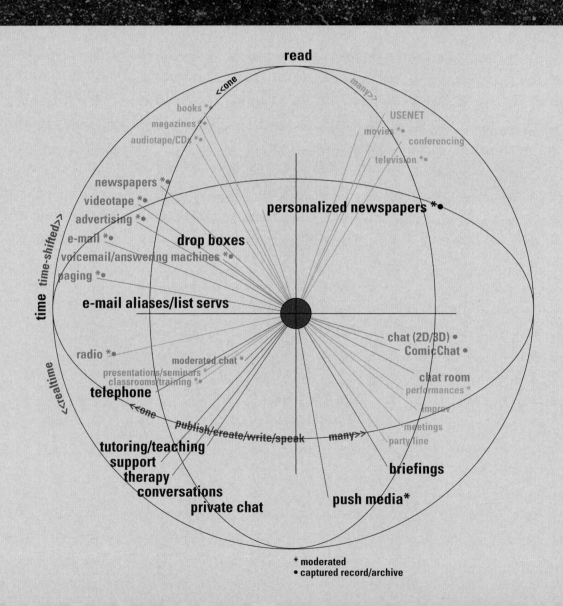

read

<<one   many>>

books *•
magazines *•
audiotape/CDs *•

USENET
movies *•
conferencing
television *•

newspapers *•
videotape *•
advertising *•
e-mail *•
voicemail/answering machines *•
paging *•

personalized newspapers *•

drop boxes

time-shifted>>

e-mail aliases/list servs

time

chat (2D/3D) •
ComicChat •

radio *•

realtime

moderated chat *
presentations/seminars *
classrooms/training *•

chat room
performances *
improv

telephone

<<one   many>>
publish/create/write/speak

meetings
party line

tutoring/teaching
support
therapy
conversations
private chat

briefings

push media*

* moderated
• captured record/archive

Chapter Contents

CHAPTER 5

What It Means to Be Creative

S. I. Hayakawa

Analyzing a concept requires some intellectual digging. We have to dig into common terms—ones that we normally take for granted. We also have to imagine a good deal of complexity beneath those common terms. In this essay, S. I. Hayakawa reveals the complexities beneath creativity. *He goes beyond merely describing creative people to breaking down the concept and showing us what it is and how it works.*

What distinguishes the creative person? By creative person I don't mean only the great painter or poet or musician. I also want to include the creative housewife, teacher, warehouseman, sales manager—anyone who is able to break through habitual routines and invent new solutions to old problems, solutions that strike people with their appropriateness as well as originality, so that they say, "Why didn't I think of that?"

A creative person, first, is not limited in his thinking to "what everyone knows." "Everyone knows" that trees are green. The creative artist is able to see that in certain lights some trees look blue or purple or yellow. The creative person looks at the world with his or her own eyes, not with the eyes of others. The creative individual also knows his or her own feelings better than the average person. Most people don't know the answer to the question, "How are you? How do you feel?" The reason they don't know is that they are so busy feeling what they are supposed to feel, thinking what they are supposed to think, that they never get down to examining their own deepest feelings.

"How did you like the play?" "Oh, it was a fine play. It was well reviewed in *The New Yorker*."

With authority figures like drama critics and book reviewers and teachers and professors telling us what to think and how to feel, many of us are busy playing roles, fulfilling other people's expectations. As Republicans, we think what other Republicans think. As Catholics, we think what other Catholics think. And so on. Not many of us ask ourselves, "How do I feel? What do I think?"—and wait for answers.

5   Another characteristic of the creative person is that he is able to entertain and play with ideas that the average person may regard as silly, mistaken, or downright dangerous. All new ideas sound foolish at first, because they are new. (In the early days of the railroad, it was argued that speeds of twenty-five mph or over were impractical because people's brains would burst.) A person who is afraid of being laughed at or disapproved of for having "foolish" or "unsound" ideas will have the satisfaction of having everyone agree with him, but he will never be creative, because creativity means being willing to take a chance—to go out on a limb.

The person who would be creative must be able to endure loneliness—even ridicule. If he has a great and original idea that others are not yet ready to accept, there will be long periods of loneliness. There will be times when his friends and relatives think he is crazy, and he'll begin to wonder if they are right. A genuinely creative person, believing in his creation, is able to endure this loneliness—for years if necessary.

Another trait of the creative person is idle curiosity. Such a person asks questions, reads books, conducts investigations into matters apparently unrelated to job or profession—just for the fun of knowing. It is from these apparently unrelated sources that brilliant ideas often emerge to enrich one's own field of work.

Finally, the creative person plays hunches. "Pure intellect," says Dr. Hans Selye, the great medical researcher at the University of Montreal, "is largely a quality of the middle-class mind. The lowliest hooligan and the greatest creator in the fields of science are activated mainly by imponderable instincts and emotions, especially faith. Curiously, even scientific research, the most intellectual creative effort of which man is capable, is no exception in this respect."

Alfred Korzybski also understood well the role of undefinable emotions in the creative life. He wrote, "Creative scientists know very well from observation of themselves that all creative work starts as a feeling, inclination, suspicion, intuition, hunch, or some other nonverbal affective state, which only at a later date, after a sort of nursing, takes the shape of verbal expression worked out later in a rationalized, coherent . . . theory."

10   Creativity is the act of bringing something new into the world, whether a symphony, a novel, an improved layout for a supermarket, a new and unexpected casserole dish. It is based first on communication with oneself, then testing that communication with experience and the realities one has to contend with. The result is the highest, most exciting kind of learning.

Writing Strategies

1. Describe the strategy Hayakawa uses to help the reader to understand the term "creative." That is, how specifically does he make the term clear to the reader?

2. Describe Hayakawa's voice—the way he sounds to the reader.

3. Would you describe Hayakawa's writing as creative? Explain what is or is not creative about his writing.

4. How does Hayakawa lead the reader from one paragraph to another? Select several paragraphs as examples for your explanation.

Exploring Ideas

1. Rate yourself on your own creativity scale. Be ready to support your claim.

2. Hayakawa says that one trait of the creative person is "idle curiosity"—asking questions, reading books, conducting investigations into matters "apparently unrelated to job or profession—just for the fun of knowing." Ask others to list several traits of the creative person, and then explain how their ideas about creativity are similar to or different from Hayakawa's.

3. In what ways is writing an essay an act of "creativity"? List Hayakawa's main points (or characteristics) of creativity and apply them to writing an essay. Which ones apply? Which ones don't?

4. Why do you think science is often seen as uncreative? What happens in school that makes students see scientific thinking and creativity as different or contrary?

Ideas for Writing

1. Based on Hayakawa's definition of "creative," who is not generally considered creative but in fact is?

2. Hayakawa's essay analyzes the concept of "creativity" or "the creative person." What other concepts might you analyze?

good teacher	great band
Thanksgiving dinner	good sermon
best friend	humanitarian
snappy dresser	nice day
bad waitress	good president
rewarding experience	parent

If responding to one of these ideas, go to the Analysis section of this chapter to begin developing ideas for your essay.

"Have It Your Way": Consumerism Invades Education

Simon Benlow

What is a student? This might sound like a silly question, but *student* can be defined in different ways. So can *education*. And the way a person defines or understands these concepts can make a difference in the way that person—and others—acts. In the following essay, Simon Benlow explores what it means to be a student and to participate in an education. Notice how Benlow narrows his focus. He doesn't talk generally about all the characteristics of education, but instead examines the important role consumerism (another concept) plays in education.

Two weeks ago, the faculty and staff received a memo regarding "National Customer Service Week." We were urged to take special efforts in serving our customers—presumably, our students. Certainly, I have no objections to extending extra efforts in helping students feel comfortable and situated in the college environment. However, I am deeply troubled (as are many, or most, instructors and professors) by use of the term "customer" to refer to students. I am concerned, in general, about the slow and subtle infiltration of consumerism into education (by companies buying access to students' brains), and I am downright hostile to the way "customer" has suddenly replaced the word (and maybe idea of) "student" in higher education. And because my concerns may seem ungrounded, I'd like to offer a brief analysis—a quick examination of the basic, and not-so-basic, differences between "customer" and "student."

"The customer is always right." We hear this hollow phrase resound through (almost) every corridor of our consumerist culture. The motive behind the phrase is painfully clear—to keep customers happy, to keep them from complaining, and most importantly, to keep them coming back. (Of course, the meaninglessness of the phrase is well known, too—for those of us who have had the displeasure of talking with Ameritech operators or "customer service" tellers at our banks.) The phrase

is meant to maintain a climate in which the substance of anyone's concerns or complaints is obfuscated by friendly and diplomatic clichés—"your business means so much to us"; "we'll do everything we can to address the problem." Ultimately, then, the goal of customer service, in this sense, is to lull customers into a sense of complacency—even though their phones may not be working or their washers are throwing sparks.

"Have it your way!" Of course, we all know the song and the friendly fried food establishment associated with this slogan. It's a harmless phrase, in and of itself, and one that works particularly well for the franchise. It suggests to customers that their particular appetites can be catered to, that their specific tastes, no matter how eccentric (within the continuum of dip n' serve fried food) can be easily satisfied. It promotes the idea that the institution will shift its entire set of processes to meet the desires of the individual.

The meal deal bargain. Recently, in our hyper-drive-thru culture, we've been given a new ticket to ride—a quicker and easier way to get fast food (and a host of other things as well): the combo or meal deal. In the old days, we had to pull up to the drive-thru board, search under "Sandwiches" and THEN go through the labor of exploring "Sides" and "Beverages." It was all too much. Now, we can simply pull up, and say a number. We don't even have to trouble ourselves with uttering all the stuff we want to eat. We just say, "#1 with a diet." The meal deal craze is, of course, not limited to fast food; it is, simply, most explicitly manifested in the fast food industry. That is, in the fast food world, we can clearly see the motives of an increasingly consumerized culture: (1) to limit the interaction between the provider and the customer, (2) to limit the time the customer has to reflect on his/her wants, and 3) to limit the energy the customer has to exert.

5   Passivity. Customers are encouraged to be passive. We are prompted in a variety of ways not to be agents of our own making. Our needs and desires are met by the work of others. As customers, we pay for someone else's work, for someone else's acts of invention, creation, and production. And we not only hire out our activities (painting our homes, cooking our dinners); we also hire out our imaginations. We don't even have to imagine what is possible. Others have already done the

imagining, created a product or service and have told us how we can use it. (They've even taken the extra step of telling us what NOT to do: "Women who are pregnant or who may become pregnant should not take, or even handle, these pills.") In short, *the world of the customer is based on intellectual inactivity;* we merely have to dial the phone, get online, say a number. We don't have to reflect, invent, produce, or research (*Consumer's Reports* has done it already). Nor do we have to shop: they will deliver. Being a customer means being driven by simple and personal desires . . . and ultimately demanding that those desires be met.

Contrary to the passive, personalizing, self-perpetuating, desire-driven customer, students are encouraged to be active. In college, students cannot simply consume knowledge. Even in its most packaged form, the textbook, knowledge must be regenerated, revised, reinterpreted, and remembered in order to be anything beyond an answer on a multiple-choice test. Students who read textbooks, literature, and articles passively will get nothing from them—it is a kind of paralyzing higher education illiteracy. Certainly, they will be able to read something aloud, or even to themselves, and maybe summarize a main point; however, they will not know how to imagine the implications or significance of a textbook chapter. (And this is what academics mean when they say, "Our students don't know how to *make meaning*.")

Students who come to college with a consumerist attitude are lost. Because they are anticipating their most basic desires will be stimulated (because that's how people are massaged into buying stuff they don't need), consumerist students come to college waiting to be tickled, waiting to see the big boom, waiting for the car chase or the sex scene, waiting for the french fry, waiting for the Cherry Coke. What they encounter, however, are rooms filled with ingredients. They see only black and white words—where they anticipate smashy colors and extravagant tools for getting their attention. In the face of pure ingredients (the stuff for making meaning), they will be confused . . . and ultimately, terribly bored.

Consumerist students (or those who have been tricked into thinking like consumers) will also have a difficult time understanding principles. Principles, established doctrines which are to be followed, or evaluated, in the processes of making knowledge, don't really exist in consumer culture (unless you count slogans as doctrines). Because everything is based on the eccentricities of the individual ("hold the pickle, hold the lettuce"), the individual need not ever think outside of his/her own desires and the reality that is created from projecting those desires onto everything and everyone in view. In higher education, principles establish how a discipline works. Physics works on principles of matter and energy. The goal of a physicist is to discover the principles and understand how they can be used. Composition works on principles—conventions of grammar and persuasion. This is not to say that all knowledge is prescribed. On the contrary, students in such classes are encouraged to invent, to break rules, to go beyond. But in order to do so, they need certain ground rules; they need to understand that certain principles exist in the world outside of their own desires. (One cannot do chemistry and simply dismiss algebra because it is distasteful.)

When I think back to the best teachers and professors in my education, I recall those who demanded everything contrary to the consumerist mentality. They insisted on active students; they made us read staggering amounts of material and then actively put that material to use; they prompted us into confusion and disorientation; they made us uncomfortable, and then, sometimes, offered paths to clarity. In short, they made us into critical, reflective agents of our own becoming, rather than passive bags of desire. Everything valuable about my education came from instructors and professors who were free from the ridiculous tyranny of consumerism.

10   There is no way higher education can counter the incredible momentum of consumerist culture. It is far more pervasive than the discourses of physics or composition studies. However, if we continue to allow the term "customer" to replace "student," I fear that students will become increasingly blind to the difference between consumerist culture and college culture. I fear they will become increasingly more confused by the expectations of college, and that in the nightmarish long run, colleges will become simply another extension of the consumerist machine in which everyone is encouraged to prepackage knowledge, to super-size grades, and to "hold" anything even slightly distasteful.

Writing Strategies

1. Evaluate Benlow's title. Is it effective?

2. How is, or isn't, Benlow's voice appropriate to his subject matter?

3. Benlow alludes throughout his essay to pop culture. Find several allusions that you think are successful and explain why. Which, if any, of his allusions do you think fail?

4. If helping Benlow with his essay, what one suggestion would you make?

5. In your view, what makes Benlow's conclusion effective or ineffective?

Exploring Ideas

1. What important distinction does Benlow make between "students" and "consumers"?

2. Interview others to find out if they think students are "customers." Then identify trends in the data you have collected. For example, do certain groups tend to give the same response, or do responses vary?

3. Explain Benlow's reasoning to several people who feel strongly that students are the "customers." Record their responses to Benlow's argument. What aspect of his argument made someone think differently? What were the most convincing, or interesting, responses to what Benlow says?

Ideas for Writing

1. Spend the next 24 hours noticing terms used in conversation, on television, in junk mail, and so on. Are any terms defined, applied, or thought of incorrectly?

2. Do members of some other group define themselves incorrectly?

If responding to one of these ideas, go to the Analysis section of this chapter to begin developing ideas for your essay.

Everything valuable about my education came from instructors and professors who were free from the ridiculous tyranny of consumerism.

What Is Education?

Petra Pepellashi

In the margins of this essay, a reader's comments point to key ideas and writing strategies.

Sometimes the most commonly held assumptions about the most common topics need to be rethought. The prevailing understanding of education, for example, is that its essence is linked to getting a good job. But as Petra Pepellashi explains, such a view, although widely accepted, is limiting and even a little tragic. In this essay, written for her first-year English writing course, Pepellashi tackles the prevailing notion of education by first revealing its historical roots. From there, she invites readers to imagine another, more humane, view of the concept.

Writing Strategies

Begins with personal testimony.

Prompts the reader to conjure a scenario, which captures the problem with the common view.

The allusion to Jefferson fleshes out a particular concept of education.

Exploring Ideas

Education is fused to career goals.

Jefferson: education should be tied to intellectual freedom.

During most of my life, I shared the common view of education as providing what I needed to learn in order to "make a good living." In this view, education defines the "correct" and "proper" way to do something: to read, to write, to add/subtract, to draw, to design, to sell, to do whatever necessary to maintain or excel in my work . . . my livelihood. The design and structure of elementary, secondary, higher education revolve primarily around building skill sets related to work/career. If in doubt about the commonly held purpose of education, try talking to a college counselor about a course path outside of a career path. A blank stare meets the inquiry. The stare represents confusion about how to construct the selection of courses without the defining purpose of a career.

Things might have been different if our system of education were more like Thomas Jefferson's vision. Jefferson felt strongly that the average unprivileged man needed to be part of the leadership bodies of the country. As historian James Conant notes, Jefferson's curriculum centered upon developing a critical mind in order to balance the interests of the common man and those of the privileged (whether the privilege came from class, status, or wealth). He was deeply troubled by the control of monarchies in Europe and worried that one of the other privileged groups could easily reign a controlling influence in our nation unless "we are not afraid to follow truth wherever it may lead, nor to tolerate any error so long as reason is free to combat it" (Conant 29). He defined the ideal curriculum of higher education as reading, writing, arithmetic, literature, rhetoric, all the sciences, philosophy, natural philosophy, and ethics. Jefferson included self examination and sincere consideration for all as crucial aspects of critical thinking. As an ardent believer in religious freedom, Thomas Jefferson felt strongly about the importance of secular education as a balance to the indoctrinating aspect of schools operated by religious organizations. Although Jefferson's concept of general public education never came to fruition, he played a major role in establishing the secular University of Virginia, with its curriculum aimed at developing a critical mind.

In fact public school as we know it today did not exist until the industrial revolution needed more highly trained workers. The founders of our school system used the Prussian system as a model, rather than what Jefferson had proposed. The Prussians initially instituted their schools in order to indoctrinate the Prussian worldview and elevate skill sets for improved soldiers and workers. Businessmen and politicians traveling in Europe were so impressed by the success of the Prussian system that they lobbied for its establishment in America (Conant 37).

Maybe we would respect authority more while blindly following authority less if education followed the Jeffersonian definition. Instead, that authority tells us the purpose of education is to succeed as a worker, and we accept the idea. Anyone who has taken Introduction to Social Psychology may remember the experiment conducted by a Midwestern teacher who assigned half her grade-school class as the blue "smart" team and the other half as the brown "dumb" team with the result that the students adhered to the assigned definitions. Amazingly, when the assignment between "smart" and "dumb" switched, it took less than a day for the students to act out their new opposite definitions. Although some may focus upon the aspect of fulfillment of expectations, the most critical factor remains that the adherence was to the expectations of the authority as definer of what "is."

5   Formal education and therefore educators function as one of the primary authorities in defining and establishing what is "correct," "fact," "truth," "commonly understood" about a wide variety of topics. The lower levels of education, elementary, secondary, and most college and university courses educate/indoctrinate the definitions established by higher education. Typically only the highest levels of education function to define, question, test, refine, and redefine the purpose, content, and context of education in the lower levels.

In addition to formal education, consider all the informal educators such as parents, family, friends, bosses, business leaders, government leaders, special interest groups, athletes, entertainers, musicians, newscasters, talk show hosts, therapists, doctors, religious leaders, etc. whose messages infiltrate our minds through stories,

---

Marginal notes (left):

The allusion to Prussians works as a contrary example to the Jeffersonian vision of education. The two different *concept*ualizations are clearly drawn here.

Allusion to the classroom experiment shows the problem with the common (Prussian) model.

Fuses together all the points made so far.

Marginal notes (right):

The system was crafted to create good workers. (Hence, good grades = good worker bees.)

We went with the Prussians and abandoned Jefferson's vision. (We gladly went with the worker bee model.)

Even though kids might not respect authority, they still obey blindly?!

Most of our academic lives are spent being obedient—learning the ropes of obedience.

magazine articles, advertising, books, TV programs, films, documentaries, radio talk shows, music, newspaper articles, websites, and more. With so many "authorities," how we evaluate and incorporate their views into our own becomes critical. All too often, the view of an "authority" eludes careful evaluation and becomes unconsciously integrated into our thinking. The danger lies not in authority. Clearly authority provides positive and necessary aspects to society such as order and structure. However, unexamined reliance on authority portends harm. Think of any atrocity throughout history and at the root are many blindly, and therefore ignorantly, following authority.

The harm in unexamined adherence appears in more subtle ways when multiple "authorities" focus our attention on work—on finding that singular career path. No doubt work represents an essential aspect of life, but I can't help but wonder if the tail is wagging the dog. Where do we investigate and define what it means to be human . . . how one relates to one's inner self, the mysteries of life, other people, animals, the planet, the cosmos, and the impact of each on the other? Shouldn't we learn about our own internal operating system before we learn applications such as work? Aren't these topics each one of us should consciously investigate in order to provide the bedrock for building a meaningful life that includes things like work?

I look around to see where one learns a process to define oneself and the criteria by which one chooses to live. I can see glimpses in poetry, in literature, in art, in music, in some sciences, and in nature, but I don't see it in middle or high school when young people are breaking away to define themselves. What tools do they have on the journey of self discovery or in developing their worldviews? In terms of higher education, one might think ethics or philosophy, but somehow they seem overly cerebral, complicated, and authority bound, focusing upon predefined *what*s instead of explorative *how*s.

Rhetoric most definitely contains the force to shake one to the bones to wake up and redefine and reconsider various aspects of one's world. I'm reminded of Jefferson's inclusion of rhetoric as an important aspect of education. However, it is an elective class taught in college, and it doesn't necessarily point one toward defining oneself and the criteria by which one chooses to live. I thought possibly religion, but it seems the most authority bound, even though the essential principles common to all religions point one down an avenue leading to self discovery and integration of a world view large

Margin notes (left):

Takes the reasoning to the next step: because authorities surround us, we must learn to think critically before/as we obey them.

Mentions the most harmful aspect of indoctrination before turning to a new set of questions.

The questions invite a new conceptualization of education.

The return to "I" creates a informal but passionate voice.

Margin notes (right):

Formal education is only the beginning. The whole society begs us to blindly follow along.

She's flipping over the whole notion of education.

She's calling for a radical new vision of education: An intensive search for meaning and self-discovery. (No more busy work!)

The new concept of education is posed as a set of questions, but the point is still focused.

enough to encompass all life. What would our human world look like if the fundamental purpose of education included educating people to define and live their highest human values for the benefit of self, people, animals, and the planet?

Maybe people would discover more life outside the job.

Work Cited

Conant, James B. <u>Thomas Jefferson and the Development of American Public Education</u>. Berkley: University of California Press, 1962.

Used by permission of the authors.

Writing Strategies

1. How does Pepellashi's personal statement in the first paragraph function in the essay? What impact does it have on the reader—and on the call to rethink education?

2. What is the relationship between Prussian history and present conceptualizations of education? Why is that relationship important to Pepellashi's point?

3. Why the focus on authority? (¶ 4–7) How does Pepellashi's description of authority figure into her claim about education?

4. Pepellashi points to ethics, philosophy, rhetoric, and religion as possible pathways for education, but she explains that each falls short in some way. What is the effect of her final paragraph—of leaving readers to imagine specifics?

5. In your view, what is Pepellashi's most analytical paragraph? Where does she best break down the specific elements or qualities of an idea? How does it serve her essay?

Exploring Ideas

1. Pepellashi is taking on the entire structure of formal schooling in this society. She's calling for a radical reconceptualization. Is such a move warranted? Why or why not?

2. How has your education been limited to the ultimate goal of getting a job?

3. What is the most quiet, least obvious, or invisible way that you obey authority? How does that obedience influence your life? How does that obedience support or oppose Pepellashi's point?

4. Pepellashi concludes ¶ 4 by writing, "Although some may focus upon the aspect of fulfillment of expectations, the most critical factor remains that the adherence was to the expectations of the authority as definer of what 'is.'" In your life, who defines *what is*?

Ideas for Writing

1. Should a country that celebrates or believes in democracy have a school system like the United States?

2. What is authority? How should it work in formal institutions like schools? How should it work in a "free" society?

If responding to one of these ideas, go to the Analysis section of this chapter to begin developing ideas for your essay.

Outside Reading

Find a written text that analyzes a concept and print it out or make a photocopy. You might focus on a concept related to your major or to a major that you are considering. (To explore a specific field or major, examine a related professional journal such as *Nutrition Health Forum, Virginia Journal of Law and Technology,* or *Journal of Teacher Education.*) To conduct an electronic search of journals and magazines, go to your library's periodical database or to InfoTrac College Edition (http://infotrac.cengage.com) For your library database, perform a keyword search, or for InfoTrac College Edition, go to the main search box and choose "keywords." Experiment by typing in various concepts, such as *art, society, industry, sportsmanship.* You might limit the search by adding *concept* to the search. (When performing keyword searches, avoid using phrases or articles such as *a, an, the;* instead, use nouns separated by *and.*) The results will yield lists of journal and magazine articles.

You can also search the Internet. Try the search engine Yahoo.com. Like most Internet search engines, Yahoo.com combines words using *and.* In the search box, try various combinations, such as those above.

The purpose of this assignment is to further your understanding of analytical writing. You may discover a text that differs considerably from the essays in this chapter (in tone, rhetorical tools, or organization). As you read through this chapter, keep the text you have discovered close by and notice the elements and strategies the writer uses. Depending on your instructor's suggestions, do one or more of the following:

1. Notice how the writer applies various strategies from this chapter. On the hard copy or photocopy of the text:
   - Highlight the thesis if it is stated. If the thesis is implied, write it in your own words.
   - Identify the major rhetorical strategies (such as narration, description, or figurative language).
   - Identify any passages in which the writer attempts to create public resonance for the topic.

2. Analyze the strategies employed by the writer. The following questions may be helpful:
   - How is the writer's voice different from the essays in this chapter?
   - How does the writer support or illustrate his or her thesis?
   - Who is the audience for this text?
   - How does the audience impact the content of the text?
   - How does the writer go beyond the obvious? (What new idea does the writer offer?)

3. Write at least three "Writing Strategies" questions for the text you found.

4. Write at least three "Exploring Ideas" questions for the text you found.

5. Write two "Ideas for Writing," such as the ones following the essays in this book, for the text you found.

INVENTION

"What does it mean that success is as dangerous as failure? Whether you go up the ladder or down it, your position is shaky."

—Tao Te Ching

Analyzing concepts involves a good deal of reflection. Valuable analysis goes beyond the first impressions a writer may have about a topic. For the writing in this chapter, you must seek out meaning beyond those initial thoughts about a concept. The following sections are designed to help you through this process: specifically, to find a particular concept (in Point of Contact), to examine the concept closely (in Analysis), to make it relevant to a community of readers (in Public Resonance), to develop a focused point (in Thesis), and to develop support for that point (in Rhetorical Tools). The Invention questions in each section are not meant to be answered directly in your final essay. They are meant to prompt inventive thinking and intensive writing.

POINT OF CONTACT

We carry concepts around with us and, for the most part, do not question them. But writers are willing to get underneath concepts that would otherwise go unquestioned. As you consider a possible topic, imagine the concepts that go unnoticed in your everyday life. To find a concept, investigate the world around you. Take a concept that goes unchallenged, uninspected. The following may prompt a possible topic:

- **Work:** Success, employment, boss, customer, profit, hours, wage, honesty, freedom, career, experience
- **School:** Education, study, discipline, learning, science, humanities, grade, teacher, student, intelligence
- **Home:** Parent, mother, father, pet, living room, divorce, values, God, marriage, privacy, faith
- **Public Life:** Friend, recreation, commitment, travel, woman, man, patriotism, romance, trash, environment
- **Sports:** Team, entertainment, audience, fan, loser, victory, competition
- **Your Major:** Someone majoring in education could analyze a concept such as learning, success, assessment, or high school. Your major itself might be seen as a concept. For example, engineering is a concept, and how one works in that field depends upon one's concept of it.

- **Television:** What does a local news program that devotes 60 seconds to world news and several minutes to sports suggest about news? What does *American Idol* suggest about America or idol? What does *The Real World* suggest about reality? What does *Sex in the City* suggest about sex? What does *The Late Show* suggest about entertainment? What does an automobile commercial suggest about excitement? What does an insurance commercial suggest about neighbors

As you reflect on the program or commercial, ask yourself if the concept is somehow oversimplified or misrepresented. Or does the program or commercial fairly represent the concept? Remember that you are not evaluating the television program, but using it to prompt an idea, to discover a concept that may need analysis and explanation.

Activity

Imagine more concepts that define your everyday life. If this can be done in a small group, take turns offering concepts until each participant has chosen a potential topic.

Do not limit yourself to familiar concepts. You might, in fact, choose a concept that is somewhat foreign to your experiences.

ANALYSIS

Analysis involves investigating particular parts, elements, or ideas within the whole. If we were to analyze an object, we might take it apart and look inside. We might, for instance, analyze a computer by opening the case and looking at the internal wires, the cards, and the connections. But when examining a concept, we cannot take off its cover and simply look inside—at least, not physically. Instead, we have to depend on intellectual inquiry. Rather than physical tools (screwdrivers or wrenches), we have to develop questions that get inside the abstraction. We have to ask questions that point to the particular elements of the concept. For example, consider *college*. To analyze the concept, we must break it down and look at particular issues: What does college suggest for people's lives? Is it a time and place for learning specific skills or for exploring boundless ideas? Is it a place for making choices or for generating options? Such questions are analytical; they help to shed light on specific issues inside the broader, more abstract idea.

Invention Questions

As you look closely at the concept you have chosen, use the following Invention questions to break it down:

- Specifically, how does it influence or change people's lives?
- What particular emotions, behaviors, or ideas are associated with it?
- What hidden role does it play in everyday life?
- Are there complexities to the concept that people overlook?

In his invention writing, Simon Benlow looks closely at the particular qualities that define student and customer. He attempts to get at root behaviors and attitudes:

How does it influence or change people's lives?

I'm dealing with two concepts: "student" and "customer." "Customer" influences people to buy things and ideas, but the concept also makes people believe certain things about themselves—that they are better off only when they have obtained some thing or some service. It makes people lazy. When people totally buy into the consumer mentality, they feel as though they should be waited on, catered to, and dealt with, no matter what the circumstances. Being a student is the opposite—or at least, being a good student is the opposite. Students have to discover meaning and to struggle through their own biases, while customers hope to have their biases fed.

What particular emotions, behaviors, or ideas are associated with it?

When consumerist students come to college, they get angry and frustrated. Their expectations about institutions have been created, in large part, from their interactions with retail. They've been advertised and sold to for most of their lives. In college when the tables are turned, when they have to do all the discovering, all the inventing, all the developing, they are often freaked out.

Benlow then develops these ideas in his essay. (See the particular development in the first half of his essay on page 140.)

Invention Workshop

As you consider the Invention questions, avoid skimming the surface of broad ideas. Enlist the help of at least two other writers. Use one of the Invention questions to launch a focused discussion. As you address the question, try to avoid chatting aimlessly about the topic (which is always tempting!). Instead, follow new ideas that surface. For example, Diana has decided to analyze *conspiracy* after watching an episode of *The X-Files* on television. In a discussion with other students, she discovers more about the concept than she initially expected:

What behaviors are associated with it [*conspiracy*]?

Diana: In the show, the conspiracy is a big network of people from various national governments who are all trying to deal secretly with aliens. It's a giant plot that involves military agencies, doctors, scientists, politicians, FBI agents, and lots of spies. It's great entertainment, but it seems so far-fetched. A conspiracy doesn't have to be so big and involved. If it were, how could it remain secret?

Linda: I know what you mean. I like that show, but I'm always wondering about the big hidden plot with the aliens. Sometimes it seems like only a small handful of people know about it, like when the conspirators, all men by the way, meet in a dark room. There's a lot of cigarette smoke and hard talk about taking control of the world. Then other episodes suggest that all kinds of people, in all parts of the world, are deeply involved.

Marcus: So the show suggests that a conspiracy is a huge underground plot where a bunch of men secretly plan to take over the world. That IS a conspiracy, right?

Diana: Yes, but can't a conspiracy be smaller than that? Does it have to involve several governments and a plan to help aliens take over the Earth?

Linda: What about these corporate executives that construct plans to grab millions of dollars before their companies go belly-up? There's a conspiracy that, maybe, develops pretty quickly—and is shared by only a few people.

The conversation is beginning to open up the concept, to go beyond the idea that Diana first encountered in the television program. This kind of exploration is the key to developing new insights. It takes writers (and their readers) beyond their opinions—and into a realm of possibilities. But Diana, Linda, and Marcus don't stop there:

Marcus: But then the accounting firms get involved, too. Then it gets bigger and bigger.

Diana: But the accountants may not be "in," so to speak; they're simply using the numbers to keep their clients afloat so that they, in turn, have jobs.

Linda: So the people don't always have to be knowledgeable about the beginnings of the conspiracy in order to participate in it.

Marcus: But those accountants are doing something suspicious too, right?

Diana: Right! But they're acting for their own self-interests. They weren't necessarily involved in the plan from the ground up.

Linda: So back to the main point: A *conspiracy* doesn't have to involve governments, dark rooms, and huge cover-ups. It can be a bunch of people doing their own thing (for various different reasons) but working, as best they can, under the covers so they keep jobs and make money.

A review of the discussion turns up the following ideas:

- A conspiracy can be much smaller than many people imagine.
- People don't have to be knowledgeable about the beginnings of the conspiracy in order to participate in it.
- Some (all?) people involved in a conspiracy may simply be acting for their own self-interests—so that they keep their jobs, for example.

These ideas, uncovered through discussion, are beginning to help Diana figure out what a conspiracy is, or can be. As Diana discusses further, even more ideas will emerge—and she must be able to manage all these ideas that are coming at her.

Thinking Further

To explore further, writers look for hidden intellectual pathways. They look and listen for statements that seem unusual, that bend thinking away from the obvious, and then start following that idea.

Imagine that Diana identifies the following statement: *Some people involved in a conspiracy may simply be acting for their own self-interests—so that they keep their jobs, for example.* This is a revelatory idea. It goes beyond, or gets underneath, the way people usually apply *conspiracy.* Now, Diana can start thinking down this path. She might ask additional questions:

- Do conspiracies require unwitting conspirators?
- Is self-interest the driving force of a conspiracy?
- Am I involved in a conspiracy? Have I ever been?

And watch what happens when Diana takes these questions and runs. She begins to discover something. The questions prompt her onward into a new intellectual zone:

Is self-interest the driving force of a conspiracy?

Yes and no. I mean, self-interest keeps people from asking the hard moral questions, like "What are the consequences of this action?" And self-interest blinds people from seeing how their own actions ripple outward. The simple process of getting through the work week, getting to the next phase, or getting that promotion keeps workers from wondering if their supporting evil enterprises, underhanded schemes, and quiet criminal activity. That's how power works. Not everyone has to be in-the-know. Conspiracies need ambitious go-getters just trying to make it in the world.

Am I involved in a conspiracy?

Until now, I had never even imagined that I might be part of a conspiracy. Am I a villain? Or a victim? Am I innocent? What is an unwitting conspirator? A conspiracy is beginning to feel more like a living being to me. It is born. It grows. It takes on certain characteristics. It has various parts. Eventually it dies off. Some parts are like a brain. Others are like feet or hands or the hair on your arms. Is the fist to blame when a punch is thrown? Or is the brain to blame? Or is it something else? Is the brain evil, or just damaged, or just thinking differently?

Diana is thinking further; she's doing the work of academic writing. She's given up simple answers and has created a new way of seeing a conspiracy. Where she may have initially seen plotting agents in smoky rooms, she now sees a whole living being. Her thinking is increasingly complex—and will likely yield a more sophisticated essay.

As you consider your own topic, explore your invention writing. Look for statements that seem unusual, that bend thinking away from the obvious, and then generate probing questions of your own.

PUBLIC RESONANCE

It is up to the writer to make a concept relevant to readers. At some level, your concept already resonates with others, because a concept is, by definition, beyond particulars. Whether it is *creativity, college,* or *student,* a concept necessarily involves others. Still, a concept is not always entirely understood—even by those who would, presumably, understand it. Consider *freedom:* As Americans, we often speak of it, sing about it, and even go to war over it, but do most Americans really understand the concept? Even though freedom is part of our collective language, we might not realize its complexities and meaning.

As you consider the social significance of your own topic, use the following questions:

- Is the concept generally agreed upon?
- Why is it important that people have an appropriate understanding of this concept?
- Does the concept need to be rethought? Why?
- What is the possible connection between the topic and some public concern?

If you choose not to directly state the public resonance of your concept, answering these questions serves another goal: to help you envision the relationship between your audience and your topic. In thinking about the public resonance of your chosen concept, you may come across your *purpose*—the reason you are writing. If you believe that the concept is often misunderstood, then the purpose of your analysis might be to educate your audience. Or if your concept is overlooked, the purpose may be to elevate the status of the concept in your reader's mind.

In the following excerpt, Simon Benlow discovers why *student,* as a concept, is necessary and why people should rethink it. Benlow could have given up early in his exploration. He could have merely stopped with "education will suffer." Instead, he tries to imagine specific effects, and in doing so, he further draws out the difference between customer and student:

Is the concept generally agreed upon?

No! That's the whole problem. Many students don't know what it means to be a student.

Why is it important that people have an appropriate understanding of this concept?

If college students really understand what it means to be a student (and not a consumerist student), their experience at college will be defined by self-discovery and enlightenment rather than petty frustration and grumbling. If colleges across America continue to confuse "student" with "consumer," education will suffer. Much of the time spent in college will be on customer service (keeping students happy) rather than challenging their beliefs, developing their minds, and broadening their horizons. Customers ultimately do not want their ideas about themselves to change; they want products and services to support what they think. If college continues down the present path, it is not hard to imagine colleges being devoid of genuinely new ideas.

Benlow's essay grows out of this thinking—out of concern for the potential harm to students and higher education. In fact, public resonance seems to drive the essay, because he initially connects a singular memo with a broader issue:

> Two weeks ago, the faculty and staff received a memo regarding "National Customer Service Week." . . . I am concerned, in general, about the slow and subtle infiltration of consumerism into education (by companies buying access to students' brains), and I am downright hostile to the way "customer" has suddenly replaced the word (and maybe idea of) "student" in higher education.

But we can see Benlow's initial thoughts most directly in the essay's conclusion (p. 141):

> There is no way higher education can counter the incredible momentum of consumerist culture. It is far more pervasive than the discourses of physics or composition studies. However, if we continue to allow the term "customer" to replace "student," I fear that students will become increasingly blind to the difference between consumerist culture and college culture.

THESIS

You probably have many different things to say about your topic, but your project will gain focus and intensity with a thesis statement, a single claim that expresses your particular view on the concept. Look over your notes from the Analysis and Public Resonance sections. Find a theme or pattern running through those notes and try to articulate that idea in a sentence. Remember that good writing *reveals* something beyond or beneath common knowledge, and good writers show the extraordinary in the ordinary. Your project might:

- Explain how particular parts or qualities make up a concept.
  - —Creativity . . . the act of bringing something new into the world . . . is based first on communication with oneself, then testing that communication with experience and the realities one has to contend with. (Hayakawa)
  - —Punk rock involves an explicit and dramatic disdain for common wisdom, popular aesthetic, and accepted manners.

- Reveal a side or layer of a concept that normally goes unnoticed.
  - —Health is not simply an internal condition but a sound relationship between body and an immediate environment.
  - —Behind the common image of trees, lakes, and loose critters, *nature* is a verb—an unyielding cyclical process.

- Show a quality that distinguishes one concept from another.
  - —Contrary to the passive, personalizing, self-perpetuating, desire-driven customer, students are encouraged to be active. (Benlow)
  - —Childhood is not pre-adulthood but an existence fundamentally distinct and characterized by a peculiar mixture of wonder and fear.

- Explain the inner workings of a concept.
  - —Formal education and therefore educators function as one of the primary authorities in defining proper intellectual behavior and the path to work. (Pepellashi)
  - —In today's use of the term, *patriotism* demands a persistent turning away from self-evaluation.

It is easy to say something broad and general about a concept—especially because concepts are, themselves, generalizations. But the goal is to reveal something specific about the concept, not to broadly announce what people may already know. One helpful strategy for narrowing and intensifying thesis statements is to write down initial statements and then ask probing questions about specific words or phrases. For example, in the following chart, the first two statements need to be narrowed and intensified. The writers can ask questions that lead to more revelatory ideas:

Education is a process of intense struggle.	**Education is a process through which students acquire knowledge.**
BROAD AND GENERAL	BROAD AND GENERAL
What type of struggle? What happens in that struggle?	**How does a student acquire knowledge? How is the student challenged?**
MORE FOCUSED AND REVELATORY THESIS	MORE FOCUSED AND REVELATORY THESIS
Education is a struggle against the intellectual conventions of the day, a struggle in which the individual attempts to escape habitual patterns of thought.	**Education involves the student in an increasingly intensive dialogue with the world.**

While the final statements are broad in scope, they show a particular process (a "struggle against conventions" and an "increasingly intensive dialogue"). These statements are rich with possibility and would help a writer to generate an intensive essay.

Evolution of a Thesis

Remember that a thesis does not materialize out of thin air. It develops over time. It may involve a long process of reflection and discussion. And often, a good thesis emerges only after a writer has thoroughly analyzed the topic. Consider the example from the Analysis section, in which Diana's topic, conspiracy, is developed through a discussion. Her thesis evolves slowly: First, she notices the idea in a television show. Then she analyzes and discovers specific elements. Finally, she refines the point in a focused statement:

- People think that conspiracy means old men meeting in a smoke-filled room and devising an evil plan, but it is far subtler than that.

- In a conspiracy, everyone involved does not have to know each other and purposely act in harmony. In fact, people in a conspiracy can simply be protecting their own interests, and in doing so, carrying out an action under society's radar.

- Although numbers of people sometimes do conspire together, what some call a conspiracy is, in truth, various people with a similar attitude acting independently in their own self-interests.

As you consider your own thesis, remember that narrower statements yield more interesting writing. At first, you might think, "I can't possibly write more than a paragraph about something so narrow." However, the process of developing the ideas will generate content for your writing. And the more focused thesis will help you to illustrate particular points rather than listing many marginally related issues.

Revision

Look back over your invention notes and thesis ideas.

Consider the following questions:

- What do people normally say or assume about the concept? How have I complicated or enriched the common way of thinking?

- What is the most revealing point I can make about this concept?

- Can I reveal the specifics in any of the terms? Can I more specifically reveal how something works?

A thesis does not materialize out of thin air.

RHETORICAL TOOLS

Examples and Contrary Examples

Each writer in this chapter puts forth a particular way of seeing a concept. And each must support that way of seeing with scenarios (hypothetical accounts), allusions (references to bits of public knowledge), and examples. Because analyzing concepts requires abstract thinking, writers must be extra careful to illustrate points with concrete examples.

For example, Benlow uses a detailed scenario to illustrate his concept of *student:*

> In higher education, principles establish how a discipline works. Physics works on principles of matter and energy. The goal of a physicist is to discover the principles and understand how they can be used. Composition works on principles—conventions of grammar and persuasion. This is not to say that all knowledge is prescribed. On the contrary, students in such classes are encouraged to invent, to break rules, to go beyond. But in order to do so, they need certain ground rules; they need to understand that certain principles exist in the world outside of their own desires. (One cannot do chemistry and simply dismiss algebra because it is distasteful.)

In some cases, writers may use details to illustrate how *not* to conceptualize an idea. They use **contrary examples** (situations that show the opposite of the writer's point) to draw stark contrast between a productive and a perilous way of thinking. For example, Benlow uses contrary examples in several paragraphs to show consumerist mentality—the opposite of his way of conceptualizing *student*. And Pepellashi explains "the common view" of education to set up her analysis that comes later in the essay:

> During most of my life, I shared the common view of education as providing what I needed to learn in order to "make a good living." In this view, education defines the "correct" and "proper" way to do something; to read, to write, to add/subtract, to draw, to design, to sell, to do whatever necessary to maintain or

excel in my work . . . my livelihood. The design and structure of elementary, secondary, higher education revolve primarily around building skill sets related to work/career.

Often it is not enough to simply mention an example. A powerful and convincing strategy is to explain in detail *how* an example or allusion reveals something relevant. For example, Benlow does not simply mention consumerist slogans; he gives detailed explanations of their significance:

> "The customer is always right." We hear this hollow phrase resound through (almost) every corridor of our consumerist culture. The motive behind the phrase is painfully clear—to keep customers happy, to keep them from complaining, and most importantly, to keep them coming back. . . . The phrase is meant to maintain a climate in which the substance of anyone's concerns or complaints is obfuscated by friendly and diplomatic clichés. . . . Ultimately, then, the goal of customer service, in this sense, is to lull customers into a sense of complacency—even though their phones may not be working or their washers are throwing sparks.

Definitions

Sometimes a definition supports a writer's take on a concept; other times, a dictionary definition (or *denotation*) is inadequate for exploring a concept's complexities. In all the essays in this chapter, for example, dictionary definitions or even common notions associated with the concepts fall short. The writers go far beyond them. They are concerned about the realm of *connotations* (meaning created by the social situations), in which society's habits and behaviors shape the meaning of concepts.

However, sometimes a dictionary definition comes in handy. Some writers begin their essays with a simple definition and then explore the connotation. Most often, the goal is not to prove a definition but to prompt readers to rethink connotations. Consider Diana's analysis of *conspiracy* (from the Analysis section). She might begin with the dictionary definition and extend the thinking. The dictionary works as a springboard. Diana uses it as a way to begin her analysis:

> Most often, a conspiracy is associated with a direct and charted plan: "We'll collect the money and stash it in the laundry baskets in the basement." In fact, the basic definition of *conspiracy* suggests a prefigured and collective act. According to the *American Heritage Dictionary,* it is "an agreement to perform together an illegal, treacherous, or evil act." However, more recent events in corporate America invite us to rethink how conspiracies work. Even a quick look at corporate fraud reveals a process in which many people, simply acting in their own self-interests, become part of a bigger covert plan that was begun without them and carries on only because they are unwilling to stand in its way.

- **Examples:** What specific examples in everyday life illustrate my point about the concept?
- **Contrary Examples:** What programs, ads, or other examples from everyday life illustrate an inappropriate or oversimplified way of understanding the concept?
- **Scenarios:** What hypothetical account could demonstrate the concept?
- **Allusions:** What person or event from history, current events, popular culture, or literature illustrates the point about the concept?

Invention Workshop

In small groups, collectively develop support for one another's projects. Each writer should announce his or her thesis to the group. Each group member then should offer at least one response to the following:

1. What specific examples in everyday life illustrate the writer's point?
2. Name something from popular culture (such as a television show, movie, advertising campaign) that illustrates the writer's point. Explain how the writer could allude to it.

3. Name something from history (a person, an event, a trend) that shows something about the writer's point.
4. Explain how the writer's point is different from how people normally think about the concept.

As the group members offer ideas, the writer should record the group members' responses so they can be integrated later. Make certain to spend equal time with each person's project.

Outside Sources

Writers often refer to other writers' ideas to substantiate points. For example, in the following passage, S. I. Hayakawa first states a point ("the creative person plays hunches") and then uses Selye's words to extend that point:

> Finally, the creative person plays hunches. "Pure intellect," says Dr. Hans Selye, the great medical researcher at the University of Montreal, "is largely a quality of the middle-class mind. The lowliest hooligan and the greatest creator in the fields of science are activated mainly by imponderable instincts and emotions, especially faith. Curiously, even scientific research, the most intellectual creative effort of which man is capable, is no exception in this respect."

This is standard practice when using outside sources. While it may be enticing to begin passages with others' words or even to use long passages from other writers, it is best to use sources to help develop or illustrate your points. In other words, be careful not to depend on others' words to make your points for you.

To find outside sources that discuss your concept, go to your library's home page and select a periodical database, such as LexisNexis, InfoTrac College Edition, or EBSCOhost, that contains lists of journal and magazine articles. Try a keyword search, and type in your concept. The search will yield lists of articles on your topic. You might also try an electronic search engine on the Internet. For instance, using Yahoo.com, type your concept in the search box. For more guidance in finding and integrating sources, see Chapter 13: Research & Writing.

ORGANIZATIONAL STRATEGIES

How Should I Begin?

Introductions depend on the tone or level of formality of the writing situation. (See more on level of formality on pages 126–127.) An analytical text written for a government agency or a corporate entity would begin formally, perhaps with a general discussion about the concept. In less formal situations, introductions vary widely, and the primary goal is to capture the reader's attention, to provoke a sense of curiosity. Among many others, here are three consistent and effective strategies:

- **Describe the common view,** which you later correct or oppose. Pepellashi begins with the common view and spends the rest of her essay promoting a different conceptualization of education:

  During most of my life, I shared the common view of education as providing what I needed to learn in order to "make a good living." In this view, education defines the "correct" and "proper" way to do something: to read, to write, to add/subtract, to draw, to design, to sell, to do whatever necessary to maintain or excel in my work . . . my livelihood.

- **Ask a pointed question.** In Hayakawa's introduction, he asks a question and then qualifies it, directing the reader's attention to a particular line of reasoning. The question thus serves a very particular purpose.

  What distinguishes the creative person? By creative person I don't mean only the great painter or poet or musician. I also want to include the creative housewife, teacher, warehouseman, sales manager . . .

  Hayakawa then spends the remainder of his essay answering the question. (This is perhaps the most important issue about raising a question: It ultimately needs to be answered!)

- **Re-create the point of contact.** Explain how you first encountered the idea. This is often more informal, since it requires some personal narration. Notice that Benlow's introduction begins with the event that provoked his need to write.

  Two weeks ago, the faculty and staff received a memo regarding "National Customer Service Week." We were urged to take special efforts in serving our customers—presumably, our students.

- **Begin with a popular reference.** Writers often invite readers into their ideas by alluding to something in popular culture, such as a television program, an advertisement, a song, a current event. This strategy instantly creates public resonance. It allows readers to enter the world of the essay through a familiar door. In her essay about conspiracy, Diana could begin with an allusion to the *The X-Files*:

  The popular program *The X-Files* stokes our suspicions of and paranoia about the government. It invites us to imagine a vast network of officials, heads of state, military groups, and secret agencies making deals with aliens. Doctors, scientists, politicians, FBI agents, and numbers of spies all share covert plans, meet in smoky, quiet rooms, and plan the future of all humans. It's great entertainment. But conspiracies are often more nuanced, less concocted, less dramatic than what *The X-Files* suggests.

When Should I Change Paragraphs?

Remember that paragraphs are tools for directing a reader's progress. Paragraphs stop the reader and refocus his or her attention on the next point. Hayakawa uses paragraph breaks between each different characteristic of a creative person. Each point has its own paragraph, its own space where it is developed and illustrated.

Paragraphs can also be used to separate specific support strategies. A writer might use paragraphs to separate several examples. Simon Benlow, for instance, dedicates four of his first five paragraphs to a particular element of the consumerist culture. Hayakawa uses paragraphs to separate different elements of creativity. Pepellashi uses paragraphs to separate historical allusions from present situations. These writers all use paragraphs to refocus the reader on a new ingredient or element in the discussion.

Paragraphs, then, tend to break:

- To shift from analyzing one element or quality to another.
- To shift from a common view to a new or uncommon view of the topic.
- To shift from one support strategy (such as allusion) to another (such as scenario).
- To shift from the past to the present.

How Should I Conclude?

As with introductions, the possibilities for conclusions are limitless. Short explanatory essays (under 1,000 words) usually do not need to summarize main points. Instead, writers often use conclusions to suggest the significance of the ideas expressed in the body of the essay. Consider the strategies used by the authors in this chapter. Hayakawa concludes by proclaiming the value of the concept:

> It is based first on communication with oneself, then testing that communication with experience and the realities one has to contend with. The result is the highest, most exciting kind of learning.

Pepellashi concludes by working through possible reconceptualizations of education. She offers the reader possibilities and then closes with a single hopeful question:

> Rhetoric most definitely contains the force to shake one to the bones to wake up and redefine and reconsider various aspects of one's world. I'm reminded of Jefferson's inclusion of rhetoric as an important aspect of education. However, it is an elective class taught in college, and it doesn't necessarily point one toward defining oneself and the criteria by which one chooses to live. I thought possibly religion, but it seems the most authority bound, even though the essential principles common to all religions point one down an avenue leading to self discovery and integration of a worldview large enough to encompass all life. What would our human world look like if the fundamental purpose of education included educating people to define and live their highest human values for the benefit of self, people, animals, and the planet?

Each strategy is different but effective. None of the writers in this chapter wastes time summarizing or "wrapping up" points that have already been made. Instead, they use their conclusions to extend their points into the reader's world (by scenarios, direct appeals, or examples).

WRITER'S VOICE

A writer's voice can make the reading experience formal or relaxed, rigorous or casual. Remember that a casual voice does not necessarily mean casual thinking. A very sophisticated analysis can be presented in a casual manner. For instance, Benlow approaches the fast food, customer service issue on its own terms. He borrows the phrases and the lowbrow tone of drive-through culture:

> In the old days, we had to pull up to the drive-thru board, search under "Sandwiches" and THEN go through the labor of exploring "Sides" and "Beverages." It was all too much. Now, we can simply pull up, and say a number. We don't even have to trouble ourselves with uttering all the stuff we want to eat. We just say, "#1 with a diet." The meal deal craze is, of course, not limited to fast food; it is, simply, most explicitly manifested in the fast food industry.

You may detect a slight shift in the last sentence—where Benlow pulls away from the drive- through language and makes a broader point about society. In this sense, Benlow's voice ebbs and flows. It adopts the casual language of consumption and then snaps, in some respects, at those same casual-sounding phrases.

> This raises an important aspect of voice, or voicing: It is far more complex than discovering a single, personal, or genuine sound. In our everyday lives, as in speech, we often shift in subtle ways, borrowing tones and phrases from popular culture, academic culture, business, entertainment, and politics. We fuse those elements into our own tongues—and it all ends up sounding like us, like the single person speaking. (But don't be fooled! Voice is often, or always, filled with the subtle tones of others.)

Activity

Closely examine the following passage from Benlow's essay. How would you describe the voice? (Consider the point about our everyday voices—how they are impacted by, or inflected with, other's tones.)

> Students who come to college with a consumerist attitude are lost. Because they are anticipating their most basic desires will be stimulated (because that's how people are massaged into buying stuff they don't need), consumerist students come to college waiting to be tickled, waiting to see the big boom, waiting for the car chase or the sex scene, waiting for the french fry, waiting for the Cherry Coke. What they encounter, however, are rooms filled with ingredients. They see only black and white words—where they anticipate smashy colors and extravagant tools for getting their attention. In the face of pure ingredients (the stuff for making meaning), they will be confused . . . and ultimately, terribly bored.

Using Figurative Language

Figurative language, such as similes and metaphors, does more than support an idea. It also adds tonality to a writer's voice. Because figurative language transforms or bends the usual meaning of words and phrases, it should bend toward the nature of the writer's voice: sobering, comic, condemning, hopeful, absurd. In other words, the nature of a simile or metaphor directly impacts how the voice sounds to readers. For instance, the first simile below would likely create a casual or even slightly humorous tone and the second, a more sophisticated or lofty tone:

> Hardcore punk singers are like public belchers—guys, primarily, with digestion problems and microphones.

> Hardcore punk singers are like angry court jesters, calling attention to their own raucous behavior while slipping in serious social commentary.

Using Allusions

Allusions are references to some public bit of knowledge (such as a historical event, a political situation, or a popular culture figure). An allusion can give a personal essay a broader and more public feeling while developing its ideas. But allusions can also help create voice. The allusions one chooses contribute to the voice created in the essay.

For example, the following allusion helps to characterize Benlow's voice—especially early in the essay when he sounds intolerant of customer life. The nature of the allusion (to a fairly unimportant matter like fast food) helps Benlow to trivialize consumer culture and appear slightly above it.

> "Have it your way!" Of course, we all know the song and the friendly fried food establishment associated with this slogan. It's a harmless phrase, in and of itself, and one that works particularly well for the franchise. It suggests to customers that their particular appetites can be catered to, that their specific tastes, no matter how eccentric (within the continuum of dip n' serve fried food) can be easily satisfied.

Promoting Curiosity

One of the primary jobs of a writer is to pique curiosity in readers. Very rarely does a writer (in any situation) seek only to tell readers what they are already thinking. Instead, writers seek to light a small fire in readers' minds, to make them want to *consider* an issue. Perhaps the most important strategy for promoting curiosity is to embody it, that is, to be curious as a writer. Curious writers make curious readers. In the following passage, from a well-known essay by Pico Iyer, the writer's own curiosity about the world drives the analysis. Iyer himself seems curious about—even awed by—language. He seems to be totally unafraid of his own imagination:

Punctuation is the notation in the sheet music of our own words, telling us when to rest, or when to raise our voices; it acknowledges that the meaning of our discourse, as of any symphonic composition, lies not in the units but in the pauses, the pacing, and the phrasing.

The person we detect through the language seems full of wonder. And it is not only the content of the passage; notice also the sentence structure. He uses long sentences to keep the reader in his perspective (as though he is holding us underwater without a breath).

> **As you consider your voice, ask yourself the following:**
>
> - What uncommon details reveal my point about the concept?
> - Can I avoid telling the reader that something is "interesting," "exciting," and so on, and instead create images or use examples that show it?
> - Can I use metaphors to make the reader see the intensity or scope or depth of the concept?
> - Can I show the reader a new way to see an everyday phenomenon?

Remember that a casual voice does not necessarily mean casual thinking.

VITALITY

It is easy to fill up pages. But good writers avoid filling. They are careful with their readers' minds. (Sentences, after all, are the only conduit between a writer's thoughts and a reader's life.) Consider the following strategies for making your final text more lively and intense.

Avoid Clichés

Clichés are tired, worn-out phrases. We hear them constantly in everyday life. We use them when there is nothing else left to say—or to make it seem like there is nothing else left to say. We read them on greeting cards, hear them in popular songs or political speeches, and even share them in casual conversations. Think of all the times you have heard phrases such as these:

> You don't know what you've got until it's gone.
> We should expand our horizons.
> Follow your dreams.
> Anything is possible.
> Children are the future.
> I believe in my heart that . . .
> Hang in there.
> Discover who you are as a person.
> People are entitled to their own opinions.

Or even consider smaller phrases that get plugged into sentences but rarely get inspected:

> the real world
> hard work
> the good life
> family values

The list goes on and on. Such common phrases are not tools for thinking—they are substitutes for thinking. Because they have been used repeatedly, and in so many different contexts, their meaning has been emptied.

Clichés blur complex thinking. They actually hide the possibility of further thought. For instance, notice the thinking that might go on behind this cliché: We should expand our horizons.

> What are horizons? How do they form? Are horizons imposed on us, or do we adopt them ourselves? If they are imposed by others, can we simply choose to expand them or do we have to break some rule? How do we know when a horizon expands? What experiences or voices or situations make them expand? Are we just as likely to shrink our horizons? Isn't that human nature? What kind of action broadens our understanding? Is it just a new experience or something else?

All of these questions suggest the complexity behind the idea. But rather than promote hard thinking, clichés invite writers and readers (both!) into quiet, unreflective agreement. In a sense, clichés are strategies for quieting the mind—the opposite goal of academic writing.

Activity

In a small group, develop a list of clichés. Share this list with the whole class to create a comprehensive list of phrases to avoid.

Avoid Stilted Language

If clichés are the common, overused phrases of the day, stilted language is the opposite: an overly elaborate jungle of clauses and phrases. Stilted language is unnecessarily elevated—and like a person walking on stilts, it makes the ideas slow and wobbly. For example:

Writer A:
People, in every walk of this big life, should query themselves about the direction of their occupational goals. And they should do this persistently, both before entering into a projected career path and while enduring the veritable ins and outs of said career path. Is it not fitting to examine the very essence of such matters, which would otherwise remain beyond our consciousness in the mundane existence of work? Certainly, we should endeavor to explore the cracks and folds of our lives and thereby free ourselves of any unknown shackles.

Here, the ideas are vague because they are stretched out over unnecessary, but pretty, phrases. The writer injects strings of needless constructions ("in every walk of this big life," "the very essence of such matters") and elaborate language ("their occupational goals," "mundane existence of work") that inflate the importance of the ideas. Writer A also mingles together two competing metaphors at the end of the passage. As readers, we are left exploring the "cracks and folds" while also freeing ourselves from "unknown shackles." Notice a less stilted approach:

Writer B:
Before entering a job, people should ask themselves if it fits their broader career plans. Even after working at a job for months or years, people should return to this question. Otherwise, the workaday lifestyle can prompt us to believe that a present career path is the best—the one that we should continue to walk.

Writer B does use a metaphor at the end, but it works here because it does not compete with other figurative language in the same sentence. Now that the ideas are less ornate, they seem less overwhelming. In fact, when they are stated more plainly, the ideas appear rather ordinary. (And this might even prompt a writer to explore the ideas further.)

These passages reveal two major problems with stilted language: (1) It jumbles ideas so that readers are left guessing or wondering; and (2) it inflates ideas so that they seem beyond exploration. Writers and readers should not be impressed with ornate language, but with intense ideas.

Essays are not performances. They are invitations to think hard.

Activity

Who can conjure the most stilted passage? Write a stilted paragraph, one that dresses up an idea in ornate wordiness, competing metaphors, and lofty sentences. And then write a more tame, less ornate version. Share both versions with the class.

PEER REVIEW

Exchange drafts with at least one other writer. Before passing your draft to others, underline the thesis, or write it above your essay. This way, reviewers will get traction as they read.

As a reviewer, use the following questions to guide your response.

1. What words or phrases in the thesis could be more focused?

2. Point out passages or sentences that could use more specific illustration. Suggest an example from everyday life that illustrates the writer's point. For example, in an essay about athletics, you might read:

   Athletics are the great motivator of many students. Without sports, many would not feel compelled to attend school at all.

   You might suggest that "the great motivator" could be illustrated more specifically, that the writer show us the particular motivating quality of sports. You might ask: "How do sports work as a motivator? What do they actually do to students?" You could also suggest a contrary example, so the writer can show contrast: "Most students experience school—the passivity, the routine, the isolation—as demotivating. Athletics, on the other hand . . ."

3. Suggest an allusion (to popular culture, literature, or history) that illustrates the writer's point. Rather than accept claims as they are, help the writer make a connection to some other time, place, or text so that the concept (whatever it is) connects to a broader set of ideas.

4. If the writer uses a dictionary definition, does he or she take you beyond that definition? The writer might rely on a dictionary to get started, but the ideas should extend beyond that definition. (Hopefully, the essay takes you beyond a definition that you could easily look up yourself.) Where do you feel that "liftoff" away from a standard definition? If there is no liftoff, where might the writer concentrate attention? If you can, offer a path beyond the definition.

5. Consider the paragraphs: Do they focus on one specific point? Point to any paragraphs that seem to stray into several ideas.

6. In which passages does the writer's voice seem most engaging? (Where do you feel yourself, as a reader, most inspired by the ideas?) Why?

7. Point to particular sentences and phrases that could gain vitality and intensity. Use the following:

   • Underline any clichés. On the back of the draft, explain how the cliché conceals or blurs thinking. Suggest an alternative to the cliché.

   • Circle any stilted language. On the back of the draft, suggest an alternative approach to the passage.

   • Consider vitality strategies from other chapters and make editorial changes on the writer's draft:

   —Help the writer experiment with sentence length and brevity. Reconstruct one paragraph, extending some sentences and abbreviating others. Try to create intensity with shorter sentences.
   —Change vague nouns to specific nouns.
   —Change *be* verbs to active verbs.
   —Change clauses to phrases.
   —Change phrases to words.
   —Combine sentences.
   —Repeat structures.
   —Intensify verbs.

8. Help the reader avoid common grammatical errors: comma splices, sentence fragments, or pronoun/ antecedent agreement.

Questions for Research

If the writer used outside sources,

• Where must he or she include in-text citations? (See pages 484–485.)

• Are quotations blended smoothly into the argument and punctuated correctly? (See pages 475–478.)

• Where could more direct textual cues or transitions help the reader? (See pages 479–481.)

• Is the Works Cited page formatted properly? (See pages 486–497.)

DELIVERY

College students are always learning new concepts, some clearly related to a chosen career, others more clearly related to everyday life. While professors and textbooks explain "academic" concepts, the rest of us explain "everyday" concepts. Distinguishing between the two is not always possible. Concepts of marketing, engineering, psychology, art, and so on affect our everyday lives, which is one reason for learning about them—even if our major is something else. The concepts learned in college are sometimes more complex or explained in greater depth. But concepts learned outside college—from childhood to old age—are often just as challenging and just as important. What might be the consequences of your essay for this chapter? That is, what effect might your ideas have on your reader's thoughts and actions?

Consider these questions:

- Will the reader better understand the issue about which you wrote?
- Is the reader likely to think or behave differently?
- What might be the benefits to others? How might others be harmed?
- Who besides your instructor might benefit from your ideas?
- How might what you wrote about be affected?
- What might be the effect of these consequences on you, the writer?

Beyond the Essay: Conceptual Mapping

A conceptual map is a graphic presentation of ideas. Using words, shapes, lines, even photographs, the creator of a conceptual map attempts to depict the complexity of ideas—how they relate, what they mean in relation to other ideas. This strategy is well suited for illustrating the various layers of a concept. For instance, in the image that opens this chapter, a conceptual map depicts cyberspace.

Now that you have taken a concept, broken it down, examined its parts and layers, and explored how it works, draw your understanding.

- Try to depict the complexity of your ideas using only key words or phrases from your essay.
- Graphically show how those words and phrases relate.
- Use lines, arrows, and other shapes to depict the relationship between ideas.
- Use colors (if possible) to group ideas or to distinguish between types of ideas.

Present your conceptual map to others. Explain how the map represents the complexity of the ideas in your essay. Also explain how the map reinforces or falls short of the essay.

See the opening image for this chapter. This conceptual map, designed by Nathan Shedroff for Cyber Geography, represents the relationships in cyberspace: With the placement of each term, line, and graphic, the designer suggests particular connections. Notice, for instance, that one of the outer spheres is "time" and it turns in tandem with "read." This suggests that time, in cyberspace, is dependent on the act of reading. This interesting relationship is part of Shedroff's particular conceptualization.

ANALYZING IMAGES

Chapter Contents

CHAPTER **6**

Writing Strategies

1. What connection does Thoman make between images and lifestyle?

2. What is Thoman's main idea, and how does the essay's title help to focus the reader on the main idea?

3. How does Thoman use history (her explanation of history) to develop the main idea? What other strategies does she use?

4. How is Thoman's essay a call to action?

5. What points do you think Thoman could provide better support for? How might you support those points?

Exploring Ideas

1. In paragraph 8, Thoman quotes Oliver Wendell Holmes as saying the "image would become more important than the object itself and would in fact make the object disposable." With others or alone, think of examples to support Holmes's point.

2. Is advertising education? Use your school library's online catalog to find sources that shed light on the relationship between advertising and education.

3. Interview others to find out how they think advertising influences them. Based on the interviews, to what degree would you say others have media awareness? (See paragraph 25.)

4. Read Plato's "Allegory of the Cave" to better help you understand Thoman's conclusion.

Ideas for Writing

1. Explore the relationship between advertising images and the economy.

2. Thoman says, "Most single commercials do not have such a direct impact. What happens instead is a cumulative effect." (¶ 15) Research this idea further, using a certain type of image to support or refute the theory.

If responding to one of these ideas, go to the Analysis section of this chapter to begin developing ideas for your essay.

Daimler-Chrysler Maybach

What does this image invite us to value?

The Mighty Image

Cameron Johnson

In the margins of this essay, a reader's comments point to key ideas and writing strategies. As you read the essay, consider how the comments might influence your own reading and writing.

Although exposed to advertising every day, most Americans are unaware of how advertisements/commercials work in their everyday lives. While ads and commercials seem harmless—or even absurd, as Cameron Johnson explains below—companies spend millions on advertising because it works. Johnson also explains the logic that keeps most people from seeing the effects of advertising in their lives.

Writing Strategies

Begins with public resonance: by addressing a flawed way of thinking among many Americans.

Introduces the issue of images.

Claims that most Americans don't realize the influence images have.

Brief analysis of images and their role in public behavior.

Develops a line of reasoning: Millions of products get purchased after a slick marketing campaign; mainstream thinking is that images don't make people buy things; we should explore this logic further.

By the time we Americans are old enough to make hard choices (what to buy, what to wear, what to drive, where to shop, where to buy our degrees, and the like), we imagine ourselves as independent, free, separate, and in control. We like to see ourselves making our own decisions. And because we are attracted to such a self-image, we believe in it. We believe it is *true*. This belief requires us to dismiss the rhetorical power of images in our lives. In fact, most people argue adamantly that they are not influenced by advertising images, that what they purchase is the choice of their own coherent and impenetrable consciousness. Some may concede that images conjure up certain feelings. They may admit, "Those images really moved me" or "That picture brought out lots of feelings in me." But other than the occasional emotional poke, images, say most Americans, have no effect on their reasoning powers—and absolutely no effect on their behaviors.

This is a peculiar stance in a culture that is submerged in advertising images—ones that are highly successful at getting millions of people to wear, drive, buy, and even fight over the same things at the same time. A quick glance at America's spending habits (millions of products suddenly get purchased directly after a slick marketing campaign) reveals the tremendous power of a finely wrought image. Still, the mainstream argument against the power of advertising goes something like this: *Images do not make people buy things. They do not make kids do drugs. They do not make people buy blue jeans or tennis shoes. They do not make adults smoke cigarettes or buy cars or jewelry.* Such statements have an obvious logical ring to them. Of course images do not *make* anyone buy anything. Pictures alone do not *make* people do things. But wait. We should explore this logic a bit further.

Exploring Ideas

To what degree are we independent, free, separate, in control?

How do images influence our thinking?

Spending habits suggest that images influence the way we think.

Pictures alone don't make people buy things. So, how does it work?

In the mainstream perspective, humans are *either* driven by media images or they are entirely independent thinkers. They *either* see something and buy a car or they decide not to buy a car. They *either* want a certain pair of blue jeans or they don't even imagine themselves wanting them. Such a perspective ignores the complexities of desire and the power of images. Of course, people do not simply run to the car lot and buy an SUV after seeing an ad in *Time*. But they consume the image and *the apparent value of the image*. When we see an image (whether it be a hairdo, a body type, or a vehicle), we also get an assumption about its worth in the culture. And this assumption stays with us. It molds into our sense of daily life. (This is, of course, why corporations spend millions of dollars to place images everywhere—so that our ideas about daily life naturally come to include the product or the image.)

Contrary to popular belief, humans are gregarious. We think and act in groups, according to historical trends. About every five years in America, kids laugh at what came five years earlier: "Look at that guy's jeans!" "Hey, check out the hairdo on her!" About every decade or so, certain social behaviors become extinct or come into favor: wearing hats, not wearing hats, getting married at 18, waiting to get married, having multiple sexual partners, being monogamous, and so on. And in the bigger spectrum of history, political consciousness changes: from thinking Indians should die to forgetting they exist, from thinking women should stay home and breed to celebrating female CEOs. How do these trends occur? How can a population make such tremendous shifts in belief in relatively short periods of time? Again, human beings don't think or make decisions in isolation. They decide on their hair, clothing, cars, homes, favorite colors, favorite body types, favorite drinks, and favorite pastimes according to the huge cultural menu of their time. Every important psychologist, anthropologist, and philosopher of the twentieth century taught us this: People do make free choices only insofar as they are free from overt oppression, *but they do not make choices that are free of culture*.

5   Take, for example, the SUV craze in the United States. Certainly, we can point to various causes for the increased sales of SUVs over the past decade: more disposable income, cheap gas prices (relative to other industrialized nations). But given the tremendous escalation of SUV sales, we might assume that significant changes have occurred: dramatic increases in snow throughout the nation, the general depletion of the highway system, rampant mudslides from coast to coast, a sudden migration from cities to

---

Further analyzes the way images work in everyday life—explaining the complexity of how images influence thinking (debunking the oversimplistic view).

Broad cultural allusions help make connections for the reader.

Uses questions *(How do . . . ? How can . . . ?)* to lead the reader to the next point.

Sharp analytical points help make distinctions and reveal the role of images in everyday life.

An extended example about SUVs to illustrate the previous point.

Consuming an image means consuming "the apparent value of the image."

Why do certain behaviors become extinct or come into favor?

People choose from a cultural menu.

Reasons why people should want to buy an SUV.

mountain hideaways, a dramatic increase in family size, a sudden discovery of free and accessible oil reserves, a sudden realization that SUVs save lives.

None of these occurred. But the opposite in each case has: People are generally moving to warmer climates and to cities; snowfall amounts are diminishing even in "snow belts"; family size is shrinking; oil is increasingly more expensive and coated in political stickiness; SUVs are involved in deadly rollover accidents; the nation is increasingly paved—perhaps the smoothest it's ever been in its paleontological history. And more roads go more places. Generally speaking, people have fewer reasons than ever to drive trucks, fewer reasons than ever to drive big people haulers, fewer reasons than ever to have four-wheel drive, fewer reasons than ever to own humungous, extra-large carrying capacity, super-low-gas-mileage vehicles. But the average suburban family is *more* likely to drive such a vehicle—one originally conceived as a tool for ranches or military operations.

Given the facts, we have to look at the mighty image. Given all the issues at hand (the history, the economics, the politics, the geography, the climate, the demographics), we must analyze what's most prevalent and powerful in our culture: advertising. Take, for example, a typical SUV ad, one for a Toyota 4Runner. The 4Runner descends a rocky cliff—a near-vertical drop—and rocky terrain stretches for miles into the background. The main text proclaims: "No intelligent life out here. Just you." (One wonders if Toyota's marketing executives are terribly ironic or terribly shortsighted.) At the bottom of the ad, a smaller message says, "Daily stops to the middle of nowhere." Certainly, most Americans live nowhere close to the middle of nowhere. Very few people will ever get to a place where they are surrounded by nothing but rocks, and even fewer will ever aim a truck down a cliff.

If we were to examine this ad and then assess the demographics of the buying public, we might guess that it's a joke—or an attempt to ruin Toyota. But the ad obviously works. It conjures up an attractive un-reality for potential consumers. We also might guess that the ad appears in an outdoors magazine—perhaps *Ranchers Quarterly, Mountain Lion News,* or *Rock Slide Specialist.* But the ad appears in *Time*—a decidedly mainstream, middle-class periodical. The vast majority of its readers commute to work on urban streets and suburban highways—and descend the gradual paved slopes of parking garages. Given the distance between readers' actual lives and the ad's imagery, Toyota may have just as logically featured the landscape of Mars.

Margin notes (left):

Develops the extended example about SUVs.

Specific examples help to influence the reader's way of thinking.

With the groundwork laid in the previous two paragraphs, Johnson emphasizes the role of the advertising image.

Specific details from Toyota 4Runner ad help drive home the idea.

Points out the logical absurdity of the Toyota 4Runner ad, while acknowledging that the ad works.

Reference to Mars points out logical absurdity.

Margin notes (right):

Why SUVs aren't a logical choice.

How prevalent is advertising in our culture? To what extent does it overcome rational thinking?

What other ads work by conjuring up "an attractive un-reality for potential customers"?

By appealing to underlying
values, logically absurd
images leave an impres-
sion.

Further analysis: The
repetition of advertising
images has an impact on
people's consciousness.

Makes final connection
between image and a set
of ideas (values, beliefs,
assumptions).

But such an image leaves an impression. It resonates with our
songs (" . . . purple mountains' majesty . . ."); it appeals to our longing for escape; it captures our desire for solitude and security; it fits
into our drive to scoff at nature. And when such imagery pounds the
average citizen relentlessly, it begins to reside in the consciousness.
It becomes familiar. Even though most Americans will never see the
top of a mountain or careen down a cliff (on purpose), they can buy
(into) the vehicle attached to the impression.

10   The image creates an *allure,* that is, an attractive association
of the thing (ridiculously large truck) with a set of ideas (escape,
individualism, America, majesty, power, etc.). That set of ideas can
be entirely divorced from reality, entirely separate from the needs of
everyday life. But everyday life doesn't matter, nor does the logic that
it might yield. The mighty advertising image makes it all irrelevant.

Advertising images appeal
to our values, desires, and
underlying beliefs—not
our logical reasoning.

Writing Strategies

1. Describe Johnson's voice as a writer, and refer to several passages for support. What is, or isn't, inviting
   about Johnson's voice?

2. How does Johnson's introduction effectively lead into
   the rest of his essay?

3. Identify one concession Johnson makes, and explain
   how he uses it to further his own argument.

4. What does Johnson imagine his readers think, and how
   would he like to change their thinking?

5. Johnson concludes paragraph 8 by saying, "Given the
   distance between readers' actual lives and the ad's
   imagery, Toyota may have just as logically featured
   the landscape of Mars." Based on the preceding paragraphs, how does (or doesn't) Johnson earn the right to
   make such a claim?

Exploring Ideas

1. Interview people outside of class to find out how they think
   advertisements influence their thinking. Then use the
   results of your interviews to support or refute Johnson's
   claim that advertisements mold our sense of daily life.

2. In his opening sentence, Johnson lists several "hard
   choices" Americans have to make. Are these really hard
   choices? What do such choices say about American culture? What do they tell the reader about Johnson?

3. In a group, explore what images Americans consume,
   settling on several key images. What do those images
   say about America?

Ideas for Writing

1. What popular image contradicts the facts (medical,
   scientific, historical, and so on)? What are the consequences of the contradiction?

2. How are advertising images effective despite their
   illogical appeals?

If responding to one of these ideas, go to the Analysis
section of this chapter to begin developing ideas for your
essay.

An Imperfect Reality

Rebecca Hollingsworth

In the following essay, Rebecca Hollingsworth, who studies art at Northwestern Michigan College, goes beyond the first glance and shows the reader how an image (an autism-awareness magazine ad) works on the consciousness of the viewer. Through analysis, Hollingsworth breaks down the particulars of an image to show how the overall ad conveys ideas, assumptions, and values, and thus influences the viewer's thinking.

Every day we hear more and more about developmental disorders that afflict children in the United States, disorders that have been misunderstood, downplayed, or ignored. With recent advances in child development and behavior studies, and, perhaps to a large extent, with the explosion of pop psychology personalities like Dr. Phil, Americans are paying more attention than ever to children's mental health. Of course, the general public isn't necessarily any more educated about developmental disorders than it was in the past, but experts and non-experts alike are now insisting that it's okay, even fashionable, to acknowledge and address the ways in which our children aren't "perfect."

One health epidemic at the forefront of public consciousness is autism, a brain disorder that impairs a person's ability to communicate, socialize, and participate in group behavior. Often surfacing by the time a child is three years old, the symptoms of autism include stifled speech and difficulty in displaying joy or affection. According to a 2007 study by the U.S. Centers for Disease Control and Prevention, about 1 in 150 American children are autistic—a staggering number that makes autism the fastest-growing developmental disorder in the United States (Rice). Since the release of these findings, nonprofit organizations across the country have been working to raise public awareness of this national health crisis. The largest of these organizations, Autism Speaks, recently launched a multimedia campaign aimed at parents of autistic, or potentially autistic, children.

The 2006 autism awareness campaign sponsored by Autism Speaks challenges common notions of the "perfect kid" by revealing how the reality of autism crushes unrealistic ideals of young American girls and boys. The campaign features a series of television, radio, online, magazine, and billboard advertisements that emphasize the prevalence of the disorder. The campaign's magazine ads show kids doing "kid things"—that is, playing dress-up for girls and playing sports for boys. In one ad (see below), a young girl adorns herself with brightly colored clothes and jewelry as proud mom looks on.

The girl wears a cropped, short-sleeved, light pink jacket unzipped to reveal a billowing fuchsia-and-black striped tie and matching fuchsia beaded necklace. She commands the attention of her mother and of us; she stands in a fashionable pose with one leg slightly bent as she looks down to tie a light pink belt around her waist. She towers above her mother, who sits in the lower-left corner of the ad, watching her daughter from the sidelines. The mother's gaze creates a direct line of vision to the young girl, drawing the viewer's eye to this fashionable focal point. Like mom, we look on as the young girl tries on one piece of clothing after another, suggested by the pink, white, and blue clothes draped over furniture in the background. The girl's jewelry—the

Odds of a child becoming a top fashion designer: 1 in 7,000

Odds of a child being diagnosed with autism: 1 in 150

Some signs to look for:

No big smiles or other joyful expressions by 6 months. | No babbling by 12 months. | No words by 16 months.

To learn more of the signs of autism, visit autismspeaks.org

AUTISM SPEAKS
It's time to listen.

chunky necklace and the dangly charm bracelet—and her sophisticated tie clash with her long, stringy pigtail braids and big white teddy bear in the background. The pink-and-white washed walls covered in a busy pastel pattern remind us that this is a child's room and that we are witnessing child's play.

5   The text of the ad jolts us into a reality that is discordant with the idealistic image. Bannered text across the bottom of the image reads, "Odds of a child becoming a top fashion designer: 1 in 7,000. Odds of a child being diagnosed with autism: 1 in 150." This startling statistic of the likelihood that this young girl—any young girl—is autistic turns our viewing experience upside down. As we watch the young girl over her mother's shoulder, we must confront the prevalence of this developmental disability in American children—and the very real possibility that our own child may be that 1 in 150.

The text of the ad goes on to educate parents about the warning signs of autism: a child's inability to show joy by six months, to babble by twelve months, and to talk by sixteen months. And all this text, along with the sobering 1 in 150 statistic, fences us off from the image. In fact, the text separates us from the scene. It's behind the mother's shoulder, but in front of our eyes. We know something she doesn't. In classic dramatic irony, we see the looming, or probable, reality that neither child nor mother can imagine in the ideal bedroom.

The sponsor's logo (a puzzle piece in the shape of a child) and slogan ("Autism Speaks: It's time to listen") appeal to a parent's responsibility to pay attention to her child's behavior, to monitor each developmental step or lack thereof, to hope for the best, to fear the worst.

And like all such ads—those that appeal to the complex tangle of parent responsibility and fear—the message begs many questions: Does autism really speak, or does it whisper? How will I know? Once I hear it, what do I do? How could autism affect my child's chances in the world? Is it curable? Is it deadly?

In this sense, the ad does what numerous other campaigns do: it scares us. But this one aims at a particularly vulnerable place: the intersection of our idealism and our fear. It contrasts deluded notions of success—defined here as becoming a top fashion designer—with a statistically harsh truth. We can no longer bask in the old *one in a million* cliché. Like the pretty imagery in the fictional bedroom, that number has been upstaged by a more demanding probability.

Work Cited

Rice, Catherine. "Prevalence of Autism Spectrum Disorders: Autism and Developmental Disabilities Monitoring Network, Six Sites, United States, 2000." <u>Morbidity and Mortality Weekly Report Surveillance Summaries</u> 56 (2007): 11 pp. 20 Feb. 2008 <http://www.cdc.gov/mmwr/preview/mmwrhtml/ss5601a1.htm>.

Writing Strategies

1. According to Hollingsworth, what does the Autism Speaks advertisement encourage us to think?

2. Hollingsworth breaks the ad down into its basic elements. Which specific elements are most important to her analysis? How, according to Hollingsworth, do the elements work on the consciousness of the reader?

3. Identify three places where Hollingsworth connects ideas for the reader, where she leads the reader from one idea to the next. Why is or isn't her strategy effective?

4. Hollingsworth generally avoids first-person pronouns in her essay. When she uses them (such as in her opening sentence and in paragraph 5), she uses the plural *we* and *us* instead of the singular *I* and *me*. What is the effect of these plural pronouns on the reader? Why might Hollingsworth have decided to use the plural instead of the singular? What is the effect created when she does use the singular *I* in paragraph 7?

5. Study Hollingsworth's use of subjects and verbs. Choose two sentences in which the verbs are especially lively, and explain how they communicate an idea that is important to the main point.

Exploring Ideas

1. In groups or alone, decide what additional detail of the image Hollingsworth could discuss. How would the additional detail strengthen her analysis?

2. Look up "dramatic irony" and explain Hollingsworth's statement: "In classic dramatic irony, we see the looming, or probable, reality that neither child nor mother can imagine in the bedroom." How is this irony important to Hollingsworth's main point?

3. With a group of peers, examine all the details of an ad, and then decide: What is the main idea of the ad? How does it encourage the viewer to think or act? How do images help the reader understand and accept the ad's main idea? How do text and image work together? Seek out and explain the importance of one hidden, or less obvious, detail.

4. How are you like an ad? What visual details have you created about yourself, and what main idea do you want these details to communicate?

Ideas for Writing

1. Hollingsworth says, "In this sense, the ad does what numerous other campaigns do: It scares us." Find a particular ad and explain how it scares us. What vulnerability does it take aim at? How does it strike fear? What does the ad achieve beyond scaring the viewer?

2. Find a print ad that you consider to be educational. How does the ad connect with the reader beyond providing educational information? How does it get the reader's attention? How does it appeal to the reader's basic values or beliefs?

If responding to one of these ideas, go to the Analysis section of this chapter to begin developing ideas for your essay.

Outside Reading

Activity

Find an Image for the Caption

1. Find an image to go with one of the captions below. Then explain the relationship between the two.

2. Share images with a group of peers, and explore how the details of each image gives the caption a different meaning.

3. How do the images speak to particular values, beliefs, and assumptions?

The American Dream

Education

Support the Troops

Success!

INVENTION

Most of the images that constitute everyday life are meant to prompt an idea or emotion—not to be analyzed. (This, say many scholars, is all the more reason to analyze them.) In developing ideas for this project, we have to work against what most images ask of us. We have to see into them, into how they work. We have to break down the parts, and then reassemble them in our own minds to understand how they impact viewers. The following sections are designed to help you through this process: specifically, to find a particular image (in Point of Contact), to examine the image closely and understand its relationship to viewers (in Analysis), to develop a focused point (in Thesis), and to develop support for that point (in Rhetorical Tools). The Invention questions in each section are not meant to be answered directly in your final essay, but to prompt inventive thinking and intensive writing.

POINT OF CONTACT

Images are everywhere. And every image contains more meaning than we might initially imagine. Explore the following possibilities to find a specific image for your own analysis:

Consider all the elements of the image: the pictures, text, colors, placement, models, clothing, blank space, audience, and even the surrounding materials such as stories and columns.

Print Advertisements Print ads range from dense collages of pictures and words to a single image with one slogan. Browse any magazine or newspaper. Also consider print advertisements that lurk in more inconspicuous places, such as your credit card bill, a public bathroom, a phone book, a calendar, and so on.

Posters Most often, posters work like billboards. They are designed to catch a passing eye—to shout loudly enough so that anyone in the vicinity will notice the message.

Internet Images The Internet offers a broad range of images, from shocking photos of war to wondrous shots of space. Do a search by entering a noun, such as "space" or "images."

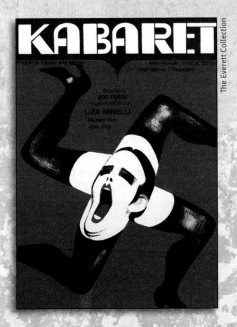

Consider sites such as Newsmap (marumushi.com/apps/newsmap) or Buzztracker.org in which stories of the world are represented graphically.

Billboards Billboards are made to distract people, to yank attention away from the road. Examine one closely to understand how it works toward that goal.

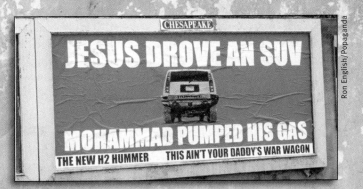

Activity

In a small group, analyze the following images. Consider content, framing, composition, focus, lighting, texture, angle and vantage point, and the significance of all the elements.

Nick Cowie/StockXchng

Library of Congress

Nate Powell/StockXchng

StockXchng

Quentin Houyoux/Stockxchng

morguefile

Invention Questions

Now examine the image you have chosen for your project. The questions below will help you analyze how the image works—how it affects viewers.

- **Content**

  What content—subject or information—is presented in the image? What are the main objects in the image? Of the main elements, which appear to be most prominent? Which are less prominent?

- **Framing**

  How is the image framed? What has been placed within the boundaries of the image? What has not been included? How do the boundaries influence your focus?

- **Composition**

  How are the elements of the image arranged? Are visual elements symmetrical (distributed evenly) or asymmetrical (not distributed evenly)? Are elements touching, overlapping, close together, or far apart? Are elements above or below each other, or to the left or the right of each other? What is in the background? What might the relationship of elements encourage someone to think?

- **Focus**

  How is the image focused? That is, what objects or areas appear most clear or sharp? What objects or areas are not clear? Is anything unusual or striking about the focus? How does the focus draw your attention? How does it affect the relationship of certain elements?

- **Lighting**

  How is the image lit? That is, what objects or areas are well lit? What areas are dark, or in shadow? Is the light harsh or soft? Is there a contrast of tones from light to dark? What is darkest, and what is lightest? How does the lighting affect what is pictured? How might different lighting change the image?

- **Texture**

  What is the texture of the image? If you could touch what is pictured, how would it feel? How does the photograph's texture relate to its content?

- **Angle and Vantage Point**

  From what angle is the photograph taken? Is it straight-on? Is it exaggerated? How does the angle affect the composition of the image? That is, are some elements more in the foreground or background? Are some more prominent?

You may, in your analysis, consider other elements as well. Colors, for example, may be subdued or bright and splashy. Such details may have significance.

Text

Images—such as photographs, diagrams, and charts—often work in conjunction with written text. In advertising or on posters, meaning is often generated by an interaction of image and text. When text accompanies an image, the two fuse into a single idea. But we can pull them apart and see how they work. For instance, Cameron Johnson examines the way text gives meaning to the image of an SUV:

The 4Runner descends a rocky cliff—a near-vertical drop—and rocky terrain stretches for miles into the background. The main text proclaims: "No intelligent life out here. Just you." (One wonders if Toyota's marketing executives are terribly ironic or terribly shortsighted.) At the bottom of the ad, a smaller message says, "Daily stops to the middle of nowhere." Certainly, most Americans live nowhere close to the middle of nowhere. Very few people will ever get to a place where they are surrounded by nothing but rocks, and even fewer will ever aim a truck down a cliff.

Many texts speak back to or depend on other texts to make meaning. That is, they exist in dialogue with other texts—a quality called *intertextuality*. Consider the following bumper sticker:

I SEE STUPID PEOPLE

This sticker makes sense alone, but has more impact if the reader knows about *The Sixth Sense,* a movie in which a young boy eerily announces, "I see dead people." If we know the original statement and its context, we are likely to see more significance in the sticker. Or imagine an advertising campaign that includes the statement, "You *Can* Always Get What You Want." While the statement makes sense, it has even more significance if we know the Rolling Stones' song, "You Can't Always Get What You Want." With the Stones' song in the background of our consciousness, the advertising slogan would have even more force. It would speak back to something that we had heard many times before.

Intertextuality adds layers of meaning to any text. When designers and advertisers make a text speak to other familiar texts, they tap into the public domain. They create public resonance.

The effectiveness of this ad depends upon the viewers' knowledge of the "Got Milk?" ad campaign.

Activity

Find an example of an image and/or text that speaks to another familiar text, and explain how the intertextuality adds a layer of meaning

Examine the image you have chosen for your project. If the image has accompanying text, answer the following questions:

- How does the text correlate with the significance of the image?

- How do content, framing, composition, focus, lighting, texture, angle and vantage point help to convey the ideas?

- Does the text echo other texts? (How does the language depend on our familiarity with other texts?)

Subtext

Not all the meaning that comes from a text is stated. Some meaning is *implied*—suggested but not clearly stated. This layer of *implication* is sometimes called *subtext*—meaning that it is under the more visible and obvious layers. Subtext might also be thought of as a collection of assumptions and hidden values, messages that are not obvious but are present nonetheless. For example, when someone asks what you do for a living, the question is about more than your actual job. It implies questions about your status, your identity, your economic situation, your schedule, even your personality. And even if you offer a short answer ("I'm in marketing"), that answer has a subtext.

Images also have subtext. Even if they have no written text, they still imply ideas. In advertising, images and text often work together to suggest a layer of subtext. The following ad relies on a layer of implication (about pleasure, about relationships, about men, about . . . ice cream).

Thank God she's late.

Häagen-Dazs

Too much pleasure?

Häagen-Dazs. Used by permission.

> **Examine the image you have chosen for your project, and answer the following questions:**
>
> - What seems to be the main idea of the image?
> - Besides the obvious statements or ideas, what subtle assumptions or beliefs are suggested by (or lurking in) the image?
> - How do content, framing, composition, focus, lighting, texture, angle, and vantage point help to convey the ideas?

Subtext is invisible, so finding it is hard work. We have to look closely at all the elements of image and text and connect them with common values and assumptions. Notice Cameron Johnson's exploration of subtext:

> **Besides the obvious statements or ideas, what subtle assumptions or beliefs are suggested by (or lurking in) the image?**
>
> To accept anything in the ad as attractive, viewers must believe they are independent—that they have lives of rugged off-road exploration. Maybe it isn't so literal. That is, people might not see themselves driving a truck down a cliff, but they have to believe in the value of rugged self-determination—let's add physical in there: rugged, physical self-determination. The ad relies on that. It only makes sense (especially within the pages of *Time* magazine!) if readers are caught up in that set of beliefs. The ad implies: "Hey . . . you're the type to bust loose and you need a vehicle to get you where you're going." (Of course, most people don't bust loose—especially the people who can afford such vehicles. Funny.)

Invention Workshop

With a group of peers, examine the Häagen-Dazs ad on this page. What seems to be the main idea of the image? Besides the obvious statements or ideas, what subtle assumptions or beliefs are suggested by (or lurking in) the image? How do content, framing, focus, lighting texture, angle, and vantage point help to convey the ideas?

Context

Analyzing an image involves examining how the image relates to its context—the things and people surrounding it. We have all seen an image of the *Mona Lisa*. But how might our response to the painting change if we saw it in the Louvre, as shown below.

Specific Context The specific context is the real physical space that surrounds the image—the building, the magazine, the neighborhood, the campus, the wall, and so on. Every image is affected by the specific context in which it appears. In these images, da Vinci's *Mona Lisa* (the world's most reproduced work of art) is surrounded by different contexts. In the first images, the crowded room at the Louvre influences how the *Mona Lisa* is viewed, what it means. In the images on the right, the *Mona Lisa* has been recontextualized (recast in different graphic surroundings, even different clothes!). The contexts drastically change how da Vinci's original image works.

Lydie/EPA/Landov Media

Beïot Tessier/Maxppp/Landov Media

Cultural Context Nothing exists without culture. Beyond the physical space surrounding an image, the broader culture provides meaning. The values and beliefs that shape everyday life also impact the way an image works—why it gets made, how it gets received.

In his analysis of an SUV ad, Cameron Johnson relies on the specific context (the magazine that published the ad) and the cultural context (the lifestyle of *Time* readers):

> If we were to examine this ad and then assess the demographics of the buying public, we might guess that it's a joke—or an attempt to ruin Toyota. But the ad obviously works. It conjures up an attractive un-reality for potential consumers. We also might guess that the ad appears in an outdoors magazine—perhaps *Ranchers Quarterly, Mountain Lion News,* or *Rock Slide Specialist.* But the ad appears in *Time*—a decidedly mainstream, middle-class periodical. The vast majority of its readers commute to work on urban streets and suburban highways—and descend the gradual paved slopes of parking garages. Given the distance between readers' actual lives and the ad's imagery, Toyota may have just as logically featured the landscape of Mars.

Jeff Greenberg/PhotoEdit

Zane Williams/Getty Images

Examine the image you have chosen for your project and answer the following questions:

- What beliefs, attitudes, or morals does it support or appeal to?
- What beliefs, attitudes, values or morals does it chafe against?
- What public concern does the image speak to?
- How might people benefit by exploring the possible meanings of the image?

In his response to the Invention questions above, Cameron Johnson comes to an easy conclusion about his image: a Toyota 4Runner.

> **What beliefs, attitudes, values, or morals does it support or appeal to?**
>
> That's easy. The image [for Toyota 4Runner] appeals to the value of independence, individualism. Americans like to think of themselves "out there" alone—doing it on the edge of the frontier. It's in our history. And . . . still . . . we're all caught up in that thinking. Many of our goods are sold to us with this basic belief in mind. We are enamored with the idea of ourselves driving across the open majesty of the country with no rules, no road, no official place to be. In the ad, the truck is aiming down a cliff (a flippin' cliff!) and no sign of civilization ruins the moment. (Apparently, that's a fun thing . . . a sign of one's independence, aiming an expensive truck down a cliff.) The print in the ad says, "No intelligent life out here. Just you." Besides that being pretty funny, it reinforces the appeal to independence. Apparently independence = off the road, off the beaten path.

Johnson is just beginning to get traction with his point. He discovers the main appeal in the ad, and the particular elements that drive the appeal.

Thinking Further

Whenever a question is easy to answer, writers should use that momentum and explore further. They should revel in the ease of the answer and then keep developing nuances, asking more questions. Notice, for instance, what happens when Cameron Johnson continues thinking. He goes beyond the initial answer (that the ad appeals to the idea of independence) and discovers the irony or absurdity of the image:

> What's weird about the appeal is this: Most people aren't at all independent. They follow rules, go to work every day, drive in the correct lanes, park in garages or metered spaces or yellow-lined areas. They trim their lawns to the exact length (about 1/2 inch within the presumed correct length for the neighborhood). They dress according to the rules of their generation. They certainly don't drive their expensive (and very clean) new trucks down cliffs. This ad (and every ad like it) is totally divorced from the real life most people lead. Most Americans are rule followers. We think what the media commentators (or government propaganda) tell us. We do what we can to stay in the lines. But the world of advertising makes it seem like we're all careening down cliffs, splashing through rivers, rockin' it out on the banks of some lake. It ain't true.

This discovery is key to Johnson's essay. That is, only after thinking further does Johnson discover the powerful insights that drive his analysis.

Invention Workshop

In a small group, use the Invention questions to explore your image in depth. First, share your image with others in your group. Then apply one of the Invention questions. Once someone in the group offers a possible answer, record the response. Someone else in the group should then continue that thinking (not moving to another topic or question) by asking how the first responder arrived at his or her point.

THESIS

The purpose of this project is to analyze how an image (or set of images) works to impact viewers. The analysis should reveal something that readers would not otherwise see or imagine. It should show the insides, the mechanics, of the image. Consider the following examples:

- Beyond the main image of the Cadillac, the sophisticated background elements make the pitch to potential consumers.
- In trendy music videos, the camera looks up from the ground at the performers, which reinforces the notion that the performers have power over, and speak down to, their audiences.
- Presidential campaign commercials rely on the imagery of middle-class America so that candidates will be seen as normal working Joes.

Notice that each statement focuses on a particular element of an image. Each also explains the significance, the meaning or impact, of that element. Take, for example, the third statement. It focuses on a particular element: *the imagery of middle-class America*. It explains how that particular element works: It casts the candidates as normal working Joes.

We can deduce that a good thesis for this project has two important qualities:

1. A focus on a particular element

2. An explanation of its significance

Look over your invention notes, and focus on a particular element (something in the content, the composition, the framing, etc.). Then try to explain its significance: how that element works to convey meaning or impact the viewer.

Common Thesis Problems

As in most writing projects, the more specific the claims, the more intensive the ideas will be. If you can point to a particular element in an image and explain how that element works, then you are probably on your way to a focused thesis. But notice the problems in the following statement. It lacks significance and focus. It targets "many" ads and offers a sweeping statement about them—they use women. The statement does not explain how something in those ads works, how they influence people, or how the individual elements create messages:

> Many *Sports Illustrated* ads use women as the main focus.

The following statement does focus on one text *(Rolling Stone)*, but it still lacks focus:

> *Rolling Stone* magazine makes one thing clear: sex sells.

Rolling Stone is a good-sized magazine—with a table of contents, record lists, pictures, ads, articles about politics, CD reviews, movie reviews, and so on. Of course, someone could associate all those elements with sex, but the project would probably lack serious analysis of particular elements. A writer with such a statement needs to look more closely at something specific in *Rolling Stone.*

Activity

Rewrite the two statements above so they are more focused. Consider the two important qualities:

1. a focus on a particular element; and

2. an explanation of its significance.

Evolution of a Thesis

Thesis statements do not always evolve in a neat fashion. They do not always progress from a broader to a more focused insight. Sometimes (maybe most times), they wander, circle back, and jump around as the writer tries to get traction. Below, we can see Johnson searching out meaning through single sentences. He is trying to connect two things: a particular element of the ad and the meaning of that element for viewers. All of the statements below are attempts, some better than others, at forging that connection.

- SUV ads, like that for the Toyota 4Runner, appeal to Americans through natural imagery.

- Ads like the one for Toyota 4Runner give a vision of life that many Americans strive for.

- Even though most Americans' lives do not resemble the natural imagery of SUV ads, that imagery appeals to what many people imagine about themselves.

- The scenic imagery of SUV ads appeals to a lifestyle that most Americans imagine for themselves but rarely realize.

- The ad for Toyota 4Runner relies on natural imagery that is far outside the experience of most Americans, but the ads still have strong appeal.

- The ad for Toyota 4Runner reveals a trend in SUV advertising: The background imagery connects to an illusive vision of American life—one that is contrary to the situation or needs of most potential consumers.

Revision

Develop a working thesis statement that includes attention to a specific element of an image and explains its significance. Then, in a small group, discuss each person's statement. Apply the following:

- Does the statement focus on a specific element (something in the content, composition, framing, angle, focus, etc.)? How could the specific element be narrower?

- Beyond the writer's statement, what is the significance (possible meaning or impact) of that specific element? (What else might it suggest about people, lifestyles, nature, America, clothing, social class, race, gender, politics, domestic life, art, music, and so on?) Be creative. Imagine that the significance is not what people initially assume!

- Make a case for the most surprising or hidden significance in the image. Make a connection that seems, at first, outrageous. Try to convince others in the group that your point is valid.

As in most writing projects, the more specific the claims, the more intensive the ideas will be.

RHETORICAL TOOLS

For analyzing images, support comes in two general categories: (1) details from the image, and (2) evidence outside of the image. The first is essential. Readers will need to see how specific claims correspond to the image itself. The second category includes a wide variety of strategies and will help provide meaningful context to your points.

Using Details from the Image

Any close analysis relies on specific details of the subject. For instance, if you are analyzing an advertisement, readers would expect to see particular features of that ad and an explanation that connects those features to your main point. In her analysis, Rebecca Hollingsworth shows the reader how details make meaning:

> Like mom, we look on as the young girl tries on one piece of clothing after another, suggested by the pink, white, and blue clothes draped over furniture in the background. The girl's jewelry—the chunky necklace and the dangly charm bracelet—and her sophisticated tie clash with her long, stringy pigtail braids and big white teddy bear in the background. The pink-and-white washed walls covered in a busy pastel pattern remind us that this is a child's room and that we are witnessing child's play.

Hollingsworth's analysis shows the power of subtle details that might get overlooked:

> As we watch the young girl over her mother's shoulder, we must confront the prevalence of this developmental disability in American children—and the very real possibility that our own child may be that 1 in 150.

Because we are looking over the mother's shoulder (at the girl from her mother's vantage point), the image confronts us with a real possibility—about American children and about *our own child.* Hollingsworth's careful analysis adds up to a main point:

In this sense, the ad does what numerous other campaigns do: It scares us. But this one aims at a particularly vulnerable place: the intersection of our idealism and our fear. It contrasts deluded notions of success—defined here as becoming a top fashion designer—with a statistically harsh truth. We can no longer bask in the old *one in a million* cliché. Like the pretty imagery in the fictional bedroom, that number has been upstaged by a more demanding probability.

Likewise, Cameron Johnson uses the details of a specific magazine ad to illustrate his thesis that advertising images are out of sync with the reality of everyday life. Notice that he does not merely mention the details; he also explains how those details illustrate his point:

> Take, for example, a typical SUV ad, one for a Toyota 4Runner. The 4Runner descends a rocky cliff—a near-vertical drop—and rocky terrain stretches for miles into the background. The main text proclaims: "No intelligent life out here. Just you." (One wonders if Toyota's marketing executives are terribly ironic or terribly short-sighted.) At the bottom of the ad, a smaller message says, "Daily stops to the middle of nowhere." Certainly, most Americans live nowhere close to the middle of nowhere. Very few people will ever get to a place where they are surrounded by nothing but rocks, and even fewer will ever aim a truck down a cliff.

Return to any notes you generated from the Analysis section of this chapter. Consider the following questions about the image:

- What details (about the content, focus, composition, framing, lighting, texture, angle, and significance) best illustrate my main point?
- What specific text best illustrates my main point?
- Does subtext help to support my main point?
- Does the context help to support my main point?

Using Other Evidence

In some ways, you are attempting to convince readers that your understanding of the image is reasonable. To this end, you can go beyond the image itself and allude to any related events, images, people, or behaviors in the present or past. Some of the readings in this chapter use cultural allusions (references to other well-known texts, films, pictures, photos, or events). For example, in his analysis of ad images, Cameron Johnson refers to broader cultural trends to support the claim that people are influenced deeply by the messages around them:

> Contrary to popular belief, humans are gregarious. We think and act in groups, according to historical trends. About every five years in America, kids laugh at what came five years earlier: "Look at that guy's jeans!" "Hey, check out the hairdo on her!" About every decade or so, certain social behaviors become extinct or come into favor: wearing hats, not wearing hats, getting married at 18, waiting to get married, having multiple sexual partners, being monogamous, and so on. And in the bigger spectrum of history, political consciousness changes: from thinking Indians should die to forgetting they exist, from thinking women should stay home and breed to celebrating female CEOs. How do these trends occur?

Consider the following questions:

- How do cultural trends or events relate to the image I am analyzing?
- Does anything in history show how the image (or type of image) has influenced people?
- Can I create a scenario (a hypothetical situation) to illustrate my point about the image?
- Can I narrate a personal experience to show something important about the image?

Research

Using a periodical database (such as InfoTrac College Edition) or an Internet search engine (such as Google), explore how others have discussed the image you are analyzing. Most likely, you won't find sources about the specific image (unless you are analyzing an historic piece of art or popular culture). However, you'll likely find sources about the type of image—whether an automobile ad, a billboard, a rural photo, and so on. For instance, if Cameron Johnson were exploring for outside sources, he might begin a keyword search with the following combinations:

sport utility vehicle *and* advertisement

sport and utility *and* vehicles *and* advertising

automobile and advertisements *and* nature

Of course, keyword searches are not an exact science. (They're not a science at all.) They are always attempts—and sometimes require several restarts with substitutions and small changes. For instance, changing automobile to car or ad to advertisement may yield significantly different results.

For more assistance with research, see Chapter 13: Research & Writing.

PEER REVIEW

Invention Workshop

Your analysis should reveal something that readers would not otherwise see or imagine. Write down what you think your analysis reveals, and then exchange drafts with at least one other writer. After reading your draft, the other writer should write down responses to the following questions:

- What did the analysis reveal? That is, what didn't I see or imagine about the image until I read the essay?

- How might the thesis be more specific and revealing? Offer particular rewording, or a whole new direction, even if you think the thesis is good as is.

- What additional details from the image might be used to strengthen or refocus the analysis?

Underline your thesis statement or write your main idea above your draft. Exchange drafts with at least one other writer.

As a reviewer, point to particular sentences and phrases that could gain vitality and intensity. Use the following guidelines:

- Underline any blueprinting passages. Suggest a strategy that keeps the reader focused on the ideas rather than on the structure of the essay.

- Check for vague pronouns. Consider use of *this, these, those, it,* and make certain that they accompany or refer to a specific noun.

- Look for sentences that can be combined through subordination. Combine two sentences in the opening paragraph, subordinating one idea to the other. Combine at least two sentences elsewhere in the essay.

- Consider vitality strategies from other chapters and make editorial changes on the writer's draft:
  - Underline any clichés. On the back of the draft, explain how the cliché conceals or blurs thinking. Suggest an alternative to the cliché.
  - Circle any stilted language. On the back of the draft, suggest an alternative approach to the passage.
  - Help the writer experiment with sentence length and brevity. Reconstruct one paragraph, extending some sentences and abbreviating others. Try to create intensity with shorter sentences.
  - Change vague nouns to specific nouns.
  - Change *be* verbs to active verbs.
  - Change clauses to phrases.
  - Change phrases to words.
  - Combine sentences.
  - Repeat structures.
  - Intensify verbs.

- Help the reader avoid common grammatical errors: comma splices, sentence fragments, or pronoun/antecedent agreement.

If you have analyzed an image for your project, what detail of the image have you overlooked? How might some quiet detail strengthen your analysis? Return to your image and the Analysis section of this chapter for help.

DELIVERY

"What was your Analyzing Images essay about?" We are often asked such questions, not only about the essays we have written, but about many other aspects of our lives. A boss may ask, "What happened last night with the customer who called back to complain this morning?" A professor may ask, "How is your writing project coming along?" A family member may ask, "How'd Cindy's softball game go?" In some cases we can simply answer, "Not much" or "Fine." But sometimes—especially when it comes to bosses and professors—we are being asked to give a briefing on an important situation.

Some briefings are impromptu. That is, we have no time to prepare and must respond on the spot. Other briefings are more formal. For example, each day the U.S. President's press secretary briefs the press on important issues. Being able to give a focused, organized, and concise briefing is a valuable skill.

Beyond the Essay: Briefings

For practice, prepare three separate briefings—or oral presentations—of your Analyzing Images essay. One briefing should be 30 seconds long, one should be one minute long, and one should be two minutes long. Your briefing should include:

- your main idea (or thesis)
- your main supporting ideas
- the most important details

Briefings often include follow-up questions, so be prepared to answer questions.

1. Write out each briefing: 30 seconds should be about 50 words, one minute about 100 words, and two minutes about 200 words.
2. Practice your verbal delivery for each briefing. Be prepared to verbally deliver the briefings, without notes.
3. To loosen up, present your 30-second briefing without notes to a classmate.
4. In small groups, present your one-minute briefing.
5. Present your two-minute briefing to the class.

Activity

Go around the room, each student describing a briefing that he or she gave at work, at school, at home, or someplace else.

1. What prompted the briefing?
2. Who was the audience?
3. What was the subject of the briefing?
4. What was the purpose of the briefing?
5. What was the method of communication?
6. What was the effect or outcome of the briefing? How was the information used?

Each student should describe a briefing unlike one that has already been described. Attempt to explore the various possibilities when it comes to audience, subject, purpose, and so on.

MAKING ARGUMENTS

Chapter Contents

CHAPTER 7

"Someone who makes an assertion puts forward a claim—a claim on our attention and to our belief."

—Stephen Toulmin

Argument is the art of persuading people how to think. This may sound absurd since most people, we hope, already know how to think, or at least *what* to think about particular issues. But with argument, we can change how people view things, even slightly, and so affect how they approach and process ideas.

Arguments come to us in different forms. We hear them given in speeches, debates, and informal discussions. We hear them every day on talk shows, in break rooms, college hallways, and public meeting places like restaurants and pubs. Arguments get delivered through action. They come explicitly in protests, parades, sit-ins, labor strikes, and elections. They also come in more subtle forms: People donate to charities (thereby expressing their favor of a particular cause); they patronize or boycott a particular store; they choose not to vote (thereby expressing their stance against the entire political process). Arguments get made through art in all media: sculpture, painting, music, and so on. And arguments are major elements of literature. For example, it has been said that Aldous Huxley's book *Brave New World* argues against the extremes of materialism and industrialization and that Kate Chopin's *The Awakening* argues for a new vision of women's identity. Even poems offer arguments: Walt Whitman's masterpiece *Leaves of Grass* argues for the value of common American workers and their common language.

People in all occupations make or deal with arguments. For example: a human resources manager for a packaging company argues in a report that more supervisors should be hired in the coming fiscal year; several department store sales associates collectively write a letter to store and regional managers in which they claim current scheduling practices minimize sales commissions; the public affairs director of a major automobile company argues that a new advertising campaign should not be offensive to a particular demographic group; the lawyers for a major computer software company argue in a district court that the company's business practices comply with federal anti-trust laws. In academia, argument is everywhere:

- The biology faculty at a state university argue for the need to study cloning and petition the administration for more leeway to do research.

- A historian argues about the number of Native Americans on the continent before European settlers so that people more deeply understand history.

- A psychologist argues that Freudian analysis is overused and that new strategies for exploring patients' psychological makeup should be further developed.
- College administrators argue for more state funds for their schools.
- Students in an architecture class argue that a particular structural design is more sound than competing designs.
- Students in a nursing program must convince others that a new staff management technique is valuable for large hospitals.

In any situation, those who can deliver the most sophisticated and engaging arguments tend to have the most influence. Of course, a sophisticated and engaging argument involves a great deal of strategy. For instance, in academic argument, blatant personal attacks, outright aggression, and sugar-coated language are not valued, nor are empty phrases ("don't question what's in my heart") and mean-spiritedness ("your ideas are simply idiotic"). But while academic writers are not out to squash an opponent or cuddle up to audiences, they do more than simply present their opinions. In providing a new way of thinking about a particular topic, academic writers must also analyze others' ideas and explain how their own claims relate to those of others.

This chapter will help you discover an argumentative topic, explore that topic in depth, develop a sophisticated argument, and communicate your argument in writing. The following essays will provide insight to various argumentative strategies. After reading the essays, you can find a topic in one of two ways:

1. Go to the Point of Contact section to find a topic from everyday life.
   or
2. Choose one of the Ideas for Writing that follow the essays.

After you find a topic, go to the Analysis section to begin developing your argument.

Why a Great Books Education Is the Most Practical!

David Crabtree

Academic writers often challenge common assumptions. David Crabtree, president and one of the founders of Gutenberg College in Eugene, Oregon, takes on the common assumption that a specialized education is the best path to a career and financial security. While many college students believe that a narrow focus on a particular set of skills will lead them to successful careers, Crabtree argues that specialization works against students' best interests. Instead, he invites readers to examine the role of "great books" (classic works of literature, philosophy, and religion) in developing a career path and a productive future. Crabtree knows what he's up against: Most people assume that studying great books is contrary to a career path in "the real world." So he begins, in the title of his essay, by taking on that assumption.

Gutenberg College is a great books college. The curriculum is designed to develop good learning skills in students; they read and then discuss in small groups the writings produced by the greatest minds of Western culture as they grappled with the most fundamental questions facing human beings of all ages. When I tell people about Gutenberg College, one of the most common responses is: "It's a good idea, but not practical." The thinking seems to be that if one had unlimited time and money, a great books education would be very good to pursue; but in the real world, food has to be put on the table, and a great books education will not do that. I am convinced, however, that a great books education is not only practical, but, in our day and age, the most practical education available.

Modern society has adopted the historically recent perspective that the purpose of education is training for the workplace. In this view, college should provide students with skills and knowledge that will prepare them to procure reasonably high-paying, satisfying employ-ment for the rest of their lives. The common wisdom says that the best way to achieve this goal is: First, as an undergraduate, select a promising occupation and major in the appropriate field of study; and second, after graduating, enter directly into the work force or attend a graduate or professional school for more specialized training. The logic seems to be that the sooner one concludes one's education and begins work in one's field, the less will be the cost of education and the better the prospects for advancement into secure, high-paying positions. While this was once a reasonable strategy, it is not suited to the economic environment currently developing.

The world is changing at a bewildering pace. Anyone who owns a computer and tries to keep up with the developments in hardware, software, and the accompanying incompatibilities is all too aware of the speed of change. This rapid change, especially technological change, has extremely important implications for the job market. In the past, it was possible to look at the nation's work force, determine which of the existing occupations was most desirable in terms of pay and working conditions, and pick one to prepare for. But the rapid rate of change is clouding the crystal ball. How do we know that a high-paying job today will be high-paying tomorrow?

A photographer told me about a talented and highly skilled artisan who touched up photographs. He was the best in our region of the country, and people knew it; because the demand for his skill was so great, he was unable to keep up with the work. A few years ago, however, this artisan suddenly closed his shop; he did not have enough work to stay in business. Due to developments in computer hardware and software, anyone with just a little training can now achieve results previously attainable by only a few highly skilled artisans. Technology had rendered this artisan's skills obsolete. And this is not an isolated case; technology is antiquating many skills.

5   One could try to avoid this fate by finding an occupation unlikely to be automated, but automation is not the only cause of job elimination. Historically, mid-management positions in large corporations provided good incomes and considerable job security.

However, AT&T's recent layoffs have drawn attention to the growing trend in American companies to eliminate mid-level managers as the companies restructure to compete better in the world market. As a result, a glut of unemployed executives are having great difficulty finding employment in their field of expertise. Most of them never dreamed they would be standing in unemployment lines.

Medicine might be a more promising field. There will always be sick people to treat, and doctors have a reputation for high pay. However, recent news reports have called into question the future of this occupation. There is an excess of doctors in the United States right now, largely due to the number of foreign medical students who decide to remain in this country after they complete their training. And physicians' incomes recently declined for the first time in decades, a change attributed to the proliferation of HMOs and managed health care providers—a trend expected to continue. To further complicate the picture, in the near future a national health care plan may rise from the ashes of President Clinton's ill-fated one. What effect such a program would have on physicians' incomes and working conditions is impossible to predict with certainty, but doctors ought not expect raises under such a plan. In light of such an uncertain future, should a student invest the time and money medical training requires? This is a tough question, but similar uncertainties lie in the future of many professions.

One could forego the traditionally desirable occupations and choose a field certain to grow and develop. Clearly the high demand for programmers, electrical engineers, and computer programmers appears to hold great promise for job security in the foreseeable future, even if one must work for several different employers over the years. However, no one in this field will be able to take his job for granted. Due to the rapid rate of technological change in the computer industry, people in this field need to be constantly learning and updating their skills to keep up with the new technology. In areas of state-of-the-art development, some companies do not want software writers or engineers over thirty-five years old because their training is out of date and they are too set in their ways to approach problems with fresh thinking. These companies prefer to replace older employees with recent graduates. Thus the longevity of one's career in this fast-changing field could be relatively short.

No matter what occupation one chooses, the future is full of question marks. Although this economic dislocation is in its early stages, statistics already indicate a high degree of instability in the job market. According to the United States government, the average American switches careers three times in his or her life, works for ten employers, and stays in each job only 3.6 years.[1]

Such unpredictability calls for a different strategy in preparing for the job market. Rather than spending one's undergraduate years receiving specialized training, one ought to learn more general, transferable skills which will provide the flexibility to adjust to whatever changes may occur. A well-educated worker should be able to communicate clearly with coworkers, both verbally and in writing, read with understanding, perform basic mathematical calculations, conduct himself responsibly and ethically, and work well with others. These skills would make a person well-suited to most work environments and capable of learning quickly and easily the requisite skills for a new career, should the need arise. Thus a hard-headed realism, with long-term economic security as the goal, would seem to dictate an undergraduate educational strategy of focusing on sound general learning skills—just what a great books education provides.

10   Therefore, a great books education makes good sense in terms of dollars spent and dollars gained when calculated over a lifetime, and, therefore, good training for the workplace. This is fortuitous, however, because a great books education is not designed with this as the primary goal. It is designed to achieve the even more practical goal historically assigned to education: to teach students how to live wisely. I say this is practical because that which helps one achieve what needs to be done is practical. Living wisely is the most important thing a person can do in his lifetime. Therefore, education with this focus is quintessentially practical.

---

[1] Sue Brower, "When You Want—or Have—to Make a Career Shift," *Cosmopolitan* Aug. 1985: 229.

Wise living means to live as one ought; in other words, to strive to achieve good goals by moral means. This statement immediately evokes an array of fundamental questions: Why are we here? What is valuable or worthwhile? What are the principles of right and wrong? Is there a God? Who is He? What is my relationship to Him? Without having seriously wrestled with these issues, one will be condemned to a life without direction or purpose. Without clearly defined and worthwhile goals, success and fulfillment are impossible. Therefore, one's answers to these questions have very important implications for how one chooses to earn a living.

Is such a goal realistic or attainable by education? It is difficult to teach a person how to live wisely. In a sense, such a skill cannot be taught; it can only be learned. The student must be challenged to think through these fundamental questions for himself; he must be an extremely active participant in his own education. We all derive our wisdom from careful reflection on our experience, and this reflection can be made more profound by considering the reflections of others who have had similar experiences. That is to say, we can benefit from the wisdom others have attained.

A great books education creates an educational environment conducive to the learning of wisdom. Classes are small, personal, and largely discussion-based. The small class size and the discussion format encourage each student to be actively involved in consideration of important issues, and they allow the course of the discussion to be tailored to the concerns of the students. The writings of the most influential thinkers of our cultural tradition are studied, which provides many thought-provoking insights into the fundamental questions. As students work to understand these writings, they develop important learning skills—reading with understanding, thinking clearly, and writing cogently—which equip them to become life-long learners.

A great books education is not for everyone. In order to benefit from such an education, a student has to be highly motivated, mature enough to realize the importance of such a focus, and self-disciplined. Whatever reasons one might have for not pursuing a great books education, it cannot be because it is not practical!

Writing Strategies

1. How does Crabtree make his main idea clear to the reader?

2. Crabtree's introduction puts his essay within a context—that is, he lets the reader know why he is writing about a great books education. Why is this strategy effective? (Many other writers only imply the argumentative context. They do not directly explain the context or the purpose. Why? When is it most helpful to directly state an essay's context and purpose?)

3. Does Crabtree clearly define a great books education? If so, how? If not, how might he have defined it more clearly?

4. What kinds of evidence (statistics, examples, allusions, personal testimony, reasoning, and so on) does Crabtree provide as support for his main idea?

5. Does Crabtree make concessions or counterarguments—that is, does he acknowledge weaknesses in his own argument or value in opposing positions (concession), or does he anticipate and respond to likely reactions to his points (counterargument)? If so, how do the concessions and/or counterarguments strengthen his argument? If not, what concessions or counterarguments might he have made?

Exploring Ideas

1. What does Crabtree mean by a "great books education"?

2. Crabtree argues that a great books education is the most practical education because the world and workforce are changing at such a rapid rate. Yet many readers disagree with him. What is at the core of these differing opinions.

3. Why else, besides practical training for a job, might a great books education be a good idea?

4. How might a great books education benefit a police officer, a nurse, an accountant?

5. What compromise might college curriculums reach between a purely great books education and purely specialized training?

Ideas for Writing

1. Crabtree argues for the practical value of a great books education, but he does not say that a great books education is for everyone. What else might you argue has practical value, even though you are not arguing that it is for everyone? (Consider a type of education, a way of doing something, a hobby, and so on.)

2. Why are we here? What is valuable or worthwhile? What are the principles of right and wrong? Is there a God? Who is He? What is your relationship with Him? How might you support or refute Crabtree's claim that "one's answers to these questions have very important implications for how one chooses to earn a living" (¶ 11)?

3. Crabtree says that "the writings of the most influential thinkers of our cultural tradition are studied, which provides many thought-provoking insights into the fundamental questions" (¶ 13). Can you think of one such insight that has influenced your thinking?

If responding to one of these ideas, go to the Analysis section of this chapter to begin developing ideas for your essay.

Cruelty, Civility, and Other Weighty Matters

Ann Marie Paulin

In the margins of this essay, a reader's comments point to key ideas and writing strategies. As you read the essay, consider how the comments might influence your own reading and writing.

As with most engaging essays, Paulin's originates in personal circumstance. (See her invention writing on pages 216, 218.) Also, as with most engaging essays, the writer extends her thinking into the public sphere. As you read "Cruelty, Civility, and Other Weighty Matters," notice how Paulin puts forth an argument while keeping herself in the background, only briefly referring to herself in the essay's introduction and conclusion. As you will see, Paulin goes beyond the increasingly common argument against media's portrayal of women; she reveals something about the subtle effects of that portrayal. Paulin, who teaches English and gender studies at Owens Community College in Toledo, Ohio, shows that a writer's voice matters—that savvy use of voice actually creates layers to an argument. That is, her voice re-humanizes the issue and the people involved. If the media have dehumanized "fat people," Paulin does more than argue against the media; she strikes back with an intense, multifaceted presence.

Writing Strategies

A strong, emphatic (but informal) voice.

"You" makes the voice more informal.

"Our" is a direct strategy to create public resonance.

This is a qualification of her argument.

Exploring Ideas

Pop culture images are simplistic.

Media images have distorted people's perceptions about life.

I swear, if I have to sit through one more ad proclaiming that life is not worth living if you aren't thin, I'll slug somebody. So much for the theory that fat people are jolly. But, contrary to what magazines, talk shows, movies, and advertisements proclaim, we aren't all a bunch of sorrowful, empty losers with no friends and no self-esteem, either. As with most complex issues—religion, politics, human relationships—most of what we see in mass media is hugely oversimplified and, therefore, wrong. So, if many of us recognize the media are notorious for getting things less than accurate, you might wonder why I let these images bother me so much. Well, if you were one of the millions of fat Americans living in a culture where you are constantly depicted as some sort of weepy loser, ill-dressed buffoon, or neutered sidekick, your good nature might wear a bit thin as well. But far more important than my ill temper is a creepy sense that these inaccurate images have shifted our vision of what is important in life way out of whack, so far out that people are being hurt. What I'm proposing here is that we need to get some perspective on this issue.

First of all, let me make it clear that I'm not advocating that everyone in America go out and get fat. According to the news media, we are doing that very handily on our own, in spite of all the messages to the contrary and the shelves of diet food in

Helps with the public resonance. It shows that Paulin is not alone.

Counterargument.

Allusion to a related news event.

Using an authority, Pipher, to support point.

every supermarket. (One of my colleagues came by today with a newspaper article on the Krispy Kreme Donut chain; evidently, Americans eat three million Krispy Kreme donuts each day. We may talk tofu, but we gobble glazed.) Americans all need to work on eating healthier and getting some exercise. Of course, the thin fanatics claim to advocate a healthy lifestyle as well, but I question how healthy people are when they are living on low-calorie chocolate milk drinks, or taking herbal supplements containing goodness knows what, or loading up on the latest wonder diet pill. Remember Fen-phen? And most diets don't work. Psychologist Mary Pipher, in her book *Hunger Pains: The Modern Woman's Quest for Thinness,* cites a 1994 study which found that "90 percent of dieters regain all the weight they lost within five years" (32). The evidence is beginning to pile up out there that being fat may not be nearly as bad for a person's health as the crazy things people inflict upon their bodies to lose weight.

But beyond these physical things, we need to get our minds straightened out. We need to get back to recognizing that a human being is a collection of qualities, good and bad, and that appearance is not the ultimate way to judge a person's character or value to society.

Yet there is definitely a prejudice against fat people in this country. Various articles and news magazine programs have reported that Americans of all sizes make far more than simple aesthetic judgments when they look at a fat person. Fat people are assumed to be lazy, stupid, ugly, lacking in self-esteem and pride, devoid of self-control, and stuffed full of a host of other unpleasant qualities that have nothing to do with the size of a person's belly or thighs. But, as anyone who has ever been the victim of such prejudice can tell you, the impact such foolish notions have on people is real and harmful. For example, Marilyn Wann, in her book *Fat! So?,* reports some alarming statistics: "In a 1977 study, half of the landlords refused to rent an apartment to a fat applicant. All of the landlords were willing to rent the same apartment to a thin applicant" (154). What does dress size have to do with whether or not you pay your rent on time? Or do landlords assume that fat people will not keep the apartments clean? Wann also cites an experiment in which "[r]esearchers placed two fake personal ads, one for a woman described as '50 pounds overweight' and the other for a woman described as a drug addict. The drug addict received 79 percent of the responses" (59). I don't even want to know what the thinking was here. And, finally, Wann points out that the average fat woman earns about $7000 less per year than her thinner sisters (80). In my case, I teach English at a community college. Jobs in academia require an

Stating an opposing view—or wrong assumption. Setting up the counter-argument.

Counterargument—she's countering the opposing view.

Millions of Americans eat poorly . . . are out of sync with the media images.

Diets don't work . . . and inflict bodily damage.

People's understanding of health has been distorted.

The study is 30 years old. Has it changed?

Marilyn Wann—fat people are discriminated against.

Real effects of prejudice. Good support.

advanced degree, so I happen to have a Ph.D., which has nothing to do with my body size, unless you want to count the weight I gained from thousands of hours sitting reading, sitting at a keyboard, sitting grading papers.

5   This weight prejudice hurts real people. When people are denied a place to live or a means of support not because of any bad behavior or lack of character or talent on their part but because of someone else's wrongheaded notions, then we need to start changing things.

The messages are particularly insidious when they suggest that being thin is more important than a man's or, more often, a woman's relationships with her loved ones or even than her health. The media churn the images out, but the public too often internalizes them. For example, in one commercial for Slim Fast, the woman on the ad is prattling on about how she had gained weight when she was pregnant (seems to me, if you make a person, you ought to be entitled to an extra ten pounds) and how awful she felt. Then there is a shot of this woman months later as a thin person with her toddler in her yard. She joyously proclaims that Slim Fast is "the best thing that ever happened to me!" The best thing that ever happened to her?! I thought I heard wrong. What about that little child romping by her heels? Presumably, there is a daddy somewhere for that little cherub. What about his role in her life? The thought that losing that weight is the most important thing that ever occurred in her life is sad and terrifying. It's even worse for the folks who share that life with her. I kept hoping that was not what she meant. I'm sure her family is really most important. But she didn't say, "Next to my baby, Slim Fast is the best thing that ever happened to me." Advertisers don't spend millions of dollars creating ads that don't say what they intend them to; this message was deliberate. Granted, this is only one ad, but the message is clear: The consumer is the center of the universe, and being thin is the only way to ensure that universe remains a fun place to live. The constant repetition of this message in various forms does the damage to the humans who watch and learn.

While we can shrug off advertisements as silly, when we see these attitudes reflected among real people, the hurt is far less easy to brush away. For instance, in her essay, "Bubbie, Mommy, Weight Watchers and Me," Barbara Noreen Dinnerstein recalls a time in her childhood when her mother took her to Weight Watchers to slim down and the advice the lecturer gave to the women present: "She told us to put a picture of ourselves on the 'fridgerator of us eating and looking really fat and ugly. She said remember what you look like. Remember how ugly you are" (347).

Margin notes (left):

Relates the problem to her personal situation. Makes the voice feel personal.

Restatement of the main idea.

Slim Fast ad that directly values thinness over family life. Good support.

This addresses an opposing point: That ads are harmless.

Margin notes (right):

The real danger of the media images.

Allusion to popular item.

Thinness ads damage minds/lives.

Keeps returning to the effects on real people—so reader can't dismiss the point.

Analysis of the opposing logic.

I have a problem with this advice. First, of course, it is too darn common. Fat people are constantly being told they should be ashamed of themselves, of their bodies. And here we see another of those misconceptions I mentioned earlier: the assumption that being fat is the same as being ugly. There are plenty of attractive fat people in the world, as well as a few butt-ugly thin ones, I might add. Honestly, though, the real tragedy is that while few people in this world are truly ugly, many agonize over the belief that they are. Dr. Pipher reported: "I see clients who say they would rather kill themselves than be overweight" (91). I never have figured out how trashing a fellow being's self-esteem is going to help that person be healthier.

People would rather die than be fat.

Ha! The writer is not above judging people . . . this creates an interesting voice.

Transition statement creates coherence between points.

Another example of this bullying comes from Pipher's book *Hunger Pains: The Modern Woman's Tragic Quest for Thinness.* Pipher recounts a conversation she overheard one day in a dress shop:

Pipher—women are psychologically damaged by the culture of thinness.

> I overheard a mother talking to her daughter, who was trying on party dresses. She put on each dress and then asked her mother how she looked. Time after time, her mother responded by saying, "You look just awful in that, Kathy. You're so fat nothing fits you right." The mother's voice dripped with disgust and soon Kathy was crying. (89)

Pipher goes on to suggest that Kathy's mother is a victim of the culture, too, because she realizes how hard the world will be on her fat daughter. Unfortunately, what she doesn't realize is how much better her daughter's quality of life would be if she felt loved by her mother. Any person surrounded by loving family members at home is much better equipped to deal with whatever the cruel world outside throws at her or him.

Follow-up to the quote makes it more engaging and relevant.

10   Dinnerstein was lucky; she had a grandmother who was very loving and supportive. Her grandmother's advice was, "Be proud, be strong, be who you are" (348). Sound advice for any child, and far more likely to produce an all-around healthy human being than a constant barrage of insults.

Another authority used for support . . . a public figure.

But the insensitivity doesn't stop when you grow up. In Camryn Manheim's book *Wake Up! I'm Fat,* the actress discusses her battle with her weight. She expected many of the difficulties she encountered from people in the entertainment industry, which is notorious for its inhuman standards of thinness for women. But when she gained some weight after giving up smoking, she was stunned when her father told her she should start smoking again until she lost the weight (78). In *The Invisible Woman: Confronting Weight Prejudice in America,* W. Charisse Goodman cites a 1987 study that concluded: "When good health practices and appearance

Camryn Manheim—the insensitivity of the industry.

norms coincide, women benefit; but if current fashion dictated poor health practices, women might then engage in those practices for the sake of attractiveness" (30). Like taking up smoking to stay slim.

Certainly everyone is entitled to his or her own opinion of what is attractive, but no one has the right to damage another human being for fun or profit. The media and the diet industry often do just that. While no one can change an entire culture overnight, people, especially parents, need to think about what they really value in the humans they share their lives with and what values they want to pass on to their children. We need to wake up and realize that being thin will not fix all our problems, though advertisements for diets and weight loss aids suggest this. Losing weight may, indeed, give a man or woman more confidence, but it will not make a person smarter, more generous, more loving, or more nurturing. It won't automatically attract the dream job or the ideal lover. On the contrary, people who allow the drive to be thin to control them may find that many other areas of their lives suffer: They may avoid some celebrations or get-togethers because of fear they may be tempted to eat too much or the "wrong" foods. They may cut back on intellectual activities like reading or enjoying concerts or art museums because those activities cut into their exercise time too much. The mania for thinness can cause a person to lose all perspective and balance in life. I know. It happened to me. My moment of revelation came about 12 years ago. I was a size ten, dieting constantly and faithfully keeping lists of every bite I ate, trying to lose 15 more pounds. While I was watching the evening news, a story came on about a young woman who was run over by a bus. I vividly recall that as the station played the footage of the paramedics wheeling the woman away on a stretcher, I said to myself, "Yeah, but at least she's thin." I've been lucky enough to have gained some wisdom (as well as weight) with age: I may be fat, but I'm no longer crazy. There are some things more important than being thin.

Margin notes:

Qualifying her main point.

Back to the personal situation and relaxed voice.

Goodman—women put health below thinness.

Being thin is not the answer to life.

The drive for thinness may shrink other parts of life.

Sanity is better than insane thinness. Conclusion ties back to the intro.

Works Cited

Dinnerstein, Barbara Noreen. "Bubbie, Mommy, Weight Watchers and Me." Worlds in Our Words: Contemporary American Women Writers. Ed. Marilyn Kallet and Patricia Clark. Upper Saddle River: Prentice, 1997. 347–49.

Goodman, W. Charisse. The Invisible Woman: Confronting Weight Prejudice in America. Carlsbad: Gurze, 1995.

Manheim, Camryn. Wake Up! I'm Fat. New York: Broadway, 1999.

Pipher, Mary. Hunger Pains: The Modern Woman's Tragic Quest for Thinness. New York: Ballantine, 1995.

Wann, Marilyn. Fat! So? Because You Don't Have to Apologize for Your Size. Berkeley: Ten Speed, 1998.

Writing Strategies

1. Why do you think Paulin refers to "overweight" people as "fat"? What is the effect of this word on the reader?

2. Paulin helps the reader to understand her main ideas by stating them at the beginning of paragraphs. Find three paragraphs in this essay that begin with the main idea. Do those sentences also connect the paragraph to the previous paragraph? If so, describe how.

3. Paulin uses written sources to support her argument. In some places she directly quotes the sources; in others she paraphrases or summarizes (that is, she puts what the source says in her own words). Find an example of each (quote; paraphrase; summary). How do you know the information is from a source? Does Paulin make that clear? Notice how Paulin introduces the information and punctuates it.

4. Paulin's conclusion does not merely summarize points she has already made. Reread the conclusion and describe how it goes beyond mere summary. What does it try to do? Is it successful?

5. Paulin seems to know that her audience needs to be nudged along to accept her point. In your view, what particular rhetorical strategy is most effective at nudging readers to see the real harm of the media's portrayal of weight?

Exploring Ideas

1. How is weight a public issue?

2. In her opening paragraph, Paulin says inaccurate images about weight "have shifted our vision of what is important in life way out of whack, so far out that people are being hurt." Then she calls for perspective. What support can you provide for her claim that our vision of what is important is out of whack? What support can you provide that people are being hurt?

3. Why should or shouldn't comedians refrain from making fat jokes about specific individuals?

4. Paulin says, "[P]eople who allow the drive to be thin to control them may find that many other areas of their lives suffer" (¶ 12). Apply her thinking to some other situation besides body weight, and explain how a particular drive has led to suffering.

Ideas for Writing

1. What point can you help Paulin make by providing different evidence?

2. What idea of Paulin's can you explore further, possibly discovering a different way of seeing it?

If responding to one of these ideas, go to the Analysis section of this chapter to begin developing ideas for your essay.

Floppy Disk Fallacies

Elizabeth Bohnhorst

Writing an essay for a class can be difficult. Among the challenges: understanding what you're being asked to do; thinking and writing adventurously without making a mistake that could hurt your grade; not sounding too much like a student writing an essay as a class requirement, even though that's what you are doing. The best student writing, like all good academic writing, puts forth a revelatory claim, has an inviting writer's voice, is to the point and well developed, and ultimately invites readers to think differently about the topic. Elizabeth Bohnhorst's essay, written for a first-semester English course at Northwestern Michigan College, is adventurous. It takes an unusual position and offers a variety of support strategies. If the essay is successful, you may feel slightly different about computer technology in education.

"Another boring PowerPoint," responds Jennifer when I ask about her day at school. I might not find these words so discouraging coming from a company executive after a long meeting or even a college student leaving an informative lecture. But these words of an eleven-year-old elementary school student leave me feeling slightly uneasy. PowerPoint presentations are intended to compel students to become more interested in the subject with the use of neon colors and moving graphic images. But these flashy additions to current educational strategies haven't fooled everyone. The text and material covered is still the same boring grammar and spelling lessons, but the educator has altered: It is a screen.

Computers can undoubtedly contribute wonders to the field of education. In fact, computer education is a must if children intend to thrive in modern society. The possibilities are endless when it comes to surfing the Web or using the thousands of educational programs currently available. These programs are capable of reading text on a computer with icons beside words that take students to a galaxy of options, icons to learn more about the era in which the text was written, fascinating facts about the author, and helpful notes about the morals of the story. But computers are being used more and more frequently as a substitute for books, blackboards, and in some cases, the teachers themselves.

America leads the world in the amount and density of computers in our public schools. In 1992, the typical high school had one computer for every ten students, while elementary and middle schools averaged thirteen students per computer ("Computers"). Compared to current numbers, the early 1990s were a time of deprivation. Some schools, such as Kent Central School in rural Connecticut, are considering funding for each student to have his or her own laptop. After visiting the school, Anne Guignon reports that "students use the computers in school, take them home each night, use the computers for homework, and soon will be able to tap into the Internet." In such situations, traditional school lingo such as "Take out a piece of paper and a number two pencil" might be replaced with "Take out your floppies and boot up your Toshibas." Unfortunately for some students, dogs cannot digest discs.

And the Texas Board of Education is only steps behind the Kent Central School. "The Texas Board of Education now has state officials seriously examining whether to give all public school students laptops instead of textbooks," states a *New York Times* investigator. The Board "is looking at $1.8 billion in projected costs for textbooks over the next six years, and . . . given technology improvements that have lowered the price of computers, it may be cheaper, to say nothing of innovative, to lease a laptop for each of the state's 3.7 million students" (Guignon).

5   Now, what could possibly be wrong with such a sophisticated device for learning? In reality, "thirty years of research on educational technology has produced almost no evidence of a clear link between using computers in the early grades and improving learning," states Michael Dertouzus, director of the MIT Laboratory for Computer Science. In fact, evidence of hazardous effects of frequent use of computers in young children is overwhelming. They do little to promote a healthy childhood. "Computers are perhaps the most acute symptom of the rush to end childhood. The national drive to computerize schools, from kindergarten on up,

emphasizes only one of the many human capacities, one that naturally develops quite late—analytic, abstract thinking—and aims to jump start it prematurely," continues Dertouzus.

Elementary schools are not only responsible for teaching children reading, writing, mathematics, and other basic skills; they also reinforce and indirectly establish guidelines for everyday behavior. Therefore, consistent use of computers in schools ultimately plants the idea in the developing mind that computers are safe, educational, and perhaps one of the most important tools of modern society. Thus, a child returns home from school after hours of staring into an illuminated box, flips through the channels of yet another illuminated box, and then proceeds to play "Final Fantasy Four" on the Macintosh for three more hours. A 1999 study by the Kaiser Family Foundation showed that children ages two to eighteen spent an average of four hours and forty-five minutes per day plugged into electronic media of all kinds. These numbers are excluding the time spent with such machinery during school hours (Dertouzus).

The emotional and social values learned during childhood are also disrupted by computerized education in elementary and middle schools. Students learn more than state capitals and multiplication; they develop a sense of social importance and are taught values of friendship and other relationships. Through interaction with peers, intimacy and companionship are only a few of the many principles computers are unable to relay to children. Dr. Stanley I. Greenspan, former director of the Clinical Infant Development Program, is concerned that the impersonal culture formulated by computerization has serious detrimental effects on children's emotional development: "So-called interactive, computer-based instruction that does not provide true interaction but merely a mechanistic response to the student's efforts," states Greenspan, can be directly linked to "the increasingly impersonal quality that suffuses the experience of more and more American children" (qtd. in Dertouzos). He also adds that lack of nurture for children at home and at school can likely result in "increasing levels of violence and extremism and less collaboration and empathy." (qtd. in Dertouzos).

"Successful education should not replace children's curiosity to explore the world around them with Internet Explorer."

Besides affecting emotional and social development in primary students, computers can also disrupt creative thinking. Like all other electronic viewing systems (television and video games), computers leave little or no room for imagination. Of course, the virtual reality computers create is often full of fantastic images. However, because imagination involves generating one's own images and ideas, consistent exposure to ready-made images only makes it more difficult for children to summon their own creativity. The intensity of the images squashes the need for intensive creativity. Educational psychologist and former school principal Jane Healy has observed that "teachers find that today's video-immersed children can't form original pictures in their mind or develop an imaginative representation. Teachers of young children lament the fact that many now have to be taught to play symbolically or pretend—previously a symptom only of mentally or emotionally disordered youngsters" (qtd. in Dertouzus). Not only do these images affect creativity and imagination; they also have potential to diffuse the sparks of curiosity. For example, if a class is learning about regional watersheds, computerized classrooms will most likely turn to the handy diagrams so conveniently laid out on the screens before the students. In a classroom that values hands-on learning techniques, a school field trip to a local stream or swamp may be an effective strategy. In short, a successful education should not replace children's curiosity to explore the world around them with Internet Explorer.

On the other hand, technology is an effective way to get kids interested in learning, considering "that there is a passionate love affair between children and computers" (Setzer). A colorful computer screen is obviously more attractive to a child than an old novel or a textbook. But this attraction is more likely a fascination with animation and sound effects rather than a genuine exploration of ideas. Dr. Valdemar W. Setzer, a professor of computer science, wonders, "What happens to a student who gets used to learning with computers? Will she be able to tolerate a normal class without all those cosmetic and video game effects?"

10   As technology's role in American society grows, we should observe its influence in public education. It is easy to consider the benefits of computerization: simplicity, standardization, and elimination of other physical controversies. But in the same light we must also consider the hazards and how important traditional education is to children. The obvious concern with traditional education is the students being "left behind" in the rush toward increasing technological advancements.

Educating students in computer skills is and should be a priority in all schools. But when it comes to teaching basic skills and allowing for intellectual development, human interaction and exploration of the real world should never come second to electronic devices. In an effort to preserve the qualities of education, we should not allow ourselves to become mesmerized by teachers that require an electrical outlet and textbooks that require a point-and-click to turn the page.

Works Cited

"Computers in American Schools, 1992: An Overview." IEA Computers in Education. 12 July 1995. 20 July 2005. <http://www.socsci.umn.edu/~iea/>

Dertouzos, Michael. "Developmental Risks: The Hazards of Computers in Childhood." The Alliance for Childhood. 20 July 2005. <http://www.allianceforchildhood.net/projects/computers/computers_reports_fools_gold_2.htm>

Guignon, Anne. "Laptop Computers for Every Student!" Education World. 19 Jan. 1998. 20 July 2005. <http://www.education-world.com/a_curr/ curr048.html>

Setzer, Valdemar W. "A Review of Arguments for the Use of Computers in Elementary Education." Southern Cross Review. 4 (2000) 20 July 2005. <http://www.southerncrossreview.org>

The obvious concern with traditional education is the students being "left behind" in the rush toward increasing technological advancements.

Writing Strategies

1. Why is or isn't Bohnhorst's introduction effective? (What particular sentences or phrases invite you into her thinking? Which do not?)

2. Why does Bohnhorst's reference to PowerPoint strengthen her argument about computers?

3. Bohnhorst is tackling a common assumption in education: that more technology is inherently good. Describe her strategy for confronting and overturning this assumption. How does she do it?

4. How does Bohnhorst apply appeals to value in her argument?

5. How does Bohnhorst deal with specific opposing ideas? Where does she reveal the shortcomings of other positions? Where does she acknowledge the value of other positions?

Exploring Ideas

1. Consider the following claims made by Bohnhorst:

   Computers can undoubtedly contribute wonders to the field of education. (¶ 2)

   In fact, computer education is a must if children intend to thrive in modern society. (¶ 2)

   With others, explore these claims further, trying to discover new ways of thinking about them. Begin by discussing whether or not you think the claims are true, and then pinpoint and explore why people disagree. After several minutes of discussion, how have the claims become more complex?

2. Interview several people who have not read Bohnhorst's argument, and find out specifically what they think computers can contribute to the field of education. Try interviewing people of various backgrounds and age groups. Following your interviews, write down any new ideas you've discovered about computers and education.

3. How might education be better in a school with fewer computers in the classroom? How might computers in the classroom actually interfere with learning? How might education be better in a *nation* with fewer computers in the classroom?

Ideas for Writing

1. What argument might you make by taking a more extreme stance on the role of computers in education?

2. How might you develop an engaging argument on this topic, based on your own experiences with technology and learning?

3. To develop your own argument, research some claim Bohnhorst makes, such as "teachers find that today's video-immersed children can't form original pictures in their mind or develop an imaginative representation" (¶ 8).

If responding to one of these ideas, go to the Analysis section of this chapter to begin developing ideas for your essay.

Whales R Us

Jayme Stayer

Good writers often invite, and sometimes force, us to confront ideas we would rather not examine. In his argument about Sea World, Jayme Stayer, sheds new light on the park. His points might seem unreasonable at first. After all, why should someone target a theme park? But Stayer's essay illustrates an important move in academic writing: uncovering the layers of meaning behind the propaganda of everyday life. Stayer, a professional musician and T.S. Eliot scholar, is a Jesuit, an order of priests and brothers in the Catholic tradition. He has taught at Texas A&M-Commerce, Universidad Centroamericana in El Salvador, and presently teaches at John Carroll University.

Mickey Mouse scares the bejesus out of me. Shamu, on the other hand, simply makes me queasy. I'm not the first to express loathing for Mickey & Co.: a giggling rodent as mascot for a nasty, litigious, multimedia *Über*-corporation. But you don't hear too many people railing against Sea World, though Shamu has a dark side too.

One of the first things to irk me at a Sea World park happened during a bird show. A perky blonde was displaying a few parrots, and she kept up a stream of banter about their feeding habits and origins. "When our ancestors came to this continent," she breezily explained to an audience chock full of non-Europeans, "they brought with them this breed of parrot from Africa." Since I'm almost certain that slaves brutally shipped to the Americas were not allowed bird cages as carry-on luggage, what she should have said was that European— not "our"—ancestors stopped off in Africa and loaded up with parrots and slaves. One needn't be a fanatical multiculturalist to be ruffled by inaccurate history and specious assumptions about an audience's makeup.

In America, unexamined notions of history and the coercive politics of majority identity go hand in hand with boorish nationalism. (See, for example, the debate over the Confederate flag and its supposed status as symbol of a unitary "Southern" culture.) Oddly, the bird show at Sea World confirmed this. Her parrots now retired, the perky woman waltzed around the stage with a bald eagle while the audience was subjected to a chummy patriotic tune. So the eagle was presented not as the largest or most impressive of birds, or as indigenous to Canada, or even as another instance of the marvels of creation, but as the Bird of American Democracy—this, in spite of the fact that eagles' politics tend to the monarchist side and that their feeding habits indicate a predisposition for brutal dictatorship. The bird becomes valued, in other words, for the cultural associations "we" Americans slapped onto it, not for any of its intrinsic properties. The eagle, in Sea World's monistic version of the world, becomes just another happy commodity—like parrots, slaves, designer clothes sweatshops—that makes America the Great Nation It Has Always Been.

But not all employees were as chipper as the bird show people. There are two types of teenagers who work at Sea World: the aggressively happy and the sullenly aggrieved. These two opposed mentalities are as old as the summer job itself: namely, the optimism of youths who want to change the world vs. the cynicism of kids who despise their jobs, resent their pay, and wouldn't give a hooey if they were fired because some enraged Yuppie did not get good service with a grovelling smile when he bought his Sno-Cone. I personally sided with the disaffected and wished I had brought copies of *The Communist Manifesto* to slip into their pockets.

5   The most important job at Sea World—and teenagers are particularly good at it—is making lots of noise. Since most Americans are terrified of being alone in a store without Muzak, Sea World willingly obliges its customers with rock-concert levels of decibels. All of the shows keep up a noxious patter complete with ear-splitting sound effects; the walkways have abrasively loud music piped over them; and even the exhibits have teenagers chained there with microphones in hand, droning their mantra of dull facts.

It is ironic that a park putatively designed to extol the wonders of nature is obsessed with high-tech wizardry and mega-voltage noise, noise, noise—even when it is extolling the wonders of nature's silence. Another talking point of the bird show featured how silently an owl could fly. The bird's flight began in blissful silence, but halfway through its flight the soundtrack faded back in with a shimmer of violins, followed by a cymbal crash when the owl landed. Even the absence of noise is packaged with noise: The owl's silence is first framed with amplified yakking (noise), then underlined as it happens (quiet noise), then punctuated (big noise) so the audience knows when to clap (make more noise).

One of the most ludicrous moments of the Shamu show was an assertion by another relentlessly cheerful teenager: "We here at Sea World believe we have the greatest jobs in the world." With its overtones of Orwellian party-speak, it was only slightly risible until she added: "We get to work with nature's most wonderful animals and contribute to the world's knowledge about them." Her jejune assumption that "world knowledge" exists as some kind of huge, accumulative spittoon—rather than a set of competing claims and shifting paradigms—was hilarious enough, particularly coming from a kid who is probably still struggling with basic algebra and who wouldn't recognize "world knowledge" if it landed on her in a heap. I imagined her logging on to a marine biology chat group and making an announcement—in all caps, no doubt—followed by an emoticon: "SHAMU DID A BACK FLIP TODAY!!! :)" Thus does the world's cup of knowledge runneth over.

And that insistent refrain of "We here at Sea World believe" was another thing that rankled me, because it was usually followed by patronizing flimflam. Some prime examples: "We here at Sea World believe that animals should not be taken from their natural habitat." Or: "We here at Sea World believe only in the use of positive reinforcement in the training of animals." The audience is supposed to believe that these are lovely sentiments. How noble that they try to find injured or orphaned animals to "befriend." How comforting to know Shamu isn't being shocked with electricity or poked in the eye when he's tired or just damned fed up with giving piggyback rides. Most disturbing was that these credos came mostly out of the mouths of the teenage staff, whose inexperience made their We-Believe proclamations ring even more hollowly.

Taken individually, some of these moments were only mildly unnerving, but there was one occurrence that stood out as gratuitous. Situated on a lake, the Sea World I visited featured a water show with ski jumps and corny skits. The theme of that year's show was *Baywatch*,

which involved—predictably enough—nubile bodies in poorly choreographed dance routines, the bold rescue of someone in the water, and the odd appearances of two buffoons (fat old man with hysterical wife), all of which was irritatingly narrated by an emcee's we-havin'-fun-yet? voice-over. At one point, the old man and his wife were "accidentally" pulled into view: the man (vertical) on skis, the woman (horizontal) with her legs wrapped around his torso. They were in the unmistakable position of sex, the two actors in a flurry of feigned embarrassment at having been "caught." (Whut in tarnation cud be more funny than ol' fat folks havin' sex? Har dee har har.) The emcee and other characters on stage slyly absolved themselves of complicity in this vulgarity by shrugging their shoulders, as if to say: "Golly, what was that all about?" Sea World, by the way, bills itself as a place for the whole family.

10   You might think that a park that sponsors PG-13 shows would divest itself of prudishness. Alas, there was more self-righteousness there than at a revival. Case in point: the shark exhibit. Before we could enter, we were forced to watch a short film about sharks; the doors to the exhibit were pointedly barred until after the film was over. The film gave us a hellfire-and-damnation scolding: you thought that sharks were human predators? WRONG. You thought sharks were abundant in the ocean? WRONG AGAIN. After airing its grievances with us—the ill-informed public—it asserted that much damage had been inflicted on these misunderstood fishies. Because we've all been shark-haters at heart, fishermen have felt free to kill them. Quivering with virtue, the film called "intolerable" the fishermen who "senselessly" destroyed the sharks, either because the sharks got caught in the nets or because the sharks fed on prized fish. With vast self-contentment Sea World then relayed how they had successfully worked to stop this great evil.

While I'm pleased to have my horror-film notions of sharks corrected, the film's smugness was unbearable. And in spite of Sea World's professed vigilance, I'm not convinced that sharks aren't still being arbitrarily killed somewhere in the world. Even so, I wonder if sharks, given the choice, would prefer to stay in a Sea World bathtub for the rest of their lives or take a chance with those fishnets.

Of the many inanities hurled at me, my favorite was an emcee's sign-off: "And remember," she intoned from a precipitously high moral ground, "before we can have peace *on* the Earth, we have to make peace *with* the Earth." Indeed. As if, in the interest of world peace, the United Nations agenda should be scuttled in favor of dotting the globe with Sea Worlds to promote feel-good vibes between humans and dolphins. Here's more glib reasoning: to make peace *with* the Earth implies the Earth was a peaceful place before we humans mucked things up. Yet the last time I looked, the Earth was full of viruses, earthquakes, predatory animals, and a survival-of-the-fittest mentality that Sea World has apparently never heard of.

And maybe it was petty of me to be irked when the woman narrating Shamu's activities insisted that whales scratch their backs on the pebbled shores when they're contented. There was captive Shamu scratching his back on the simulated shore. The audience oohed and aahed. Nevermind that Shamu had been explicitly directed to scratch his back, and that to have disobeyed would have resulted not in a whack on the head (lucky for him) but in the withholding of food (not so lucky). Is that contentment then? With the help of an extraordinarily costly visual aid, the audience was expected to "learn" a fact of whale behavior that could be shown only at the cost of candor.

Sea World, I realized after an afternoon of learning very little, was a place that was desperately trying to present itself as a place where education occurs. And for twenty-some bucks, your educational experience goes roughly like this: You can give up an afternoon of watching vapid TV shows and take your whole family to watch a skit based on a vapid TV show. You get to ogle busty women and hirsute men. You get to have constant noise crowd out any independent thoughts that might be percolating to the surface of your brain. You get to harbor the illusion that America is a happy, white, European family, as well as a leading maker of world knowledge, and that Sea World is largely responsible for such happiness and abundance. You get to imagine you hold the key to world peace (remember to give the dog a kiss when you get home). You get to indulge in patriotic goosebumps ("the *American* eagle!"), have your heart-strings jolted ("Ah—Shamu's happy to be

"Sea World . . . was desperately trying to present itself as a place where education occurs."

here!"), get your sluggish sense of morality jump-started ("*baaaad* fishermen, *gooood* sharkie"). And if you're willing to invest another three bucks, you can fling a sardine at dolphins that have been petted to within an inch of their lives. Best of all, at the end of the day you get to go home with the vaguely self-congratulatory feeling that you've *learned* something, by God.

15   I'm an educator, and I pay close attention when someone is trying to teach me something. So on my way out of Sea World, I asked myself what I had learned. Like a student who has crammed for an exam, I was able to recall lots of idiocies, but could only say I had truly learned two things. (1) Thanks to the film, I learned that sharks attack humans only when provoked, and, (2) thanks to their anthropomorphizing skits, I learned that sea otters are cute little buggers. Even if these elements were judicious pedagogical objectives (which they are not), they still don't add up to anything resembling education. In fact, the entire experience of Sea World is suspiciously similar to the exact opposite of education: mind control.

It was only in retrospect that I realized that these annoyances were related: the high-pitched entertainment and trivial sexual jokes, the shut-up-and-listen attitude, the constant noise and verbal presence, the Big Brotherly refrains of exactly what "We here at Sea World believe." These are all rhetorical strategies of a government diverting its citizens, masking something it doesn't want the public to know. And what is it that Sea World doesn't want its customers to think about?

In a review lambasting Disney World, an author hilariously describes the ideology of the place as "benign fascism": The streets are immaculately clean; the worker bees wear impossibly happy smiles; the rides and trains run on time; and every day, the gloved hero appears on parade, where the hordes worship him and his lickspittles with songs and fireworks. The author's comparison of Mickey to Mussolini is more than just amusing: He ties it into his critique of how history is portrayed at the Epcot center. Because Disney does not want to offend any of its ethnically and racially diverse customers (Sea World: take note), their film on American history carefully controls the emotional barometer of its vacationers. The Disney film of American history is whitewashed to the point of banality, and such central topics as the atomic bomb, racial conflict, and imperialist genocide are entirely avoided. The point is that fascists, benign or not, always have political and economic reasons for telling history the way they do. And like Disney World and other fascist operations, Sea World likes to keep a tight grip on what and how its visitors think.

Take, for example, the "we-believe-animals-should-be-treated-in-this-way" gestures that continually crop up. These assertions pose as facts the audience ought to memorize in preparation for an exit quiz. Yet the nervous tic of emphasizing the politically correct means of treating animals in captivity belies Sea World's uneasiness with the larger, unasked question: Should we even have animals in captivity for our bourgeois amusement? Nowhere in their literature, exhibit signs, or rehearsed prattle of their miked minions is this basic question broached or answered.

Part of the way Sea World can get away with ignoring the obvious fact that these animals are there for our entertainment is that it nervously insists that it is a place of science and research, and disingenuously implies that entertainment easily meshes with education and research. While I scoff at the idea that important research gets done at Sea World, the problem isn't really with what kinds of knowledge Sea World makes, or how much, or how important it is. Rather, the problem is Sea World's communication of that knowledge, or to be more explicit, their refusal to level with its visitors about its real cultural role and worth. If they would fess up to the fact that Sea World is essentially a playground and not a classroom, that might be a start towards a real educational experience.

20   Sea World keeps up its image of itself as a classroom by propagating signs with facts and statistics on them. These factoids—and their Post-it Note ubiquity—are a peculiar manifestation of "textbook knowledge": boring chunks of data unconnected to any larger, compelling theme. There were a plethora of facts swimming around at Sea World and a dearth of ideas, which is why I couldn't remember anything at the end of my day. Like the eager student who has a bad teacher, I was given no complex or interesting framework inside of which ideas jostled about; so I was reduced to cramming lists of unconnected information in preparation for a never-to-be-taken exam.

I'm not suggesting that Sea World become a place that sponsors round-table discussions of animal rights and lets biology students present their theses during Shamu intermissions. But I do think that instead of slavishly subscribing to popular notions of science, Sea World might call them into question. This is what real education does.

As it stands, none of our deeply rooted cultural beliefs are explored or challenged at Sea World. After a trip there the visitor is likely to keep thinking that facts are equivalent to knowledge; that America is synonymous with Europe; that science and technology are the greatest goods imaginable; that education means being fed a list of facts in a condescending manner; and that sated, docile fish—who decorously eat buckets of non-cute sardines—are practically vegetarians.

A skit in which a lovably frisky sea otter has its head chomped off by a hungry predator is not the kind of bloody epiphany Sea World is likely to promote. Imagine the screams of the unsuspecting children. Imagine the lawsuits of offended suburbanites who like their nature sanitized and safe. But imagine, too, how such a moment would educate an audience about the dangers of humanizing certain animals at the expense of others. Such a skit might end with a question to the audience about why its government enacts laws to protect the habitat of owls but not of insects or low-income humans.

The only cultural assumption that was seriously challenged at Sea World was the premise of *Jaws*—and that was much too heavy-handed, not to mention incorrect, as events in Florida have shown. It turns out that sharks *will* attack idle swimmers. It should come as no surprise that a capitalist venture like Sea World can't even get its basic facts straight. Neither can the tobacco industry seem to grasp what everyone else knows about nicotine addiction. Nor is Disney equipped to navigate the treacherous waters of American history.

25   Surely the most real moments at Sea World occurred when the fascists lost control, for example, when the staff had trouble getting the animals to obey their directions. Such glitches in the program put their slapstick routines and canned jokes on hold, and forced them to talk to the audience about fixing this problem. It also gave the teenage apparatchiks an opportunity for some inspired ad-libbing, disburdening them from their less endearing lecture notes.

If the ideology of Disney is benign fascism, then the ideology of Sea World is exploitative spectacle masquerading as education. Too occupied with obscuring the real moral, environmental, and scientific issues at stake, Sea World is constitutionally incapable of teaching respect for nature. Love of nature is spiritually informed and politically assertive. It is not the kind of passive, sentimental quackery Sea World prefers, and it cannot be taught with the crude tools in Sea World's lesson plans: glib moralizing, base pandering, and clichés masquerading as insights.

But in the last analysis, Sea World—to paraphrase Auden—makes nothing happen. Sea World is a reflection of American culture: a consequence, not a cause; a mirror of consumerist desires, not a promoter of political change via education. The American traits Sea World reflects most clearly are its gullibility and irrationality. It's a consolation, albeit a small one, to consider that Americans are likewise gullible to the very real beauty of nature. It's that kind of openness—and not Sea World's preaching—that makes the connection between humans and dolphins seem worth investigating. It's less of a comfort to consider another analogy between Americans and marine life that Sea World leaves unexplored: America's exorbitant arms race, its rape of the environment, its valorization of guns and violence, its giddy, media-fueled acclamation of the death sentence that disproportionately murders minorities: Are these not strikingly similar to the fierce logic of the food chain? Screw the little guy; I'm hungry and more powerful.

So my advice is to go to Sea World anyway. Even inside the ideological frame where they are forced, the creatures there—including the teenagers—are amazing, hilarious, and terrifying. Who can remain unimpressed when a mammal the size of a Mack truck lifts itself out of the water? As for Sea World itself: If, aided by earplugs and skepticism, you can ignore what they're trying to teach you, you just might learn something.

Work Cited

Alexander, Maxwell. "Promise Redeemed: At Long Last Mickey." <u>Johns Hopkins Magazine</u> Apr. 1995: 5.

Writing Strategies

1. What word would you use to describe the voice of this essay—humorous, serious, urgent, angry, light, or something else? Identify several passages to support your description.

2. Stayer is trying to call Sea World out—to reveal something disingenuous or fake about the park's rhetoric. In your own words, what is Stayer trying to reveal?

3. How does counterargument function in this essay? Point to particular passages in which Stayer is countering some opposing claim and explain how that passage figures into the overall point of the essay.

4. How does Stayer use Sea World to make broader points about American culture?

5. How does Stayer's conclusion work on the audience? Describe what the conclusion does for readers—how it reinforces or develops a kind of relationship between Stayer and the reader.

Exploring Ideas

1. What new way of thinking does Stayer introduce? (Consider his points about education, entertainment, theme parks, even American popular culture.)

2. Based on this essay, how are Stayer's thoughts, values, beliefs, or feelings similar to or different from yours?

3. Stayer argues, "If the ideology of Disney is benign fascism, then the ideology of Sea World is exploitative spectacle masquerading as education." In small groups, paraphrase this sentence. How does this point work in Stayer's overall argument?

4. How does Stayer's thinking go beyond one's initial ideas about entertainment parks?

Ideas for Writing

1. What public place—such as Sea World—presents itself in a way that is different from what you know (or suspect) about that place?

2. What public place presents itself honestly and accurately?

If responding to one of these ideas, go to the Analysis section of this chapter to begin developing ideas for your essay.

If, aided by earplugs and skepticism, you can ignore what they're trying to teach you, you just might learn something.

Outside Reading

Find a written argument and print it out or make a photo-copy. You might find an argument about a social or politi-cal issue in a general readership publication (such as *Time, Newsweek,* or the *New York Times*). For an argument related to your major, explore an academic journal such as *Journal of the American Medical Association, Texas Nursing,* or *Psychol-ogy of Women Quarterly.* To conduct an electronic search of journals and magazines, go to your library's periodical data-base or to InfoTrac College Edition (http://infotrac.cengage. com). For your library's database, perform a keyword search, or go to the main search box for InfoTrac College Edition and select "keywords." Enter word combinations such as *debate and community, opinion and politics, argument and politics, debate and sports, argument and art.* (When perform-ing keyword searches, avoid using phrases or articles such as *a, an, the;* instead, use nouns separated by *and.*) The search results will yield lists of journal and magazine articles.

You can also search the Internet. Try the search engine Dogpile.com. Like most Internet search engines, Dogpile combines words using *and.* In the search box, try various combinations, such as those above.

The purpose of this assignment is to further your under-standing of argument and to introduce a broad range of argumentative strategies. As you are probably discovering, argument appears in many different places and in many dif-ferent contexts. Even among the essays in this chapter, argu-ments range in tone, style, length, and strategy. As you read through this chapter, keep the written argument you have discovered close by and notice the elements and strategies the writer uses. Depending on your instructor's suggestions, do one or more of the following:

1. Notice how the writer applies various strategies from this chapter. On the hard copy or photocopy:

   - Highlight the thesis if it is stated in the argument. If the thesis is implied, write it in your own words.

   - Highlight the major support strategies, and write "support" next to each one in the margin.

   - Highlight any passages in which the writer addresses other opinions on the topic, and write "counterargu-ment" or "ca" next to each one in the margin.

   - Highlight any passages in which the writer grants value to another position, and write "concession" or "c" in the margin.

2. Analyze the strategies employed by the writer. The fol-lowing questions may be helpful:

   - Does this text seem more or less argumentative than the readings in this chapter? Why?

   - How does the writer support his or her argument?

   - Who is the audience for this argument?

   - How does the audience impact the kinds of things said in the argument?

3. Write at least three "Writing Strategies" questions for the argument.

4. Write at least three "Exploring Ideas" questions for the argument.

5. Write two "Ideas for Writing," such as the ones follow-ing the essays in this book, for the argument.

INVENTION

Academic audiences demand more than "three reasons why I believe X" arguments. They want to experience more in an argument than a writer's personal beliefs; they want to learn a new way of thinking about a topic. So academic writers often look for a new stance, a way to make people rethink an issue entirely. In general, a successful argument creates a new position on a familiar topic or offers a position on a fresh topic. And good writers do not merely *choose* topics; instead, they *build* topics from the novel and surprising moments of everyday life.

The following sections are designed to help you develop ideas for your argument: specifically, to discover a topic (in Point of Contact), develop particular points about the topic (in Analysis), make it relevant to a community of readers (in Public Resonance), focus your position (in Thesis), and create support for that position (in Rhetorical Tools). The questions in each section will help you generate intense ideas and start writing. Your responses to the Invention questions may take you in a variety of directions, and some of your responses may get left behind. That is to be expected in academic work—or in any work that seeks to discover something valuable.

POINT OF CONTACT

Some situations in everyday life are obviously significant—what they mean for our lives, or for the lives of others, is apparent. When our country goes to war or when a new president is elected, for example, most Americans understand the significance. Many situations, however, are far more subtle; their potential meaning is hidden by life's hustle and bustle. To understand their meaning, we must stop in our tracks and focus on them. Use the following suggestions and questions to explore possible topics. If a question seems engaging to you, or if you associate some emotion or idea with the question, start writing. Ask yourself: "Can I change someone's mind about this situation or issue?"

School What lurking attitude is ruining the learning process? If we're a country of progress, why should history be taught anyway? How is mainstream fashion brainwashing even the smart kids? Will football be the end of serious public education? How was *Napoleon Dynamite*'s portrayal of high school right on target? How are high schools destroying students' ability to cope with the first year of college?

Work Do my co-workers get along? Do supervisors treat workers fairly? Are the work expectations fair? Are the hours fair to workers? Do fellow workers do a good job? What hidden forces or assumptions work against productivity?

Home What does my neighborhood layout suggest about being a human? How does the layout of my house or apartment or dorm help me to be a better person? What is the central appliance in my living space? Does that support my goals as a person? Should more people have gardens? Why?

Community Does my town know what to do with teenagers? Does the water taste funny? Does my town offer ample mass transit? How does the police force function—as keepers of the peace or something else? How important are trees?

Pop Culture How does *American Idol* impact popular music? Can a democracy seriously thrive without a good punk scene? Should we be leery or supportive of a whole channel dedicated to food? What does the Discovery Channel do for science? Why aren't there any fun shows about language and writing?

Your Major Look through a current journal in your field to find controversial issues: Are entry-level personnel in my field treated fairly? Is some research in my field or major controversial? Is my field undervalued by the public? Has my field changed any of its practices, for better or worse, in recent years? Should my field be more diverse (in gender and/or ethnicity)?

Activity

Make a list of other questions that draw attention to troubling situations in the world around you. What attitude or basic assumption lies beneath some troubling behavior or policy? Ask yourself: What behavior or situation or policy is wrong? What could be different? What could be better than it is?

Question everything, especially those things that seem unquestionable.

IMAGE:BAGDAD 02APR2003

ANALYSIS

Analysis cracks open the layers of a topic—and helps a writer to see more than his or her initial thoughts about it. Without analysis, writers may find themselves with little new to say. As you answer the Invention questions, avoid answering too quickly. Instead, use the questions to search for deeper understanding, which will then translate into more intensive writing. Allow time and space for your own thinking to develop.

Invention Questions

- What is the particular point of crisis or tension?
- How has the situation (or condition, behavior, policy) come about, and why does it continue?
- What are the effects of the situation (or condition, behavior, policy)?
- Why do I have an opinion on this topic?
- Why is this belief valuable?

Try to go beyond broad complaints and vague generalities.

Ann Marie Paulin looks beneath the initial tension or problem and discovers a hidden layer. She goes beyond being "angry" and discovers that media trends indirectly support, even "encourage," mistreatment and incivility:

Why do I have an opinion on this topic?

I have been fat since I was a kid. For about two days in my twenties I starved my way down to a size ten, thereby earning this head-turning compliment from the guy I was then dating: "You'd be a real fox if you'd just lose a few more pounds." I've had complete strangers say the most astonishing things to me on the street. For example, on my way through a parking lot to get to my car, I passed a young man who looked over at me and shouted: "I don't !@#$ fat chicks!" Who was asking? While these behaviors have sometimes hurt me, they mostly make me angry. And when I look around at the society in which I live, I don't see any signs that this kind of behavior is discouraged. Indeed, the media seems to suggest that fat people, by their very existence, seem to deserve contempt and abuse.

How has this situation come about?

Where it gets tricky is that by the media's definition, damn near everyone is fat. How has this situation come about? I'm not sure, but I've watched it develop. When my mother was young, a size ten or twelve was a respectable dress size. When I was in my twenties, a size eight was a respectable size. Now, you must be a size four, two, or even better, a zero to be considered thin. Now, a six-foot-tall model who wears a size twelve dress is considered plus size. She only gets her photo in Lane Bryant ads and such. It's as if society has completely forgotten the concept of "normal size," and so a person is either thin (if you can count all her bones when she appears in a bathing suit) or she's fat. And that leaves the majority of women believing they are fat and hating themselves for it.

Paulin's thinking shows how writers work: In the process of analyzing ideas, they create various possible writing directions. However, as they begin to develop their projects, they become more focused and revelatory; they grab onto one point and take it somewhere. They go beyond the common complaints and reveal a particular quality, effect, or layer of the issue.

Invention Workshop

Enlist the help of another writer in answering one of the Invention questions. Use the question to initiate a discussion. Explore further by questioning one another's responses to the questions. For example, Jack is focusing on his high school education. Notice how the discussion with Marcus goes beyond Jack's initial response:

What is the particular point of crisis or tension?

Jack: My high school education was inadequate. I graduated with a B average and I came to college having to take developmental courses before I could even begin taking credit courses.

Marcus: But is that the high school's fault?

Jack: Well, if I couldn't cut the mustard in entry-level college courses, why did I get mostly Bs in high school? It seems like something's out of whack.

Marcus: OK. So the standards are too low in high school?

Jack: Yeah, I think so.

Marcus: Were you ever warned about the standards in college?

Jack: Sure. All the time, teachers would scare us with things like "Wait 'til you get in college; you've got to work constantly to keep your grades up."

Marcus: But did anyone ever share specifics with you? Did you know what kinds of writing, for instance, you would be doing in college?

Jack: Not really. It's all been a big surprise.

Marcus: Maybe that's the issue: High school students (and maybe teachers and administrators) don't really know what kinds of things go on in entry-level college courses.

Jack: Yes—and so there's this huge gap in between, and some students fall right into it.

It would be easy to reinforce Jack's initial idea—the inadequacy of high school—by sharing examples of bad teachers or rotten classes, but Marcus and Jack do better. They develop the initial idea into something more specific and revealing: the gap between high school and college standards.

Thinking Further

Analysis is not about answering a question and finding an answer. The real insights lie beneath the answers. Return to your responses to the Invention questions and try to find the most valuable ideas:

- What statements reveal something specific?
- Which statements or phrases seem new to you?
- Which statements or phrases make a new connection, one that you had not considered before?

Now, you can take the statements or phrases forward and use them to develop increasingly intense ideas for your argument. If nothing stands out at this point, consider reapproaching the Invention questions, and invite another person to join your exploration. And this time, deliberately take the ideas further:

- What behavior, policy, or quality is at the heart of the topic? (What is beneath the tension you initially discovered?)
- What attitude, value system, or assumption rests beneath the actions of people who are involved?

Good writing goes further than the writer or reader initially expects.

PUBLIC RESONANCE

Writers transform issues or personal concerns into arguable topics, issues that matter in some way to other people. Making a personal concern resonate with a public issue is simply a process of extension. To this end, the following Invention Questions can be used as springboards from personal concerns to public issues. For example, examine the following question: *Is my living situation conducive to my goals as a student?* You may have answered: "Yes. I live at home with my parents and commute to school." Your situation is not unique. Many college students struggle with their living situations—with the decision of living on campus, in a nearby apartment complex, or at home with their parents, away from the campus altogether. This decision involves more than a simple personal choice. It has something to do with college funding, with the success of college students, with the entire college experience. In this sense, your situation resonates with a more public issue. The initial (more personal) question might evolve into a more public question: *Is it beneficial for college students to live at home while going to school?*

As you consider your own topic, use the following questions:

- Who might care about this issue? Why?
- Who *should* care about this issue? Why?
- How are my readers involved in this issue? How *could* they be involved?
- What group of people might understand or sympathize with my situation?
- Is this issue an example of some trend?
- Why is it important that others hear my opinion about this issue?
- What else has been said about this issue, and how are my ideas different?

Public resonance is key in Ann Marie Paulin's project. Her essay shows that the more a topic affects people, the more attention it may deserve. In her responses to the Invention Questions, she explores the hidden messages in ads and the unstated assumptions lurking in the public domain. Paulin's responses show her making connections between her own situation and many others. By extending her thinking outward, she is developing the public dimensions of her idea:

Who might care about this issue? Why?

This is certainly a very public issue because it is almost impossible to escape the media: magazines, newspaper ads, billboards, radio, TV, movies, ads plastered in public restrooms and on the walls of buses, ads in your e-mail every day. And every one of those images that deals with weight or beauty makes it clear that to be fat is completely unacceptable and completely fixable if only a person tries hard enough and buys the right products.

Now, if this were just an issue of vanity, it might be something that could be shrugged off. But it goes much deeper than that. If you really pay attention to those ads, their real message is often that if you are fat, no one will love you. Your husband will leave you (if you ever manage to get one to begin with). Your children will be ashamed of you. Your friends will give up on you. You will be alone and unloved because you are fat. That is the message that really hits us where we live. Who wants to be some lonely outcast? We must conform to whatever it takes.

And so, most of us try the diets, the pills, the exercise classes, the wonder machines, and sometimes even more extreme measures like stomach stapling surgery. But in spite of all the time, money, and effort we expend, most of us are still fat. If you look at the studies done, the results are all about the same: Anywhere from 90% to 98% of the people who lose weight gain it all back within five years.

Sometimes writers need to go beyond the *actual* effects or consequences of an issue and *imagine* the possible ways others are involved. Consider the following: A writer is arguing about college students living at home. The issue seemingly affects only college students, and maybe their parents. But the writer makes the issue resonate with many other potential readers by transforming a personal issue into a more public one:

> How college students live is not simply a matter of personal choice and comfort. It is a public issue, a public education issue. At the federal, state, and local levels, Americans are increasingly focused on the out-of-school living conditions of elementary and secondary students. Whenever people talk about the quality of education, invariably they end up discussing the living situation of students—the stability of their homes, the qualities of the neighborhoods. Why? Because people are beginning to realize that education does not occur in a vacuum, that how and where students live impact how they learn. But for some reason, we don't seem to be concerned once students are in college. Consequently, millions of college students swarm off to school every fall, often without deeply considering the implications of where they will live. And when millions of dollars of loans and grants go down the drain when students fail out their first year, we don't seem to ask the same questions we ask about elementary and secondary students.

Research

Consider using outside sources to help you invent—to help you imagine the hidden values, assumptions, and attitudes people have about the topic. Discover what has been said about your topic, what people have argued, why they have taken certain positions, or why they have ignored it altogether. (See pages 456–462 for help with finding sources.)

Going from Private to Public

Private Concern:

Why do ads for dieting products make me, an overweight person, so angry?

Public Concern:

Why should more people be concerned about the common portrayal of overweight people?

THESIS

An argumentative thesis invites debate or suggests that opposing claims exist. For example:

> But far more important than my ill temper is a creepy sense that these inaccurate images [about body type] have shifted our vision of what is important in life way out of whack, so far out that people are being hurt.

The process of narrowing down an argument to an intensive single sentence helps writers to understand the heart of their idea. At an early stage in your project, you need not settle into an exact wording, but trying to generate a focused statement can help you focus—and help your ideas gain intensity.

An argumentative thesis should have four qualities:

Arguability It should be arguable. That is, an arguable thesis should take a stand on an issue that has two or more possible positions. If you can conceive of other possible positions on the topic, you are probably in arguable territory.

Scope It should be appropriately narrow. Scope can be addressed by asking narrow enough questions. Be careful of broad questions: *Is my town boring?* To answer such a question, one would have to consider all of the town's complexities, all of its goings-on, all of its people, all of its places, and so on. However, the question *Does my town offer sufficient activities for teens?* is more easily answerable—and ultimately arguable.

Public Resonance It should address an issue that resonates with the readers. A good argument addresses a concern that others have *or that a writer thinks they should have.* In other words, a thesis should express something that matters (that has some significance) to readers. It should involve others.

Revelation Academic writers attempt to do more than argue for their own opinions. They try to *reveal* an unfamiliar topic or reveal a new layer to a familiar topic. *Revelatory* thesis statements change readers' (and the writer's) thinking because they show something new. They clear away the mundane thinking and reveal the roots of an issue. Often, revelatory thesis statements:

- Include a reference to the opposition.
- Overturn or contradict popular opinion.
- Show a particular effect or relationship.
- Uncover a hidden layer.

Activities

1. Transform the following into revelatory thesis statements:
   - The Internet has changed the world.
   - Video games are bad for kids.
   - Sixteen-year-olds who commit crimes should be punished as adults.

2. In a small group, choose one of the following topics and develop at least one revelatory argumentative statement:
   - Leash laws in your town
   - The process for choosing presidential nominees
   - Product placement in movies
   - The cost of college textbooks
   - High school English courses

Evolution of a Thesis

A writer can always increase the focus and revelation of a thesis. The following idea evolves into an increasingly sophisticated point:

- College students benefit from living at home.
- Traditional college students still need the support structure of their home lives to deal with the new challenges of college.
- Because college culture demands intense intellectual and social change from high school culture, traditional college students need the support structure of home.

The first statement announces a simple opinion. The second narrows in on a specific tension: "the new challenges of college." But the statement is still a bit vague, and the idea will intensify with even more focus on that tension. The third statement brings us up close to the primary tension and shows us something that might otherwise escape our awareness: the "intense intellectual and social change" between high school and college culture. The reader of the last two theses, especially the third, has been given a novel insight about schooling. In this way, revelatory thesis statements are more than personal opinion; they are particular and persuasive insights.

Common Thesis Problems

The Question Problem A question is not a thesis, because it offers no stance. People sometimes use questions to imply a stance: *Isn't that the point of college? Why can't you be like your sister?* But this is generally an informal strategy—something people do in everyday talk. A formal argumentative stance should suggest a particular position amidst a realm of many others.

The Obvious Fact Problem An argument that simply announces a commonly known condition is no argument at all. Imagine someone arguing: *Many people go to college for their futures; Americans love cars;* or *Space exploration is expensive.* Such statements do not invite opposition because they are widely held beliefs. They are safe statements about the condition of our civilization. But the statement *Space exploration is too expensive to continue at its present pace* invites opposition.

The Personal Response Problem Argument depends upon the presence of several other perspectives peering at the same topic. However, when people proclaim a personal response (about their tastes, likes, dislikes, or desires), they merely make public their own state of mind. "I really liked the movie" is not an argumentative stance. It is a statement about a person's tastes. But the statement, "Johnny Depp's portrayal of a wayward pirate illustrates his superior range as an actor" invites opposition. Other positions can engage the point critically.

Revision

Before moving on, try to express the main point of your argument in a single sentence. Then evaluate the statement using the following questions:

- How is the statement arguable? (What other positions might be taken?)
- Can the statement be narrower? (What words are too vague or broad?)
- With what public issue or concern does the statement resonate?
- How does the statement reveal a unique insight or hidden layer of the issue?

You might also exchange your working thesis statement with two to three peers and use these questions to generate helpful responses.

RHETORICAL TOOLS

Crafting an essay, or any written text, is a recursive process: Writers move back and forth, drafting, rethinking, redrafting. It is not a simple step-by-step journey through a chapter. But all writers benefit from a large collection of strategies, various tools they can use according to their particular needs, situations, and voices. The strategies in this section will help you build a sophisticated and engaging text—one that emerges from your particular ideas.

Academic argument involves four basic ingredients or elements:

- Main claim/Thesis
- Support
- Counterargument
- Concession

MAIN CLAIM/THESIS · SUPPORT · COUNTERARGUMENTS · CONCESSION

Cengage Learning

Support

Support gives substance and legitimacy to an argumentative claim and comes in a variety of forms. Consider the following as a collection of usable support strategies, a toolbox for persuading readers of your position, despite the particular topic.

Examples Specific cases or illustrations of a phenomenon. (See Paulin ¶ 6.)

Allusions References to history, science, nature, news events, films, television shows, or literary texts. (See Crabtree ¶ 5, Paulin ¶ 2.)

Personal Testimonies/Anecdotes Individual accounts or experiences. (See Paulin ¶ 1–2, Bohnhorst ¶ 1.)

Scenarios Hypothetical or fictionalized accounts. (See Crabtree ¶ 6.)

Statistics Information (often given as numerical value) collected through experimentation, surveys, polls, and research. (See Paulin ¶ 4, Bohnhorst ¶ 3.)

Authorities References to published (most often written) sources. (See Paulin ¶ 2, Bohnhorst ¶ 5.)

Facts Agreed-upon events or truths, or conclusions drawn from investigation. (See Crabtree ¶ 5.)

Additionally, arguments depend on appeals, which make a con-nection between the topic and the audience's thought process. In fact, appeals have such rhetorical force that they give meaning to and can even dominate over other forms of evidence. The first three appeals below (to logic, emotion, and character) are often discussed using three classical Greek terms: *logos* (for logic), *pathos* (for emotion), and *ethos* (for character). These are sometimes referred to as the Classical appeals.

Appeal to logic relates the argument to the audience's sense of reason or creates a line of reasoning for the audience to follow. (See Crabtree ¶ 9–11, Paulin's conclusion, Bohnhorst ¶ 10–11.)

Appeal to emotion relates the argument to an emotional state of the audience, or attempts to create a particular emotional state in the audience. (See Paulin ¶ 1.)

Appeal of character relates the argument to a quality of the author/speaker. (See Paulin ¶ 1.)

Appeal to need relates the argument to people's needs (spiritual, economic, physical, sexual, familial, political, etc.).

Appeal to value Relates the argument to people's values (judgments about right/wrong, success, discipline, selflessness, moderation, honesty, chastity, modesty, self-expression, etc.). (See Crabtree ¶ 9, Bohnhorst ¶ 7–8.)

The appeal to logic, or *logos,* is the most valued appeal in formal argument. It requires the arguer to establish premises—claims that must be accepted in order for the main claim (or conclusion) to be acceptable. One example is the *syllogism,* which asserts two premises and a conclusion: A is true and B is true; therefore, C must also be true. The other two Classical appeals, *pathos* and *ethos,* have worked into everyday English usage: e.g., *He has a particularly engaging* ethos. *The newspaper dramatized the* pathos *of the events.*

Too often, writers limit themselves by assuming that facts and statistics are the primary support tools for a good argument, when the truth is that facts and statistics are merely a fragment of what's possible—and what's most valuable. Writers have the whole world of culture and history within reach. They can make connections (allusions) to historical or current events, literary texts, science, nature, and their personal lives. For example, perhaps you see a connection between your topic and a recent news event. You could briefly explain details of the event and then describe what it means for your topic—how it reveals something significant and ultimately validates your opinion. The same thing goes for a movie, an ad, or a historical event. For instance, imagine a writer developing the argument about college residence policies. He might bring popular culture to his aid:

> In movies and popular television shows, college is nearly always portrayed as a raucous social engagement. The typical movie college student (like those in *American Pie* or *Animal House*) is a dormitory, apartment, frat or sorority house dweller who thrives or suffers in the family-free environment. The whole point of college in mainstream movies is to create a living situation in which the students just tread the line between responsible participation in society and utter immersion in bohemian life. It's no wonder that going to college seems synonymous with "going away" to college. When students long to avoid living in the chaotic social climate of campus life, they are working against more than some college policies. They are working against popular culture.

If you see a connection, especially one that others might not see, it can create a new way of thinking about the topic.

Use the following questions to develop allusions, testimony, and scenarios for your argument:

- Does a historical situation or trend (say, the rise of a particular fashion, organization, or individual) illustrate something about my topic?
- How has popular culture treated my topic? Does it show up in television shows, movies, or commercials? If so, how is it characterized, mishandled, or celebrated?
- Have fictional characters illustrated something important about the topic or some behavior related to it?
- How does nature (animals, life cycles, plants, biological processes, and so on) demonstrate something about my topic?
- What has science taught people about my topic?
- Do any news events illustrate my point or stance?
- What have I witnessed or experienced that illustrates my point?
- What hypothetical situation could illustrate my point?
- What do other writers or authorities on the matter say about the topic?

When using authorities, writers must formally document the use of any information, ideas, and expressions taken from sources. For an extended explanation of formal documentation and integration of sources, see Chapter 13: Research & Writing.

Now, imagine how using appeals can help your argument. The various appeals can be applied to nearly any topic. Notice how a writer might tie an argument about college students to broader values—family intimacy and self-determination:

> Going to college should not have to mean going away to college. The intellectual commitment required of a student should not necessarily require a domestic commitment. Coming into an institution should not necessarily mean abandoning the intimacy of family. And entering college should not mean entering a compulsory social climate. But policies that require first-year students to live on campus impose a domestic and social arrangement onto students.

The most valued strategy in formal academic argument is the appeal to logic—or what is often called a *line of reasoning*. When writers create a line of resaoning, they create an intellectual path for readers—several steps (sometimes called premises) that lead to the writer's thesis. Consider the topic from the previous section: college students living at home. If we want to convince readers to believe that colleges should not require students to live on campus, we might create the following line of reasoning:

a. The shift from high school to college culture is significant.

b. Many students experience a kind of culture shock in the transition.

c. This culture shock negatively impacts their academic performance.

Each of these statements requires further explanation, examples, illustration, evidence, and appeal. In other words, this line of reasoning might require several lengthy passages of text. But if the readers could accept each claim, then they would be led directly to the main point—that college policies should not require on-campus residence for all first-year students.

As you consider your own topic, use the following questions to develop appeals:

- What line of reasoning can I create for the reader to follow? What premises do readers have to accept before they accept my thesis?

- How can I connect the topic to people's values (sense of right and wrong, success, discipline, selflessness, moderation, honesty, chastity, modesty, self-expression, etc.)?

- How can I connect the topic to people's basic needs (spiritual, economic, physical, sexual, familial, political, etc.)?

- How can I connect the topic to people's emotions (fear, hope, sadness, happiness)?

- Does my life (my role in a relationship, on a job, in school, on a team) lend credibility to my position on this topic?

Activity

Generate a variety of appeals for each of the following claims:

- Although war illustrates human cruelty and malice, it also illustrates human compassion and sympathy.

- Most proponents of capital punishment fail to consider the impact on the executed person's loved ones.

- Democracy cannot thrive in a two-party system.

- Excessive marketing leads to a lack of civility and respect among citizens.

Counterargument

Counterarguments anticipate and refute claims or positions that oppose those being forwarded by the writer. Writers must anticipate and account for positions outside of or opposed to their own claims(s) and include reasoning to off-set that potential opposition. For example, a savvy teenager who wants to attend a party will imagine his parents' concerns and work them into his argument about why he should be allowed to go. A politician will anticipate her opponent's position on an issue and formulate her speech accordingly.

The most successful arguers are good counterarguers. They address and even dismantle the specifics of opposing claims. In her essay, Ann Marie Paulin counterargues by summing up advice given to Barbara Dinnerstein: "She told us to put a picture of ourselves on the 'fridgerator of us eating and looking really fat and ugly. She said remember what you look like. Remember how ugly you are." In the paragraph that follows this advice, Paulin explains why she disagrees:

> I have a problem with this advice. First, of course, it is too darn common. Fat people are constantly being told they should be ashamed of themselves, of their bodies. And here we see another of those misconceptions I mentioned earlier: the assumption that being fat is the same as being ugly. There are plenty of attractive fat people in the world, as well as a few butt-ugly thin ones, I might add. Honestly, though, the real tragedy is that while few people in this world are truly ugly, many agonize over the belief that they are. Dr. Pipher reported: "I see clients who say they would rather kill themselves than be overweight" (91). I never have figured out how trashing a fellow being's self-esteem is going to help that person be healthier.

In academic argument, opposing claims are vital. Instead of ignoring or fearing them, good writers *use* them to develop points. In developing your argument, try to address opposing claims. Doing so will make your own argument more complex, more developed, and more persuasive.

- Who might disagree with my position? Why?
- What reasons do people have for disagreeing with me?
- What would support an opposing argument?

Invention Workshop

The Devil's Advocate This activity is designed to generate counterarguments. The process involves an intensive group exchange. Follow these steps:

- Assemble writers into small groups (three or four per group work best).
- Each writer should have his or her thesis statement (main argumentative claim) written down.
- The first writer should read his or her thesis statement aloud to the group.
- Taking turns, each group member then should attempt to refute the position given in the statement. The idea is to play devil's advocate, to complicate the writer's ideas.
- The writer should record each opposing claim that is offered.
- After everyone in the group has given an opposing claim to the first writer, the second writer should recite his or her thesis, and the process begins again.

Using Counterargument to Qualify Your Thesis

Thesis statements become narrower and more meaningful when they include an understanding of the broader argument (others' positions on the subject). Let's examine the opposition to a working thesis: *College students benefit from living at home while attending school.* Many college students insist that living away from home during college helps to define "the college experience." They might develop an argument using personal or anecdotal evidence. They might illustrate personal (hence, intellectual) growth that comes from living away from home, away from one's family, away from familiar turf. They might point to stories in literature in which a character leaves her or his homeland to seek knowledge or wisdom in the world and gains insight only because of the new surroundings. They might point to movies in popular culture that promote that same idea. We would do well to consider these points, and perhaps work against some of them directly. We might even include part of the logic into our own thesis: *Despite the attraction of living away from home and experiencing life in unfamiliar territory, college students benefit from living at home while attending school.*

Concession

While counterarguments refute objections, concessions acknowledge the value of others' claims. Put another way, if the writer says that an objection or alternative is wrong, the response is a counterargument; but if the writer says that the objection or alternative is right, that response is a concession.

Concession is a vital aspect of academic argument. Notice how Crabtree concedes a point in the conclusion of his essay. Although he argues for the value of a great books education throughout his essay, he does concede that it demands a particular kind of commitment:

A great books education is not for everyone. In order to benefit from such an education, a student has to be highly motivated, mature enough to realize the importance of such a focus, and self-disciplined. Whatever reasons one might have for not pursuing a great books education, it cannot be because it is not practical!

Concessions might acknowledge the limitations of, or make clear boundaries for, the writer's own argument. In this case, they are sometimes called *qualifiers*. When giving a speech on the evils of corporate tax evasion, a senator qualifies her statements: "Granted, most companies in America pay taxes responsibly, but we must focus on those few rogue and politically powerful companies." When arguing for a salary increase, a union leader acknowledges a point made by the opposition: "We understand that economic times ahead could be perilous and that a salary increase could make the company more financially vulnerable to outside forces, but the future of the company certainly depends upon the well-being of its loyal employees."

Conceding in academic argument does not make an argument wishy-washy. In fact, a good concession shows that a writer has a broad sense of his or her claims—that they fit into a larger context. A good writer might discuss the logic of another position and show, *to some degree,* how that position has validity. This does not mean that the writer's own point is weak; on the contrary, it means that his or her point is so strong and valid that it can even acknowledge the soundness of other positions. (See more on this in the Writer's Voice section.)

Consider the following questions for your argument:

- Are there other valid positions that one could take on my topic?
- Are there legitimate reasons for taking another position on this topic?
- Does my argument make any large, but necessary, leaps?

Caution: Logical Fallacies Ahead

Logical fallacies are flaws in the structure of an argument that make the claims invalid. A fallacy is a falsehood, so a logical fallacy is a logical falsehood that makes no sense within a given situation. For example, consider this familiar line:

> If you break a mirror, you'll have seven years of bad luck.

We may recognize this as superstition. In academic terms, it is called *faulty cause/effect*. That is, the broken mirror does not actually cause misfortune in one's life. The statement seems categorically faulty. However, the success (or logic) of any argument depends on the particular situation. All argumentative statements exist in situations that give those statements credibility. (If someone's entire fortune were tied to a mirror, then the previous statement would be more logical!) Statements are logical or illogical based on the situation.

In academia, recognizing logical fallacies is part of being a critical thinker in all disciplines. There is no quicker way to make readers of your own work suspicious than committing any fallacies (listed on the next page) when making an argument.

Activities

A. What logical fallacies might you overhear in everyday situations? Consider the following scenarios: a customer trying to return an item; a store clerk trying to sell an extended warranty; a teacher explaining why a student cannot receive credit for a late assignment; a student arguing that he or she should receive a better grade; two politicians debating a tax cut; a husband explaining why he should go fishing with his cousin all weekend.

B. In groups, write an example for each of the fallacies listed in this chapter.

C. In groups, write short argumentative essays loaded with logical blunders. Someone in each group should read the completed essay aloud, and the class should attempt to point out and name the fallacies.

D. Explain the problem with the logic in the internet bumper stickers, and name the fallacy.

YOU DESERVE WHAT YOU ACCEPT

IF ALL ELSE FAILS STOP USING ALL ELSE

NEVER BELIEVE GENERALIZATIONS

DON'T BLAME ME. *I voted.*

CONCEIVE. BELIEVE. ACHIEVE.

POLITICAL CORRECTNESS IS A DISEASE

STRIP MINING PREVENTS FOREST FIRES

Ad hominem (Latin for *to the person*) Attacks a person directly rather than examining the logic of the argument.

- We cannot possibly consider Ms. Smith's proposal because she is a Catholic.
- Mr. Mann's argument is suspicious because he is a socialist.

Strawperson Exaggerates a characteristic of a person or group of people and then uses the exaggeration to dismiss an argument.

- Islamic fundamentalists are crazy. They only want to destroy Americans. We cannot accept their claims about imperialism.
- Environmentalists are radical. They want to end everyone's fun by taking cars and boats away.

Faulty cause/effect Confuses a sequential relationship with a causal one. Assumes that event A caused event B because A occurred first.

- Since the construction of the new baseball stadium, homelessness in the downtown area has decreased.
- The tax cut made energy rates drop.

Either/or reasoning Offers only two choices when more exist.

- Either we destroy Russia or it will destroy us.
- The American people will choose to control their own lives or give away their wills to socialist candidates.

Hasty generalization Draws a conclusion about a group of people, events, or things based on insufficient examples (often, the logical flaw behind racist, sexist, or bigoted statements).

- Men are too possessive. My ex-boyfriend would never let me go out alone.
- French people are rude. When I went to France, the civilians grunted French statements when I asked for help.

Non sequitur (Latin for *it does not follow*) Skips several logical steps in drawing a conclusion.

- If we do not trash the entire tax code, the downtown area will slowly deteriorate.
- A new baseball stadium downtown will help with the homelessness problem.

Oversimplification Does not acknowledge the true complexity of a situation or offers easy solutions to complicated problems.

- If we could give kids something to do, they wouldn't get depressed.
- This credit card will end all of my financial problems.

Slippery slope Assumes that a certain way of thinking or acting will necessarily continue or extend in that direction (like a domino effect). Such an argument suggests that once we begin down a path, we will inevitably slip all the way down, and so the effects of a particular action or idea are exaggerated.

- If the college makes students take more mathematics, the next thing we know, advanced calculus and quantum physics will be requirements for all graduates.
- If North Vietnam succeeds in making South Vietnam communist, it will eventually threaten the shores of the United States of America.

False analogy Makes a comparison between two things that are ultimately more unlike than alike. The differences between the things make the comparison ineffective or unfair, or the comparison misrepresents one or both of the things involved.

- Writing is like breathing: You just do what comes naturally.
- Like Galileo, Bill Clinton was breaking new ground, but no one understood him.

Begging the question Attempts to prove a claim by using (an alternative wording of) the claim itself.

- Girls should not be allowed into the Boys' Military Academy because it is for boys only.
- All cigarette smoking should be banned from public places because I believe it in my heart.

ORGANIZATIONAL STRATEGIES

How Should I Begin?

As with all essays, the sky is the limit. Remember some of the basic introductory tools (anecdote, provocative question, shocking statement). Remember, too, that introductions not only create focus for the topic, but also establish the tone of the essay. They are the invitation to *start* thinking. But if an introduction is flat, typical, or vague, it is an invitation to *stop* thinking. Notice this typical, vague introduction:

> There are many critical issues facing today's public schools. They have to consider violence, financial constraints, teacher training, drugs, and student apathy, just to name a few. But in this difficult era, educators have become enamored with a saving grace: technology. Computers are everywhere in our public schools. But the problem is that the technology isn't the saving grace that it seems. Schools should rethink their allegiance to computers.

This introduction illustrates a few critical mistakes. First, the writer begins with a statement that nearly everyone knows. It is not an invitation to think rigorously or explore an issue. Second, it is far too broad for the reader to get traction. Third, because the introduction begins so broadly, it makes at least two large intellectual leaps in the goal of getting to the writer's thesis at the end. Fourth, the attempt to place the thesis at the end of the paragraph makes all the other information seem contrived and formulaic.

To the contrary, in her essay Elizabeth Bohnhorst takes us directly to the critical issue, showing a specific example. She does not need to rush through several vague statements to suggest her position on the issue. She makes it indirectly from the outset:

> "Another boring PowerPoint," responds Jennifer when I ask about her day at school. I might not find these words so discouraging coming from a company executive after a long meeting or even a college student leaving an informative lecture. But these words of an eleven-year-old elementary school student leave me feeling slightly uneasy. PowerPoint presentations are intended to compel students to become more interested in the subject with the use of neon colors and moving graphic images. But these flashy additions to current educational strategies haven't fooled everyone. The text and material covered is still the same boring grammar and spelling lessons but the educator has altered: It is a screen.

Bohnhorst does go on in her essay to speak about computer technology in general, but here she focuses on a specific program, PowerPoint, which gives her argument, and her readers, a focal point.

Activity

Check the essays in this chapter. Notice the difference among introduction strategies. Do the introductions help to establish the tone in each essay?

Where Should I Put Counterarguments?

Counterarguments can be tricky, but they need not be. First, they can be placed anywhere in a paper: at the beginning, throughout the body, and even at the conclusion. You might explain an opposing point and then counter, explain another opposing point and then counter. (Depending on the amount of detail given to each counter, each point might be an entire paragraph, or more, with supporting evidence.)

Opposing Point A

Your counterargument

Opposing Point B

Your counterargument

Opposing Point C

Your counterargument

Some writers use a turnabout paragraph for counterarguments. A turnabout paragraph begins with one point and then shifts to an opposing or alternative point while giving the reader a clear sign of the shift. For example, you might begin a paragraph explaining an opposing position, and then counterargue in that same paragraph. In the following example, the opposing claim (that global warming is not a real problem) is addressed within the paragraph. The paragraph also includes the change of direction ("This argument, however . . ."):

> Some people argue that global warming is not a problem at all. They suggest that all the discussion about the ozone layer is merely fear-mongering by left-wing political activists. This argument, however, ignores the volumes of evidence compiled by scientists (many of whom are Nobel Prize winners) from around the world—scientists from different cultures, from different religious contexts, from different political systems, and with different political agendas. The amount of data they have collected and the sheer din of their collective voices ought to be enough to convince people that global warming is much more than the delusions of a few environmental groups.

You might decide that the opposing viewpoint(s) require significant explanation, and that it would be best to keep them grouped together. Therefore, you might devote a chunk of space at the beginning of your paper before countering:

Opposing Point A

Opposing Point B

Opposing Point C

Your counterargument to A

Your counterargument to B

Your counterargument to C

You also might decide that your argument only needs a single main counterargument. That counter might come after you have given your supporting evidence and appeals, or it might even begin the argument. Or several opposing claims might be discussed, and addressed, in one paragraph. (See Paulin ¶ 2.)

Activity

Examine the essays in this chapter for counterarguments. Notice their different organizational strategies.

How Should I Make Transitions?

Regardless of your general organization strategy, make certain to cue the reader when giving a counterargument. It is important that the reader understand when the focus is shifting from counter to main argument. You might begin a paragraph with an opposing viewpoint: "Some opponents might argue that. . . ." If so, you will need to shift the reader back to your logic: "But they do not understand that. . . ." Here is a list of some strategic transitions when doing counter argument:

On the other hand,

Contrary to this idea,

Although many people take this stance,

However, (; however,)

Despite the evidence for this position,

But

Also, remember that transitions can wait. While developing rough drafts, writers often wait to add the glue between paragraphs. Rather than fret over difficult transition statements, they move ahead with their arguments and return later to fill in gaps. (For more on transitions, see page 91.)

WRITER'S VOICE

Argument need not be cast as an act of aggression or belligerence. While arguments are sometimes heated and intense, they need not attempt to belittle their opponents. In fact, the fastest way to alienate, or turn off, a reader is to sound narrow-minded, mean, arrogant, or intimidating. A good argument attracts readers and engages those who might oppose the claims being made; a bad or unsuccessful argument loses readers. Here are some strategies for maintaining a cool tone—one that invites readers rather than alienates them.

Making Concessions

Conceding or qualifying a point can make an argument seem more controlled and more inviting; therefore, even when writers have a very strong conviction, they will often acknowledge the value of some other point or the limits of their own argument. Imagine the following argument:

> First-year college students are not mature enough to live on their own, without the guidance of parents and the familiarity of home turf. Dorm life is a celebration of self-destruction and disorientation. The social distractions draw students away from the real purpose of college and defeat even the most focused and determined students. Colleges should rethink the requirements for first-year students to live on campus.

While these claims unfairly generalize college students (see *logical fallacies*) and threaten the logical soundness of the argument, they also project a hasty or pushy voice. Such unqualified claims create a certain character in readers' minds—someone who is overly anxious and forceful. But the same argument can be cast with a different voice (which uses concession). The following paragraph acknowledges some value in dorm life and, as a result, seems fairer and less alienating:

> Dorm life does hold some value for young students. It can create a climate of inquiry and academic engagement. However, many young college students are overcome by the utter freedom, lack of genuine guidance, and constant social distractions. And too many students who would otherwise succeed in their first years at college are suffering or failing because they are forced to live on campus. Colleges should, at least, begin to reevaluate requirements for on-campus living.

While conceding can create a more engaging voice, conceding unnecessarily, or too often, can have negative results. Imagine the same argument, but with a distracting degree of concession:

> Living in dorms can be the best thing possible for a college student; however, dorm life can also defeat many students. Sometimes, even the brightest and most determined students can be overcome by the social distractions. Although it all depends on the individual student's personality and upbringing, college dorm life can actually work against the whole purpose of going to college. Certainly, each college should consider the characteristics of its own student body, but policies that require students to live on campus should be reevaluated.

All the concessions undermine the importance of the argument. The voice behind the text seems concerned about offending potential readers. But, ironically, such writing makes readers feel distant or detached from the ideas. Because the writer seems uncommitted, readers have no reason to engage the ideas. (Be cautious not to concede away your argument—and your level of commitment.)

Avoiding Harsh Description

It is often easy to use the most emotionally loaded terms to describe something or someone, to proclaim an opposing view as "dumb" or "evil." Such description, however, is most often exaggerated, and suggests that the writer has not fully investigated the subject. In the following, Paulin does not attack the media and the diet industry with aggressive adjectives, but argues that they damage people's lives. This is a far more sophisticated and useful strategy than merely dismissing them with a simple negative word or phrase:

> Certainly everyone is entitled to his or her own opinions of what is attractive, but no one has the right to damage another human being for fun or profit. The media and the diet industry often do just that. While no one can change an entire culture overnight, people, especially parents, need to think about what they really value in the humans they share their lives with and what values they want to pass on to their children.

Talking with, Not Arguing at, Readers

An academic argument is not an argument with readers. It is a *conversation with readers about an argumentative position.* And if that conversation is compelling, the reader may find that position valuable. In other words, argumentative writing speaks with the reader about a particular position or set of positions and attempts to make one position more logical and/or valuable than others.

To help visualize the role of the writer and reader, imagine the following: The writer sits beside the reader, pointing at and directing attention to a set of claims. The writer does not sit in front of and point his or her finger at the reader. This may seem like a subtle difference, but notice how it may change a passage. In the example below, David Crabtree speaks to the reader about the need for workers in America to be intellectually capable of changing work environments. He does not command the reader:

> Such unpredictability calls for a different strategy in preparing for the job market. Rather than spending one's undergraduate years receiving specialized training, one ought to learn more general, transferable skills which will provide the flexibility to adjust to whatever changes may occur.

But imagine a different approach if Crabtree had talked at us directly. In the following, the writer tries to convince the reader ("you") to change his or her behavior. Rather than speak with the reader about an issue, this passage targets the reader's own behavior, which is generally avoided in academic writing:

> Such unpredictability should make you realize the need to be ready for a shifting job market. Rather than spending undergraduate years receiving specialized training, you ought to learn more general, transferable skills which will provide the flexibility to adjust to whatever changes may occur.

VITALITY

While the editing strategies in other chapters can be applied here, argumentative writing has potential difficulties of its own. Because argument is such a common everyday practice, writers have to be especially mindful of some informal habits that can make formal written argument less intense and vital.

Avoid Unnecessary Attention to *I*

In argumentative writing, it is especially tempting to use the first-person pronouns *I, me,* and *my.* As in the following two sentences, personal pronouns can distract the reader from the argument itself and bog down the sentences:

> I think that social security ought to be tied to the marketplace.

> It is my personal belief that social security should not be a gamble.

In each of these sentences, the main idea is subordinated in a *that* clause. *I* statements such as these are unnecessary in argumentative writing because the claims are already attributed to the writer. By simply attaching his or her name to an essay, the writer has already implied "I believe." Saying it again is redundant.

However, writers do occasionally choose to insert personal pronouns. When dealing with several claims or outside sources, writers may insert the first-person pronoun in order to make a clear distinction between their own thoughts and others', as Paulin does:

> For instance, in her essay, "Bubbie, Mommy, Weight Watchers and Me," Barbara Noreen Dinnerstein recalls a time in her childhood when her mother took her to Weight Watchers to slim down and the advice the lecturer gave to the women present: "She told us to put a picture of ourselves on the 'fridgerator of us eating and looking really fat and ugly. She said remember what you look like. Remember how ugly you are."
>
> I have a problem with this advice. First, of course, it is too darn common.

Paulin could also have avoided the first-person pronoun:

> But this advice is dangerous to young women.

But she chose the first-person pronoun, perhaps because it is less formal and coincides with the personal voice she has established in her essay. While it is good practice to avoid unnecessary use of first-person pronouns, writers like Paulin can make effective, occasional use of it.

Writers also use *I* for personal narratives—telling a story or anecdote involving their own experiences. Such uses are legitimate and important. Narratives draw attention to the relevant experience of the writer, which requires use of the first-person pronoun.

Unnecessary *I* Statement

> I think that history should be taught with more attention to the lives of everyday people.

Appropriate Personal Narrative

> When I was in high school, my history courses focused almost exclusively on big battles and big governmental moments.

Avoid Unnecessary Attention to *You*

The second-person pronoun *you* refers directly to the reader—the person holding your text and reading from it. And because academic essays are invitations to a broad audience (to instructors, peers, and even the broader community of thinkers that they represent), *you* is generally avoided. Like the first-person singular pronouns *(I, me, my), you* distracts the reader from the issue at hand. But *you* is especially hazardous in academic writing because it makes writers shift into the imperative mood—the mood of commands. Here, the writer shifts focus and mood:

> Political parties do their best to keep people from closely examining issues. Instead, they wash over complexities and invite voters to stand on one side or another. You should consider your allegiance to any political party.

The first two sentences focus on political parties, people, and voters. But the final sentence shifts and suddenly speaks at the reader. To most academic audiences, this shift is unacceptable. (See more about speaking *with* versus *at* the reader in Writer's Voice.)

Avoiding first- and second-person pronouns keeps the writer, and therefore the reader, focused on the ideas— on the argument itself.

Vitalize with Verbs

Verbs are the engine of a sentence. And they are the agent of motion for the reader's mind: They move the reader's thoughts. Weak verbs make for little movement. In the following, the first sentence depends on a weak verb:

> Telemarketers are bad for home life.

> Telemarketers have diminished the sanctity of the home.

The verb of the first sentence, *are,* is often called a *linking verb.* When linking verbs act as the main engine of a sentence, they limit what's possible. Often, they corner the writer into using a vague adjective, in this case *bad.* The second sentence uses an active and more intensive verb: *diminished.* The second sentence creates a more engaging image. In the following sentences, linking verbs actually create unnecessary layers and clauses. Notice how each can be tightened and vitalized with an *active verb*:

> The problem with this *is* that the house is too expensive for our budget.
> <u>Vitalized</u>: Here's the problem: the cost of the house *exceeds* our budget.

> The committee *is* not prone to allowing everyone *to be* as free with their money as they want.
> <u>Vitalized</u>: The committee will probably not *allow* everyone to *spend* resources freely.

Using active verbs rather than linking verbs vitalizes writing. This is not to say that using linking verbs is always a mistake. (Sometimes, they are necessary.) However, changing to more active verbs can dramatically impact your writing, creating more focused statements, more intensive ideas, and more revelatory thinking.

ACTIVITY

Revise and vitalize the following sentences. Try replacing the linking verb first and see how that impacts your decision about other parts of the sentence:

1. Energy drinks may give you wings but they are not helping students to focus.

2. It's going to be a long time before that cat is home again.

3. The arguments against global warming are often full of strawperson fallacies, which are fallacies that unfairly characterize a person or group of people.

4. Presidential candidates seem to be getting more mean-spirited as time goes by, but elections early in American history were often deeply hostile as well.

PEER REVIEW

Exchange drafts with at least one other writer. Before passing your draft to others, underline the thesis, or write it on the top of your essay. This way, reviewers will get traction as they read. Reviewers should use the following questions to guide a helpful response:

1. Could the thesis be more narrow and revelatory? How? (What words or phrases are too broad?)

2. Can you think of another cultural, literary, historical, or political allusion that relates to the writer's position?

3. How well can you follow the writer's line of reasoning? (See appeals to logic, page 245.) Imagine the line of reasoning as though it is a stone path. If the path is well laid out, you should feel a stone at every step. If it is not, you might miss a step; you might feel like some intellectual step is missing.

4. Suggest specific points that the writer should concede or qualify. For instance, the writer's position might seem too extreme; the claims might include too many people or a large, diverse group without making any distinctions. Point out such claims, and help the writer to see the need to acknowledge subtlety, complexity, and exceptions.

5. Can you imagine another opposing point that the writer could address in a counterargument? While the writer may have dealt with several opposing positions, you might think of an additional issue that should be addressed.

6. Consider the writer's voice. Circle passages or sentences that shift mood and speak *at*, rather than *with*, the reader. Suggest an alternative strategy or phrasing.

7. Do paragraphs focus on one main point? Point to sentences in paragraphs that stray from the initial idea put forth in the paragraph.

8. What is the most engaging passage in the draft so far? Why?

9. Check for sentence vitality.

   • Where can the writer change linking verbs to active verbs?

   • Where can the writer avoid drawing attention to *I* and *you*?

   • Consider vitality strategies from other chapters:

     —Help the writer change unnecessary clauses to phrases.

     —Help the writer change unnecessary phrases to words.

     —Point to expletives (such as *there are* and *it is*).

     —Help the writer change passive verbs to active verbs for more vitality.

     —Help the reader avoid common grammatical errors: comma splices, sentence fragments, or pronoun/antecedent agreement.

Questions for Research

If the writer used outside sources,

• Where must he or she include in-text citations? (See pages 484–485.)

• Are quotations blended smoothly into the argument and punctuated correctly? (See pages 475–478.)

• Where could more direct textual cues or transitions help the reader? (See pages 479–481.)

• Is the Works Cited page formatted properly? (See pages 486–497.)

DELIVERY

Academic essays are not merely vehicles for communicating thought. They are intellectual playing fields—places for writers and readers to discover something. Those discoveries do not exist in the vacuum of an essay; they resonate outward through the lives of the writers and readers. An argument essay in particular sets out to assert something about the world, and that assertion is bound to impact reality—because people live according to the arguments they accept.

Now that you have written an argumentative essay, respond to the following:

- How do your claims challenge something in your life? The lives of your friends and family?

- Do your words support mainstream intellectual life? Or does your essay challenge something about the way most people live and think?

- What particular groups, organizations, or people should read your essay? How might it impact their behavior?

Beyond the Essay: The Open Letter

Argumentative essays have changed the world. They've started revolutions, supported religious movements, initiated new scientific organizations, spotlighted atrocities, and prompted a broad range of political events. But sophisticated arguments can impact the world through other genres.

The open letter is closely related to the essay. It is aimed at a particular audience, a particular reader or set of readers, but it also resonates with a broader audience. An open letter draws both writer and reader, and an otherwise private discussion, into a public setting—a powerful move! For example, Martin Luther King, Jr.'s "Letter from Birmingham Jail" was originally aimed at nine fellow clergy members, but the letter also speaks to millions of others. In effect, King performs a response to a particular audience for a broader audience. The conversation occurs between a few particular people, but the issues and claims involve many. Or consider the apostle Paul's letters to the Romans that now constitute part of the New Testament.

They have become known to millions of readers, but they were originally aimed at a particular group of people. Or more currently, newspapers and magazines often print open letters to the president, to an editor, or to corporate heads.

Because letters are written with a particular audience in mind, they may draw attention to specifics about the readers' life, such as specific behaviors, policies, attitudes, or events. The writer may then draw out the significance, explaining the impact on or meaning for others.

Return to your essay and imagine a particular person or group of people who should read and accept your claims. Then develop an open letter addressed to that particular audience

The following questions may help shape your ideas:

- Who has the power or authority over the issue?
- How can you make a specific connection between them and the issue?
- To what specific behavior, attitude, event, or policy can you draw attention?
- What is the public significance of that behavior?

> "People don't operate based on reality. They operate based on their perceptions of reality. And with language, we can change those perceptions."
>
> —David Hawes

RESPONDING TO ARGUMENTS

Chapter Contents

CHAPTER 8

"We hold these truths to be self-evident, that all men are created equal, that they are endowed by their Creator with certain inalienable rights, that among these are life, liberty, and the pursuit of happiness."

—The Declaration of Independence

Arguments are all around us. They lurk in nearly every behavior and event of our lives, and we often respond to arguments that hover but are not stated directly. Imagine an American citizen protesting nuclear energy; she carries a sign that says, "Nuclear energy ≠ clean energy!" Her sign is a response to the argument that nuclear energy is cleaner than energy from oil and coal. The protester is not responding to a particular text or person, but to an argument made by many people (such as politicians) in many different contexts. The sign actually evokes (or brings to mind) this argument and directly refutes it. Someone might also respond to an advertiser's argument that cigarettes promote social and physical pleasures. Such an ad argues that a certain brand of cigarette provides pleasure beyond inhaling the smoke and feeling the nicotine, and a writer might (quite easily) argue the opposite.

In academia, writers most often respond to arguments that are formally delivered (in an essay or editorial). They respond to a particular text or person and to particular statements or claims:

- A psychologist responds to Freud's theory of ego development, explaining that such a theory is not valuable in treating female patients.

- A political science student supports a revised historical account of U.S. foreign policy that holds Henry Kissinger partly responsible for atrocities in Chile during the 1970s.

- Law students respond to a Supreme Court ruling that upholds the rights of law enforcement officers to detain citizens for traffic violations. They argue that the ruling erodes protections against "unreasonable search and seizure."

- An English professor reviews a controversial new book and defends its claims against rampant consumerism.

As these examples suggest, responding to an argument does not necessarily mean disagreement. The initial argument (whether a court ruling, a book, an essay, or a historical account) provides the position on a topic. A writer has many options beyond agreement or disagreement. For instance, he or she might agree with the initial argument and extend the ideas with additional points, disagree with a particular point, redefine the issue, or point out some logical flaws.

As you can imagine, this is a somewhat more sophisticated task than what we examined in Chapter 7, Making Arguments. However, responding to arguments is an engaging activity, one that is not only vital to and valued in academia, but also necessary for maintaining a democracy.

Although a writer can respond to many different kinds of argument, this chapter primarily focuses on arguments that are formally delivered. The chapter will help you discover and analyze an argument, develop a sophisticated argumentative response, and communicate your position in writing. Read the following essays, which illustrate a variety of arguing strategies. After reading the essays, you can find an argument in one of several ways:

1. Go to the Point of Contact section to find an argument from everyday life.
2. Choose one of the Ideas for Writing that follow the essays.
3. Respond to any argumentative essay from another chapter in this book.

After you find a topic, go to the Analysis section to begin developing your response.

What Orwell Didn't Know

George Lakoff

George Orwell, the pen name of Eric Arthur Blair (1903–1950), was a journalist, novelist, and political commentator famous for his most popular works, *Animal Farm* (1945) and *1984* (1949), two influential novels that have been required reading in many high school and college courses. Like *Animal Farm* and *1984,* Orwell's essay "Politics and the English Language" (1946) has been required reading for many college students. As George Lakoff (1941–), a professor of cognitive linguistics at the University of California, Berkeley explains in the essay below, Orwell argues that inaccurate language leads to "political propaganda and its effects." While Lakoff commends Orwell's essay for its important contribution, his response labels it an anachronism because, as Lakoff explains, those in his profession have "learned a lot about the brain, the mind, and language since then."

George Orwell will forever be a hero of mine. When I read *1984* in high school, I became sensitized to the workings of propaganda. After more than forty years as a linguist and cognitive scientist, I remain sensitized.

When I first read "Politics and the English Language" as an undergraduate in the late 1950s, I loved it. Nearly fifty years later I find it an anachronism. Why? I, and those in my profession, have learned a lot about the brain, the mind and language since then. Orwell's essay belongs to an earlier time, a time that lacked our deepening understanding of how the human brain works.

Orwell suffered from what we might now call the "Editor's Fallacy": Bad habits of "foolish thought" and inaccurate, slovenly, dull, pretentious, ungraceful, and meaningless language—the "decay of language"—lead to political propaganda and its effects. If we just "let the meaning choose the word," he claimed, we would all be saved. This is not only false, it is dangerously naïve.

Orwell fell into traps—false views of language: *Meanings are truth conditions. Words have unitary meanings. If people are told the truth, they will reason to the right conclusions—unless they are stupid or ignorant. And ignorance can be cured by truths conveyed in good prose.*

5 All of that is false. Yet progressives still fall into those traps. Even you, dear reader, may have fallen into them. And even *I* am trying to cure ignorance via truths conveyed in good prose. I am banking on cognitive dissonance—yours! Dissonance between the real brain and the apparent mind. Intellectuals are confident they know their own minds, though they realize they don't know their own brains. But their brains betray their confidence in their minds. Neuroscience and cognitive science reveal a far more interesting picture than Orwell could have guessed.

Probably 98 percent of your reasoning is *un*conscious—what your brain is doing behind the scenes. Reason is inherently emotional. You can't even choose a goal, much less form a plan and carry it out, without a sense that it will satisfy you, not disgust you. Fear and anxiety will affect your plans and your actions. You act differently, and plan differently, out of hope and joy than out of fear and anxiety.

Thought is physical. Learning requires a physical brain change: Receptors for neurotransmitters change at the synapses, which changes neural circuitry. Since thinking is the activation of such circuitry, somewhat different thinking requires a somewhat different brain. Brains change as you use them—even unconsciously. It's as if your car changed as you drove it, say from a stick shift gradually to an automatic.

Thought is physical in another way. It uses the brain's sensory-motor system. Imagining moving uses the same regions of the brain as moving; imagining seeing uses the same regions of the brain as seeing. Meaning is mental simulation, activating those regions of the brain. Reasoning from A to B is the neural activation of the mental simulation of B, given the mental simulation of A. Mental simulation, like most thought, is mostly unconscious.

Thought is structured, in large measure, in terms of "frames"—brain structures that control mental simulation and hence reasoning.

10 You think metaphorically, perhaps most of the time. Just by functioning with your body in the world as a child, you learn at least hundreds of simple "conceptual metaphors"—metaphors you think with and live by. For example, Quantity is understood in terms of Verticality (More is Up), and the words follow along:

prices rise and fall, skyrocket and hit bottom. Why? Because every day of your life, if you pour water into a glass, the level rises. You experience a correlation between quantity and verticality. In your brain, regions for registering verticality and quantity are activated together during such experiences. As a result, activation spreads, and circuits linking Verticality to Quantity are formed. Those circuits constitute the metaphor More is Up in your brain. As a child lives in the world, his or her brain acquires hundreds of such "primary" conceptual metaphors that are just there waiting to be used in everyday thought.

We have high-level moral worldviews—modes of reasoning about what's right and wrong—that govern whole areas of reason, both conscious and unconscious, and link up whole networks of frames and metaphors.

Cultural narratives are special cases of such frames. They stretch over time and define protagonists and antagonists—and heroes, victims, and villains. They define right and wrong, and come with emotional content. And most important, we all live out cultural narratives—with all their emotionality and moral sensibility. We even define our identities by the narratives we live by.

What are words? Words are neural links between spoken and written expressions and frames, metaphors, and narratives. When we hear the words, not only their immediate frames and metaphors are activated, but also all the high-level worldviews and associated narratives—with their emotions—are activated. Words are not just words—they activate a huge range of brain mechanisms. Moreover, words don't just activate neutral meanings; they are often defined relative to conservative framings. And our most important political words—*freedom, equality, fairness, opportunity, security, accountability*—name "contested concepts," concepts with a common shared core that is unspecified, which is then extended to most of its cases based on your values. Thus conservative "freedom" is utterly different than progressive "freedom," as I showed in detail in *Whose Freedom.* Liberals such as Paul Starr, in *Freedom's Power,* unselfconsciously use their own version of freedom, as if there were no other version. Not understanding conservative "freedom" and pointing out its problematic nature greatly weakens one's effect.

A few words in political language can activate large portions of the brain: *War on Terror, tax relief, illegal immigration, entitlements* (turned to conservative use by Ronald Reagan), *death tax, property rights, abortion on demand, cut and run, flip-flop, school choice, intelligent design, spending programs, partial birth abortion, surge, spreading freedom, private accounts, individual responsibility, energy independence.*

15   When they are repeated every day, extensive areas of the brain are activated over and over, and this leads to brain change. Unerasable brain change. Once learned, the new neural structure cannot just be erased: *War on Terror* be gone! It doesn't work. And every time the words are repeated, all the frames and metaphors and worldview structures are activated again and strengthened—because recurring activation strengthens neural connections. Negation doesn't help. "I'm against the War on Terror" just activates the *War on Terror* metaphor and strengthens what you're against. Accepting the language of issue and arguing the other side just hurts your own cause.

Can you counter such brain change? There are two possibilities. First, you can try to mark the idea—as silly, immoral, stupid, and so on—by having lots of people say so over a long period of time. That's what conservatives did with "liberal," starting back in the 1960s when most people wanted to be liberals. *Tax and spend liberal, liberal elite, liberal media, limousine liberal,* and so on repeated over and over slowly got across the idea to lower- and middle-class Republicans that liberals were elite, financially irresponsible, and oppressing poor conservatives. And it undermined liberals' confidence in themselves.

The second strategy is to provide an alternative honest framing—either by inhibiting what is in the brain or by bypassing it. Done honestly, it is righting history. Done dishonestly, it is "rewriting history." Conservatives have done this with the Vietnam War: We lost because we didn't use enough force—*"We had one hand tied behind our backs."*

Neither is quick or easy.

Today, sophisticated right-wing propaganda is very well-written—the editor in Orwell would love David Brooks's prose. Mind control works via brain change, through the effective use of well-written language to activate not just frames, conceptual metaphors, and emotions, but whole worldviews. When the language is repeated and the words become just "the normal way you express the idea," then even the best people in the media get sucked in. Journalists have to use words people understand, and they have to use the words most people normally use to express the ideas they are writing about. As a result, they often have no idea that they are using conservative language, which activates a conservative view of the world as well as the conservative perspective on the given issue. They are rarely aware that in doing so, they are helping conservatives by strengthening the conservative worldview in the public's mind, and thereby accelerating brain change.

20   Once a member of the public has undergone brain change, he or she then thinks as a conservative on the issue. Not convinced rationally, just subject to the techniques every marketer uses. Is free will being exercised? The very idea of "free will" has been changed.

Orwell wasn't aware of how brains, minds, and language really work, nor was anyone else in 1947. But we don't have that excuse today. Yet even the very best of our news media are stuck in the same traps. Every now and then a result about the brain will leak out into the *Science Times* or *Discover,* only to be forgotten the next week. But what we know about the brain, the mind, and language barely ever makes it to the front page or opinion pages where politics is discussed. The ghost of Orwell still haunts our very best news and political opinion media.

Orwell's old-fashioned views about reason and language also haunt the Democratic Party. But there are promising developments. Presidential candidate John Edwards has rejected the very term *War on Terror* as an inappropriate metaphor and a means to grab power. In the Democratic debate in New Hampshire in June 2007, the questions Wolf Blitzer of CNN asked were all framed from a conservative viewpoint. Democratic candidate Barack Obama stepped forward and rejected *one* of the conservatively framed questions as "specifically designed to divide us."

In another positive development, progressives have been saying out loud that conservatism itself is the problem. Robert Borosage, in the *The American Prospect,* staunchly argues from a progressive worldview, "Conservatives cannot be trusted to guide the government they scorn. Not because they are incompetent or corrupt

(although corruption and incompetence abound), but because they get the world wrong."

This is half right. But it ignores the thousands of conservative "successes" from *their* point of view, which Borosage cites as "failures." In hundreds of cases (excepting Iraq—a big exception), conservatives would say that George W. Bush got the world right—because he changed the world as he wanted to.

25   If Democrats think that those who voted for Bush will consider all those "successes" as failures, they might just find a way to lose the next election. Moral: To counter conservatism, you have to understand, and publicly discuss the problems with, the conservative moral worldview. And to do that, you need to know how largely unconscious worldviews work.

Conservatives think tanks, over thirty-five years, started with the conservative worldview and showed how to apply it everywhere on every issue, and even beyond issues in the acts of governance—cutting regulating budgets, reassigning regulators, using the courts to redefine the laws, changing the facts on Web sites, eliminating libraries. New Democratic think tanks haven't helped much. The problem is that they are *policy* think tanks. They mistakenly think that "rational" programs and policies constitute political ideas. They don't understand unconscious thought. It's the unspoken ideas behind the programs and the policies—the worldviews, deep frames, metaphors, and cultural narratives—that need to be changed in the public mind. Only one progressive think tank, the Rockridge Institute, is even working in this direction. Its handbook for progressives, *Thinking Points,* applies the study of mind to the cause of truth.

Is it legitimate to use the real mechanisms of mind—worldviews, frames, metaphors, emotions, images, personal stories, and cultural narratives—to tell important truths? Hell, yes! It is usually the only way that works. Al Gore's movie, *An Inconvenient Truth,* uses all those mechanisms of mind and heart—and it works. Had it just given facts and figures unframed, it would have flopped.

It is time to exorcise Orwell's ghost. We all need to understand how the brain, mind, and language really work. We need to apply that knowledge effectively to make truths meaningful and give *truths* the power to change brains. Our democracy depends on a clear and open understanding of the political mind.

Writing Strategies

1. Describe Lakoff's opening strategy. How does it set the tone for the essay?

2. What does Lakoff disagree with George Orwell about? To Lakoff, why is the disagreement important?

3. Lakoff says, "Thought is physical." Summarize his explanation, and then explain how this idea is important to Lakoff's main point.

4. As part of his response, Lakoff defines *words*. How is his definition important in helping the reader understand and accept his main idea?

5. According to Lakoff, what are the real mechanisms of mind, and why should they be used to tell important truths?

Exploring Ideas

1. Lakoff says, "You think metaphorically, perhaps most of the time." Summarize Lakoff's explanation, and then come up with an original example of metaphorical thinking that supports Lackoff's point.

2. Explain Lakoff's idea that cultural narratives are frames.

3. With a group of classmates, come up with an original example to illustrate Lakoff's claim that "[a]ccepting the language of issue and arguing the other side just hurts your own cause."

4. Why does Lakoff think "[o]nce a member of the public has undergone brain change, he or she then thinks as a conservative on the issue"?

5. Do some research on think tanks to become more informed about what they are. What is the purpose of a think tank? Why are think tanks important to Lakoff's response?

Ideas for Writing

1. Respond to an older way of thinking that has played an important role in your development, but that now needs to be revised in some important way.

2. In groups or alone, generate ideas for an essay by creating at least ten titles, filling in the blanks: What _____ Didn't Know About _____.

If responding to one of these ideas, go to the Analysis section of this chapter to begin developing ideas for your essay.

Entitlement Education

Daniel Bruno

We often respond to the people (and arguments) that we agree with the most. In the following essay, Daniel Bruno agrees with most of the original argument. His introduction explains: "But he fails, it seems, to emphasize enough a most harmful effect of this sense of entitlement." Bruno's response will not disagree, but will *emphasize* a crucial point in an attempt to make the reader more aware of it.

Writing Strategies

Overall summary of original argument.

Main response to the original argument.

(Attention to "I") Bruno's thesis, and distinction between his argument and the original.

Turnabout paragraph.

Analysis of several possible arguments about the results of student entitlement.

In his book *Generation X Goes to College,* Peter Sacks describes, among other things, the sense of entitlement that some students in today's consumerist culture have toward a college education. One entire chapter explores this issue alone, providing examples of this "sense" and looking into its "humble beginnings." Sacks shows how consumerism has invaded education, leading some students to expect good grades for little effort. But he fails, it seems, to emphasize enough a most harmful effect of this sense of entitlement. The biggest problem, as I see it, is that although students are able to graduate from high school (and even some colleges) with minimal effort, those students may find themselves cheated in the long run.

How might they be cheated? One might argue that students get cheated because entitlement doesn't go on forever. At some point it stops. For example, a college graduate with a marketing degree, but especially weak thinking or writing skills, may find himself disadvantaged on the job. It is not that his boss puts her foot down; instead, the job does. Our student finds himself not well prepared for it. He gets cheated because he is disadvantaged at his job—a job that he paid money to learn how to do. Of course the point isn't about marketing majors. The same is true of students in any field. (Marketing is just what came to mind.)

One might also claim that students will be cheated because their lives will somehow *be less.* This argument claims that a person's intelligence contributes to his quality of life. Here we must remember that "intelligence" is not just "knowledge." Instead, it is being able to use knowledge, to make connections and figure things out, to see causes and solve problems. A person may have much knowledge— that is, he may have accumulated a lot of facts—but not have much intelligence . . . or so the argument goes. As one goes from first grade to twelfth, from twelfth grade to college, and from freshman to senior, education shifts focus from mere accumulation of information (knowledge) to application of information (intelligence). And while we may accumulate more knowledge as a senior in college than

Exploring Ideas

Entitlement: Expecting to get good grades for little effort.

Cheated out of adequate job preparation.

Cheated out of quality of life.

Intelligence = being able to use knowledge.

we did as a senior in high school, the focus in college has (or should have) shifted from mere knowledge to intelligence—that is, to the ability to make good use of one's knowledge.

Other standard arguments claim other ways students might be cheated. For example, we might feel sorry for someone who doesn't get a joke—or a reference. Allusions to literature, history, philosophy, and so on allow us to say much in few words. But does the listener understand? If a person is unaware of common references—the Battle of the Bulge, Normandy, Existentialism, T. S. Eliot, World War I, Rasputin, John the Baptist, Gandhi, apartheid, Jonas Salk, Johnny Appleseed, Lewis and Clark, the Trail of Tears, slavery, the Donner Party, and so on—he misses out on conversations, on meaning, on *connecting with his fellow inmates.* Of course, here one might counter that you don't need to know all of these things. And, I agree, you don't. People tend to hang out with people who have similar interests and tastes.

5   One more argument claims that because we live in a democracy, we must be well-educated. Since all the citizens are responsible for the government, our forefathers promoted public education so that all citizens—not just the wealthy and elite—would know how to read and write. Thomas Jefferson wrote,

> I know no safe depository of the ultimate powers of society but the people themselves; and if we think them not enlightened enough to exercise their control with a wholesome discretion, the remedy is not to take it from them, but to inform their discretion by education. This is the true corrective of abuses of constitutional power. (278)

In what ways can educated citizens correct abuses in a democracy? A person's way of life, his purchases and activities—not just a person's vote or protest march—is part of the responsibility. Thus, consumers and neighbors and co-workers and so on should behave responsibly and think intelligently. It is our responsibility as citizens of a democracy.

True enough, these are all ways that students who are allowed to just slide by end up getting cheated. But another way (and one less talked about) strikes me as being far more offensive. This reason hinges on the fact that many students are not just sliding by.

In *Generation X Goes to College*, Peter Sacks illustrates that all of today's college students cannot just be thrown in the same big barrel. In describing the modern/post modern clash in education, he spends the majority of his time talking about those students who are underprepared, who lack the basic study skills required in academic work, and who demonstrate little real commitment to their own education. Yet, he does not discuss this problem in isolation.

He also mentions another type of student. For example, he introduces the reader to Marissa and Carol: "As very good students, [their] views] were virtually excluded by The College in order to accommodate the whiners and complainers" (61). And he says they "suffered not only educationally" (63). In addition to discussing specific good students, an entire chapter presents survey results about students' attitudes toward education. While he makes claims such as "nearly a quarter of the students . . . harbored a disproportionate sense of entitlement," this very statement tells the reader that a full three-quarters (that is, three out of four) students *do not* "harbor a disproportionate sense of entitlement" (54–59). He wraps up the book by focusing on another student, Andie, who he describes as "a good student, constantly picking [his] brain for information and feedback on her work" (186–87). His final paragraph, before the Epilogue, says, "Let's create a system that encourages people like Andie at least as much as the ones who don't give a damn" (187). Thus, Sacks shows that today's students are a more diverse group—in skill level, background, and attitude toward education—than has ever before been gathered together in the college classroom.

Now when we connect two things—the present grade-inflated, entitlement-driven education system that has got a foothold in most of America's high schools and colleges AND the diversity in skill and attitude toward education of today's college students—two problems appear.

10   One problem is that the motivated students are not being as challenged as they could be. Although their situation is not ideal, it is far from hopeless. They have at least three options: (1) take advantage of the easy system and learn a little along the way; (2) motivate themselves, working harder (and learning more) than the system requires them to; and (3) attend a more academically rigorous school (of course such schools still exist, though they are likely to cost more to attend).

While motivated students suffer in our too-lax system, so do the un- (or under-) motivated ones. And these students, who need our help the most, are the ones most cheated. As Sacks says, "I now believe the students are the real victims of this systematic failure of the entitlement mindset" (189). The students who are allowed to slide by, who are content to slide by, who perhaps don't even realize that they are sliding by because sliding by is all they know— those students find themselves arriving at college less prepared and less motivated than the "better students." And what happens next? Sadly, the gap between these two groups grows even wider.

The motivated student with good study skills (the one who has had at least an adequate high school education) attends class, takes notes, understands reading assignments, follows instructions, devel-

---

Left margin annotations:

Quotations illustrate particular points of the original. A properly used colon—to introduce a quote with words that could be punctuated as a sentence—provides coherence. The reader knows immediately the relationship of the words on the left and right of the colon. Quotation marks provide coherence by making clear that the words inside them are from a source.

More summary of the original argument.

Transition paragraph.

Sacks's quotation supports Bruno's argument.

Right margin annotations:

1/4 students feel entitled.

3/4 students do not.

Diversity in skill and attitude.

Motivated students are cheated.

Under-motivated students are cheated.

Gap between students grows bigger.

ops even better habits of mind, gains even more knowledge, and learns ways of making that knowledge work for her and her fellow humans. But in a system where B's are average and C's might indicate that although a student "tried" she did not demonstrate understanding or skill, the poorer students continue to advance through the system while remaining trapped at the bottom. Their level of thinking does not change much, while that of their better-prepared peers does.

Scenarios are the main support tool.

The injustice, then, has been done to the students (as Sacks says, the students are the victims). While the student has happily skipped (or unhappily slogged) along through sixteen years of formal education, she is allowed, if she wants, to come away with very little in terms of education. She is allowed, unfortunately, to escape practically unscathed by learning. The problem, of course, is that the two students have entered college on different academic levels and the one on the higher level has graduated on an *even higher* level while the one on the lower level has remained pretty much the same.

Sacks and Bruno argue the same point.

Students would do well to look around them, at the room full of fellow classmates. They should imagine that many of those students will be graduating one day. And they should imagine the students in the classroom next door and across the hall and in all the other buildings on campus. They will be graduating, too. They should also imagine all those students at the more than 4,000 other colleges throughout the country: Ohio State, Michigan, Michigan State, Findlay College, Iowa State, Oklahoma A&M, The University of Utah, California This or That. (*The Chronicle of Higher Education*'s 2000–2001 "Almanac" lists 4,096 colleges in the United States.) Many of those students are well-prepared, working hard, and developing even better habits and thinking skills.

They do not even realize they are being cheated.

The statistic creates some alarm for student readers.

15 In our competitive world, the sad truth is that even some of the very good students, though their college dreams were to be doctors and lawyers and pharmacists and engineers, will be waiting tables. Don't get me wrong: There is no shame in that. The point is, that's not why they went to college. The truth is that for some students, college will be a tough uphill climb (a climb that could have been avoided with a more adequate high school education). A sadder truth, I am afraid, is that because of skills and attitudes developed in high school, for some students the reality of genuine learning (as opposed to just getting by) might already be too late.

Competition for jobs and status.

Qualifier.

The "I" draws attention to Bruno's personal concern.

It's too late for many!

Works Cited

"Almanac." The Chronicle of Higher Education. 18 Oct. 2000 <http://chronicle.com/free/almanac/2000/almanac.htm>.

Sacks, Peter. Generation X Goes to College. Chicago: Open Court, 1996.

Writing Strategies

1. Are you able to understand Bruno's response to Peter Sacks, even if you have not read *Generation X Goes to College*? What helpful background information does Bruno provide? What other information might have been helpful?

2. Bruno defines "intelligence" in his essay. How is this definition important? Might he have deleted this definition without damaging his essay?

3. What is Bruno's main idea? Does he state it explicitly or imply it? Why is or isn't his strategy successful?

4. Explain how Bruno's essay has public resonance. That is, how is what he says important to others besides himself?

5. What evidence does Bruno provide to support his claim? Does he refer to statistics, outside sources, experience, logical reasoning? What other kind of evidence might he have provided?

Exploring Ideas

1. With a group of peers, explore through discussion how the education system you have experienced is or is not "too lax." Provide specific examples.

2. What is the purpose of education in elementary school? What is the purpose in high school? What is the purpose in college? After you write out responses, explore further with a group of peers: What else might be the purpose, or a purpose, of education?

3. How might high school better prepare students for college? How might it better prepare them for life?

4. Bruno says, "[academically] poorer students continue to advance through the system while remaining trapped at the bottom" (¶ 12). Explore Bruno's claim further: Is it true? Can you provide examples for support? Why do some students get trapped at the bottom? Is it okay for them to be trapped there? What if anything should be done about this?

Ideas for Writing

1. What does Bruno get wrong?

2. If you agree with Bruno, what new and important point might you add?

If responding to one of these ideas, go to the Analysis section of this chapter to begin developing ideas for your essay.

Cengage Learning

Reality Check

Alison Hester

While some responses point out how an argument is wrong, others spotlight the particular value of an argument. Do Americans ignore reality? In the essay below, Alison Hester, an English major at Northern Michigan University, illuminates Jayme Stayer's claim that they do. Stayer's challenging essay (226–230) uncovers layers of meaning that a reader at first might have difficulty accepting. Our initial response might be: Why criticize an amusement park? How can such criticism be worthwhile? Using the Invention questions in this chapter, Hester helps the reader understand and accept Stayer's claims.

Sea World is a place where humans can come to a better understanding of animals and experience the tranquility and magnificence of nature. To some, this is a valid and heartfelt statement about Sea World. But to others, such as author Jayme Stayer, it is not only a false statement, but one that masks a perilous underscoring issue of American culture. In his essay "Whales R Us," Jayme Stayer bravely exposes the truth behind Sea World's lofty statements and divulges the well-hidden realities of Sea World. Stayer steps apart from the crowd to reveal that what is deemed normal and satisfactory in society is actually the opposite, which, in turn, compels his readers to come to terms with reality.

In America we have produced a society that allows its citizens to ignore reality. We buy designer clothing made by children in sweatshops, drive cars that are impractical but stylish and status-setting, and permit the majority of the our population to pay little to no attention to other countries' governments or issues. Living in a country without reality is easy and pleasant and upholds our American way of life. Stayer discusses ignoring reality, shows us its destructiveness, and divulges underlying dangers in his darkly humorous analysis of Sea World.

Jayme Stayer reveals the multitude of falsehoods in Sea World. He shows how Sea World is not a representation of nature's tranquility but a bombardment of noise and underdeveloped factoid presentations. Throughout his essay, Stayer accuses Sea World of a plethora of inexcusable blunders. He turns their lofty statements about contributing to "world knowledge" (329) and making "peace with the earth" (330) against themselves to expose their blatant hypocrisy and lack of knowledgeable statements. Stayer chuckles at the idea of world knowledge being something fixed, an "accumulative spittoon" (329), and corrects this hasty, generalized outlook by explaining that world knowledge is in actuality "a set of competing claims and shifting paradigms" (329). Stayer challenges the idea that we can prospectively make peace with the earth by reminding us the world isn't innately peaceful but a place of "viruses, earthquakes, predatory animals, and a survival-of-the-fittest mentality" (330). He criticizes their mindless skits while suggesting that sex is a reality that family viewers should not have to face at Sea World. As the essay continues, it takes on a more serious nature. Stayer decides to dig even deeper into the design of Sea World to reveal its true intentions.

Stayer brings his reader's attention to the issue of Sea World's focus on education. After a thorough analysis and discussion of Sea World's "education," Stayer concludes that what takes place isn't education at all, but a form of "mind control" (331). Stayer has discovered that all of the microphones, manipulated applauding, and silly skits are there for no other purpose than to distract viewers from the reality of what they are witnessing. Sea World has decided what their audience needs to see, hear, and think in order to enjoy their visit. They make sure to keep bad thoughts out by replacing them with noise, "heartfelt" slogans, and the conjured proof of the captive animal's happiness and contentment. Sea World carefully sidesteps another harsh reality, which Stayer brings to the surface.

5   The animals at Sea World are there solely for our entertainment. In order for Sea World to hide this reality, they inform their audience of all the education that occurs at Sea World. The problem is, as Stayer points out, that "Sea World's communication of that knowledge, or to be more explicit, their refusal to level with its visitors about its real cultural role and worth" (331) is the most pressing issue of all. Sea World has decided for the better of the audience's entertainment to conceal the truth behind why Sea World even exists and instead base everything on education that doesn't even take place. What does this say about Americans and entertainment?

POINT OF CONTACT

In this chapter, the point of contact is an actual argument. You will be responding to an explicit argument that someone else has formulated or to an argument that is expressed by many people. Remember that an argument need not be an essay; arguments are also made by advertisements, posters, and billboards. To find an argument that may relate directly to the goings-on of your life and community, examine the following options:

- **Local/City/Campus Newspapers:** Search the editorial pages and letters to the editor for arguments.

- **National Newspapers:** Publications such as the *New York Times, USA Today,* and *The Wall Street Journal* have editorial pages and columnists who offer arguments on various political and social issues.

- **Magazines:** Popular weeklies (such as *Newsweek, The Nation, Time, US News and World Report*) and monthly or quarterly magazines (such as *Utne Reader* or *The New Republic*) are filled with argumentative articles and personal columns on social and political issues.

- **A Publication from Your Major** (such as *Education Journal, Nursing, Applied Science and Engineering*): Examine not only main articles, but also reviews and personal columns.

- **Disciplinary Databases** (databases that focus on specific disciplines): Go to your library and check the electronic databases for your major or a closely related one.

- **Websites:** Go to your favorite search engine and enter topical keywords (*dogs, skateboards, economy,* etc.). You might find argumentative sites or pages more quickly if you combine potential topics with words such as *law, policy, argument, crisis,* or *debate.*

| Search the Web: | dogs and law and debate | **Search** |

You can also focus your search on arguments made by bloggers by using blog searchers such as Google Blog Search (blogsearch.google.com), or a blog directory such as the one found at technorati.com.

Choose an argument that interests you and that you can address with some authority. Once you have found a potentially interesting argument, answer the following question:

- Why does the argument interest me?
  —Because something or someone has been omitted?
  —Because something or someone has been misrepresented?
  —Because I disagree or agree with it?
  —Because it raises an important issue that should be further discussed?
  —Because it changed my mind on a topic?
  —Because it is potentially important (helpful or dangerous)?

Remember that you need not strongly disagree or agree with a particular argument. A powerful response often comes from a slight agreement or disagreement.

ANALYSIS

To analyze the argument in front of you, it may help to think of that argument as having two layers: the elements of argument and the underlying warranting assumptions.

The First Layer:
The Four Elements of Argument

Thesis—the primary assertion, or main claim, about the topic.

Support—what gives substance and legitimacy to a claim.

Counterargument—refuting the claims or positions that are opposed to the ones being forwarded in the argument.

Concession—acknowledging the value of other claims.

The Second Layer:
Warranting Assumptions

Claim—an argumentative position, or thesis, being put forward.

Grounds—the support for the position.

Warranting Assumption—the idea, often unstated, that connects the claim and grounds.

Explicit: stated directly in the text

Implied: not stated, but suggested by supporting points

The First Layer: The Four Elements of Argument

Thesis Before we can respond to an argument, we must know *exactly* what is being argued. That is, we must figure out the thesis, the particular stance the writer takes on the topic. Finding the thesis for a written argument can be trickier than it seems. While some essays have explicit theses (stated directly), others are implied (not stated, but suggested by the supporting points). Most often, in sophisticated academic essays, the thesis does not come at the end of the first paragraph. Instead, it comes along later, after the debate has been explained—and even after other perspectives have been addressed. Once we locate the thesis (or understand it based on the details of the argument), we can then see how it is supported.

Support Initially, the thesis might seem outlandish, but good support strategies will invite readers to accept even the most extreme thesis statements. Remember that support comes in a variety of forms:

Statistics	Scenarios
Authorities	Appeal to Logic
Facts	Appeal to Emotion
Examples	Appeal of Character
Allusions	Appeal to Need
Personal Testimonies/Anecdotes	Appeal to Value

Depending on the medium of the argument (essay, poster, etc.), the support may be varied. Or the writer may depend on a single key support strategy. Remember that all these support strategies can help create a powerful argument. (Don't be fooled into believing that statistics are the only certain support strategy.) The key question, however, lies in their connection to the thesis. We might ask: *How well does the support strategy connect to the thesis?* Or, *Given this argument, how appropriate is the support strategy?* For a detailed explanation of support strategies, see page 243 in Chapter 7.

Counterargument Sophisticated arguments counterargue. That is, they anticipate and refute opposing claims. In fact, the success of an argument may depend on its counterarguments—on the ability of the writer to fend off opposing claims. Remember a key counterargument strategy, the turnabout paragraph, in which a writer explains an opposing perspective and then responds directly.

Concession Concessions acknowledge the value of opposing claims. Writers who concede acknowledge that others' positions may offer some insight outside of the writers' own claims. When writers concede points, their arguments do not lose force; instead, they appear more fair-minded. A writer who concedes shows that he or she has considered a range of other ideas.

Invention Questions

Now, examine the argument to which you are responding. To fully understand the first layer of the argument, answer the following questions:

- What is the main claim/thesis?
- What are the means of support for the main claim?
- Do the support strategies sufficiently prove the thesis?
- How does the argument address opposing claims? Are those claims sufficiently refuted?
- Does the argument concede to outside positions? What is the effect of those concessions?
- Does the writer define the issue correctly?

Here, Daniel Bruno responds to one of these Invention questions. He uses the question as a springboard to discover a specific shortcoming in Sacks's book:

Does the writer define the issue correctly?

Sacks defines the issue correctly as far as he defines it. Entitlement education has the negative effect that he says it does, but he fails, it seems, to discuss or focus on an important aspect of the issue, which is that some students, who don't have an entitlement mentality, learn a great deal in school while others, who do, don't learn a great deal, or very much at all. The students who have the entitlement mentality slide by while their classmates are learning more and more. The gap between the two groups widens. So, what does this mean to those students who feel entitled to good grades because they showed up (high school) or paid the tuition (college)? They get grades, but did they learn anything? Did they get an education?

Rogerian Argument

Rogerian argument is based on the work of Carl Rogers (1902–1987), who is best known for his contributions to clinical psychology and psychotherapy. Rogers's ideas about mutual understanding, trust, and supportive rather than competitive rhetoric have become key concepts in argument. According to Rogerian argument, arguers should first try to understand opposing views. In "Communication: Its Blocking and Its Facilitation" (1952), he writes, "The next time you get into an argument . . . stop the discussion for a moment and for an experiment, institute this rule. 'Each person can speak up for himself only after he has first restated the ideas and feelings of the previous speaker accurately, and to that speaker's satisfaction.'" This means that "before presenting your own point of view, it would be necessary for you to really achieve the other speaker's frame of reference—to understand his thoughts and feelings so well that you could summarize them for him." This sounds simple, but isn't. Rogers says, "But if you try it you will discover it one of the most difficult things you have ever tried to do. However, once you have been able to see the other's point view, your own comments will have to be drastically revised." According to Rogers, doing this takes courage: "If I enter, as fully as I am able, into the private world of a neurotic or psychotic individual, isn't there a risk that I might become lost in that world?"

As you respond to an argument for this chapter, first accurately summarize it. For help, ask a group of classmates to suggest where you might be misrepresenting the original argument.

The Second Layer: Warranting Assumptions

Beneath the first, most visible, layer of an argument lurk warranting assumptions: the beliefs that connect points in an argument. Warranting assumptions are the root system of an argument; although they most often go unstated, they are as important as the most directly worded points. And when we dig up warranting assumptions and investigate them closely, we can decide for ourselves if they are reasonable.

We need intellectual tools for digging up assumptions. Philosopher Stephen Toulmin has developed a powerful analytical system for this job. In his perspective, every argument has a structure with interrelated parts. Using this, we can see how those parts relate, and how well they function. Here are the three basic elements:

Claim: The main argumentative position (or thesis) being put forward.

Grounds: The support for the position (evidence, examples, illustrations, etc.).

Warranting Assumption: The idea, often unstated, that connects the claim and the grounds—or that justifies the use of the grounds for the claim.

Three Basic Elements of Argumentative Statements

Claim
▲
Warranting Assumption
▼
Grounds

The warranting assumption lies (often hidden) between the claim and the grounds. See how the elements work in the following example:

Claim: Sport utility vehicles are dangerous.

Grounds: Many different models roll over easily.

Warranting Assumption: **Vehicles that roll over easily are dangerous.**

The assumption lies between the claim and the grounds, connecting them logically.

In this example, the rollover frequency of SUVs supports the claim that they are dangerous. The warranting assumption (vehicles that roll over easily are dangerous) lies between the claim and the grounds. The assumption is entirely acceptable; few people would challenge it. But consider a different argument:

Claim: Sport utility vehicles are valuable to the average American driver.

Grounds: The extra-large carrying capacity and four-wheel drive capability meet traveling needs.

Warranting Assumption: Extra-large carrying capacity and four-wheel drive are valuable for the average American driver's traveling needs.

The assumption here is less acceptable. Someone might argue against this warranting assumption on the grounds that the average American driver does not need extra-large carrying capacity and four-wheel drive, and that these aspects are actually unnecessary for most drivers. Stating the assumption thus reveals a particular weakness in the argument and provides an opportunity to respond.

Dissecting arguments in this fashion allows for various critical opportunities. Writers can focus attention on (take exception or agree with) two different layers of an argument: grounds and/or assumptions. Consider, for example, the first claim: *Sport utility vehicles are dangerous.* Although the assumption *vehicles that roll over easily are dangerous* is acceptable, the grounds for the claim *many models roll over easily* can be challenged. Someone might agree with the assumption but cite statistics showing that only a few models are prone to rollover accidents.

Claim:	Sport utility vehicles are dangerous.	
Grounds:	Many different models roll over easily.	(Questionable)
Warranting Assumption:	Vehicles that roll over easily are dangerous.	(Acceptable)

Responding with such statistics could help a writer challenge the original argument. In this case, the responding writer would be challenging the grounds. For other arguments, both the grounds and assumption might be arguable:

Claim:	The environment is not in danger from human influence.	
Grounds:	The environment is supporting the Earth's population today.	(Questionable)
Warranting Assumption:	The present human population directly illustrates the health of the environment.	(Questionable)

Here, both the grounds and the warranting assumption are questionable. While the grounds could be refuted on their own terms (by illustrating the vast numbers of people starving throughout the world), the more interesting response might point to the warranting assumption. The mere presence of people, of course, does not indicate the health of the environment. Someone, for instance, might point to dramatic increases in skin and other cancers to illustrate the effects of greenhouse gases and environmental contamination. In this case, discovering the warranting assumption would allow a responding writer to point out a flaw in the logic.

Activity

In groups, decide on the warranting assumption for the following claims and explain why each assumption is acceptable or questionable.

Claim: Consumerism is out of control in American life.
Grounds: Many people are going into debt to pay for luxury items.

Claim: America is losing a sense of community and social connectedness.
Grounds: The number of bowling teams has steadily decreased in the past 20 years.

Claim: People rely too much on technology that puts us out of touch with our neighbors and our own bodies.
Grounds: Leaf blowers are increasingly popular.

Now go to the argument you have chosen to examine and answer the following questions. They will help you to develop a response.

- What is the warranting assumption?
- Is the assumption acceptable or arguable?
- Can I prove that the assumption is incorrect?
- What else does the author of the argument assume (about life, identity, society, people's behavior, time, politics, human nature, etc.)?

PUBLIC RESONANCE

Public resonance refers to the way in which a topic (or argument) relates to a community. In most cases, any published argument that you find will already have public resonance, especially if it comes from a newspaper, magazine, or journal. Your job, however, is not complete. As a responding writer, you can draw attention to the effects of the original argument on its readers and on the community at large.

To develop public resonance, examine the argument to which you will respond, and answer the following questions:

- Has the argument had an impact on readers? Any specific person or people?
- How *could* the argument affect people (negatively or positively)?
- What other issues or situations does the argument relate to or address?
- How can I relate the argument to the needs/wants of my audience (or anyone who is involved in the topic)?

Invention Workshop

In a small group of writers, use one of the Invention questions to start a discussion about your topic. First, briefly explain the original argument (the argument to which you are responding) to your group members. Then pose the question. (It may be helpful to write the question on a board or have all group members focus on this page so the question does not get lost in the discussion.)

Diana is responding to Ward Churchill's essay "Crimes Against Humanity." In a discussion with peers, her argument takes on several layers. Notice how Diana's thinking begins to extend beyond her initial reaction. At first, she is simply offended by Churchill's argument—a gut reaction. But then she starts to consider the public effects of that reaction. This is an important intellectual turn. It is easy to have a gut reaction, but good writers ask questions about the feelings they have. Like Diana, they seek out intellectual turns.

How could the argument affect people (negatively or positively)?

Diana: Churchill's argument made me mad, and I think it may do the same to a lot of people. It basically suggests that everyone who supports certain professional sports teams is somehow tied to genocide.

Jack: I think that's his point, isn't it?

Diana: Yes, and I don't buy it, and I don't think most people would.

Jack: Does that mean that most people are right, or that most people don't see their own racism? Like Churchill says, during World War II most Americans were okay with the racist stereotypes of Japanese people. So, does that make such stereotyping okay?

Diana: Of course not. But making such an extreme point as Churchill seems counterproductive. When he comes out and says that wearing a Cleveland Indians baseball hat is like committing genocide, I think he's setting himself up for a certain amount of disagreement.

Marcus: But is he really making the connection that clearly?

Diana: Well, maybe not, but I think most people would see it that way . . . and they wouldn't like it.

Jack: Maybe that's an important point. Churchill's argument is probably more involved than what people want to hear.

Diana: And that's usually the case with arguments about race. But, still, calling mainstream America racist and making a connection between a national pastime and the Holocaust is going too far.

Jack: Why? Are you afraid of offending mainstream Americans who like sports?

Diana: No. I just wonder how valuable it is.

Jack: But isn't that what mainstream America said to the civil rights activists of the '60s? They didn't want activists to be offensive or confrontational, but most people are not going to change their thinking unless they are moved deeply—and sometimes that means they have to be offended.

Diana: So you're saying that mainstream America needs to be pushed before it will accept new ideas? Maybe.

Jack: Yeah, I think that's been shown throughout history. People don't just change their minds and suddenly become more enlightened.

In the following excerpt, Daniel Bruno explores *what* and *how* people might think about the topic of student entitlement. Here, Bruno has narrowed in on a particular issue from the original argument (Peter Sacks's book about college students). It's not merely that students shouldn't feel entitled to high grades. Bruno goes further and discovers the double jeopardy of entitlement: Those who feel entitled are "missing out" on their own educations:

How can I relate the argument to the needs/wants of my audience (or anyone who is involved in the topic)?

Some students feel entitled, which means expecting a good grade automatically, without working or learning anything. Some don't. The wants of the entitlement students are different than their needs. They want a grade or degree but need to learn and work. Interestingly, the students who feel entitled are the ones missing out, while the ones who don't feel entitled benefit. Maybe the students who believe they are entitled would benefit from thinking about the students who think differently, the ones who they will be competing against in the future, the ones who perhaps will be better prepared and have a better work ethic. The entitlement-minded students may find out too late that others are working hard and developing good skills and attitudes.

Research

What have others said about your topic? If you are responding to a specific text (like an article or a book), go beyond that author's views and seek out other perspectives. Examine your invention writing and seek out keywords. Enter them into a periodical database search. (Remember that periodical databases, such as InfoTrac College Edition, rely on keywords rather than phrases.) Enter main nouns linked together with *and*. If you have no luck, keep changing the nouns; try replacing them with synonyms. For instance, Bruno might enter: *students and college and entitlement*. Then, he might try: *students and college and attitude*. He might replace *attitude* with *achievement, success, study skills, apathy,* or a combination of these.

> As a responding writer, you can draw attention to the effects of the original argument on its readers and on the community at large.

THESIS

Responding to arguments is complicated because another set of claims must be engaged. But do not let those other claims confuse you. Resist chasing ideas throughout the original argument, and instead focus on a particular issue and then springboard into your own reasoning. Your argument might do one or more of the following:

- Redefine the issue according to your understanding.

    Sacks shows how consumerism has invaded education, leading some students to expect good grades for little effort. But he fails, it seems, to emphasize enough a most harmful effect of this sense of entitlement. (318)

- Argue for the value of a particular point or assumption in the original text.

    In "Technology, Movement, and Sound," Ed Bell argues against our culture's increasing love affair with technology. The real value of his argument is its focus on the relationship between personal technology and public effects.

- Argue against a particular point or assumption in the original text.

    Simon Benlow insists that students are increasingly more consumerist in their approach to education, but consumption is not inherently passive or anti-educational.

- Extend the original argument to include a broader set of ideas.

    A great books education is practical, as David Crabtree argues; however, it is not practical because it makes one "wise," as he suggests. Instead, a great books education develops key intellectual skills that, in turn, help students succeed in various academic and professional pursuits.

- Narrow the argument and suggest an important emphasis.

    As Jayme Stayer argues in "Whales R Us," theme parks such as Sea World are a "reflection of American culture . . . not a promoter of political change." His argument shows us that mainstream American culture may entirely lack a language for political change.

As you can see in these statements, it is not enough to say "I disagree" or "I agree." Instead, a project such as this benefits from a more focused point—one that shows something (important, harmful, inaccurate, valuable, etc.) in the original argument.

Use the following questions to help generate the thesis of your argumentative response:

- With what *particular* point do I agree or disagree?
- How are my assumptions different from or similar to those of the writer?
- How is the original argument too narrow or too exclusive?
- What particular point in the original argument might readers fail to see? Why is it so important?
- How can I extend or broaden the original argument?

Resist chasing ideas; instead, focus on a particular issue.

Evolution of a Thesis

Diana's thesis (first developed in the Public Resonance section) focuses on how people might respond to Churchill's argument. In the following, notice how her idea evolves from summary, to gut reaction, to analytical insight:

- In "Crimes Against Humanity," Ward Churchill argues that the use of Native American symbols for sports teams is racist.

  Summary

- Churchill's argument made me mad, and I think it may do the same to a lot of people. It basically suggests that everyone who supports certain professional sports teams is somehow tied to genocide.

  Gut reaction

- Mainstream America might need to be pushed before it will accept new ideas.

  Analytical insight

- Churchill's "Crimes Against Humanity" reminds us that mainstream opinions often do not change unless they encounter shocking, even offensive, claims.

  Focused statement

Diana goes from summary statement to a gut reaction to an analytical statement about that reaction to an insight about mainstream opinions. Throughout this intellectual journey, she discovers something specific about Churchill's argument and its potential effect on readers. Diana also moves from dismissing the argument to revealing a quality in it.

Thinking Further

Writers may decide that their gut reaction to an argument will suffice as a thesis statement. However, while gut reactions get a writer started, they are often too vague. The following statements show what someone might feel directly after reading Paulin's, Crabtree's, or Churchill's arguments. While these initial feelings are valuable, they are only the beginning:

- Ann Marie Paulin's argument is right on target.
- David Crabtree's argument is important for college students to hear.
- In "Crimes Against Humanity," Ward Churchill is just making a mountain out of a molehill.

Now, those initial reactions must be explored. The writers might ask:

- What particular idea or assumption of Paulin's argument is insightful or valuable? Why is it insightful or valuable?
- Why is Crabtree's argument important? What particular aspect is valuable to college students?
- Why might the issue really be a mountain?

In asking such questions, the writers can take their gut reaction to the next level—to more focused ideas:

- Ann Marie Paulin reveals the quiet everyday prejudices against overweight people.
- David Crabtree's argument correctly challenges the common misconception that college courses translate directly into real-world experience.
- Churchill describes a view of American history and sports that most people do not consider.

Revision

With a group of peers, explore your thesis statements. Each group member should share his or her thesis in turn. Then the group should collectively attempt to narrow it by asking questions like those above. Go after broad adjectives (*valuable, wrong, irresponsible, good, intense,* etc.). Try to prompt the writer to give specific descriptors or explanations.

Also, check out the Common Thesis Problems in Chapter 7 on page 241. The same problems may lurk in this project as well. Make certain to avoid them!

RHETORICAL TOOLS

Even though you are responding to someone else's argument, you are still creating your own argument. Consider all the argumentative strategies introduced in Chapter 7.

Using Support

Remember that you have the whole world beyond the original argument to support your points. You can use various forms of evidence (such as personal testimony, examples, and facts, as well as allusions to history, popular culture, and news events) and appeals.

- What particular examples from everyday life show my point?

- Does a historical situation or trend (say, the rise of a particular fashion, organization, or individual) illustrate something about my topic?

- How has popular culture treated my topic? Does it show up in television shows, movies, or commercials? If so, how is it characterized, mishandled, or celebrated?

- How has literature (novels, poetry, drama, short stories) dealt with my topic? Have fictional characters illustrated something important about the topic or some behavior related to it?

- How does nature (animals, life cycles, plants, biological processes, and so on) demonstrate something about my topic?

- How can this topic relate to people's sense of logic? What line of reasoning can I create for the reader to follow?

(See pages 242–249 in Chapter 7: Making Arguments, for more help in developing evidence and appeals for your argument.)

Counterarguing

Good writers try to address specific opposing claims. Notice, for example, how Alison Hester responds to an opposing position:

> Those who believe that Sea World truly does support education and living harmoniously with the earth's creatures inevitably disagree with Stayer's arguments and disdainful outlook on Sea World.
>
> Some might argue that Sea World is really a place of education. This would mean that there is no mind control and Stayer's argument falls. If Sea World really is based around teaching, learning, and the transfer of knowledge then Stayer must have made countless inaccurate observations. That would mean that all the whale's back flips and the dolphin's synchronized jumps were not the point of the show, but rather the actual facts about the whales and the dolphins were. This is obviously not so. People go to Sea World to see these sea creatures perform magnificent shows and create presumed warm connections between humans and nature. Sea World is not about the animal's vanishing habitats, or their family dynamics, or even how we can help these animals. Although these subjects might be footnotes at Sea World, the real purpose is undeniably entertainment.
>
> We would like to believe that Sea World is simply a fabulous way to learn. But after reading Stayer's essay, having the realities of Sea World revealed, one cannot deny that he makes a strong case.

As you develop your own argument, examine the particular points of the original argument with which you disagree or find fault.

Consider the following questions for your own argument:

- Apart from the author of the original argument, who might disagree with my position? Why?

- What reasons do people have for disagreeing with me?

- What evidence would support an opposing argument?

Conceding and Qualifying Points

When responding to argument, a writer should be especially mindful of giving credit to others' points. For example, in Bruno's response to Peter Sacks's book, he acknowledges several important elements of Sacks's argument:

> His final paragraph, before the Epilogue, says, "Let's create a system that encourages people like Andie at least as much as the ones who don't give a damn" (187). Thus, Sacks shows that today's students are a more diverse group—in skill level, background, and attitude toward education—than has ever before been gathered together in the college classroom.

Answering the following questions will help you to see possible concessions for your own argument:

- Does the original argument make any valid points?
- Does my argument make any large, but necessary, leaps? (Should I acknowledge them?)
- Do I ask my audience to imagine a situation that is fictional? (Should I acknowledge the potential shortcomings of a fictional or hypothetical situation?)
- Do I ask my audience to accept generalizations? (Should I acknowledge those generalizations?)

Remembering Logical Fallacies

Logical fallacies are logical stumbles—gaps or shortcomings in reasoning. Examine the original argument closely to determine if it is free of fallacies. Finding logical fallacies in an argument can help you to generate a response. For example, in the following passage, the writer points to a logical shortcoming in the original argument:

> Smith argues that incoming college students cannot handle the intellectual rigors of academia. He characterizes an entire generation as "undisciplined and whimsical." But like all arguments about entire generations, Smith's depends upon a hasty generalization. The truth about today's college students is far more complex than Smith's assertions, and any statement that seeks to characterize them as a whole should be looked upon with suspicion.

See a list and examples of logical fallacies in Chapter 7, page 249.

Invention Workshop

Need some help? Borrow the brains of your peers. In a small group, share thesis statements, and then use the following questions to generate ideas for one another's arguments.

Support

- Can you offer the writer a scenario to support his or her stance?
- What popular cultural, historical, or literary references come to mind as you consider this topic—and the writer's stance?

Counterargument/Concession

- What valid points or perspectives does the original argument offer? (If the writer takes an opposing position, should he or she concede?)
- Why might the writer be wrong (oversimplifying, mischaracterizing, misjudging)?

ORGANIZATIONAL STRATEGIES

Should I Quote the Original Argument?

Quoting is like putting a spotlight on a key passage. Responding writers sometimes want to draw attention not only to a point, but also to the particular way the author delivered it. A quote can flag the shortcoming in the original text:

> In her argument, Ross claims banks "only share customers' personal information with affiliated companies" (43). However, an "affiliated company" in the present economic environment can be any company with which a bank does business. Because most financial institutions are parts of huge conglomerates, they can be justified in "sharing" information with a practically unlimited number of companies seeking to exploit people and invade their personal lives. In other words, Ross's argument only further conceals the exploitive policies of many financial institutions.

Sometimes writers quote the original argument to illustrate the importance or value of a particular point, or to extend an idea. Notice Bruno's quotation of Peter Sacks:

> While motivated students suffer in our too-lax system, so do the un- (or under-) motivated ones. And these students, who need our help the most, are the ones most cheated. As Sacks says, "I now believe the students are the real victims of this systematic failure of the entitlement mindset" (189). The students who are allowed to slide by, who are content to slide by, who perhaps don't even realize that they are sliding by because sliding by is all they know—those students find themselves arriving at college less prepared and less motivated than the "better students." And what happens next? Sadly, the gap between these two groups grows even wider.

Here, Bruno builds his argument from Sacks's point. That is, he begins with Sacks's idea, and then goes further to show the greater extent of the problem.

Using quotation can be a powerful strategy in drawing attention to key passages. However, be careful not to quote too often. Rather than quote the original argument (or any outside source), you may choose to summarize or paraphrase. The exact language of a source is often unnecessary and can be a distraction. Notice how Hester restates information from Stayer's original argument in her own words by summarizing or paraphrasing, but quotes a few key words:

> Jayme Stayer reveals the multitude of falsehoods in Sea World. He shows how Sea World is not a representation of nature's tranquility but a bombardment of noise and underdeveloped factoid presentations. Throughout his article, Stayer accuses Sea World of a plethora of inexcusable blunders. He turns their lofty statements about contributing to "world knowledge" (329) and making "peace with the earth" (330) against themselves to expose their blatant hypocrisy and lack of knowledgeable statements. Stayer chuckles at the idea of world knowledge being something fixed, an "accumulative spittoon" (329), and corrects this hasty generalization outlook by explaining that world knowledge is in actuality "a set of competing claims and shifting paradigms" (329). Stayer challenges the idea that we can propsectively make peace with the earth by reminding us the world isn't innately peaceful but a place of "viruses, earthquakes, predatory animals, and a survival-of-the-fittest mentality" (330). He criticizes their mindless skits while suggesting that sex is a reality that family viewers should not have to face at Sea World. As the essay continues, it takes on a more serious nature. Stayer decides to dig even deeper into the design of Sea World to reveal its true intentions.

Activity

In groups or alone, examine the excerpt above. Why might Hester have decided to quote when she did?

Quotation, using the exact words of a source, puts a spotlight on another writer's language. It allows writers to integrate especially important phrasing or passages. Quotes match the source word for word and are placed within quotation marks.

Paraphrase is a detailed rewording of the original source using your own words and expressions and conveying the detail and complexity of the original text. Although different from the source in organization, sentence structure, and wording, a paraphrase matches the meaning of the original passage. Paraphrased information is not placed within quotation marks.

Summary, like paraphrasing, involves expressing a source's idea in your own words instead of the source's words, but unlike paraphrasing, summary removes much of the detail. Summarized information is not placed within quotation marks.

For more information on quoting, summary, and paraphrase, see Chapter 13: Research and Writing.

Invention Workshop

With a group of peers, examine the argument to which each group member is responding.

1. What specific language from the argument might the writer quote? Why?

2. What ideas should be summarized in a sentence or two?

3. What ideas should be paraphrased (detailed restatement in the responder's own words)?

How Should I Structure My Response?

The structure of your essay largely depends on what you intend to address from the original argument. You can use some standard organization strategies for argument essays, such as:

Point A (from original argument)
Your evaluation and response

Point B (from original argument)
Your evaluation and response

Point C (from the original argument)
Your evaluation and response

Of course, you also might have points D, E, F, and so on. And each of your evaluations and responses can vary in length, from a sentence to several paragraphs, depending on the main point of your essay.

You might decide that the opposing viewpoint requires significant explanation, and that it would be best to keep all your points grouped together rather than separating them with passages from the original:

Point A (from original argument)
Point B (from original argument)
Point C (from original argument)
Your evaluation and response to A
Your evaluation and response to B
Your evaluation and response to C

Remember that the turnabout paragraph (see page 251) is a good strategy for counterargument. A turnabout paragraph begins with one point, and then changes directions, giving the reader a clear indication of that change.

WRITER'S VOICE

Rogerian Argument

Because argument can potentially create hostility and turn people away from each other, Carl Rogers developed an argumentative perspective that emphasizes building connections between different positions (as shown on page 279). People who use Rogerian argument look for similarities rather than differences between arguments. Such a strategy creates an engaging voice—one that invites exploration of ideas rather than harsh dismissals. All the writers in this chapter establish common ground with the argument to which they are responding.

> George Orwell will forever be a hero of mine. When I read *1984* in high school, I became sensitized to the workings of propaganda. After more than forty years as a linguist and cognitive scientist, I remain sensitized.
>
> When I first read "Politics and the English Language" as an undergraduate in the late 1950s, I loved it. Nearly fifty years later I find it an anachronism. Why? I, and those in my profession, have learned a lot about the brain, the mind, and language since then. Orwell's essay belongs to an earlier time, a time that lacked our deepening understanding of how the human brain works.

Even though his essay will show how Orwell was wrong, George Lakoff begins by acknowledging the value of Orwell's ideas and explaining that they are understandably flawed because since Orwell's time we have developed "a deepening understanding of how the human brain works." Daniel Bruno takes a similar approach:

> In his book *Generation X Goes to College,* Peter Sacks describes, among other things, the sense of entitlement that some students in today's consumerist culture have toward a college education. One entire chapter explores this issue alone, providing examples of this "sense" and looking into its "humble beginnings."

Sacks shows how consumerism has invaded education, leading some students to expect good grades for little effort. But he fails, it seems, to emphasize enough a most harmful effect of this entitlement. The biggest problem, as I see it, is that although students are able to graduate from high school (and even some colleges) with minimal effort, those students may find themselves cheated in the long run.

Rogers suggests that before responding, one should accurately restate the ideas being responded to. Notice how Bruno establishes common ground by summing up and acknowledging the value of the idea to which he is responding.

Invention Workshop

With a group of classmates, seek out the common ground between your argument and the argument to which you are responding. How might you use similarities in thinking as a way of getting at the key difference?

The Invisible/Present "I"

Writers often wonder if they should use the first-person pronoun *I*. Using *I* may be especially tempting in argumentative writing. However, many academic disciplines favor writing that does not draw attention to the writer (to the *I*). And writing for English courses, which often focuses on personal insights and reflection, avoids unnecessary attention to *I* as well. This is because argumentative writing implies or assumes the presence of the writer. In other words, every claim or position in a paper that is not attributed to some other source belongs to the writer; therefore, phrases such as "I think that," "In my opinion," or "I believe" are often unnecessary.

However, the first-person pronoun occasionally can be used to make a distinction between an outside argument and the writer's own opinion. If the writer is dealing with several ideas or outside opinions, he or she might decide that using the first-person pronoun refocuses attention on the main argument. For example, notice how Bruno uses "I" in his introductory paragraph, which is excerpted on page 290:

> The biggest problem, as I see it, is that although students are able to graduate from high school (and even some colleges) with minimal effort, those students may find themselves cheated in the long run.

Activity

If you are enrolled in multiple courses, ask each instructor about his or her stance on first-person pronouns in writing. You might also ask about the standard practice of your major, or examine a professional journal in your field of study to see how (and how often) first-person pronouns are used.

Consider Tone

If you are responding to a specific argument, you are encountering a tone (the color or mood of a writer's voice). Sometimes writers who are responding to an argument choose to mimic the tone of the original argument. In other words, if you are responding to a very sober and formal argument, you might do well to respond in kind. On the other hand, changing the tone of a discussion can be a powerful rhetorical tool. When writers want to challenge an argument, they may not only argue against the ideas but also shift the tone to their own particular liking. For example, imagine a politician arguing against the comedic rants of Howard Stern.

The politician might put forth a very sober argument against Stern—thereby arguing on her own ground rather than on Stern's comedic turf. The opposite is often done: Many writers (and public figures) argue informally to challenge a seemingly formal argument. Consider programs such as *The Daily Show with Jon Stewart* and *Saturday Night Live* or Michael Moore's film *Roger & Me.* They respond to "serious" political arguments by spoofing them—by revealing their flaws and deliberately changing their tone.

As you examine your chosen argument (the one to which you are responding) and your own position, consider tone. Ask yourself the following:

- Has the tone been established by someone else's argument?
- Do I want to change the tone slightly, or dramatically?
- What effect would a change in tone have on the argument?

Changing the tone of a discussion can be a powerful rhetorical tool.

VITALITY

For any essay project, boiling down text is a key strategy. When writers approach a final draft, they benefit from taking time away and then returning to the draft with one goal in mind: to make it more concise and intensive. This requires the willingness to boil away unnecessary phrases, clauses, and sentences. To help you make decisions at the sentence level, consider the following.

Avoid Over-Embedding

Sometimes sentences can become over-embedded, or jumbled by too many overlapping clauses. In the following sentences, notice how dependent clauses (those beginning with *that, because, if, how, which, what,* etc.) keep you from linking the main ideas in the sentence:

1. The problem that Thoreau has with the government that depends upon the majority is that the majority often fails to think of what is right and what is wrong.

2. King wonders if because the white moderate assumes the wrong thing about time, they will not want to change society for the better for all people.

3. The moderate does not consider about the way time really works to the goals of evil.

Good writers delete unnecessary words and sentences.

In each case, the sentence offers a long clause where a specific noun would help the reader connect ideas. For example, in the first sentence, we have to traverse two *that* clauses before we know what "the problem" is. The clauses overlap, piling up on us as we try to connect the subject ("the problem") and its verb ("is"). The sentence might be rewritten:

> According to Thoreau, a government of the majority has a key problem: Majorities often fail to distinguish between right and wrong.

Notice that the revised sentence contains fewer clauses and phrases. Instead, it relies on more direct connections between nouns and verbs.

Activity

Rewrite the second and third sentences to the left. Try to avoid overlapping clauses.

Break Bad Habits

Developing as a writer involves identifying and breaking bad habits. Some writers are surprised to learn that they have picked up their worst habits from previous writing courses. For example, instead of working to boil down text, they try to stretch it out. This raises the question: If I am supposed to delete unnecessary phrases, clauses, and sentences, how can I make my essay long enough? The answer is: Invention!

The parts of the writing process (and the sections of this textbook) are not entirely separate from each other; they are all connected. Vitality, for example, relates to invention. As writers work to make their writing more lively, they delete not only phrases, clauses, and sentences, but examples, paragraphs, and entire sections when possible. Good writing packs a punch: Instead of taking longer to say less, good writing says more in fewer words. To reach the required length, writers don't simply dig up a lot of facts, statistics, or examples; instead, they complicate their thinking through analysis. As you boil down your essay, complicate your thinking by revisiting the Invention questions in this chapter.

Clean Up Attributive Phrases

Attributive phrases connect an author and his or her ideas: *According to Biff Harrison; in Jergerson's argument; as Jacobs points out* and so on. Because you are dealing with another text, you may need to draw consistent attention to the author's words and use attributive phrases. But be cautious of clumsy phrasing such as the following:

1. In "Letter from Birmingham Jail," by Martin Luther King, Jr., King writes about how society can be unjust.

2. In Jayme Stayer's perspective, Sea World reveals the shallowest qualities of American culture. He believes that "[t]he American traits that Sea World reflects most clearly are its gullibility and irrationality."

3. Ann Marie Paulin wrote an essay about incivility and obesity. It is called "Cruelty, Civility, and Other Weighty Matters."

Each of these sentences makes a similar error: Each draws an unnecessary degree of attention to the act of writing or to the author's thoughts. Each could be boiled down. For the first sentence, Martin Luther King, Jr., only needs mentioning once:

1. In "Letter from Birmingham Jail," Martin Luther King, Jr. writes about injustice.

For the second sentence, a colon can replace "he believes that." (Generally, a colon says to readers, "Here's the quotation that proves my point," so it can replace any statement that suggests this idea.)

2. In Jayme Stayer's perspective, Sea World reveals the shallowest qualities of American culture: "The American traits that Sea World reflects most clearly are its gullibility and irrationality."

For the third, the fact that Paulin wrote the essay does not need to be stated. It is better to imply the point:

3. Ann Marie Paulin's essay "Cruelty, Civility, and Other Weighty Matters" shows the deeply personal impact of media images.

Generally speaking, writers do not need an entire sentence or clause to name a title or make a connection between a writer and her words. It is sufficient to use possessive phrases, such as "Paulin's essay."

Try Absolutes!

Absolute phrases—which consist of a noun, modifiers, and often a participle—modify an entire clause or sentence, not just a word or phrase. Absolutes can help intensify ideas—weaving them together to create a more sophisticated, yet concise, sentence. Consider the following two sentences:

> The beauty pageant had finally concluded and the whole ordeal had finally come to an end. Cindy Bosley could now escape the desperate feelings around her.

Although these sentences are correct and functional, they can be combined with an absolute phrase. The verbs of the first sentence will be omitted, the ideas slightly compressed into an absolute phrase and attached to the clause:

> The beauty pageant concluded and the whole ordeal finally over, Cindy Bosley could escape the desperate feelings around her.

If they are used intermittently, and sparingly, absolute phrases can add subtle variety to an essay. They help writers (and their readers) escape the march of subject/verb, subject/verb sentence patterns.

Activity

With a partner, turn two sentences in your draft into one by creating an absolute phrase.

PEER REVIEW

Exchange drafts with at least one other writer. Before exchanging, underline your thesis (or write it on the top of the first page) so that others will more quickly get a sense of your main idea.

Use the following questions to respond to specific issues in the drafts:

1. Can any phrases or terms in the thesis be narrowed? If so, circle them and make some suggestions for more focus.

2. Is the main idea of the original argument sufficiently summarized? (Could the summary be shorter? How?)

3. Where could the writer support broad statements with specific evidence (allusions, examples, facts, personal testimony, scenario)? Writers often fall into the habit of making broad claims that should be illustrated. For instance, someone might argue, "All students learn differently." But such a statement needs to be supported with specifics. Otherwise, a reader has no reason to accept it, no reason to see it as true.

4. Where might the writer oversimplify the original argument/issue or mischaracterize the original author's position? (Look especially for ad hominem or strawperson logical fallacies. See page 249.)

5. What paragraphs shift focus? Where do you sense gaps in the lines of reasoning? How could the writer fill those gaps?

6. Circle any clichés or overly broad statements that could be transformed into specific and revelatory insights.

7. Consider sentence vitality:

- What sentences are over-embedded? (Point to any clauses that overlap with other clauses, causing a disconnect between ideas.)

- Examine attributive phrases. Point out unnecessary phrases or sentences that could be boiled down.

- Consider vitality strategies from other chapters:

   —Where can the writer change linking verbs to active verbs?

   —Where can the writer avoid drawing attention to *I* and *you*?

   —Help the writer change unnecessary clauses to phrases.

   —Help the writer change unnecessary phrases to words.

   —Point to expletives (such as *there are* and *it is*).

   —Help the writer change passive verbs to active verbs for more vitality.

   —Help the reader avoid common grammatical errors: comma splices, sentence fragments, or pronoun/antecedent agreement.

Questions for Research

If the writer used outside sources:

- Where must he or she include in-text citations? (See pages 484–485.)

- Are quotations blended smoothly into the argument and punctuated correctly? (See pages 475–478.)

- Where could more direct textual cues or transitions help the reader? (See pages 479–481.)

- Is the Works Cited page formatted properly? (See pages 486–497.)

DELIVERY

Just as we discuss (or explore ideas) with others, we play out discussions internally, in our own minds. And the ideas, the thoughts and opinions, that we express outwardly to others often originate in our own internal dialogues.

Have you ever considered how you explore ideas internally through imaginary dialogue with others?

- For several days keep a journal, jotting down imaginary (internal) discussions you have. (To do this, you will have to catch yourself having one of these internal discussions. Remember, you have them often throughout the day, so often that you may have trouble stepping back and noticing one. Instead of simply thinking, you will have to step back and *think about your thinking*.)

Then examine the content of your internal dialogues:

- What is the purpose of each discussion? (Does it have a thesis?)
- How, in the discussion, are you responding to an argument?
- How do your ideas develop?
- Is the imaginary discussion helpful or counterproductive?
- How does your thinking (from the imaginary discussion) play out externally?

Consider the invention writing you did for the essay in this chapter. You may have relied on written responses to Invention questions, public dialogue, internal dialogue, or previous internal dialogues (before you began the assignment).

- Which did you rely on most? And which might you have utilized more?
- Identify several key points in your essay and explain how they developed. What role did writing in response to chapter questions, public dialogue, internal dialogue, or previous dialogue (prior to the assignment) play in the development of those points?
- If you can recall internal dialogues, describe how they worked:
  —Who were your imaginary discussion partners?
  —What was the nature of the discussion? Cooperative? Combative? Something else?
  —What new thinking emerged from the imaginary discussions?

Beyond the Essay

1. Find or create an image that responds to an argument.

   - What response does the image make to the argument?
   - How do particular visual elements help to make the response?

2. Find or create an image that corresponds to the argument you made in your essay for this chapter.

EVALUATING

Chapter Contents

CHAPTER 9

"The trouble with normal is it always gets worse."

—Bruce Cockburn

Evaluating is the act of judging the value or worth of a given subject. We make informal judgments constantly throughout our daily lives: We decide that we like a particular car more than another, or that one song on the radio is better than another. Such evaluations are informal because they involve little analysis; that is, we do not usually take the time to thoroughly analyze each song we hear on the radio as we are sweeping through stations. We also take part in formal evaluation, a process that goes beyond an expression of likes and dislikes: Teachers must evaluate student performance; jury members must evaluate events, people, and testimony; voters must evaluate political candidates; members of unions must evaluate contracts; managers must evaluate employees; executives must evaluate business proposals; citizens must evaluate laws and lawmakers. In such situations, mere personal tastes cannot dictate evaluative decisions. Instead, a formal process—sometimes entirely intellectual, sometimes organized in visible steps—is necessary for sound evaluation.

The ability to make formal evaluations is essential to academic thinking and writing:

- Biologists at a national conference evaluate the success of a particular molecular research process.

- Law enforcement students are assigned to evaluate a new highway safety program.

- Crime lab scientists evaluate a particular procedure for gathering evidence.

- University civil engineers evaluate a downtown rezoning plan.

- English professors evaluate a new textbook for the department literature courses.

- Education faculty members and graduate students evaluate the state's controversial new standardized tests.

- Art students evaluate a set of paintings from the early Modernist era.

Much literary work is also evaluative. William Copeland's book *Generation X,* for example, may be viewed as an evaluation of the culture created by the baby boomer generation. Toni Morrison's *Jazz* may be seen as an evaluation of 1920s culture. And Jonathan Swift's *Gulliver's Travels,* perhaps one of the most famous examples of evaluative literature, critiques (or satirizes) political and economic institutions of eighteenth-century England.

Whether one is an author, jury member, civil engineer, or voting citizen, the person who can evaluate well and make judgments outside of his or her personal tastes is able to make valuable decisions, to help distinguish the best course of action, to clarify options when many seem available. And in a culture that is increasingly filled with choices (among political candidates, retirement plans, religious paths, and lifestyles, to name just a few), it is increasingly important for the literate citizen to evaluate well.

The essays in this chapter all make judgments and, in doing so, present their subjects to the reader in a particular light. In other words, each writer gives an opinion about a subject (be it a computer program, a television show, etc.) and then supports that opinion by showing selected details of the subject. While the writers give some form of overview (some general summary about the subject), they also focus the reader's attention on the details that support their judgments. This is fair play. In drawing attention to certain details (and ignoring others), they are simply creating argumentative positions—the positions they want the reader to accept. Notice, also, that the writers tend to draw on support outside their subjects; that is, they refer to other like subjects to show particular points, which gives credibility to their judgments.

This chapter will help you develop a formal evaluation of a particular subject and communicate your evaluation in writing. The following essays will provide valuable insight to various evaluation strategies. After reading the essays, you can find a subject in one of two ways:

1. Go to the Point of Contact section to find a topic from your everyday life. **or**

2. Choose one of the Ideas for Writing that follow the essays.

After finding a subject, go to the Analysis section to begin developing the evaluation.

Goodbye, Cruel Word:
A Personal History of
Electronic Writing

Steven Poole

Steven Poole has contributed articles to the *Guardian,* the *Times Literary Supplement,* and the *New States-man.* His books include *Unspeak* and *Trigger Happy.* This blog entry, from September 2007, describes Poole's divorce from Microsoft Word and the intellectual evolution that led him to abandon Word for a new platform. The author uses British spelling throughout his essay.

For the first time, I no longer have a copy of Microsoft Word installed on either of my computers. That's some change. I wrote my first two books and many hundreds of articles in Word. But I'm writing my third book in an inexpensive yet wonderful piece of Mac-only software written by a single person instead of a "business unit" at Redmond. Scoured of Word, my computers feel clean, refreshed, relieved of a hideous and malign burden. How did it come to this?

I remember when Word was all clean and sci-fi and inspiring, on the sharp monochrome screens of late-1980s and early-1990s Macs. When I was at university, hardly anyone owned a computer. We wrote our final dissertations on Mac Classics running Word in the college Computer Room. Afterwards, when I began to write for newspapers, the first electronic writing tool I owned was a Brother LW-20.

For some reason the fact that this is called an *Elektrische Schreibmaschine* in German makes me feel all nostalgic for the ultrasmooth Kraftwerk future it seems I was living back then without even realising it, tapping out theatre reviews on a six-line green LCD (not even backlit), and then watching the typewriter daisywheel chatter back and forth to print a hard copy that I would then take to the library and send to the *TLS* [*Times Literary Supplement*] or the *Independent* via a facsimile machine, at 10p per page.

After a while I was able to buy a black-and-white PowerBook 520 running Word 5:

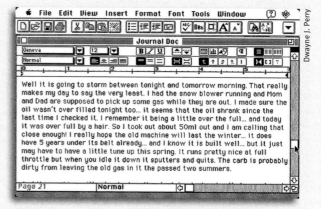

Many people agree that revision 5.1a, specifically, was the best version of Word that Microsoft has ever shipped, combining utility and minimalist elegance with reliability. Sadly for me, although it wasn't strictly necessary, after a few years and a colour Performa I "upgraded" to Word 98, and somehow the magic was gone. Yes, I turned off all the crappy lurid toolbars and tried to make the compositional space as simple as possible, but by this time Word was stuffed with all kinds of "features" that let you print a pie-chart on the back of a million envelopes or publish your cookery graphs to your "world wide web home-page", and it already felt to me that Word was only grudgingly letting me write nothing but, you know, *words.* [Poole's book] *Trigger Happy* got out of Word 98 and onto the streets, but not without routine crashes and the occasional catastrophic loss of a few finely honed paragraphs.

5   I was still somehow brainwashed, though, as perhaps many people still are today, into believing that Word was the "serious" word-processor: the *professional* tool for anyone who did heavy lifting with language. Part of the reason for Microsoft's success in this propaganda trick, I think, was its brilliant choice of file-name extension. Think about it: .doc. That means "document." A .doc just *is* a document, right? And a document has to be a .doc. Stands to reason. Anything else would look amateurish. If they had called their files .mwd or something, we might have all jumped ship a lot sooner.

Anyway, through inertia, through not even thinking about whether alternatives existed, I continued to stick with Word. And then, like a cunning crack dealer, Microsoft threw me a freebie twist that had me hooked anew. It was Live Word Count, which (IIRC) appeared in Word v. X.

Ah, Live Word Count. When pretty much everything you write has a word-limit attached, and you realise after long and tragic experience that exceeding that limit will not cause the editor to expand the space available to you in tribute to your genius but will instead cause the sub-editors unerringly to home in precisely on the bits that *must not be cut* if the article is still to make any sense and *cut them,* then you need to know at every stage how much you have written, and how much you have left to go. With Live Word Count, there was no longer any need to hit a key combination every 10 seconds to check the word-count (which was often a way of procrastinating). The word count was permanently right there in the toolbar, updating as you typed. It was a beautiful thing, a real boon to anyone who wrote to predetermined length. So I couldn't leave Word now, could I?

(In the mean time, I also had one of these [a Psion Series 5]. It was for filing articles while travelling, but I often preferred to write on that machine, with its small monochrome LCD, even when my desktop or laptop Mac was available. So something, some unexamined preference, was percolating in my mind. Eventually the Psion broke, and nothing as good has replaced it as an ultramobile writing tool. So much for progress.)

Anyway, a few more years, and eventually *Unspeak* got out of Word v. X on my PowerMac G5 and on to the streets, but not without routine crashes and the occasional catastrophic loss of a few finely honed paragraphs. (Sound familiar?) And then I began to feel a vague dissatisfaction. My eye started roving. I would check out the other word-processors walking down the street, observing their smooth lines and lithe swing, imagining what it would be like to be with them instead.

10   Crucially, Live Word Count became available in a range of other programs. (Amazingly, though, it seems that PC users did not get a live word count from Microsoft until Word 2007.) Mac users can now get it pretty much anywhere. The guitar-rocking genius at Transparent Head even hacked me up a version of TextEdit that had a live word count in a floating window.

The second crucial thing was an answer to prayers I hadn't even known I was praying. It was Full-Screen

Mode, which I first discovered in WriteRoom.[1] Write-Room's slogan is "distraction-free writing," and it does just what it says on the tin. Your entire screen is blacked out, except for the text you are working on. I now use WriteRoom for all my journalism. When I'm working, the screen of my MacBook looks like this:

Courtesy of Steven Poole

Pretty old-skool, huh? It's perfect: far less temptation to switch to a browser window, much better concentration on the text in front of you. WriteRoom has a "typewriter-scrolling mode," so that the line you are typing is always centred in the screen, not forever threatening to drop off the bottom, and what you have already written scrolls rapidly up off the top of the screen, dissuading you from idly rereading it. It's a bit like the endless roll of typewriter paper on which Jack Kerouac wrote *On the Road.*

So WriteRoom allows me to turn my whizzy modern computer into the nearest equivalent possible (allowing for modern conveniences like backup to the internet and so on) to my old Brother typewriter and its six-line LCD. The focus is on the words and nothing else. Except for that line you can just make out at the bottom left of the screen. That's the Live Word Count.

Microsoft Word still uses the metaphor of the page, the computer screen that imitates a blank, bounded sheet of physical paper. For me, this is outdated and unimaginative. It has become a barrier rather than a window. And there is always the distraction of changing font and line-spacing, jumping ahead too quickly to imagining

---

[1] WriteRoom is Mac-only, but PC users can try a similar experience with JDarkRoom.

the text as a visual, physical product instead of a process, a fluid semantic interplay. Instead, turning my Mac-Book into a kind of replica 1980s IBM machine, with the words glowing and hovering in an interstellar void, is liberating: as though I am composing the Platonic ideal of a text that might eventually take many different forms.

Through WriteRoom I then discovered Scrivener, a more sophisticated program with excellent features for managing very large documents or document collections: like a book. I couldn't have written *Unspeak,* with its many hundreds of footnotes, in WriteRoom; but I could have in Scrivener. I'm writing my next book in Scrivener, and a significant part of my enjoyment of the process is that I'm not doing it in Word, so somehow it doesn't feel so much like cubicular, fluorescent-lit *work.* And it can also do Platonic simplicity. When working on a chapter, I set Scrivener up to give me exactly the same full-screen orange-on-black view as my WriteRoom environment above, with one exception: the Live Word Count doesn't appear unless you mouse over the bottom of the screen. Which is perfect for writing a book, where length is not crucial on a paragraph-to-paragraph basis, and it eliminates the last possible distraction from your mindworld.

15   And imagine trying the following with Microsoft—when I first used Scrivener I was a bit irritated that the cursor was a thin blinking line, which I found interfered with my new-found writing Zen. So I posted on the programmer's forum saying could we please maybe have the same square, non-blinking block cursor as you get in WriteRoom? With the next beta, he had done it. That's customer service.[2]

Am I not worried that WriteRoom and Scrivener, delightful though they are, are small products from tiny outfits, not "supported" by the corporate might of a large company such as Microsoft? No, I'm not. Because actually my writing is now more secure. Instead of a bloated proprietary file format like .doc, both programs use accessible formats—.txt, .xml, .rtf [3]—that (as far as one can predict these things) will be readable forever. My new book is one big "project" in Scrivener, but under the hood each chapter is a universally accessible .rtf file, which can be opened and used in a multitude of other programs.

The last question is one of interoperability, and on first sight it's a serious one. Surely if everyone else is using Microsoft Word and we are sending documents back and forth to each other, then I need to use Microsoft Word too? I imagine that kind of reasoning sells the majority of new copies. But for me it doesn't matter at all. If I just need to read a Word document, I can open it in pretty much any Mac program. If I need to exchange files back and forth using comments or Track Changes, I can do that through Google Apps or Pages. If someone really insists on sending me a Word document so festooned with all its formatting "features," tables, graphics, and so on that it doesn't work in another program, I am just likely to respond: What the fuck?

So that's how it is now. I write within the pure, glowing universes of Scrivener and WriteRoom. I send articles to the *Guardian* as plain-text rather than .doc. I am confident that I will be able to open those articles and the chapters of my book again, if I want to, in 30 years' time. And now a 1,000-word review weighs 4K instead of 30K. I weep at all the innocent electrons I wastefully killed over the years, sending those massive, lumbering Word documents through the Internet. I apologise for my particle profligacy. I have learned my lesson. Goodbye, cruel Word.

---

[2] As Scrivener's creator relates, he emailed Jesse Grosjean, Writeroom's author, wondering how he did the block-cursor thing; very generously, Grosjean just gave him the code, and even recommends Scrivener on his own website.

[3] RTF is actually proprietary, originally developed by DEC and now owned by Microsoft, but it's so widespread now that (fingers crossed) they won't be able to break it.

Writing Strategies

1. Although Poole's subtitle characterizes the blog entry as a personal story, it is also a public evaluation of Microsoft Word. What passages or particular strategies make this more than a personal story?

2. How does Poole deal with opposing positions or concerns? How does he counterargue or concede in his argument?

3. Every evaluation relies on criteria—standards of judgment that allow the evaluator to weigh specifics of the topic. For instance, a good film should have a gripping plot, believable characters, and so forth. A consumer product should be comprehensible, practical, and so on. What are Poole's criteria? Even though he doesn't list them, what standards does he seem to apply in his evaluation of Microsoft Word?

4. Describe Poole's voice. How does it make you more or less apt to adopt his argument?

5. What organizational strategies can you detect in this argument? For instance, how are paragraphs used to develop and separate ideas?

Exploring Ideas

1. Based on Poole's argument, why do you think consumers get brainwashed by technology?

2. On the surface, this blog entry is about Microsoft Word, but what's behind that? What human habits and sociological phenomena does Poole invite us to consider?

3. After reading Poole's personal word-processing history, why might someone insist on the value of Microsoft Word?

4. How does Poole's evaluation support the notion that simpler is better? Point out particular passages or claims.

Ideas for Writing

1. Consider a popular consumer product that just doesn't cut it but that people still purchase. What qualities or aspects have people learned to ignore or live with? Why don't they abandon the product for a better one?

2. Are you a Mac or PC fan? Develop an evaluative argument that defends or celebrates one of the two platforms.

If responding to one of these ideas, go to the Analysis section of this chapter to begin developing ideas for your essay.

Scoured of Word, my computers feel clean, refreshed, relieved of a hideous and malign burden.

The Andy Griffith Show: Return to Normal

Ed Bell

In the margins of this essay, a reader's comments point to key ideas and writing strategies.

Evaluations invite readers to see why something is valuable or deficient. To do this, a writer may propose a new standard of judgment (a criterion) upon which the evaluation is based. For example, a writer might suggest that a television show should not only entertain but also *comfort* its audience. In this essay, Ed Bell, a writing instructor, does just that, first establishing comfort as a potential criterion for a prime-time television sitcom, then arguing how well *The Andy Griffith Show* meets that criterion.

Writing Strategies

Introduction discusses what sitcoms do (their purpose): instruct, entertain, comfort. Evaluation of show can be based on how well the shows do this.

Main claim: "More than any other sitcom . . ."

Criteria for evaluation. How *Andy Griffith* differs from other shows—it's more comforting because things return to normal.

Develops argument by discussing what happens in other shows: Things work out okay, but we can tell a new crisis will loom.

From those early days of Lucy and Ricky to our own Dharma and Greg, situation comedies have been part of American culture. And for all the advancements, it still seems like the plots of most of them are something cooked up by Lucy who dragged along Ethel and got caught (and ultimately forgiven) by Fred and Barney . . . uh . . . Fred and Ricky, I mean. Whether or not these shows instruct is, I suppose, debatable. But what is not debatable is that over the past 50 years they have entertained millions. And, I would suggest, through that very act of entertaining us, they have comforted us—the most comforting of them all being *The Andy Griffith Show*.

More than any other sitcom, *The Andy Griffith Show* leaves its viewers with a sense that everything is all right. While *Three's Company* or *Dharma and Greg* or *MASH* may also wind things up happily after 30 minutes, there is—even though the complication of that particular week's crisis has been worked out—always a sense on those shows that things are not quite right. Yet *The Andy Griffith Show* leaves us with the feeling that, even though our friends sometimes get big-headed ideas or strangers from Raleigh come driving or dancing or swindling their mixed-up way into our peacefulness, life will eventually return to normal, all warm and wonderful.

On *Three's Company* or *Seinfeld* or *Friends*, things work out in the end. The friends are getting along just fine, but we can see that they are bound for another conflict in a week or so. Though this week's crisis has worked itself out, the pace of their lives or their natural temperaments or their complicated living conditions are still spinning wildly and we know next week they're in for trouble again. On *Dharma and Greg* or *Green Acres* or *I Love Lucy* (even on *The Dick Van Dyke Show*), the family has once again survived, but as with the shows about friends, on the shows about families there seems to be only temporary comfort in the happy ending. Dharma

Exploring Ideas

Connects to life of viewer: Do sitcoms instruct? How?

Okay, but there must be "other" shows like *Andy*—such as *Leave It to Beaver*.

and Greg are still bound for a divorce. Lisa, on *Green Acres,* is only putting up with the farm life a little while longer and Oliver loves it so much that he is never going back to the city. Though she is ironically more suited to the place than he is, she longs always to live elsewhere. No one could possibly put up with all Lucy's scheming. And as for Richard and Laura Petrie, the most stable of our sample couples, to the average American they seem only a step away from falling into the New York swinger crowd. On *MASH* or *Hogan's Heroes* or *Gomer Pyle,* they are either at war or could be. There's little real and lasting comfort in these folks who are gathered together out of necessity so far from home. Yes, they're buddies and that's nice, but it's all so temporary.

This doesn't exhaust all the sitcoms or all the types, but it does set up the reasons that *The Andy Griffith Show* comforts us more than the others. The show's main character, Andy, is full of southern wisdom. He is quiet and listens and makes better decisions in the midst of all the madness than we could have. That is comfort number one: Someone—the general, the man in charge, *the sheriff*—has things under control. All the madness results from one of three things: either intruders, but Andy gets rid of them after they have caused only a little trouble; or just boys (Opie and sometimes his friends) going through what is natural to go through growing up, but Andy deals with this expertly, too; or ego, ambition, and pride—usually Barney is having the trouble here, though it could be Aunt Bea or one of the others. Andy understands all of this, though not so well or right away that the show isn't a little bit interesting. The plot is better than most sitcoms: There is always a solution that takes a little while to get to, and we believe it when we finally do.

5   What's most comforting about this show, however, is that things return to normal. That is, *The Andy Griffith Show* offers us a normal that can be returned to. With *Andy Griffith* we get a sense that the complication has blown through like a summer thunderstorm, instead of us getting the sense that a little blue sky has blown through a place where it is otherwise always thunderstorming. The characters are at home. They're not strangers thrown together, and they haven't been transplanted in some strange land (such as Hooterville, New York City, or Postmodern America). They are familiar with their surroundings and like (both "similar to" and "fond of") each other. The zaniness on *Andy Griffith* could just as well not ensue . . . but it does. On all those other shows, it must ensue. How couldn't it?

The situation itself—small-town people in a small town—is comforting. The show develops this sense with Andy's quiet wisdom, but also with the integrity of the wacky supporting characters.

Margin notes:

This seems to go beyond initial thinking. (I've never thought about it.)

Author concedes that there are other sitcoms and other types of sitcoms.

Goes beyond initial thinking here. Gets specific. Show provides comfort because someone's wise. Madness because of:
1) intruders,
2) natural growing up,
3) ego, ambition, pride.

Develops argument through specific analysis of *The Andy Griffith Show.* Shows specifically why/how AG comforts us.

Main idea: Says what is most comforting about the show (relates to title of essay).

This seems to go beyond initial thinking: Things are normal and get wacky, instead of things generally just being wacky.

All of them to some degree are like Barney—a liability and an asset all at once. They are, like us, good people flawed. We are all familiar with the show's gentle theme song, whistled as Andy and Opie walk along with fishing poles. And the black and white camera shots are always perfectly composed, like a photo we'd see in *Life* magazine. The dialog is quiet, engaging, funny, real. For 30 minutes we are practically back in the womb of Mayberry—a place that doesn't exist, but does. It is a place that, whether we ever felt it as a child or not, as adults we feel that we once knew. We can feel it now, and *The Andy Griffith Show* captures what we all now think that we once felt back then.

> Connects to reader (public resonance): They are, like *us*, good people flawed. The use of "we" (though not required) helps make this connection.

> Is this true? Doesn't it have to ensue because of Barney, etc.?

> The situation itself (small-town life) contributes to comforting.

Not all sitcoms set out to comfort, though all do set out to entertain. Some, such as *All in the Family* or *Soap* or *Will and Grace,* might even set out to challenge us, to make us think. But *The Andy Griffith Show,* I believe, sets out to entertain and comfort and it succeeds as no other show ever has . . . or ever will. *The Cosby Show* could only circle in *Andy's* orbit. The reason is, I suppose, because the times have changed. Today an attempt to create the comfort of Mayberry (an attempt to say your small-town life is idyllic) would somehow fail. It would seem a lie without any of the twenty-first-century issues (drugs, pregnancy, homosexual kissing), without any of the edgy technology, the music, the rapid-fire slick wit, the self-aware writing and directing. Mayberry exists, cliché as it sounds, in our hearts. The show, like no other, captured what we want to remember, whether it happened or not. It tells us that blue skies are normal.

> Concession/Qualifier: Not all sitcoms set out to comfort. Some may even do the opposite.

> The show captures something. What is it?

> Concludes by providing a possible reason why *The Andy Griffith Show* is more comforting than today's shows.

> Connects to viewers because it is comforting. Assures viewer that blue skies, not storms, are normal. (Even if this is not true? Is it?)

Writing Strategies

1. What criteria (standards of judgment) does Bell use to evaluate *The Andy Griffith Show*? List several other criteria he might have used but didn't.

2. Highlight any background or summary information necessary to understand Bell's evaluation. Where does such information appear? Why is it helpful? Where might more or less background information have been presented?

3. If workshopping Bell's essay, what suggestion would you make, and why?

4. Would you say that Bell's essay is an argument? Why or why not?

Exploring Ideas

1. How does Bell's essay encourage the reader to think differently about TV sitcoms?

2. How does Bell's essay encourage the reader to think differently about entertainment?

3. Think of three television shows that might impact the quality of the viewer's life. Explain how each show might influence the way that people think or act.

Ideas for Writing

1. What television show is overestimated or underestimated? Why do audiences have the wrong take on it?

2. Examine a popular website and try to discover an element of the design that people may not usually consider—font use, spatial arrangement, color scheme, and so on. How does that particular aspect positively or negatively impact the overall effect of the site?

If responding to one of these ideas, go to the Analysis section of this chapter to begin developing ideas for your essay.

CBS/Landov Media

"The situation itself—small town people in a small town— is comforting."

Star Trek: Where No Man Has Gone Before

Jaren Provo

Most people have a favorite television program, but few of us consider how that program resonates with broader cultural trends—how it speaks to, addresses, or challenges common biases and prejudices. In this essay, Jaren Provo takes a close look at *Star Trek*. She goes beyond merely celebrating its attributes; she evaluates *Star Trek* according to the role it has played in shaping attitudes about and within popular culture. Provo wrote this essay for her first-semester college writing course. Now an English major at Arizona State University, she plans to study English literature and history in graduate school.

"The greatest danger facing us is ourselves, and irrational fear of the unknown. But there's no such thing as 'the unknown,' only things temporarily hidden, temporarily not understood." –Captain James T. Kirk

Since its stunning and innovative debut in 1966, *Star Trek* has given modern culture a new promise for the future, one of peace, cooperation, and tolerance not seen in such tenacity or splendor before or since. Yet, despite the significant cultural contribution *Star Trek* has made, many see this legendary universe as unreachable, non-applicable, influencing only the stereotypical Klingon-quoting, uniform-donning, convention-going fan. However, this view is false. *Star Trek* empowers mainstream America to imagine a future of hope-filled opportunity rather than horrific obliteration.

Each of us is familiar with *Star Trek* in some manner, whether it be the phrase "Beam me up, Scotty" (which, actually, was never said verbatim in the series), the *USS Enterprise,* the . . . very . . . long pauses . . . of William Shatner's portrayal of Captain Kirk, or its groovy theme music. *Star Trek* is best described, by Roddenberry himself, as the 1960's television show set "close enough to our own time for continuing characters to be fully identifiable as people like us, but far enough into the future for galaxy travel to be fully established" ("*Star Trek* Is"). It is not until much later in the fran-

chise that we realize *Star Trek* is set in the 2260s AD, focusing on the crew and voyages of the starship *Enterprise* as it carries out its five-year mission of peaceful exploration. As the *Enterprise* travels through space, it encounters various worlds with attributes reminiscent of Earth, and discusses numerous issues of political, social, and human nature. *Star Trek* shows us, through a cast of recurring dynamic characters and a space-oriented view, a reflection of humanity and its possibilities.

The specific focus here is Roddenberry's first series, the original series (or what Trekkies refer to as TOS). There have been five television spin-off series and ten movies deriving their roots from TOS, but each successive reiteration of *Star Trek* brings an even more commercialized version of Roddenberry's standard-defying innovation. In these new series, special effects have replaced meaningful plots; de rigueur characters have replaced dynamic ones. Roddenberry's vision rose above the need for believable explosions, unrecognizable aliens, and shoot-em-up alien-invader plots, such that *Star Trek* struggled to remain on the air during its short (but syndicate-able) three-year stint; it was a vision that broadcasting officials placed little promise in, as it was most certainly not a mainstream science fiction show.

But this vision was so powerful and so magnificent that it opened an avenue to engage humans in their own universe. While popular culture at the time focused on the individual and his or her worldly place in society, *Star Trek* expanded the horizons of the human mind toward the furthermost reaches of space. In the *Star Trek* future, there are no physical boundaries or burdens, for the greatest, most inaccessible reaches of the universe are merely a warp speed away, the unknown cultures of a million worlds much like Earth are open for communication and exploration. Indeed, one of the core principles of *Star Trek* is the "parallel worlds concept"—that there are billions of planets with conditions comparable to Earth that could harbor similar social, ecological, and humanlike development ("*Star Trek* Is"). It is this principle that shapes the core mission of the *USS Enterprise* herself: "to boldly go where no man has gone before."

5   And in so doing, the humans of the twenty-third century do not have to face a decimated, physically and culturally broken world similar to those in many recognizable pop culture realms, such as *Terminator* or *The*

Matrix. Instead, they are a functioning global culture. These individuals are able to realize their own humanity by exploring and relating to alien cultures in the depths of the universe, offering aid and relief to struggling civilizations, but willing to observe and maintain the customs of the native peoples. This core idea constitutes the Prime Directive, a predominant theme throughout *Star Trek*. The Prime Directive advocates involvement with, but not indoctrination of, other cultures (unless there is a lack of a progressing, stable culture). To each world the *Enterprise* travels, it promotes a mission of peace and negotiation, rather than conquest.

Through this process, humans become increasingly tolerant of groups within their own species. Bigotry or intolerance in any form is seen as a horrendous trait and a mark of low character. On the bridge of the *Enterprise,* such individuals as an African woman, Asian American man, Scottish engineer, pointed-eared alien without emotions, nationalistic Russian youngster, and even an Iowan hunk with a rhythmically related speech deficiency are regular residents, each respected for his or her own talents and merit as a member of the crew. Even representatives of such backgrounds as German, French, Irish, Indian, British, Native American, and more are seen frequently on the *Enterprise*. Jeff Greenwald, author of *Future Perfect: How "Star Trek" Conquered Planet Earth,* echoes this idea: "[*Star Trek*] has given us a model of a truly multicultural world, where all races and creeds are afforded equal respect and rights" (qtd. in Schrof 8). Together, this diverse and accepting group explores the human condition, such items as the role of good and evil (in such episodes as "The Savage Curtain" and "The Enemy Within"), maturity and age (in the episodes "Miri," "Charlie X," and "The Deadly Years"), and an ambition-free life ("This Side of Paradise").

However, some feel that *Star Trek*'s diverse cast is not as accepting and multicultural as it appears. In his piece, "Carved From the Rock Experiences of Our Daily Lives: Reality and *Star Trek*'s Multiple Histories," Lincoln Geraghty concedes that TOS casts "token" minority members as crew and is deficient because of its lack of an openly homosexual crewmember (161). In this way, he argues, *Star Trek* repeats the "mistakes other popular television series made" (161). However, it is important

to observe the cultural climate of the 1960s, especially in popular media. If indeed minority groups were portrayed, they were often playing roles of servants (Asian Americans), slaves (African Americans), or senseless and vicious warriors on the Western plains (Native Americans). The latter was not often represented by those from this culture; often, individuals of Italian descent were given the roles of Native Americans. Though perhaps not main characters with substantial parts (with the exception of Spock, who is an alien and would in a sense be considered a member of a "minority" group), these individuals are not degraded, but are respected on the merit of their performance and contributions to the ship itself. These individuals also took on a more active role as *Star Trek* progressed; in the third season, *Star Trek* was even so bold as to portray the first interracial kiss on television ("Plato's Stepchildren"). Given the exclusive nature of the times, *Star Trek*'s role was an advanced platform (unlike other pop culture outlets) upon which racial, ethnic, and gender acceptance could be built.

Together, these humans learn from past mistakes, attempting to avoid their occurrence in other cultures developing in similar manners (as in the episodes "Patterns of Force" and "A Taste of Armageddon"). Indeed, as William Blake Tyrrell states in his 1977 article (around the peak of *Star Trek*'s syndication-led revival), "*Star Trek* creates a future world where the glories of the past are pristine and the failures and doubts of the present have been overcome. It gives us our past as our future, while making our present the past, which . . . is safely over and forgotten" (qtd. in Geraghty 167). But in *Star Trek*, the past is not so much forgotten as it is no longer dwelled upon; it is often revisited for comparative and developmental purposes. Humanity in the future does not degrade; it matures and refines itself toward a more ideal form.

Notably absent from *Star Trek*'s list of qualities is the predominant science fiction theme regarding space aliens: "When they come, they'll destroy us all." This permeated view is reflected in numerous locales, such as *Independence Day, Invasion of the Body Snatchers,* and H.G. Wells' *War of the Worlds*. Yet in *Star Trek*, the first contact with aliens is a diplomatic one, in which logical, peaceful Vulcan representatives come to Earth to note their presence and encourage future technological development. After this contact, more connections are forged with other alien worlds, such that the United Federation of Planets develops (with a flag suspiciously reminiscent of that of the United Nations) to promote peaceable cooperation among these cultures. Alien cultures are not (generally) out to conquer Earth and all of humanity in a blazing inferno of death and destruction, but are civilized, developing worlds willing to forge ties with others in the universe to assure mutual survival.

10   Also uncharacteristic of *Star Trek* but common in the sci-fi realm is the element portraying humans as slaves of technology, hopelessly existent only in body. This concept is perhaps most prevalent in the *Matrix* trilogy. Yet *Star Trek* foretells humans as harnessing the resources of technology to propel themselves outward into space, to explore, to contact, to impact in a positive way. The transporter and warp drive allow for expedient, efficient movement among planets and realms; the communicator (predecessor to the flip-phone?) and universal translator aid in interpersonal and intercultural contact; the scientific tricorder (a handheld programmable scanning device) and ship's scanners enhance exploration purposes; and medical tricorders and unknown, but apparently technical, whirring devices devised from salt 'n' pepper shakers exist for medical purposes. True, some matters of technology are dangerous and destroy human independence, such as the M-5 Multitronic Computer in the episode "The Ultimate Computer." Essentially, this device is meant to save lives by replacing the human presence on a starship, yet it manages to entirely control the ship and destroy hundreds of innocent lives in the process. However, this technology is not typical, and ends up being destroyed. M-5 reminds us to maintain a fine balance between technology serving and subverting humankind.

Some, however, disagree with the assertion that *Star Trek* promotes a palate of peace, tolerance, and diplomacy, pointing to the predominant enemy throughout the series: the Klingon Empire. They observe the constant conflict between the Klingons and the Federation, between their opposing interests of complete colonization and diplomatic cooperation. Certainly the Federation is not peaceful toward or tolerant of this group of aliens. Yet, the Klingon Empire is an imperialistic, dictatorial force of conquest interested in destroying the

diplomatic network of the Federation and its promotion of freedom and democracy. Actions taken against the Klingons are in matters of defense, not of aggression, and peace negotiations between the Klingons and Federation persist throughout and beyond the series. Eventually, internal political movements bring the dictatorial regime to its knees, and even the Klingons themselves are incorporated into the Federation.

Many also claim that *Star Trek* is merely a scripted TV show, unrealistic and inaccessible to all but the most obsessive fans. However, *Star Trek* has reached and influenced some of the leaders of technology and society, including individuals such as Bill Gates, several NASA scientists and engineers, and even the late Dr. Martin Luther King, Jr. The message of *Star Trek* resonates through these and other individuals familiar with *Star Trek*'s ideals, such that all in society are influenced by this series. Many outlets in society and the media also carry *Star Trek*'s concepts into their settings on an entertainment level. Considering entertainment's pivotal role in our society (take, for instance, the large number of individuals who gain current events knowledge from comedy shows such as *The Daily Show, The Tonight Show with Jay Leno,* and *Saturday Night Live*), the sheer entertainment quality of *Star Trek* brings it into our everyday lives. Furthermore, the core concepts of *Star Trek* are not fictional and far-reaching, but are based on events and themes within the Vietnam War era and relating to the human condition.

Imagine a world in which *Star Trek* is absent. We would miss more than the phrases "He's dead, Jim" and "Beam me up, Scotty", more than warp drive and the same men in red shirts dying before the introductory theme each week. Our culture would be void of a revolutionary promise, a promise of tolerance, peace, exploration, and humanity in our future. Without *Star Trek*, modern pop culture would be filled only with bleak visions for tomorrow, of aliens ruthlessly invading and destroying Earth, of a humanity decimated and barely clinging to the edge of existence, of survival depending upon backstabbing and cruelty. *Star Trek* is one of the few (perhaps the only) candles flickering in the darkness of popular apocalypticism, a guarantee of a secure future where tomorrow may not be such a horrible thing after all.

15   We must be sure not to violate the magnitude of *Star Trek* and its whispers of truth for the days ahead. We must not be intolerant of that which heralds a tolerant tomorrow, doubtful of a harbinger of hope, or disparaging toward a beacon of peace or humanity. The zeitgeist bestowed upon our culture by *Star Trek* must be appreciated for its complexities and considered in its hopeful message to the people of today.

Works Cited

Geraghty, Lincoln. "Carved From the Rock Experiences of Our Daily Lives: Reality and Star Trek's Multiple Histories." European Journal of American Culture. 21 (2002): 160-177. Academic Search Elite. EBSCO. Osterlin Lib., Northwestern Michigan College. 8 Apr. 2008 <http://search.epnet.com/>.

Schrof, Joannie M. "A World of Trekkies." U.S. News and World Report. 29 June 1998: 8. Academic Search Elite. EBSCO. Osterlin Lib., Northwestern Michigan College. 7 Apr. 2008 <http://search.epnet.com/>.

"Star Trek Is." Memory Alpha. 8 Apr. 2008. <http://memory-alpha.org/en/wiki/Star_Trek_is...>.

Writing Strategies

1. How does Provo address the common dismissal about "Trekkies"?

2. Although she does not state them directly in the essay, what can you infer about Provo's criteria (standards of judgment)? In other words, in her view, what makes a good television program? Why does *Star Trek* meet those standards?

3. How does Provo counterargue? Describe how particular counterarguments add dimension and value to her essay.

4. Provo's points often sound extremely positive—as though she cannot imagine a downside to the topic. Where does Provo qualify or concede to some other point of view? Why might she be justified in such glowing praise of the program?

5. How does Provo's sentence structure influence her voice? Focus on a particular paragraph and explain how the sentences impact the "sound" of the argument.

Exploring Ideas

1. Provo argues that television programs are more than entertainment: "Considering entertainment's pivotal role in our society (take, for instance, the large number of individuals who gain current events knowledge from comedy shows such as *The Daily Show, The Tonight Show with Jay Leno,* and *Saturday Night Live*), the sheer entertainment quality of Star Trek brings it into our everyday lives. Furthermore, the core concepts of *Star Trek* are not fictional and far-reaching, but are based on events and themes within the Vietnam War era and relating to the human condition." What current television dramas attempt to deal with the current political and cultural tensions of our era? How do they succeed or fail?

2. Provo celebrates *Star Trek* because it challenged racial prejudices of the 1960s. Do you think television can genuinely challenge or overturn common assumptions about race or gender? Why or why not?

3. Provo argues that most science fiction in popular culture, other than *Star Trek,* predicts a future of "horrific obliteration." What recent movies or television programs reinforce Provo's point? Do any challenge her notion?

4. From ancient times to the present, civilizations imagine other nations, tribes, people, or species as inherently wicked or debased. Oral stories, religious traditions, novels, and popular movies often characterize some faraway, unknown group as hostile, weird, or even corrupt. How does *Star Trek* fit into that long tradition?

Ideas for Writing

1. What particular program works to break down common prejudices or stereotypes? How does it succeed or fall short?

2. Consider a current commercial or ad campaign. How does it subtly reinforce negative stereotypes about people? Why don't viewers tend to acknowledge that quiet stereotypes?

If responding to one of these ideas, go to the Analysis section of this chapter to begin developing ideas for your essay.

Outside Reading

Find a written evaluation, and make a photocopy or print it out. You might find an evaluation of a government policy or politician in a news magazine (such as the *National Review* or *Slate*). General readership magazines such as *Spin* and *Rolling Stone* regularly feature reviews of movies, music CDs, and performances. Your local city or campus newspaper may feature reviews of movies, music, and restaurants.

To conduct an electronic search of journals and magazines, go to your library's periodical database or to InfoTrac College Edition (http://infotrac.cengage.com). For your library database, perform a keyword search, or for InfoTrac College Edition, go to the main search box and click on "keywords." Type in subjects that interest you (such as *books, political policy, music, restaurant*) and combine that keyword with an evaluative term *(critique, review, evaluation),* such as *book and review, political and policy and critique, restaurants and reviews, hip-hop and music and review.* (When performing keyword searches, avoid using phrases or articles such as *a, an, the;* instead, use nouns separated by *and.*) The search results will yield lists of journal and magazine articles. This same strategy can be used with a newspaper database.

You can also search the Internet. Try the search engine Altavista.com. Like most Internet search engines, Altavista.com combines words using *and.* In the search box, try various combinations, such as those above.

The purpose of this assignment is to further your understanding of evaluation and to introduce a broad range of evaluation strategies. As you are probably discovering, evaluation appears in many different places and in many different contexts. But despite the subject or the audience, some elements of evaluation are consistent. As you read through this chapter, keep the written evaluation you have discovered close by and notice the elements and strategies the writer uses. Depending on your instructor's suggestions, do one or more of the following:

1. Notice how the writer applies various strategies from this chapter. On the hard copy or photocopy:
   - Highlight the thesis if it is stated. If the thesis is implied, write it in your own words.
   - Identify (or write in the margins) the criteria, or standards of judgment, the writer uses to judge the subject.
   - Identify any counterarguments or concessions (elements of argument from Chapter 7).

2. Analyze the strategies employed by the writer. The following questions may be helpful:
   - Do you believe the writer uses appropriate criteria? Why?
   - How does the writer support his or her judgment about the subject?
   - Who is the audience for this evaluation?
   - How does the audience impact the kinds of things said in the evaluation?

3. Write at least three "Writing Strategies" questions for the evaluation.

4. Write at least three "Exploring Ideas" questions for the evaluation.

5. Write two "Ideas for Writing," such as the ones following the essays in this book.

INVENTION

"I criticize by creation . . . not by finding fault."

—Marcus Tullius Cicero

Invention is the primary strategy for generating new ideas. As you work through the following sections, imagine possibilities beyond your initial thoughts. The Point of Contact section will help you to find a subject for the evaluation; Analysis will help you to develop particular points about the subject; and Public Resonance will help you to make it relevant to a community of readers. The Thesis and Rhetorical Tools sections will help you develop a specific claim and support it appropriately. As in the other chapters, the Invention questions in each section are not meant to be answered directly in your final written assignment. They are meant to prompt reflection and discovery; however, your answers may translate directly into your drafts.

POINT OF CONTACT

An evaluator needs to have particular insight into his or her subject, so choose something that you can examine carefully. Your instructor may provide subjects, or you can use the suggestions and questions below to seek out and focus on a particular subject.

- **Visit a Place** (such as a restaurant, movie theater, night club, amusement park, college classroom or campus, shopping mall, grocery store, etc.). Gather information about the place. How do people behave? What behavior is tolerated, supported, ignored? What is on the walls? How does this influence the mood of the place? How much open space is available? Is the place empty, crowded, stuffy, clean, lonely, isolated, intense?

- **Attend an Event** (such as a carnival, circus, beauty pageant, dance, tractor pull, art show, concert, poetry reading, company meeting, college class, etc.). What happens before the event? What is the mood? How are the participants treated during the event? What kinds of interaction occur during the event? Where does the event take place? What impact does the location have on the event?

- **Investigate a Person** (such as a government official, doctor, religious leader, talk show host, roommate, professional athlete, work supervisor or manager, work associate, etc.). Evaluating a person can be tricky because it is easy to fall into an explanation of one's likes and dislikes. Instead, focus on the qualities or actions of the person in terms of his or her particular position or title. Is he or she willing to listen to people? For how long? What does he or she do while listening to someone? How do people respond or react to this person? Are people comfortable around this person? Is this person entertaining, enlightening, engaging, comforting, informative, energizing (or the opposite of any of these)?

- **Watch a Movie or Show** (such as a motion picture, sitcom, documentary, television drama, music video). Gather information and details, going beyond simple likes and dislikes. Does the dialogue reveal something about the characters that their actions do not? What kinds of graphic or sexually explicit images appear? Is the movie/show humorous or frightening in some way? How? What message(s) does the movie/show offer? Does the movie/show have stereotypes (of rich people, poor people, women, men, racial groups, children, the elderly)?

- **Read a Text** (such as a book, article, poster, letter, website, etc.). Consider texts from your major. In this case, go to one of the journals for your major, or to a database in your library. In some ways, evaluating a text is easy because it can be examined closely without having to rewind or travel somewhere. However, a written text can be a complicated mass of elements. What is the main idea or main argument of the text? What kind of evidence or support is used? How formal is the language? What is the tone of the text? If the text is an argument, does it address counterarguments? Does it use concession? What strategies are used to draw the reader into the ideas of the text?

Once you've focused on a subject, take notes. Record as much information about the subject as possible.

Like a detective, gather all the information you can. Ask hard questions. Ask weird questions.

ANALYSIS

Imagine taking your car to a mechanic because you heard a strange knocking sound when you accelerate. As you pull into the garage, the mechanic smiles and exclaims, "Hey, nice car! I love Ford Mustangs! There's nothing wrong with *that* car." Obviously, you'd be a bit disoriented, and maybe a little grumpy. You would also probably complain: "Hey, I want you to tell me what's wrong with the car—tell me why it's making that sound!" The problem with this scenario is that the mechanic does no analysis and uses no *criteria* (the standards on which judgments are based). The evaluation of the car is based on the mechanic's own likes and dislikes.

Or imagine reading a review of a fine Italian restaurant. While ignoring the wine list, entrees, and presentation of the food, the reviewer gives the restaurant a very low rating because of a limited number of ice cream flavors. In this scenario, the reviewer uses the *wrong* criteria. The reviewer evaluates a fine dining establishment with criteria for judging an ice cream shop. This would be similar to judging a historical drama negatively because it is not funny: Historical dramas are not necessarily supposed to be funny, nor are fine Italian restaurants supposed to have wide varieties of ice cream.

Two challenges for evaluating:

1. Creating criteria.
2. Creating appropriate criteria.

Discovering the Purpose of the Subject

The first analytical step is to discover the subject's purpose or goal—to understand, in other words, what the subject is attempting to achieve. We can only develop criteria and then evaluate a subject if we know the subject's purpose and audience. For example, we can evaluate a movie only if we understand what the movie is attempting to do: to succeed as a comedy for teens, to maintain high action for adults, or to retell a classic fairy tale for children. Evaluating something means understanding what that subject is attempting to do.

Invention Questions

While the specifics you recorded from the Point of Contact section tell what your subject *does*, the following Invention questions will help you discover the *purpose* of your subject and criteria for the evaluation:

- What does this subject try to achieve? (Be specific. For example, an Italian restaurant may be attempting to provide an elegant dining experience with a particular ethnic cuisine. This is different from the goal of a general chain restaurant such as Denny's, which attempts to provide economically priced food from a general menu.)

- What do other like subjects try to achieve? (Think about subjects similar to yours—other teachers, other comedic movies, other restaurants, and so on.)

- What is the subject's audience? (Whom does your subject attempt to engage or attract?) If you have not already considered the audience, imagine who might use, benefit from, and interact with the subject.

- What goals *should* this subject, or all subjects like it, have? (It might be argued, for instance, that a restaurant should attempt to elevate the dining experience, to transform the mundane act of eating into a cultural and social event. Once this criterion is established, someone might then use it to judge a particular restaurant.)

In Ed Bell's invention writing, he grapples with the idea of entertainment—what it does and should do for its audience:

What does this subject try to achieve?

The Andy Griffith Show is a sitcom (situational comedy). It tries to entertain people. If people are entertained, they will continue watching the show. That's the basic idea. But entertain how? Some shows entertain through violence, others drama, some through sex, and so on. Sitcoms try to entertain through comedy, but not just comedy. There has to be something even more specific than just comedy. Comedy how? What kind of comedy? *The Andy Griffith Show* has a particularly comfortable, slow pace to it. One might say that the show tries to entertain, but in a relaxing, maybe even comforting way.

What is the subject's audience?

The original audience for this show was the general American public in the 1960s, I imagine. Perhaps the show's producers had some more specific demographic in mind. But at the time, most people got three stations—NBC, CBS, and ABC. Americans tuned in to watch one of three shows. Looking back, it may be difficult, yet interesting, to imagine the audience. I imagine it being a simpler time. I wonder if such a show could even be created today, or if it would seem unrealistic, fake, insincere. The audience today is different but still likes the show. For some reason, the show has maintained its appeal (perhaps because it's just pleasant, comforting). Maybe there's something valuable about creations from the past.

Applying Criteria to the Subject

Now that you have a sense of the subject's purpose, you can begin making specific evaluative points. Answering the following questions will provide you with the raw material for your evaluation.

Refer to your notes from the Point of Contact section and answer the following:

- In what particular ways does the subject achieve its goal? What specific parts, tools, or strategies help the subject to achieve its goal? (For example, a restaurant depends upon such things as servers, atmosphere, and interior design, in addition to the actual food.)
- In what particular ways does the subject fall short of achieving its goal?
- What goals does the subject ignore?
- How does the subject compare to and contrast with other similar subjects?
- What is unique about your subject's approach or strategy to achieving its goal?

In his exploration of *The Andy Griffith Show,* Bell discovers the main point of his essay:

In what particular ways does the subject achieve its goal? What specific parts, tools, or strategies help the subject to achieve its goal?

The subject achieves its goal through the characters—Andy, Barney, Opie, Aunt Bea, etc. These characters are nice, in some cases quirky, small-town folk. Andy, the sheriff, is the rock, the most reasonable one. It also achieves its goal through plot. The small-town characters are placed (or find themselves) in situations (situation comedy). The madness swirls around Andy, and he is always able to sort things out. The setting is important too: small town. Mayberry is like one of the characters. And the cinematography: the black and white artistically framed shots contribute to the characters, plot, setting. They are all conveyed through the cinematography (not sure if "cinematography" is the right word.)

How does the subject compare to and contrast with other similar subjects?

More recent sitcoms take on issues. *All in the Family* comes to mind. That sitcom changed things a little. It opened up the range of what a situational comedy can be or do. As for shows more like it that do not attempt to take on cultural issues as *All in the Family* did, they are all pretty much the same: standard situations, basic character types, and so on. It seems that these shows always begin with some normal, comfortable scene; then something happens to create confusion or turmoil; then it gets sorted out in the end. If it's different at all, maybe *The Andy Griffith Show* returns to normal. Or, said another way, maybe the normal that it returns to is a different kind of normal—a normal that is more comfortable and lasting. (We might call this type of normal "Mayberry.") That is to say, other sitcoms of the time such as *Hogan's Heroes* or *Gomer Pyle* (and later ones like *MASH* or *Three's Company*) don't really start or end with a "normal" situation. Instead, with those shows you have inevitable trouble always bound to emerge.

What is unique about your subject's approach or strategy to achieving its goal?

I'm beginning to think that what's unique is the starting place and ending place of the show. While all these sitcoms open with a pleasantly normal situation that gets complicated then sorted out, the beginning and ending scenes for *The Andy Griffith Show* suggest that there is a standard, normal type of life that occasionally gets turned upside down. The other sitcoms—take *Three's Company* for example—have as a basis an inherently unstable situation: Jack and the girls are lying to Mr. Roper about their living situation (this is similar to *Bosom Buddies*).

As you consider your own writing project, try to see the subtle, almost hidden, mechanics of the subject. Ask yourself: What's going on beneath the surface? (And what's going on beneath that?)

PUBLIC RESONANCE

A meaningful evaluation considers how the subject affects or influences people—how it resonates with people's lives and concerns. For example, a movie critic might argue that children's movies carry the responsibility of developing notions of right and wrong. Or someone might suggest that a restaurant affects the health and well-being of a community and influences the image of a neighborhood. Ultimately, it is up to the writer to reveal the influence of a subject.

- How does the subject influence people's lives (their health, attitudes, living conditions, etc.)?
- Why is this subject important in people's lives?
- What do people expect from the subject?

Invention Workshop

With at least one other writer, use one of the Invention questions to launch an intensive and focused discussion about your subject. Try to go beyond your first thoughts on the subject. For example, Linda, who is evaluating a new restaurant in her town, transcends her initial thoughts. Her discussion leads to a more complicated understanding of the subject and its relationship to people's lives:

Why is this subject important in people's lives?

Linda: That's easy . . . a restaurant serves people food. And people need food.

Marcus: But do restaurants just provide food?

Jack: No, they also provide service—someone bringing you the food. And they also make eating a social event.

Linda: But that isn't the important part.

Marcus: Well, it isn't the main part, but I'd say people need that social aspect in their lives, and eating is naturally a social activity. That's what's so enjoyable about eating out—you get to feel social.

Linda: But eating is also a personal thing, right? It's about the home and family, too.

Jack: I would say that restaurants are important because they provide a place where people can feel slightly special—like they're somewhere besides their living room with a bowl of cereal. They make eating feel elevated.

Linda: If that's the case, what's the deal with all these restaurants saying they're "just like home"?

Marcus: Well, that's the goal of those chain restaurants, which really aren't like home at all. They're trying to make people feel close to home.

Linda: So these restaurants provide something psychologically to people. I guess that's why restaurants spend so much on atmosphere and advertising.

Marcus: So what about the particular restaurant Chunky's? Does it make people feel "at home"?

Linda: Not really. It feels like a chain restaurant that's attempting to not feel like a chain restaurant.

Linda has discovered something beyond the obvious about the subject's purpose: Restaurants aren't simply about food; they are also about familiarity. (There's an important psychology to food service!) This discovery could impact how she evaluates the particular restaurant.

In Bell's invention writing, the public resonance is tied to the main discovery he makes in Analysis. In the following excerpt, he narrows in on the actual thesis of the essay:

Why is this subject important in people's lives?

It is some people's favorite TV show, a show that they grew up watching and that gives them a certain feeling. It makes them feel good. It makes them feel at home. The same could be said about *Star Trek* or *Will and Grace* or other shows. Specifically, *The Andy Griffith Show* goes beyond being funny in the way that it presents what people might like to think of as "normal." Life is full of all sorts of characters (some wacky, some annoying) and all sorts of situations or complications arise, and in all sitcoms (maybe not all, but probably) the conflict is resolved. But *The Andy Griffith Show* seems to suggest that the resolution is normal, whereas other shows suggest that conflict or tension is normal.

THESIS

An evaluation makes a judgment about a subject. An evaluative thesis statement gives focus to that judgment: The thesis sheds light on a particular element of the subject. For instance, a movie has many elements, such as characters, plot, cinematography, themes, special effects, and dialogue. A thesis can help create focus, telling the reader that the evaluation will deal primarily with plot, not character development and costumes:

> The movie's plot is unnecessarily confusing.

An evaluative thesis need not be completely positive or completely negative. It need not, for example, claim that a particular movie is absolutely great or downright rotten. Many evaluative thesis statements are a mixture of judgments. A statement might concede some value but focus primarily on a shortcoming as in the following:

> While the movie's cinematography is engaging, the plot is unnecessarily confusing.

> Although the student government has been more public than in previous years, it has still failed to address the student body's most significant concerns.

> Even with the new ensemble tricks, which provide an interesting layer of ear candy, Ebenezer Typhoon's new collection of songs still lacks any substantive message.

> The menu at Robinson's Grill may lack diversity, but it does what so many other restaurants cannot: deliver a genuinely local dining experience.

Evolution of a Thesis

A good thesis gives focus to an entire project. Linda's evaluation of a restaurant (in the Public Resonance section) gains focus as she works to craft a thesis. First, she discovers the subject's purpose. Then, while exploring public resonance, she discovers another, less obvious, layer. From there, she refines the idea into an evaluative claim:

- Chunky's attempts to give people a variety of good food and friendly service.

- People like to feel attached to their surroundings, to the places they shop and eat. Therefore, restaurants such as Chunky's try to create the illusion that diners are patronizing a friendly neighborhood grill.

- Although Chunky's attempts to make people feel comfortable in a small neighborhood grill, it doesn't work very well.

- Although Chunky's attempts to make people feel comfortable in a small neighborhood grill, the atmosphere and food still seem prepared by a distant corporate chef.

Linda's thesis evolved as she worked through the complexities of the subject. She discovered a subtle gap between the restaurant's purpose and the actual dining experience. This insight reveals something that might otherwise go unnoticed.

To focus your evaluation and generate a thesis, answer the following:

On what particular value or shortcoming do I want to focus?

Common Thesis Problems

The blurry focus problem A sufficiently narrow focus can mean all the difference between intensive and bland writing. First, a writer needs to hone in on a particular subject, such as a particular band, a particular college campus or program. But that is often not enough. As in the following examples, the specific subjects still do not provide intensive points:

- Green Day is a great punk band.
- Big River Community College is a good school.

These statements need more focus. The writers could examine more particular elements (such as the themes of Green Day's songs or the accessible class times at Big River). Or the writers could develop more vital statements by avoiding the broad predicates "is a great . . ." and "is a good. . . ."

The obvious fact problem The goal of evaluative writing is to help readers see the subject in a new light—to help them see some particular value or shortcoming. But writers sometimes fall into the trap of stating the obvious:

- Howard Stern offends people.
- Although some purists did not like it, the *Lord of the Rings* trilogy made a lot of money at the box office.

Both of these statements announce common knowledge, facts about the radio shock jock and the Peter Jackson movies. But neither statement offers an evaluation. The stated facts say nothing about the value or shortcoming of the subjects. Offending people, for instance, may be a good thing. And making lots of money may not mean much about the movies' artistic success.

The noncommittal problem An evaluation is an argument; therefore, the writer should put forth a position. But it may be tempting to back away from the evaluation and to let the reader make up his or her own mind about the subject. The following examples back away; they lack a committed stance:

- The new building will please some and offend others.
- It's up to all readers to decide whether they appreciate Kingsolver's *The Bean Trees* or not.

The noncommittal problem is related to a broader issue: Some writers are afraid of pushing too hard. They want to avoid forcing readers into a perspective. While this seems like a legitimate concern, we should remember that readers need not be *forced* into an opinion or new perspective. Instead, they can be invited, lulled, guided, nudged, or attracted. Writers should seek to make their opinions so attractive, reasonable, enlightened, and compelling that readers feel as though they must adopt them. In short, don't fear commitment! Readers are waiting around for their minds to be changed.

Revision

Share the thesis statement for your essay with two other writers. As you look over their statements, look for all three common problems: blurry focus, obvious fact, and noncommittal. Suggest strategies for narrowing and intensifying the statements.

RHETORICAL TOOLS

An evaluation puts forth a particular, and potentially debatable, opinion about a subject. And when any debatable opinion is put forth, it should be supported.

Support about the Subject

Most of the claims made in evaluations are supported with specific information about the subject itself. The writer points out particular details that illustrate the main idea and show the value or shortcoming of the subject. For example, Ed Bell describes particular features of *The Andy Griffith Show:*

> The show's main character, Andy, is full of southern wisdom. He is quiet and listens and makes better decisions in the midst of all the madness than we could have. That is comfort number one: Someone—the general, the man in charge, *the sheriff*—has things under control. All the madness results from one of three things: either intruders, but Andy gets rid of them after they have caused only a little trouble; or just boys (Opie and sometimes his friends) going through what is natural to go through growing up, but Andy deals with this expertly, too; or ego, ambition, and pride—usually Barney is having the trouble here, though it could be Aunt Bea or one of the others. Andy understands all of this, though not so well or right away that the show isn't a little bit interesting. The plot is better than most sitcoms: There is always a solution that takes a little while to get to, and we believe it when we finally do.

For your evaluative claims, be sure to use details about your subject. As you develop support, ask the following:

Which details best show my point about the subject's worth or shortcomings?

Caution: Beware of Too Much Summary

A writer should present some basic facts about, or summarize, the subject as part of the evaluation. The presentation or summary of the subject should *not* constitute the majority of an evaluation, but should offer only the relevant details about the subject. For example, an evaluation using the thesis *While the movie's cinematography is engaging, the plot is unnecessarily confusing* would not devote long passages to the dress or appearance of the characters. Such information would be unnecessary and irrelevant to the evaluation.

Support Outside the Subject

As explained in Chapter 7, writers have the world of history and culture at their disposal. This applies to evaluation as well. Although evaluative writing depends primarily on details about the subject at hand, writers may also refer to outside issues/ideas/subjects to substantiate their claims. To prove a point about the subject, the writer can borrow from other moments in history, from science, nature, popular culture, or merely point out other like subjects. For example, Jaren Provo goes beyond her topic, *Star Trek,* to reinforce her thesis:

> Many also claim that *Star Trek* is merely a scripted TV show, unrealistic and inaccessible to all but the most obsessive fans. However, *Star Trek* has reached and influenced some of the leaders of technology and society, including individuals such as Bill Gates, several NASA scientists and engineers, and even the late Dr. Martin Luther King, Jr. The message of *Star Trek* resonates through these and other individuals familiar with *Star Trek*'s ideals, such that all in society are influenced by this series. Many outlets in society and the media also carry *Star Trek*'s concepts into their settings on an entertainment level. Considering

entertainment's pivotal role in our society (take, for instance, the large number of individuals who gain current events knowledge from comedy shows such as *The Daily Show, The Tonight Show with Jay Leno,* and *Saturday Night Live*), the sheer entertainment quality of Star Trek brings it into our everyday lives. Furthermore, the core concepts of *Star Trek* are not fictional and far-reaching, but are based on events and themes within the Vietnam War era and relating to the human condition.

To develop claims using outside support, consider the following questions:

- Does a historical situation or trend (such as the rise of a particular fashion, organization, or individual) illustrate something about my topic?

- Does my topic or situation appear in any movies or television shows? If so, how is it handled?

- Does my topic appear in any works of literature? If so, how is it handled?

- Has science taught us anything about my topic?

- Have I witnessed or experienced someone or something that illustrates my point?

- Can I construct a scenario to illustrate my point?

Counterarguments and Concessions

Evaluations can also involve counterarguments and concessions (see Chapter 7, pages 246–247). Because evaluations are argumentative, they must acknowledge that other opinions (other judgments about the subject) are possible. In another passage from Provo's essay, she explains an opposing position, and then in a classic turnabout paragraph, she counters:

> However, some feel that *Star Trek*'s diverse cast is not as accepting and multicultural as it appears. In his piece, "Carved From the Rock Experiences of Our Daily Lives: Reality and *Star Trek*'s Multiple Histories", Lincoln Geraghty concedes that TOS

casts "token" minority members as crew and is deficient because of its lack of an openly homosexual crewmember (161). In this way, he argues, *Star Trek* repeats the "mistakes other popular television series made" (161). However, it is important to observe the cultural climate of the 1960s, especially in popular media. If indeed minority groups were portrayed, they were often playing roles of servants (Asian Americans), slaves (African Americans), or senseless and vicious warriors on the Western plains (Native Americans). The latter was not often represented by those from this culture; often, individuals of Italian descent were given the roles of Native Americans. Though perhaps not main characters with substantial parts (with the exception of Spock, who is an alien and would in a sense be considered a member of a "minority" group), these individuals are not degraded, but are respected on the merit of their performance and contributions to the ship itself.

Invention Workshop

The Devil's Advocate

This activity is designed to generate counterarguments. The process involves an intensive group exchange. Follow these steps:

- Assemble writers into small groups (three or four per group work best).

- Each writer should have his or her thesis statement (main evaluative claim about the subject) written down.

- The first writer should read his or her thesis statement aloud to the group.

- Taking turns, each group member then should attempt to refute the position given in the statement. The idea is to play devil's advocate, to complicate the writer's ideas.

- The writer should record each opposing claim that is offered.

- After everyone in the group has given an opposing claim to the first writer, the second writer should recite his or her thesis, and the process begins again.

ORGANIZATIONAL STRATEGIES

How Should I Include Support Outside of the Subject?

Like any support tool, the possibilities are limitless. You might reference another similar subject briefly to help describe something, as Jaren Provo does:

> Also uncharacteristic of *Star Trek* but common in the sci-fi realm is the element protraying humans as slaves of technology, hopefully existent only in body. This concept is perhaps most prevalent in the *Matrix* trilogy.

The reference to the *Matrix* movies is quick. It serves only to describe an alternative view, and so the attention on the original subject, *Star Trek,* is only briefly interrupted or broken. However, sometimes writers, such as Ed Bell, want to put more attention on something other than the original subject, and so develop a new paragraph entirely:

> From those early days of Lucy and Ricky to our own Dharma and Greg, situation comedies have been part of American culture. And for all the advancements, it still seems like the plots of most of them are something cooked up by Lucy who dragged along Ethel and got caught (and ultimately forgiven) by Fred and Barney . . . uh . . . Fred and Ricky, I mean. Whether or not these shows instruct is, I suppose, debatable. But what is not debatable is that over the past 50 years they have entertained millions. And, I would suggest, through that very act of entertaining us, they have comforted us—the most comforting of them all being *The Andy Griffith Show.*

When Should I Change Paragraphs?

When considering paragraphs, it may be helpful to think of a television documentary of the Civil War: The camera pans across an old battlefield while the host's voice narrates events. Then the scene breaks, and the camera focuses on a city that housed the soldiers; then the scene breaks again to focus on plantations that encircled a key battlefield. And when an in-depth analysis is in order, the camera shifts to a studio where the host sits talking with us about the deeper significance of the scenes; that is, the camera focuses on the speaker, so that she or he can expound on one issue.

Paragraphs in an evaluation can work similarly. They can break when the writer wants the reader to focus on a new aspect of the subject, and they can even shift whenever the writer wants to give an extended analysis of a particular point. For example, Jaren Provo uses paragraphs as mini-analytical sections. Each focuses on a particular attribute of her topic. Notice how the first sentence of three paragraphs helps the reader to tune in on that attribute:

> ¶ 8 Together, these humans learn from past mistakes, attempting to avoid their occurrence in other cultures developing in similar manners . . .

> ¶ 9 Notably absent from *Star Trek*'s list of qualities is the predominant science fiction theme regarding space aliens: "When they come, they'll destroy us all."

> ¶ 10 Also uncharacteristic of *Star Trek* but common in the sci-fi realm is the element portraying humans as slaves of technology, hopelessly existent only in body.

How Should I Deal with Counterargument?

As in any argument, counterargument can be addressed in an unlimited number of ways. It may depend on the nature of your subject and on your position. If you are taking a relatively controversial stance or one that is not often taken, you should be prepared to counterargue. For example, imagine a writer giving a negative evaluation of *Good Morning, America,* a popular and seemingly harmless television program. In this turnabout paragraph, the writer briefly addresses an opposing view ("Certainly, many would argue that . . . ") and then immediately counters ("But the problem is not . . . "):

> Good Morning, America confuses news with feel-good entertainment. Like an evening sitcom, its primary goal seems to be making the viewer feel that all is right with the world—or, specifically, all is right with the shiny happy middle-class world in America. Certainly, many would argue that feel-good shows are a plus and that a morning show devoted to gloom and doom would be a great disservice. <u>But</u> the problem is not with the feel-good mood. It is that Good Morning, America postures itself as a quasi-news program, so any "news" that is given is ultimately framed by dimwitted celebrities making gratuitous appearances and exercise tips for the on-the-go lifestyle. The show smears news of the world across the same screen as the movie of the week. It's newstainment.

But you might decide to develop an opposing view for an entire paragraph and then counter in a new paragraph:

> opposing position ¶
> your counterargument ¶

And if the topic required attention to more opposing points, the pattern can be repeated:

> opposing position ¶
> your counterargument ¶
>
> opposing position ¶
> your counterargument ¶

Activity

Make a Plan

Now that you have the basic elements of your evaluation, map out your evaluation. Will you state your main judgment in the introduction? Where and how will you address counterarguments? Do you have to include much support outside the subject? What about allusions? Counterarguments? Concessions? In developing her evaluation of Chunky's (see p. 320), Linda might develop the following map:

Intro: personal testimony about a dining experience

¶ Description of the walls—signs and various "old" artifacts

¶ "Fun" wait staff and "Happy Birthday" song

¶ Menu, entry names, and their appeal

¶ Food, the seasoning

¶ What a local restaurant should attempt, what atmosphere it should create

Integrate the Jackson article here.

¶ What eating in public means, what people pay for

Integrate the psychology article here.

¶ Opposing position: consistency—the "no surprises" value of corporate food.

Counterargument: the need for intimacy and locality. Integrate second quote from psychology article.

¶ Opposing position: cost—the corporate restaurant offers more deals for families.

Counterargument: that's an illusion that doesn't work out at the final bill.

¶ Concessions: Corporate restaurant chains are not inherently evil.

Conclusion: Nearly everything about public life is defined by corporate slogans, aesthetic, and service. (Add allusions) People need a break from places like Chunky's. We can only swallow so much before our taste buds are ruined for good.

WRITER'S VOICE

A good evaluation can be strongly worded without being stilted. A productive evaluation, like a good argument, attracts readers and engages those who might oppose the claims being made; a bad or unsuccessful evaluation loses readers. Here are some strategies for maintaining a cool but engaging tone.

Avoiding Harsh Description

It is often easy to use the most emotionally loaded terms to describe something or someone, to proclaim a subject "ridiculous" or "dumb." Such description, however, is usually exaggerated, and suggests that the writer has not fully investigated the subject. Be cautious of dismissing a subject by using especially harsh words. Imagine the following passage in which a writer evaluates a government official:

> Mayor G. is out of his mind. He has no understanding of the political spectrum and no concept of city governance. He is just some crazy, power-hungry man looking for a soapbox to stand on. If the city really understood the depth of his insanity, it would kick him out of office immediately.

Such language is not only full of logical fallacies, but it also reveals the writer's unfocused aggression more than revealing an interesting and important point about the mayor. Such language distracts readers from the subject, but a successful writerly voice should prompt the reader to investigate the subject closely.

Avoiding the Enthusiasm Crisis

On the other hand, be careful not to overwhelm your reader with enthusiasm. If a writer comes off too amused or too enthralled with a subject, readers may react with suspicion. Imagine a glowing evaluation of a political candidate:

> Zelda Brown is the best politician the country has seen. She has a perfect record as a community leader. Her insights into state politics are responsible for the American dream we are all living.

Certainly, any conscious and critical reader would recognize such claims as overblown and ungrounded. Too much enthusiasm alienates a reader in the same way as excessive negativity does.

Exploring the Boundaries

Some writers perform. Their language suggests, "Look at what I'm saying, and how I'm saying it!" Some writers lay low. Their language says, "I'm here, but only to give you some information." Some writers hide. Their language says, "I hope no one sees me in this essay." Every writer has a comfort zone, the place where he or she feels most at ease. The problem is that our most comfortable voices are not always the most appropriate for the situation, and they do not allow us to explore language. In some situations, the intensely performative writer may need to be invisible and understated. The writer hiding behind sentences may occasionally need to step forward and be noticed.

The best writers in all disciplines, occupations, and walks of life are not locked into a voice. They can work with various voices, depending on the writing situation. As you consider your own voice and your own habits, imagine breaking from your comfort zone. Explore the following:

Asides Writers often use parentheses or dashes to make an aside comment or ask a rhetorical question. The material separated by parentheses or dashes is often a more intimate or personal note (something one might share only with the person sitting closest at the table). These often help create a particular voice because they reveal insights that are less public, or even less directly related to the main idea, than other information. In the following passage, Jaren Provo makes two asides:

> After this contact, more connections are forged with other alien worlds, such that the United Federation of Planets develops (with a flag suspiciously reminiscent of that of the United Nations) to promote peaceable cooperation among these cultures. Alien cultures are not (generally) out to conquer Earth and all of humanity in a blazing inferno of death and destruction, but are civilized, developing worlds willing to forge ties with others in the universe to assure mutual survival.

The first, longer aside effectively winks at the readers. It nudges us in the shoulder as if to say, "On the down-low, we know what that's all about, eh?" The second offers a slight qualifier. Because *generally* is set apart from the main part of the sentence (in parentheses), it slows the reader down a bit and makes Provo's voice feel slightly more cautious, more present, more aware of us—her readers. In fact, we might even say that all asides function in this way: to make the writer feel more in touch, more in cahoots, with readers.

Intensive Description When writers stay abstract and general, when they do not commit to particulars, their voices remain less visible. Abstraction often hides the writer's voice. But when writers characterize their subjects by using particular and focused words, their voices become recognizable. For instance, throughout his essay, Steven Poole commits to specific details about his topic:

> Pretty old-skool, huh? It's perfect: far less temptation to switch to a browser window, much better concentration on the text in front of you. WriteRoom has a "typewriter-scrolling mode," so that the line you are typing is always centred in the screen, not forever threatening to drop off the bottom, and what you have already written scrolls rapidly up off the top of the screen, dissuading you from idly rereading it. It's a bit like the endless roll of typewriter paper on which Jack Kerouac wrote *On the Road*.

His specific descriptions create a sense of his emotional relationship with the topic. We understand more than his formal comments about Microsoft Word; we also feel a layer of emotion. Ed Bell's description also impacts his voice in his own essay. The intensive description does more than describe the show; it also develops the tone of the essay:

> Yet *The Andy Griffith Show* leaves us with the feeling that, even though our friends sometimes get big-headed ideas or strangers from Raleigh come driving or dancing or swindling their mixed-up way into our peacefulness, life will eventually return to normal, all warm and wonderful.

Revision

As you consider your own writing, revise abstract passages and describe your subject with intense details.

SEARCHING FOR CAUSES

Chapter Contents

CHAPTER 10

"All human beings should try to learn before they die what they are running from, and to, and why."

—James Thurber

When something happens in a community, everyone wants to know why. Why did the apartment building catch on fire? Why did the incumbent mayor's campaign lose momentum? Why are so many kids absent from school? What causes the traffic jam on I-95 every day? Why did the stock market suddenly drop? Why did the terrorists attack? Of course, everybody has guesses, but it takes a close analysis to discover the possible causes of such phenomena. Fire officials inspect the ashes of a burned apartment building; political scientists examine candidates' speeches and poll results; civil engineers look closely at travel patterns and highway capacity; economists deliberate over consumption trends and overseas markets. In all these cases, the people searching for causes are detectives attempting to find answers amidst a dizzying array of possibilities.

The search for causes constitutes much of the workload in many occupations. Doctors, of course, diagnose patients (looking for the cause of particular symptoms). Psychologists try to understand the causes of personality disorders or behavioral problems. Business executives hold weekly meetings and discuss the causes of production failures. Education specialists work with children to find the cause of scholastic problems. And, as you can imagine (or as you may have witnessed), the search for such causes is not easy. Any number of factors can contribute to an effect. Take, for example, low proficiency test scores in public schools: School administrators might argue that poor teaching is the cause; teachers may point to poor parenting and discipline problems in the classroom; parents may point to bullying on school grounds or drug abuse; others might point to the tests themselves as the cause. The search for this cause, as it turns out, is a heated debate.

In academia, students spend much of their time studying causes:

- In an engineering class, students try to discover what causes one generator to produce more energy than another.

- Educational psychology students discuss why a particular student has lost all motivation.
- In history and economics seminars, students study economic conditions of the 19th century and debate the causes of the American Civil War.
- A class of physics students tries to determine the cause of black holes.

It might even be said that academia prepares people to understand causes in different fields—that is, that the study of a particular discipline gives students the critical perspectives necessary for asking the right questions (to find the right answers) within their fields. But despite the particular field or discipline, the process of discovery (of focusing and analyzing) is much the same, and the act of communicating one's discoveries is key in every situation.

This chapter will help you focus on a particular topic (a behavior, event, trend), discover a possible cause, and then develop an argument in favor of that particular cause. The following essays will provide valuable insight to necessary writing strategies. After reading the essays, you can find a topic in one of two ways:

1. Go to the Point of Contact section to find a problem from your everyday life. or
2. Read the following essays and choose one of the Ideas for Writing that follow.

After finding a subject, go to the Analysis section to begin developing the evaluation.

Outside Reading

Find an essay or report that explores causes, and print it out or make a photocopy. To explore a specific field or major, search a related professional journal, such as *Nutrition Health Forum, Law Technology,* or *Education Journal.* Keep an eye out for titles of articles that begin with *why.* You might also find articles about causes in local and national newspapers. For journal or newspaper articles, go to your library's home page, and then choose a magazine or periodical database. (Choose one that says "full text" in the title.) Using a keyword search, enter *cause and* plus any noun that interests you, such as *cause and flu, cause and recession, cause and global warming, cause and traffic jams.*

You can also search the Internet. Try a Google search, but go to Google's special search for government studies and reports: www.Google.com/unclesam. At the search box, type any topic of interest, and *cause.* (In Google, Boolean operators such as *and* are unnecessary.) The search results will yield only government-sponsored studies and reports.

The purpose of this assignment is to explore the range of possibilities for writing. You may discover a text that differs considerably from the essays in this chapter (in tone, rhetorical strategies, or organization). As you read through this chapter, keep the text you have discovered close by, and notice the elements and strategies the writer uses. Depending on your instructor's suggestions, do one or more of the following:

1. Notice how the writer applies various strategies from this chapter. On the hard copy or photocopy:
   - Highlight the thesis if it is stated. If the thesis is implied, write it in your own words.
   - Identify the major rhetorical strategies (appeals, evidence, counterargument, concession, etc.).
   - Identify any passages in which the writer attempts to create public resonance for the topic.

2. Analyze the strategies employed by the writer. The following questions may be helpful:
   - How is the writer's voice different from the essays in this chapter?
   - How does the writer support or illustrate his or her thesis?
   - Who is the audience for this text?
   - How does the audience impact the kinds of things said in the text?
   - How does the writer go beyond the obvious? (What new idea does the writer offer?)

3. Write at least three "Writing Strategies" questions for the text you found.

4. Write at least three "Exploring Ideas" questions for the text you found.

5. Write two "Ideas for Writing," such as the ones following the essays in this book, for the text you found.

- Educational psychology students discuss why a particular student has lost all motivation.

- In history and economics seminars, students study economic conditions of the 19th century and debate the causes of the American Civil War.

- A class of physics students tries to determine the cause of black holes.

It might even be said that academia prepares people to understand causes in different fields—that is, that the study of a particular discipline gives students the critical perspectives necessary for asking the right questions (to find the right answers) within their fields. But despite the particular field or discipline, the process of discovery (of focusing and analyzing) is much the same, and the act of communicating one's discoveries is key in every situation.

This chapter will help you focus on a particular topic (a behavior, event, trend), discover a possible cause, and then develop an argument in favor of that particular cause. The following essays will provide valuable insight to necessary writing strategies. After reading the essays, you can find a topic in one of two ways:

1. Go to the Point of Contact section to find a problem from your everyday life. **or**

2. Read the following essays and choose one of the Ideas for Writing that follow.

After finding a subject, go to the Analysis section to begin developing the evaluation.

Outside Reading

Find an essay or report that explores causes, and print it out or make a photocopy. To explore a specific field or major, search a related professional journal, such as *Nutrition Health Forum, Law Technology,* or *Education Journal.* Keep an eye out for titles of articles that begin with *why.* You might also find articles about causes in local and national newspapers. For journal or newspaper articles, go to your library's home page, and then choose a magazine or periodical database. (Choose one that says "full text" in the title.) Using a keyword search, enter *cause and* plus any noun that interests you, such as *cause and flu, cause and recession, cause and global warming, cause and traffic jams.*

You can also search the Internet. Try a Google search, but go to Google's special search for government studies and reports: www.Google.com/unclesam. At the search box, type any topic of interest, and *cause.* (In Google, Boolean operators such as *and* are unnecessary.) The search results will yield only government-sponsored studies and reports.

The purpose of this assignment is to explore the range of possibilities for writing. You may discover a text that differs considerably from the essays in this chapter (in tone, rhetorical strategies, or organization). As you read through this chapter, keep the text you have discovered close by, and notice the elements and strategies the writer uses. Depending on your instructor's suggestions, do one or more of the following:

1. Notice how the writer applies various strategies from this chapter. On the hard copy or photocopy:
   - Highlight the thesis if it is stated. If the thesis is implied, write it in your own words.
   - Identify the major rhetorical strategies (appeals, evidence, counterargument, concession, etc.).
   - Identify any passages in which the writer attempts to create public resonance for the topic.

2. Analyze the strategies employed by the writer. The following questions may be helpful:
   - How is the writer's voice different from the essays in this chapter?
   - How does the writer support or illustrate his or her thesis?
   - Who is the audience for this text?
   - How does the audience impact the kinds of things said in the text?
   - How does the writer go beyond the obvious? (What new idea does the writer offer?)

3. Write at least three "Writing Strategies" questions for the text you found.

4. Write at least three "Exploring Ideas" questions for the text you found.

5. Write two "Ideas for Writing," such as the ones following the essays in this book, for the text you found.

INVENTION

"One great cause of failure is lack of concentration."

—Bruce Lee

Invention is an act of discovery. It involves opening all the intellectual cases we have closed in everyday life. It involves asking questions where we had assumed we knew the answers. For this chapter, invention involves asking why something occurs (or has occurred) and going beyond the first (and second) guess. In Point of Contact, ask adventurous questions to find a topic. In Analysis, imagine unseen causes. In Public Resonance, consider the ways your topic extends outward and affects the public. In Thesis, focus your ideas to a particular insight, and in Rhetorical Tools, explore a range of possible support strategies. The Invention questions in each section are not meant to be answered directly in your final written assignment. In fact, as you work through the sections, avoid simply answering them and then moving on. Instead, use them to explore and to develop revelatory ideas.

POINT OF CONTACT

The search for a cause begins with a question: Why did something happen? Why does something continue? What causes some phenomenon? The following questions can help you to explore possible topics. After you have decided on a particular topic, go to the Analysis section to continue your search for causes.

Work

- Why are some sections/groups/teams more successful than others?
- Why is workplace efficiency up or down?
- Why are profits for the company or organization up or down?
- Why are some workers more content or fulfilled than others?

Local Events

- Why is urban sprawl taking place in your community?
- Why is a local sports team winning or losing?
- What makes one school perform better than others?
- Why are some areas of town more policed than others?
- Why do so many yards look the same?

Social Trends

- What causes road rage? Teenage rebellion? Conformity to fashion trends?
- Why are the elderly isolated?
- Why is depression on the rise in the United States?
- Why do Americans love sport utility vehicles?
- Why does the condition of streets change throughout a city?
- Why doesn't anyone care about the future?

Campus Issues

- Why do college students binge drink?
- Why do some students cheat? Procrastinate?
- What causes boredom?
- Why are some classes more difficult for large numbers of students?

Politics

- Why do younger generations tend not to vote?
- Why does a certain community consistently vote Democratic or Republican?
- Why do minority voters tend toward Democratic candidates?

Your Major

- What has caused the field to thrive (or deteriorate) in recent years?
- What has fueled a recent debate in the field? Why has the debate continued?
- Find the cause of a phenomenon in your field, for example:
  —*History:* a revolution, a military victory or loss
  —*Art:* a style (such as impressionism), an artistic revolution
  —*Geology:* mudslides, a volcanic eruption
  —*Biology:* an organism's short life span
  —*Criminal Justice:* a jury decision, a Supreme Court decision to hear a case
  —*Business Marketing:* the success or failure of a marketing campaign
  —*Architecture:* the appeal of a recent building design, the change in mid-20th-century buildings

Activity

In a group (in class, on a listserv, or in a chatroom), generate more options for seeking out a topic. Share your ideas with the class.

ANALYSIS

Now that you have a topic (any phenomenon from the above or from your own set of questions), the next step is to begin searching for possible causes. (We use the term *phenomenon* here to refer to anything you are exploring—any behavior, event, situation, attitude, issue, idea, and so on.) You may already have some guesses about the cause. But keep an open mind. Any single phenomenon can be a consequence of many factors, both physical and abstract.

Invention Questions

Respond to the following questions and refer back to your notes as you continue the process.

- What events or behaviors led to the phenomenon?
- What social conditions or prevailing attitudes led (or could lead) to the phenomenon?
- What economic conditions led to the phenomenon?
- What state of mind or psychological need may have led to the phenomenon?
- What are all the possible reasons someone would carry out this behavior?

With several other writers, use one or two of the Invention questions to initiate a discussion about your topics. Even though some questions might seem irrelevant, do not dismiss them quickly. Explore the impact of each question on your topic. For example, in the following workshop, Jack develops his initial thoughts about this topic: why people join cults.

What state of mind or psychological need may have led to the phenomenon?

Jack: These people are obviously sick—mentally ill.

Diana: What kind of mental illness?

Jack: I don't know . . . probably some kind of schizophrenia or something.

Diana: But a lot of the people who join cults are otherwise productive members of society—with jobs, families, homes, social responsibilities. I've even heard that some cults attract people who are smarter than average. It doesn't seem like these people are downright mentally ill—at least in the way most people talk about mental illness.

Jack: So if they aren't sick in some way, why would they possibly leave behind their families and friends, give all their money to a group of strangers, and lose their identities?

Marcus: Well, I've heard that a lot of those people don't have friends—they're lonely.

Jack: How can people be lonely if they have families and jobs?

Marcus: Working a job and supporting a family doesn't necessarily make someone truly connected to others. Think about mid-life crises—where people run out and have wild flings or buy ridiculously expensive sports cars. They're obviously unfulfilled.

Jack: But wouldn't you say that joining a cult is a little more extreme than buying a car or having an affair?

Diana: Sure, but remember that a lot of people long for something more than sex and fast cars. They wonder what's out there, what their purpose is, what's beyond this life.

Jack: And religious cults have all those answers—well, at least that's the argument.

Diana: Yeah, so the whole issue may be related to loneliness and longing rather than sickness.

Thinking Further

Now for the fun part: taking your new ideas and exploring them further. For example, in his dialogue with Diana and Marcus, Jack's thinking evolves:

Beginning of the dialogue: Sick people join cults.

End of the dialogue: Loneliness and longing, which run rampant in mainstream culture, drive people to wonder what they're missing. This is where cults come in.

With this new understanding, Jack might come to more insightful conclusions about the perspective of people who join cults:

> I guess in the eyes of a potential cult member, a cult doesn't look like a cult. I mean, a group doesn't hang a "Cult" sign on the door. They don't say, "Hey!! Join our cult!! We'll all kill ourselves next year! It'll be great!!" No. A cult is merely a group of people who offer a web of relationships and a clear purpose in life. Isn't that why people go to college even though they hate it?! Isn't that why people join the Army?? A clear sense of purpose?!! Is college a kind of cult? Is the Army?!! Here's the message of both institutions: "Leave behind everything—your family, etc. Come here. Stay with us. And . . . you have to follow our strict schedule of events. But in the end, you'll be way better off." Holy crap! We're a culture of . . . cults.

Jack's continued exploration of why people join cults has taken him into new intellectual territory. He is exploring the relationship between something he thinks is dangerous (cults) and something he thinks is normal (college, the army).

Use the following questions to think further:

- How has your understanding of the cause developed? What new idea has entered your thinking?
- Why didn't you think about this before?

In Leonard Kress's invention notes, he explores some personal behaviors from the past in his attempt to determine what caused his bulimic behavior. Here, Kress begins to note the gap between common assumptions about bulimia and his own experience. And that gap is important, even vital, for Kress's analysis:

What caused your behavior as a child?

I have seen some discussion about high school wrestlers—I even recall a friend who subsisted on popsicles for two days to "make weight" and who occasionally vomited in the boys' room, both with the coach's approval. But children? Young boys? This didn't seem to fit the mold. I have these vivid images of places where I vomited, of scenes I caused, of my parents' quiet exasperation.

Research

Find an outside source (a website, article, or book) about your concept. (Consult Chapter 13: Research & Writing, to help you explore.) The author(s) of the source may have a different understanding of the causes. Summarize the main points of the source, then answer the following questions:

- Does the source suggest a cause for the phenomenon?
- If not, does the source imply or assume a cause?
- Does the source account for the most direct cause?
- Does the source account for indirect or multiple causes? Hidden causes?

PUBLIC RESONANCE

Some topics automatically resonate with public concerns or interests. For example, Jamie Bentley's essay discusses how our love of consumption harms the environment, causes individual economic problems, and contributes to the breakdown of the family. But other topics may seem more difficult to connect with. Local or intensely personal topics, for instance, may seem less linked to broader concerns. Who would think that childhood vomiting could be an interesting topic or make for a valuable essay? But Leonard Kress makes his own vomiting experience resonate (in more than one way) with readers:

> My brother and sister were silent, too, as though my barfing were a perfectly acceptable alternative to an after-dinner mint, a toothpick, a wet-wipe wrapped like a condom. Perhaps they were too busy stashing away the details of the affront, safekeeping for a time of need—like Aesop's despicable, self-righteous ant. I can only imagine the hay they might have later made by simple melodramatic evocations of the sounds of my gagging, as it echoed in tiny bathrooms. The deep, throaty sound of plosively expelling vomit. "Well, whatever I did can't be as gross and disgusting as THAT," I can hear them repeating over and over till they got what they wanted. Or did they have their own equally disgusting but self-customized techniques of catharsis and orgasm back then—I wondered. Does everyone, I still wonder? And how could a "D" in French or a detention or a missed meal or a dent in the car compare with what I did, over and over and over?

In this paragraph, Kress broadens the scope, including his siblings and "everyone." He makes the connection for us: Not everyone throws up for catharsis, but, he supposes, everyone may have some technique for experiencing relief, release, or comfort. This broader scope does not mean that Kress is losing focus—he is bringing others into the issue. As a writer, he knows that his job is to invite others into his exploration, into his search for causes.

Imagine how your topic involves others who are not directly associated with it. Use the following questions to help generate a sense of public resonance for your topic:

- What are the effects of this phenomenon?
- Whom does it affect? How does it affect them?
- How does it affect people indirectly?
- How does my position or understanding relate to popular perspectives on the topic?

In his exploration, Leonard Kress looks outward and compares his personal search with "pop psychology." He decides that his personal experience (and intellectual response) is different than what he sees in the media. But he doesn't therefore decide that his topic has no public resonance. Instead, he decides to explore the contrast between his experience and common characterizations.

How does your position or understanding relate to popular perspectives on the topic?

In writing this, I guess I am caught in the popular mania of confession. I consider myself to be a fairly private person, but all around I see people (in books, articles, on TV, etc.) revealing the most personal and embarrassing details about their lives. And doing so with relish. The fact that this piece deals with childhood makes it somewhat easier, of course. This is as close as I came to a taboo subject—and it intrigues me that my experience was so different from the media and pop psychology take on eating disorders and adolescent girls.

Kress's move here is vital to academic writing: When a writer discovers contrast or tension between his own experience and that of others, he has discovered something worth exploring more—something worth writing about.

Like Kress's topic, Jack's topic of cult membership might seem to only affect specific people—cult members, their families, maybe the communities surrounding the cult. But Jack goes further than that and imagines the broader and subtler factors:

How does it affect people indirectly?

If people are drawn to cults through deep loneliness, then cults potentially relate to everyone—that is, anyone who cares about family, friends, the quiet neighbor, etc. Our days are filled with constant inattention to others. Most people choose their narrow paths (their jobs and their small circle of friends) and leave everyone else. Many of us will go weeks without truly acknowledging anyone outside of our little circles. Rarely do we invite the quiet guy from work out with us; rarely do we call our cousin to see how she's doing. We leave lonely people behind us every day.

Jack could even explore further, examining the messages that popular culture sends to people: that we must have intense social engagement to achieve happiness and fulfillment, that solitude should be avoided, that excitement and purpose should define every minute of our lives. Jack would then be exploring the culture surrounding cults. He would be thinking like a sociologist, and assuming that any one behavior is linked to a broad system of attitudes, messages, and group behaviors.

Activities

1. Make a conceptual map of your ideas thus far. Graphically display the elements: the event, behavior, trend, the most direct cause, other possible causes, and even the public resonance. (See pages 133, 134, and 167 for ideas about of conceptual maps.)

2. Present your ideas to a small group of peers. Explain specifically how the phenomenon is caused. Also, explain the public resonance: how this phenomenon relates to the concerns and lives of others. Start a follow-up discussion about the phenomenon by asking the group members to consider how it affects their lives.

Is your thinking out of sync with conventional wisdom? If so, you may have discovered something important!

THESIS

The kind of writing done in this chapter is both analytical and argumentative. Each author of the chapter readings offers an analysis of the topic and an argument for his or her understanding of the cause. Each author has a thesis that focuses on the causes or set of causes most responsible for the phenomenon. As you consider your main point, examine all possible avenues. (You may even begin writing and drafting before your ideas take shape.) Your thesis might:

- Argue for a particular cause.

  Professional sports have gotten more violent because of the intensity of sports coverage in the media.

- Argue that several factors equally cause the phenomenon.

  Writing proficiency among American high school students continues to diminish because of a broader cultural disinterest in reading and a fundamental misunderstanding of language.

- Argue against an apparent cause or widely held belief and for a less obvious or more complicated cause.

  People drive gas guzzlers not because they are selfish and insensitive, but because they are uneducated about their real choices.

  The music industry is losing profits not because college kids are insatiable thieves, but because the industry has not evolved with the listening habits of the new generation.

As you consider your topic, decide on your emphasis:

Will it be important to thoroughly describe several causes or to focus on one?

Evolution of a Thesis

Your main idea may not come into focus immediately. Notice how Jack's thesis evolves from his initial thoughts into a sophisticated point.

Jack focuses on a particular phenomenon:

- What makes people leave everything and everyone behind and join cults?

He uses the Invention questions on page 354 to probe for causes:

- *What state of mind or psychological need may have led to the phenomenon?* Some form of mental disease makes people join cults.

He works through his initial thoughts and discovers a less obvious cause:

- Deep loneliness and lack of purpose in life cause people to leave their families and join cults.

Jack struggles to integrate public resonance into his understanding of the cause:

- The deep loneliness and loss created in our society cause people to crave belonging and purpose in their lives, and cults can meet those needs.

- The deep loneliness and loss fostered by our hurried society create desperate searches for belonging and purpose, and cults sometimes fulfill those needs.

Activity

Reflect on how your main idea, like Jack's, came into focus:

- What phenomenon did you focus on?
- What Invention question(s) did you use to probe for causes?
- What less obvious cause did you discover?
- How did you integrate public resonance into your understanding of the cause?

Common Thesis Problems

Perhaps the two most common thesis problems are psychological, striking before the writer ever touches a key or marks a paper.

1. **Fear of Ongoing Invention:** Some writers assume that thesis statements are fixed, unchangeable structures that must be strictly adhered to throughout a writing project. As they draft ideas and generate support for their initial point, they avoid asking hard questions and making new connections; that is, they fear continued invention once they've started drafting. But thesis statements are not traps. They are merely statements that help writers focus and intensify their thinking *as they are writing*. The human brain functions in new ways once serious writing and shaping begin; therefore, writers should allow their own writing to help them with new ideas.

2. **Fear of Commitment:** In contrast to the above fear, some writers avoid committing to a focused statement. They wander around without attempting to establish a particular idea, without digging in to a specific intellectual place. Such wandering, if it goes on for too long, often leads to shallow ideas (saying lots of different things about lots of different things). Although invention is key throughout the process, invention is not general wandering. Better ideas come when writers dig in their intellectual heels.

For more related common thesis problems, see Chapter 7, page 241.

Revision

Write out responses to these questions: *Am I afraid of ongoing invention? Why? Am I afraid of commitment? Why?* Then discuss your responses with a group of classmates.

1. How many people in your group have a fear of, or resistance to, ongoing invention or commitment?
   - What reasons do group members give for their fear of, or resistance to, ongoing invention? (What caused their fear or resistance?)
   - What reasons do group members give for their fear of, or resistance to, commitment? (What caused it?)

2. Discuss how each group member arrived at his or her thesis for this chapter's essay. Which group members might have committed to a rigid thesis too early? Choose an Invention question from earlier in the chapter that they should explore further for ongoing invention.

3. For group members who have trouble committing to one idea, help them focus their statement. Choose an Invention question they should explore to help narrow and deepen their thoughts.

Thesis statements are tools for narrowing and intensifying our ideas.

RHETORICAL TOOLS

Remember that you are not simply explaining a cause. You are arguing that a particular cause (or set of causes) could be responsible for a phenomenon, and you also are arguing that your understanding of the cause/effect relationship is worth considering. Therefore, consider the support strategies of argument (from Chapter 7: Making Arguments).

In the essays for this chapter, the writers use a broad range of support strategies. Kress, for instance, depends on information collected in his own everyday life (personal testimony and anecdotes) to support his argument. Personal experience (in the form of narration) is his primary support. He also uses authorities (outside sources). Deborah Tannen uses authorities, testimony, allusions, and examples. And all the writers rely heavily on appeals to logic in order to show the cause/effect relationships between the possible cause and the phenomenon itself.

Use the following questions to develop support for your thesis:

- How can I illustrate the relationship between the cause and the effect? (What line of reasoning can I use?)
- Does a historical event or figure help to show the cause?
- Can I allude to a similar phenomenon (with a similar cause) to support my point?
- Does a literary work (novel, poem, drama) or popular culture text (movie, television program, song) support my point?
- How do other writers discuss this cause?
- Does something in nature (in animal or plant life) support my point?
- Has anyone done scientific study on this phenomenon? Does it support my point?
- Have I witnessed or experienced someone or something that illustrates my point?
- Can I construct a hypothetical situation that illustrates my point?

Integrating Authorities (Outside Sources)

Outside sources must be carefully integrated into your own argument; that is, they must genuinely interact with your own claims. For instance, notice how Deborah Tannen uses the claims of other researchers. Since her own observations resonate with others' conclusions, her claims do not rest exclusively on outside sources. Like all good writers, she does not depend on the sources, but uses them to show how her own ideas fit into a broader discussion on the topic:

> The pattern was observed by political scientist Andrew Hacker in the late '70s. Sociologist Catherine Kohler Riessman reports in her new book *Divorce Talk* that most of the women she interviewed—but only a few of the men—gave lack of communication as the reason for their divorces.

Immediately after referring to other sources, she mentions her own research:

> In my own research, complaints from women about their husbands most often focused not on tangible inequities such as having given up the chance for a career to accompany a husband to his, or doing far more than their share of daily life-support work like cleaning, cooking, social arrangements and errands. Instead, they focused on communication . . .

Research should relate directly to the writer's claims. Tannen, or any of the writers in this chapter, could appear unbelievable if her claims were disconnected from her research. Imagine if Tannen had gone on in her essay to claim that "women are better talkers than men." Nothing in her research, at least as it is reported to us, would suggest such a conclusion. So, despite years of research, Tannen would lose credibility. However, Tannen's claims are appropriately focused and illustrated by the observations she shares with her readers. In other words, readers accept ideas when the support seems proportional and related to the claims.

See Chapter 13: Research & Writing for further guidance in integrating and documenting sources.

Counterarguing

Counterarguments defend against opposing claims. Writers must anticipate and account for positions outside of or opposed to their own claims(s) and include reasoning to offset that potential opposition. In many cases, writers must contend directly with arguments that forward another cause. Leonard Kress, for example, argues against common views and explains the way his position differs from others'. Here, Kress points to authorities who seem to miss the mark:

> I also locate "Determinants of Adolescent Obesity: A Comparison with Anorexia Nervosa," in *Adolescence* (1988), which claims that "both anorexics and the obese are characterized by overprotectedness and enmeshment, resulting from a poor sense of identity and effectiveness." After a whole week of research, this seems to be the extent of my findings. I can find nothing to urge me to go beyond the abstracts, nothing at all, though I type in "eating disorder," "vomiting," "obesity," "abnormal psychology," "gluttony," "disgusting and destructive behavior"—always cross-referenced with "childhood."

Because Kress mentions these other causes (or other takes on the phenomenon), we get the sense that he has a broad understanding of the topic—he is not simply guessing at a cause, but has explored other possibilities.

Use the following questions to develop counterarguments:

- What other causes could be attributed to this phenomenon? (Why are these other causes less acceptable or less valid?)
- What other reasons do people have for disagreeing with me?
- What support will most effectively respond to opposing positions?

Conceding

Concessions acknowledge the value of positions or claims other than those being forwarded by the writer. Remember that a good writer (with a broad understanding of the topic) is able to concede the value of some points or qualify his or her own points well.

As you consider your own argument, your own position about a cause, use the following questions to develop concessions and qualifiers:

- Are there legitimate reasons for taking another position on this topic?
- Does the argument make any large, but necessary, leaps?
- Do I ask my audience to accept generalizations?

Invention Workshop

The goal here is to play devil's advocate—to give each writer opposing positions to consider and possibly counterargue or concede.

- Each writer should announce his or her thesis.
- Group members should take turns offering responses to the first two Invention questions in each box on this page. Counterargument: What other causes could be attributed to this phenomenon? What other reasons do people have for disagreeing with me? Concession: Are there legitimate reasons for taking another position on this topic? Does my argument make any large, but necessary, leaps?

The goal for this workshop is to expose ideas that were hidden from writers. While it may be tempting to discuss one opposing position in-depth, at this point avoid discussion or debate until all group members have responded to each essay.

ORGANIZATIONAL STRATEGIES

Where Should I Explain the Phenomenon?

As with any argument, the elements of your essay can be arranged in many ways. One tendency among writers, whether using narrative, examples, or illustrations, is to detail the phenomenon (the behavior, event, trend) before getting into a discussion of causes. Notice how Kress's description of the phenomenon leads the reader into his discussion of the cause:

> I remember standing breathless and exhilarated in the hotel lobby, the rest of my family still in the dining room finishing their evening meal. I'm not sure whether or not they can see what I see—the thin gray broken line on the carpet, leading all the way to the back entrance. This time I don't make it out to the patio, the swimming pool, down to the beach, inundated this summer with jellyfish and jelly lichen, Portuguese Man O'War. If only they would leave their table, they could easily find me by following the half-digested dinner rolls and the masticated but intact sirloin morsels, the bitter tomato-broth they soak in. Hansel, whom I imagine to be about my age (seven and a half), couldn't have left a better trail for him and his sister to follow back to their woodland cottage. Even if the birds had pecked it clean, that bile-stain would still remain, like a stripe dividing a country highway. We are here in Miami Beach to visit my grandparents, Ada and Max, and since they live in a tiny apartment, we are staying in this beachfront hotel, more luxurious than we are used to. It occurs to me that only the desk clerk has been following my whole grand performance with any interest. Whatever others there might be carefully and kindly turn away their gaze. But the desk clerk glances over to me and across the lobby, as if surveying both the damage and the cause of it. I recognize that smirk and wonder, was he a vomiter too? I don't have a clue and don't really care; he assiduously computes the cleaning bill.

How Should I Deal with Other Causes?

Other causes, those that are different than yours, can help develop counterarguments; you can argue against other causes in favor of the cause you put forth. For example, Jack may point to a possible cause of cult membership (mental illness), but refute that idea in favor of another (loneliness). In this case, the argument that mental illness causes people to join cults is an opposing position—one that the writer counters:

> Some may argue that people join cults because they are mentally ill, nuts, freaked out. It is easy to write off cult members as lunatics. They willingly cast away their families and friends, give all of their life belongings to a bunch of strangers, wear uniform-like apparel, and sometimes even cut their hair to match the group. In short, they throw away their identities, something next to insanity in a culture that honors individualism as the greatest good. However, insanity may not be the main reason people join cults. In fact, many cult members are highly intelligent, entirely reasonable, and healthy individuals. But they long for something, something that everyone longs for—belonging and purpose.

If you have potential counterarguments, remember some standard strategies from Chapter 7: Making Arguments. Counterarguments might come directly after opposing points in counterpoint, point, counterpoint, point manner. Depending on the amount of detail given to each counter, each point might be an entire paragraph, or more, with supporting evidence:

Opposing Point A
Your counterargument

Opposing Point B
Your counterargument

How Should I Include Outside Sources?

If you have already gathered some information and know how you want to use it, keep in mind that any information from your research should only be included as part of your purpose for the paper. In other words, *be careful not to include information just for the sake of including it.* Notice how Tannen uses outside sources to support her argument (in ¶ 3) and to explain the phenomenon (in ¶ 7):

> The pattern was observed by political scientist Andrew Hacker in the late '70s. Sociologist Catherine Kohler Riessman reports in her new book *Divorce Talk* that most of the women she interviewed—but only a few of the men—gave lack of communication as the reason for their divorces. Given the current divorce rate of nearly 50 percent, that amounts to millions of cases in the United States every year—a virtual epidemic of failed conversation.
>
> In the April [1990] issue of *American Psychologist,* Stanford University's Eleanor Maccoby reports the results of her own and others' research showing that children's development is most influenced by the social structure of peer interactions. [...]

Tannen doesn't just insert outside information. She integrates it by concisely stating the source: Sociologist Catherine Kohler Riessman reports in her new book *Divorce Talk* that . . . . In the April [1990] issue of *American Psychologist,* Stanford University's Eleanor Maccoby reports . . . . Integrating outside information involves first, choosing information that helps the reader understand and accept your position and then, working it smoothly into the argument.

Invention Workshop

In your research thus far, have you found any outside sources that help to explain other perspectives on the cause? With a group of peers, discuss how you might use outside sources to explain other perspectives. If you haven't come across any outside sources that explain other perspectives, discuss what specific sources (journals, online databases, personal interviews) might offer other perspectives.

Also, discuss how you might use outside sources to help explain the phenomenon. What specific sources might be especially helpful?

If you have used outside sources, see Chapter 13: Research & Writing, for guidance on integrating and documenting them.

How Should I Use Paragraphs?

As in all academic prose (the language that scholars use to communicate ideas), paragraphs are used to cluster information. But we should also think of paragraphs as rhetorical tools—strategies for focusing and refocusing readers' attention. In this sense, paragraphs focus readers on a single idea, point, or example. For an argument about causes, a single paragraph might focus readers on a single illustration of a cause, an outside source that argues for a particular cause, a personal narrative that coincides, or counters the outside source, or a concession to an outside perspective.

Remember that the turnabout paragraph is a good tool for addressing opposing views. It often begins by expressing an opposing position (one different than the writer's) and then turns to counter that position. For example, see Jack's paragraph on the previous page. Rather than turnabout in the same paragraph, you can also begin a new paragraph when counterarguing.

Paragraphs are rhetorical tools— strategies for focusing and refocusing readers' attention.

WRITER'S VOICE

Creating Credibility

You are now familiar with many different tools for creating an engaging voice. As earlier chapters discuss, good writers are inviting and curious; they avoid preachiness and hostility. Writers also need to create a sense of credibility, the quality that makes points believable. In argumentative writing, and especially in more complicated types such as in this chapter, credibility is very important so readers consider your claims.

A credible voice is not necessarily commanding or domineering. It might simply be very logical or insightful. Deborah Tannen offers a slice of her own research to ground her claims and create credibility. Some writers, such as Leonard Kress, use personal experience to build credibility. In his essay, we get the sense that he may know more about the behavior than many of the supposed experts because of his experience. It is not his reference to *The Encyclopedia of Pediatric Psychology* that gives credibility to Kress's voice; rather, it is the manner in which he uses that information to highlight his own understanding. By the time Kress discovers the important passage in the encyclopedia, he has established his own credibility:

> . . . I could simply will the partially chewed hearty chunks of meat and potato up from their sour churning stock. It felt so good! *The Encyclopedia of Pediatric Psychology* (1979) reports that children who vomit, farfetched as it sounds, even "those who have learned society's aversions . . . can overcome such scruples and experience vomiting as cathartic, even orgasmic."

Activity

With a group of peers, discuss Bentley's voice: Does it project credibility? Why or why not? Refer to several passages to support your response.

Remember that you can be credible by your examination of personal experiences as well as of others' research. In considering your own writing, ask yourself the following:

- How will my own experiences or insights create credibility?
- How might outside sources add to my credibility?

Projecting Wonder

Some people assume that a sense of credibility means that the writer is unquestionable and unquestioning. However, credibility should not diminish a sense of curiosity. Even though the writers in this chapter have justification for speaking authoritatively about their topics (from research and observation), they also create a sense of curiosity, even wonder. Sometimes, the most authoritative voice is also the most curious. For example, Leonard Kress is curious even though he has reason to be certain about his claims:

> I often wonder now what led me to such disgusting behavior—what might lead any child to such disgusting behavior. Like any good 21st-century questioner/researcher, I go to the Internet, hopeful that a search of current medical literature will provide answers and understanding. So I begin my search, seated in front of my computer.

Now think of your own topic and your stance on it. Ask yourself the following:

- What about my topic is mysterious or unknown?
- How does my topic extend beyond usual perceptions or conventional thinking?
- What details or ideas associated with my topic might make the reader curious?

Avoiding Preachiness

Because this essay is argumentative in nature, it could potentially invite accusatory language. However, remember that most readers do not accept language that demeans people or tells people what they need. For example, in her essay "When Bright Girls Decide That Math Is a 'Waste of Time'," Susan Jacoby maintains a reflective and analytical voice:

> In saying that scientific and mathematical ignorance is a self-inflicted female wound, I do not, obviously, mean that cultural expectations play no role in the process. But the world does not conspire to deprive modern women of access to science as it did in the 1930s, when Rosalyn S. Yalow, the Nobel Prize–winning physicist, graduated from Hunter College and was advised to go to work as a secretary because no graduate school would admit her to its physics department. The current generation of adolescent girls—and their parents, bred on old expectations about women's interests—are active conspirators in limiting their own intellectual development.

Jacoby does not attack adolescent girls and their parents. Instead, she explains the complicated cultural process by which they accept their own low expectations in scientific and mathematical proficiency. Jacoby's analysis is not a blame game, but an examination of cause and effect. Imagine if Jacoby became accusatory toward adolescent girls and their parents:

> Girls should know better than to dump math and science classes. They need to realize that math and science are important for their intellectual development, and that dropping these courses means they will remain behind their male counterparts in many occupations. Their decision to replace math and science courses with drama and art shows their lack of responsibility.

Such language does nothing to help a reader understand the phenomenon or accept a particular cause; it merely spouts opinions about behavior. This passage also moves away from an argument about why something occurs to an argument against certain people. Most often, academic writing avoids telling readers what people should do and instead shows readers the value or liability of certain behavior.

Activity

1. In small groups, discuss how you might create credibility or project wonder for your essay.
2. Support your thesis by writing a paragraph that creates credibility or projects wonder.
3. Consider why you should or should not include the paragraph you wrote for #2 in your final essay.

As you consider your own voice, avoid condemning people or behaviors. Instead, try to explain why situations occur or why people act in a particular way. This strategy will help create a voice that is reflective and analytical, rather than condemning.

VITALITY

Academic writing should be clean and intense. Sentences should be sophisticated enough to prompt intensive thinking but concise enough to keep the reader moving briskly. Lively sentences can be any length—but they should not bog down the reader. It's a fine line: A long engaging sentence can help the reader experience an intense idea, but a long rambling phrase can confuse a reader thoroughly. This section focuses on that fine line. On one hand, we should avoid unnecessarily difficult phrases; on the other, we can intensify sentences by deliberately adding a series of clauses.

Avoid Strings of Phrases

Writers sometimes string together several prepositional phrases. (A prepositional phrase begins with a preposition, such as *in, of, between, on, beside, behind, for,* and so on.) Too many prepositional phrases (even two in a row) can slow down the reader. You might think of it as a matter of momentum: Verbs propel readers through sentences. So when too many phrases pile up, the sentence slows down. Without verbs, the meaning thickens up, the sentence gets muddy, and the reader gets bogged down. That's why good writers avoid clustering together too many phrases.

The following sentence begins with three prepositional phrases:

> The celebration of the holiday at the end of the month will attract many tourists to the town.

If the sentence is revised to have fewer prepositional phrases, the verb *(will attract)* will be closer to the beginning, and the sentence becomes less muddy:

> At the end of the month, the holiday celebration will attract many tourists to the town.

Activity

Rewrite the five following examples. Try to avoid using strings of prepositional phrases, but also try to keep all the information in the sentences.

1. The solving of this problem of racial segregation involves several steps that the people of the United States ought to understand.

2. Because of the nonviolent actions of the protestors in the courtyard, the city council arranged an emergency meeting.

3. The environmental group argued against the increased use of toxic chemicals for the development of the area golf courses.

4. Our present strategy creates the transition from imagining the world as a place full of attainable riches to thinking of the world as a place full of human resources.

5. The end of the first chapter of the book on migrating birds lists several different species and their geographical patterns.

A string of phrases or clauses is not always bad. In fact, good writers intentionally line up several phrases or clauses. What's the difference between a confusing string of phrases and a powerful series of phrases? The answer lies in *repetition:* Good writers use repeating patterns to reinforce ideas.

Intensify with a Series

A series of words creates a pattern for readers. When a chain of words is lined up, readers make an automatic intellectual connection among those words. We most often see single words in a series:

> The land flattens itself out and creates a sense of <u>openness</u>, <u>emptiness</u>, and <u>space</u>.

But phrases can also be put in a series:

> The land flattens itself out and creates <u>a feeling of openness</u>, <u>a sense of emptiness</u>, and <u>an eyeful of space</u>.

Skillful writers can even put entire clauses in a series. Here, the repeating clauses create an intellectual pattern for the reader. They set up a way of thinking—and pull the reader briskly through the images:

> They live in a place <u>where the fields lie uninterrupted</u>, <u>where the houses take the full brunt of the wind</u>, <u>where the horizon simply evaporates</u>.

The same strategy can be applied to any topic:

> The feelings of paranoia increase because the victims are often socially isolated, because they often live far from family, and because they seldom understand the nature of their condition.

> In spring, when the temperatures stay consistently above freezing, when the rain becomes nearly constant, and when the daylight overtakes the darkness, mammalian activity increases sharply.

The previous examples rely on three clauses in each series. Of course, a series can extend far beyond three clauses, but the same effect can be created with only two clauses. To reinforce a way of thinking, writers often use two of the same type of clause. Here, Leonard Kress uses a double clause pattern to emphasize and develop thinking:

> I often wonder now <u>what led me to such disgusting behavior</u>—<u>what might lead any child to such disgusting behavior</u>.

Avoid Expletives

Strings of phrases and extra words can begin to build up and choke the life out of one's writing. To help keep things lively, writers learn to delete unnecessary words, such as expletive constructions. Expletives begin with *there* or *it* and are followed by a form of *to be* (*is, are, was, were,* etc). Not every expletive construction should be replaced, and not every *there* or *it* followed by a form of *to be* functions as an expletive. Notice how the following sentences can be revised to remove the expletive and make the writing more clean and intense:

> There were women who perceived such responses as belittling and unsupportive. But there were boys who seemed satisfied with them.

> Women perceived such responses as belittling and unsupportive. But boys seemed satisfied with them.

> It is these differences that begin to clarify why women and men have such different expectations about communication.

> These differences begin to clarify why women and men have such different expectations about communication.

Invention Workshop

In small groups, each group member should share several pages of recent writing. Go through each member's writing looking for unnecessary and excessive use of expletives. Rewrite the sentences.

PEER REVIEW

Now get help from other writers. Before exchanging drafts with at least one other writer, underline your main idea (your thesis) or write it on the top of your draft.

As a peer reviewer, use the following questions to respond to specific issues in the draft.

1. Can any phrases or terms in the thesis be narrowed? If so, circle them and make some suggestions for more focus. Does the thesis avoid the common problems? (See pages 359 and 366.)

2. Can you follow the writer's line of reasoning? Do you accept the cause the writer asserts? Why or why not?

3. What other support strategies could the writer employ? (Consider examples, allusions, scenarios, and so on. See pages 243 and 360.)

4. Do any paragraphs shift focus from one point about the subject to another? Write "shifts focus" in the margins.

5. If the writer uses outside sources, are they integrated smoothly into the argument? (See pages 471–478, in Chapter 13: Research & Writing, for specific strategies.)

6. Consider the writer's voice.

   a. Identify any passages that seem preachy. (See page 365.)

   b. Does the writer seem credible? What passages support your decision? (See page 364.)

   c. Identify a passage that seems flat, without intensity. Suggest a strategy for the writer to create a sense of wonder. (See page 364.)

7. As a reviewer, point to particular sentences and phrases that could gain vitality and intensity. Use the following:

   a. Look for confusing strings of phrases. Suggest a revision.

   b. Rewrite a passage of the draft, and use a series of phrases or clauses to intensify an idea.

   c. Consider vitality strategies from other chapters:

   - Look for unnecessary, interrupting clauses and phrases. Underline them and/or draw an arrow to show where the phrase or clause can be moved.

   - Rewrite a sentence and create more intensity with a repeating pattern.

   - Cross out wordy phrases and write in more concise options.

   - What sentences are overembedded? (Point to any clauses that overlap with other clauses, causing a disconnect between ideas.)

   - Examine attributive phrases. Point out unnecessary phrases or sentences that could be boiled down.

   - Where can the writer change linking verbs to action verbs?

   - Where can the writer avoid drawing attention to *I* and *you*?

   - Help the writer change unnecessary clauses to phrases and phrases to words.

   - Point to expletives (such as *there are* and *it is*).

   - Help the writer change passive verbs to active verbs for more vitality.

DELIVERY

In academia, at work, and at home, understanding causes can have serious consequences. Exploring and writing about issues is likely to have consequences for the reader, the writer, and their community as a whole. What are the possible consequences of the essay you wrote for this chapter?

Consider these questions:

- Will the reader better understand the issue about which you wrote? Is the reader likely to think or behave differently as a result?
- What might be the benefits to others? How might others be harmed? Who besides your instructor might benefit from your ideas?
- What are the possible effects on you, the writer?

Beyond the Essay

Explore a photo (or image) essay How does the photo essay "Road Salt," below, encourage people to think about a cause? How do the four images work together to make some point? What other images might the writer have used, and why? What other order might the images have been placed in?

Create a photo (or image) essay Use at least four images to encourage people to think about a cause. Select and arrange the images carefully, and then in writing explain how the images work together to make your point.

Road Salt

PROPOSING
SOLUTIONS

PROZAC ®Weekly™

fluoxetine hydrochloride **90 mg**

Control No./Exp. Date

7RC09P / FEB 1 2010

3   0002-3004-01 7

Chapter Contents

CHAPTER 11

Xian Studio, LLC/MorgueFile

How to Say Nothing in 500 Words

Paul Roberts

College has a particular set of problems and a corresponding set of familiar solutions. For the college writing student, the recurring problem is fulfilling an assignment on time. And many (most?) students have accumulated strategies for "knocking out" or "getting through" the chore. But, as Paul Roberts argues, those familiar strategies work against students. The common solutions for getting through a writing assignment actually create another problem—bad grades. Roberts first names and illustrates the common solutions (or writing strategies) and then offers an alternative path for better dealing with college writing assignments.

It's Friday afternoon and you have almost survived another week of classes. You are just looking forward dreamily to the weekend when the English instructor says: "For Monday you will turn in a five-hundred-word composition on college football."

Well, that puts a good hole in the weekend. You don't have any strong views on college football one way or the other. You get rather excited during the season and go to all the home games and find it rather more fun than not. On the other hand, the class has been reading Robert Hutchins in the anthology and perhaps Shaw's "Eighty-Yard Run," and from the class discussion you have got the idea that the instructor thinks college football is for the birds. You are no fool. You can figure out what side to take.

After dinner you get out the portable typewriter that you got for high school graduation. You might as well get it over with and enjoy Saturday and Sunday. Five hundred words is about two double-spaced pages with normal margins. You put in a sheet of paper, think up a title, and you're off:

Why College Football Should Be Abolished

College football should be abolished because it's bad for the school and also for the players. The players are so busy practicing that they don't have any time for their studies.

This, you feel, is a mighty good start. The only trouble is that it's only thirty-two words. You still have four hundred and sixty-eight to go, and you've pretty well exhausted the subject. It comes to you that you do your best thinking in the morning, so you put away the typewriter and go to the movies. But the next morning you have to do your washing and some math problems, and in the afternoon you go to the game. The English instructor turns up too, and you wonder if you've taken the right side after all. Saturday night you have a date, and Sunday morning you have to go to church. (You can't let English assignments interfere with your religion.) What with one thing and another, it's ten o'clock Sunday night before you get out the typewriter again. You make a pot of coffee and start to fill out your views on college football. Put a little meat on the bones.

Why College Football Should Be Abolished

In my opinion, it seems to me that college football should be abolished. The reason why I think this to be true is because I feel that football is bad for the colleges in nearly every respect. As Robert Hutchins says in his article in our anthology in which he discusses college football, it would be better if the colleges had race horses and had races with one another, because then the horses would not have to attend classes. I firmly agree with Mr. Hutchins on this point, and I am sure that many other students would agree too.

One reason why it seems to me that college football is bad is that it has become too commercial. In the olden times when people played football just for the fun of it, maybe college football was all right, but they do not play college football just for the fun of it now as they used to in the old days. Nowadays college football is what you might call a big business. Maybe this is not true at all schools, and I don't think it is especially true here at State, but certainly this is the case at most colleges and universities in America nowadays, as Mr. Hutchins points out in his very interesting article. Actually the coaches and alumni go around to the high schools and offer the high school stars large salaries to come to their colleges and play football for them. There was one case where a high school star was offered a convertible if he would play football for a certain college.

Another reason for abolishing college football is that it is bad for the players. They do not have time to get a college education, because they are so busy playing football. A football player has to practice every afternoon from three to six and then he is so tired that he can't concentrate on his studies. He just feels like dropping off to sleep after dinner, and then the next day he goes to his classes without having studied and maybe he fails the test.

(Good ripe stuff so far, but you're still a hundred and fifty-one words from home. One more push.)

Also I think college football is bad for the colleges and the universities because not very many students get to participate in it. Out of a college of ten thousand students only seventy-five or a hundred play football, if that many. Football is what you might call a spectator sport. That means that most people go to watch it but do not play it themselves.

(Four hundred and fifteen. Well, you still have the conclusion, and when you retype it, you can make the margins a little wider.)

These are the reasons why I agree with Mr. Hutchins that college football should be abolished in American colleges and universities.

5   On Monday you turn it in, moderately hopeful, and on Friday it comes back marked "weak in content" and sporting a big "D."

This essay is exaggerated a little, not much. The English instructor will recognize it as reasonably typical of what an assignment on college football will bring in. He knows that nearly half of the class will contrive in five hundred words to say that college football is too commercial and bad for the players. Most of the other half will inform him that college football builds character and prepares one for life and brings prestige to the school. As he reads paper after paper all saying the same thing in almost the same words, all bloodless, five hundred words dripping out of nothing, he wonders how he allowed himself to get trapped into teaching English when he might have had a happy and interesting life as an electrician or a confidence man.

Well, you may ask, what can you do about it? The subject is one on which you have few convictions and little information. Can you be expected to make a dull subject interesting? As a matter of fact, this is precisely what you are expected to do. This is the writer's essential task. All subjects, except sex, are dull until somebody makes them interesting. The writer's job is to find the argument, the approach, the angle, the wording that will take the reader with him. This is seldom easy, and it is particularly hard in subjects that have been much discussed: College Football, Fraternities, Popular Music, Is Chivalry Dead?, and the like. You will feel that there is nothing you can do with such subjects except repeat the old bromides. But there are some things you can do which will make your papers, if not throbbingly alive, at least less insufferably tedious than they might otherwise be.

Avoid the Obvious Content

Say the assignment is college football. Say that you've decided to be against it. Begin by putting down the arguments that come to your mind: it is too commercial, it takes the students' minds off their studies, it is hard on the players, it makes the university a kind of circus instead of an intellectual center, for most schools it is financially ruinous. Can you think of any more arguments, just off hand? All right. Now when you write your paper, make sure that you don't use any of the material on this list. If these are the points that leap to your mind, they will leap to everyone else's too, and whether you get a "C" or a "D" may depend on whether the instructor reads your paper early when he is fresh and tolerant or late, when the sentence "In my opinion, college football has become too commercial," inexorably repeated, has brought him to the brink of lunacy.

Be against college football for some reason or reasons of your own. If they are keen and perceptive ones, that's splendid. But even if they are trivial or foolish or indefensible, you are still ahead so long as they are not everybody else's reasons too. Be against it because the colleges don't spend enough money on it to make it worthwhile, because it is bad for the characters of the spectators, because the players are forced to attend classes, because the football stars hog all the beautiful women, because it competes with baseball and is therefore un-American and possibly Communist-inspired.

There are lots of more or less unused reasons for being against college football.

10   Sometimes it is a good idea to sum up and dispose of the trite and conventional points before going on to your own. This has the advantage of indicating to the reader that you are going to be neither trite nor conventional. Something like this:

> We are often told that college football should be abolished because it has become too commercial or because it is bad for the players. These arguments are no doubt very cogent, but they don't really go to the heart of the matter.

Then you go to the heart of the matter.

Take the Less Usual Side

One rather simple way of getting into your paper is to take the side of the argument that most of the citizens will want to avoid. If the assignment is an essay on dogs, you can, if you choose, explain that dogs are faithful and lovable companions, intelligent, useful as guardians of the house and protectors of children, indispensable in police work—in short, when all is said and done, man's best friends. Or you can suggest that those big brown eyes conceal, more often than not, a vacuity of mind and an inconstancy of purpose; that the dogs you have known most intimately have been mangy, ill-tempered brutes, incapable of instruction; and that only your nobility of mind and fear of arrest prevent you from kicking the flea-ridden animals when you pass them on the street.

Naturally personal convictions will sometimes dictate your approach. If the assigned subject is "Is Methodism Rewarding to the Individual?" and you are a pious Methodist, you have really no choice. But few assigned subjects, if any, will fall in this category. Most of them will lie in broad areas of discussion with much to be said on both sides. They are intellectual exercises, and it is legitimate to argue now one way and now another, as debaters do in similar circumstances. Always take the side that looks to you hardest, least defensible. It will almost always turn out to be easier to write interestingly on that side. This general advice applies where you have a choice of subjects. If you are to choose among "The Value of Fraternities" and "My Favorite High School Teacher"

and "What I Think About Beetles," by all means plump for the beetles. By the time the instructor gets to your paper, he will be up to his ears in tedious tales about a French teacher at Bloombury High and assertions about how fraternities build character and prepare one for life. Your views on beetles, whatever they are, are bound to be a refreshing change.

Don't worry too much about figuring out what the instructor thinks about the subject so that you can cuddle up with him. Chances are his views are no stronger than yours. If he does have convictions and you oppose him, his problem is to keep from grading you higher than you deserve in order to show he is not biased. This doesn't mean that you should always cantankerously dissent from what the instructor says; that gets tiresome too. And if the subject assigned is "My Pet Peeve," do not begin, "My pet peeve is the English instructor who assigns papers on 'my pet peeve.'" This was still funny during the War of 1812, but it has sort of lost its edge since then. It is in general good manners to avoid personalities.

Slip out of Abstraction

If you will study the essay on college football [near the beginning of this essay], you will perceive that one reason for its appalling dullness is that it never gets down to particulars. It is just a series of not very glittering generalities: "football is bad for the colleges," "it has become too commercial," "football is big business," "it is bad for the players," and so on. Such round phrases thudding against the reader's brain are unlikely to convince him, though they may well render him unconscious.

15   If you want the reader to believe that college football is bad for the players, you have to do more than say so. You have to display the evil. Take your roommate, Alfred Simkins, the second-string center. Picture poor old Alfy coming home from football practice every evening, bruised and aching, agonizingly tired, scarcely able to shovel the mashed potatoes into his mouth. Let us see him staggering up to the room, getting out his econ textbook, peering desperately at it with his good eye, falling asleep and failing the test in the morning. Let us share his unbearable tension as Saturday draws near. Will he fail, be demoted, lose his monthly allowance, be forced to return to the coal mines? And if he succeeds, what will be his reward? Perhaps a slight ripple of applause

when the third-string center replaces him, a moment of elation in the locker room if the team wins, of despair if it loses. What will he look back on when he graduates from college? Toil and torn ligaments. And what will be his future? He is not good enough for pro football, and he is too obscure and weak in econ to succeed in stocks and bonds. College football is tearing the heart from Alfy Simkins and, when it finishes with him, will callously toss aside the shattered hulk.

This is no doubt a weak enough argument for the abolition of college football, but it is a sight better than saying, in three or four variations, that college football (in your opinion) is bad for the players.

Look at the work of any professional writer and notice how constantly he is moving from the generality, the abstract statement, to the concrete example, the facts and figures, the illustrations. If he is writing on juvenile delinquency, he does not just tell you that juveniles are (it seems to him) delinquent and that (in his opinion) something should be done about it. He shows you juveniles being delinquent, tearing up movie theatres in Buffalo, stabbing high school principals in Dallas, smoking marijuana in Palo Alto. And more than likely he is moving toward some specific remedy, not just a general wringing of the hands.

It is no doubt possible to be too concrete, too illustrative or anecdotal, but few inexperienced writers err this way. For most the soundest advice is to be seeking always for the picture, to be always turning general remarks into seeable examples. Don't say, "Sororities teach girls the social graces." Say, "Sorority life teaches a girl how to carry on a conversation while pouring tea, without sloshing the tea into the saucer." Don't say, "I like certain kinds of popular music very much." Say, "Whenever I hear Gerber Sprinklittle play 'Mississippi Man' on the trombone, my socks creep up my ankles."

Get Rid of Obvious Padding

The student toiling away at his weekly English theme is too often tormented by a figure: five hundred words. How, he asks himself, is he to achieve this staggering total? Obviously by never using one word when he can somehow work in ten.

20 He is therefore seldom content with a plain statement like "Fast driving is dangerous." This has only

four words in it. He takes thought, and the sentence becomes:

> In my opinion, fast driving is dangerous.

Better, but he can do better still:

> In my opinion, fast driving would seem to be rather dangerous.

If he is really adept, it may come out:

> In my humble opinion though I do not claim to be an expert on this complicated subject, fast driving, in most circumstances, would seem to be rather dangerous in many respects, or at least so it would seem to me.

Thus four words have been turned into forty, and not an iota of content has been added.

Now this is a way to go about reaching five hundred words, and if you are content with a "D" grade, it is as good a way as any. But if you aim higher, you must work differently. Instead of stuffing your sentences with straw, you must try steadily to get rid of the padding, to make your sentences lean and tough. If you are really working at it, your first draft will greatly exceed the required total, and then you will work it down, thus:

> It is thought in some quarters that fraternities do not contribute as much as might be expected to campus life.

> Some people think that fraternities contribute little to campus life.

> The average doctor who practices in small towns or in the country must toil night and day to heal the sick.

> Most country doctors work long hours.

> When I was a little girl, I suffered from shyness and embarrassment in the presence of others.

> I was a shy little girl.

> It is absolutely necessary for the person employed as a marine fireman to give the matter of steam pressure his undivided attention at all times.

> The fireman has to keep his eye on the steam gauge.

You may ask how you can arrive at five hundred words at this rate. Simple. You dig up more real content. Instead of taking a couple of obvious points off the surface of the topic and then circling warily around them for six paragraphs, you work in and explore, figure out the details. You illustrate. You say that fast driving is dangerous, and then you prove it. How long does it take to stop a car at forty and at eighty? How far can you see at night? What happens when a tire blows? What happens in a head-on collision at fifty miles an hour? Pretty soon your paper will be full of broken glass and blood and headless torsos, and reaching five hundred words will not really be a problem.

Call a Fool a Fool

Some of the padding in freshman themes is to be blamed not on anxiety about the word minimum but on excessive timidity. The student writes, "In my opinion, the principal of my high school acted in ways that I believe every unbiased person would have to call foolish." This isn't exactly what he means. What he means is, "My high school principal was a fool." If he was a fool, call him a fool. Hedging the thing about with "in-my-opinion's" and "it-seems-to-me's" and "as-I-see-it's" and "at-least-from-my-point-of-view's" gains you nothing. Delete these phrases whenever they creep into your paper.

The student's tendency to hedge stems from a modesty that in other circumstances would be commendable. He is, he realizes, young and inexperienced, and he half suspects that he is dopey and fuzzyminded beyond the average. Probably only too true. But it does-n't help to announce your incompetence six times in every paragraph. Decide what you want to say and say it as vigorously as possible, without apology and in plain words.

25 Linguistic diffidence can take various forms. One is what we call euphemism. This is the tendency to call a spade "a certain garden implement" or women's underwear "unmentionables." It is stronger in some eras than others and in some people than others but it always operates more or less in subjects that are touchy or taboo: death, sex, madness, and so on. Thus we shrink from saying "He died last night" but say instead "passed away," "left us," "joined his Maker," "went to his reward." Or we try to take off the tension with a lighter cliché: "kicked the bucket," "cashed in his chips," "handed in his dinner pail." We have found all sorts of ways to avoid saying "mad": "mentally ill," "touched," "not quite right upstairs," "feebleminded," "innocent," "simple," "off his trolley," "not in his right mind." Even such a now plain word as "insane" began as a euphemism with the meaning "not healthy."

Modern science, particularly psychology, contributes many polysyllables in which we can wrap our thoughts and blunt their force. To many writers there is no such thing as a bad schoolboy. Schoolboys are maladjusted or unoriented or misunderstood or in the need of guidance or lacking in continued success toward satisfactory integration of the personality as a social unit, but they are never bad. Psychology no doubt makes us better men and women, more sympathetic and tolerant, but it doesn't make writing any easier. Had Shakespeare been confronted with psychology, "To be or not to be" might have come out, "To continue as a social unit or not to do so. That is the personality problem. Whether 'tis a better sign of integration at the conscious level to display a psychic tolerance toward the maladjustments and repressions induced by one's lack of orientation in one's environment or—" But Hamlet would never have finished the soliloquy.

Writing in the modern world, you cannot altogether avoid modern jargon. Nor, in an effort to get away from euphemism, should you salt your paper with four-letter words. But you can do much if you will mount guard against those roundabout phrases, those echoing polysyllables that tend to slip into your writing to rob it of its crispness and force.

Writing Strategies

1. Is Roberts's essay engaging (or inviting)? That is, does it make you want to read on? Why or why not?

2. What strategy does Roberts use to make the problem clear to the reader? Must he convince his reader of a problem before offering a solution? Explain.

3. Roberts supports his points by giving specific examples. Did any stand out to you? Without rereading, recall several examples, and then connect them to the main points they illustrate. Why might those examples have stood out to you?

4. Are Roberts's headings helpful? Should, or might, he have used more? When might *you* use headings (love letters, business reports, college essays, shopping lists)? What drawbacks do headings have?

5. Roberts uses lively language. Identify at least five lively words or expressions that struck you as you read. What makes these expressions lively? What is the value of such lively language?

Exploring Ideas

1. What is the purpose of Roberts's essay?

2. Have you experienced the problem that Roberts describes? Discuss with several classmates or others outside of class any difficulties you have had coming up with ideas for an essay. Take notes on what people say as you explore this problem. Then draw conclusions: Why do some people have a hard time coming up with good ideas for their essays?

3. How does writing an essay help students to develop worthwhile thinking skills?

4. How might Roberts's ideas be important beyond merely writing an essay? That is, how might they be of value in schoolwork that does not involve essay writing; how might they be of value in the workplace; and how might they be of value in everyday life?

5. Why is Roberts's essay, first published in 1958, still relevant today?

Ideas for Writing

1. What can you tell someone how to do? Avoid a simple step-by-step instructional approach, and instead make worthwhile points that could benefit your reader.

2. How can a student succeed either (a) at college, (b) at his or her freshman year of college, or (c) at the first two weeks of college? Narrow your focus to suit your comfort level. For example, if you have been in college only a few months, you may not feel comfortable telling others how to succeed for all four years.

If responding to one of these ideas, go to the Analysis section of this chapter to begin developing ideas for your essay.

Attending to the Word

Deirdre Mahoney

Our culture's response to illiteracy and low academic performance has involved sweeping proposals: more standardized testing, more teacher accountability, required master's degrees for all K–12 teachers, better buildings, newer textbooks, more administrators, no more art and music classes, and so on. But writing instructor Deirdre Mahoney invites us to look very closely at reading. In this argument, we are invited to analyze the act of reading, to understand the intellectual nuances of engaging text. And then, we might more readily accept a less sweeping, more elegantly basic solution.

Today's college students are suffering, and unnecessarily so. I see them arrive in my writing classes each semester eager and determined, but all too often the motivation and passion dissipate when they come face-to-face with—well—words on the page. This is distressing for both them and me. My students are not illiterate by any means, as they successfully broke the code of sound-to-symbol in the earliest elementary years. Since that time, they've continued to learn in public and private school systems or they've been home-schooled. They're educated and plenty adept at moving through the system. But I'm not convinced any of this means they are capable of truly committing to a book, an essay, or any document requiring sustained focus and labor-intensive thinking and doing. And what interferes most with their abilities to focus and commit? Lack of a pencil in hand while attempting to read, contemplate, and retain the text on the page.

When I tell my students the only way to read a book is with pencil gliding freely across the page (no highlighters please), they look stymied. Selected passages ought to be underlined, I maintain, and tricky vocabulary circled. Further, I suggest that handwritten symbols in the form of stars, asterisks, squiggly lines, question marks, brackets, and the like warrant placement alongside their personal comments posted in the margins. After all, the white space on the printed page could use the company. My students offer good enough reasons, however, for *not* writing in their books: (1) Writing in

books during the K–12 years is absolutely taboo, they tell me, and they've been successfully trained to do as told; (2) Some college bookstores won't buy back textbooks with extensive personalized annotations and markings. Students need cash at semester's end, so they dutifully comply. But how is any of this non-writing good for thinking and learning? I'm pretty sure it's not. We might find the current state of affairs particularly worrisome if we frame the problem this way: In an attempt to educate, it seems that educators and a whole lot of other well-meaning adults have worked successfully to ensure disengagement with the printed word, often during the most formative and critical years of literacy acquisition.

"Don't write in the book." Even though I remain convinced this is perfectly awful advice, the mantra remains standard, announcing itself from every corner of our culture. A few years back Kathie Coblentz, New York Public Library cataloger and author of *The New York Public Library Guide to Organizing a Home Library,* disclosed to a *New York Times* reporter her penchant for scribbling notes on the pages of books in her *private* collection. My elation was short-lived when the reporter amiably cautioned readers *not* to do the same (Braden). But why not, especially if the scribbler is also the owner? Think about this (mis)guiding principle for a moment and you too may share my distress and bewilderment.

I've been scribbling in books for years (lightly and in pencil, I might add) but I'm not nearly as self-disciplined as bibliophile Kathie Coblentz, as I write in books I borrow from libraries. There. I've said it. At a later date, I sometimes borrow the book again and am greeted by my previously penciled notes still etched softly in the margins. Two important things seem to occur in this moment. First, I'm promptly reacquainted with my previous thoughts and, second, I'm often surprised at how much my thinking has shifted since the previous visit to the page, a sure sign that the human mind is in a constant state of making meaning as it constructs and then reconstructs itself.

5   So, I think the problem is clear. Our system of educating, parenting, and nurturing unwittingly conspires to ensure students' disciplined detachment from words on the page. In other words, creating disengaged adults begins early. My proposal is simple and not particularly original, but I'll reiterate it nonetheless. Those

of us committed to raising and teaching need to raise and teach differently. For starters, we need to insist that from the earliest stages of literacy acquisition all humans—especially the tiniest in size and age—be invited to scribble fervently as they explore books. If we take into account the opening statement in Maryanne Wolf's *Proust and the Squid: The Story and Science of the Reading Brain,* it becomes apparent that humans could use an assist. Wolf avows forebodingly, "We were never born to read" (3). Ditto for writing. Out of necessity, it seems, resourceful adults looking for ways to enhance overtaxed memories found their way to literate practices. In doing so, the human brain began to evolve in ways probably not intended in the original blueprint. That is, in the process of teaching oneself to read and write, the brain began to reinvent itself, thus enhancing human development and evolution. Experts concur that coding and decoding symbols enhances thought and conscious-ness, which in turn literally alters brain matter. In other words, what we do with our brains determines what our minds are or what they might become.

We are born with the capacity for language built into our genetic code. It's simple enough. People aim to foster human connection, and speech makes itself apparent in children eager to converse soon after birth. Without any overt instruction, the youngest of tots uses speech to assert needs and preferences, often doing so in the form of the familiar toddler command: "More cookie" or "Me hold you." In short order, the toddler strings phrases together and begins to verbalize inces-santly with anyone willing to stop and chat a bit. So the advent of spoken language seems straightforward enough, but literacy acquisition, or the ability to read and write, remains a stellar unintended achievement and a considerable cognitive coup if there ever were one. Depending on how we do the math, our ability to pen language goes back five thousand years or so, half that if we're talking specifically about the creation of the Roman alphabet. If we consider that humans were vocalizing perhaps as far back as one hundred thousand years before stumbling on to technologies for captur-ing memory in print, we recognize the veritable brevity of the written word. And although a relatively recent human innovation, the written word has enhanced the mind's cognitive prowess.

Again, in *Proust and the Squid,* Wolf writes, "Read-ing can be learned only because of the brain's plastic design, and when reading takes place, that individual brain is forever changed, both physiologically and intel-lectually" (5). In his essay "Writing Is a Technology that Restructures Thought," esteemed twentieth-century theorist Walter Ong informs the reader, "[W]riting is utterly invaluable and indeed essential for the realization of fuller, interior, human potentials. Technologies are not mere exterior aids but also interior transformation of consciousness . . ." (23). Neuroscientist and Nobel Prize winner Eric R. Kandel confirms in his memoir *In Search of Memory: The Emergence of a New Science and Mind* that "Today, most philosophers of mind agree that what we call consciousness derives from the physi-cal brain . . ." (378). Kandel cautions, however, that all this business of consciousness is "more complicated than any property of the brain we understand" (379). Current neuroscience, complete with functional mag-netic resonance imaging (fMRI) and other fancy tools, seems to substantiate Ong's and Kandel's claims. So if the specialists are correct in their collective assertion that literate acts transform consciousness (we might call it "knowingness") and brain construction, why would anyone choose to read a text *without* a pencil grasped firmly in hand? Why not enthusiastically dot the text with penciled symbols and words as matter of habit? More importantly, why wouldn't the "pencil to page" mantra become the preferred teaching strategy of par-ents and educators everywhere?

I'm passionate about penciling, but this doesn't mean I disapprove of today's sophisticated technologies. Not at all. Like most, I often wonder how we func-tioned effectively before the arrival of the word proces-sor, cable television, fancy phones, and the Internet. No doubt about it: Current technologies provide us with unprecedented speed and convenience, perfectly timed supports for life in the twenty-first century. I'm grateful everyday for their availability; however, the loyal pen-cil, an archaic invention if there ever were one, contin-ues to garner my full support. The graphite-enhanced wooden stick offers definite advantages. It slows my reading and thinking, allowing opportunity to interact more purposefully with words on the page. Addition-ally, I'm sure the sensual aspect of sharpened graphite pressing softly against textured paper plays a key role in arousing the neurons. The pencil draws me into the text and invites my active participation, and when my voice appears as light markings on the page it becomes clear that I've assumed my required role in the conversation. The bright yellow #2 meandering along the page ushers me from passivity to activity. Call me sentimental or just demanding, but I want my students to join me in leaving traces on pages. After all, what might be lost in the process? Certainly not enhanced brain development, sustained focus, or heightened awareness. Let the scribbling begin.

Works Cited

Braden, Carole. "A Bibliophile, 3,600 Friends, and a System." New York Times Online. 10 Feb. 2005. 6 April 2008. <http://www.nytimes.com>.

Kandel, Eric R. In Search of Memory: The Emergence of the New Science of Mind. New York: Norton, 2006.

Ong, Walter. "Writing Is a Technology that Restructures Thought." Literacy: A Critical Sourcebook. Ed. Ellen Cushman, Eugene R. Kintgen, Barry M. Kroll, and Mike Rose. Boston: Bedford, 2001. 19–31.

Wolf, Maryanne. Proust and the Squid: The Story and Science of the Reading Brain. New York: Harper, 2007.

present in the act of grasping the use and yet isn't present.—For we say that there isn't any doubt that we understand the word, and on the other hand its meaning lies in its use. There is no doubt that I now want to play chess, but chess is the game it is in virtue of all its rules (and so on). Don't I know, then, which game I want to play until I *have* played it? or are all the rules contained in my act of intending? Is it experience that tells me that this sort of game is the usual consequence of such an act of intending? so is it impossible for me to be certain what I am intending to do? And if that is nonsense—what kind of super-strong connexion exists between the act of intending and the thing intended?——Where is the connexion effected between the sense of the expression "Let's play a game of chess" and all the rules of the game?—Well, in the list of rules of the game, in the teaching of it, in the day-to-day practice of playing.

198. "But how can a rule shew me what I have to do at *this* point? Whatever I do is, on some interpretation, in accord with the rule."— That is not what we ought to say, but rather: any interpretation still hangs in the air along with what it interprets, and cannot give it any support. Interpretations by themselves do not determine meaning.

"Then can whatever I do be brought into accord with the rule?"— Let me ask this: what has the expression of a rule—say a sign-post— got to do with my actions? What sort of connexion is there here?— Well, perhaps this one: I have been trained to react to this sign in a particular way, and now I do so react to it.

But that is only to give a causal connexion; to tell how it has come about that we now go by the sign-post; not what this going-by-the-sign really consists in. On the contrary; I have further indicated that a person goes by a sign-post only in so far as there exists a regular use of sign-posts, a custom.

199. Is what we call "obeying a rule" something that it would be possible for only *one* man to do, and to do only *once* in his life?— This is of course a note on the grammar of the expression "to obey a rule".

To understand a sentence means to understand understand a language means to be master of a tech

200. It is, of course, imaginable that two peop tribe unacquainted with games should sit at a c through the moves of a game of chess; and even with mental accompaniments. And if *we* were to see it were playing chess. But now imagine a game according to certain rules into a series of actions ordinarily associate with a *game*—say into yells an And now suppose those two people to yell and sta ing the form of chess that we are used to; and that their procedure is translatable by suitable r chess. Should we still be inclined to say they we What right would one have to say so?

201. This was our paradox: no course of act mined by a rule, because every course of action accord with the rule. The answer was: if everyth to accord with the rule, then it can also be made o And so there would be neither accord nor conflict

It can be seen that there is a misunderstanding he that in the course of our argument we give one another; as if each one contented us at least for thought of yet another standing behind it. Wh there is a way of grasping a rule which is *not* an in is exhibited in what we call "obeying the rule" a in actual cases.

Hence there is an inclination to say: every act rule is an interpretation. But we ought to restrict tion" to the substitution of one expression of th

202. And hence also 'obeying a rule' is a prac is obeying a rule is not to obey a rule. Hence it i a rule 'privately': otherwise thinking one was ob the same thing as obeying it.

Writing Strategies

1. Closely examine Mahoney's introduction. How does the first paragraph focus our attention on a particular aspect of a broader problem? In your own words, explain how this problem is more specific than illiteracy.

2. Trace the logic of the essay (the line of reasoning) and explain each intellectual step leading to the solution.

3. In ¶ 5, Mahoney refers to a source (Wolf) and then extends the point: "Wolf avows forebodingly, 'We were never born to read' (3). Ditto for writing." Why is this step critical to Mahoney's line of reasoning?

4. How does Mahoney's use of personal testimony fit into the argument? (Could the argument function without that testimony?)

5. Focus on particular passages in which Mahoney deals with some opposing position or concern. Describe her tactic. How does she deal with that opposition? Does she deflect, take apart, destroy, neutralize, calm, or something else?

Exploring Ideas

1. Mahoney claims that most of her students have learned how to "move through the system" of education without really attending to language. How does this resonate with your own experience? Why is simply "moving through the system" a bad thing?

2. In Mahoney's words, "Our system of educating, parenting, and nurturing unwittingly conspires to ensure students' disciplined detachment from words on the page. In other words, creating disengaged adults begins early." Give a specific example or practice or scholastic behavior that encourages students to be detached "from words on the page."

3. After walking us through her line of reasoning, Mahoney wonders: "So if the specialists are correct in their collective assertion that literate acts transform consciousness (we might call it 'knowingness') and brain construction, why would anyone choose to read a text *without* a pencil grasped firmly in hand?" Try to imagine why people would choose to read without a pencil in hand. What reasons, besides those Mahoney counters, might people have for ignoring her solution?

4. Mahoney argues that reading with a pencil "slows [her] reading and thinking, allowing opportunity to interact more purposefully with words on the page." What type of opportunity is this? What is *opportunity* during the reading process?

5. Describe the specific way that you attend to text. Do you skim, occasionally skim, or read closely? How would you characterize your interaction with words on the page? Are they strangers passing by? Are they people you're desperately trying to know?

Ideas for Writing

1. Point out and attempt to solve another particular layer or aspect of illiteracy in America.

2. What other problem could be solved with something elegantly simple—like a pencil?

If responding to one of these ideas, go to the Analysis section of this chapter to begin developing ideas for your essay.

Reverence for Food

Rachel Schofield

In the margins of this essay, a reader's comments point to key ideas and writing strategies.

Writers, thinkers, activists, parents, and some politicians have argued about America's bad diet for years. Thousands of voices jeer junk food, fast food, and fake food. So Rachel Schofield, who wrote the following essay for her first-year college writing course, works to show a new dimension to a common argument. She does not simply reinforce what readers likely know about junk food; instead, she reveals a problem with the way mainstream culture views and obsesses over food.

Writing Strategies

Exploring Ideas

The typical American meal today is fast and convenient. Microwave dinners, frozen pizza, hot pockets, fast food, soda. It's mostly fake food, even though our waistlines seem to say otherwise. Economists and historians agree that the advent of processed foods after World War II contributed to the downfall of the family farm and rise of the factory farm. And many argue that it has also contributed, if not outright caused, America's current obesity epidemic. But we've heard these arguments before. Aside from the obvious health and economic concerns, what are the deeper consequences of eating such processed foods? America's food system, with its fast convenience foods, disconnects us from food's source, resulting in less reverence for food and decreased respect for nature itself.

Acknowledges and then goes beyond the usual arguments about obesity and diet.

It's more than obesity and bad diets. It's disconnection from the earth.

Historically, humans have worshipped the earth and gods of agriculture and fertility. There is a common myth among many cultures that the earth is the giver of life, and in a very literal sense, it is true. Food comes from the earth, and we require it for sustenance. Many great civilizations flourished under these gods, recognizing their connection to the earth and giving thanksgiving for its sacred bounty. In the past, we revered the earth, nature, and food because we could directly see that our lives depended on them. Most of the population worked the fields and witnessed the divinity of the soil as it miraculously produced their daily bread. Today our lives still depend on nature's produce, but most of us have lost our connection. In losing our reverence, we have allowed for the birth of Frankenfoods.

Because we no longer value nature, we've created monstrous foods. We're playing God . . . and failing.

Appeal to tradition: our ancestors may have had the right relationship to the earth.

Jump forward (or should I say backward?), and today's food is fast, cheap, and easy. The prostitute of processed food has replaced the revered goddesses who once nurtured our crops. Our blind faith in science has led us to a world where humans re-create in the lab what already exists in nature. We mutilate the natural into virtually unrecognizable forms. Enter high-fructose corn syrup—a highly

Prostitute vs. Goddess (the powerless vs. the powerful).

The writer builds up the point with her own line of reasoning before giving the info from the source.

processed, unnatural liquid. A complicated and convoluted method of chemical alchemy is utilized to create this all-too-artificial sweetener:

> First, cornstarch is treated with alpha-amylase to produce shorter chains of sugars called polysaccharides. Alpha-amylase is industrially produced by a bacterium, usually *Bacillus sp.* Next, an enzyme called glucoamylase breaks the sugar chains down even further to yield the simple sugar glucose. Unlike alpha-amylase, glucoamylase is produced by *Aspergillus,* a fungus, in a fermentation vat where one would likely see little balls of *Aspergillus* floating on the top. The third enzyme, glucose-isomerase . . . converts glucose to a mixture of about 42 percent fructose and 50–52 percent glucose with some other sugars mixed in . . . liquid chromatography takes the mixture to 90 percent fructose. Finally, this is back-blended with the original mixture to yield a final concentration of about 55 percent fructose . . . . (Forristal)

Brings the info from the source to a crescendo.

If we literally are what we eat, then we're all full of junk.

As unappetizing as vats of floating fungus and bacterial enzymes may sound, Americans are blissfully consuming more and more of this revolting substance. "Since its introduction in the early 1970s, the cheap sweetener's use has jumped 4,000 percent; it's now showing up in everything from sodas to steak sauce" (Callahan). Our food comes more and more from chemical concoctions rather than the earth; we have lost our sense of connection with the very thing that sustains us. We make the distance between life-giving nature and ourselves greater through over-processing our food. In some kind of strange twist of logic, we actually make our food less nutritious.

Again, the paragraph builds to a climactic statement.

Our food choices are increasingly illogical . . . and weird.

5   Food still enables us to survive, but we no longer revere it. Some would disagree, citing the weight problems engorging our country. We see food 24/7 on TV, hear about it on the radio, see it advertised on billboards, and even in Internet pop-ups. Advertising works. We buy what we see, yet the low nutrition levels in our highly processed foods leave our bodies starving for more, and we only give them more junk. We can see the preeminence of food in the dedication of temples to food all along our highways; fast food chains are more popular than ever. However, there is a difference between obsession with food and reverence for it. Our fast food restaurants and freezer aisles are brothels where impure, chemically altered food is bought and sold. Almost gone are the days when honest, unadulterated food can be purchased by the American family.

A turnabout paragraph of sorts!

Obsession with fake food ≠ reverence for the real thing.

How can Americans have reverence for food when we have so many artificial consumables surrounding us? And to complicate the

So . . . we can't revere what's fake.

The quote supports this step in the line of reasoning: Americans are stuck in our obsession with fake food.

problem, "Compare the price of a grapefruit to that of a pack of strawberry-flavored Twizzlers" (Zinczenko). It seems that processed food is almost always cheaper and more accessible than wholesome fresh foods. What can a struggling American family do when the only thing they can afford is cheap processed food?

Turnabout paragraph: an alternative solution and its potential shortcoming.

David Zinczenko of *Men's Health* proposes that we put a sin tax on unhealthy and unnatural foods. What if "OJ cost less than that *high-fructose* horror known as Sunny Delight? Wouldn't America be a little bit healthier?" (Zinczenko) But a tax on the powerful agribusiness industry, with its already entrenched team of lobbyists in Washington, seems a long way off. Eric Roston of *Time* magazine states: "Although U.S. taxpayers subsidize American farmers generously—to the tune of $20 billion a year—that's not likely to change anytime soon. Besides, corn is so cheap that even a farm policy that doubled the crop's price might make only a marginal difference in grocery-store prices."

A new tax won't solve the problem.

Another turnabout paragraph: alternative solution and its shortcoming.

Another solution comes from Arkansas governor Mike Huckabee. He has proposed "a plan whereby food stamps would be worth more when they're applied to healthy foods" (Zinczenko). This is a great idea, and I commend the governor for doing so. But this is just a superficial jab. It does not address the origin of the problem: lack of reverence for nature and food.

A real solution has to go to the root of the problem.

Another turnabout: explains the ideal and why it won't work.

The ultimate cure for our lack of connection to nature would be for each person to grow his or her own food. We would be in the fields, dealing directly with the earth itself. We would relearn the lost art of cultivation: how to care for the earth and provide for its needs so it can do likewise for us. One-on-one interaction with nature herself would be the best way of rejuvenating our reverence for food. However, this ideal is neither practical nor possible for the vast majority of people. Why is that so? Because we would have to drastically alter our consumer lifestyles. We would have to take time out of our busy day and spend it at what many see as the mundane task of digging in the dirt.

The ideal never seems to work out.

10   Before we can begin, we must change the way that we think about the earth. It is not some dead mass of matter, but rather a complex interconnection of life. Far from being boring, farming is an entrance into life itself. We can begin to take baby steps toward the ideal. Americans can buy food from their local organic stores. Better yet, they could get to know the people who grow their food. And, whenever possible, Americans should start their own gardens. Once we experience its creation firsthand, it is almost impossible not to have a healthy respect for all the time, effort, and hope embodied in the art of farming.

The solution to our food problem: change our thinking about the earth itself!

The solution is qualified—in "baby steps." This is more acceptable than a grand recalibration of all food items.

Works Cited

Callahan, Maureen. "Sugar Smack." <u>Health</u> Oct. 2006: 150–52.
 Academic Search Elite. 28 March 2007.
 <http://search.ebscohost.com.proxy.nmc.edu>.

Forristal, Linda Joyce. "The Murky World of High Fructose Corn
 Syrup." <http://www.westonaprice.org/motherlinda/cornsyrup.html>.

Roston, Eric. "The Corn Connection." <u>Time</u> 7 June 2004: 83.
 Academic Search Elite. 28 March 2007.
 <http://search.ebscohost.com.proxy.nmc.edu>.

Zinczenko, David. "Food Fight!" <u>Men's Health</u> 1 June 2006: 22+.
 Academic Search Elite. 28 March 2007.
 <http://search.ebscohost.com.proxy.nmc.edu>.

Writing Strategies

1. How does Schofield get us to see something beyond the obvious: that junk food is bad?

2. How are appeals to value operating in Schofield's argument?

3. What is Schofield's line of reasoning? Trace the backbone of the argument—its basic steps—through the paragraphs, and characterize each step in one sentence.

4. What is Schofield's solution? How does it address the heart of the problem?

5. How does Schofield deal with potentially opposing positions? Point to particular passages in which she counters or concedes.

Exploring Ideas

1. Schofield argues that other solutions, such as Governor Huckabee's, are "superficial." Why is it important to discover the origin, the root cause, of a problem before proposing a solution?

2. Schofield argues that the solution begins with an intellectual change: "Before we can begin, we must change the way that we think about the earth." How is such a change possible?

3. Why do you suppose "we" (mainstream Americans) have lost reverence for the earth, for nature, for real food? What particular cultural, economic, or political forces caused this?

4. In everyday life, we are invited to revere flags, sports heroes, politicians, our alma maters, and sometimes religious figures. What would it mean to revere food? And who might take offense to this notion?

5. Schofield makes a distinction between obsession and reverence. In your own words, how would you describe that distinction? What is the fundamental difference between obsessing and revering?

Ideas for Writing

1. Schofield argues that mainstream American culture has forsaken food. What other basic or fundamental thing has mainstream American culture forsaken? What problem has this created? How do we solve it?

2. What other specific social problem can we solve simply by readjusting our perspective?

If responding to one of these ideas, go to the Analysis section of this chapter to begin developing ideas for your essay.

Outside Reading

Find a text that proposes a solution, and make a photocopy or print it out. Solutions for social problems are often published in general readership publications *(Time* or *Newsweek)* and in national or local newspapers (on opinion pages). More in-depth solutions might appear in monthly or quarterly journals *(Utne Reader* or the *New Republic).* You also might find an interesting solution related to your major. For that, explore academic journals such as *Criminal Law Forum, Engineering,* or *Elementary School Journal.* To conduct an electronic search of journals and magazines, go to your library's periodical database or to InfoTrac College Edition (http://infotrac. cengage.com). For your library database, perform a keyword search, or go to the main search box for InfoTrac College Edition and choose "keywords." Enter word combinations such as *problems and schools, problems and flying, problems and food, solutions and sewage, solutions and farms,* and so on. (When performing keyword searches, avoid using phrases or articles such as *a, an, the.)* The search results will yield lists of journal and magazine articles.

You can also search the Internet. Try the search engine Yahoo.com. Like most Internet search engines, Yahoo! combines words using *and.* In the search box, try various combinations, such as those above; however, if using *solutions* in your search, be cautious of the many business and corporate sites in the search results.

The purpose of this assignment is to further your understanding of writing that proposes solutions. As you are probably discovering, such writing is sometimes very argumentative, and other times appears to be neutral; however, even the most neutral-sounding text offers a position—a stance that requires support. As you read through this chapter, keep the text you have discovered close by and notice the elements and strategies the writer uses. Depending on your instructor's suggestions, do one or more of the following:

1. Notice how the writer applies various strategies from this chapter. On the photocopy or hard copy:
   - Identify the passage that most clearly states the problem and write "problem" in the margin.
   - Identify the passage that most clearly states the solution and write "solution" in the margin.
   - Identify the passages in which the author offers support for the solution and write "support" next to each one in the margin.
   - Find any passages in which the writer addresses other opinions on the topic and write "counterargument" or "ca" next to each one in the margin.
   - Find any passages in which the writer grants value to another position (or alternative solution) and write "concession" or "c" in the margin.

2. Analyze the strategies employed by the writer. The following questions may be helpful.
   - Does this text seem more or less argumentative than the readings in this chapter? Why?
   - How does the writer support his or her proposed solution?
   - Who is the audience for this argument?
   - How does the audience affect the kinds of things said in the argument?

3. Write at least three "Writing Strategies" questions for the text you found.

4. Write at least three "Exploring Ideas" questions for the text you found.

5. Write two "Ideas for Writing," such as the ones following the essays in this chapter.

INVENTION

"No problem can withstand the assault of sustained thinking."

—Voltaire

For this chapter, your topic will be a particular problem—some situation that needs to be changed or an idea that needs to be rethought. Be wary of global problems like hunger, poverty, or racism. They are not unapproachable or unsolvable, but such big problems usually have local or particular expressions, and it is the local or particular that is often the most appropriate place to start. Focusing on a particular problem also sets the ground for a manageable solution. For example, solving financial difficulty for single-parent students is more manageable than solving poverty in general.

The following sections are designed to help you through the invention process: specifically, to discover a problem (in Point of Contact), to develop an understanding of its causes and develop a possible solution (in Analysis), to make it relevant to a community of readers (in Public Resonance), to develop a focused statement about the problem and solution (in Thesis), and to develop support for your argument (in Rhetorical Tools). The Invention questions in each section are not meant to be answered directly in your final written assignment. They will, however, help you to think further into your topic, to develop intense claims and insightful points.

POINT OF CONTACT

Social problems are not necessarily physical or material; they can be intellectual, spiritual, or psychological. Consider problems related to bad policies (all first-year students must live on campus), narrow thinking (a government administration that assumes energy must come from fossil fuels), or troubled systems (a bureaucracy in which all decisions must be made at the executive level before action can be taken).

Writers often do best with topics with which they are familiar, or with which they can become familiar. To discover particular problems, consider the different circles of your life. Use the following suggestions and questions to help dig up a problem that you, as a writer, witness or experience; and attempt to see problems that others might disregard. See the problems that lurk behind the obvious. If one of the suggestions prompts you to see a problem, begin by recording details—that is, try to explain the particulars of the problem.

School

- Are students missing too many classes?
- Do my instructors communicate poorly with students?
- Are my peers lazy?
- Are enough courses offered to students?
- Do instructors give enough or too many exams?
- Did my high school education adequately prepare me for college?
- Is the curricular gap between high school and college too wide?

Community

- Are the elderly people in my family or community isolated?
- Do people in my neighborhood ignore one another?
- Are there too few animals in people's lives? (Too many?)
- Does traffic in my community interfere with daily life?
- Are billboards tasteless or boring?
- Are there too many chain stores or strip malls in my community?

Government

- Does the city government do enough for children? For senior citizens?
- Does state government overlook the particular needs of my community?
- Are citizens sufficiently involved in local government?
- Do average citizens know how tax dollars are spent?
- Are there enough minorities in public office?

Television

- Is prime-time television too adolescent?
- Are sports televised too often?
- Is there something wrong with the way sports are televised?
- Are talk shows tasteless, moronic, or disrespectful?
- Has art been abandoned by popular culture?

Your Major

- What are the problems related to employment in my field?
- What about job security? Safety for the workers? Safety for the public?
- Are there problems with government regulations?

Activity

Now go beyond these suggestions. In groups or alone, develop more strategies for encountering and exploring social problems. Imagine what might be wrong, or what can be better than it is.

ANALYSIS

Problems

Any solution must address the causes of a problem. There-fore, analyzing a problem to discover all possible causes is essential to developing a good solution. Often the causes of a problem are not clear, however. A problem may originate from an abstract source, such as a long tradition, a widely held attitude, or a flawed assumption. And writers must search through such abstractions to find the possible causes.

Invention Questions

To understand the full complexities of your problem, respond to the following questions:

- What are the causes of the problem?
- What are the most troubling or alarming images associated with the problem?
- What are its short-term effects? Long-term effects?
- What other situation (event, attitude) does this problem resemble?

In her invention writing, Deidre Mahoney explores her topic: students' inability to read intensively and critically. Her own language takes her somewhere. Here, she discovers that the problem is one of commitment—or even the relationship her students have with text:

> **What are the most troubling or alarming images associated with the problem?**
>
> Here's what's troubling and distressing: Each semester I meet many college students who mean well and want to succeed but who are entirely removed from the printed word. That is, they know how to read . . . to a point. These students often associate reading with glancing or skimming and that's it. Sometimes they skip the reading assignments entirely. So here we have it—adults who really don't understand what it means at all to commit to a text. These are students who don't fully realize that

decoding sophisticated texts (or even somewhat sophisticated texts or even just slightly sophisticated texts) will take focus and self-discipline and perhaps, even, a whole lot of time. They don't seem to fully understand that engaging in literate practices, especially on the college level, requires all kinds of ongoing, serious application and hard work. Really hard work.

What are its short-term effects? Long term effects?

The effects are complicated. Often it takes students weeks into a semester before they come to terms with the gravity of the situation. Until that time, they may continue to do the same exercise day in and day out (glancing and skimming), hoping for a different outcome—that of the easily earned revelation. But, of course, success doesn't work that way. Significant challenges most often require commitment to a task not easily begun or completed. So, what are the short-term effects? Failure, decimated confidence, learned helplessness, and hopelessness.

Generally speaking, college students who commit—who are willing to attend to words on the page and to embrace the challenge of analyzing a text seriously and laboriously—can begin to train their minds to function differently and more effectively. They might begin to experience access to ideas that they've previously not had the abilities to know or retain. They might discover liberation, confidence, and their own abilities—they might come to understand that the human mind can be trained.

Research

You may respond to the Invention questions on different levels, first providing your own initial responses, and then gathering information from outside sources. Such sources may include friends, coworkers, family members, websites, articles, and books. (Consult Chapter 13: Research & Writing, to help you explore.) As you research, look not just for ideas that support your initial responses but, more importantly, for ideas that might change the way you think.

Solutions

Before settling on a solution, consider how the solution will work, how it will address the causes of the problem, and how it might fail. Answers to the following questions will be vital to developing your solution and to making it persuasive to readers. While you will benefit from understanding all of the following issues, your readers may need some points emphasized over others. Ask yourself what points seem least obvious, or most debatable, to your audience.

Respond to the following questions to develop your solution:

- What action will best address the causes of the problem?
- What might stand in the way of this action?
- How will the action change the situation?
- Does this solution have potential shortcomings or limitations?

Again, Mahoney's invention writing takes her thinking into the complexities. She begins with the most fundamental acts of learning to read:

What action will best address the causes of the problem?

We need a culture shift. We need to think differently about the printed word and our relationship to it. We need to assume that we are always teaching reading and learning how to read throughout our lives—just as we do in the earliest stages of development. Three-year-olds read the same book over and over. They request we read it to them over and over. They want to retell it over and over. They read it (in their own way) to themselves over and over. Three-year-olds seem to understand the notion of tenacity and commitment. We need to do a better job of teaching students that reading and thinking are labor-intensive, by design.

We must allow students the right to underline and scribble in books.

What might stand in the way of this action?

Students, often to their credit, are managing too much at once. Where I teach, many must earn money to put themselves through school and pay the bills. Their academic schedules are full, and they allot themselves so much time for this course and that course. So it's important to point out that students are not afraid to take on significant challenges, but I think what they don't fully understand is that they have to adopt a different vision for themselves—they must begin to imagine themselves as capable readers of complex texts.

At this point, Mahoney is thinking in brave terms: a cultural shift! She's imagining that people could begin *thinking* differently (which is certainly more difficult than implementing a policy or action).

In analyzing the specific problem, Mahoney is also exploring broader cultural trends. She's exploring public resonance! It is important to realize that insights about public resonance may come at any time during the invention process. Since the process of exploration and discovery cannot be divided simply into separate steps or stages (analysis, public resonance), one must always be on the lookout for insights.

A solution might change the *intellectual* environment so that *physical* changes can take place later.

PUBLIC RESONANCE

Some topics may seem difficult to connect to a broad public concern, but good writers bring *seemingly* marginal topics into the center of public consciousness. The problem you have chosen may obviously affect (or potentially affect) a community or society at large. However, no matter how much your problem involves or affects people, you still must make it known.

As you consider your own topic, respond to the following questions to help develop public resonance:

- Who should care about this issue? Why?
- What particular community, place, or thing does this issue affect?
- How might my reader(s) be involved in this issue?
- Why is it important that others hear my opinion about this issue?

In Mahoney's invention writing, she picks up on a point from her Analysis responses. Some core ideas are gaining momentum: Children and adults alike must develop *intellectual tenacity* as part of literacy.

Who should care about this issue? Why?

Parents, educators, and anyone who cares about books and ideas should care, especially all of us who want to see our kids succeed in school.

How might my reader(s) be involved in this issue?

Parents who save and save for their kids' college education and who think they are preparing their kids for college and beyond might most need to hear this message, as they might be the ones who are not seeing how important it is to help their children fall in love with words—from the earliest years—and then to continue to foster that relationship throughout the school years. All too often, I sense that parents believe we are off the hook once we've created literacy in our children, but that's actually just the beginning. Without fostering the relationship or constantly celebrating intellectual tenacity, we fall short in our jobs.

Invention Workshop

The public resonance may not be clear at first, but working through all the possibilities can help your topic to expand in interesting ways. Enlist the help of other writers, and in a small group, answer one of the questions for your topic. As a group, work at collectively building a sophisticated answer to the question.

In the following, Marcus has discovered a problem in his community: Elderly people in nursing homes and senior living centers are isolated from others. In a discussion with peers, Marcus develops his initial thinking:

What group of people might understand or sympathize with this situation?

Marcus: Primarily the elderly. Senior citizens are primarily concerned about this issue, and as medical advances allow people to live longer, it seems like we all should be worried—because we'll all be old someday.

Linda: But shouldn't the younger generations be concerned about the isolation of the elderly, too—I mean beyond just caring about themselves as they age?

Diana: Yeah . . . even if they don't care, it seems like stuffing the elderly away from mainstream society can't be a good thing, for anybody.

Marcus: It's like we are ignoring a huge group of people—the group that probably has the most insight and experience about big social problems.

Linda: And I would even say personal and family problems. I know in my family, it was always my grandmother who understood everyone's problems and could talk through them without getting angry or mean. She was the one that gave everyone a sense of direction.

Marcus: So when society shuts away its elderly, maybe the biggest victims are the younger generations. Of course, it's bad for the elderly, but in a more indirect and long-term way, maybe their absence from mainstream society is an even bigger wrong. Maybe the younger generations feel the effects in the long term without their patience, insights, and experience.

THESIS

A thesis for this project should offer a specific strategy for addressing a specific problem. The following examples show a range of possible strategies:

- If the sales associates at Dalworth's had more discretion over break time, the management/employee tension would decrease significantly.
- The budget crisis at Midland State College can only be addressed with a tuition increase.
- Small group work can help writers get beyond their frustration with invention.
- The degradation of rural areas cannot be stopped with peaceful public rhetoric. Significantly higher gasoline taxes would, however, keep people from building homes farther away from their jobs.
- If the country could begin to take back the airwaves from corporate interests, democracy might then begin to flourish.
- When America's hunters and fishermen see their shared interests with strong environmental groups, their combined political force will help counter the unchecked movement into wildlife areas.

Thesis statements tend to go off track for a few consistent reasons. Before committing to a statement (to something that may impact everything hereafter!), see the Common Thesis Problems in Chapter 7 (page 241), which overlap with this chapter.

Evolution of a Thesis

Notice how a thesis might evolve out of the invention process. Marcus's topic (isolation of the elderly) can be developed into a focused and sophisticated point. He begins by articulating the problem. Then he tries to make the problem more specific. Finally, he works to integrate the solution:

- In the long run, younger generations may feel the effects of the elderly's isolation.
- Older generations are isolated—their experiences, insights, and wisdom cut off from the people who need it most: everyone else.
- We have to make our grandparents the center of our families, not the marginal human satellites they are presently.
- Because older generations are isolated, their experiences, insights, and wisdom cut off from those who need them most, families should rethink how grandparents figure into everyday life.
- The lost experiences, insight, and wisdom of the older generations can only be reintegrated into culture through families; therefore, each family should work to place its grandparents at the center of everyday life.

Try to express your own problem and your solution in a sentence or two before moving on.

Revision

Could your thesis be narrower? Writers sometimes seek out problems that are simply too big: hunger, racism, sexism, political deceit, and so on. But such giant problems have too many causes and too many forms. Writers are more apt to create a focused argument and offer an important insight if they take on a specific problem—one that can be located in a particular place and time. Before moving on, make certain that your problem is narrow—as narrow as possible.

RHETORICAL TOOLS

Remember that proposing a solution is a form of arguing. In fact, the process may involve two layers of argument: (1) persuading the reader about the nature or degree of the problem and (2) showing the value of a particular solution. The goal is not necessarily to convince readers that only one solution is possible, but that a particular solution to an important problem has merit.

Although the act of proposing solutions can vary greatly, good proposal essays have certain key elements (which you have already begun to develop):

- **Problem:** Includes illustrations or examples, an explanation of causes, and a picture of short- and long-term effects.
- **Solution:** Includes an explanation of how that solution will address, confront, or stop the causes of the problem.
- **Counterargument:** Addresses concerns about or opposing claims to the solution or the articulation of the problem.
- **Alternative Solutions:** Include any other potential strategies for addressing the problem. Articulating alternative solutions requires an explanation of why these are less desirable than the main solution being offered.
- **Concession/Qualifier:** Acknowledges any possible shortcomings of the solution, or concedes value to some opposing claim or alternative solution.

Proposing Solutions: The Double-Layer Argument

1. Argue about the nature of the problem.
2. Argue for the value of your solution.

The development of these elements depends upon your particular problem and solution. Some problems, for instance, require significant explanation; that is, you might need to work hard just to make the reader aware of the complexities of the problem. Or perhaps you have a problem that is rather apparent (such as abandoned buildings plaguing an entire section of town). Consider how your audience may view the problem, and make certain to convince your readers to see the problem as you do.

Also, remember the strategies from Chapter 7, Making Arguments. Writers have the whole world of culture, history, and science within reach. By alluding to key historical moments, relevant literary texts, news events, or popular culture figures, a writer can make claims more persuasive to readers or show that his or her position is shared by others.

Use the following questions to help construct supporting points for your argument (and see the examples in the chapter readings):

- Does a historical situation or trend (the rise of a particular fashion, organization, or individual) illustrate something about my topic? (See Schofield ¶ 4–5.)
- Has science taught us anything about my topic? (See Mahoney ¶ 5–7.)
- Have I witnessed or experienced someone or something that illustrates my point? (See Mahoney ¶ 1 and 4.)
- Can I construct a hypothetical situation that illustrates my point? (See Roberts ¶ 1–9.)

Discovering Counterarguments and Alternative Solutions

In proposing a solution, you are arguing that a problem exists and that a particular solution will address it. But someone might argue with you about several different points: that the problem is no problem at all, that your solution will not work, that your solution is inappropriate—too costly, inhumane, unmanageable, and so on. A good arguer addresses those possible objections. And an especially sophisticated writer can dig into opponents' assumptions. (See Mahoney ¶ 2–3.)

Every problem has many possible solutions, and a good writer acknowledges other possibilities. But acknowledging solutions other than your own involves explaining their shortcomings. That is, as you mention other solutions, you must also make it clear that they are not as valuable as yours for some reason. Other solutions, for instance, might be less efficient, more dangerous, less ethical, less manageable, or simply inadequate. (See Schofield ¶ 7–8.)

Considering other solutions can also help you understand the strengths and shortcomings of the solution you are promoting. For instance, a solution to Marcus's problem (from the Public Resonance section), isolation of the elderly, might involve refiguring the concept of the nuclear family to include grandparents, uncles, aunts, and cousins. Only in reconceptualizing the basic family unit, he might argue, will elderly members of society find more genuine social engagement. But he might also address other solutions, such as programs that bring together schoolchildren and nursing home residents. According to his argument, such solutions might fall short of creating deep and lasting relationships for the elderly.

Apply the following questions to your own proposal:

- Who might not see this as a problem? Why?
- Why might my solution not work?
- What other solutions could be (or have been) attempted?
- Why is the solution I am proposing better or more effective?

Avoiding Logical Fallacies

Logical fallacies are flaws in the structure of an argument that can make readers call the claims into question. (See further explanation of logical fallacies in Chapter 7, pages 248–249.) In proposing solutions, be especially cautious of the following fallacies: faulty cause/effect, non sequitur, and slippery slope. When considering the possible long-term effects of a solution, writers may make any of several logical errors:

- Creating an effect unrelated to the factors of the present (**faulty cause/effect**).
- Skipping several logical steps between a cause and a possible effect (**non sequitur**).
- Extending present circumstances to their most dramatic or disastrous conclusion without sufficient logical clause (**slippery slope**).

Consider Marcus's topic: *Mainstream society isolates the elderly.* It might be valuable for Marcus to project the long-term effects of this problem. However, he should be cautious; it may be tempting to overstate the effects.

Logically sound

- Without the insight of older generations, mainstream society may continuously forget the social crises of the past and have to re-live many burdens.
- As older generations are further isolated, the difficulties they have lived through are isolated with them. And without constant real-life reminders in our midst, younger generations are likely to ignore a past that is not written by official voices of history.

Logically unsound

- America will have to go through another two world wars because it has completely forgotten the past.
- Everyone will eventually think like children without the elderly in everyday life.
- Society will eventually keep everyone over 50 years old locked away.

ORGANIZATIONAL STRATEGIES

How Should I Separate Problem and Solution?

Many elements go into a proposing solutions text: the problem, illustrations or support for the problem, the solution, support for the solution, the alternative solutions, shortcomings of those solutions, counterarguments, and concessions. These can be arranged in any imaginable order. Here are two standard strategies:

- Problem
  Examples/Illustrations

- My Solution
  Examples/Illustrations

- Alternative Solution
  Explanation
  Shortcoming

- Alternative Solution
  Explanation
  Shortcoming

OR

- Problem

- Alternative Solution A/Shortcoming

- My Solution

- Alternative Solution B/Shortcoming

- My Solution

- Alternative Solution C/Shortcoming

- My Solution

But the arrangement of elements depends on the topic. Some problems demand more attention, others less. Some solutions need significant explanation and support, others less. If the problem is fairly obvious—if readers will accept it as a problem—then it will not require lengthy supporting passages, counterarguments, concessions, and so on. But if the problem is subtle—if readers are not likely to accept that it's a problem in the first place—then it will demand lengthy explanation. Writers must ask themselves two questions:

- Will readers easily accept this as a problem? (If not, I'll have to persuade them.)
- Will readers easily accept the solution? (If not, I'll have to persuade them.)

If the problem is a violent elementary school playground, the writer may not have to work diligently to make a case. (Readers are not apt to dismiss such a problem.) But if the problem is a quiet form of institutional racism, then the writer will have to take more time (more paragraphs) to reveal the problem.

When the solution involves many meticulous steps, it needs significant explanation. In the Roberts essay, for example, the problem, the task of writing a 500-word essay, is presented quickly. The solution is developed with specific details, specific how-to strategies:

- ¶ 1-3: Description of the problem
- ¶ 4: Alternative Solution
- ¶ 5-6: Shortcoming of the Alt Solution
- ¶ 7–27: Roberts' Solution with Examples and Illustrations

How Should I Include Counterarguments?

Counterarguments (responses to those opposing your claims) often are arranged in separate paragraphs. You might develop a counter in an entire paragraph—explaining why, for example, some people are opposed to your understanding of the problem. Then, in a new paragraph, you might explain why your understanding is most appropriate or correct or valuable. Some writers use the *turnabout paragraph* for counterarguments. A turnabout paragraph begins with one point and then changes directions at some point, always giving the reader a clear indication of that change. For example, you might begin a paragraph with an opposing claim, and then counterargue in that same paragraph, as in the following passage from Rachel Schofield's essay:

> Food still enables us to survive, but we no longer revere it. Some would disagree, citing the weight problems engorging our country. We see food 24/7 on TV, hear about it on the radio, see it advertised on billboards, and even in internet pop-ins. Advertising works. We buy what we see, yet the low nutrition levels in our highly processed foods leave our bodies starving for more, and we only give them more junk. We can see the preeminence of food in the dedication of temples to food all along our highways; fast food chains are more popular than ever. However, there is a difference between obsession with food and reverence for it. Our fast food restaurants and freezer aisles are brothels where impure, chemically altered food is bought and sold. Almost gone are the days when honest, unadulterated food can be purchased by the American family.

Counterarguments can also be addressed in a subtler manner. In the following paragraph, Mahoney creates a kind of back and forth between her solution (using a pencil to read) and resistance to it:

> When I tell my students the only way to read a book is with pencil gliding freely across the page (no highlighters please), they look stymied. Selected passages ought to be underlined, I maintain, and tricky vocabulary circled. Further, I suggest that handwritten symbols in the form of stars, asterisks, squiggly lines, question marks, brackets, and the like warrant placement alongside their personal comments posted in the margins. After all, the white space on the printed page could use the company. My students offer good enough reasons, however, for *not* writing in their books: (1) Writing in books during the K–12 years is absolutely taboo, they tell me, and they've been successfully trained to do as told; (2) Some college bookstores won't buy back textbooks with extensive personalized annotations and markings. Students need cash at semester's end, so they dutifully comply. But how is any of this non-writing good for thinking and learning? I'm pretty sure it's not. We might find the current state of affairs particularly worrisome if we frame the problem this way: In an attempt to educate, it seems that educators and a whole lot of other well-meaning adults have worked successfully to ensure disengagement with the printed word, often during the most formative and critical years of literacy acquisition.

Such a strategy helps writers to deal directly with resistance by developing specific reasoning for that resistance. It's much like sitting down with the opposing team and working through the logic of disagreement.

Where Should I Put Alternative Solutions?

Alternative solutions, those strategies other than the one forwarded by the writer, can come early or late in an essay. Some writers acknowledge other possibilities soon after their introductions. Notice Roberts's strategy: In his scenario, a student hands in an essay using typical get-it-done strategies and receives a "D." The hypothetical writing process of the student is the alternative solution, which, Roberts argues, is not a very good one. He explains this after showing us the hypothetical paper on college football:

> On Monday you turn it in, moderately hopeful, and on Friday it comes back marked "weak in content" and sporting a big "D."

Once Roberts shows the negative side of such a strategy, he goes on to give a detailed solution to the problem of writing assignments.

WRITER'S VOICE

Because proposing a solution is an argumentative process, the Writer's Voice strategies from Chapter 7: Making Arguments, apply here as well (see pages 252–253). But proposing solutions brings with it some particular concerns and strategies. The following strategies will help you develop and maintain an engaging writer's voice.

Creating Reasonable Tone

It might be said that *tone* is the way a writer treats readers. In argumentative writing, tone is vital to maintaining readers' interest. One that is too emotional can overwhelm; one that is condescending is apt to alienate. When proposing solutions, writers must be careful not to force problems *at* readers. Instead, it is the writer's job to present a problem and illustrate its significance *for* readers. For example, notice Mahoney's strategy for making the reader understand the significance of a problem:

> Today's college students are suffering, and unnecessarily so. I see them arrive in my writing classes each semester eager and determined, but all too often the motivation and passion dissipate when they come face-to-face with—well—words on the page. This is distressing for both them and me. My students are not illiterate by any means, as they successfully broke the code of sound-to-symbol in the earliest elementary years. Since that time, they've continued to learn in public and private school systems or they've been home-schooled. They're educated and plenty adept at moving through the system. But I'm not convinced any of this means they are capable of truly committing to a book, an essay, or any document requiring sustained focus and labor-intensive thinking and doing.

It would be easy, or at least tempting, for Mahoney to scream and shout at her readers about students' disengagement from the written word. Imagine the following:

> Today's college students cannot read closely or intensively. They might want to perform well in their classes, but their hopes have been dashed by a careless educational system. They are victims in the worst sense. By the time they've reached my classes, very few of them will be able to learn how to read at the college level. The rest will be left behind. We've forgotten our most vulnerable population—our children.

This passage is over the top. It forces the problem at its readers and demands that they feel a particular emotion. Mahoney's passage is less confrontational, while still intense. She does not make emotional demands on the reader; instead, she presents the strengths and weaknesses she sees in her students and leaves the reader to reflect on them.

Inviting the Reader

Writerly invitations are phrases that promote curiosity in readers, phrases that entice them to examine a particular topic.

Question Asking the right question can make a reader concerned about the subject: *Why are the computer labs at University Hall a problem? How safe is the drinking water in our community?* In her essay, Schofield invites the reader to consider hard questions that bring the reader into the center of the problem:

> How can Americans have reverence for food when we have so many artificial consumables surrounding us? And to complicate the problem, "Compare the price of a grapefruit to that of a pack of strawberry-flavored Twizzlers" (Zinczenko). It seems that processed food is almost always cheaper and more accessible than wholesome fresh foods. What can a struggling American family do when the only thing they can afford is cheap processed food?

Group Inclusion A writer can include potential readers in a relevant group (small or large) that is affected by the subject. Mahoney creates a collective us—a group that is interested in raising and teaching children:

> So, I think the problem is clear. Our system of educating, parenting, and nurturing unwittingly conspires to ensure students' disciplined detachment from words on the page. In other words, creating disengaged adults begins early. My proposal is simple and not particularly original, but I'll reiterate it nonetheless. Those of us committed to raising and teaching need to raise and teach differently.

Statement A simple claim that calls the reader's attention to the matter is often the most effective. Notice Mahoney's strong statement at the beginning of her essay:

Today's college students are suffering and unnecessarily so.

Considering Verb Mood

There are three moods in English: *indicative* (used for stating facts or statements about the world), *subjunctive* (used to express conditions that are not facts, such as a recommendation, a wish, a requirement, or a statement contrary to fact), and *imperative* (used for issuing commands or suggestions). Many passages in this text are in the imperative mood. (Find one right now.) Rather than informing the reader about possible ways to act (as in the subjunctive), imperative mood orders the reader to act.

Imperative mood is not often used in academic essays or formal proposals because it puts the reader in the position of action. Of course, there are exceptions. Roberts's essay is written, almost entirely, in the imperative mood. Because his strategy is to give his audience the particular steps to solving a problem, the imperative mood is appropriate. It is also appropriate because his audience is very specific—college writers. He assumes that the audience has (or will have) a personal encounter with the problem.

But be careful with imperative mood. It can often diminish the intensity of a good argument. Because imperative mood draws attention to the reader (to you), it must necessarily draw less attention to the topic. The goal of most academic writing is to keep intensive focus on the topic, to build a compelling idea for would-be readers, not to go after the particular person holding the essay. In the following, notice how the first sentence focuses on the reader rather than the topic. In other words, the energy of the sentence goes toward a nameless and invisible "you," while the second and third sentences draw more attention to the topic:

- **Imperative Mood:** While reading, use a pencil to better engage the nuances of a text.
- **Indicative Mood:** Reading with a pencil helps students to engage the nuances of a text.
- **Subjunctive Mood:** If students would use a pencil while reading, they could better engage the nuances of a text.

The differences may seem subtle but the three sentences radically change the role of a reader. In an imperative sentence, the reader is called upon—insisted upon. In indicative and subjunctive sentences, the reader joins the writer in a mutual examination of the topic. And because academic writing celebrates that mutual examination, indicative and subjunctive are used most often.

Activity

Draft a paragraph that makes your topic inviting to the reader. Apply one of the three strategies:

1. Ask an important question.

2. Include the reader in an affected group.

3. Call attention to the matter with a strong statement.

VITALITY

In his essay "How To Say Nothing in 500 Words," Paul Roberts offers college students sound advice. The problem students face: a standard college assignment that requires a certain page length. The solution Roberts proposes: less obvious approaches and less usual positions.

Avoid the Obvious Content

In his essay, Roberts argues that writers should avoid saying what everyone knows. He urges writers to make a list of the first ideas that come to mind on any topic, and then to avoid those initial ideas: "If these are the points that leap to your mind, they will leap to everyone else's too. . . ." Even at the sentence level, writers can avoid the obvious. They can trim out the statements that readers will simply infer on their own. Notice the following obvious content:

> It is wrong when people cheat others. And when the Enron executives cheated thousands of employees out of their pensions, they ruined retirement years for many families.

The entire first sentence is unnecessary, and it detracts from the intensity of the ideas. When writers force such obvious statements onto readers, they make readers less involved. Obvious statements actually tell readers to turn off!

Get Rid of Obvious Padding

Padding occurs when writers stuff their sentences with unnecessary material. The sentences become longer but contain no added meaning. In his essay, Roberts begins with a brief sentence and a simple idea: "Fast driving is dangerous."

The brief idea then gains words but no meaning:

> In my humble opinion though I do not claim to be an expert on this complicated subject, fast driving, in most circumstances, would seem to be rather dangerous in many respects, or at least so it would seem to me.

The padded sentence is full of unnecessary qualifiers and attention to the writer. While qualifiers can be valuable and first-person pronouns can be important, they can be overused. They can slow down sentences and inflate simple ideas so they sound important.

But when writers begin pruning and trimming their essays, when they really get good at vitalizing their sentences, their drafts are apt to shrink. This may seem like bad news if the goal is, in fact, to reach a certain length requirement. But Roberts again gives good advice:

> Instead of taking a couple of obvious points off the surface of the topic and then circling warily around them for six paragraphs, you work in and explore, figure out the details. You illustrate. You say that fast driving is dangerous, and then you prove it. How long does it take to stop a car at forty and at eighty? How far can you see at night? What happens when a tire blows? What happens in a head-on collision at fifty miles an hour? Pretty soon your paper will be full of broken glass and blood and headless torsos, and reaching five hundred words will not really be a problem.

So it all comes back to invention. Developing more intensive ideas from the beginning means writers can avoid padding.

Call a Fool a Fool

Academic audiences value intensity and directness. But some writers may avoid directly stating points. Roberts gives the following scenario:

> The student writes, "In my opinion, the principal of my high school acted in ways that I believe every unbiased person would have to call foolish." This isn't exactly what he means. What he means is, "My high school principal was a fool." If he was a fool, call him a fool. Hedging the thing about with "in-my-opinion's" and "it-seems-to-me's" and "as-I-see-it's" and "at-least-from-my-point-of-view's" gains you nothing. Delete these phrases whenever they creep into your paper.

PEER REVIEW

Exchange drafts with at least one other writer. Before passing your draft to others, underline the thesis, or write it above your essay. This way, reviewers will get traction as they read.

As a reviewer, use the following questions to guide your response:

1. After reading the draft, do you believe that the problem the writer describes is worthy of attention? Do you think it's a problem worth solving? If not, what might the writer do to make the problem more significant? (Consider the Public Resonance section of the chapter.)

2. Do you think the writer's solution is appropriate for the problem? Will it address specific causes? Is it manageable? Realistic? Humane?

3. Try to imagine a reason why the writer's solution will not work. What unforeseen forces or variables should the writer consider?

4. What other solutions might be as or more productive in solving the problem?

5. Consider the organization of the essay. Do any paragraphs shift focus without sufficient cues? Do you feel like any paragraphs move away from their initial points without taking you along? Point to specific places in the essay that move too abruptly from one idea to another.

6. How would you describe the writer's tone? (See page 400.) Do you feel invited into the topic, or do you have to work at keeping your attention focused? (Is the writer's voice too flat, too uninteresting, too typical?) Rewrite a short passage of the draft using a different voice. Help the writer to imagine how a different voice might sound.

7. Consider sentence vitality:

   a. Help the writer to avoid obvious content. Circle any sentences or passages that seem obvious to you. (Write "obvious?" next to the passage.)

   b. Help the writer to avoid padding. Underline phrases that inflate simple ideas and draw out sentences unnecessarily.

   c. Help the writer to "call a fool a fool." Rewrite any phrases or sentences that seem to hedge, that circle around a more direct and intense wording.

   d. Consider vitality strategies from other chapters.

Academic audiences value intensity and directness.

DELIVERY

The real value of everything in this book lies in how you apply it to real-life situations. To do this, imagine the essay as a sort of practice field, and see all the lessons you learn from writing an essay as important knowledge you can now apply in your everyday life—at work, at home, at school, and everywhere else. What problems do you and others face in real life? And what are the possible solutions?

- Do you drive too far to work?
- Are you strapped financially?
- Why, surrounded by modern conveniences, don't you have enough free time?

Consider the essay you wrote for this chapter:

- Will the reader better understand that a problem exists?
- How might others act differently from reading your essay?
- How did writing the essay help you, the writer, with the problem?

Beyond the Essay

The comic on the following page encourages you to express the idea from your essay in some other form: a letter, speech, and so on.

Why?

Students sometimes see education—or certain college courses such as this one—as separate from their actual lives. However, the course is not only related to your major; it is, more importantly, related to your *life*. Writing courses such as this one go out into the real world and bring that real world back into the classroom.

Such courses look at what really goes on in everyday life, and they present what goes on (invention strategies, rhetorical strategies, and so on) in an organized way. College courses gather and organize the untidy ideas of disorganized real life, and they present those ideas in an orderly, more graspable way. Admittedly, the college writing course can be a confusing and seemingly irrelevant place. But if you can remember that the invention and delivery strategies in this book are a description (not a prescription) of how everyday people think and communicate effectively, you can more successfully fuse schoolwork and real life. This fusion is the intended purpose of all education.

A student's job is to connect classroom work to everyday life.

A student's job is to connect everyday life to classroom work.

"We must therefore look in the most obscurest corners and summon up courage to shock the prejudices of our age if we want to broaden the basis of our understanding of nature."

—Carl Jung

Living in a society demands a certain degree of conformity. As individuals in a society, we conform to laws, clothing styles, hairstyles, and even culinary tastes (most Americans like french fries but not raw oysters). We also conform to ways of thinking; we learn to follow intellectual conventions. This is not to say that we all think alike, not by a long shot, but we do buy into conventional modes or patterns of thought that, on the one hand, allow us to participate in shared knowledge but, on the other hand, limit intellectual possibilities.

Mainstream thought invites us to accept a particular view of reality, and with it, certain assumptions. Consider the following:

- Progress involves technological advancement.
- The past is behind us.
- People who make lots of money are successful.
- Poor people are worse off than rich people.
- We make individual choices.
- Time is constant.

Such ideas are what we might call *common sense,* in that they represent widely held, and largely unexamined, beliefs. But some people have examined and even challenged such common ideas. For example, thinkers such as Wendell Berry challenge the idea that human progress necessarily involves increased dependence on technology; several important religious figures (Jesus, Buddha, Mohammed) overturned the inherent value of monetary riches; and Albert Einstein showed the world that time is not constant but relative. We might say that such figures transcend and challenge commonsense thinking. They call into question those beliefs that rest beneath layers of intellectual practice and everyday life. They show us questions where we may have assumed solid answers.

People who transcend conventional thinking are not *radical* in the sense that they want to destroy mainstream life. (We are not talking here about anarchists, religious zealots, or specific political positions.) Rather, they are radical *thinkers:* They escape conventional thought patterns. While convention calls on us to think within the lines, radical thinkers work to see beyond those lines, and then communicate what ideas are possible. Their writing seeks to reform conventional thinking.

Radical thinking is not necessarily a matter of topic choice; in fact, topics are not, in themselves, radical. Radical thinking involves an adventurous *approach* to a topic and offers a new way to think. For example, in 1784, Benjamin Franklin first put forth the idea of daylight savings time. After waking at an unusually early hour in the morning and finding that the sun had risen, he imagined that people could change their clocks to coincide with sunrise throughout the seasons.

In 1543, Nicolaus Copernicus challenged the conventional theory that the Earth is the center of the universe. He defied church law and common sense of the day and claimed that the Earth rotates around the sun. History is filled with such intellectual adventurers, those who transcended norms to see relationships beyond the obvious, to find meaning outside of cultural norms, and to imagine perspectives beyond the present:

- W. E. B. Dubois argued against mainstream thinking about African Americans' place in society. While most politicians, educators, and civic leaders walked a moderate line, assuming that black people in America could thrive in subservient positions, Dubois imagined that African Americans should act as leaders for national and global change.

- Psychologist Carl Jung broke away from his colleague Sigmund Freud (and the conventional wisdom of the psychological community) to argue that human unconscious is, in part, a collective rather than an individual phenomenon.

- Georgia O'Keeffe transcended artistic conventions by focusing on the organic. While art and popular culture were increasingly transfixed on the abstract, O'Keeffe sought out the most pure and basic forms of identity in images such as flowers and landscapes.

Radical thinkers have changed how laws, government, and institutional policy work. People such as Thomas Jefferson, Mahatma Gandhi, Eleanor Roosevelt, Martin Luther King, Jr., and Martin Luther articulated ideas and policies that were beyond conventional thinking of their times.

In academic study and everyday life, methods often evolve because real people transcend the common sense of their fields; that is, they imagine the possibilities beyond what is assumed. The people who are able to think beyond *what is* and to conjure images of *what could be* are those who most often provide direction for improvement in the quality of daily work and daily life. As you explore this chapter, remember that all those people who have helped bring about change are those who first had to imagine a reality beyond the status quo.

This chapter will help you transcend conventional thought, focus on a particular topic, develop a focused thesis, and communicate your ideas in writing. The following essays will provide valuable insight to various strategies. After reading the essays, you can find a topic in one of two ways:

1. Go to the Point of Contact section to find a topic from everyday life.
   or
2. Choose one of the Ideas for Writing following the essays.

After finding a subject, go to the Analysis section to begin developing your thoughts.

Why Doesn't GM Sell Crack?

Michael Moore

A common assumption in mainstream America is that society should work for the advancement of business. People don't often assume (or say) that a democratic society should come first and that business should advance society. In fact, whenever such a notion comes up, it is often cast away with scorn. In this essay, Michael Moore applies a line of reasoning (appeal to logic) to pull readers away from the most common assumptions about business.

People in the business world like to say, "Profit is supreme." They like chanting that. "Profit is king." That's another one they like to repeat. They don't like to say, "I'll pick up the check." That means less profit. Profit is what it's all about. When they say "the bottom line," they mean their *profit.* They like that bottom line to contain a number followed by a lot of zeroes.

If I had a nickel for every time I heard some guy in a suit tell me that "a company must do whatever is necessary to create the biggest profit possible," I would have a very big bottom line right now. Here's another popular mantra: "The responsibility of the CEO is to make his shareholders as much money as he can."

Are you enjoying this lesson in capitalism? I get it every time I fly on a plane. The bottom-line feeders have all seen *Roger & Me,* yet they often mistake the fuselage of a DC-9 for the Oxford Debating Society. So I have to sit through lectures ad nauseam about the beauties of our free market system. Today the guy in the seat next to me is the owner of an American company that makes office supplies—in Taiwan. I ask the executive, "How much is 'enough'?"

"Enough what?" he replies.

5   "How much is 'enough' profit?"

He laughs and says, "There's no such thing as 'enough'!"

So, General Motors made nearly $7 billion in profit last year—but they could make $7.1 billion by closing a factory in Parma, Ohio, and moving it to Mexico—that would be okay?"

"Not only okay," he responds, "it is their duty to close that plant and make the extra $.1 billion."

"Even if it destroys Parma, Ohio? Why can't $7 billion be enough and spare the community? Why ruin thousands of families for the sake of *$.1* billion? Do you think this is *moral?*"

10   "Moral?" he asks, as if this is the first time he's heard that word since First Communion class. "This is not an issue of morality. It is purely a matter of economics. A company must be able to do whatever it wants to make a profit." Then he leans over as if to make a revelation I've never heard before.

"Profit, you know, is supreme."

So here's what I don't understand: if profit is supreme, why doesn't a company like General Motors sell crack? Crack is a *very* profitable commodity. For every pound of cocaine that is transformed into crack, a dealer stands to make a profit of $45,000. The dealer profit on a two-thousand-pound car is less than $2,000. Crack is also safer to use than automobiles. Each year, 40,000 people die in car accidents. Crack, on the other hand, kills only a few hundred people a year. And it doesn't pollute.

So why doesn't GM sell crack? If profit is supreme, why not sell crack?

GM doesn't sell crack because it is illegal. Why is it illegal? Because we, as a society, have determined that crack destroys people's lives. It ruins entire communities. It tears apart the very backbone of our country. That's why we wouldn't let a company like GM sell it, no matter what kind of profit they could make.

15   If we wouldn't let GM sell crack because it destroys our communities, then why do we let them close factories? *That, too,* destroys our communities.

As my frequent-flier friend would say, "We can't prevent them from closing factories because they have a right to do whatever they want to in order to make a profit."

No, they don't. They don't have a "right" to do a lot of things: sell child pornography, manufacture chemical weapons, or create hazardous products that could conceivably make them a profit. We can enact laws to prevent companies from doing anything to hurt us.

And downsizing is one of those things that is hurting us. I'm not talking about legitimate layoffs, when a company is losing money and simply doesn't have the cash reserves to pay its workers. I'm talking about companies like GM, AT&T, and GE, which fire people at a time when the company is making record profits in the billions of dollars. Executives who do this are not scorned, picketed, or arrested—they are hailed as heroes! They make the covers of *Fortune* and *Forbes*. They lecture at the Harvard Business School about their success. They throw big campaign fund-raisers and sit next to the President of the United States. They are the Masters of the Universe simply because they make huge profits regardless of the consequences to our society.

Are we insane or what? Why do we allow this to happen? It is *wrong* to make money off people's labor and then fire them after you've made it. It is *immoral* for a CEO to make millions of dollars when he has just destroyed the livelihood of 40,000 families. And it's just plain *nuts* to allow American companies to move factories overseas at the expense of our own people.

20 When a company fires thousands of people, what happens to the community? Crime goes up, suicide goes up, drug abuse, alcoholism, spousal abuse, divorce— everything bad spirals dangerously upward. The same thing happens with crack. Only crack is illegal, and downsizing is not. If there was a crack house in your neighborhood, what would you do? You would try to get rid of it!

I think it's time we applied the same attitudes we have about crack to corporate downsizing. It's simple: If it hurts our citizens, it should be illegal. We live in a democracy. We enact laws based on what we believe is right and wrong. Murder? Wrong, so we pass a law making it illegal. Burglary? Wrong, and we attempt to prosecute those who commit it. Two really big hairy guys from Gingrich's office pummel me after they read this book? Five to ten in Sing Sing.

As a society, we have a right to protect ourselves from harm. As a democracy, we have a responsibility to legislate measures to protect us from harm.

Here's what I think we should do to protect ourselves:

1. Prohibit corporations from closing a profitable factory or business and moving it overseas. If they close a business and move it within the U.S., they must pay reparations to the community they are leaving behind. We've passed divorce laws that say that if a woman works hard to put her husband through school, and he later decides to leave her after he has become successful, he has a responsibility to compensate her for her sacrifices that allowed him to go on to acquire his wealth. The "marriage" between a company and a community should be no different. If a corporation packs up and leaves, it should have some serious alimony to pay.

2. Prohibit companies from pitting one state or city against another. We are all Americans. It is no victory for our society when one town wins at another's expense. Texas should not be able to raid Massachusetts for jobs. It is debilitating and, frankly, legal extortion.

3. Institute a 100 percent tax on any profits gained by shareholders when the company's stock goes up due to an announcement of firings. No one should be allowed to profit from such bad news.

4. Prohibit executives' salaries from being more than thirty times greater than an average employee's pay. When workers have to take a wage cut because of hard times, so, too, should the CEO. If a CEO fires a large number of employees, it should be illegal for him to collect a bonus that year.

5. Require boards of directors of publicly owned corporations to have representation from both workers and consumers. A company will run better if it has to listen to the people who have to build and/or use the products the company makes.

For those of you free-marketers who disagree with these modest suggestions and may end up on a plane sitting next to me, screaming, "You can't tell a business how it can operate!"—I have this to say: Oh, yes, we can! We legally require companies to build safe products, to ensure safe workplaces, to pay employees a minimum wage, to contribute to their Social Security, and to follow a host of other rules that we, as a society, have deemed necessary for our well-being. And we can legally require each of the steps I've outlined above.

25 GM can't sell crack. Soon, I predict, they and other companies will not be able to sell us out. Just keep firing more workers, my friends, and see what happens.

Use of description to paint a picture.

and that you know the names and effects of toxins that only our most advanced scientists understood. No doubt, you must regard even the most basic food ingredients with scrutiny. I imagine that the sun is no longer personified in children's drawings with a gentle smile and happy radiant beams, but is, instead, something to avoid at all costs. (I imagine that you cannot possibly imagine how we once "bathed" in sun rays for recreation.)

I imagine that your everyday lives are filled with the consequences of our political naïveté. Perhaps the countries that provided our laborers, those we so boldly referred to as "Third World," have by now demanded a change in the world order. Perhaps they are now capable of responding to years of exploitation; perhaps they have escaped the economic imperialism of the twentieth century; or, perhaps their numbers ultimately afforded them the ability to resist their tyrants—who served them up as objects to our "globally minded" leaders. Or perhaps our greed for oil became so great that we no longer concealed our desire to control entire regions of the world. Perhaps, the hidden global tensions of the late twentieth and early twenty-first centuries came to full realization, and you are living in the aftermath.

International policies/politics figure in, too.

Every age has its dissonant voices. But as it shrinks into the past, its internal tensions and dissonant voices fade, and the telescopic lens of history sees it as a unity. And certainly, this fate will befall our time. The material conditions created by our time will frame us all as guilty, as complicit in the deterioration of a socially and environmentally uninhabitable world. And this is no defense of our dissonant voices—those who tried to warn us. They too enjoyed our opulence. As a collective mass of consumers, we all created the conditions that you presently endure—whatever they may be.

We are all guilty. Even those who object to the current lifestyle contribute to it, participate in it. We must be a part of our culture while at the same time resisting it.

Concession: Dissonant voices (such as Benlow) enjoyed opulence, too.

5   Although it is probably impossible, I hope you do not look back and characterize us as purely self-serving and wicked, but as trapped in our own enterprise. We were a young culture with no parents. In fact, we stumbled over ourselves to appear perpetually immature and restless. We packaged restlessness, and sold it in the form of hair dyes, fake breasts, and sexual stimulants. Like a mass of delirious adolescents, we made ourselves increasingly giddy, posing for ourselves and for one another, posing in every aspect of our lives: our homes, travel, clothes, food, water, and vacations. It was a mammoth parade of teenage delirium that began in New York, wormed through every tiny town of the Midwest, and wrapped around itself in dizzying perpetual circles on the beaches of California. As it came through every town, no one could resist it. It banged and clamored and woke everyone from dreamy isolation, and so even the most ascetic types found themselves playing along in some small way.

Figurative language: "we stumbled over ourselves"

Examples supporting the argument.

We are a young culture. America is a country like a child, without parental control. Our parents are children. Our leaders are like children in the world. As a country, we lack discipline and foresight.

"Perhaps" shows Benlow's exploration of the issue.

We grew outward and consumed everything because we told ourselves that we could, because our parents said we could, and because their parents said we should. Relentless growth was part of our mythology. It was hard-wired into our daily lives and our nightly dreams. Perhaps it was our conflated notion of private property that eclipsed our potential concern for those outside our fences or beyond our calendar years. Perhaps it was our bloated pride at overcoming nature; we were utterly smitten by the idea that nature could rarely infringe on our desires to move whimsically about the world. Perhaps it was some instinctual drive to outdo others—to surpass the luxuries of past generations. Perhaps it was all of these that blurred our collective vision of the future. Had we been able to look beyond our giant, ballooned notions of self, property, and progress, perhaps we would have been able to foresee something or someone out there in the distance.

Very formal language— seems like a funeral.

Although you cannot possibly imagine it, we were, generally, an agreeable people: We knew how to celebrate, how to have a parade, how to draw a crowd, how to break seating capacity records. And if you could return to our time, I would make a dubious wager that you, too, would find it difficult to resist the lure of our lifestyle, the attraction of our conveniences. And if we had been able to imagine you as real people, even as our own distant progeny, rather than a simple euphemism ("the future"), we certainly would have acted differently. Although we probably would not have relented in our give-it-to-me-now race for more, we would have taken a solemn moment to raise a toast and drink to your hardship.

Conclusion: Any humans tempted by our times would be likely to go along, too.

We are guilty, but nice, people.

. . . we're also ridiculous.

Writing Strategies

1. Evaluate Benlow's introduction. How does or doesn't it invite the reader into the essay?

2. Benlow organizes his essay by dividing his apology into several major sections. What is the purpose of each major section?

3. Describe Benlow's voice as a writer, and refer to several passages to support your description.

4. If workshopping Benlow's essay, what would you tell him? What do you like most about his apology? What one suggestion would you make?

5. Discuss your workshopping ideas (from #4 above) with several classmates. How are your ideas similar to or different from your classmates' ideas?

Exploring Ideas

1. In a paragraph or two, describe how Benlow sees contemporary American culture.

2. How is the way that you see contemporary American culture similar to or different from the way Benlow sees it?

3. Consider your initial reactions to Benlow's essay. What points did you most agree or disagree with? What ideas did you not understand?

4. Ask others if they feel future generations deserve an apology and, if so, for what. Record their responses and compare them to Benlow's essay. How are their views similar to or different from Benlow's and your own?

Ideas for Writing

1. Imagine that Benlow's essay and one of yours will be read by future generations. What would you like to say to future generations?

2. What idea of Benlow's might you expand on?

If responding to one of these ideas, go to the Analysis section of this chapter to begin developing ideas for your essay.

Used by permission of the authors.

Unemployed and Working Hard

Simon Wykoff

Radical thinkers help others re-imagine conventional ways of thinking. In the following essay, written for his first-year writing class, Simon Wykoff provides carefully selected details from an average day to help others re-imagine the common stereotype of the "lazy bum." Using personal testimony and a few outside sources, Wykoff flips the stereotype upside down.

A common stereotype in today's society is that of the lazy bum. People see a homeless man on the side of the road, waiting for handouts, and assume that's all he ever does. In reality, this couldn't be farther from the truth. As the painter Willem de Kooning once said, "The trouble with being poor is that it takes up all of your time." This is absolutely true, and I think you'll find that homeless people are incredibly busy doing the most important job to all of us: surviving.

According to a fact sheet available from the National Coalition for the Homeless, the best approximation of the total number of homeless people comes from a study done by the National Law Center on Homelessness and Poverty, which states that roughly 3.5 million people in the United States will experience homelessness every year ("How Many" 2-3). For most of my childhood, my father was one of these many homeless people. While growing up, I spent a large amount of my time living on the streets with him. I can tell you from my experiences that the process he went through every day in order to find food and shelter was one of the roughest "jobs" I have ever seen.

Before I begin, something you need to understand is that my father did not make use of services like shelters during his many years of homelessness. His opinion, which I have seen held by many other homeless people, was that these services were usually crowded, of poor quality, and often more dangerous than simply living on the streets. While this did make life more difficult in some ways, he (and I) felt it kept him safer in the end.

The first thing my father did upon waking up was check his belongings. Depending on the place he was sleeping, there was a good chance that something could have been stolen from him in the middle of the night. It was not uncommon for him to find the clothes in his backpack gone, or to discover that he was missing money he had stashed away.

5   After checking through his items, he would look over the money he had remaining from his efforts on the previous day. If he had enough, he would buy himself breakfast, usually at one of the cheaper coffee shops around town. If he had no money, he went to the dumpsters behind several bakeries in the town to fish out the four-day-old bread they had thrown away. If the bread wasn't moldy, it was his morning meal.

Once he had some food in his belly, he usually tried to locate a current paper. This often meant waiting around in coffee shops until someone left one on the table after their breakfast. Sometimes this step could take him hours, but he was determined not to waste the precious money on a newspaper when he could get it for free with patience.

As soon as he had the paper, he thumbed through it, looking for jobs he could feasibly apply to. Due to his particular circumstances, he was without official identification. This, of course, made the search much more difficult. If he found something, he would tear off the piece of the paper and store it to refer to later.

I should interject here and explain how he got around the city. While my father was homeless, he was lucky enough to have a bicycle, which he treasured beyond everything else. It's not uncommon in a larger city to have the place you get food, the place you sleep, and the place you go to try and earn money be miles and miles apart. Because of this, even on a bike my father spent a considerable amount of time traveling. He would often ride from one end of the city to the other several times a day. This takes an incredible amount of endurance, especially when you are doing it on an empty stomach, as he often was. Many times, just a trip from the place he was sleeping to the closest bakery in the morning was a marathon!

The next thing he did after looking for job opportunities was to get money in order to buy food for the rest of the day. While you may see many homeless panhandling, I think people don't realize that a large number of homeless actually do small-time work for their daily bread. As mentioned in an online editorial, the homeless these days are increasingly working menial tasks for extra cash, or just to survive (Hilton). For all the people you see standing outside of stores with signs, others are playing instruments on street corners, gathering cans for recycling, or washing windows.

10 My father fell into the category of musicians. To make money, he sat in a high-traffic area and played his pennywhistle for the people passing by. He didn't heckle pedestrians, or openly beg. He didn't even display a sign. He was simply a man on the street with an upturned hat in front of him, playing Irish jigs.

After a few hours of tiring playing, my father went off to buy his lunch and dinner for the day. He had no place to store food, like a refrigerator, so he was forced to buy items that wouldn't perish. His diet was made up largely of things like chips, bread, and vegetables that could be eaten raw. This was hardly an ideal diet, but he managed nonetheless.

After he finished his lunch, my father went looking for things he could sell or use himself. The best way for him to do this was dumpster diving. He would go to the areas of town where the richer college students lived, and wade through the communal dumpsters for things like VCRs or microwaves that could be carried to nearby stores and sold. This was often difficult work, as he had to strap any large items to the back of his bicycle and ride with them for some time.

Once he finished searching through the dumpsters, he went on to his next task, applying for any jobs he had found in the paper. This was difficult, as most of the places he could apply to were on the edges of town, away from the college districts. He would ride all the way across town to submit his barren resume, only to have it rejected.

Finally, as his arduous day neared an end, my father looked for a place to sleep at night. This was not always easy, and he had to switch locations fairly often. If he didn't, he would begin to raise the suspicions of the property owner, or become a target for the more dangerous people on the streets.

As you can see, my father's day was far from that simplistic stereotype of the bum who sits on street corners all day and waits for people to help him out. What people don't seem to realize is that to survive on the streets, you have to take things into your own hands. You need to have perseverance, stamina, and a little bit of luck. Though it may seem outlandish, I think you'll find that many homeless people work just as much, or more, than you.

Works Cited

Hilton, G. Dan. "Designer Java for a Regular Joe." Homeless Man Speaks. 2 Nov. 2006. 8 Nov. 2007 <http://homelessmanspeaks.wordpress.com/facts-arguments-nov-2-2006/>.

"How Many People Experience Homelessness?" National Coalition for the Homeless. Aug. 2007. 8 Nov. 2007 <http://www.nationalhomeless.org/publications/facts/How_Many.pdf>.

Koonig, de Willem. The Quotations Page. 14 Nov. 2007 http://www.quotationspage.com/quote/27636.html.

Writing Strategies

1. How is Wykoff's essay a response to conventional thinking?

2. What is Wykoff's thesis?

3. What support strategies does Wykoff use to help the reader understand and accept his thesis?

4. Choose one paragraph from Wykoff's essay and explain why it is especially effective in helping the reader re-imagine the homeless.

5. Identify several details and explain how they help bring Wykoff's narrative to life.

6. How does Wykoff organize his essay? What other organizational strategy might he have used?

Exploring Ideas

1. What important qualities does Wykoff's father have? What other qualities might be important to surviving as a homeless person?

2. What skills are most important for the survival of someone who isn't homeless?

3. With a group of peers, explore Wykoff's closing sentence: "Though it may seem outlandish, I think you'll find that many homeless people work just as much, or more, than you." Does that seem outlandish? Do group members agree with Wykoff's statement?

Ideas for Writing

1. What common stereotype couldn't be further from the truth?

2. What don't people realize?

If responding to one of these ideas, go to the Analysis section of this chapter to begin developing ideas for your essay.

Used by permission of the authors.

Outside Reading

Find a written text that you believe illustrates radical think-ing, and make a copy or print it out. While radical think-ing sometimes appears in popular or general readership publications (*Time, Newsweek,* the *New York Times,* and so on), such periodicals usually appeal to conventional think-ing. You might have better luck exploring less mainstream sources, such as academic journals in art, science, commu-nication, religion, political science, and so on. To conduct an electronic search of journals and magazines, go to your library's periodical database or to InfoTrac College Edition (http://infotrac.cengage.com). For your library database, per-form a keyword search, or for InfoTrac College Edition, go to the main search box and choose "keywords." Enter word combinations such as *radical and ideas and science, innova-tive and business and ideas, revolutionary and medical and health, avant-garde and physics* (or any topic combined with synonyms for *radical*). (When performing keyword searches, avoid using phrases or articles such as *a, an, the;* instead, use nouns separated by *and.*) The search results will yield lists of journal and magazine articles.

You can also search the Internet. Try the search engine Lycos.com. Like most Internet search engines, Lycos.com combines words using *and.* In the search box, try various combinations, such as those above. Unlike periodical data-bases, Internet search results will contain sources that are sell-ing products and services. Be cautious of such sites.

As you will see, writers in many disciplines write and think on the edge of conventional wisdom and, as you will probably discover, any topic can be approached radically. Writing that transcends conventional thought varies widely in tone, style, length, and strategy. As you read through this chapter, keep the text you have discovered at hand and notice the elements and strategies the writer uses. Depending on your instructor's suggestions, do one or more of the following:

1. Notice how the writer employs various rhetorical strate-gies. On the hard copy or photocopy:
   - Highlight the thesis if it is stated. If the thesis is implied, write it in your own words.
   - Highlight the most radical claims.
   - Highlight any passages in which the writer attempts to bridge conventional wisdom with radical thinking.
   - Identify any counterarguments (passages in which the writer anticipates and refutes opposition) or conces-sions (passages in which the writer grants value to another position).

2. Analyze the strategies employed by the writer. The fol-lowing questions may be helpful:
   - In what ways does the writer transcend or challenge conventional thinking?
   - How does the writer persuade the reader to see his or her vision?
   - Who is the audience for this text?
   - How does the audience impact the kinds of things said in the argument?
   - How would you describe the writer's voice?

3. Write at least three "Writing Strategies" questions for the text that you found.

4. Write at least three "Exploring Ideas" questions for the text you found.

5. Write two "Ideas for Writing," such as the ones follow-ing the essays in this book, for the text that you found.

INVENTION

"Uncertainty can be your guiding light."

—U2

On the one hand, the focus of this chapter may seem rather abstract; we are, after all, attempting to imagine new intellectual ground. On the other hand, these ideas can have their beginnings in familiar, everyday terrain. While the goal may be to extend thinking beyond familiar ideas, we can still start with everyday life.

For this chapter, nothing is more important than the act of invention. As in previous chapters, the writer should attempt to discover something particularly interesting or valuable—or even bizarre. Unlike previous chapters, the ultimate goal is to escape conventional thinking and to imagine something entirely outside of common intellectual activity. The following sections are designed to help you through this process: specifically, to discover a topic (in Point of Contact), to develop particular points about the topic (in Analysis), to make it relevant to a community of readers (in Public Resonance), to invent a focused position (in Thesis), and to develop support (in Rhetorical Tools). Use the Invention questions in each section to explore further. Good luck!

POINT OF CONTACT

The prompts on this page are designed to generate possible writing topics. Fill in the blanks with as many possibilities as you can until you find an engaging topic. As you explore each category, you might imagine particular situations or people to help you start exploring ideas. But do not confine yourself to practical situations or personal experiences. Imagine the possibilities beyond your experiences.

Imagining new connections We are taught (directly and indirectly) to see some things as inherently related and others as entirely disconnected. But radical thinkers can see connections that are not normally seen. Radical thinkers might see an important connection between the economy and nature, oceans and people, or music and politics. Imagine various possibilities, and fill in the blanks to the following statements:

> Most people do not see the connection between _____ and _____.

> Even though it is not apparent, _____ and _____ are deeply connected.

Imagining different possibilities The policies and procedures of society often blind us to alternatives. Imagining those alternatives might reveal a new way to live. For example, someone might imagine something even better than democracy, or a new way to fund college, or an alternative to war. Fill in the blanks with possible ideas:

> Presently, most people _____, but they could _____.

> Presently, the law requires that people must _____, but the law could state that _____.

Questioning common sense Living in a society means participating in common practices and beliefs. But a common belief is not always the best belief. Imagine possibilities for the following and fill in the blanks:

> Most people in my community want _____ without examining the underlying meaning.

> I have always been taught to think _____, but now see a different way.

Exploring the past and future A radical vision is one that sees beyond the confines of the present. A radical thinker might imagine what the world would be like if the American Revolution had not occurred, or how work in America will be defined in 50 years. As you imagine time beyond the present, fill in the blanks for the following:

> In the past, people's perspective of _____ was fundamentally different from our present understanding.

> In the future, people will probably understand _____ differently than we do.

Going to the root The term *radical* comes from the Latin *radix,* which means *root* or *source.* Radical thinking might be seen as a process of finding the root or essence. For example, someone might explore the essence of womanhood or manhood, the true meaning of growing old, or the essence of education. Fill in the blanks to the following questions:

> What is the essence of _____?

> What is the most fundamental quality of _____?

Activity

In a small group, use the categories in this section to ask more questions. After generating more questions within these categories, try to create more categories, and then create several questions for each category. Do not stop generating questions until everyone participating has encountered a potential topic.

ANALYSIS

The intellectual activity in this chapter involves *theory*—reasoning that is divorced from practical or physical particulars. When people theorize, they explore the realm of ideas and assumptions and make generalized claims. For example, when Sigmund Freud theorized about the nature of the unconscious, he was not making guesses about his own mind, but that of the *human* mind. He theorized that psychological ailments emerge from childhood crises. His theory, like all theories, could be applied to particular situations; he used the general notion to help cure problems within specific patients.

Everyone has theories (general accounts or concepts that inform how we receive ideas and act on the world), but theories are usually not discussed openly. They most often lie undetected in our minds. For instance, people may have a theory about knowledge acquisition; that is, they may have a general account of how people come to know things. This theory may be fairly complicated and may involve memory, experience, and language use—but rarely do people examine such theories closely and ask hard questions: *How does language acquisition relate to knowledge acquisition?* Doing theory, then, is the act of examining and developing our concepts. As you can imagine, theorists take little for granted. They are not willing to accept the answers they have been given, but look around them and imagine what other answers may be possible.

Activity

Group Theory

Doing theory requires a degree of intellectual play, as well as some deliberate and constructive probing. With several peers (online or in the classroom), choose one of the following topics:

- The difference between men and women
- When a child becomes an adult
- The relationship between individual and community
- The relationship between humans and nature

Each participant should explain his or her theory about the topic in one minute—or one paragraph if using e-mail or instant messaging. After each participant has a turn, start again: Everyone should take another turn and build upon or speak back to particular points made in the previous round. After the second round, start again. After several rounds, each participant should write a brief paragraph explaining how the theory session changed, developed, confirmed, expanded, or highlighted his or her ideas.

Theorists discuss what others avoid . . . or ignore.

Now, *theorize* about your topic: The strategy here is to explore freely, beyond prior assumptions or quick answers. (Ponder your topic for as long as possible before coming to any conclusions. Perhaps keep a notepad with you for a day or for several days, while you continue to rethink your ideas. Record even the most offbeat or seemingly irrelevant notions.)

Invention Questions

The following questions may help you discover meaning or make connections:

- What is the basic or essential quality of the topic?
- How does the topic affect or influence thinking?
- How does conventional thought or practice keep people from a radical perspective on this topic?
- What is the origin of the topic?
- What do people normally not consider about the topic?

Make certain to extend your thinking when answering these questions. In fact, you might not *answer* the questions at all, but begin a process of exploration that could continue in your writing. For example, Linda, a business major, has chosen to explore the *essence of business*. In a discussion with peers, she begins a true exploration of the topic:

What is the basic or essential quality of the topic?

Linda: Well, I wonder if this topic can even be thought about radically, but let's try it: I think the basic quality of business is competition.

Marcus: Competition with other people?

Linda: Yes . . . I think so. Other people or companies— or even countries.

Marcus: For that matter, what about towns and communities?

Linda: Yeah, I guess so. Towns and communities do compete for customers, for market, for tourism dollars.

Diana: So are all these people and communities competing for money?

Linda: Ultimately, yes. But at first, they are competing for more customers or clients.

Marcus: So . . . is it always about more customers? More money?

Linda: Well, I'd think so. Certainly, for retail stores, the daily goal is getting more people through the doors and to the cash register than the store across the street.

Diana: What if we looked at it like the companies are living organisms? I just saw something about bears on the Discovery Channel: every summer and fall, before hibernation, the bears try to consume as much food as possible. But they also need to conserve their strength. They don't want to exert a lot of energy while trying to eat all this food. The ultimate goal isn't the amount of food. It's survival. The bears are competing for food, like salmon, but the essence of their competing is survival.

Linda: So . . . back to business . . . companies are not necessarily competing for just money; they're competing for survival, for life.

Marcus: That makes a lot of sense. Surviving in business involves making a lot of money (more than others), but it also involves conserving. Think about it: Companies that are out just to make a lot of money go down quickly because they didn't conserve.

The important moment here is Diana's brave reference to the Discovery Channel. While bears and business have little in common, Diana is thinking about the essence of things—how entities stay alive. Her inventive connection makes the group rethink the essence of business. And now Linda's thoughts on the essence of business are beginning to take flight. She is going beyond the quick, easy response and exploring some hidden dynamics of business. If she continues developing these ideas, she could transcend conventional wisdom and make valuable discoveries.

Thinking Further

Everyday language is filled with sayings that suggest indisput-able truths. They are often widely used but unexamined, and so often conceal more truth than they communicate. These sayings, sometimes called *clichés,* might even misguide our thinking. Consider the following: *What doesn't hurt you only makes you stronger. Bigger is better. Back to the basics. Boys will be boys.* Such clichés might get in the way of exploring your own topic, but they can also mark the exact spot where radical thinking most needs to be done.

The following questions may help you work around conventional thinking:

- Can you think of any clichés related to your topic?
- How do they limit thinking?
- Might the opposite of the cliché be true?

Activity

In a small group, share topic ideas. Then list the common sayings, assertions, and opinions related to each topic. In this collective brainstorm, try to capture all the conventional wisdom associated with each topic. What do people normally think, feel, and say about each? What are the common opinions, complaints, and hopes? The goal is to give each writer a clear sense of the conventional so that he or she can think beyond it.

Clichés are intellectual bubbles. Pop them, and there's nothing there.

In his invention writing about the future, Simon Ben-low explores the present:

What do people normally not consider about the topic?
People do not normally consider pollution and the future because nothing in our popular culture invites us to, unless it's some silly movie inviting us to imagine a post–world war future, or a not-so-silly documentary that we forget about as soon as the lights come back up. In general, we're not asked to consider how our present wants will influence anyone beyond ourselves. The presiding language of our culture is filled with provocations to be fulfilled, to be happy (i.e., buy lots of things and drive a new car). We keep building/buying bigger and bigger vehicles, and consider our actions only (only!) when gas prices go up. In other words, the general trend in buying goods is to wrap ourselves in as much luxury as our wallets allow.

Benlow then goes further when he thinks about the language we use in everyday life. He tries to get beyond the common phrases (such as "the future") that hide complexity:

Can you think of any clichés related to your topic?
Maybe "the future" itself is a cliché. If a cliché hides or glosses over complexity, that phrase ("the future") hides something. It hides the people out there in the distance . . . the real people who'll no doubt have to deal with our wants! When we say "the future" or "posterity" or "our children," we're just glossing over the real people who'll be living with policies and laws and practices that emerge from our overindulgence. "Make sure to wear your air mask, Connor." "Oh, I left it at school yesterday." And then, of course, if anyone today brings up things like breathing nontoxic air or drinking clean water, they get deemed "environmentalists," "tree huggers," "liberals," etc. These terms are ways of dismissing the present and the future . . . real humans with real lungs and kidneys. We've become a culture of lunatics.

PUBLIC RESONANCE

A topic that has public resonance taps into the concerns of many or makes a connection to public conditions or interests. In one sense, your topic may already have public resonance. Because you are theorizing (exploring more general ideas rather than particular situations), your topic may easily connect to others. However, radical thinking always runs the risk of alienating others. When a writer transcends conventional wisdom, he or she must also do the work of inviting others into the new vision, which is no small task (consider Galileo's fate!).

> **Use the following questions to help connect your ideas to your readers' concerns:**
>
> - What is conventional thought on the topic?
> - What nonconventional claims have been made about the topic?
> - What keeps people from understanding the thing/idea in nonconventional ways?
> - How would a new understanding of the topic help people? (Who, particularly, would a new understanding help?)

In his invention writing, Simon Benlow goes beyond naming "conventional thought." He tries to explain the nature of present thinking, how it works, how it is limited:

What is conventional thought on the topic?

The thing is . . . there is no conventional thought on this matter. People do not genuinely think about the future—in the specific and local sense. They don't imagine their lives affecting their grandchildren's world. People have been lulled into a present-tense-only mentality. Sure, most parents try to provide for their children . . . but they don't imagine how their lives (outside of creating a savings account) will affect the world that their children (and their children's children's children) will inhabit. In general, people in America spend most of their time thinking about their own financial existence, and the future earning power of their children. But they do not think about

the air, the land, the water of the world 50 years, or 100 years, from now . . . and they don't imagine how present global politics might impact the future.

Writers who make radical (or new) claims cannot simply dismiss the beliefs of others; they must build an intellectual bridge between conventional thought and new thought. In a sense, this is the primary objective of the writing in this chapter.

When making adventurous claims, it is especially important to make these connections, so your ideas have genuine significance and are more than vague abstractions. Notice how Michael Moore makes a connection to his readers:

> I think it's time we applied the same attitudes we have about crack to corporate downsizing. It's simple: If it hurts our citizens, it should be illegal. We live in a democracy. We enact laws based on what we believe is right and wrong. Murder? Wrong, so we pass a law making it illegal. Burglary? Wrong, and we attempt to prosecute those who commit it.

Moore's broader point, about the injurious consequences of corporate downsizing, could be presented in abstract terms—and very few people would be engaged. But Moore attempts to make the issue about Americans, about people who live and work in this democracy.

Writers like Moore (and all the other writers in this text) work to make a connection between their readers and the bigger social/political/natural world. When that connection is made, the writing gains a sense of purpose and significance.

"Everything that can be invented has been invented."

—Charles H. Duell. Commissioner, U.S. Office of Patents, 1899.

THESIS

Remember that a thesis provides focus for both writer and reader. For the kind of writing done in this chapter, a thesis is especially important. Since the ideas are potentially abstract and far-reaching, a strong focus will keep the text from wandering. (While the goal may be to invite readers to wonder, a writer should keep readers from wandering.)

The following statements all work to transcend or speak back to conventional thinking. Each focuses on a particular topic, acknowledges or suggests a conventional view, and offers an alternative way of seeing:

- Behind our desire to drive bigger vehicles and own bigger homes lurks more than an attraction to personal success; it is, rather, a deep hostility toward other people and the environment.

- While a glass ceiling may prevent women from climbing the ladder of success, women and men both would have a better quality of life if they participated on the lower rungs only.

- Though *Jeopardy* is often perceived as a test of intelligence, it is really a test of knowledge. A better test of intelligence is *Survivor* or *The Amazing Race,* which requires more analytical thinking skills.

- More gunfights and car crashes actually make a movie duller, not more exciting.

- Because people have come to believe it is the ultimate power, modern medicine has ironically done more harm than good in most people's lives.

- It is commonly thought that the North defeated the South in the Civil War. In fact, the South now controls the American government.

- Even just a cursory look at one's own life will turn up evidence that every American's primary function these days is to consume.

- While the American school system prepares citizens for employment, it allows (and perhaps encourages) them to be helpless against propaganda.

- Farmers or dogcatchers as politicians would serve the people better than professional politicians do.

- A president who doesn't understand why terrorists might fly planes into buildings is ultimately far more dangerous than the terrorists are.

- The poor are better off than the wealthy.

- Had the electric guitar not been invented, the accordion would have continued its reign as the most popular instrument among American youth.

- Although students should feel comfortable in a college classroom, the uneasiness some students feel is necessary to learning.

- All animals, not just humans, should be given the right to life, liberty, and the pursuit of happiness.

- Because of credit and debt, most Americans today are unknowing slaves to the wealthy.

- College professors aren't any smarter than the average Joe.

- Eggs are more valuable than gold.

- Mundane tasks, like weeding a garden or doing the dishes, are a form of meditation that most Americans should indulge in more often and more earnestly.

- The way that Americans communicate with each other is a bigger threat than terrorism.

Activity

Choose five of the statements on this page. Describe how each statement is or is not radical. Does it transcend or speak back to some particular conventional way of thinking? Does it reveal something usually overlooked or dismissed? How does the wording and construction of each sentence help the reader to see something new?

Evolution of a Thesis

Do not be in a hurry to solidify your thesis. As you write and think, ideas will evolve—and the *evolution* of ideas is the goal of academic writers. In the following example, Linda's ideas transform over a period of time. She started trying to discover the essence or root of business. In her early discussion with peers (see the Analysis section, page 427), she made a big leap and discovered an alternative way of thinking, as illustrated in the move from the first and second statements. More focused and inventive thinking led her to the final statement.

Linda begins with a widely held understanding of her topic:

- The essence of business is making money.

She develops a position different from conventional thinking:

- Like any organism, the essence of business is survival.

Linda shapes the idea as she writes:

- Beneath the everyday affairs of making money, the essence of business is survival, which involves consuming and conserving.

Because this chapter invites you beyond your initial opinion, you might be wondering: *Am I supposed to give my opinion, or what?* This is a fair question. A radical statement is an opinion insofar as a single writer is offering a new way to see a topic. But it is more than a personal opinion. It is a writer's attempt at rethinking something—and a writer's invitation to others to rethink something.

Revision

How do you know that your opinion is speaking back to conventional views? How do you know that you've gone far enough in your thinking? To answer these questions, you might enlist the help of others in reevaluating your thesis. In a small group, present your topic. Have the group describe all the conventional opinions they can imagine. Then present your thesis and explain why you think it responds to or transcends conventional thinking. The group members should then ask:

- Does the thesis uncover something new?
- Does it offer a new way of seeing the topic?
- If not, what is holding it back?

A radical statement is more than a personal opinion. It is a writer's invitation to others to rethink something.

RHETORICAL TOOLS

"Adventure is worthwhile in itself."

—Amelia Earhart

The primary objective for this writing is to communicate a new vision on your topic. This will take some sound explaining tactics. But you will also need to persuade your reader that your vision, your adventurous new way of thinking, is valuable, and this will take a broad range of tools.

Using Narration

Narration draws readers into a set of events. A narrative or story can help writers illustrate a broader point; and when making adventurous claims, a narrative can help bridge the gap between conventional and radical ideas. You might also consider anecdotes or testimonials (brief and often personal accounts) to illustrate points. Throughout his essay, Simon Wykoff uses narration to help the reader understand his broader point about how hard some homeless people work:

> Once he had some food in his belly, he usually tried to locate a current paper. This often meant waiting around in coffee shops until someone left one on the table after their breakfast. Sometimes this step could take him hours, but he was determined not to waste the precious money on a newspaper when he could get it for free with patience.
>
> As soon as he had the paper, he thumbed through it, looking for jobs he could feasibly apply to. Due to his particular circumstances, he was without official identification. This, of course, made the search much more difficult. If he found something, he would tear off the piece of the paper and store it to refer to later.

Using Description

Writers making adventurous or radical claims must consider the intellectual positions of their audience. Because readers may have no mental pictures of the ideas being put forth, it is up to the writer to sufficiently describe or characterize ideas. Notice Benlow's description, which helps the reader to see evidence of his claims:

> Nearly every person of every town had his or her own internal combustion engine lawn mower, leaf blower, snow blower, hedge trimmer. Nearly every home and vehicle had air conditioners. And beyond these "utilities," we had hordes of trinkets, recreational instruments, and pleasure devices that all, eventually, had to lie in waste somewhere when our fickle appetites refocused on the new faster-smoother-quicker-shinier-more-interactive-more-believable-gadget.

Using Figurative Language

Literal description is sometimes insufficient to communicate the depth of an idea. This is when writers turn to figurative language, such as similes and metaphors, which help to represent complex or particularly abstract ideas. Notice Benlow's simile, which develops into a metaphor:

> Like a mass of delirious adolescents, we made ourselves increasingly giddy, posing for ourselves and for one another, posing in every aspect of our lives: our homes, travel, clothes, food, water, and vacations. It was a mammoth parade of teenage delirium that began in New York, wormed through every tiny town of the Midwest, and wrapped around itself in dizzying perpetual circles on the beaches of California.

As it came through every town, no one could resist it. It banged and clamored and woke everyone from dreamy isolation, and so even the most ascetic types found themselves playing along in some small way.

Using Definitions

Although radical thinking does not depend on dictionary definitions, writers can use definitions to communicate complex ideas. In fact, defining and redefining terms is at the heart of radical thinking. In Moore's essay, he indirectly defines "democracy" and then applies that definition to his argument:

> We live in a democracy. We enact laws based on what we believe is right and wrong. Murder? Wrong, so we pass a law making it illegal. Burglary? Wrong, and we attempt to prosecute those who commit it. . . .
>
> As a society, we have a right to protect ourselves from harm. As a democracy, we have a responsibility to legislate measures to protect us from harm.

Argumentative Support

When making adventurous claims, writers must possess a broad range of support strategies.

Evidence

- **Statistics:** Information (often given in numerical value) collected through experimentation, surveys, polls, and research.
- **Authorities:** References to published (usually written) sources.
- **Facts:** Agreed-upon events or truths.
- **Examples:** Specific cases or illustrations of a phenomenon.
- **Allusions:** References to history, news events, films, television shows, science, nature, or literary texts.
- **Personal Testimonies/Anecdotes:** Individual accounts or experiences.
- **Scenarios:** Hypothetical or fictionalized accounts.

Appeals

- **Appeal to Logic:** Relates the argument to the audience's sense of reason.
- **Appeal to Emotion:** Relates the argument to the audience's emotional state, or attempts to create a particular emotional state in the audience.
- **Appeal of Character:** Relates the argument to a quality of the author or speaker.
- **Appeal to Need:** Relates the argument to people's needs (spiritual, economic, physical, sexual, familial, political, etc.).
- **Appeal to Value:** Relates the argument to people's values (judgments about right and wrong, success, discipline, selflessness, moderation, honesty, chastity, modesty, self-expression, etc.).

In "Why Doesn't GM Sell Crack?" Michael Moore relies on several appeals:

- **Appeal to Logic:** If a company must do "whatever is necessary to create the biggest profit possible," and selling drugs like crack makes a big profit, then companies should just sell crack.
- **Appeal to Logic:** Crack is illegal because it harms lives and destroys communities. Likewise, removing a major employer for the sake of profit harms communities. Therefore, removing a major employer for the sake of profit should be illegal.
- **Appeal to Value (fairness or moderation):** CEO salaries shouldn't be more than 30 times that of the workers.
- **Appeal to Value:** If workers lose jobs, CEOs shouldn't prosper.

Counterargument

Counterarguments anticipate and refute opposing claims or positions. Especially when their claims are unconventional or challenging, writers must anticipate and account for positions outside of or opposed to their own. Depending on the position being taken and the kind of claims being put forth, some writers may need to counter many points. For example, we might say that Michael Moore is counter-arguing throughout his essay. He is speaking directly back to the claim that corporations should be able to do whatever they deem necessary to generate profit. Notice how Moore's opening paragraph sets up his essay as a counterargument that refutes this position:

> People in the business world like to say, "Profit is supreme." They like chanting that. "Profit is king." That's another one they like to repeat. They don't like to say, "I'll pick up the check." That means less profit. Profit is what it's all about. When they say "the bottom line," they mean their *profit*. They like that bottom line to contain a number followed by a lot of zeroes.

Notice how Simon Wykoff, like Moore, uses his introduction to help the reader understand his essay as a counterargument to conventional thinking:

> A common stereotype in today's society is that of the lazy bum. People see a homeless man on the side of the road, waiting for handouts, and assume that's all he ever does. In reality, this couldn't be farther from the truth. As the painter Willem de Kooning once said, "The trouble with being poor is that it takes up all of your time." This is absolutely true, and I think you'll find that homeless people are incredibly busy doing the most important job to all of us: surviving.

Concession

While counterarguments refute objections, concessions acknowledge the value of others' positions or claims. Even though a text making radical claims may not be openly argumentative, by definition it seeks to overturn conventional ideas. For this reason, concessions can be essential to engaging potentially apprehensive readers. Notice Simon Benlow's concession below. Most of Benlow's essay condemns his own generation, but he offers this small note, suggesting that people were more weak than evil. Without such a concession, readers might reject Benlow's ideas as purely antagonistic:

> Although it is probably impossible, I hope you do not look back and characterize us as purely self-serving and wicked, but as trapped in our own enterprise. We were a young culture with no parents.

Toulminian Analysis

Stephen Toulmin's framework for analyzing arguments (claim, warrant, grounds) may be valuable for revealing the shortcomings of conventional thought. (See a more detailed explanation of Toulminian analysis on pages 278–281.) The first step of revolutionary thinkers often is to critique the logic of widely held beliefs. And Toulminian analysis allows writers to show previously unexamined assumptions. For example, Michael Moore's analysis reveals the assumptions (or what he calls "attitudes") beneath the laws of our society. Once he discovers that the basic motivation for enacting laws is to protect society from harm, he can apply that to corporate behavior:

> I think it's time we applied the same attitudes we have about crack to corporate downsizing. It's simple: If it hurts our citizens, it should be illegal. We live in a democracy. We enact laws based on what we believe is right and wrong. Murder? Wrong, so we pass a law making it illegal. Burglary? Wrong, and we attempt to prosecute those who commit it. . . .
>
> As a society, we have a right to protect ourselves from harm. As a democracy, we have a responsibility to legislate measures to protect us from harm.

Outside Sources

Radical or adventurous claims do not exist in a vacuum; they exist alongside other similar claims and discoveries. While Wykoff develops his argument primarily through a personal narrative about his father, notice how he reinforces this position with an outside source:

> The next thing he did after looking for job opportunities was to get money in order to buy food for the rest of the day. While you may see many homeless panhandling, I think people don't realize that a large number of homeless actually do small-time work for their daily bread. As mentioned in an online editorial, the homeless these days are increasingly working menial tasks for extra cash, or just to survive (Hilton). For all the people you see standing outside of stores with signs, others are playing instruments on street corners, gathering cans for recycling, or washing windows.

Remember that the primary goal is to bring potential readers into your new vision, not to leave them behind.

Research vs. Mesearch

It is often easy to find outside sources that confirm our positions and support our worldviews. But such work, what we might call *mesearch*, misses the spirit and goal of *research*, which is to explore beyond our own initial suppositions, to read and re-think topics. Researching can be an inventive process—one that catapults us beyond initial ideas.

Avoid:

- Collecting statistics without questioning them, reflecting on them, evaluating their significance.
- Limiting your exploration to sources that share your opinion or perspective.
- Merely "proving" your position with others' words.

Try:

- Gathering perspectives from a variety of sources.
- Closely examining writers who oppose your perspective or who see the world differently.
- Directly addressing the unstated assumptions and values in the sources. Try to discover what the writers value, hope for, or dismiss. What is their basic view of the world, and how does that influence their approach to the topic?

ORGANIZATIONAL STRATEGIES

How Should I Begin?

The important point to remember in this chapter is that the writing must move the readers outside of their comfortable intellectual positions. Readers tend to associate highly conventional writing structure with conventional thinking. So if writers want to move readers beyond conventional thinking, they might do well to explore alternative introduction strategies.

Consider an introductory strategy you would not typically use: anecdote, scenario, allusion, figurative language, question. For any of these introduction strategies, remember that an opening paragraph should not only establish the tone of a text; it should also create an intellectual climate that is developed throughout the text.

Examine the essays in this chapter, and decide if or how the introductions help to invite the readers into a new way of thinking.

How Should I Make Connections to Conventional Thinking?

Conventional ideas are those you are trying to transcend or challenge. You might treat them as you would treat opposing arguments, using paragraphs to distinguish between conventional and radical ideas in the same way as you would for counterargument.

> Conventional thinking ¶
> New radical thinking ¶
> Conventional thinking ¶
> New radical thinking ¶

Or you might use the turnabout paragraph (see page 251). For example, consider Linda's topic (in the Analysis section), the essence of business. In making a connection to conventional thinking, she could use a paragraph that shifts to her new ideas. Notice the turnabout in the middle of the paragraph below, where the direction shifts and the new way of thinking is introduced:

Money seems to be the thing that drives business. It seems to be the ultimate goal, the bottom line, the thing that is pursued every hour of every day. We might even say that money itself is the essence of business. It is, after all, the life source of every business enterprise, from the major international retail chain to the small-town Ma and Pa restaurant. However, money is merely the engine—the thing that sustains and develops business. It is not the essence. The essence of business is the same as the essence of a living organism: the struggle for survival. And when survival is the root of business, an exaggerated focus on money can actually put the nail in the coffin.

How Should I Conclude?

Apprehensive readers might see radical claims as irrelevant, even dangerous, so writers must be vigilant about connecting to readers. Conclusions are especially important places for making those connections and for making the claims in the text relevant and valuable to the world shared by the writer and readers. You might say that a conclusion is where the writer uses *the most dramatic or direct means for connecting the idea to the reader*. Notice, for instance, Benlow's conclusion; he offers a scenario and an image that reinforce the main idea of the essay:

> And if you could return to our time, I would make a dubious wager that you, too, would find it difficult to resist the lure of our lifestyle, the attraction of our conveniences. And if we had been able to imagine you as real people, even as our own distant progeny, rather than a simple euphemism ("the future"), we certainly would have acted differently. Although we probably would not have relented in our give-it-to-me-now race for more, we would have taken a solemn moment to raise a toast and drink to your hardship.

Examine the conclusions of the other essays in this chapter. Decide how each conclusion creates a connection to the shared world of the writer and reader.

WRITER'S VOICE

Inviting the Reader

No matter how radical or challenging the ideas, a writer should attempt to bring the reader into a new vision. Even if the writer wants to overtly condemn conventional wisdom (and sometimes such a move is necessary), he or she should craft a voice that invites a reader into the ideas. Notice, too, that writers sometimes condemn *ideas* or *actions*, but are less inclined to attack *people*. After all, people should not necessarily be blamed because they think conventionally. (And attacking people creates a harsh voice, which prompts readers to dismiss writers' ideas.)

Moore, for instance, condemns conventional wisdom, but avoids antagonizing or belittling the reader. He speaks to a collective *we*, presumably Americans who participate in democracy. Notice that he does not condemn people for allowing corporations to "downsize"; instead, he argues for what can be done: "Here's what I think we should do to protect ourselves." He invites readers into his hopes rather than condemning us for believing a particular way.

Considering Formality

While some writers tend toward a formal, sober tone, others use comedy or informality to connect with readers. Moore is informal. His voice is appropriate because he does not usually write for an exclusively academic crowd. Instead, Moore attempts to engage large, mainstream audiences. He creates an informal tone with subtle jokes:

> If I had a nickel for every time I heard some guy in a suit tell me that "a company must do whatever is necessary to create the biggest profit possible," I would have a very big bottom line right now.

He also draws attention to himself:

> Two really big hairy guys from Gingrich's office pummel me after they read this book? Five to ten in Sing Sing.

And Moore addresses the audience directly, a move not usually made in more formal writing:

> For those of you free-marketers who disagree with these modest suggestions and may end up on a plane sitting next to me, screaming, "You can't tell a business how it can operate!"—I have this to say: Oh, yes, we can!

As you consider your own voice, remember to stay consistent throughout your text. If you are wondering about the degree to which you can explore levels of formality, ask your instructor about the range he or she deems appropriate.

Projecting Wonder

While writers need to create a sense of authority and credibility, they also need to project wonder or curiosity. If a writer is curious about the world and about the topic at hand, the reader will be inclined to explore with an open mind. Writers can invite exploration by suggesting possibilities, rather than forcing absolute statements or fixed answers. For example, in her essay "The Menstrual Cycle," notice how Christianne Northrup's introduction is a call to, even a celebration of, what could be: a deeper understanding of "inner knowing." The claims themselves provide wonder and an engaging writerly presence:

> The ebb and flow of dreams, creativity, and hormones associated with different parts of the [menstrual] cycle offer us a profound opportunity to deepen our connection with our inner knowing. This is a gradual process for most women, one that involves unearthing our personal history and then, day by day, thinking differently about our cycles and living with them in a new way.

This is a powerful lesson for all writers: Drawing attention to the extraordinary creates interesting writing—and interesting writers!

VITALITY

Creating vitality in writing means creating life—making language feel lively and real to the humans who engage it. (Remember, readers are real humans who are swirling around in their own messy lives.) When language is intensive enough, it draws us inward to the ideas. Consider the following strategies, which may fall outside the normal or "safe" academic sentence patterns.

Try the Stylistic Fragment

Sentence fragments are grammatical errors. They occur when a writer punctuates a phrase or dependent clause as though it were a full sentence. Here are some examples of sentence fragments:

Fragment errors

- By writing on the sidewalk in colored chalk and then hiring an airplane to write the message in the sky.

- Because the grand opening of the hotel coincided with the holiday parade and the community's main fund-raising festival.

- Just when Marvin flummoxed the toss and flailed wildly at Herdie's aunt, who was then experiencing an intestinal expression.

None of the above can stand alone as full sentences. This is not because of the content, but because of the grammatical structure. None of them are independent clauses.

But some writers venture into fragments intentionally. They deliberately craft fragments because breaking the conventions calls the reader out of a comfortable intellectual pattern. Notice the (underlined) stylistic fragments in the following passages.

Stylistic fragments

- At some point in its life cycle, business must conserve. <u>Like a lion or a bear. Like any organism.</u>

- Sooner, rather than later, evaluating performance will not be the enterprise of faculty. It'll be the work of outside corporations. <u>Profit hounds. Performance peddlers.</u>

- <u>When everything seems broken. When nothing seems fixable. When persistent crisis looms.</u> These are the conditions that make political parties comfortable. Then, they can further etch their agendas into the masses by detailing the wrongs of the other party.

The underlined fragments are technically incorrect. But the writers decided to use the unconventional to help create vitality and intensity.

Activities

1. Discuss why the three stylistic fragments are deliberate rather than simple errors.

2. In a small group, create a passage that integrates one or several stylistic fragments. Share the passage with the rest of the class, and explain how the fragment adds life to the ideas.

Deliberately Break Some Other Rule

Grammar is a set of conventions—a code agreed upon and supported by institutions within a culture. But all codes are toyed with. People who know the codes of a culture well intentionally tamper . . . for one of several reasons:

- They want to explore the limits of language and not simply use it.

- They want to assert some sense of individuality—something beyond their complicity in rules.

- They want readers to share in a brief moment of non-conformity.

And, believe it or not, academia is a perfect place for intellectual rule breaking. In fact, many would argue that the job of academia is to make certain that students know the rules so well that they can break them with grace and purpose. Playing with the conventions of language helps us to better understand what's possible, intellectually speaking. Keep in mind that rule breaking should not be a mere game of self-indulgence. It should increase the vitality of the text and increase the reader's understanding of your ideas.

As you look over your writing, consider some sentence-level rule. Break it. Make certain you explore this option with your instructor. Also make certain you understand your own motives!

Give Your Essay an Engaging Title and Sharpen Your Opening Sentence

An engaging title helps to capture the reader's interest, suggest the writer's position on the topic, and establish a tone for the essay. It gets the essay off to a good start. While some titles leap into the writer's mind like a gift out of nowhere, others emerge slowly over time as the writer invents and revises.

Activities

1. With a group of peers, discuss the titles in this chapter: "Why Doesn't GM Sell Crack?," "An Apology to Future Generations," "Unemployed and Working Hard." Which title is most engaging and why? How does each title reflect the tone of its essay?

2. With a group of peers, discuss possible titles for your essays for this chapter. Have fun suggesting alternative titles that capture interest, suggest the writer's position, and establish tone.

Like titles, opening sentences can either engage or alienate a reader. For example, an obvious, general opening sentence, such as "There are many kinds of people in the world," can send a reader the unintended message that the rest of the essay will communicate equally obvious, and therefore uninteresting, ideas. The obvious opening sentence has created this expectation in the reader's mind.

Activities

1. With a group of peers, discuss the opening sentences for Moore's, Benlow's, and Wykoff's essays. How does each sentence encourage the reader to keep reading?

2. Browse through the other chapters in this book, reading the opening sentences of their essays. Which opening sentence is most engaging? Why?

3. With a group of peers, discuss the opening sentences for your essays for this chapter. First, decide whether each opening sentence is specific and engaging or general and obvious. Then have the group discuss how to make it sharper.

Share a brief moment of nonconformity with your readers.

BASIC CONCEPTS

Why Get Information from Sources?

How do you know what you know? Where did you learn it? In everyday life, we pick up information, use it, and pass it along to others when we think they might benefit from it. For example, we might tell a friend that we think she would enjoy seeing a certain movie or art exhibit, and to convince her of it we might provide some evidence for our claim. The evidence would not be formally documented: We might informally refer to an article we had just read about it, or we might pass on anecdotal evidence based on personal experience. We are basing our claim (our assertion or opinion) on something—and we can call that something *a source of information.*

In college and workplace writing, sources are used in the same basic way as in everyday life. While we use them in our writing to support claims, a source does not always have to agree with our opinion. Instead, a writer might provide information from a source and then respond to it, or counterargue, by showing how he or she thinks the information is wrong. Or the writer might use the source in a variety of other ways—such as to provide necessary background information or to illustrate another interesting way of thinking about the matter.

Issues to Consider and Discuss

- When and why do people refer to sources in everyday life?
- How might sources contribute to a writer's credibility?
- Why should information gained from a source be documented?
- When is informal documentation acceptable?
- How can a researcher evaluate the reliability of information from a source?

When to Get Information from Sources

Writers may do research throughout the writing process. For example, getting information from sources is helpful for exploring the topic early in the process, as well as late in the process for developing certain points. Toward the end of the writing process, finding statistics, an appropriate quotation, or some other type of evidence to insert into the right place can be just the thing needed to "top off" part of your essay. But sources are also helpful—more helpful, probably—early in the writing process when exploring an idea. (See What Is Inventive Research? below.) Sources provide valuable new information that is likely to alter a writer/reader's early ideas about a topic and raise new and interesting questions. Many academic and workplace assignments require significant research *prior to any serious drafting.*

What Is Inventive Research?

Inventive research is a discovery process in which the researcher is open to a wide range of sources and ideas. Inventive researchers are adventurous. Rather than only reading the most accessible source (say, the first on a database list), they read others that at first may seem irrelevant. Rather than seeking only those sources that are in line with their initial thinking, inventive researchers explore articles that may be opposed to their original positions. They go after essays with strange titles; they crack open dusty books and surf obscure websites. Inventive researchers take a particular posture as they encounter sources. They do more than simply read or listen. They also look beneath the meaning of each keyword or phrase; they go back in history to find the origin of words, attitudes, and beliefs related to the topic; they imagine how their topic resonates with some broader set of rules or earlier cases; they make comparisons to other situations or topics while reading and researching; they read for hidden arguments.

Where to Get Information from Sources

A source can be an interview, a TV show, a movie, a newspaper, a magazine, a scholarly article in a professional journal, a book, and so on. Sources can be thought of as (1) primary, or firsthand accounts, and (2) secondary, or information from another, often primary, source of information. While primary sources (an interview; an experiment, survey, or study; a historical document; correspondence) are often useful and/or necessary, secondary sources save writers the trouble of going out and conducting interviews or experiments (often a time-consuming and expensive process) when others have already done so. Using secondary sources means wisely taking advantage of research other people have done. (See more about finding sources on pages 456–462. And also see Primary Research on pages 447–454 and Secondary Research on pages 455–467.)

What Is Plagiarism?

Plagiarism—failing to acknowledge, or give credit to, a source of information—is intellectual theft. It involves using either (1) an idea or (2) the manner of expression of another person as if it is the writer's own idea or manner of expression.

Plagiarism can take many forms and may be either intentional or unintentional. For example, knowingly turning in another person's paper and claiming it as one's own work is a serious form of academic dishonesty likely to have a severe consequence, such as damage to one's reputation and expulsion from school. Other times, however, writers plagiarize accidentally because they are unaware of the rules. They do not know, for example, that the ideas taken from a source, even if not quoted directly, must be documented.

Just as it is every driver's responsibility to know and obey the rules of the road (for his or her own benefit as well as for the benefit of others), it is every writer's responsibility to know the rules of documentation. To avoid plagiarism, you must acknowledge your source (also referred to as "citing" or "crediting" the source) whenever you express someone else's idea, opinion, or theory, or whenever you provide information such as a fact or statistic that is not common knowledge.

If you use the exact words of the source, you must indicate that by putting them within quotation marks—and also by crediting the source (using quotation marks alone does not count as crediting the source). If you use information from a source but express it in your own words (called *paraphrasing* or *summarizing*), you should not put the information inside quotation marks, but you still must credit the source. (See more about plagiarism on page 472.)

Why Document Sources?

There are at least three good reasons for documenting sources:

- To be honest. When presenting others' opinions, research, or manner of expression, writers give credit to, or acknowledge, their sources.

- To gain credibility. If a source is credible (see Evaluating Sources, pages 463–467), then the writer's claims gain credibility. Many times writers are not experts on their subject matter; however, they can write confidently about their subjects as a result of sources. Also, writers are taken more seriously if they appear well-informed, having "done their research."

- To provide readers with more information. Listing sources provides readers access to more information. This allows readers to explore the subject matter further.

What's a Good Research Topic?

Using research in a writing project should not change some fundamental principles: The project should still be focused and revelatory. Like any academic writing project, a research essay should develop a new topic or offer a new insight on a familiar topic. It may be tempting to choose a familiar issue (such as abortion) and then report what many others have said. But most often, the job of the researcher is not to *compile* outside sources but to *use* particular insights or information from sources. (This is a big difference.)

Sometimes, a writer may begin a research project and discover very little information or that much of the research does not support his or her initial opinion. But a lack of information is not a bad sign. In fact, it offers writers an opportunity to ask interesting questions and make valuable intellectual connections. Instead of dumping the topic or shifting focus, the writer can:

- Explore what has been said about similar topics and make a comparison in his or her essay.

- Use opposing positions to create counterarguments in his or her own writing.

- Research the history of the topic to see how people's opinions evolved.

- Research the cultural context (the popular, institutional, religious, and scientific activities surrounding the topic itself) and ask: *Why have people not written much about it?*

It might be helpful to think not of *research* topics but of *writing* topics. When a writer generates a topic from a particular situation or intellectual place (a particular point of contact), then he or she can move outward from there—searching out sources that help create public resonance or a historical perspective.

Formal versus Informal Documentation

In academic and professional writing, information from sources may be documented formally or informally, depending upon the situation. Some writing requires in-text documentation that corresponds with a Works Cited page; other writing does not. "My mother said it is raining," is an example of informal documentation. The information from the source is that *it's raining*. The source is *my mother*. In-text documentation and a Works Cited page are unnecessary here. But more formal writing situations require more formal documentation.

Research is another form of invention.

PRIMARY RESEARCH

Academic writers do both *primary* and *secondary* research. In primary research, information is gathered firsthand by the researcher. That is, the researcher interacts directly with the subject(s) and is engaged in the activities and behavior of the thing being studied. A writer doing primary, or field, research makes observations or does experiments, interviews, and surveys. He or she participates in the original actions of gathering data.

OBSERVATION

In *detached observation,* the researcher attempts to stay removed or distant from the subject(s). In other words, the researcher tries to remain uninvolved so that his or her conclusions are not influenced by personal attachment to the subject(s). In detached, or what is sometimes called *scientific,* observation, researchers attempt to generate conclusions that others would also generate under the same conditions in the same situation. Findings generated from detached observation usually do not involve the researcher's personal situation or perspective; therefore, the first-person pronouns *I* and *we* are usually absent from the writing.

In *participant observation,* on the other hand, the researcher interacts with the subject(s). The researcher acknowledges, and even draws attention to, the interaction and how it influences the information gathered. Here, the conclusions may depend on the presence of the researcher. Annie Dillard's essay "Living Like Weasels" depends upon her interaction with the subject. What Dillard learns and ultimately communicates about weasels is a result of her brief participation in the weasel's existence:

> The weasel was stunned into stillness as he was emerging from beneath an enormous shaggy wild rose bush four feet away. I was stunned into stillness twisted backward on the tree trunk. Our eyes locked, and someone threw away the key.

Participant observation, however, must be carried out with a consideration for the subjects involved. A researcher must not attempt to change or adversely affect the subjects or the environment.

Field Notes

Regardless of the type of observation, whether participant or detached, nothing is more important than good field notes. Good researchers do not rely on memory. After the initial observation, field notes become the primary source of interaction. Because researchers cannot return to the particular time and place of the observation and cannot re-live the experience itself, they must rely on ample notes that capture all possible details, nuances, and impressions. Field notes can be taken in a variety of ways, which may depend on the researcher and the research situation. Notice the range of details in the excerpts from field notes below. Also notice the observers' focus—and strategies for making connections between elements:

> The Apartment
> Second Fl.
> June 1, 2008
>
> The thermostat in the apartment reads 84 degrees (at 11 P.M.). The air conditioner is on, but produces only cool—not cold or air-conditioned— air. If turned on high, the air conditioner eventually blows a fuse. But if

on high, it still only produces cool, not cold, air. Needs freon. A 20-inch box fan blows warm air around, not really cooling the place off much. If on medium or high, it makes too much noise. On low, as it is now, it is quiet, yet not very helpful. The television is loud, in order to be heard over the fan and air conditioner. Windows are closed. If open, street noise becomes a problem. Outside on the ground, it is much cooler, comfortable even, but this is a second-floor apartment with a poor, at best, air conditioner.

Sam's Diner
Palmer Street
May 18, 2008

At Sam's, the cooks (two men) are fully visible to the customers in the seating area. The grills, the cutting boards, the prep tables, the refrigerators, canisters, and utensils are all in plain view of customers. One of the two cooks, with a dark beard, is slicing meat (what appears to be ham), and the other is frying a sandwich. They are talking and laughing.

There are three servers, all women. One (wearing blue jeans) is standing behind the counter, by the cash register, occasionally joining in the conversation with the cooks, and also filling ketchup bottles. Another (with a long ponytail) is talking with a table of customers. She seems acquainted with them and the three customers are all engaged in the conversation with her. The other server (with brown glasses) is getting drinks for another table of customers (of four people). She is the only one of the staff moving throughout the diner. At 11:24 A.M., three tables are full. The remaining tables are empty.

Between 11:30 and 12:10 the dining area fills. All but two tables are taken by customers. The workers, servers, and cooks have stopped talking among themselves and are focused on different jobs.

12:14: Twelve tables are full and five people are seated at the counter. The first server (in blue jeans) attends to them, and seems to be exclusively in charge of the cash register. The other two (ponytail and brown glasses) are now both moving quickly from tables to the kitchen area.

The cooks are both at grills, their backs turned away from the customers (and servers) for long periods of time. (They only turn around quickly to place a finished plate on the pickup counter—and are not talking.)

Field notes allow the writer to return to the scene and find new connections or see meaning he or she did not see initially. Without field notes, an observer can only return to mental pictures. Because the human mind remembers selectively, those pictures will hold only details that initially had meaning, so the observer is left exploring a narrow and selective list of details—essentially, exploring his or her own memory. This significantly narrows the chances of discovering something new. The surprising and valuable connections that can be made through observation occur because the observer notices a subtle connection or a hidden pattern—and these connections and patterns do not necessarily exist in an observer's selective memory.

Activity

Examine the essays in Chapter 4: Observing. Do they signal detached or participant observation?

INTERVIEWS

At a basic level, interviewing involves gathering information from a single person. But it can mean a great deal more. Good interviewers seek to engage interviewees in intensive conversations. They probe for knowledge and ideas, but they also allow interviewees to explore and develop ideas. A good interview, like a good essay, goes beyond basic knowledge; it provides insight.

Asking the Right Questions

Good interview questions create focus, yet allow interviewees to explore. While they may seek out specific information (data, facts, dates), interview questions should go beyond collecting basic knowledge. (In fact, asking interviewees basic information that can be retrieved through print sources undermines the interview process.) A more valuable strategy is to prompt interviewees to reflect on the meaning of issues or to make connections between ideas. Notice the difference between the following:

What's it like being a doctor?

How has working in the medical field influenced your personal life?

The first question does not focus attention on any particular issue; the interviewee could talk about anything related to the profession. The second question, however, draws attention to a particular issue, asking the interviewee to consider a particular relationship. It is more specific than the first question, but still calls for a certain degree of exploration.

Asking Follow-up Questions

Following up on answers is the interviewer's most powerful research tool. While a survey can only ask a list of preformulated questions, an interview can follow a line of thought that comes from an interviewee's response.

Imagine the following scenario, in which a researcher is interviewing a civil engineer:

Interviewer:	Is being a civil engineer interesting?
Engineer:	Sure. I get to deal with all kinds of people and very real situations.
Interviewer:	Is being a civil engineer hard?
Engineer:	Well, some of the work can be difficult. Trying to figure in all the variables in a given project can be a mathematical nightmare.

> Interviewer: What would you tell someone who wants to become a civil engineer?

Here, the interviewer comes up short in several ways. First, the questions are mundane. As worded here, such questions would probably not yield focused and insightful answers; they prompt the engineer to respond in general terms. They are surface questions (the kind one might ask at a party), which yield short and uncomplicated answers. Also, the interviewer ignores opportunities to follow up. After the engineer's first responses, the interviewer could have asked about the "very real situations" or the "mathematical nightmare" but leaves both ideas and, instead, moves to the next question. This interview does not probe for insight or engage the thoughts of the interviewee, but merely poses a list of unrelated questions. However, notice the following example:

> Interviewer: How is a civil engineer important to society?
>
> Engineer: Well, civil engineers conceptualize living space for the public. They envision what it might be like to live in particular place, say, a downtown area, and then lay out plans to make a park, an intersection, even an entire downtown livable— and they do it all while considering how an area will grow and how people's needs may change.
>
> Interviewer: So, civil engineers have to be visionaries?
>
> Engineer: Yes! They are not simply figuring formulas about buildings and zones and land; they are imagining what it might be like to live and work within a given area in the present and future.
>
> Interviewer: And they do all this while accommodating the demands of city officials?

Here, the interviewer starts with a more insightful question. While the first interviewer depends on a vague concept ("interesting"), the second interviewer seeks out the meaning of a potential relationship (between civil engineers and society), and consequently receives an insightful response. Also, the interviewer in the second scenario springboards from the engineer's answers ("So, civil engineers have to be visionaries?"), thereby extending initial thoughts. The second interview evolves, even within a short amount of time.

Using Interviews

Ideas from an interview can be incorporated into various writing situations and purposes. An interview can be used to support claims made in argument, to help explain an idea, or even to help explain the history or significance of some topic. In the following example, notice how the information helps support an idea:

Most often the water sewers can withstand the runoff from storms, but the past season has illustrated the inadequacy of the current sewer system. According to Harold Johnston, Director of Utilities, the sewer system was overwhelmed twice in the past three and a half months, and the result was that untreated sewage flowed out into Silver Lake. When an overflow occurs and untreated water spills into the natural water system, the high amounts of bacteria affect the wildlife and jeopardize the health of swimmers and water enthusiasts. In essence, anyone or anything in the lake for days after an overflow is swimming in sewage.

Here, the writer is trying to persuade readers that the water treatment system in her town is inadequate. The claim made by the Director of Utilities supports the idea. Although the writer probably collected extensive information about the treatment system, she only used one particular point in this paragraph because it directly supports the main idea. (Other information might be used in different passages.)

Planning an Interview

When setting up an interview, be sure to respect the interviewee's position and accommodate his or her schedule. Researchers should never impose themselves on potential interviewees. Use the following hints and strategies:

- Always request an interview well in advance of your own deadlines.
- When making a request, introduce yourself and the reason for the interview: Explain the nature of your research and how the interview will be integrated.
- Beforehand, negotiate a reasonable amount of time for the interview (such as 30 minutes)—and stick to it so as not to impinge on the interviewee's time.
- Plan out the method of recording responses—writing, audiotaping, or videotaping. Ask the inter-viewee if his or her answers can be recorded, and if his or her name can be used in the research.
- At the end of the interview, thank the interviewee for his or her time, and leave promptly.

SURVEYS

While an interview is based on an individual's ideas and knowledge, a survey attempts to find public opinion on a topic. An interview is driven, in part, by the interviewee; his or her insights may influence the direction or emphasis of the interview. But with surveys, the researcher prearranges the direction and emphasis with carefully formulated questions.

Generating Questions

In generating survey questions, a researcher should consider three points:

1. Questions should not lead the respondent to an answer. Good survey questions avoid influencing the respondents' thinking about the issue. For instance, a question that asks *Is our current president completely out of touch with public opinion?* leads the respondent toward a negative evaluation of the president. Such questions prompt respondents to take up a certain position even before answering. A better approach is to state the question without leading the respondent; for example: *Is the current president in touch with labor issues in America?*

2. Questions should narrow the focus of the respondents on a particular topic. While good survey questions should not influence the respondents' thinking on an issue, questions should create a particular focus. For instance, a question that asks *Has the president taken an appropriate stance on international trade?* is more focused than *Do you like our current president?*

3. Questions should use common or unspecialized language. Because survey respondents may come from different walks of life, survey questions should avoid technical jargon or specialized terminology.

Choosing Respondents

Surveyors must consider the demographics (or particular characteristics) of their potential respondents.

What is the age range in the respondent group?

What is the racial makeup of the respondent group?

What is the gender makeup of the respondent group?

What is the occupational makeup of the respondent group?

What is the geographical origin of the respondent group?

Sample Survey: Working Hours

Please respond to the following questions. Use the back if you need more space.

1. Do you currently hold a full-time or part-time job? If so, what is the nature of the work?

2. If you work part-time, how many hours per week?

3. How many hours per week are you contracted to work? (Or how many hours per week are you supposed to work, according to the job description?)

4. How many hours per week do you normally work (at or away from the job site)? Do you work weekends?

5. How much time do you spend preparing for and/or traveling to and from work? (Feel free to give specifics.)

6. Is overtime mandatory or voluntary at your job? (What kinds of incentive are offered for overtime?)

7. Do you feel sufficiently compensated for the work you do? Why or why not?

People's occupations, gender, ethnicity, age, and geography impact their understanding of the world—and how they are likely to respond to any particular issue. For instance, imagine a survey about college life: If all the respondents are college instructors, the answers will probably reflect certain biases and assumptions—which may be entirely different than those of students or people not associated with college life.

Recording and Using Responses

Responses can be recorded in a variety of ways. Perhaps the easiest means is to elicit written responses by asking the respondents to write or check off their answers. But if that is not possible, the researcher must do the recording by writing or taping. (If you plan to tape answers, either on video or audio equipment, you must always ask the respondents' permission.)

Survey responses are most often used to show public opinion about a topic or to illustrate common trends in everyday life. A writer researching work issues among students at her college might discover important trends:

> While many students take a full course load, they also work late on weeknights and throughout the weekends. In an informal survey, 24 of 35 respondents reported that they work at least 25 hours each week—and 21 of those 35 work over 30 hours each week. One student explained her situation bluntly: "No one told me that a full load of classes would compete with my work schedule. I thought I could do both, but it's nearly impossible."

Notice that the writer uses the information from the survey to enhance the significance, or the public resonance, of her topic. She sets up the idea in her first sentence, and then plugs in the information from the survey.

The sample survey on this page offers room for the respondents to write in answers and to develop their thoughts. You could imagine someone responding to this survey fairly quickly because the questions are limited in number and fairly simple. While it could offer some valuable insights about working hours, it is also limited in its scope, like all surveys. Because this survey does not ask for personal information from the respondents (age, sex, education, etc.), the researcher should be careful not to make broad statements about salary and job satisfaction in America, but to stay focused on the amount of time people dedicate to their jobs.

SECONDARY RESEARCH

In secondary research, the researcher explores the thoughts, theories, or findings of others, through print and electronic sources. Whether a writer is arguing, explaining, or evaluating, sources can give depth and sophistication. However, sources should not replace other means of support and development (anecdotes, allusions, scenarios, appeals, examples, and so on)—they should work in conjunction with these other strategies. In short, print and electronic sources should be thought of as another set of writerly tools for inventing, developing, and delivering ideas.

The research process can be broken into five major steps:

1. Finding sources
2. Evaluating sources
3. Processing ideas
4. Integrating sources
5. Documenting sources

This might seem like an easy chronological path, but the entire research process should be seen as an act of invention. Good writers do *inventive research,* approaching the process as an archeological journey in which each source is a potential link to some idea, some springboard, that might further develop their understanding and stance on a subject. They see each text, whether a book, newspaper, or website, as a hypertextual connection to another idea.

FINDING SOURCES

The first rule of finding secondary sources is: *Don't give up.* Many writers are surprised to find how much information is out there. No matter how esoteric a topic, chances are that a great deal has been written about it. The key to doing research is finding the right path—or paths—to information. And because of interconnected library resources, print reference guides, and electronic networks, the paths are many.

It is important to remember that writers rarely find sources that neatly overlap, or completely agree with, their own positions. In fact, research should not be seen as a process of seeking out agreement, but as a process of bringing together various kinds of information, viewpoints, and arguments. Sometimes, writers do not find any sources that share their position on a specific topic. Instead, they discover sources that partially overlap in some way. All of these sources, then, help to give dimension to the writer's ideas. In the following chart, notice that supporting evidence (for instance, some fact or statistic that backs up the writer's stance) is only one possibility. Other sources will help to round out the ideas—and create a richer project.

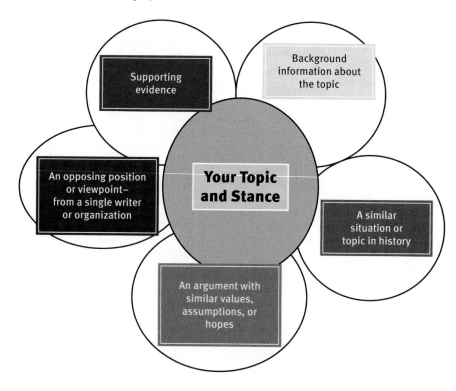

Supporting evidence

Background information about the topic

An opposing position or viewpoint—from a single writer or organization

Your Topic and Stance

A similar situation or topic in history

An argument with similar values, assumptions, or hopes

For example, consider the topic *light pollution*. Imagine that a writer begins the research process with a vague sense of her position—that too much light hinders most people from seeing the night sky. A quick search of the Web and periodical databases will likely yield some sources that share her position. She might find statistics on the number of Americans who cannot see constellations other than the Big Dipper. And she might also find background information about the topic: when it became a concern for astronomers, or how much it impacts plant life. But then she can go further. In some invention work, the writer may discover that the night sky is important because it bestows a sense of wonder and humility in people. In her research, she could seek out sources that celebrate the power of wonder—a sociologist who argues that civilizations without a deep sense of wonder quickly fade from history, or a religious scholar who argues for the value of humility. Perhaps she even finds some rationale for parking lots that are lit all night from a major retailer. She then develops a counterargument to address that rationale. In her reading, she might also discover a similar but related issue—noise pollution and its effects on agriculture. Although this information about noise pollution may not directly support her main claim, it may show a trend in history—that people have always battled the slow invasion of technology into the natural world. All of these sources could help to develop an insightful and rich argument.

Sources of Information

Secondary sources include books, periodicals (journals, magazines, and newspapers), government documents, reference books (such as dictionaries and encyclopedias), audiovisual materials, and websites. They give a researcher a broader understanding of a topic. In many ways, the process of reading and analyzing secondary sources is a process of invention: The writer is generating new ideas and perspectives, which, in turn, make writing more interesting and engaging (for both writer and reader).

When exploring a topic, writers should use different types of sources—not just books, not just websites. For example, books, although they contain a lot of information and are easy to find, can contain too much information to sort through, thus taking up a lot of the researcher's time. Books can also be outdated; a journal or magazine article might be shorter, more current, and more focused on your particular topic. Websites, too, are easy to find but are not always the most accurate source and may not always be up to date. An online article found through a library database can be more relevant and reliable even though it may take a bit more effort to find.

Activity

1. Consider your own topic. Draw a circle in the middle of a page with your topic and stance (if you have one). Then, in separate circles, write out possibilities for the following: background information; supporting evidence; similar situations or topics in history; the values, assumptions, and hopes underlying your position; opposing positions and the people or groups that might hold them.

2. Enlist the help of others. In an invention workshop format, enlist the help of several peers. Each writer should explain his or her topic and stance. Then the group should offer possible ideas for the different circles.

After writing down possible directions, circle the nouns (such as *constellations, wonder, parking lots, noise pollution*). These can be keywords in your initial database research.

Activity

Explore your library's home page, focusing on it as a gateway to useful information. Describe how you get from the library home page to a book, journal, or newspaper; encyclopedias, maps, or almanacs; other useful websites; and so on.

Books are found by searching a library's catalog. While most libraries have electronic catalogs (which allow for author, title, subject, or keyword searches), many academic libraries also have catalogs that are linked to other libraries, so people can check titles not only at that particular location but also in all other connected libraries. Through such services, library users can then order books to be delivered to a desired location.

Online catalogs can be easier to search by keeping some points in mind. Adding words narrows a search, while using fewer words broadens the scope. For instance, "economics" by itself tells the catalog to find any and all works with "economics" in the title or description. (At Northwestern Michigan College, this search yielded 1,387 works.) "Economics and consumers" narrows the search (and yielded 9 works—a much more reasonable number to browse.)

Indicates status or availability and the location (a particular section in the library).

The call number.

The title of the book.

The author.

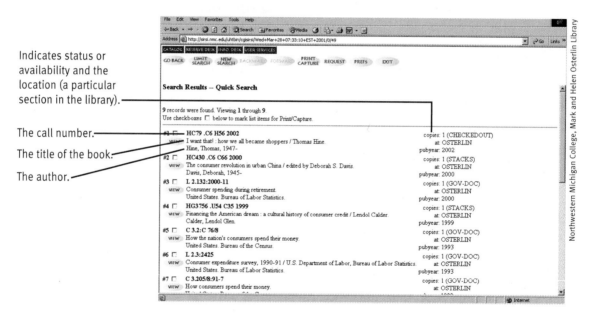

When you have obtained a promising book, the best strategy is to read through the introductory and concluding chapters. (Introductions and conclusions most often give a broad understanding of the main argument and ideas of the text.) Also, consider edited books (a collection of chapters or articles by different authors) in your search. Edited books, which are very common in academia, often cover a very specific topic and offer many different perspectives from various authors.

Periodicals include magazines (for a general audience), journals (for a specialized audience), and newspapers. (Some periodicals, such as *Ladies Home Journal* and the *Wall Street Journal,* are called journals, but are, in fact, magazines or newspapers.) Popular magazines, such as *People* or *Rolling Stone,* offer information about mainstream news or popular culture events but rarely provide indepth analysis of issues, and even more rarely deal with issues outside of major social and political topics.

Scholarly journals, which are usually specific to one discipline (such as English, writing, business, marketing, and so on), offer very detailed analyses and well-developed opinions on a seemingly endless range of topics. The writing in academic journals is most often well-researched and documented, so it tends to be more reliable than that of popular magazines.

Is It a Journal or a Magazine?

At first glance, journals and magazines may look a lot alike. But closer inspection will reveal significant differences. Generally, journals are written for academic or highly specialized readers, and the articles put forward new theories or practices in a particular field of study (sociology, psychology, nursing, English, chemistry, history, etc.). Magazines are written for general readers, who may have a particular interest (cycling, running, gardening, and so on). If you are not certain what kind of periodical you have, use the following criteria:

Journals

- Seek to advance knowledge in a *field of study*.
- Deal with principles, theories, or core practices in an academic discipline.
- Are associated with a particular discipline or field of academic study.
- Have few advertisements, which usually appear only at the beginning and end (not between or among articles).
- Have few colors and flashy pictures (unless they are related to a study or article)

Magazines

- Report information/news or offer how-to advice.
- Offer the latest technique in a hobby or sport.
- May appeal to readers with a particular *interest*.
- Have advertisements throughout the pages, even interrupting articles.
- Tend to have more colors and pictures.

Newspapers are most valuable for highly publicized topics—those that are or have been visible to the public eye, such as political events, public figures, national or local disasters, and significant cultural events. Most academic and public libraries have newspaper databases with access to past editions. Many newspapers also have websites. *USA Today*, for example, can be accessed online through a simple keyword search *(USA Today)* or by entering the URL www.usatoday.com. Explore local newspapers for regional and local events, and national newspapers such as the following for national or world events: *Afro American, American Banker, Amsterdam News, Atlanta Journal-Constitution, Boston Globe, Chicago Tribune, Christian Science Monitor, Denver Post, Detroit News, Houston Chronicle, Los Angeles Sentinel, Los Angeles Times, Muslim Journal, New York Times, San Francisco Chronicle, St. Louis Post Dispatch, Times-Picayune [New Orleans], USA Today, Wall Street Journal, Washington Post.*

Periodicals are listed on electronic databases, such as InfoTrac and EBSCO-host, which are often available at public and academic libraries. These periodical databases usually contain the most reliable and credible periodicals because they have already been evaluated according to certain academic standards. In other words, unlike searching the Internet, you will not have to sift through pornography sites, advertisements, and a limitless array of unedited blogs. Instead, you will encounter lists of previously published and edited articles. Also, these articles will have been paid for by an institution (a college or library), so you will not be asked for personal or credit card information to access them. (Chances are: if you are using a college library database, your tuition has already helped to pay for the information!)

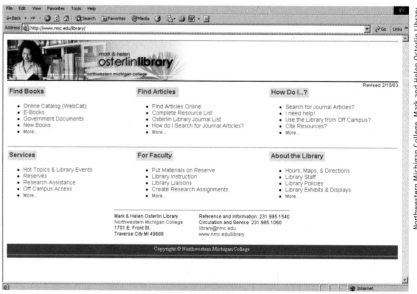

Most databases give the option of doing *an author search, a title search, a subject search,* or *a keyword search*. Do an *author search* if looking for works by a particular author; do a *title search* if you already know the title of the specific work. *Subject searches* are organized by headings (such as *agriculture, government, gender*), and will usually produce many sources for a particular topic. *Keyword searches* are most helpful after you have generated a list of possible words and phrases related to your topic. Not only can keyword searches help to open up intellectual possibilities, they can also be used to focus a search. For example, the keyword search for "weight" on one library's online catalog produced 804 entries. Narrowing the search by typing "weight and body" produced only 146 entries. Thus, if you know you are looking for information about weight and the body, "weight and body" allows you to find the relevant sources without having to sort through all the others. Typing "weight or body" produced 3,993 entries. And typing "weight and body and media" produced just one entry. Typing "body weight" produced 93, and typing "bodyweight" produced none.

Database searches can be made more efficient by using the following words (called *Boolean operators*):

- Using *and* between words narrows a search by finding documents containing multiple words—*weight and body.*

- Using *or* between words broadens a search by finding documents with either word in a multiword search—*weight or body.*

- Using *and not* between words finds documents excluding the word or phrase following "and not"—*weight and not body* (that is, *weight* only, without any references to *body*).

- Using *near* between words finds documents containing both words or phrases that are near, but not necessarily next to, each other—*weight near body.*

Also, remember that a simple keyword search can turn up thousands of returns or "hits." Narrowing one's focus by typing "weight and body and media," for example, will eliminate irrelevant returns found by typing just "weight."

Government documents include reports, transcripts, pamphlets, articles, speeches, books, maps, films, and more. While the U.S. government is the nation's largest publisher, state and city governments publish as well. Such documents, which can be of great value in one's research, can be found online with keyword searches, or by going directly to the Government Printing Office (GPO) website at www.access.gpo.gov.

Activities

1. Compare Internet search engines. Enter the same keyword sets into a variety of engines and compare the number of hits. For example, a Google search for *dogs* yielded 260,000,000 returns, *dogs and cats* 9,730,000; a Yahoo! search for *dogs* yielded 806,000,000 returns.

2. Try several different keyword approaches for each of the following questions: In what ways might organized sports harm the young children who participate in them? What is the impact on the environment of people relocating to Western states? What novel written in the last half of the 20th century has been most influential?

3. List the different types of sponsors for websites that you found. For example, did you find government-sponsored websites? Websites created and maintained by businesses? Individuals? Nonprofit organizations?

Reference books such as dictionaries, encyclopedias, and almanacs can be helpful, but should not be relied upon as one's only sources for a college research paper. (Doing so may indicate a researcher's inability to find a range of sources.) Reference materials are usually found in a library's reference room or reference area and often cannot be checked out. They can be located, as with other library materials, by searching the library's catalog of holdings or by asking the reference librarian.

Audiovisual materials include videos, CDs, DVDs, films, photographs, records, cassettes, microfilm, and microfiche, and the increasing number of downloadable video and audio files on the Web. For example, the Academy of American Poets offers videos of poets reciting their work; organizations such as Amnesty International offer video reports, and a long list of governmental sites now include recorded speeches and video updates.

The World Wide Web, or Web, is made up of many websites created and maintained by all types of organizations and individuals. A home page, which greets the user upon arriving at a website, usually contains links to the other pages of that site or to other, external sites. Websites can be found by (1) typing in the known address (or URL) of the site (such as www.whitehouse.gov) or (2) doing a subject or keyword search.

Searching or surfing the Web basically means skimming through different websites using search engines. That is, you type in a keyword (usually a noun) or phrase, and the search engine scans the World Wide Web for related sites. All search engines are not the same. Some, for example, attempt to be faster, while others attempt to be more comprehensive. Here are some popular search engines:

http://www.google.com	http://lawcrawler.findlaw.com
http://www.ask.com	http://www.lycos.com
http://www.altavista.com	http://www.monstercrawler.com
http://www.allonesearch.com	http://www.webcrawler.com
http://www.yahoo.com	http://search.aol.com
http://www.dogpile.com	

Worthwhile information can be found on websites, yet researchers must beware. Because of the open nature of the Web, much information is likely to be unreliable. Thus, good evaluating skills (discussed in the next section) are essential.

EVALUATING SOURCES

Sources should be reliable, relevant, timely, and diverse. Weak or unreliable sources introduce weakness or unreliability into a writing project. Thus, evaluating sources before using them is key.

Relevance

A source that is relevant is appropriately related to the writer's particular topic. A writer's first inclination may be to find those sources that directly support his or her thesis statement; that is, sources that speak directly about the writer's particular subject and that espouse his or her particular stance on it. However, this is very limiting—especially since the research process might develop or change how a writer thinks about a subject. Sources do much more than back up someone's opinion. They might help to explain the complexities of the subject; explain the history of the subject; explain the writer's position; support the writer's position; show claims that oppose the writer's; show claims that are different from the writer's.

Because sources can be used in a variety of ways, a source that seems only remotely related to your project might, in fact, be extremely valuable in the long run. Consider the following example: A writer is researching voting practices in his community and wants to make a claim about low voter turnouts in recent elections. He finds a newspaper article about a local school, scheduled for demolition, that had previously been used as a voting location. This article at first might seem unhelpful. After all, how does this particular school relate to voting trends in the community? It may, in fact, suggest a great deal about voting. That is, one of the factors in voter turnout is proximity to voting locations. This article might therefore show a trend in declining number of voting locations. The same writer might find a government Web page about the history of voting in his state. At first this source may not seem valuable because the writer is primarily concerned with recent voter activity. However, the history may provide some clues about the system itself, about the reasons for establishing Tuesdays as election days, about the number of constituents in a given area—all potentially valuable factors in understanding the complexities of recent voter turnout.

Consider the following questions for the sources you find:

- Does the source speak directly to my specific topic?
- How does the source help to clarify some broader or related point?
- How does the source help to explain the history or complexities of the topic?

Paragraph transitions: Integrating outside sources can make a text more sophisticated, but it can also create confusion if the writer does not make clear connections between points. Because outside sources often increase the complexity of a text, *paragraph transitions* (sentences and phrases that join the content of paragraphs and show the logical connections) become vital to a coherent paper. Transition statements usually begin paragraphs and act as bridges from one paragraph to the next. The following sentences, which all begin paragraphs, act as bridges from previous points:

> Not all farmers, however, agree with Johnson's strategy.

> Despite this overwhelming amount of evidence, some teachers refuse to acknowledge the way gender and race figure into the classroom.

> But all of the discussion on war distracts voters from significant domestic issues that will impact everyday life in the present and future.

> Because of Smith's recent book, many researchers have begun focusing their attention on the ways technology will change our ability to communicate.

Blending in the Source Information

In the following paragraph, notice how Daniel Bruno blends together, or integrates, what he thinks and what his source says. He (1) states his main idea *(Sacks illustrates that all of today's college students cannot just be thrown in the same big barrel)*, (2) directs the reader to the source *(he spends; he says; he mentions)*, (3) provides the information from the source that supports or explains his idea (in this paragraph, Bruno both quotes and summarizes the source), and (4) concludes by commenting on the information. Writers need not include these four steps every time they use information from a source, but it can be helpful to frequently rely on these four elements: (1) the writer's main idea, (2) reference to the source, (3) information from the source, (4) the writer's commentary.

> In *Generation X Goes to College,* Peter Sacks illustrates that all of today's college students cannot just be thrown in the same big barrel. In describing the modern/post-modern clash in education, he spends the majority of his time talking about those students who are underprepared, who lack the basic study skills required in academic work, and who demonstrate little real commitment to their own education. Yet, he does not discuss this problem in isolation. He also mentions another type of student. For example, he introduces the reader to Marissa and Carol: "As very good students, [their views] were virtually excluded by The College in order to accommodate the whiners and complainers" (61). And he says they "suffered not only educationally" (63). In addition to discussing specific good students, an entire chapter presents survey results about students' attitudes toward

education. While he makes claims such as "nearly a quarter of the students
. . . harbored a disproportionate sense of entitlement," this very statement
tells the reader that a full three quarters (that is, three out of four) students
do not "harbor a disproportionate sense of entitlement" (54–59). He wraps
up the book by focusing on another student, Andie, who he describes as "a
good student, constantly picking [his] brain for information and feedback
on her work" (186–87). His final paragraph, before the Epilogue, says,
"Let's create a system that encourages people like Andie at least as much
as the ones who don't give a damn" (187). Thus, Sacks shows that today's
students are a more diverse group—in skill level, background, and attitude
toward education—than has ever before been gathered together in the college classroom. (322)

Notice how the references to sources cue the reader that the text is moving to
an idea from a source. Writers use cues, also called *attributive phrases* (such
as *according to, says, explains,* etc.), to help readers see when ideas are from a
source. Notice Ann Marie Paulin's strategies below. She first makes a point about
diets—they don't work. And then she offers a source and a quotation to support
that point. In this case, the reader knows why the quotation is offered: to give
credence to her claim about diets:

> And most diets don't work. Psychologist Mary Pipher, in her book *Hunger
> Pains: The Modern Woman's Quest for Thinness,* cites a 1994 study which
> found that "90 percent of dieters regain all the weight they lost within five
> years" (32). The evidence is beginning to pile up out there that being fat
> may not be nearly as bad for a person's health as the crazy things people
> inflict upon their bodies to lose weight. (260)

Planting a Tree

You might think of integrating sources as planting a tree. First, the hole
should be dug. (One cannot simply plop a tree onto the ground.) Then,
after the hole is prepared, the tree can be dropped into place. But the
job is not done! The planter must fill in the hole, pack good dirt back into
that space, and water it, making certain that the roots of the tree are nes-
tled into the new soil. Likewise, a writer must first set up the idea—not
simply plop the ideas from a source into a paragraph. Then, the information (summary, paraphrase, quotation) can be integrated smoothly into
the writer's own language. Finally, the writer should then consider how to
fill in and reinforce the connectedness of the source and his or her own
points.

MLA STYLE

Different disciplines rely on different styles of documentation. The two most common styles are MLA (Modern Language Association) and APA (American Psychological Association). English and humanities use MLA. Like other documentation styles, MLA depends on two basic components: (1) an in-text citation of a work and (2) a list of works cited at the end of the text. These two components function in the following ways:

- In-text citations let a reader know that particular ideas come from a particular source.
- In-text documentation corresponds to the complete bibliographic information provided at the end of the text.
- In-text citations lead the reader directly to the corresponding Works Cited page.
- Done correctly, the in-text reference lists the first word(s)—whether it be the author's last name or the article title—plus the page reference of the citation on the alphabetized Works Cited page. This allows the reader to easily locate the source in the list of works.
- The Works Cited page provides complete information for finding all formal sources.
- This complete information is provided only once and comes at the end of the entire text so that it doesn't interfere with ease of reading.

In-Text Citation

In-text documentation involves referencing the original text in parentheses within the actual sentences of your text; because it uses parentheses, it is sometimes called *parenthetical citation*. In general, for MLA style, in-text citations should include the author's last name (unless it is given within the sentence) and page number of the source from which the cited material is taken (unless the source is electronic and lacks page numbers).

> "After months of exhausting research, they had finally come to understand the problem with their design" (Smith 82).

A space separates the name and the page number.

The end punctuation comes after the citation.

An in-text citation must occur whenever a writer:

- Quotes directly from a source.
- Paraphrases ideas from a source.
- Summarizes ideas from a source.
- References statistics or data from a source.

If the author is referred to in the sentence, his or her name can be omitted from the citation.

> Emphasizing her point, Miller demands that "it is now time for something drastic to change here on campus" (43).

If the source has no author, use the first word or phrase of the source's title and punctuate accordingly (quotation marks for an article and underlining for books).

> The oil had spread over much of the shoreline and had "already begun its death grip on a vast array of wildlife" ("Black Death" 54).

If the source has two or three authors, use the last name of all authors.

> (Lunsford, Olin, and Ede 158)

If you have more than one work by the same author, insert the title of the work after the author name, followed by the page number.

> (Faigley, <u>Fragments of Rationality</u> 43)

If you are citing material that is already quoted in the source, cite the source in which you found the quotation and add "qtd. in" before the author's name or title.

> (qtd. in Smith 82)

If you want to acknowledge more than one source for the same information, use a semicolon between citations within one set of parentheses.

> (Lunsford and Ede 78; Smith 82)

If you have an electronic source with no page numbers, simply exclude the page number from the citation. Do not add page numbers, and do not use those that a computer printer assigns.

> According to Martha Smith, "untold numbers of children are negatively affected by the proficiency test craze."

Works Cited

Works Cited pages list the sources that are directly cited in the text. In general, the first piece of information in the Works Cited entry should correspond directly with the in-text citation. For example, notice the relationship between the in-text citation for King, below, and the entire bibliographic information in the Works Cited page:

> People must create change because "progress never rolls in on wheels of inevitability" (**King** 130).

The in-text reference refers the reader to the Works Cited page at the end of the essay, where complete bibliographic information allows the reader to locate the source.

> Smith 4
>
> Works Cited
>
> **King**, Martin Luther, Jr. "Letter from Birmingham Jail."
> A World of Ideas: Essential Readings for College
> Writers. Ed. Lee A. Jacobus. Boston: St. Martin's,
> 2004. 121–37.

Entries in Works Cited pages must follow strict formatting guidelines, but the process is easy if you know the formulas involved.

Bibliographic information for books is contained on the title page and the copyright page (the back side of the title page). The title page contains the full title of the book, the author(s), the publishing company, and the city of publication. The copyright page contains date(s) and any edition numbers. Go to the title and copyright pages of this text, and find all the information you would need to cite it as a source.

- Author name(s) comes first and is inverted (last name first), with a comma between last and first names.
- Title of the work comes directly after author name. All words in titles are capitalized except prepositions (such as *on, in, between*), articles (*a, an, the*), coordinating conjunctions (*and, but, for, nor, or, so, yet*), and *to* in infinitives (such as *to run, to go*).
- If no author is listed, the title comes first.
- Article titles are in quotation marks, while the sources in which they appear (newspapers, books, journals, and magazines) are underlined.
- Publication information follows the title of the source.
- Copyright or publication date comes last. But if the source is an article, then page numbers come last. If the source is electronic, the date of access and URL come last.
- Periods come after names of people (authors, editors, translators), after titles, the year of publication, and at the end of all entries.

BOOKS

Single author

┌─ **Author's name:**
    As for all sources in MLA format,   ┌─ **The title:**
    single author names are inverted.   Book titles are underlined.

Howell, Mark D. <u>From Moonshine to Madison Avenue:</u>

    <u>A Cultural History of the NASCAR Winston Cup</u>.

    Bowling Green: Bowling Green State U Popular P, 1997.

City of publication:
If multiple cities are listed on the title page of the book, give only the first.

Publishing company:
Publishing companies are always found on the title page of the book. List them in shortened form, directly after the city. A colon separates the city of publication and the publisher.

Date of publication:
The date usually appears on the copyright page, which is the back side of the title page in a book. Always use the most recent date listed. Use a comma between the publishing company and the date of publication.

Two or more authors

Vasta, Ross, Marshall M. Haith, and Scott A. Miller. <u>Child</u>

    <u>Psychology: The Modern Science</u>. New York: Wiley, 1995.

For more than three authors, you may avoid listing all the names and simply add *et al.,* Latin for "and others" after the first name.

Johansen, Sturla, et al.

Corporate author or government publication

Modern Language Association. <u>MLA Style Manual and Guide to</u>

    <u>Scholarly Publishing</u>. 3rd Ed. New York: MLA, 2008.

United States. Office of Consumer Affairs. <u>2003 Consumer's</u>

    <u>Resource Handbook</u>. Washington: GPO, 2003.

If an author is not given for a government publication, list the name of the government first, followed by the agency. The title follows, and then the publication information. Many federal publications are published by the Government Printing Office (GPO).

Subsequent editions

Wicks-Nelson, Rita, and Allen C. Israel. <u>Behavior Disorders of Childhood</u>. 3rd ed. Upper Saddle River: Prentice, 1997.

Find the edition information on the title page of the book, and place the information in the entry directly after the title or the editor, if there is one. Use the abbreviations *2nd ed., 3rd ed.*, and so on, or *Rev. ed.* for "Revised edition," depending on what the title page says.

Republished book

Tolkien, J. R. R. <u>The Hobbit</u>. 1937. New York: Ballantine, 2003.

Older books may be published by a company different than the original publishers, or a hardcover book may be republished in paperback. In this case, insert the original publication date after the title, and then give the recent publisher and date.

Edited book

Foucault, Michel. <u>The Foucault Reader</u>. Ed. Paul Rabinow. New York: Pantheon, 1984.

Add *Ed.* after the title of the book, followed by the editor's name, not inverted. Since *Ed.* here means "Edited by," not "Editor," it should never appear as "Eds." even if there is more than one editor.

Translated book

Bakhtin, Mikhail. <u>Problems of Dostoevsky's Poetics</u>. Trans. Caryl Emerson. Minneapolis: U of Minnesota P, 1984.

Add *Trans.* after the tile of the book followed by the translator's name, not inverted.

ARTICLES

Articles appear in newspapers and periodicals (journals or magazines). While newspapers are usually published daily, magazines are usually published weekly or monthly, and journals are published quarterly or even biannually.

Article in magazine

Author name:
Regardless of the type of source, the author name is inverted. The same rules apply for all sources.

Article title:
Article titles are always in quotation marks.

Murphy, Cullen. "Lines in the Sand." <u>Vanity Fair</u> Jan. 2008:

60+.

Page numbers:
End with the specific page number(s) on which the article appears. If the article covers consecutive pages, include the range (such as *52–75*). If the page numbers are not consecutive, include the first page number, immediately followed by a plus sign (such as *64+*). Place a colon after the date and before the page numbers.

Periodical title:
The title of the magazine, journal, or newspaper is underlined.

Publication date:
Include month and year directly after the title of publication. For weekly or biweekly magazines, include the date (day, month, and year). (For all types of sources, abbreviate all months except May, June, and July.)

Article in a journal paginated by volume

Crow, Angela. "What's Age Got to Do with It? Teaching Older Students in the Computer-Aided Classrooms." <u>Teaching English in the Two-Year College</u> 27 (2000): 400–15.

Most academic journals number the pages of each issue continuously through a volume. The second issue does not begin with page 1, but with the number after the last page of the previous issue. For these sources, the volume number comes directly after the title. The year is in parentheses, followed by a colon and the inclusive page numbers.

Activity

Decide which type of periodical (magazine or journal) may have published the following articles, and in groups or as a class, discuss the reasoning behind your decisions:

"Heading for the Mountains: An Exciting Getaway for the Whole Family"

"Climactic Shifts in the Mountain Region"

"Coach Fired, Team Responds"

"Enzymes, Nutrition, and Aging: A Twenty-Year Study"

"The Latest in Deep Water Bait"

"Re-inventing the Microscope"

"The Epistemology of Literature: Reading and Knowing"

Article in a newspaper

McWhirter, Sheri. "Bird Die-Offs Spur Set of Guidelines."

Record Eagle [Traverse City] 20 May 2008: A3.

After the author, if one appears, list the title of the article and the publication information. Exclude introductory articles *(A, An, The)* from publication titles. Add the city name in square brackets if it does not appear in the title of the newspaper and the newspaper is local. Add section letters before the page numbers. As with magazine articles, if the page numbers are not consecutive, list the first page number, immediately followed by a plus sign.

Scholarly article reprinted in an anthology (such as a college textbook)

Faigley, Lester. "Judging Writing, Judging Selves." College

Composition and Communication 40 (1989): 395–412.

Rpt. in Landmark Essays on Voice and Writing. Ed. Peter

Elbow. Davis: Hermagoras, 1994. 107–20.

First use the basic article format with the information of the original publication. Then add *Rpt. in* (abbreviation for "Reprinted in") and include the information for the anthology. End with the page numbers on which the article appears.

Encyclopedia article

Esposito, Vincent J. "World War II: The Diplomatic History of

the War and Post-War Period." Encyclopedia Americana.

Intl. ed. 2000.

Like all sources, begin with an author name (inverted) if one is given. (Check for author names at the beginning or end of the article.) Put the title of the article in quotation marks, and underline the encyclopedia title. End with the edition and year.

ELECTRONIC SOURCES

Often, websites do not list authors. But when they do, author names should be documented as they are for print sources (inverted at the beginning of the entry). Like print sources, websites also have publication information, but it is different in nature: While a book, for instance, has a publishing company, a website is sponsored by an institution or organization (unless the site is a personal site). Website entries should include: the title of the site (underlined), the date of publication or the date of the most recent update (if available), the name of the sponsoring institution or organization, the date when the researcher accessed the site, and the Uniform Resource Locator (URL), or the Internet address.

URLs can be excessively long and cumbersome. Rather than reproduce a URL that bleeds onto several lines of text, give the URL for the previous page in your search, so the reader can easily access the document by typing in the title or the author name. (When adding the URL to your citation, break it only after a slash [/] and do not add hyphens.) And with electronic sources especially, remember the basic principle behind documentation: *to provide a guide for finding the sources you used.*

The purpose of citing sources: To provide a guide for finding the sources you used.

Official website

Robin Flies Again: Letters Written by Women of Goucher
    College, Class of 1903. Ed. Sarah Pinsker. 1999. Goucher
    Coll. 20 June 2008 <http://meyerhoff.goucher.edu/library/
    robin>.

Sierra Club. June 2008. 1 June 2008. <http://www.sierraclub.org>.

Begin with the title of the site (underlined). If the site has no title, offer a description, such as *Home page* (not underlined) in its place. Next, give the name of the site's editor (if available), the date of electronic publication or the latest update (if available), and the name of any sponsoring or supporting institution or organization. Always end with the date that you accessed the site and the URL.

Personal home page

Good, Melissa. Merwolf's Cave. 2007. 10 June 2008
    <http://www.merwolf.com/>.

Begin with the creator's name, followed by the title (or *Home page* if no title is given), the most recent update, the date of access, and the URL.

Document from website (author and date stated)

Sacks, Bo. "How Magazines Can Survive." <u>Media Bistro</u> 15 Dec.
2006. 12 July 2008 <http://www.mediabistro.com/articles/
cache/a9304.asp>.

Begin with the author name, followed by the title of the particular document (in quotation marks), the title of the entire site (underlined), the date of last update or publication (if given), the hosting organization (if not cited earlier), the date of access, and the URL.

Document from website (no author or date stated)

"Astrology." <u>Wikipedia</u>. 8 May 2008 <http://en.wikipedia.org/
wiki/Astrology>.

Begin with the title of the particular document (or article), and follow the same rules as the previous entry.

Magazine article retrieved from a database

Stanglin, Douglas, and Amy Bernstein. "Making the Grade."
<u>U.S. News and World Report</u>. 4 Nov. 1996: 18. <u>Academic
Search Elite</u>. EBSCOhost. Northwestern Michigan Coll.,
Osterlin Lib. 4 June 2008 <http://www.epnet.com/>.

First cite as a print article. Then list the name of the database, the name of the publishing service (if known), the name of the library, the city and state if useful, the date of access, and the URL. (Use a direct link to the article if possible. Otherwise, use the URL of the database's home page.) Notice that databases do not always list the entire page range of an article. In that case, list the initial page number, followed by a hyphen, a space, and a period.

Journal article retrieved from a database

Clifford, Edwards H. "Grade Inflation: The Effects on Educational Quality and Personal Well-Being." <u>Education</u>.
120 (2000): 538. <u>Academic Search Elite</u>. EBSCOhost.
Northwestern Michigan Coll., Osterlin Lib. 4 June 2008
<http://www.epnet.com/>.

Follow the guidelines for a magazine article retrieved from a database, but make certain to format the publication information accordingly: volume (year): page range.

Article in online journal

Kingma, Mireille. "Nurses on the Move: Historical Perspective

and Current Issues." <u>Online Journal of Issues in Nursing</u>.

31 May 2008. 14 June 2008 <http://www.nursingworld.org/

MainMenuCategories/ANAMarketplace/ANAPeriodicals/

OJIN.aspx>.

Follow the format for print articles. After the date of publication, give the range of pages or paragraphs (abbreviated as *pars.*) if they are numbered in the article. At the end of the entry, add the date of access and the URL.

Online book

Shaw, Bernard. <u>Pygmalion</u>. New York, 1916. <u>Bartelby.com:</u>

<u>Great Books Online</u>. 9 June 2008 <http://bartleby.com/138/

index.html>.

Follow the format for print books. Underline the title of the website. If the book is part of an online scholarly project, which is often the case, include the sponsoring institution. At the end of the entry, add the date of access and URL.

Abstract

Barton, Ellen. "Resources for Discourse Analysis in Composition

Studies." <u>Style</u> 36.4 (2002): 575–95. Abstract. <u>InfoTrac</u>

<u>College Edition</u>. InfoTrac. 10 July 2008 <http://

infotrac.thomsonlearning.com>.

Use the format approriate for the type of source (book, article, etc.) and add the descriptor *Abstract* before the title of the database, hosting institution or library (if applicable), date of access, and URL.

E-mail

Wells, Carson. "Recent Behavior." E-mail to Anton Chigurh.

23 Nov 2007.

Begin with the author, followed by the title (the word or phrase from the subject line of the e-mail) in quotation marks, the descriptor *E-mail to,* and the recipient's name. If you were the e-mail's recipient, insert *E-mail to author.* End with the e-mail's date.

Listserver posting

Brandywine, Jacob. "Raising Standards." Online posting. 21 Apr. 2005. Writing Program Forum. 4 May 2005 <http:// writingforum@nmc.edu>.

Follow the format for e-mail, but use the descriptor *Online posting*. Then give the date of the posting, the name of the listserver or forum, the date of access, and the electronic address of the listserver (if known) or the e-mail address of the moderator (in angled brackets).

CD-ROM

The Trigonometry Explorer. CD-ROM. Chevy Chase: Cognitive Technologies, 1996.

If no author is given, use the editor, compiler, or translator's name, with the abbreviation *(ed., comp., trans.)*. If none of these are listed, begin with the title, followed by the descriptor *CD-ROM*. End with publication information (city, publishing company, date).

Part of CD-ROM

Allen Edmonds Shoes. Advertisement. Comp21: Composition in the 21st Century, The Composition of Everyday Life. CD-ROM. Boston: Wadsworth, 2006.

If citing a portion of a CD-ROM, begin with the author of that particular section (if one is listed), the title of the section, and then follow the format for a CD-ROM entry.

Online encyclopedia

"India." Columbia Encyclopedia. 2003. Yahoo!. 5 June 2008. Path: Reference; Encyclopedia; Columbia Encyclopedia; India; India History.

As with a print encyclopedia, begin with the title of the article if no author is available. Then list the title of the encyclopedia, the publication date (if available), the name of the online service, and the date of access. If you found the source through a sequence of related topics, add *Path:* and give the words in your search sequence, separated by semicolons.

OTHER SOURCES

Brochure

Masonic Information Center. <u>A Response to Critics of</u>
    <u>Freemasonry</u>. Silver Spring: Masonic Services Assn.: n.d.

Give information in the same format as a book. Use abbreviations to indicate missing publication information: *n.p.* (no publisher or no place), *n.d.* (no date of publication), and *n. pag.* (no page numbers).

Personal interview

Mossbacher, Delaney. Personal interview. 4 Mar. 2008.

Begin with the name of the interviewee, inverted. End with the interview date.

Personal letter or memo

Bosley, Cindy. Letter to author. 15 Nov. 2004.

Like all sources, begin with the author name (inverted). Then give the title or description of the letter. End with the date.

Published letter

Tolkien, J. R. R. "To Christopher Tolkien." 18 Jan. 1944.
    Letter 55 of <u>The Letters of J. R. R. Tolkien</u>. Ed. Humphrey
    Carpenter and Christopher Tolkien. New York: Houghton,
    2000. 67–68.

After the date of the letter, give the number of the letter, if available. List the information of the source in which the letter was published, according to the correct format for the source. (In other words, if the letter is published in a book, as above, follow the book format.)

Television program

"A Streetcar Named Marge." <u>The Simpsons</u>. FOX. WAGA,
    Atlanta. 10 Oct. 2007.

Begin with the title of the episode or segment (in quotation marks). Underline the title of the program. Name the creator, producer, director, narrator, performer, or writer (if known), network, call letters, and city of the television station (if appropriate and available). End with the broadcast date.

Film

Monty Python's The Meaning of Life. Dir. Terry Jones. 1983.

DVD. Celandine, 2004.

After the title (underlined), list the director, the year of original release (if relevant), the type of medium on which you viewed the film (such as *DVD* or *Videocassette*), the distributor, and the year of release or re-release.

Musical composition

Strauss, Johann. Tales from the Vienna Woods, waltz op. 325.

Begin with the composer's name (inverted). Underline the title of the work. Do not underline the form, number, or key of the work.

Sound recording

Coldplay. "Yes." Viva La Vida. Capitol, 2008.

Begin with the artist's name. Then list the title of a particular song or section (in quotation marks), the collection title (underlined), the recording company, and the year of release. All of this information is available on the product sleeve or insert. If the recording is not on compact disc, list the medium *(Audiocassette, Audiotape, LP)*, followed by a period, before the recording company.

Lecture or speech

Obama, Barack. "Change That Works for You." Raleigh.

9 June 2008.

Begin with the speaker's name (inverted). Then list the title of the presentation (in quotation marks), the name of the meeting and sponsoring organization (if applicable), the location of the lecture or speech, and the date.

Advertisement

ShopForChange.com. Advertisement. <u>Utne Reader</u>. July–Aug.

    1999: 34.

Begin with the company or product name, followed by *Advertisement*. Then list the relevant publication information. For instance, if the ad appears in a periodical, list the information in the appropriate format and end with the page number.

Work of art (painting, sculpture, photograph)

O'Keeffe, Georgia. <u>Evening Star No. VI</u>. Georgia O'Keeffe

    Museum, Santa Fe.

Include the artist's name (inverted), the title of the work (underlined), the collector or institution that houses it, and the city where it is held.

Performance

<u>Twelfth Night</u>. By William Shakespeare. Dir. William Church.

    Harvey Theater, Interlochen, MI. 28 June 2008.

Begin with the title (if applicable), the author of the performed work (if applicable), the director, the performers (if available), the site of the performance, and the date.

Wetherbee 5

escalates. To use a cliché, "monkey see, monkey do." Humans <u>are</u> primates, after all—in Lessing's words, "we are group animals"—so humans mimic popular behavior (48). Once a trend gains popularity, social pressure colossally adds to its momentum; it's that simple. For my own example (this was before I became rebelliously anti-logo), I recall the desire to wear Airwalk shoes as a middle-schooler, the longing for miniature insignias to dot my socks just above the ankles. These things were cool. Social pressure—there's no avoiding it.

But enough with the how of the matter—corporate enthusiasm and the psychology of conformity explain that simply enough. The more pressing question is why? Why did the phenomenon of logo-wearing appear in the first place? Logos on employee attire and company-owned vehicles—sure, those make complete sense. Nobody's questioning those who wear logos to advertise their own businesses. But what prompted the pioneers of the logo-wearing movement to plaster other people's logos across their backpacks, sweatshirts, and jeans?

The answer is frightening: If clothing reflects cultural identity, and my generation wears corporate logos on its clothing, then my generation must identify with corporations. I, therefore, am a member of the Corporate Generation. How precisely did we come to identify with corporations? That's a difficult question with particularly elusive details. However, one can hardly ignore the correlation between the logo-wearing phenomenon and the general rise of corporate America—the symbiotic existence of Washington and big business, the sweeping deployment of Wal-Marts against local enterprises. Corporate America has engraved its mark on this nation, including this nation's youth. My generation, we have been branded.

What's scarier, though, is how well we have adapted to our brands. To best describe my generation's passion for corporate logos, one must employ a word that evades the dictionary. The extraordinary novelist Kurt Vonnegut, in his book <u>Cat's Cradle</u>, first introduced the much-needed term *granfalloon*. *Granfalloon* describes a group of people

The writer follows the quotation with personal testimony—wrapping the outside sources into his own argument.

Transition paragraph—to a more "frightening" insight.

All the support, thus far, leads here: the "corporate generation."

Wetherbee 6

bound by a hollow cause, who have nothing genuinely significant in common—"a seeming team that [is] meaningless in ways God gets things done," as Vonnegut puts it (91). "Hazel's obsession with Hoosiers around the world was a textbook example of a . . . granfalloon," Vonnegut elaborates. "Other examples of granfalloons are the Communist party, the Daughters of the American Revolution, the General Electric Company, the International Order of Odd Fellows—and any nation, anytime, anywhere" (91–92). With this in mind, one could aptly accuse my generation of assembling itself into a brand-based granfalloon.

I try to like my generation—sometimes successfully. But this is too much. First, the premise uniting my generation's granfalloon is positively ludicrous. Much worse than Vonnegut's examples, our cause has no deep and philosophical criticism. No, ours is blatantly nutty: We willingly advertise corporations with which we have no affiliation whatsoever. Furthermore, brand-name attire is usually more costly than "plain" clothes, clothes that don't advertise—and we buy it anyway! We financially go out of our way to advertise other people's corporations. It's borderline insanity! Don't we realize we're doing their work for them? Don't we get it?—we're advertising for them; they should be paying us!

And it goes deeper. Recall that clothing also reflects individual identity. The Corporate Generation's members still seek to express their individual identities, but even this is often achieved through logo-wearing. Some wish to show off their wealth by wearing pricey brands. Some wish to boast their acute tastes in fashion. Some think the Nike swoosh just looks so damn cool. So, the Corporate Generation has broken itself into sub-granfalloons: the Nike-wearers, the Abercrombie-wearers, etc. And this is our individual expression—brand selection. On marches the rich kids' granfalloon, wearing its seventy-dollar Tommy Hilfiger jeans. On marches the in-crowd girls' granfalloon, signifying its lofty social altitude with Roxy sweatshirts and pink Adidas shoes. And on

Even literature helps to make the point. (Good writers find the connections between culture, literature, history, film, and their secondary sources.)

The writer maintains a strong but playful voice—even among the sources and allusions.

The writer intensifies the point by using the terms from his sources.

Wetherbee 7

marches the wannabe jocks' granfalloon, t-shirts and warm-up pants plastered with any number of athletically oriented logos. This is my generation.

We don't use the symbol the way other generations have. Symbols are wildly effective in triggering ideas—the two-fingered V, the black armband, the holy cross. Past generations have used symbols effectively to represent specific movements and ideas; they have personalized symbols. The peace sign, for example, originally stood specifically for nuclear disarmament, its design very possibly inspired by the semaphore code positions for N and D (Liungman 253). The anti-Vietnam War movement personalized the emblem in the late '60s—its meaning was slightly altered to fit a new cause. But our emblems still mean "Nike," "Adidas," and "Reebok." The matter would vastly change if we were to use corporate logos against corporations—protesters have adopted this ironic spirit by wearing old army jackets to anti-war rallies. But irony is not our intention. We provide good publicity.

And let us take a moment to consider what we're publicizing. By and large, these corporations we advertise fall short of refined virtue; their methods are often questionable, to say the least. Nike, for example—undoubtedly among the worst offenders—remains a long-time target of human rights groups. A report from 2000 entitled "Sweatshops Behind the Swoosh" alleges that "Nike [factory] workers in China . . . put in 12-hour days and seven-day weeks and earn $1.50 for every pair of shoes they turn out—which Nike sells for $80–$120" (qtd. in "The Swoosh"). Furthermore, the report directly asserts that "the deplorable conditions in Nike factories are Nike's fault. In a global economy with no rules that protect workers, it is companies such as Nike [that] direct the global sweatshop in industries such as clothing and footwear" (qtd. in "The Swoosh"). Ouch! So Nike is not quite a monument to morality and good will toward men, and other corporations face similar charges. Names like Adidas, Gap, Reebok, and many more can also be associated with the third-world sweatshop, and it doesn't even end there. Abercrombie, for instance,

The source helps to prove a small supporting point.

He follows the info from the source with a direct response—which resonates with his voice.

Wetherbee 8

faces accusations of racial discrimination in its hiring policies. Do we really want to pay top dollar to advertise for the Abercrombies and Nikes of the world, to essentially do their work for them? If it isn't absurd enough to willingly advertise other people's companies in the first place, we're advertising companies with distinctly sinister backgrounds.

In all fairness, however, Nike and other corporations have undertaken efforts to improve working conditions since 2000. But this hardly justifies the small fortunes we pay to do their advertising work for them. It seems unlikely, anyway, that these sweatshop-based corporations would have taken any virtuous steps in the absence of scalding pressure from humanitarian groups. They have no excuses. They exploited their impoverished workers.

My generation, let us not reward such exploiters, even if they have shown a little progress. At the very least, let them do their own advertising.

I have to give my generation a bit of credit, though—not every company logo worn may directly reflect a granfalloon. Paintball enthusiasts, for instance, may wear the logo of a certain paintball equipment company—thus the logo reflects their identities as paintballers. And wearing the Atari logo may be a genuine expression of proud nerdiness, though even this logo has been trivialized by widespread popularity. These groups may qualify as granfalloons, too, by Vonnegut's standards, but at least their status is debatable. The Nike-wearers, the Roxy-wearers, the Adidas-wearers, the Abercrombie-wearers, though—they're only expressing their membership in the Corporate Generation, a certain granfalloon among granfalloons.

Indeed, Aldous Huxley may have foreseen the Corporate Generation in his 1932 novel <u>Brave New World</u>, a depiction of an ultra-consumerist future in which *Ford* has replaced God: "Ford! Ford! it was too revolting . . ." (91). Had Huxley only lived to witness the upsurge of Nike and its compatriots, perhaps he'd have found a more contemporary replacement for Ford—"[Nike! Nike!] it was too revolting . . ." Or perhaps

The source ("The Swoosh") prompts several paragraphs of writer's commentary.

Speaking directly to his generation makes the essay slightly informal.

He consistently points to corporate logo examples.

Wetherbee 9

Another novel helps
illustrate the point. And
the writer helps make the
connection between the
fictional and the real.

The historical allusions
now contrast with the
present generation.

"Adidas! Adidas!" or "Reebok! Reebok!" After all, we have taken our logo-wearing perilously near a religious status. Perhaps we're out to make Huxley a prophet, to attain the dystopia of his vision. It's a farfetched notion, but here we are—marching steadfastly onward, proudly adorned by our favorite corporate insignias. This is my generation.

And to you, my generation, I offer this challenge: We can do better. We're still the young generation; we're supposed to rebel against the machine. We're supposed to rally against the aged fat cats who watch us from lofty offices—cigars dangling from their lips; disgusted, aghast, and mortified by our presence. We're supposed to strike blows for humanity. We're supposed to be out to change the world.

Rather, we're blithely buying into the schemes of those aged conservatives in their towering office buildings. Some youth of the nation we are.

So what happened to the creativity of youth? Look at how the hippie kids dressed. It may have been eccentrically colorful and a little too LSD-inspired, but at least it was their style. Look at how the '70s kids dressed. Brown and orange may be a thoroughly nasty color combination, but at least it was theirs. Look at how the original punks dressed. They may have been crude, vulgar, and downright revolting, but at least it was their crudeness. At least it was their vulgarity, their downright revoltingness.

These corporate logos—they aren't ours. They belong to old men in grey suits, sweatshop-perpetuators, violators of human rights, crushers of the little guy. Our adornment of these logos plainly exposes our shortcoming as the young generation. We aren't even trying. We actually wear the mark of the enemy—all that the young generation, by definition, is supposed to oppose. Nike is not ours. Adidas is not ours. Reebok is not ours. Billabong is not ours. Roxy is not ours. Abercrombie is not ours. No corporate entities are ours.

So let's be damn sure we aren't theirs.

Wetherbee 10

Works Cited

Anderberg, Kirsten. "Corporate Logos and Protest Signs." <u>Eat the State!</u> 26 Feb. 2003.

     20 Apr. 2008 <http://www.eatthestate.org/07-13/CorporateLogosProtest.htm>.

Huxley, Aldous. <u>Brave New World</u>. New York: Harper, 1969.

Knutsen, Jim. "Making Your Mark." <u>Searcher</u> 12 (2004): 56. <u>Academic Search Elite</u>.

     EBSCOhost. Northwestern Michigan Coll., Osterlin Lib. 24 Apr. 2008

     <http://www.epnet.com/>.

Lessing, Doris. "Group Minds." <u>Prisons We Choose to Live Inside</u>. New York: Harper,

     1988. 47–62.

Liungman, Carl G. <u>Dictionary of Symbols</u>. New York: Norton, 1991.

"The Swoosh and the Sweats." <u>Nation</u>. 22 May 2000: 7. <u>General Reference Center Gold</u>.

     InfoTrac. Northwestern Michigan Coll., Osterlin Lib. 30 Apr. 2008

     <http://infotrac.galegroup.com/>.

Vonnegut, Kurt. <u>Cat's Cradle</u>. New York: Delta, 1998.

The first element in each entry (usually the last name of the author) appears in the text.

APA STYLE

The American Psychological Association (APA) documentation style is used in psychology, nursing, education, and related fields. But while the format is somewhat different from MLA, the strategies for finding, evaluating, and integrating sources remain the same. And even the basic principles of documentation remain the same across styles: The information in the in-text citation should correspond directly with the References page (the APA equivalent of a Works Cited page).

- In-text (or parenthetical) citations provide unobtrusive documentation of specific information.

- In-text citation lets a reader know that particular ideas come from a particular source.

- In-text citation corresponds to the complete bibliographic information provided at the end of the text.

- In-text citations lead the reader directly to the corresponding References page.

- Done correctly, the in-text citation is the first word(s)—whether the author's last name or the article title—plus year of publication and the page number of the citation on the alphabetized References page. This allows the reader to easily find the appropriate source on the References page.

- The References page provides complete information for finding the source.

- This complete information is provided only once and comes at the end of the entire text so that it doesn't interfere with ease of reading.

- This complete information should allow the reader to find the source easily.

In-Text Citation

Like MLA style, in-text documentation for APA involves referencing the original text in parentheses within the actual sentences of your text. An in-text citation must occur whenever a writer:

- Quotes directly from a source.
- Paraphrases ideas from a source.
- Summarizes ideas from a source.
- References statistics or data from a source.

For direct quotes, APA in-text citations should include the author name, date (year only) of the source, and page number from which the cited material is taken. Include the author name in the citation unless it is given within the sentence.

> "After months of exhausting research, they had finally come to understand the problem with their design" (Smith, 2008, p. 82).

p. or *pp.* comes before the actual page number(s).	End punctuation comes after the parenthetical citation.	Commas separate elements within the parentheses.

Writers using APA style often include the date directly after the author's name in the sentence.

> Emphasizing her point, Miller (2000) demands that "it is now time for something drastic to change here on campus" (p. 43).

If the source has no author, use the first word or phrase of the source title and punctuate the title accordingly (either with quotation marks or italics).

> "Even though most of the nation's coastal shorelines can no longer sustain a full range of sea life, the vast majority of Americans seem unconcerned" ("Dead Seas," 2001, p. 27).

If the source has two authors, use the last name of both authors. (Notice that APA style uses &, an ampersand, for in-text citations and the References page.)

(Lunsford & Ede, 2004, p. 158)

If the cited material is quoted in another source, cite the source in which you found the quotation and add *as cited in* before the author name or title.

(as cited in Smith, 2008)

If you want to acknowledge more than one source for the same information, use a semicolon between citations within one set of parentheses. The sources should be listed in alphabetical order.

(Lunsford & Ede, 1984; Smith, 2008)

Electronic Sources Many electronic sources (Web pages, for instance) do not have page numbers, but page numbers may appear on the hard copy. Unless the original source has page numbers, omit them from the in-text citation. Instead, either use the paragraph number (with ¶ or *para.*), if provided, or, if the source has headings, use the heading plus the paragraph number of the source. Electronic texts (especially Web pages) may lack authors; in that case, follow the same formula as with print sources and use the title of the source in the citation.

(Vince, 2005, Blood to Brain section, para. 2)

References

In general, the rule for in-text citation is that the information given should align with the first piece of information in the References list. The References list gives sources that are directly cited in the text. (Bibliographies, on the other hand, list all the sources that a writer may have read and digested in the process of researching the project.) Entries in a References list must follow strict formatting guidelines, but the process is easy if you know the formulas involved.

The most basic idea in referencing sources is that the information in the in-text citation should correspond with the first piece of information given in the References list. For example, notice how the citation from Stremlow's essay (on page 518) corresponds with the entry from her References list:

Some 91.2 million people choose to make a New Year's resolution each year (**Wrightson**, 1992, p. 19).

Vultures 9

References

Wrightson, C. (1992, November/December). Vital statistics. *Health, 6* (6), 19. Retrieved from http://www.ebscohost.com/

The following pages show specific formatting for different types of sources, but the following rules apply for all sources:

- Author names come first. Last name first, followed by first initial of first name (and first initial of middle name, if given).
- The date comes in parentheses directly after the author names.
- Title of the work comes directly after the date. Article titles are always in regular type, while the sources in which they appear—newspapers, magazines, and journals—are italicized. (Only the first letter of the article title or subtitle is capitalized unless there are proper nouns.)
- If no author appears, the title comes first.
- Publication information follows the title of the source.
- If the source is an article, page numbers come last. If the source is electronic, the retrieval information comes last.

BOOKS

All of the necessary information for books can usually be found on the title page, which is inside the front cover.

General format for books

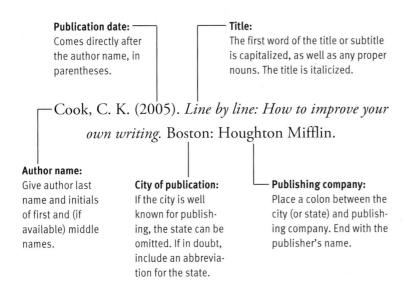

Publication date:
Comes directly after the author name, in parentheses.

Title:
The first word of the title or subtitle is capitalized, as well as any proper nouns. The title is italicized.

Cook, C. K. (2005). *Line by line: How to improve your own writing.* Boston: Houghton Mifflin.

Author name:
Give author last name and initials of first and (if available) middle names.

City of publication:
If the city is well known for publishing, the state can be omitted. If in doubt, include an abbreviation for the state.

Publishing company:
Place a colon between the city (or state) and publishing company. End with the publisher's name.

Two or more authors

Vasta, R., Haith, M. M., & Miller, S. A. (2005). *Child psychology: The modern science.* New York: Wiley.

Add all additional author names, also inverted, before the title. Use an ampersand (&), not *and,* between the names.

Corporate author

American Automobile Association. (2007). *Tour book: New Jersey and Pennsylvania.* Heathrow, FL: Author.

Use the name of the corporation for the author name. If the corporate author also published the text, write *Author* for the publisher.

Subsequent editions

Lauwers, J., & Shinskie, D. (2004). *Counseling the nursing mother* (4th ed.). Sudbury, MA: Jones and Bartlett.

Find the edition information on the title page of the book, and place the information in parentheses directly after the title. Use abbreviations: *2nd ed., 3rd ed.,* etc., or use *Rev. ed.* for "Revised edition."

Edited book

Foucault, M. (1994). *The Foucault reader* (P. Rabinow, Ed.). New York: Pantheon.

After the title, add the editor's name (first initial and last name) and *Ed.* (for "editor"). Use *Eds.* (for "editors") if the book has more than one editor.

Translated book

Bakhtin, M. (2004). *Problems of Dostoevsky's poetics* (C. Emerson, Trans.). Minneapolis, MN: University of Minnesota Press.

Add the translator's name (first initial and last name) and *Trans.* (all in parentheses) after the title of the book.

ARTICLES

Articles appear in newspapers and periodicals (journals or magazines). While newspapers are usually published daily, magazines are usually published weekly or monthly, and journals are published quarterly or even biannually.

Article in a magazine

Buchanan, M. (2004, November 20). A billion brains are better
than one. *New Scientist, 184,* 34–37.

Include the date (year, month, day) directly after the author name. Do not abbreviate months. Give the volume number in italics after the magazine title.

Article in a newspaper

Bush: Shift superfund costs to taxpayers. (2002, February 24).
The Blade, p. A7.

If no author appears, give the title of the article first, followed by the date. After the title of the newspaper, add section letters before the page numbers.

Article in a journal paginated by volume

Crow, A. (2003). Risky behavior among youth: A study of
American teens. *American Psychologist, 58,* 400–415.

Most academic journals number the pages of each issue continuously through a volume. The second issue does not begin with page 1, but with the number after the last page of the previous issue. For these journal articles, place the volume number in italics directly after the journal title, and before the page numbers.

Article or chapter in an edited book

Mickelson, R. A., & Smith, S. S. (1991). Education and the
struggle against race, class, and gender inequality. In E.
Disch (Ed.), *Reconstructing gender: A multicultural anthology*
(pp. 303–317). Mountain View, CA: Mayfield.

After the author and date, give the title of the article or chapter. Then write *In* and the first initial and last name of the editor(s). The abbreviation *Ed.* or *Eds.* (in parentheses) should follow the editor(s). End with the title of the book, the page numbers in which the article appears, and the publication information.

Encyclopedia article

Esposito, V. J. (2000). World War II: The diplomatic history of the war and post-war period. In *Encyclopedia Americana* (9th ed., Vol. 29, pp. 364–367). Danbury, CT: Grolier.

Begin with the author (if given) and date. Then give the title of the article. The name of the encyclopedia (after *In*) should be in italics. The edition number, volume number, and page number(s) should be in parentheses.

"**Consistency in reference style is important, especially in light of new technologies in database indexing.**"

–*APA Style Guide*

ELECTRONIC SOURCES

As with print sources, citations for electronic sources require author(s), date, title, and publication information. Authors and titles are formatted in the same manner as print sources. The difference occurs with publication information, which often calls for the date of access (date on which you retrieved the information) and the URL or the database name. (When adding the URL to your citation, break it only before slashes [/] and do not add hyphens.)

After the initial publication information, add *Retrieved,* the date, *from,* and the URL or the name of the database. However, the *APA Style Guide* says, "no retrieval date is necessary for content that is not likely to be changed or updated, such as a journal article or book." Especially with electronic sources, remember the basic principle behind citing sources: *to provide a guide for finding the sources you used.* Therefore, the most direct route to the source should always be used in the entry.

Website

Pinsker, S. (Ed.). (1999). *Robin flies again: Letters written by women of Goucher College, class of 1903.* Retrieved from Goucher College, Julia Rogers Library Web site: http://meyerhoff.goucher.edu/library/robin

Sierra Club. (2008, June). Retrieved June 10, 2008, from http://www.sierraclub.org

As with all sources, begin with the author's or editor's name(s) (inverted), if available, and the date of electronic publication. Give the title of the site (italicized). If the information is likely to change or be updated, write *Retrieved* and then the date of access, followed by *from* and the name of the source or its URL.

Document from website (author and date stated)

Sacks, B. (2006, December 15). *How magazines can survive.*
    Retrieved July 12, 2008, from Media Bistro:
    http://mediabistro.com/articvles/cache/a9304.asp

Begin with the author name (normal APA format), followed by the date (in parentheses), the title of the specific document (in italics), the word *Retrieved* and the access date, and finally *from,* the website name, and the URL. (Note that APA style uses "Web site" in the References.)

Document from website (no author or date stated)

Astrology. (n.d.). Retrieved May 8, 2008, from Wikipedia:
    http://en.wikipedia.org/wiki/Astrology

Begin with the title. In place of the date, write *n.d.* in parentheses for "no date." Then, give the title of the specific document (if applicable), *Retrieved* and the access date, and finally *from,* the website name, and the URL.

Personal home page

Good, M. (7). *Merwolf's cave.* Retrieved June 10, 2008, from
    http://www.merwolf.com/

Begin with the creator's name, followed by the date of the most recent update, the title, *Retrieved,* the date of access, *from* and the URL.

Journal or magazine article retrieved from a database

Boyd, N. G. (2002). Mentoring dilemmas: Developmental
    relationships within multicultural organizations. *Journal of*
    Occupational & Organizational Psychology, 75(1), 123–125.
    Retrieved from http://www.ebscohost.com

First cite as a print article. Then write *Retrieved from* and the home page URL of the database. Since this article has been published, no retrieval date is needed.

Article in an online journal

If the online journal is exactly the same as the print version (which is most common for academic journals), then follow the format for print articles, but conclude the entry with *Retrieved from* and the URL:

Crow, A. (2000). What's age got to do with it? Teaching older students in computer-aided classrooms. *Teaching English in the Two-Year College, 27*(4), 400–415. Retrieved from http://www.ncte.org

Online book

Shaw, B. (1916). *Pygmalion.* Retrieved from http://bartleby.com/ 138/index.html

Follow the format for print books, but exclude the original print publication information. End with the URL.

Abstract

Fitterman, B. (2006). *Post-conviction DNA testing* (NCJ No. 220975) [Abstract]. Retrieved from National Criminal Justice Reference Service database.

Include either the database name or the database URL, but not both.

Text with a DOI

Birmingham, P. (2008). Elated citizenry: Deception and the democratic task of bearing witness. *Research in Phenomenology 83*(2), 198–215. doi: 10.1163/156916408X286969

Some publishers have begun assigning Digital Object Identifiers (DOIs) to electronic sources. These take the place of URLs and database names. If you find a DOI for a source, enter *doi,* a colon, and then the identifier.

OTHER SOURCES

Brochure

Masonic Information Center. (n.d.). *A response to critics of free-masonry* [Brochure]. Silver Spring, MD: Masonic Services Association.

Use *n.d.* to indicate no date, which is often necessary for brochures. After the title, add the descriptor *Brochure* in brackets before the publication information.

Personal interview or letter

(L. Jackson, personal communication, March 4, 2002)

APA style recommends citing personal communications only with an in-text citation—not in the References list. In the in-text citation, give the name of the interviewee, the title *personal communication,* and the date.

Television program

Martin, J. (Writer), & Moore, R. (Director). (1992). A streetcar named Marge [Television series episode]. In A. Jean & M. Reiss (Producers), *The Simpsons.* Los Angeles: Twentieth Century Fox.

Begin with the name and title of the scriptwriter, then the name and title of the director and the date. Give the title of the episode or segment followed by the producer and the title of the program (italicized). End with the location of the broadcasting company and the company name.

Government publication

U.S. Census Bureau. (2002). *Statistical abstract of the United States* (122nd ed.). Washington, DC: U.S. Government Printing Office.

If no author is given, use the government agency as the author, followed by the date, the title (in italics), and the publication information that appears on the title page. If no publication information appears and the publication is a federal document, you can assume that it was published by the Government Printing Office in Washington, D.C.

Vultures 7

month on advertising directly after the holiday season (Murphy, p. 12). Their method preys on consumers' internal thoughts about inadequacy and worth, specifically the ones that surround the holidays. Knowing that this is the most fertile time in which to implant this faulty reasoning, they increase their budgets and, in turn, succeed in creating a customer that they previously didn't have. This type of strategic marketing is not exclusive to the diet/health industry but it is probably the most obvious to the average consumer. Clearly, strategic marketing that preys on our existing vulnerability (or need) during the holiday season promotes great profit.

Even the tobacco industry recognizes and reacts to the trends of New Year's resolutions in our society by increasing their marketing during the months of January and February (Basil et al., 2000). But they aren't trying to increase profit; clearly, one can infer that their marketing seeks to counter the impact of smoking cessation during the New Year. In an article from *Advertising Age,* Mercedes Cardona (1998) outlines how SmithKline Beecham, the company in charge of NicoDerm and Nicorette, is "following the dieter's recipe" by taking "advantage of a tendency among smokers to choose the beginning of the year as the kick off for their attempts at quitting" (1998). According to a Gallup poll, half of the smokers who aim to quit begin their attempts on New Year's Day (as cited in Cardona). Smoking cessation companies increase their advertisements in an attempt to maximize their profit by exploiting this tendency.

This is not to say that companies should not cater to our needs during the season, but they shouldn't have to create them. As in the above scenario, Sarah doesn't have the best confidence in herself, but she can ignore her inadequacies until they are thrown in her face by the diet industry. This is how advertising works; this is its purpose. In our capitalistic society, competition is key and an edge on the market is the best way to increase profit.

Maybe consumers can't stop advertising from affecting us, but we can tip the balance by at least understanding and accepting its power to do so. We, the consumers, push this art of advertising forward by participating in the process. Looking at our clothes,

Paragraphs 14–17 all work to support the same point about money, advertising, and the strategic marketing.

The references to sources always give information about the writer's identity or the publication. This boosts reliability.

A concession paragraph.

Vultures 8

our houses, our cars, our refrigerators, and our lifestyles, we must accept the effects of advertising and level with them. As Doris Lessing argues, "It is one thing to admit it, in a vague uncomfortable way . . . but quite another to make that cool step into a kind of objectivity" where consumers can say, "'let's admit it, examine and organize our attitudes accordingly'" (1998, p. 50). Think about that on New Year's and choose wisely at the stroke of midnight.

References

Basil, M. D., Basil, D. Z., & Schooler, C. (2000). Cigarette advertising to counter New Year's resolutions. *Journal of Health Communication, 5* (2), 161–174. Retrieved from http://www.ebscohost.com

Cardona, M. M. (1998, December 21). Nicorette, NicoDerm CQ ads tied to New Year's resolutions. *Advertising Age, 69* (51), 4. Retrieved from http://www.ebscohost.com

Lessing, D. (1988). Group minds. *Prisons we choose to live inside* (pp. 47–62). New York: HarperCollins.

Murphy, I. P. (1997, February 3). Marketers help consumers to keep their resolutions. *Marketing News, 31* (3), 12–13. Retrieved from http://www.ebscohost.com

New Year's resolutions: Why do we make them when we usually don't keep them? (2003, December 5). Retrieved December 6, 2008, from http://newsinfo.iu.edu/news/page/normal/1206.html

Spethmann, B. (1995, November 6). Lean mean New Year. *Brandweek, 36* (42), 1. Retrieved from http://www.ebscohost.com

Wrightson, C. (1992, November/December). Vital statistics. *Health, 6* (6), 19. Retrieved from http://www.ebscohost.com

The conclusion avoids mere summary—and offers a new way to think about our own attitudes.

The sources are listed in alphabetical order—each corresponding to the appropriate format. (Pages 510–517 show APA formatting for articles, books, and so on.)

FREQUENTLY ASKED QUESTIONS

What if I Don't Know What Type of Source I Have?

This question often comes up when researching electronic sources. Most online research methods lead to either periodicals (journals, magazines, and newspapers) or websites. (Online books are generally not in the same search paths as periodicals.) If you have an electronic source and are not sure if it is a website or a periodical, check the top of the first page for publication information. If the text has a volume or issue number, or date information, it is most likely a periodical. Also, an electronic article most often lists the title of the magazine or journal at the top of the first page.

How Do I Tell the Difference between a Journal and a Magazine?

In general, a magazine is published more often than a journal. Magazines are published every week *(Time, Newsweek)*, every other week, or every month. Magazines are written for nonspecialized, or *general,* readership, whereas journals are written for readers with a specialized field of knowledge (such as nursing, engineering, or pharmacology). While magazines attempt to inform or entertain the public about various (sometimes even eccentric) topics, journals attempt to investigate particular ideas, theories, or situations within a discipline or field of study. Check the publication information to see how often the periodical is published, and look at the table of contents to see if the articles are written for general or specialized readers. (See page 459.)

How Do I Find the Publication Information?

Publication information for books can be found on the title page. The front of the title page has the full title, the publisher, and the city of publication, and the reverse (or copyright page) includes the copyright dates and any edition information. For periodicals, the volume and issue number usually appear at the bottom of each page and are often printed on the first page inside the cover along with the table of contents. (However, some periodicals fill the first few pages with advertisements.) Websites can be more tricky. If the author, last update, or sponsoring institution does not appear on the opening (or home) page, scroll down to the bottom of the page (or look on the menu for *Information* or *About Us*).

How Do I Know the Page Numbers of an Electronic Source?

Generally, electronic sources do not have page numbers—and documentation styles do not require page numbers for websites or online journal articles. Sometimes, however, a print source will republish its contents electronically and retain page numbers. (In other words, the source appears online exactly as it does in print.) In that case, simply use the page numbers as they appear.

Should I Use APA or MLA or What?

MLA (or Modern Language Association) style is used by writers in the humanities and literature (such as English and communications). APA (or American Psychological Association) style is used by writers in the medical field, education, and, of course, psychology. CMS (or Chicago Manual of Style) is used by writers in humanities fields, such as religion, history, and philosophy. The sciences (such as physics and chemistry) have particular styles as well. When writing for an academic audience, you should always ask what style to use. Some instructors want their students to use a particular style, regardless of their major or field of study.

Why Are There Different Documentation Styles?

The different styles have emerged over the course of years. They have developed because different research techniques sometimes call for a particular type of documentation. As academic fields grow, they develop and reward particular research strategies—and one documentation style cannot always account for those strategies.

Standard Abbreviations

MLA	APA	
ed.	Ed.	= Editor or Edited by
eds.	Eds.	= Editors
ed.	ed.	= Edition, usually associated with a number (4th ed.)
Rev. ed.	Rev. ed.	= Revised edition
n.d.	n.d.	= No date
n.p.	n.p.	= No publisher or no place
n. pag.	n. pag.	= No page numbers
trans.	Trans.	= Translator
p.	p.	= Page number
pp.	pp.	= Page numbers
no.	No.	= Number
pars.	para.	= Paragraphs
vol.	Vol.	= Volume

ANTHOLOGY: EVERYDAY RHETORIC

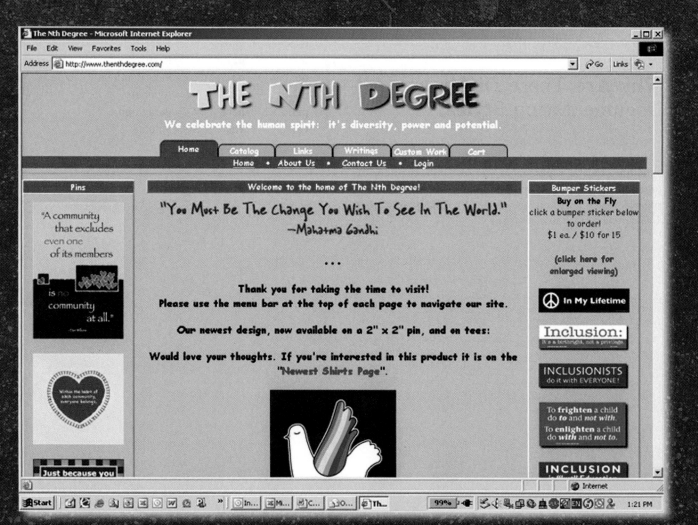

Chapter Contents

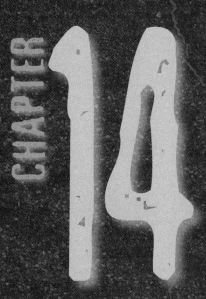

CHAPTER 14

Remembering Who You Were

A *Beat* Education

Leonard Kress

It's easy to list the things we know. But it's impossible to list the things we do not know. Occasionally, people get a direct glimpse of the gaps in their learning and come face to face with the huge, dangerous, unruly reality beyond their knowing. For Leonard Kress, a poet and professor at Owens Community College in Toledo, Ohio, this moment came on a hobo-like trip to Chicago. As you read this essay, notice his allusion to the Beats—a group of influential writers and thinkers from the mid-twentieth century who lived hard and traveled throughout America, who dramatized freedom and intellectual revolution. Like Kress, many writers, musicians, artists, and scholars were influenced by the Beats and the world they imagined. (Kress's writing also appears in Chapter 10.)

At 20 I was convinced that the single most important experience, without which my education would remain shamefully incomplete, was that of hopping a freight. Doubtless, my sense of education at that time (as well as my sense of what constituted good writing) was more than mildly seasoned by huge doses of the Beats—Allen Ginsberg, Gregory Corso, William Burroughs, Kenneth Patchen, LeRoi Jones, and, of course, Jack Kerouac. That these writers were at the time considered non-scholarly, marginal, and were all but vilified by my literature teachers made them, I'm sure, that much more irresistible. I would merely open a page at random—a short story, say Kerouac's "Railroad Earth"—and find myself filled with wonder and admiration and conviction: this was sacramental:

> Remembering my wonder at the slow grinding movement and squee of gigantic boxcars and flats and gons rolling by with that overpowering steel and dust clenching closh and clack of steel on steel, the shudder of the whole steely proposition, a car going by . . . the frightening fog nights in California when you can see thru the mists the monsters slowly passing . . . when those wheels go over your leg they don't care about you.

I did manage, once at least, to imitate the Beats. I was staying with some friends in Grand Rapids, Michigan, when I decided, receiving little or no discouragement from them, to seek out the local freight yard. I figured I would ride the rails in whichever direction they took me—unconcerned as I was with notions of destination and arrival. Unable to summon up any practical or procedural advice on how to begin from Kerouac's disjointed and out-of-control prose, I simply searched for a site full of boxcars and cabooses and lanes upon lanes of tracks.

It was early morning and the yard seemed deserted, so I brazenly set forth. I had no fear of the dreaded railway dicks, no sense of the danger of heavy machinery, but I did carry with me a bright blue rucksack, a sense that all would go well if I only abandoned myself to the open road. As hoped for and expected, a figure appeared out of nowhere. I assumed he was something of a tramp or hobo—I had the sense at least not to ask him about his vocation—and he quickly took me under his grimy wing. With no exchange of words, we managed to cross over several tracks, duck out of sight of the hollering switchers, and second-guess the direction of cars clanking over shuntings. He knew which trains were already made up and ready to pull out, and which might sit for hours filling up with unbearable heat from the morning sun. He led me to one, sitting on the outer tracks, mostly a string of lime-dusty hoppers interspersed with empty boxcars—doors flung invitingly wide open! I rushed in front of him, tossed my rucksack in, and was about to hoist myself inside, when he grabbed my leg and tackled me down to the rails. I was too shocked to resist; he pinned me to the railroad ties and moved his head in real close to mine. Just when I was sure that he was about to slit my throat, he released his grip and delivered what seemed to be a prepared speech about hopping freights. "Don't never board a still train," I remember him saying, "they shut them doors when the train's pulling out. You get stuck in there, you roast, you just roast, that's all there is to it."

Although I was a bit chastened from the stern warning, which at the time didn't seem to be warranted, and covered with brush and gravel burns from the take-down, I felt that I had just participated in some arcane initiation rite and passed through it successfully, the bearer of some sort of *tramp-gnosis*. If I were to characterize it now, I might say that it seemed to be a particular mix of the medieval Franciscan ideal, International Workers of the World notions of brotherhood and solidarity . . . and my own middle class suburban naïveté.

5   We strode together—in some sort of unacknowledged sync—farther down the line, to a spot beyond the cluster of workers' shacks and railroad paraphernalia. Ducking in a trackside ravine almost as if we were kids playing backyard war, we waited until the freight began its slow grinding movement, almost overwhelmed by what Kerouac called that *overpowering steel dust and clenching closh and clack of steel on steel, the shudder of the whole steely proposition*. . . . We waited, nodding as each car rolled past, until a boxcar with unshut doors presented itself to us. Then we sprung up, tossed our packs inside and scissor-jumped our way in.

While I was making myself comfortable, shifting around on a sift of rust and pebbles, dangling my legs over the side, my companion leaped off, barely losing his footing, and rushed off. I didn't know why he left. I thought at first that he had forgotten something, later that he was trying to set me up—for what, though, I couldn't imagine. He just disappeared, and though the train was barely snailing along, I was afraid to jump down after him. As it picked up speed, however, I regretted not taking that chance, as my dangling legs were almost sheared off by a switching signal the boxcar curved past.

The ride itself was unbelievably jittery and uncomfortable. I couldn't open the can of beans I'd brought along, and the slices of bread I'd stuffed into my rucksack fell onto the floor and coated themselves in rust-flecked grease. The freight did, however, grant me a spectacular view of the setting sun as it ambled ever so slowly along the banks of Lake Michigan. And it did ease through innumerable small town backyards where children ran alongside, not easily winded, cheering both the train and me on. Even young mothers waved shyly while they pinned banner-like sheets onto their clotheslines.

Almost half a day later, around midnight, the train crunched into Chicago, where I hopped off, exhausted and exhilarated. As my shaky train-legs hit the gravel of the roadbed, I thought I heard a threatening shout, so I ran, tripped mostly, over the 50 or so tracks and platforms and switchings, down a steep embankment. Right into the middle of some rundown neon-shod shopping strip near 95th Street on the South Side—bars and liquor stores and boarded-up groceries, card readers, barber colleges, and storefront churches, groups of men hanging on the corners drinking from passed-around rumpled paper bags. Here was a whole gallery of street life like nothing I'd ever seen. Somehow the rickety freight ride and all that drama and lure of the past two days quickly dissipated, replaced by an urgent sense of new gaps in my learning, of new educational possibilities.

Writing Strategies

1. Through his use of vivid language, Kress shows himself riding the rails. Identify several fresh expressions that appealed to you. Was it "shifting around on a sift of rust and pebbles" (¶ 6) or "he grabbed my leg and tackled me down to the rails"? (¶ 3) Explain how several expressions helped bring his experience to life for you.

2. How else might Kress have vividly described his experience for the reader? Write two or three additional sentences of description, and explain why each one is successful at describing the scene.

3. Describe Kress's voice as a writer. What does he sound like? Provide several examples from the essay (particular word choices, for example) that support your description. How is, or isn't, Kress's voice appropriate for an essay about hopping a freight train?

4. If workshopping Kress's essay, how would you answer the following questions: What do you like most about the essay? What do you like the least about it? What suggestion do you have for the writer?

5. Kress refers (or alludes) to several poets and writers in the essay. Explain the effect of these allusions: how they help to illustrate a point, how they influenced you as you read.

Exploring Ideas

1. How does the way Kress talks about education invite the reader to think differently about the subject?

2. How is Kress's essay part of a larger discussion? What is the general subject matter—or issue—of that larger discussion?

3. What educational experiences can you remember that might help you think further, and differently, about this topic?

4. Interview several people about an important learning experience of their own. How many people's experiences included

formal education settings? How many didn't? How were others' experiences similar to or different from yours or Kress's? How might these responses help you better understand and write about an educational experience of your own?

For help inventing your own writing project, see the Point of Contact section on pp. 44–45.

✖ ✖ ✖

The Greatest Gift

Samantha Tengelitsch

Emotions have a way of hiding in the past and concealing the complexities of life from ourselves and others. But writing can break open the past, unravel the truth, and show us what we're made of. Samantha Tengelitsch, who bravely wrote this essay for her first-semester English course at Northwestern Michigan College, cracks open the past. She finds insight about motherhood in an odd place: a puppy. As you read this essay, consider the intellectual risks the writer takes and how she uncovers big emotions in little places. Tengelitsch reminds us of something that is easy to forget: Every event in our lives impacts every other event in our lives.

Let me say first, I am flexible. In birth, I stretched for the little being who unfolded from within me. In the months preceding her birth, I read every book on babies, pregnancy, on labor, breastfeeding, bonding and diapering; if it had been written, I had read it, preparing to stretch further, in my thinking, in my way of being. Curiously, I can't recall a single true-to-the-topic book on motherhood. And after the birth of our daughter, there all at once appeared an obvious and enormous gap in my education.

Immediately following the birth, I was bombarded by family and friends, armed with cameras and Hallmark cards, all anxious to see the new baby. Even the strange relations who only appear at weddings and at funerals came from all around, smothering me with noisy talk when what I wanted most in the whole world was to curl up into myself and discover who I had become.

I was nothing like the women I saw on television or in magazines. Never were they caught in their pajamas in the afternoon, or in milk-stained t-shirts, eyes the color red, dark splotches below. I had stretch marks in places I hadn't realized stretch marks would appear. I loved my child with a fierceness unlike anything I had ever experienced before, but in this, I felt lost. When my husband returned to work and the busy distraction of family finally petered out, I found myself alone for the first time. Suddenly, I could stretch no further. I felt isolated and vulnerable. While images surrounding me in the media were of happy, bubbling mothers and babies, I sat alone on the couch in despair, waiting for my husband to return home from work day after day; writhing with envy at the fun my single or child-free friends seemed to be having without me. I was starving for adult conversation, but with family and friends scattered across the country, I didn't feel like I could call back the troops. *Bring your damn cameras,* I thought, anything to relieve me from this monotony someone tricked me into believing was supposed to be bliss.

It was then I abandoned my worldly ambitions and fell into a dull routine that consisted of playing with baby, changing diapers, preparing food, cleaning house, and watching television. I began studying *Martha Stewart.* This woman was legendary in her perfection. I watched her make birthday cakes, pull together astonishing flower arrangements from her impeccable gardens and make every evening special with an elaborate table setting. I, like many women, both envied and hated her for this.

5   My neighbor was a Martha. She, too, had recently given birth to a healthy baby girl, but somehow she survived unscathed. I watched from my living room window as she carefully tucked her baby into the car seat and went out for groceries each day. Her house was immaculate, dinner was on the table every night by five and she even had time to garden. I couldn't see then through the veil of expectations placed upon me by Martha and others before her, that this woman was older, wiser, and far more emotionally and financially prepared for motherhood.

So, while the country sat glued to their televisions following the attacks of September 11th, I sat glued to mine, searching for some answer as to who I was supposed to be. What is a mother after all?

I can now say with certainty that motherhood is a progressive transition, an evolution of acceptance of self.

We immerse ourselves in images of perfection: women who can do no wrong, who require no help, who never ask for help. We are not taught to ask for help. I remember that the case of the woman in Texas who killed her children was in the news at this time and I hated myself because I *empathized* with the woman. How could I feel that way? What kind of horrible person was I to empathize with what the papers labeled a *monster*? I knew I wasn't sick and that my child was not in danger, but I felt her isolation, her desperation and I wanted to reach out to her, but it was too late.

My husband never once ignored my growing vulnerability. He was desperate to help. That winter, a few weeks before the holiday, he brought home a special gift. He carried it through the door, under his arm like the morning paper. It was a puppy, wrapped carefully in a big green bow. I know he saw me in my depressed heap on the couch and wanted, like me, to do anything to help me surface from the sea of hormones and emotions, the complexity of which frightened even him. This snuggly, black and white puppy, he hoped, would end my depression.

I was elated at first to have a dog in the house, but soon the cold Michigan winter won over my countless potty-training attempts. (The dog obviously preferred the warmth of our house when relieving herself.) I awoke suddenly to the realization that my problems were now compounded by the puppy. It was then, while mopping up pee in our kitchen that I made my first decision, not as the girl who wanted to keep her Christmas puppy, but as a woman *and* mother. The dog would have to go. I picked up my daughter and held her close, for the first time savoring the sweet smell of her breath and the way her little body fit so perfectly into mine. She snuggled down and fell blissfully asleep, her head resting on my shoulder. The change was almost undetectable, but she felt it too. Her body relaxed as did mine for the first time in months. I glowed, now face to face with my new identity as a mother and, for the first time, accepting this as such.

10   A few years later, Martha Stewart was arrested for committing securities violations. I noticed many people seemed elated with the news of her arrest: Their enthusiasm was the result of witnessing this image of perfection finally topple. It was like watching the people of the former Soviet Union tear down the busts and statues of Stalin and Lenin. Martha Stewart, guilty as charged by the imperfect women of America for aiding the real criminal, the media, in its unyielding and misleading representation of women and motherhood. And there were others before her: June Cleaver, guilty; Carol Brady, guilty; Barbie, guilty; NBC, CBS, ABC, guilty, guilty, guilty.

If only I had realized earlier how unfair it was to compare myself and my baby to these fictional characters, I would have saved myself the agony of unwarranted expectations and the feeling of stubborn independence that blocked me from asking others for help. This is my experience—only I can claim it. *All of it,* the imperfections and the beautiful wisdom born out of the sacred transition of woman to mother. If only I could have realized then that the real perfection exists not in the glamour-hungry media but in our own imperfection; in our uniqueness as women and as mothers.

Show me motherhood as it really exists. Why simplify such a diverse and powerful, womanly transition? Show me the midnight feedings, talk to me about sore nipples, breastfeeding, sleeplessness. Let us honor the restless abandonment of ourselves for our new identities as mothers. Let us recognize the wisdom of our elders and pass it on to the next generation of women through the simple act of putting down the camera and doing a load of laundry, or by holding the baby while a mother takes a long-deserved shower or nap. Let us ask for help and surround ourselves with other women, mothers. Let us be comfortable enough in our womanly bodies to embrace motherhood.

The real gift I received that holiday was not the little puppy, but what my experience inspired: growth, wisdom, the ability to stretch further than ever before, to be swallowed whole, to surrender, evolve, and accept my new role as a mother. This wisdom alone was the greatest of all gifts.

Writing Strategies

1. How do certain details of Tengelitsch's introduction set up the main idea that comes later in her essay?
2. How does Tengelitsch use cultural references (to Martha Stewart, to "the woman in Texas") to develop her main idea?
3. How is the essay's title a unifying device throughout the essay?

4. If workshopping this essay, what major strength would you point out? What suggestion would you make for improving the essay, and why?

Exploring Ideas

1. In groups, explore how the puppy impacted Tengelitsch's thinking.
2. Tegelitsch says, "I was nothing like the women I saw on television or in magazines." (¶ 3) In addition to the specific examples she mentions, what specific media images can you think of that Tengelitsch, and other mothers, should not compare themselves to? What media images may be helpful to new mothers?
3. What other roles, in addition to motherhood, are a "progressive transition, an evolution of acceptance of self"? (¶ 7)

For help inventing your own writing project, see the Point of Contact section on pp. 44–45.

Explaining Relationships

We Love Them. We Hate Them. We Take Them.

Abigail Zuger

In all occupations, relationships are mysterious, troubling, and controversial. And professionals in all walks of life find themselves stumped by the relationships that seem most common and mundane. In this essay, published in the *New York Times* in December 2004, Abigail Zuger, a physician, explores the relationship among doctors, patients, and the pills that bind them.

There were eight of us crowded into the exam room as an exasperated patient and I tried to figure out why he was feeling weak and tired and itchy and nauseated and almost fainted in the subway Thursday night.

Two of us, the patient and I, were human beings. The rest had no voices, bodies or personalities in the ordinary sense of the word, but they played a role in the discussion that was just as vigorous and important as if they did.

They were, of course, my patient's pills. Or rather, they were my pills: the pills I gave him. Or rather, they were Merck's pills and Pfizer's and GlaxoSmithKline's and a couple of generic manufacturers'. They were the Food and Drug Administration's pills, too, released into our little sphere only with that agency's blessing.

But mostly, the pills were the patient's and mine, and we tussled over them with all the wishful thinking and hidden agenda of estranged parents haggling over the kids. The blue capsule? He'd been taking it for years, with good results. It seemed unlikely to be causing

problems now. The new white capsule I gave him last month, the one I figured was making him sick?

5   "I love it," he said. "Makes me feel like myself. Can't live without it."

The big white tablet from last spring?

"I just look at one and I feel sick," he said. "I hate them and I'm not taking them anymore. The end."

"You'll wind up in the hospital without them," I said for the sixth time in six months. "Please, bear with them. There's nothing else to use."

But I knew perfectly well he had probably stopped taking them regularly months ago, and would never swallow one again.

10   When he left the room, I gazed for a few moments at the single prescription he had left sitting on the desk. The big white tablet. Such a good pill. Cheap, safe and effective, if a little hard on the stomach. How I loved that modest, hardworking pill. Of course, I had never put one into my mouth, but it was still one of my favorites. How could he reject it, reject me, out of hand like that?

The nation's use of prescription drugs is soaring, a government report said this month, and the relationships we all have with those little pieces of matter, our pills, are becoming ridiculously tangled.

Medical anthropologists have written at length about how medications "commodify" health, fostering the illusion that it is something bought and sold at market. In doctors' offices and in medicine cabinets, though, a reverse process takes place: We all anthropomorphize pills right back from commodities to willful agents of good or evil. For patients, they can be saviors,

Zuger   **535**

We Love Them. We Hate Them. We Take Them.

or assassins. For doctors, the voodoo is even stronger. Medicines are our prosthetics, at once utterly foreign (we are unlikely to take them ourselves, and may not even know what they look like) yet so much a part of us that we can barely function without them.

For those of us in specialties without scalpels or scopes, they are our only tools (if you don't count all the good advice). Inevitably, we evolve idiosyncratic patterns of prescribing, favorite combinations, pills we love or hate. The pills become our friends, our servants, our agents, ourselves.

Of course, that artistry and control is all an illusion. We flex our dosing muscles at a remove too far from the actual ingestion to be in control of anything, and we are in turn controlled by forces we never see. One moment we are signing for Vioxx, confident and enthusiastic; the next moment, it disappears, and we are left to explain why. One moment we are prescribing a patient's big white tablet, happy that we are practicing medicine of the highest quality by protecting him from bad things. The next, we discover once again that little known fact: There is a placebo effect for doctors, too.

15   Pity the doctor who thinks that prescribing a drug is the same thing as treating a patient, and the patient who agrees. Some never learn otherwise. The rest of us slowly wake up to the fact that the prescription is just the beginning, sometimes not even that. Without constant discussion and re-evaluation, we might as well all be writing poetry on those prescription forms.

After a month without the big white pills my patient said he felt a lot better. I, of course, was no longer practicing quality medicine, and felt a lot worse. His stomach talked to him. The statistics of what would happen to him without the pills talked to me. The pills, for once, were silent. Perhaps the best we could do, under the circumstances, was keep talking to each other.

Writing Strategies

1. How is Zuger's opening strategy ("There were eight of us crowded into the exam room . . .") important to the rest of her essay?
2. Zuger begins her essay with a narrative. At what point does she leave the narrative, and why?

3. What conclusions does Zuger come to at the end of her essay? What would she like her reader to consider?
4. Zuger's essay was published in the *New York Times,* a daily newspaper with a general readership. How might Zuger have presented her ideas differently if her essay were
   - written for an academic journal?
   - written for a college writing course?
   - an advertisement?

Exploring Ideas

1. In groups, explore the following:
   - Medical anthropologists have written at length about how medications "commodify" health, fostering the illusion that it is something bought and sold at the market. (¶ 12)
   - What evidence can you provide to support the statement?
2. Why do Americans take so many pills? Generate as many reasons or possibilities as you can. Then explore them further through discussion. Which reasons are most valid or least valid? Are any just the tip of the iceberg?
3. In paragraph 14, Zuger says doctors are "controlled by forces we never see." What does she mean? How much are, or aren't, doctors in control?

For help inventing your own writing project, see the Point of Contact section on pp. 80–81.

■ ■ ■

What the Honey Meant

Cindy Bosley

It is easy to see ourselves moving steadily ahead in time. But Cindy Bosley, poet, novelist, and writing teacher, invites us to see how the past circles up into our lives— and how the people from our past linger in the present. In this essay, Bosley's present relationship with her husband involves her past relationship with her father. While the essay is highly narrative, it is also highly analytical, making intense connections between single moments throughout Bosley's life. And these connections help to reveal significant meaning in a simple honeycomb. (Bosley's writing also appears in Chapter 2.)

My husband disappeared out the back door with an empty bowl in his hand. I did not see him leave, but a few moments later, he came back in and asked me to shut my eyes. I did as he asked. When I opened them, he stood in front of me holding out a bowl of fresh honey and a piece of the comb which had been pulled away from the hive and was still running with the buttery sweet liquid of all my best memories. My husband might as well have gone out just then and shoved his hand, in brown bear fashion, through the stinging, angry bees to release this small brick of honeycomb for all the love and gratitude I felt toward him at that moment. He stood there holding out to me a bowl filled with my life as it should have been, and I wept.

When I think of honeycomb, I think of my father. I first tried a small bite, and then more and more by the spoonful, the day before my father left. He had brought the honey home from a guy at work, he said, and so he set the brick in its jar onto the counter, and found a spoon for himself, plunged the spoon into the hexagon cells and pulled it away with a *suck*. And then he went back for more. I stood over the jar of honeycomb marveling at it—the many sections of honey, the yellowish layer of beeswax sealing the liquid in, the small brown and black flecks of flower remnant, or bee poop, I guessed. My father said nothing to me, and he did not offer me his spoon, but when I got off my chair to get one from the drawer, I stood over the honey jar again waiting for permission, and he said, "Wanna try it?" with surprise and, I think, a little joy, as if it hadn't occurred to him before to offer some to others. That was the way he was. And I ate and ate and ate. I loved the wax like gum, how it stayed behind in my mouth long after the honey part was gone, swallowed, tasted, and replaced with another spoonful.

When my father left that night, I was sleeping and he did not say good-bye. In the years to come as he came and went, moving in and out like a college boy from a dormitory, I would learn that this was how he did things. That first morning, though, I did not know anything had happened, but like a too bulky winter coat a kid inherits from an older sibling, that morning when I woke, the house just *felt* different—a little bigger, a little old. The rooms were quieter. It's hard to believe that was possible, the new quiet, since my father was a too quiet man to begin with, but it was *quiet*. And the browns and golds of our '70s decor were browner, and deeper gold. And my mother was in her bedroom on the phone trying to muffle hard crying. And my younger sister was watching *Land of the Lost*, while my brother played with his Tinker Toys. Something had happened,

and I didn't have to ask anyone what that was. The sun was a sawblade in the sky.

I didn't quite know what to feel about this. Part of what I felt was certainly excitement. *Wow. Our dad's gone. Wow.* I also felt a puncture, very small like a needle, that I couldn't locate inside me. And I was, I think now, terrified at the new development that no one had yet explained to me though it was nearing lunch time, though it was time for someone to talk.

5   I finally had to ask the obvious question, but I didn't know how these things were supposed to go—I had imagined other families, more loving families, sitting down together to talk over the coming changes with the children well before they happened, or maybe even a day before they happened. I had imagined other families dealing with it in other ways—the father kissing the children a special goodnight when he knew he would not be there the next day when they woke up, or maybe he would not save the trauma for the night or morning, but ease out in the smooth part of the afternoon, lots of hugs and tears, but at least the witnessing of leave-taking. And then I remembered the honeycomb.

And if I say: I went to the kitchen to look for something. Like a small and pitiful gesture of his helplessness and regret, there on the counter was a spoon he'd left beside the jar of honey, and I knew he meant it for me.

It feels one way.

But if I say: I went to the kitchen to look for the jar of honey. When I saw the counter, I saw there was nothing there, and I suppose I expected that. He must have taken it with him.

That feels another way.

10   But what really happened is that I did not have to ask my obvious question, "What happened with Dad?" And I did not have to bother looking for the honey because, yes, he left it—it simply wasn't that important to him. And no, there was no symbolic spoon or other invitation, *Eldest Daughter, please eat*, nearby. What happened was that I took a bite of honey and then I joined my sister and brother, two and ten years younger, watching Saturday morning cartoons together on the black, brown, white carpet, patterned in such a wild way that it was quickly making my head ache.

I heard my mother tell the story five or six times that morning, with different details and emphasis, to the people she talked to most easily. She had moved from the heavy weight of the red and black paisley bedroom to the dimness of the kitchen, a room the sun rarely ventured into, like all the dark rooms of our house. She told Aunt Edith that he better damn well get his stereo cabinet out of this house today. She moaned her money fears to Patty, and there was a hitch in my heart when I heard her mention my violin lessons. While she talked to Marlene, I heard several female names come flying, and with Darla, I understood more clearly that there was somehow another woman involved. What had happened I never did learn exactly, but my father had moved out overnight. Everything felt brand new. And there was a jar half-full of honey in the kitchen that no one but me wanted to eat.

When my husband brought his bowl of honeycomb to me that bright, grown-up day in the kitchen, I did not think *Father.* I did not think *Childhood.* I did not think *Old Pain.* But my husband knows my stories well enough to understand what it might mean to me, and when he heard our neighbor at the door that morning telling him to come get some of this amazing honey someone had given him, my husband knew enough to grab a bowl and bring me some.

Everyone I know has aches so deep that small triggers bring tears to their eyes. The honey gift was clearly that trigger for me. I like to think I cried because seeing that bowl of honey made me miss my father. Or maybe I cried because I don't yet understand all that happened in my life back then, or why people can do the things they do to each other. Maybe I cried because my husband loves me that much, enough to know what the honey would mean. But I do know one thing: I sure do like honey. I wept to see that honey just for me.

Writing Strategies

1. In paragraph 3, Bosley offers the reader details about physical goings-on:
   - –And the browns and golds of our '70s decor were browner, and deeper gold. And my mother was in her bedroom on the phone trying to muffle hard crying. And my younger sister was watching *Land of the Lost,* while my brother played with his Tinker Toys. Something had happened, and I didn't have to ask anyone what that was. The sun was a sawblade in the sky.
   - –What purpose do these details serve? What point, if any, might they communicate to the reader?

2. Notice how Bosley uses her introduction and conclusion (about honey) to frame her essay. Is her framing technique effective? What are such a technique's effects on the reader? Can you think of any situations in which this framing technique would be ineffective?

3. Paragraphs 7 and 9 are very short—one sentence each. What effect does their brevity have on the reading of the essay? Why does she offer these particular ideas in one-sentence paragraphs?

4. How does Bosley develop her main idea—with narration (storytelling), description, or both? In what other ways does she develop it?

5. Identify at least one use of figurative language such as hyperbole, metaphor, understatement, or allusion and explain why it is effective.

Exploring Ideas

1. In a paragraph, explain what the honey means to Bosley. Include in your explanation how the honey comes to have the meaning for her that it does.

2. Revise the paragraph you wrote for #1 and share it with several classmates. Discuss the differences between your paragraphs.

3. How does Bosley's essay encourage the reader to think about everyday things, such as honey?

4. In what ways might you respond to Bosley's essay? What kinds of responses does it invite? List several possibilities and discuss them with your peers.

5. Talk to old friends and relatives and visit places from your past (a playground, old school, church, and so on). Through writing, explore the memories or emotions you experience.

For help inventing your own writing project, see the Point of Contact section on pp. 80–81.

❧ ❧ ❧

Dog-Tied

David Hawes

We are surrounded by interesting, complex, and puzzling relationships—which we rarely examine closely. In "Dog-Tied," David Hawes explores the relationship he has with his dog, Logan. His essay prompts the rest of us to consider similar relationships. Hawes's essay demonstrates the curious mind at work, looking not just from the owner's point of view but from the pet's as well.

I realize this is an odd paraphrase of the Beatles, but it certainly seems fitting: I have a dog, or should I say, my dog has me? Often it seems unclear which of us is in charge in this arrangement. As I once explained to a non-dog owner, "Logan and I have a symbiotic relationship: I feed him, walk him, bathe him, take him to the vet, give him his heartworm and flea-and-tick medicines, buy him treats, pet him, and play with him. And what does he do? He lets me." This past summer I even bought him a kiddie pool to lay in when he got too hot. He is, after all, a retriever, so he likes water. Not to mention that he has this hairy coat on all the time that he can't take off when he's too warm. Do I spoil him? Of course I do. Isn't that the whole point of having a dog?

On the other hand, I realize some people don't see things the way I do. Just this morning I saw a man walking his dog past the front of my house. In a loud and commanding voice he kept saying, "Heel! Heel!" Obviously he wanted his dog to make no mistake about who was in charge. However, I did notice that the man kept up his commands all the way down the street. Maybe the dog's name is "Heel." I think most people, though, have a tendency to spoil their dogs. Just go to any pet store and look at the vast array of foods, toys, beds, and treats, not to mention the shampoos and skin treatments.

It wasn't always this way, of course. Dogs were originally domesticated so they could help with the work. And some dogs are still workers, helping herd the sheep or bring in the cattle. But I have to believe these true "working dogs" are a small minority. I think most dogs these days, at least in this country, lead a fairly pampered life, so it certainly gives a different meaning to the old sayings about "a dog's life" and "working like a dog." Personally, I'd love to work as much as my dog does.

Sometimes, though, I have to wonder about him liking his pampered life. Sometimes when he's in a really deep sleep, his legs jerk violently, like he's running. Is he dreaming about retrieving ducks and quail? When fall comes, do those longing looks he gives me mean he's wondering when I'm going to get the shotgun out so he can do what he was bred to do? When he lies down with his head between his paws and heaves one of the heavy dog sighs, is he wishing he could be running through a field somewhere, sniffing out the game? Does he feel like something is missing from his life, but he's not sure what it is? And worst of all, does he blame me for what's missing?

5   I worry about these things sometimes, but not too much, I guess, because when I leave for work in the morning and he looks very sad, or when I get home from work and he wiggles all over the place in his happiness to see me, or when he comes into the bedroom and lies beside me first thing in the morning waiting for his wake-me-up belly rub, it seems like maybe this relationship is working out OK.

Writing Strategies

1. How does Hawes convey his main idea? Does he state it explicitly or imply it? Does he develop it through narration, description, explanation, or a combination of the three?
2. Hawes describes his relationship with Logan as "symbiotic." Is this a good word choice? Explain. If it is not, what one word would you use to describe their relationship?
3. Is Hawes's essay engaging—that is, do you as a reader become interested and want to read on? If so, carefully consider why. If not, why not?
4. If workshopping Hawes's essay, how would you answer the following questions: What is the essay's biggest strength? What is the essay's biggest weakness? What one recommendation would you make?
5. Write a new introduction and conclusion for Hawes's essay, and then compare it with one a classmate wrote. Discuss the different strategies you chose and the advantages and disadvantages of both.

Exploring Ideas

1. Describe the relationship between Hawes and his dog.
2. Describe the relationship you have with a dog, another pet, a stray or wild animal, or some other life form, such as your prize orchids, herb garden, and so on.
3. To further explore people's relationships with other life, interview at least five people about their relationship with any non-human life form.
   a. Begin by considering what you want to know. For example, you might ask them to describe the relationship in general, explain what they find rewarding about it, explain what they find frustrating about it, and so on. In groups or alone, compose several clear and purposeful questions that will encourage informative responses.
   b. Conduct the interviews, being certain to accurately record the responses. Then look for interesting ideas that help you to learn something new about people's relationships with other life. Write down the two or three most interesting ideas you discovered, and explain what you think is interesting about them.
4. How might you respond to Hawes's essay without writing about dogs or pets? What relationships can you use to illustrate your main idea?

For help inventing your own writing project, see the Point of Contact section on pp. 80–81.

■ ■ ■

Friend or Foe?

Dean A. Meek

In "Friend or Foe?" Dean Meek explores his relationship with alcohol and with addiction. Meek not only analyzes how his addiction began, how it ended, and how it impacted his life; by casting his addiction as a relationship, he helps us to open our minds and perhaps look at the broader subject—*addiction*—differently. As you read, notice how Meek provides relevant narrative details to shed light on the relationship.

As a boy growing up in suburban Indiana, I still remember the feelings of loneliness and alienation. I was always bigger than the other children in my class and they often made fun of my husky build. This was a feeling that I would carry with me through my teenage years, a feeling of not fitting in and being ashamed of the way I looked. However, this would all change once I was introduced to that great healer of all, the one thing that could right all wrongs and change my life forever. From the moment I took my first drink of alcohol, it was obvious we were meant to be together. We were akin to the likes of Steve Yzerman and Brendan Shanahan or Terry Bradshaw and Lynn Swann. Together we were unstoppable and feared nothing.

It all started on a lovely fall day my freshman year of high school. Although this day started no different than all the previous, it would drastically change all the days to come. Prior to school I was standing outside and was approached by Cool Jim. Cool Jim was a very popular kid in school; he was happy-go-lucky and very outgoing. He wasn't afraid of anyone or anything and really had a way with the ladies.

"Would you like to buy a bottle of wine?" said Cool Jim.

"No, I'm not into that," I replied, while leaning against the building and smoking a cigarette.

5   "That's cool," commented Jim as he made his way down the side of the school.

Finishing my smoke, I watched Jim stop and talk to all the people; he had so many friends. On the way to my first class, I still recall thinking to myself how lucky Cool Jim was to have so many friends and such self-esteem. "If I could only be more like him, life would be great!"

Later that morning, I passed Jim in the hall between periods.

"Still got that wine!" Jim said.

Before I could respond, a thought came over me: "If I want to be more like Jim, then maybe this is one way to get started."

10   "How much?" I replied.

"Five dollars, it's top shelf," said Jim.

"I'll take it!"

During lunch, I went for a walk with my newfound friend, a bottle of Mad Dog 20/20. As I opened that classy metal cap, it was as if I had transformed into manhood. At first the taste was quite bitter but the more I indulged, the better the flavor became. Walking back to school, my face seemed to become numb and that numbness continued throughout my entire body. "That's it!" I thought. This is what I had been searching for all my life. This new comrade of mine would shelter me from those unbearable feelings of loneliness and disgust.

That evening while lying in bed, I had a strange feeling come over me. In a matter of seconds it was obvious to me that my new friend would revisit me. In the bathroom praying at the porcelain altar, I somehow had the crazy notion this was all worthwhile. This physical pain was nothing compared to the emotional turmoil I endured. Kindly, I would trade an upset stomach for the feeling of fearlessness.

15   Through the years we stuck together and were completely inseparable. Occasionally we would find ourselves in a sticky situation but nonetheless we were best of friends.

Then came the day that would begin an unexpected metamorphosis. It was Sunday morning and I bowled on a league at 11:00 a.m. As with every Sunday, soon as the clock hit 12:00 noon, it was party time. The bar would start selling alcohol and more importantly, I would begin coming out of my shell. By the middle of the second game, I was back on top and feeling good. Sure, my bowling would suffer but who cares? It was just for fun and lots of it. Then after bowling, we headed into the bar and continued throwing down the suds. Shortly after that, I have no memory of what was to come.

The next morning as I opened my eyes, the glare of bright lights blinded me. The glare magnified the pounding in my head, which had become as certain as the rising of the morning sun. While rubbing my eyes, I noticed a shadow hanging over me. Startled by the image, I fought to gain my faculties. As my eyes began to focus, the image became clear. It was that of a rather large police officer. Overwhelmed by the fear and confusion of not knowing what had happened, I visually scanned the room for answers. I was in a hospital room and at the foot of my bed stood my parents: they were clearly upset and on edge. Placing her hand on my leg, Mom said: "Just relax. You are going to be all right." I tried to speak but could not. It felt as if my heart was pounding in my throat and I was trembling in fear. Then the officer said: "The charges are DUI and leaving the scene of an accident."

"DUI, for what?" I exclaimed.

"Just keep your mouth shut," replied my mother forcefully.

20 After the officer had left the room, my parents informed me that I had hit three cars in the parking lot of the bowling alley. Then, I had continued on to hit two more parked cars and a telephone pole: Thankfully no one was hurt. This was where the police and EMTs had found me. Furthermore, the 1965 Mustang that I had cherished was totaled and I was facing some very serious legal issues. "How could this be?" I thought. The one thing that had removed my emotional turbulence was now the cause of all this. Well, that thought was short-lived. Maybe I overdid it a little and needed to exercise some control, but quitting was definitely out of the question!

Several months had passed and I lay awake in bed suffering from an anxiety attack. Feelings of loneliness and disgust flowed through me like the Maumee River through Toledo, Ohio. How could I be lonely? After all, I had a wife and four daughters. How could anyone be lonely? Nevertheless, I was and the one true friend that could always be counted on was failing me. Those same emotions of that teenage schoolboy came rushing back. Where drinking once removed them, it now magnified those demons. I could run no more. Those emotions now compounded with alcoholism would be the end of me. I only had two choices left: I would either get help or commit suicide and there were no other options. Thankfully, I chose treatment and, with the help of my wife, was admitted to a program that same day.

That was a few 24 hours ago and life is much better today. That once shy high school boy has matured into a recovering alcoholic. After giving up the alcohol, I again faced those evil emotions but this time I faced them head-on. You see, nothing external could mend this torn soul. It had to be fixed internally. As for my old friend, he is now my foe. I see him around but only from a distance. Sometimes, I think he would like us to rekindle those burning desires we once shared but I refuse. As for those schoolboy feelings of loneliness and shamefulness, gratitude and pride have since replaced them and the yearning to be a part of the crowd is no more.

Writing Strategies

1. Describe Meek's voice, and identify several passages to support your description. How does his voice influence your response to the essay?
2. In your own words, write down what you think Meek's main idea is, and then discuss what you wrote down with several classmates. How were your understandings of the main idea similar or different?
3. Identify several passages in which Meek personifies (gives human characteristics to) his foe. What is the effect of these passages? How are they, or aren't they, successful?
4. How else might Meek have begun and ended his essay? Discuss different approaches with a group of classmates, considering the advantages and disadvantages of each.

Exploring Ideas

1. Briefly summarize Meek's relationship with alcohol, including how/why it began, the nature of the relationship, and its current status.
2. How does Meek's essay encourage the reader to think about alcohol?
3. What "friend or foe" relationships have you had or do you have? Consider, but do not limit yourself to, substances, activities, habits, people, thoughts, and so on. You might discover less-obvious relationships through discussion with relatives, friends, classmates, and co-workers, or by looking through personal belongings.
4. How might writing about one of your "friend or foe" relationships (#3) help you or others? What might be the consequence of such an essay?

For help inventing your own writing project, see the Point of Contact section on pp. 80–81.

Observing

Planting a Tree

Edward Abbey

Edward Abbey, author of *Desert Solitaire* (1968) and other books, is a careful observer. In "Planting a Tree," Abbey shares his observations *and* his insights. The observational details go beyond merely reporting. Instead, he analyzes his observations, and puts forth ideas about what they mean, or might mean.

My wife and I and my daughter live (for the moment) in a little house near the bright, doomed city of Tucson, Arizona. We like it here. Most of the time. Our backyard includes a portion of the Sonoran Desert, extending from here to the California border and down into Mexico. Mesquite trees grow nearby, enough to supply fuel for the Franklin stove when the nights are cold, enough to cook the occasional pork chop, or toast the tortilla, on the grill under the decaying Chinese elm.

Out back is the dry creekbed, full of sand, called a "wash" in this country, winding through the trees and cactus toward the Tucson Mountains five miles away. We'll climb those hills yet, maybe. Rattlesnakes live in the rocky grottoes along the wash. Sometimes they come to the house for a social call. We found one coiled on the Welcome mat by the front door Sunday evening. Our cat has disappeared.

There are still a few bands of javelina—wild semi-pigs—out there. They come by at night, driving the dogs into hysterics of outrage, which the javelinas ignore. Coyotes howl at us when they feel like it, usu-ally in the mornings and again around sundown, when I rile them some with my flute—they seem partial to "Green-sleeves," played on the upper register. We have an elf owl living in a hole in the big saguaro cactus by the driveway, and three pygmy owls, bobbing and weaving like box-ers, up in the palm at evening. There are packrats in the woodpile and scorpions under the bark of the logs; I usually find one when I'm splitting firewood.

So it's pretty nice here. We'd like to stay for a while, a lifetime or two, before trying something else. But we probably won't. We came down here from Utah four years ago, for practical reasons, now satisfied. We are free to leave whenever we wish.

5   The city remains at a comfortable distance. We hear the murmur of it by day, when the wind is from the east, and see its campfires glow by night—those dying embers. The police helicopters circle like fireflies above Tucson, Arizona, all night long, maintaining order. The homicide rate hangs steady at 3.2 per diem per 1,000,000, including lowriders, dope peddlers, and defenseless winos. All is well. Eighteen Titan missile bases ring the city, guarding us from their enemies. The life expectancy of the average Tucsonan, therefore, is thirty minutes—or whatever it takes for an ICBM to shuttle from there to here. Everything is A-OK. We sleep good.

Still, the city creeps closer, day by day. While the two great contemporary empires are dying—one in Afghanistan and Poland, the other in Vietnam, Iran, Nicaragua, El Salvador. And though I welcome their defeat, their pain and fear make them more dangerous than ever. Like mortally wounded tyrannosaurs, they thrash about in frenzy, seeking enemies, destroying thousands of innocent lives with each blind spasm of reaction. And still the city creeps closer. I find a correla-tion in these movements. I foresee the day when we shall be obliged to strike camp, once again.

Where to this time? Home to Utah? Back to Appa-lachia? On to Australia? Down the river of eternal recur-rence? It doesn't matter too much. There is no final escape, merely a series of tactical retreats, until we find the stone wall at our backs, bedrock beneath our feet.

Ah well, enough of this skulking rhetoric. Before we go we will plant a tree. I cleared away some ragweed yesterday, dug a thigh-deep hole this morning, and planted a young budding cottonwood this afternoon. We soaked the hole with well water, mixed in the peat moss and the carefully set-aside topsoil, and lowered the root ball of the sapling into its new home. The tree shiv-ered as I packed the earth around its base. A shiver of pleasure. A good omen. A few weeks of warm weather and the little green leaves will be trembling in the sun-light. A few good years and the tree will be shading the front porch and then the roof of the house. If the house is still here. If someone, or something, as I hope, is still enjoying this house, this place, this garden of rock and sand and paloverde, of sunshine and delight.

We ourselves may never see this cottonwood reach maturity, probably will never take pleasure in its shade or birds or witness the pale gold of its autumn leaves. But somebody will. Something will. In fifty years Tucson will have shrunk back to what it once was, a town of adobe huts by the trickling Santa Cruz, a happier place than it is now, and our tree will be here, with or without us. In that anticipation I find satisfaction enough.

Writing Strategies

1. How does Abbey convey his main idea? Does he state it explicitly or imply it? In your own words, write a thesis statement (a statement of the main idea) for "Planting a Tree."
2. Notice Abbey's use of concrete language ("Tucson, Arizona"; "mesquite trees"; "Franklin stove"; "pork chop"; "tortilla"; "decaying Chinese elm"). Identify specific language that you found to be effective or ineffective in his essay. Explain why you think the specific language did or did not work.
3. Abbey describes his own rhetoric as "skulking." What does he mean? What, if anything, does the writer's own commentary about his rhetoric tell you about the writer?
4. Abbey uses figurative language throughout his essay; for example, he compares the city lights to campfires glowing and police helicopters to fireflies. How are these comparisons consistent with the overall content and tone of "Planting a Tree"?

Exploring Ideas

1. In one paragraph, summarize what Abbey is saying in this essay.
2. How is the way that you see "the city" similar to or different from the way Abbey sees it?
3. How is the way you see "planting a tree" similar to or different from the way Abbey sees it?
4. What does your response to this essay tell you about the way you see things? That is, whether you agree with Abbey, disagree, or have some other response, what does that response tell you about your own outlook on the world?

For help inventing your own writing project, see the Point of Contact section on pp. 114–115.

■ ■ ■

Gombe

Jane Goodall

Jane Goodall is known for her pioneering work in primatology—the study of primates. She has written a number of books about her experiences with chimpanzees; "Gombe" was originally published in *Through a Window* (1990). Goodall, like other writers in this section, carefully selects certain details to help the reader understand the larger point of her essay. As you read, notice how Goodall's description of the chimpanzees paves the way for general points that she will make in the essay's last seven paragraphs.

I rolled over and looked at the time—5.44 a.m. Long years of early rising have led to an ability to wake just before the unpleasant clamour of an alarm clock. Soon I was sitting on the steps of my house looking out over Lake Tanganyika. The waning moon, in her last quarter, was suspended above the horizon, where the mountainous shoreline of Zaire fringed Lake Tanganyika. It was a still night, and the moon's path danced and sparkled towards me across the gently moving water. My breakfast—a banana and a cup of coffee from the thermos flask—was soon finished, and ten minutes later I was climbing the steep slope behind the house, my miniature binoculars and camera stuffed into my pockets along with notebook, pencil stubs, a handful of raisins for my lunch, and plastic bags in which to put everything should it rain. The faint light from the moon, shining on the dew-laden grass, enabled me to find my way without difficulty and presently I arrived at the place where, the evening before, I had watched eighteen chimpanzees settle down for the night. I sat to wait until they woke.

All around, the trees were still shrouded with the last mysteries of the night's dreaming. It was very quiet, utterly peaceful. The only sounds were the occasional chirp of a cricket, and the soft murmur where the lake caressed the shingle, way below. As I sat there I felt the expectant thrill that, for me, always precedes a day with the chimpanzees, a day roaming the forests and mountains of Gombe, a day of new discoveries, new insights.

Then came a sudden burst of song, the duet of a pair of robin chats, hauntingly beautiful. I realized that the intensity of light had changed: dawn had crept upon me unawares. The coming brightness of the sun had all but vanquished the silvery, indefinite illumination of its own radiance reflected by the moon. The chimpanzees still slept.

Five minutes later came a rustling of leaves above. I looked up and saw branches moving against the lightening sky. That was where Goblin, top-ranking male of the community, had made his nest. Then stillness again. He must have turned over, then settled down for a last snooze. Soon after this there was movement from another nest to my right, then from one behind me, further up the slope. Rustlings of leaves, the cracking of a little twig. The group was waking up. Peering through my binoculars into the tree where Fifi had made a nest for herself and her infant Flossi, I saw the silhouette of her foot. A moment later Fanni, her eight-year-old daughter, climbed up from her nest nearby and sat just above her mother, a small dark shape against the sky. Fifi's other two offspring, adult Freud and adolescent Frodo, had nested further up the slope.

5   Nine minutes after he had first moved, Goblin abruptly sat up and, almost at once, left his nest and began to leap wildly through the tree, vigorously swaying the branches. Instant pandemonium broke out. The chimpanzees closest to Goblin left their nests and rushed out of his way. Others sat up to watch, tense and ready for flight. The early morning peace was shattered by frenzied grunts and screams as Goblin's subordinates voiced their respect or fear. A few moments later, the arboreal part of his display over, Goblin leapt down and charged past me, slapping and stamping on the wet ground, rearing up and shaking the vegetation, picking up and hurling a rock, an old piece of wood, another rock. Then he sat, hair bristling, some fifteen feet away. He was breathing heavily. My own heart was beating fast. As he swung down, I had stood up and held onto a tree, praying that he would not pound on me as he sometimes does. But, to my relief, he had ignored me, and I sat down again.

With soft, panting grunts Goblin's young brother Gimble climbed down and came to greet the alpha or top-ranking male, touching his face with his lips. Then, as another adult male approached Goblin, Gimble moved hastily out of the way. This was my old friend Evered. As he approached, with loud, submissive grunts, Goblin slowly raised one arm in salutation and Evered rushed forward. The two males embraced, grinning widely in the excitement of this morning reunion so that their teeth flashed white in the semi-darkness. For a few moments they groomed each other and then, calmed, Evered moved away and sat quietly nearby.

The only other adult who climbed down then was Fifi, with Flossi clinging to her belly. She avoided Goblin, but approached Evered, grunting softly, reached out her hand and touched his arm. Then she began to groom him. Flossi climbed into Evered's lap and looked up into his face. He glanced at her, groomed her head intently for a few moments, then turned to reciprocate Fifi's attentions. Flossi moved halfway towards where Goblin sat—but his hair was still bristling, and she thought better of it and, instead, climbed a tree near Fifi. Soon she began to play with Fanni, her sister.

Once again peace returned to the morning, though not the silence of dawn. Up in the trees the other chimpanzees of the group were moving about, getting ready for the new day. Some began to feed, and I heard the occasional soft thud as skins and seeds of figs were dropped to the ground. I sat, utterly content to be back at Gombe after an unusually long time away—almost three months of lectures, meetings, and lobbying in the USA and Europe. This would be my first day with the chimps and I planned to enjoy it to the full, just getting reacquainted with my old friends, taking pictures, getting my climbing legs back.

It was Evered who led off, thirty minutes later, twice pausing and looking back to make sure that Goblin was coming too. Fifi followed, Flossi perched on her back like a small jockey, Fanni close behind. Now the other chimps climbed down and wandered after us. Freud and Frodo, adult males Atlas and Beethoven, the magnificent adolescent Wilkie, and two females, Patti and Kidevu, with their infants. There were others, but they were travelling higher up the slope, and I didn't see them then. We headed north, parallel with the beach below, then plunged down into Kasakela Valley and, with frequent pauses for feeding, made our way up the opposite slope. The eastern sky grew bright, but not until 8.30 a.m. did the sun itself finally peep over the peaks of the rift escarpment. By this time we were high above the lake. The chimpanzees stopped and groomed for a while, enjoying the warmth of the morning sunshine.

10   About twenty minutes later there was a sudden outbreak of chimpanzee calls ahead—a mixture of pant-hoots, as we call the loud distance calls, and screams. I could hear the distinctive voice of the large, sterile female Gigi among a medley of females and youngsters. Goblin and Evered stopped grooming and all the chimps stared towards the sounds. Then, with Goblin now in the lead, most of the group moved off in that direction.

Fifi, however, stayed behind and continued to groom Fanni while Flossi played by herself, dangling from a low branch near her mother and elder sister. I decided to stay too, delighted that Frodo had moved on with the others for he so often pesters me. He wants me to play, and, because I will not, he becomes aggressive. At twelve years of age he is much stronger than I am, and this behavior is dangerous. Once he stamped so hard on my head that my neck was nearly broken. And on another occasion he pushed me down a steep slope. I can only hope that, as he matures and leaves childhood behind him, he will grow out of these irritating habits.

I spent the rest of the morning wandering peacefully with Fifi and her daughters, moving from one food tree to the next. The chimps fed on several different kinds of fruit and once on some young shoots. For about forty-five minutes they pulled apart the leaves of low shrubs which had been rolled into tubes held closely by sticky threads, then munched on the caterpillars that wriggled inside. Once we passed another female—Gremlin and her infant, little Galahad. Fanni and Flossi ran over to greet them, but Fifi barely glanced in their direction.

All the time we were climbing higher and higher. Presently, on an open grassy ridge we came upon another small group of chimps: the adult male Prof, his young brother Pax, and two rather shy females with their infants. They were feeding on the leaves of a massive *mbula* tree. There were a few quiet grunts of greeting as Fifi and her youngsters joined the group, then they also began to feed. Presently the others moved on, Fanni with them. But Fifi made herself a nest and stretched out for a midday siesta. Flossi stayed too, climbing about, swinging, amusing herself near her mother. And then she joined Fifi in her nest, lay close and suckled.

From where I sat, below Fifi, I could look out over the Kasakela Valley. Opposite, to the south, was the Peak. A surge of warm memories flooded through me as I saw it, a rounded shoulder perched above the long grassy ridge that separates Kasakela from the home valley, Kakombe. In the early days of the study at Gombe, in 1960 and 1961, I had spent day after day watching the chimpanzees, through my binoculars, from the superb vantage point. I had taken a little tin trunk up to the Peak, with a kettle, some coffee and sugar, and a blanket. Sometimes, when the chimps had slept nearby, I had stayed up there with them, wrapped in my blanket against the chill of the night air. Gradually I had pieced together something of their daily life, learned about their feeding habits and travel routes, and begun to understand their unique social structure—small groups joining to form larger ones, large groups splitting into smaller ones, single chimpanzees roaming, for a while, on their own.

15   From the Peak I had seen, for the first time, a chimpanzee eating meat: David Greybeard. I had watched him leap up into a tree clutching the carcass of an infant bushpig, which he shared with a female while the adult pigs charged about below. And only about a hundred yards from the Peak, on a never-to-be-forgotten day in October, 1960, I had watched David Greybeard, along with his close friend Goliath, fishing for termites with stems of grass. Thinking back to that far-off time I relived the thrill I had felt when I saw David reach out, pick a wide blade of grass and trim it carefully so that it could more easily be poked into the narrow passage in the termite mound. Not only was he using the grass as a tool—he was, by modifying it to suit a special purpose, actually showing the crude beginnings of tool-*making*. What excited telegrams I had sent off to Louis Leakey, that far-sighted genius who had instigated the research at Gombe. Humans were not, after all, the *only* tool-making animals. Nor were chimpanzees the placid vegetarians that people had supposed.

That was just after my mother, Vanne, had left to return to her other responsibilities in England. During her four-month stay she had made an invaluable contribution to the success of the project: she had set up a clinic—four poles and a thatched roof—where she had provided medicines to the local people, mostly fish-

Bettman/CORBIS

taken them off to eat in the bush. Once he had discovered bananas he had returned for more and gradually other chimpanzees had followed him to my camp.

One of the females who became a regular visitor in 1963 was Fifi's mother, old Flo of the ragged ears and bulbous nose. What an exciting day when, after five years of maternal preoccupation with her infant daughter, Flo had become sexually attractive again. Flaunting her shell-pink sexual swelling she had attracted a whole retinue of suitors. Many of them had never been to camp, but they had followed Flo there, sexual passions overriding natural caution. And, once they had discovered bananas, they had joined the rapidly growing group of regular camp visitors. And so I had become more and more familiar with the whole host of unforgettable chimpanzee characters who are described in my first book, *In the Shadow of Man.*

20 Fifi, lying so peacefully above me now, was one of the few survivors of those early days. She had been an infant when first I knew her in 1961. She had weathered the terrible polio epidemic that had swept through the population—chimpanzee and human alike—in 1966. Ten of the chimpanzees of the study group had died or vanished. Another five had been crippled, including her eldest brother, Faben, who had lost the use of one arm.

At the time of that epidemic the Gombe Stream Research Centre was in its infancy. The first two research assistants were helping to collect and type out notes on chimp behavior. Some twenty-five chimpanzees were regularly visiting camp by then, and so there had been more than enough work for all of us. After watching the chimps all day we had often transcribed notes from our tape recorders until late at night.

My mother Vanne had made two other visits to Gombe during the sixties. One of those had been when the National Geographic Society sent Hugo van Lawick to film the study—which, by then, they were financing. Louis Leakey had wangled Vanne's fare and expenses, insisting that it would not be right for me to be alone in the bush with a young man. How different the moral standards of a quarter of a century ago! Hugo and I had married anyway, and Vanne's third visit, in 1967, had been to share with me, for a couple of months, the task of raising my son, Grub (his real name is Hugo Eric Louis) in the bush.

ermen and their families. Although her remedies had been simple—aspirin, Epsom salts, iodine, Band-Aids and so on—her concern and patience had been unlimited, and her cures often worked. Much later we learned that many people had thought that she possessed magic powers for healing. Thus she had secured for me the goodwill of the local human population.

Above me, Fifi stirred, cradling little Flossi more comfortably as she suckled. Then her eyes closed again. The infant nursed for a few more minutes, then the nipple slipped from her mouth as she too slept. I continued to daydream, re-living in my mind some of the more memorable events of the past.

I remembered the day when David Greybeard had first visited my camp by the lakeshore. He had come to feed on the ripe fruits of an oil-nut palm that grew there, spied some bananas on the table outside my tent, and richly deserved rewards, whatever the occasion. It takes an enormous amount of energy to maintain the kind of denial necessary to protect an alcoholic from his or her self-loathing. It is so painful to face the deep belief that one is worthless, unlovable, that many alcoholics, especially male alcoholics, seek refuge in grandiosity—which is, after all, a form of self-hatred. The alcohol advertisers know this—and play on it in ad after ad.

Finally, what is addiction if not a *desire for more connection*? Unfortunately, it is a connection that makes human connection and real intimacy difficult, if not impossible. "More . . . more . . . more . . . gin taste," one ad declares. More gin taste simply means more gin, of course. "More" is even the name of a cigarette brand. "Absolut Attraction," says an ad featuring a cocktail glass leaning toward a bottle of vodka. People are not even present and yet the ad still implies a promise of greater connection.

Most often, the intimate connection that the alcohol ads offer is a sexual experience. Countless ads feature couples passionately embracing with suggestive copy such as, "May all your screwdrivers be Harvey Wallbangers," "Wild things happen in the 'oui' hours," and, "Is it proper to Boodle before the guests arrive?" "If the French can do this with a kiss . . . ," asks an ad featuring a man passionately kissing a woman's neck, "imagine what they can do with a vodka!" Given that the vodka is called Grey Goose, I hate to think.

35   Of course, alcohol has long been advertised to men as a way to seduce women. An ad for Cherry Kijafa from the 1970s features a virginal young woman dressed entirely in white and the headline "Put a little cherry in your life." Such double entendres abound, ranging from a cocktail called "Sex on the Beach" to an ad featuring a young man dressed as a fencer declaring, "I'm as sure of myself on each thrust as I am when choosing my scotch." In a series of suggestive print and television ads in the 1980s, Billy Dee Williams promised that Colt 45 malt liquor "works every time." Years later a radio ad, also for malt liquor and also targeting young African-American men, said, "Grab a six-pack and get your girl in the mood quicker. Get your jimmy thicker with St. Ides malt liquor." Imagine—our kids are growing up in this kind of environment and some people think it's enough

to tell them to "just say no" to sex. "Get your jimmy thicker" but keep it in your pants?

An extremely erotic 1999 ad for Kahlua pictures a milkmaid lasciviously pouring milk all over her leg. Her head is tossed back and her eyes closed, as if she were in the throes of orgasm. The goosebumps on her leg are obvious as is the erect state of her exposed nipple. "Anything goes" is the tagline.

Using sex to sell alcohol certainly isn't new. What is new in recent years is the promise in alcohol ads of a sexual relationship with the alcohol itself. No longer a means to an end, the drink has become the end. "You never forget your first girl" is the slogan for St. Pauli Girl's beer. "Just one sip of St. Pauli Girl's rich, imported taste is the start of a beautiful relationship." "Pilsner is a type of beer," says an ad featuring a beautiful young woman, "kind of like Rebecca is a type of woman." The ad concludes that it would be great to meet either one in a bar.

"Six Appeal" is the slogan for an ad that features a six-pack of beer and the copy, "The next time you make eye contact with a six-pack of Cold-Filtered Miller Genuine Draft Longnecks, go ahead and pick one up. You won't be disappointed!" In a 1998 Bud commercial, a group of women are standing in a bar and, nodding toward some leering guys, talk about how men think about "it" every eight seconds. But it turns out that the guys are ogling bottles of Bud. An Absolut ad features the top part of a woman's leg clad in a black silk stocking with a garter in the familiar shape of the Absolut bottle. This focus on one part of the female body, this dismemberment, is common in ads for many products, but especially so for alcohol. The image draws men in, but there is no person, not even a whole body to distract them from the focus of the ad, the bottle.

Women are increasingly encouraged to think of the bottle as a lover too. "If your man won't pour, I will," says an ad for cognac which features the bottle rakishly leaning toward the woman. Another ad pictures a bottle of whisky in a drawstring pouch with the tagline "Smooth operator." In an ad for an Italian wine called Florio, a beautiful and sultry woman says, "For 15 nights I have been with Florio. Never once was it the same." This reminds me of a joke I used to make about my drinking years—that perhaps I had had the same conversation every night over and over again and just didn't know it!

40 In the early 1980s Campari ran a series of ads featuring celebrities such as Geraldine Chaplin and Jill St. John talking lasciviously about their "first time." "There are so many different ways to enjoy it," Chaplin says. "Once I even tried it on the rocks. But I wouldn't recommend that for beginners." The sophomoric campaign used the slogans, "The first time is never the best," and, "You'll never forget your first time." One of the ironies of this campaign is that alcoholics usually do remember their first drink and often romanticize it. For this reason, there's a saying among alcoholics that we should remember our last drunk, not our first drink.

A rawer version of the sexualization of the product was a campaign for the subtly named Two Fingers tequila. Every ad in the campaign featured an older man caressing a beautiful younger woman and saying such things as, "This woman, she is like my tequila. Smooth, but with a lot of spirit," and, "Señor, making good tequila is like looking for a good woman." One of the ads further describes the woman as "the only other love Two Fingers had besides his tequila." Given their age difference, it seems that Two Fingers spent most of his life in love with tequila.

A strange campaign for Hiram Walker liqueurs personifies the product in a series of ads. In one a beautiful young woman says, "Hiram Walker knows the way to Kokomo." She continues, "He took me there late last night. I hadn't packed a bag. But he said all I needed was the right attitude." Another ad in the campaign features a fairly distraught young man saying, "Who is this Hiram Walker guy anyway?" He goes on to say, "My girlfriend couldn't stop talking about him. 'He's spirited . . . and sophisticated . . . and fun. Everything a man should be!' I said, 'Listen, it's him or me. Make up your mind.' She said, 'I want you both.'" The young man ends up having some Hiram Walker, saying, "If you can't beat him, join him." Sadly, this is an attitude many people adopt when dealing with alcoholics.

In this case, the man is introduced to the drink by the woman. Usually, in life and advertising, it is the other way around. Women and girls are usually introduced to alcohol and other drugs by their boyfriends, who generally are older and more experienced. Women often use the drugs to please their men, to have a common activity, or simply to make the relationship bearable.

The advertisers sometimes encourage women to drink in order to keep company with drinking men. "Share the secret of Cristal," says a beautiful woman. The copy continues, "The Columbians kept it to themselves. Men mostly drank it straight. I thought it was pretty tough stuff 'til the night I met him in Miami and he persuaded me to try CRISTAL & O.J. on ice. Very nice!" Often, as in this ad, the man is urged to drink the product straight while the woman is encouraged to cut it with juice, orange juice in this case, or soda (a more "feminine" approach).

45 The increasing sexualization of alcohol in ads parallels the progression of the disease of alcoholism, in which alcohol plays a more and more important role. Alcohol is used initially by many people as an attempt to increase confidence, especially sexual confidence, and for some a drink or two can lead to greater relaxation and less inhibition (although intoxication usually reduces sexual responsiveness). For the alcoholic, however, alcohol eventually becomes the most important thing in life and makes other relationships, including sexual relationships, more difficult, if not impossible. Thus, the ads move from a soft-core promise of sexual adventure and fulfillment with a partner to a more hard-core guarantee of sexual fulfillment without the trouble of a relationship with a human being. Alcohol becomes the beloved. And when alcohol is the beloved, relationships with people—with lovers, children, friends—suffer terribly.

One of the most chilling commercials I've ever seen is a 1999 one for Michelob. It opens with an African-American man and woman in bed, clearly just after making love. A fire is blazing and romantic music is playing. "Baby, do you love me?" the woman asks. "Of course I do," the man replies. "What do you love about me most?" she asks. The man looks thoughtful, "Well, Michelob, I love you more than life itself." "What did you call me?" the woman asks indignantly. "I called you Theresa," he replies. "No, you did not," she says, leaping from the bed. "You just called me Michelob. I'm outta here." "Wait, wait," the man says. "What?" she asks. "While you're up," the man says, "could you get me a Michelob?" On the surface, this commercial is intended to be funny, of course. But on a deeper level, and I believe intentionally

2. Kilbourne says, "As always, the mythology presented in the alcohol ads is exactly the opposite of the truth about alcohol." (¶ 24) According to Kilbourne, why can this strategy be successful?

3. Write down one statement Kilbourne makes that you disagree with. Then explore the statement further (through research, invention writing, and discussion with others), trying to change your own thinking about it.

4. What picture does Kilbourne paint of advertising?

For help inventing your own writing project, see the Point of Contact section on pp. 186–187.

■ ■ ■

Cartoons 'n Comics: Communication to the Quick

Joy Clough

Like any art form or highly publicized text, a comic strip is far more than meets the (untrained) eye. It is a complex form of communication, with a set of conventions and a shared history. The comic strip artists practice a particular set of rhetorical tools—different tools than we might see or use for academic writing. In the following essay, Joy Clough, president of the Chicago Community of the Sisters of Mercy of the Americas, explains how comics appeal to readers by connecting with human psychology and the particular culture of the times.

The comics. They may be worth a glance as you check your horoscope. They may provide a chuckle as you sip your morning coffee. But seriously? You can't take the comics seriously!

Au contraire. The comics are taken quite seriously—by fans whose complaints deluge any newspaper that dares cancel a strip, by semi-literate adults who can find in them a sort of pictographic "Ann Landers," and certainly by historians and analysts of popular culture who regard the "funnies" as a revelatory aspect of cultural history.

The comics, say these experts, offer a cross-section of human psychology and capture significant snatches of American life and mores.

The Comics as History

A look at the evolution of the comic strip shows how the "funnies," in their own way, record history. The "Yellow Kid," born in 1895 in the *New York World,* is generally accepted as the first comic character. A violent, gangster-talking figure, the Kid would probably be banned from today's papers. His comments and struggles, however, echoed reality for the city's slum dwellers. Though the Kid died, comics, with their solid psychological appeal, were here to stay.

5 By the Roaring Twenties, such still-familiar strips as "Mutt and Jeff" and "Gasoline Alley" were populating newspaper pages. "Gasoline Alley" made comic strip history by introducing realism and allowing its characters to age. In keeping with the decade, some strips incorporated the emancipated woman. "Nancy," "Winnie Winkle," and "Blondie" (a high-fashion model) were all born in this era.

The Crash and the troubled '30s saw the rise of action comic strips. "Dick Tracy," "Terry and the Pirates," and "Buck Rogers" could take charge and set things right.

With the war in Europe spreading to the U.S., the 1940s became the decade of the comic strip superhero. Welcome "Superman" and "Wonder Woman," both vigorous fighters in the Allied cause. The comics stepped out of newspapers into books of their own with the creation of additional heroes: Batman, Captain Marvel, the Green Lantern.

The 1950s, by and large, grew reflective. Comment could be humorous or biting. "Li'l Abner" grew in popularity. "Pogo" and "Peanuts" offered observations on politics and life. The humorous side of the daily lives of ordinary mortals became the subject of such strips as "Dennis the Menace" and "Beetle Bailey."

If the '60s were an era of protest and questioning, the comics felt the mood. As "Doonesbury" was born, superheroes went into a sharp decline. The self-doubting and reluctant Peter Parker (alias Spiderman) is one of the few superheroes of recent vintage.

The Comic Appeal

10 Old-timer or newcomer, the comic strips apparently owe their ongoing appeal to solid psychology. They mirror human life and respond to the human

spirit. When life is bleak, a laugh can help. When life is dull, adventure spells relief. When life seems stupid, humor-become-satire makes its point. When life is lonely, romance provides connections.

These are, in fact, the four major responses the comics offer. Humor strips like "Momma," "Marmaduke," "Hi and Lois," "Hagar," and "For Better or For Worse" allow us to laugh at life's petty but persistent frustrations.

Adventure series like "Steve Canyon," "The Amazing Spiderman," and the perennial "Dick Tracy" and "Superman" spin stories that keep us wondering (but not worrying) about what will happen next.

Comment comics, including "Doonesbury" and "Peanuts," strike with satire at political, social, or human pretensions.

Romance or soap opera strips like "Mary Worth," "Brenda Starr," and "Dondi" provide a cast of caring characters with which to people our private worlds.

15 This unique media form has marched out of the "funny papers" to an expanded social role: to educate and irritate, tickle and tease, inform and reform.

The comics' universal appeal to the human psyche is strengthened by their universal distribution. Long before television or radio provided cross-country communication links, comic strip characters were known nationally.

They were fantasy figures inciting the imagination. They were mythic heroes proving in varied situations that right overcomes might. They were storybook characters authorized for adults, reflections of daily life, witty crusaders in a variety of causes, 20th-century successors to the likes of King Arthur and Robin Hood.

An American Art Form

Such literary connections come naturally to the comics, which, as an art form indigenous to America, have verbal as well as visual components. No serious discussion of the "funnies" can proceed far without including words like satire, allegory, fable, personification, comedy (in the classical sense), myth, pun, allusion. All these aspects of literary art exist in the comic strip.

However, it is primarily as a visual art form that the comics have made their contribution. They borrowed and refined the tools of the political cartoonist. Before movies were commonplace or television was conceived,

Robert Crumb/The Everett Collection

comic strips were the storyboards from which later script writers would learn.

20 Panel by panel, they set the scene, introduced the characters, unfolded the action. Comic artists taught movie serial makers how to build to a climax and bring the audience back next week.

The strips developed their own "language" or signals: word balloons indicated dialog; sentences strung across a frame suggested narration; and the very way words were printed "produced" sound effects! Any wonder, then, that comic strips have spawned television series and vice versa?

In the enriching mix of today's media, comic strip characters continue to command considerable attention. They entertain us, exercise our fantasy, and reflect wryly on the way life is. They are multiplying. They are leaping off the pages of our papers to live on our movie screens.

In doing so, they continue, like living beings, to adapt to the times. Popeye has proved capable of touching several million Gypsies, Poles, Slavs, homosexuals, and other *untermenschen* (subhumans).

The sole offense for which the accused was ordered put to death was in having served as publisher/editor of a Bavarian tabloid entitled *Der Sturmer* during the early to mid-1930s, years before the Nazi genocide actually began. In this capacity, he had penned a long series of virulently anti-Semitic editorials and "news."

15   Stories, usually accompanied by cartoons and other images, graphically depicted Jews in extraordinarily derogatory fashion. This, the prosecution asserted, had done much to "dehumanize" the targets of his distortion in the mind of the German public. In turn, such dehumanization had made it possible—or at least easier—for average Germans to later indulge in the outright liquidation of Jewish "vermin." The tribunal agreed, holding that Streicher was therefore complicit in genocide and deserving of death by hanging.

During his remarks to the Nuremberg tribunal, Justice Jackson observed that, in implementing its sentences, the participating powers were morally and legally binding themselves to adhere forever after to the same standards of conduct that were being applied to Streicher and the other Nazi leaders. In the alternative, he said, the victorious allies would have committed "pure murder" at Nuremberg—no different in substance from that carried out by those they presumed to judge—rather than establishing the "permanent benchmark for justice" which was intended.

Yet in the United States of Robert Jackson, the indigenous American Indian population had already been reduced, in a process which is ongoing to this day, from perhaps 12.5 million in the year 1500 to fewer than 250,000 by the beginning of the 20th century. This was accomplished, according to official sources, "largely through the cruelty of Euro American settlers," and an informal but clear governmental policy which had made it an articulated goal to "exterminate these red vermin" or at least whole segments of them.

Bounties had been placed on the scalps of Indians—any Indians—in places as diverse as Georgia, Kentucky, Texas, the Dakotas, Oregon, and California and had been maintained until resident Indian populations were decimated or disappeared altogether. Entire peoples such as the Cherokee had been reduced to half

their size through a policy of forced removal from their homelands east of the Mississippi River to what were then considered less preferable areas in the West.

Others, such as the Navajo, suffered the same fate while under military guard for years on end. The United States Army had also perpetrated a long series of wholesale massacres of Indians at places like Horseshoe Bend, Bear River, Sand Creek, the Washita River, the Marias River, Camp Robinson, and Wounded Knee.

20   Through it all, hundreds of popular novels—each competing with the next to make Indians appear more grotesque, menacing, and inhuman—were sold in the tens of millions of copies in the U.S. Plainly, the Euro American public was being conditioned to see Indians in such a way so as to allow their eradication to continue. And continue it did until the Manifest Destiny of the U.S.—a direct precursor to what Hitler would subsequently call *Lebensraumpolitik* (the politics of living space)—was consummated.

By 1900, the national project of "clearing" Native Americans from their land and replacing them with "superior" Anglo American settlers was complete; the indigenous population had been reduced by as much as 98 percent while approximately 97.5 percent of their original territory had "passed" to the invaders. The survivors had been concentrated, out of sight and mind of the public, on scattered "reservations," all of them under the self-assigned "plenary" (full) power of the federal government. There was, of course, no Nuremberg-style tribunal passing judgment on those who had fostered such circumstances in North America. No U.S. official or private citizen was ever imprisoned—never mind hanged—for implementing or propagandizing what had been done. Nor had the process of genocide afflicting Indians been completed. Instead, it merely changed form.

Between the 1880s and the 1980s, nearly half of all Native American children were coercively transferred from their own families, communities, and cultures to those of the conquering society. This was done through compulsory attendance at remote boarding schools, often hundreds of miles from their homes, where native children were kept for years on end while being systematically "deculturated" (indoctrinated to think and act in the manner of Euro Americans rather than as Indians). It was also accomplished through a pervasive foster home and adoption program—including blind adoptions, where children would be permanently denied information as to who they were/are and where they'd come from—placing native youths in non-Indian homes.

The express purpose of all this was to facilitate a U.S. governmental policy to bring about the "assimilation" (dissolution) of indigenous societies. In other words, Indian cultures as such were to be caused to disappear. Such policy objectives are directly contrary to the United Nations 1948 Convention on Punishment and Prevention of the Crime of Genocide, an element of international law arising from the Nuremberg proceedings. The forced "transfer of the children" of a targeted "racial, ethnical, or religious group" is explicitly prohibited as a genocidal activity under the Convention's second article.

Article II of the Genocide Convention also expressly prohibits involuntary sterilization as a means of "preventing births among" a targeted population. Yet, in 1975, it was conceded by the U.S. government that its Indian Health Service (IHS), then a subpart of the Bureau of Indian Affairs (BIA), was even then conducting a secret program of involuntary sterilization that had affected approximately 40 percent of all Indian women.

The program was allegedly discontinued, and the IHS was transferred to the Public Health Service, but no one was punished. In 1990, it came out that the IHS was inoculating Inuit children in Alaska with Hepatitis-B vaccine. The vaccine had already been banned by the World Health Organization as having demonstrated a correlation with the HIV syndrome, which is itself correlated to AIDS. As this is written [March 1993], a "field test" of Hepatitis-A vaccine, also HIV-correlated, is being conducted on Indian reservations in the northern plains region.

25   The Genocide Convention makes it a crime against "humanity" to create conditions leading to the destruction of an identifiable human group, as such. Yet the BIA has utilized the government's plenary prerogatives to negotiate mineral leases "on behalf of" Indian peoples paying a fraction of standard royalty rates. The result has been "super profits" for a number of preferred U.S. corporations. Meanwhile, Indians, whose reservations ironically turned out to be in some of the most mineral-rich areas of North America, which makes us the nominally wealthiest segment of the continent's population, live in dire poverty.

Library of Congress

By the government's own data in the mid-1980s, Indians received the lowest annual and lifetime per capita incomes of any aggregate population group in the United States. Concomitantly, we suffer the highest rate of infant mortality, death by exposure and malnutrition, disease, and the like. Under such circumstances, alcoholism and other escapist forms of substance abuse are endemic in the Indian community, a situation which leads both to a general physical debilitation of the population and a catastrophic accident rate. Teen suicide among Indians is several times the national average.

The average life expectancy of a reservation-based Native American man is barely 45 years; women can expect to live less than three years longer.

Such itemizations could be continued at great length, including matters like the radioactive contamination of large portions of contemporary Indian Country, the forced relocation of traditional Navajos, and so on. But the point should be made: Genocide, as defined in international law, is a continuing fact of day-to-day life (and death) for North America's native peoples. Yet there has been—and is—only the barest flicker of public concern about or even consciousness of, this reality. Absent any serious expression of public outrage, no one is punished and the process continues.

A salient reason for public acquiescence before the ongoing holocaust in Native North America has been a continuation of the popular legacy, often through more effective media. Since 1925, Hollywood has released more than 2,000 films, many of them rerun frequently on television, portraying Indians as strange, perverted, ridiculous, and often dangerous things of the past. Moreover, we are habitually presented to mass audiences one-dimensionally, devoid of recognizable human motivations and emotions: Indians thus serve as props, little more. We have thus been thoroughly and systematically dehumanized.

30   Nor is this the extent of it. Everywhere we are used as logos, as mascots, as jokes: "Big Chief" writing tablets, "Red Man" chewing tobacco, "Winnebago" campers, "Navajo" and "Cherokee" and "Pontiac" and "Cadillac" pickups and automobiles. There are the Cleveland "Indians," the Kansas City "Chiefs," the Atlanta "Braves," and the Washington "Redskins" professional sports teams—not to mention those in thousands of colleges,

high schools, and elementary schools across the country, each with their own degrading caricatures and parodies of Indians and/or things Indian. Pop fiction continues in the same vein, including an unending stream of New Age manuals purporting to expose the inner works of indigenous spirituality in everything from pseudo-philosophical to do-it-yourself styles. Blond yuppies from Beverly Hills amble about the country claiming to be reincarnated 17th-century Cheyenne Ushamans ready to perform previously secret ceremonies.

In effect, a concerted, sustained, and in some ways accelerating effort has gone into making Indians unreal. It is thus of obvious importance that the American public begin to think about the implications of such things the next time they witness a gaggle of face-painted and war-bonneted buffoons doing the "Tomahawk Chop" at a baseball or football game. It is necessary that they think about the implications of the grade-school teacher adorning their child in turkey feathers to commemorate Thanksgiving. Think about the significance of John Wayne or Charleton Heston killing a dozen "savages" with a single bullet the next time a western comes on TV. Think about why Land-o-Lakes finds it appropriate to market its butter with the stereotyped image of an "Indian princess" on the wrapper. Think about what it means when non-Indian academics profess—as they often do—to "know more about Indians than Indians do themselves." Think about the significance of charlatans like Carlos Castaneda and Jamake Highwater and Mary Summer Rain and Lynn Andrews churning out "Indian" bestsellers one after the other, while Indians typically can't get into print.

Think about the real situation of American Indians. Think about Julius Streicher. Remember Justice Jackson's admonition. Understand that the treatment of Indians in American popular culture is not "cute" or "amusing," or just "good, clean fun."

Know that it causes real pain and real suffering to real people. Know that it threatens our very survival. And know that this is just as much a crime against humanity as anything the Nazis ever did. It is likely the indigenous people of the United States will never demand that those guilty of such criminal activity be punished for their deeds. But the least we have to expect—indeed to demand—is that such practices finally be brought to a halt.

Writing Strategies

1. Describe Churchill's voice as a writer. Refer specifically to several sentences that support your description. Then explain how Churchill's particular writer's voice might affect his reader. What seems to be Churchill's strategy regarding his writer's voice?

2. Identify places in Churchill's essay where he anticipates his reader's thoughts. How is he able to anticipate them, and how successful is he at responding to them?

3. Describe Churchill's evidence. What type of evidence is it: personal anecdotes, literary allusions, observations, logical reasoning, historical allusions, or something else? What particular evidence did you find most convincing? What evidence did you think fell short?

4. Consider Churchill's opening and closing strategies. How successful are they? How else might he have gotten into and out of his essay?

Exploring Ideas

1. While some people argue that the use of Native American names, images, and symbols is harmless, others argue that it is actually a tribute to Native Americans. Why does Churchill think it isn't a tribute? What values, beliefs, or assumptions create the difference of opinion?

2. Take Churchill's side and respond to the following statement: "I am Irish, and I'm not offended that Notre Dame's mascot is a leprechaun."

3. Why shouldn't a school or team change their name from Redskins to Bears?

4. Search the Internet for websites against the use of Native American names for sports teams. How are the arguments put forth on such sites more effective or less effective than Churchill's argument?

For help inventing your own writing project, see the Point of Contact section on pp. 234–235.

◼ ◼ ◼

Beware of Drug Sales

Therese Cherry

Extensive use of outside sources can be difficult in a short essay. The writer's voice can easily be drowned out by reliance on statistics and authorities, and the writer's own line of reasoning can be sidetracked by secondary sources. But Therese Cherry manages to use sources in her essay while maintaining a consistent voice and a coherent line of reasoning. Cherry wrote this essay for a first-semester English course at the University of Toledo. The topic emerged from her field of study. At the request of her instructor, she expressed the ideas of the essay in a letter that appears at the end of this essay.

Prescription drug ads are everywhere. You can't turn on the TV or open a magazine these days without finding out if Claritin is "right for you" or being told to ask your doctor about Viagra. Obviously, the makers of prescription drugs want the public to know that there are pills to cure what ails us, and that they don't mind making a little money off our relief. This is how business is run, spending money to make money, marketing the product so that as many consumers as possible are aware of it and will buy it. However, it seems that pharmaceutical companies have taken their role a bit far, marketing their drugs so aggressively that they are actually creating the demand for them. In an industry that sells cars, an ad campaign that sold cars to people who hadn't even realized they wanted to buy one would definitely be a triumph. But to advertise prescription drugs to the extent that people who don't even need them want to buy them is irresponsible and dangerous.

According to the United Nations International Narcotics Control Board (INCB), advanced countries are overdosing on quick-fix pills to ease "non-medical" problems like fat and stress ("Rich States"). INCB also stated that mood-altering drugs are often prescribed for social problems, such as unemployment or relationship problems ("Prescription"). Consumers around the globe are taking medication for this disease called life. The fact that people are spending their hard-earned money on medicine they do not need is bad enough, but the harm these unnecessary drugs can do is a much bigger issue. Yet the drug companies keep on telling us, "It's okay, just ask your doctor." The problem is, the doctors don't have all the answers, either.

Some statistics cited by the FDA reported that toxic reactions to marketed drugs are estimated to cost more than 30 billion dollars per year and to be among the ten leading causes of death in the United States (Pomper 6). So if these drugs are having these kinds of negative effects on people, why are doctors prescribing them? For one, pharmaceutical companies are advertising more aggressively than they have in the past, in part because of loosened restrictions. In 1997 the FDA caved to heavy pressures from the industry, which made it possible for drug companies to advertise on TV without spending huge chunks of time describing side effects (Pomper 6). Now that drug companies can market directly to consumers, suddenly patients are telling their doctors what drugs they want to use. A recent study published by *Health Affairs* reported that three-quarters of the respondents who saw a drug on TV and asked their doctors for it were successful (Pomper 6).

Another reason these drugs are being prescribed is because some doctors are influenced to prescribe drugs which are marketed more aggressively, according to the January 2000 *Journal of the American Medical Association*. And since the most heavily advertised drugs tend to be the newest drugs, the long list of possible side effects cannot be known. In fact, six new drugs approved since mid-1996 have been pulled off the market, and 150 deaths were linked to the drugs before they were pulled (Pomper 8).

5   Perhaps the most unjust and appalling fact about this considerably new trend of pharmaceutical peddling is the industry's knowledge of the damage this marketing technique is causing to the health of the public: "Even people in the industry will concede off the record that groups acting as advertising agents for manufacturers should be subject to FDA regulations" (Pomper 10). The INBC stated in its 2000 report that there was a "continuing existence of aggressive sales methods and even some cases of financial support to various advocacy groups to foster sales" and appealed to the pharmaceutical industry to demonstrate social responsibility and voluntary cooperation ("Rich States"). We all need to make this same appeal to the drug companies. A business has every right to turn a profit, but should it really be at the risk of good health? Without your health, money means nothing. So, until the pharmaceutical industry can agree with that, buyer beware.

Works Cited

Pomper, Steven. "Drug Rush." <u>Washington Monthly Online</u>. May 2000: 6–10. 23 Jan. 2002 <http://www.washingtonmonthly.com/features/2000/0005.pomper.html>.

"Prescription Drugs 'Over-Used.'" <u>BBC News Online</u>. 21 Feb. 2001. 21 Jan. 2002 <http://news.bbc.com.uk/low/english/heath/newsid_1182000/1182115.stm>.

"Rich States Overdosing on Feel-Good Pills." <u>Dawn the Internet Edition</u>. 21 Feb. 2001. 21 Jan. 2002 <http://www.dawn.com/2001/02/21/int13.htm>.

Writing Strategies

1. What strategy, or strategies, does Cherry use to draw the reader's attention to the point of her essay?

2. What type of evidence does Cherry provide to support her claim? How successful is her evidence? What other evidence might she have provided?

3. Identify any concessions Cherry makes in this essay. That is, where does she acknowledge the validity of a differing viewpoint?

Exploring Ideas

1. In groups, explore Cherry's claim: "A business has every right to turn a profit, but should it really be at the risk of good health?" (¶ 5) Consider each part of her claim:
   - Does a business have every right to turn a profit? What businesses don't?
   - What businesses, besides major pharmaceutical companies, threaten their customers' health?
   - How do pharmaceutical companies actually threaten their customers' health?
   - What businesses should be prohibited from advertising on television and why?
   - What legal businesses should be illegal? What illegal ones should be legal?

   After exploring through discussion, in what ways has the issue become more complex?

2. Is it all right for Americans to take prescription drugs to ease non-medical problems like fat and stress (¶ 2)? What problems should prescription drugs be used for? Consider the following problems: fat, stress, attention, anger, worry, doubt, blood pressure, fear, vision, hearing, sleep, energy, income. Add several more items to the list and explore their relationship to the prescription drug solution.

3. Why do Americans take so many prescription drugs?

For help inventing your own writing project, see the Point of Contact section on pp. 234–235.

▨ ▨ ▨

This professional letter is based on the invention strategies Therese Cherry used to write the previous essay (pp. 579–580).

205 West 5th Street
Kenmore, OH 46904
(213) 555-9086
April 22, 2005

Ruth Weisheit, Public Affairs Specialist
Brunswick Resident Post
Food and Drug Administration
3820 Center Road
Brunswick, OH 44212

Dear Ms. Weisheit:

As a concerned citizen and patient, I have become very alarmed at the growing addiction to prescription drugs in the United States. Though the medical advancements of our time are to be applauded, it seems that stricter regulations on the marketing and prescribing of these drugs may be in order to help ensure public health.

According to the United Nations International Narcotics Control Board, advanced countries are overdosing on quick fix pills to ease non-medical problems like fat and stress. The INCB also reported that mood-altering drugs are often prescribed for social problems, such as unemployment or relationship problems. Not only are many of these drugs being prescribed unnecessarily, they are increasingly dangerous. According to Steven Pomper's May 2000 article "Drug Rush" in the *Washington Monthly Online,* toxic reactions to marketed drugs are estimated to cost more than 30 billion dollars per year and to be among the ten leading causes of death in the U.S. Six new drugs approved since mid-1996 have been pulled off the market, and 150 deaths were linked to these drugs before they were pulled.

Although part of the problem involves unnecessary prescriptions being written, the aggressive marketing of these drugs appears to play a key role in this addiction issue. "Drug Rush" also reported that in 1997, the FDA loosened restrictions on the marketing of pharmaceutical companies, due in large part to heavy pressure from the pharmaceutical industry. This made it possible for drug companies to advertise on T.V. without spending huge chunks of time describing risks and side effects. And the 2000 *Journal of the AMA* has researched and shown findings that doctors are influenced to prescribe drugs that are marketed more heavily. Recent studies in *Health Magazine* stated that three-quarters of the respondents who saw one of these ads on T.V. and asked their doctors to prescribe it were successful.

Apparently, many factors have contributed to this growing epidemic, but none so fully or irresponsibly as the marketing companies that are pushing these drugs. The INCB stated in its 2000 report that there was a "continuing existence of aggressive sales methods and even some cases of financial support to various advocacy groups to foster sales" and appealed to the pharmaceutical industry to demonstrate social responsibility and voluntary cooperation. Even people in the industry will concede off the record that groups acting as advertising agents for manufacturers should be subject to FDA regulations. Since this voluntary cooperation does not seem likely, I would like to know what actions the FDA, as well as other organizations, are taking to curb the aggressive sales tactics of these pharmaceutical drugs.

The growing use of new and heavily marketed drugs for the ease of social conditions is not going to just go away. I am concerned about this issue and would like to learn how I can get involved with organizations that understand the importance of placing stronger restrictions on advertisers. Thank you for taking the time to address my concerns and I would appreciate any information you can send me.

Sincerely,

Therese Cherry
Therese Cherry

Writing Strategies

1. How does Cherry support her main idea?
2. Describe Cherry's writer's voice, using several sentences from her letter to support your description.
3. Give some examples of good sentence vitality in Cherry's letter.

How would Jesus drive?

This bumper sticker provides a rich study in rhetoric. On the surface, it speaks to drivers and suggests that drivers in general and the reader in particular might consider driving differently. It alludes to the teachings of Jesus and, as Jesus taught, stops short of judging others—instead asking them to consider their own actions. (Imagine a bumper sticker that said, "Hey! You oughta drive like Jesus, you stupid jerk!") And it prompts readers to apply a philosophy (a belief system or a religious principle) to the way they treat other drivers (other people)—and themselves. (Are they relaxed, angry, at peace, stressed out?) So at a deeper level, the sticker connects the present act of driving and an overriding philosophy or approach to life.

Of course, to some people the bumper sticker may simply be amusing. To others, it may be offensive or make no sense at all. And to some, it may serve as an important reminder, helping them to better live what they believe.

Someone reading the bumper sticker might feel that it convicts him or her of bad or inconsiderate driving. Or the reader might think it is a critique of other drivers. Or both.

While on one level the bumper sticker is talking about operating a motor vehicle, referencing Jesus, especially for certain readers, elevates the question—particularly the meaning of the word "drive." Those who are used to reading religious texts on different levels are bound to extend their thinking outward, to other aspects of their lives. (How would Jesus drive on the highway? How would Jesus drive through life?)

The decision to place a bumper sticker on a car and to drive around with it, parking in parking lots, speeding down the highway, or pulling into your own driveway, involves considering all the rhetorical issues above—and more.

For help inventing your own writing project, see the Point of Contact section on pp. 234–235.

How would Buddha drive?

How would Lao Tzu drive?

How would Moses drive?

How would Muhammad drive?

_____ ?

Responding to Arguments

Is Hunting Ethical?

Ann F. Causey

We can become entrenched in our own way of thinking, and argument can be antagonistic: two sides battling to the death. Or an argument can be an open exploration, as we challenge our own way of thinking and try to accept an idea before rejecting it. "Is Hunting Ethical?" illustrates how a writer can step back and analyze an argument or debate, acknowledge the value of more than one way of thinking, and create a path for better understanding.

The struggling fawn suddenly went limp in my arms. Panicked, I told my husband to pull the feeding tube out of her stomach. Though Sandy had quit breathing and her death was clearly imminent, I held her head down and slapped her back in an attempt to clear her trachea. Warm, soured milk ran from her mouth and nose, soaking my clothes and gagging us with its vile smell. I turned Sandy over in my arms, and my husband placed his mouth over her muzzle. While he blew air into her lungs, I squeezed her chest as a CPR course had taught me to do for human infants in cardiac arrest.

After a minute or so I felt her chest for a pulse. Nothing at first, then four weak beats in rapid succession. "She's alive! Keep breathing for her."

My husband gagged, then spit to avoid swallowing more of the soured milk, and continued his efforts to revive Sandy. I kept working her chest, hoping that through some miracle of will she would recover. Come on, Sandy, wake up. Please wake up!

Sandy never woke up. My husband, a wildlife biologist, and I had nursed over two dozen white-tailed deer fawns that summer for use in a deer nutrition and growth study he was conducting. Most of the animals were in poor shape when we got them. People around the state found them—some actually orphaned, others mistakenly thought to be abandoned. After a few days of round-the-clock feedings, the fun gave way to drudgery and frustration. That's when they would call their county conservation officer, who in turn called us.

5   All the animals we raised required and got from us loving care, attention, and patience, no matter how sick or recalcitrant they may have been. All were named, and we came to know each one as an individual with unique personality traits and behavior patterns. Though most lived to become healthy adults, each fatality was a tragic loss for us, and we mourned each and every death.

The afternoon Sandy died, however, was not convenient for mourning. We were going to a group dinner that evening and had to prepare a dish. Through tears I made a marinade for the roast. While the meat smoked over charcoal and hickory, we brooded over Sandy's death.

When the roast was done, we wiped away our tears, cleaned up, and went to the dinner. Our moods brightened as our roast was quickly gobbled up, and the evening's high point came when several guests declared that our roast was the best venison they'd ever eaten. The best deer meat. Part of an animal my husband, an avid hunter, had willfully killed and I had gratefully butchered, wrapped, and frozen—a deer that once was a cute and innocent little fawn . . . just like Sandy.

If any one word characterizes most people's feelings when they reflect on the morality of killing an animal for sport, it is "ambivalence." With antihunters insisting that hunting is a demonstration of extreme irreverence for nonhuman life, thoughtful hunters must concede, albeit uncomfortably, the apparent contradiction of killing for sport while maintaining a reverence for life. Yet I know of few hunters who do not claim to have a deep reverence for nature and life, including especially the lives of the animals they seek to kill. It seems that this contradiction, inherent in hunting and increasingly the focus of debate, lies at the core of the moral conundrum of hunting. How can anyone both revere life and seek to extinguish it in pursuit of recreation? The opponents of hunting believe they have backed its proponents into a logical corner on this point, yet the proponents have far from given up the battle for logical supremacy. Is either side a clear winner?

None who know me or my lifestyle would label me "antihunting." Most of the meat in my diet is game.

And many is the time I've defended hunting from the attacks of those who see all hunters as bloodthirsty, knuckle-dragging rednecks.

10   Yet I have on occasion found myself allied with antihunters. But it's an uneasy and selective alliance, my antihunting sentiments limited to diatribes against such blatantly unethical behavior as Big Buck contests, canned Coon Hunt for Christ rallies, and bumper stickers proclaiming "Happiness Is a Warm Gutpile."

There is also a subtler reason for my concerns about hunting, stemming, I believe, from my disappointment with the responses of many hunters and wildlife managers to questions concerning the morality of hunting. In the interest of enlivening and, I hope, elevating the growing debate, it is these moral questions, and their answers, I wish to address here.

To begin, I should point out some errors, common to ethical reasoning and to the current debate, that we should do our best to avoid. The first is confusing prudence with morality. Prudence is acting with one's overall best interests in mind, while morality sometimes requires that one sacrifice self-interest in the service of a greater good.

While thorough knowledge is all that's required to make prudent decisions, the making of a moral decision involves something more: conscience. Obligations have no moral meaning without conscience. Ethical hunters do not mindlessly follow rules and lobby for regulations that serve their interests; rather, they follow their consciences, sometimes setting their own interests aside. In short, ethics are guided by conscience.

Another important distinction is between legality and morality. While many immoral activities are prohibited by law, not all behavior that is within the law can be considered ethical. The politician caught in a conflict of interest who claims moral innocence because he has broken no laws rarely convinces us. Nor should hunters assume that whatever the game laws allow or tradition supports is morally acceptable. The ethical hunter is obligated to evaluate laws and traditions in light of his or her own moral sense. Conscience is not created by decree or consensus, nor is morality determined by legality or tradition.

15   Finally, it's all too tempting to dismiss the concerns of our opponents by questioning their motives and cre-

dentials instead of giving serious consideration to the questions they raise. Hunters do hunting no favors by hurling taunts and slander at their opponents. The questions raised about hunting deserve a fair hearing on their own merits. Consideration of antihunting messages must not be biased by personal opinions of the messengers, nor should hunters' efforts remain focused on discrediting their accusers. Rather, ethical hunters must undertake the uncomfortable and sometimes painful processes of moral deliberation and personal and collective soul-searching that these questions call for.

The first difficulty we encounter in addressing the morality of hunting is identifying and understanding the relevant questions and answers. To me, the most striking feature of the current debate is the two sides' vastly different understanding of the meaning of the question, Is hunting a morally acceptable activity?

Those who support hunting usually respond by citing data. They enumerate the acres of habitat protected by hunting-generated funds; how many game species have experienced population increases due to modern game management; how much the economy is stimulated by hunting-related expenditures; how effectively modern game laws satisfy the consumptive and recreational interests of the hunting community today while assuring continued surpluses of game for future hunters; and how hunters, more than most citizens, care deeply about ecosystem integrity and balance and the global environment.

While these statements may be perfectly true, they're almost totally irrelevant to the question. Antihunters are not asking whether hunting is an effective management tool, whether it's economically advisable, or whether hunters love and appreciate nature. Rather, they're asking, Is it ethical to kill animals for sport? Are any forms of hunting morally right?

The hunter says yes; the antihunter says no, yet they are answering entirely different questions. The hunter answers, with data, what he or she perceives as a question about utility and prudence; the antihunter, though, has intended to ask a question about morality, about human responsibilities and values. It's as if one asked what day it is and the other responded by giving the time. While the answer may be correct, it's meaningless in the context of the question asked.

20   The point is that moral debates, including this one, are not about facts but about values. Moral controversy cannot be resolved by examination of data or by appeal to scientific studies.

An obsession with "sound, objective science" in addressing their opponents has led many hunters not only to avoid the crucial issues but to actually fuel the fires of the antihunting movement. Animal welfare proponents and the general public are primarily concerned about the pain, suffering, and loss of life inflicted on hunted animals, and the motives and attitudes of those who hunt. They're offended by references to wild animals as "resources." They're angered by the sterile language and, by implication, the emotionally sterile attitudes of those who speak of "culling," "controlling," "harvesting," and "managing" animals for "maximum sustained yield." And they're outraged by those who cite habitat protection and human satisfaction data while totally disregarding the interests of the sentient beings who occupy that habitat and who, primarily through their deaths, serve to satisfy human interests.

Antihunters insist that nontrivial reasons be given for intentional human-inflicted injuries and deaths—or that these injuries and deaths be stopped. An eminently reasonable request.

Even when hunters acknowledge the significance of the pain and suffering inflicted through hunting, they too often offer in defense that they feel an obligation to give back more than they take, and that hunters and wildlife professionals successfully have met this obligation. Granted, it may be that the overall benefits to humans and other species that accrue from hunting outweigh the costs to the hunted. Nevertheless, this utilitarian calculation fails to provide moral justification for hunting. Is it just, hunting's detractors ask, that wild animals should die to feed us? To clothe us? To decorate our bodies and den walls? To provide us with entertainment and sport?

These are the questions hunters are being asked. *These* are the questions they must carefully consider and thoughtfully address. It will not suffice to charge their opponents with biological naïveté, as theirs are not questions of science. Nor will charges of emotionalism quiet their accusers, since emotion plays an integral and valid part in value judgments and moral development. Both sides have members who are guided by their hearts, their minds, or both. Neither side has a monopoly on hypocrisy, zealotry, narrow-mindedness, or irrationalism. Opposition to hunting is based in largest part on legitimate philosophical differences.

25   It has been said that hunting is the most uncivilized and primitive activity in which a modern person can legally engage. Therein lies ammunition for the biggest guns in the antihunters' arsenal; paradoxically, therein also lies its appeal to hunters and the source of its approval by many sympathetic nonhunters.

Hunting is one of few activities that allows an individual to participate directly in the life and death cycles on which all natural systems depend. The skilled hunter's ecological knowledge is holistic and realistic; his or her awareness involves all the senses. Whereas ecologists study systems from without, examining and analyzing from a perspective necessarily distanced from their subjects, dedicated hunters live and learn from within, knowing parts of nature as only a parent or child can know his or her own family. One thing necessary for a truly ethical relationship with wildlife is an appreciation of ecosystems, of natural processes. Such an appreciation may best be gained through familiarity, through investment of time and effort, through curiosity, and through an attitude of humility and respect. These are the lessons that hunting teaches its best students.

Not only have ethical hunters resisted the creeping alienation between humans and the natural out-of-doors, they have fought to resist the growing alienation between humans and the "nature" each person carries within. Hunters celebrate their evolutionary heritage and stubbornly refuse to be stripped of their atavistic urges—they refuse to be sterilized by modern culture and thus finally separated from nature. The ethical hunter transcends the mundane, the ordinary, the predictable, the structured, the artificial. As Aldo Leopold argues in his seminal work *A Sand County Almanac*, hunting in most forms maintains a valuable element in the cultural heritage of all peoples.

Notice, though, that Leopold does not give a blanket stamp of moral approval to hunting; nor should we. In fact, Leopold recognized that some forms of hunting may be morally depleting. If we offer an ecological and evolutionary defense for hunting, as Leopold did and as many of hunting's supporters do today, we must still ask ourselves, For which forms of hunting is our defense valid?

The open-minded hunter should carefully consider the following questions: To what extent is shooting an animal over bait or out of a tree at close range after it was chased up there by a dog a morally enriching act? Can shooting an actually or functionally captive animal enhance one's understanding of natural processes? Does a safari to foreign lands to step out of a Land Rover and shoot exotic animals located for you by a guide honor your cultural heritage? Does killing an animal you profess to honor and respect, primarily in order to obtain a trophy, demonstrate reverence for the animal as a sentient creature? Is it morally enriching to use animals as mere objects, as game pieces in macho contests where the only goal is to out-compete other hunters? Is an animal properly honored in death by being reduced to points, inches, and pounds, or to a decoration on a wall? Which forms of hunting can consistently and coherently be defended as nontrivial, meaningful, ecologically sound, and morally enriching?

30   Likewise, we who hunt or support hunting must ask ourselves: Does ignoring, downplaying, and in some cases denying the wounding rate in hunting, rather than taking all available effective measures to lower it, demonstrate reverence for life? Does lobbying for continued hunting of species whose populations are threatened or of uncertain status exemplify ecological awareness and concern? Is the continued hunting of some declining waterfowl populations, the aerial killing of wolves in Alaska, or the setting of hunting seasons that in some areas may sentence to slow death the orphaned offspring of their legally killed lactating mothers, consistent with management by hunters—or do these things verify the antihunters' charges of management primarily *for* hunters?

These questions and others have aroused hunters' fears, indignation, defensive responses, and collective denial. Yet no proponent of ethical hunting has anything to fear from such questions. These are questions we should have been asking ourselves, and defensibly answering, all along. The real threat comes not from outside criticism but from our own complacency and uncritical acceptance of hunting's status quo, and from

our mistaken belief that to protect *any* form of hunting, we must defend and protect *all* forms. In fact, to protect the privilege of morally responsible hunting, we must attack and abolish the unacceptable acts, policies, and attitudes within our ranks that threaten all hunting, as a gangrenous limb threatens the entire body.

The battle cry "Reverence for Life" has been used by both sides, at times with disturbing irony. Cleveland Amory, founder of the Fund for Animals, described in the June 1992 issue of *Sierra* magazine the perfect world he would create if he were appointed its ruler: "All animals will not only be not shot, they will be protected—not only from people but as much as possible from each other. Prey will be separated from predator, and there will be no overpopulation or starvation because all will be controlled by sterilization or implant."

A reverence for life? Only if you accept the atomistic and utterly unecological concept of life as a characteristic of individuals rather than systems.

But neither can all who hunt legitimately claim to hold a reverence for life. In a hunting video titled "Down to Earth," a contemporary rock star and self-proclaimed "whack master" and "gutpile addict" exhorts his protégés to "whack 'em, stack 'em, and pack 'em." After showing a rapid sequence of various animals being hit by his arrows, the "master whacker" kneels and sarcastically asks for "a moment of silence" while the viewer is treated to close-up, slow-motion replays of the hits, including sickening footage of some animals that clearly are gut shot or otherwise sloppily wounded. A reverence for life? Such behavior would seem to demonstrate shocking *irreverence,* arrogance, and hubris. As hunters, we toe a line between profundity and profanity and must accept the responsibility of condemning those practices and attitudes that trivialize, shame, and desecrate all hunting. To inflict death without meaningful and significant purpose, to kill carelessly or casually, or to take a life without solemn gratitude is inconsistent with genuine reverence for life.

35   To be ethical, we must do two things: We must *act* ethically, and we must *think* ethically. The hunting community has responded to its critics by trying to clean up its visible act: We don't hear many public proclamations of gutpile addictions anymore; we less

frequently see dead animals used as hood ornaments while the meat, not to be utilized anyway, rapidly spoils; those who wound more animals than they kill are less likely nowadays to brag about it; and, since studies show that the public opposes sport hunting as trivial, hunters are coached to avoid the term "sport" when they address the public or their critics.

What's needed, though, for truly ethical hunting to flourish is not just a change of appearance or vocabulary but a change of mindset, a deepening of values. Hunters may be able to "beat" antihunters through a change of tactics, but to win the wrong war is no victory at all. Some morally repugnant forms of hunting are *rightfully* under attack, and we can defend them only by sacrificing our intellectual and moral integrity. We should do all we can to avoid such "victories." Hunters must reexamine and, when appropriate, give up some of what they now hold dear—not just because doing so is expedient but because it's *right*. As T. S. Eliot, quoted by Martin Luther King, Jr., in his "Letter from Birmingham Jail," reminds us, "The last temptation is the greatest treason: To do the right deed for the wrong reason."

Can anyone give us a final answer to the question, Is hunting ethical?

No.

For one thing, the question and its answer depend heavily on how one defines "hunting." There are innumerable activities that go by this term, yet many are so different from one another that they scarcely qualify for the same appellation. Moreover, there is no one factor that motivates one hunter on each hunt; nor is there such a thing as the hunter's mind-set.

40   Second, and even more important, is the recognition that in most cases one cannot answer moral questions for others. Two morally mature people may ponder the same ethical dilemma and come to opposite, and equally valid, conclusions. The concept of ethical hunting is pluralistic, as hard to pin down as the definition of a virtuous person. Unlike our opponents, we who are hunting proponents do not seek to impose a particular lifestyle, morality, or spirituality on all citizens; we merely wish to preserve a variety of options and individualities in all our choices concerning responsible human recreation, engagement with nature, and our place in the food web. It's doubtful that any one system, whether it be "boutique" hunting, vegetarianism, or modern factory farming, is an adequate way to meet the ethical challenges of food procurement and human/nonhuman relationships in our diverse culture and burgeoning population.

Like education of any sort, moral learning cannot be passively acquired. In fact, the importance of answering the question of whether hunting is ethical is often exaggerated, for the value of ethics lies not so much in the product, the answers, as in the process of deep and serious deliberation of moral issues. To ponder the value of an animal's life versus a hunter's material and spiritual needs and to consider an animal's pain, suffering, and dignity in death is to acknowledge deeper values and to demonstrate more moral maturity than one who casually, defensively dismisses such ideas.

No matter the result, the process of moral deliberation is necessarily enriching. Neither side can offer one answer for all; we can only answer this question each for ourself, and even then we must be prepared to offer valid, consistent moral arguments in support of our conclusions. This calls for a level of soul-searching and critical thinking largely lacking on both sides of the current debate.

Today's ethical hunter must abandon the concept of hunting as fact and replace it with the more appropriate concept of hunting as challenge—the challenge of identifying and promoting those attitudes toward wildlife that exemplify the values on which morally responsible hunting behavior is based. Heel-digging and saber-rattling must give way to cooperation, to increased awareness and sensitivity, to reason and critical analysis, and to honest self-evaluation and assessment.

The Chinese have a wonderful term, *wei chi,* that combines two concepts: crisis . . . and opportunity. The term conveys the belief that every crisis presents an opportunity. I submit that the hunting community today faces its greatest crisis ever and, therein, its greatest opportunity—the opportunity for change, for moral growth, for progress.

Writing Strategies

1. Do you consider Causey's opening narrative (¶ 1–7) to be effective? Explain how her opening is or is not a strength of her essay.
2. How does Causey make the purpose of her essay clear to the reader?
3. Examine Causey's essay for coherence. Provide several examples of how she connects ideas for the reader. What different strategies does she employ?
4. What writing decisions does Causey make to avoid alienating hunters? What decisions does she make to avoid alienating nonhunters?
5. What, if anything, about Causey's essay alienated you as a reader? Why?

Exploring Ideas

1. What is Causey trying to accomplish with this essay?
2. What points do you find most interesting, and why? Which of Causey's ideas make you think differently?
3. Interview various people to find out their views on hunting. Record their responses, and then write several paragraphs explaining how others' views are similar to or different from Causey's.
4. What issues, in addition to hunting, can Causey's ethical approach be applied to? That is, what issue do others discuss in terms of data or legality when you feel the issue should be ethics?

For help inventing your own writing project, see the Point of Contact section on pp. 270–271.

■ ■ ■

Letter from Birmingham Jail

Martin Luther King, Jr.

Martin Luther King, Jr. wrote "Letter from Birmingham Jail" in response to a public statement signed by eight white Alabama clergymen. The statement, "A Call to Unity," was a response to nonviolent protests against segregation in Birmingham. (Notice how King's letter is a response to a response, and thus, a contribution to an ongoing discussion.) This type of letter is referred to as an "open letter," because the writer intends it to be read by a wide audience, not just the individuals to whom it is addressed. King's letter, dated April 16, 1963, was first published as "Letter from Birmingham Jail" on June 12, 1963 in *The Christian Century* and on June 24 in *The New Leader*.

AUTHOR'S NOTE: This response to a published statement by eight fellow clergymen from Alabama (Bishop C. C. J. Carpenter, Bishop Joseph A. Durick, Rabbi Hilton L. Grafman, Bishop Paul Hardin, Bishop Holan B. Harmon, the Reverend George M. Murray, the Reverend Edward V. Ramage and the Reverend Earl Stallings) was composed under somewhat constricting circumstance. Begun on the margins of the newspaper in which the statement appeared while I was in jail, the letter was continued on scraps of writing paper supplied by a friendly Negro trusty, and concluded on a pad my attorneys were eventually permitted to leave me. Although the text remains in substance unaltered, I have indulged in the author's prerogative of polishing it for publication.

April 16, 1963

MY DEAR FELLOW CLERGYMEN:

While confined here in the Birmingham city jail, I came across your recent statement calling my present activities "unwise and untimely." Seldom do I pause to answer criticism of my work and ideas. If I sought to answer all the criticisms that cross my desk, my secretaries would have little time for anything other than such correspondence in the course of the day, and I would have no time for constructive work. But since I feel that you are men of genuine good will and that your criticisms are sincerely set forth, I want to try to answer your statement in what I hope will be patient and reasonable terms.

I think I should indicate why I am here in Birmingham, since you have been influenced by the view which argues against "outsiders coming in." I have the honor of serving as president of the Southern Christian Leadership Conference, an organization operating in every southern state, with headquarters in Atlanta, Georgia. We have some eighty-five affiliated organizations across the South, and one of them is the Alabama Christian Movement for Human Rights. Frequently we share staff, educational and financial resources with our affiliates. Several months ago the affiliate here in Birmingham asked us to be on call to engage in a nonviolent direct-action program if such were deemed necessary. We readily consented, and when the hour came we lived up to our promise. So I, along with several members of my staff, am here because I was invited here. I am here because I have organizational ties here.

But more basically, I am in Birmingham because injustice is here. Just as the prophets of the eighth century B.C. left their villages and carried their "thus saith the Lord" far beyond the boundaries of their home towns, and just as the Apostle Paul left his village of Tarsus and carried the gospel of Jesus Christ to the far corners of the Greco-Roman world, so am I compelled to carry the gospel of freedom beyond my own home town. Like Paul, I must constantly respond to the Macedonian call for aid.

Moreover, I am cognizant of the interrelatedness of all communities and states. I cannot sit idly by in Atlanta and not be concerned about what happens in Birmingham. Injustice anywhere is a threat to justice everywhere. We are caught in an inescapable network of mutuality, tied in a single garment of destiny. Whatever affects one directly, affects all indirectly. Never again can we afford to live with the narrow, provincial "outside agitator" idea. Anyone who lives inside the United States can never be considered an outsider anywhere within its bounds.

5   You deplore the demonstrations taking place in Birmingham. But your statement, I am sorry to say, fails to express a similar concern for the conditions that brought about the demonstrations. I am sure that none of you would want to rest content with the superficial kind of social analysis that deals merely with effects and does not grapple with underlying causes. It is unfortunate that demonstrations are taking place in Birmingham, but it is even more unfortunate that the city's white power structure left the Negro community with no alternative.

In any nonviolent campaign there are four basic steps: collection of the facts to determine whether injustices exist; negotiation; self-purification; and direct action. We have gone through all these steps in Birmingham. There can be no gainsaying the fact that racial injustice engulfs this community. Birmingham is probably the most thoroughly segregated city in the United States. Its ugly record of brutality is widely known. Negroes have experienced grossly unjust treatment in the courts. There have been more unsolved bombings of Negro homes and churches in Birmingham than in any other city in the nation. These are the hard, brutal facts of the case. On the basis of these conditions, Negro leaders sought to negotiate with the city fathers. But the latter consistently refused to engage in good-faith negotiation.

Then, last September, came the opportunity to talk with leaders of Birmingham's economic community. In the course of the negotiations, certain promises were made by the merchants—for example, to remove the stores' humiliating racial signs. On the basis of these promises, the Reverend Fred Shuttlesworth and the leaders of the Alabama Christian Movement for Human Rights agreed to a moratorium on all demonstrations. As the weeks and months went by, we realized that we were the victims of a broken promise. A few signs, briefly removed, returned; the others remained.

As in so many past experiences, our hopes had been blasted, and the shadow of deep disappointment settled upon us. We had no alternative except to prepare for direct action, whereby we would present our very bodies as a means of laying our case before the conscience of the local and the national community. Mindful of the difficulties involved, we decided to undertake a process of self-purification. We began a series of workshops on nonviolence, and we repeatedly asked ourselves: "Are you able to accept blows without retaliating?" "Are you able to endure the ordeal of jail?" We decided to schedule our direct-action program for the Easter season, realizing that except for Christmas, this is the main shopping period of the year. Knowing that a strong economic- withdrawl program would be the by-product of direct action, we felt that this would be the best time to bring pressure to bear on the merchants for the needed change.

Then it occurred to us that Birmingham's mayoral election was coming up in March, and we speedily decided to postpone action until after election day. When we discovered that the Commissioner of Public Safety, Eugene "Bull" Connor, had piled up enough votes to be in the run-off we decided again to postpone action until the day after the run-off so that the demonstrations could not be used to cloud the issues. Like many others, we waited to see Mr. Connor defeated, and to this end we endured postponement after postponement. Having aided in this community need, we felt that our direct-action program could be delayed no longer.

10   You may well ask: "Why direct action? Why sit-ins, marches and so forth? Isn't negotiation a better path?" You are quite right in calling for negotiation. Indeed, this is the very purpose of direct action. Nonviolent direct action seeks to create such a crisis and foster such a tension that a community which has constantly refused to negotiate is forced to confront the issue. It seeks so to dramatize the issue that it can no longer be ignored. My citing the creation of tension as part of the work of the nonviolent-resister may sound rather shocking. But I must confess that I am not afraid of the word "tension." I have earnestly opposed violent tension, but there is a type of constructive, nonviolent tension which is necessary for growth. Just as Socrates felt that it was necessary to create a tension in the mind so that individuals could rise from the bondage of myths and half-truths to the unfettered realm of creative analysis and objective appraisal, so must we see the need for nonviolent gadflies to create the kind of tension in society that will help men rise from the dark depths of prejudice and racism to the majestic heights of understanding and brotherhood.

The purpose of our direct-action program is to create a situation so crisis-packed that it will inevitably open the door to negotiation. I therefore concur with you in your call for negotiation. Too long has our beloved Southland been bogged down in a tragic effort to live in monologue rather than dialogue.

One of the basic points in your statement is that the action that I and my associates have taken in Birmingham is untimely. Some have asked: "Why didn't you give the new city administration time to act?" The only answer that I can give to this query is that the new Birmingham administration must be prodded about as much as the outgoing one, before it will act. We are sadly mistaken if we feel that the election of Albert Boutwell as mayor will bring the millennium to Birmingham. While Mr. Boutwell is a much more gentle person than Mr. Connor, they are both segregationists, dedicated to maintenance of the status quo. I have hope that Mr. Boutwell will be reasonable enough to see the futility of massive resistance to desegregation. But he will not see this without pressure from devotees of civil rights. My friends, I must say to you that we have not made a single gain for civil rights without determined legal and nonviolent pressure. Lamentably, it is an historical fact that privileged groups seldom give up their privileges voluntarily. Individuals may see the moral light and voluntarily give up their unjust posture; but, as Reinhold Niebuhr has reminded us, groups tend to be more immoral than individuals.

We know through painful experience that freedom is never voluntarily given by the oppressor; it must be demanded by the oppressed. Frankly, I have yet to engage in a direct-action campaign that was "well timed" in the view of those who have not suffered unduly from the disease of segregation. For years now I have heard the word "Wait!" It rings in the ear of every Negro with piercing familiarity. This "Wait" has almost always meant "Never." We must come to see, with one of our distinguished jurists, that "justice too long delayed is justice denied."

We have waited for more than 340 years for our constitutional and God-given rights. The nations of Asia and Africa are moving with jetlike speed toward gaining political independence, but we still creep at horse-and-buggy pace toward gaining a cup of coffee at a lunch counter. Perhaps it is easy for those who have never felt the stinging darts of segregation to say, "Wait." But when you have seen vicious mobs lynch your mothers and fathers at will and drown your sisters and brothers at whim; when you have seen hate-filled policemen curse, kick and even kill your black brothers and sisters; when you see the vast majority of your twenty million Negro brothers smothering in an airtight cage of poverty in the midst of an affluent society; when you suddenly find your tongue twisted and your speech stammering as you seek to explain to your six-year-old daughter why she can't go to the public amusement park that has just been advertised on television, and see tears welling up in her eyes when she is told that Funtown is closed to colored children, and see ominous clouds of inferiority beginning to form in her little mental sky, and see her beginning to distort her personality by developing an unconscious bitterness toward white people; when you have to concoct an answer for a five-year-old son who is asking: "Daddy, why do white people treat colored people so mean?"; when you take a cross-county drive and find it necessary to sleep night after night in the uncomfortable corners of your automobile because no motel will accept you; when you are humiliated day in and day out by nagging signs reading "white" and "colored"; when your first name becomes "nigger," your middle name becomes "boy" (however old you are) and your last name becomes "John," and your wife and mother are never given the respected title "Mrs."; when you are harried by day and haunted by night by the fact that you are a Negro, living constantly at tiptoe stance, never quite knowing what to expect next, and are plagued with inner fears and outer resentments; when you are forever fighting a degenerating sense of "nobodiness" then you will understand why we find it difficult to wait. There comes a time when the cup of endurance runs over, and men are no longer willing to be plunged into the abyss of despair. I hope, sirs, you can understand our legitimate and unavoidable impatience.

15   You express a great deal of anxiety over our willingness to break laws. This is certainly a legitimate concern. Since we so diligently urge people to obey the Supreme Court's decision of 1954 outlawing segregation in the public schools, at first glance it may seem rather paradoxical for us consciously to break laws. One may well ask: "How can you advocate breaking some laws and obeying others?" The answer lies in the fact that there are two types of laws: just and unjust. I would be the first to advocate obeying just laws. One has not only a legal but a moral responsibility to obey just laws. Conversely, one has a moral responsibility to disobey unjust laws. I would agree with St. Augustine that "an unjust law is no law at all."

Now, what is the difference between the two? How does one determine whether a law is just or unjust? A just law is a man-made code that squares with the moral law or the law of God. An unjust law is a code that is out of harmony with the moral law. To put it in the terms of St. Thomas Aquinas: An unjust law is a human law that is not rooted in eternal law and natural law. Any law that uplifts human personality is just. Any law that degrades human personality is unjust. All segregation statutes are unjust because segregation distorts the soul and damages the personality. It gives the segregator a false sense of superiority and the segregated a false sense of inferiority. Segregation, to use the terminology of the Jewish philosopher Martin Buber, substitutes an "I-it" relationship for an "I-thou" relationship and ends up

relegating persons to the status of things. Hence segregation is not only politically, economically and sociologically unsound, it is morally wrong and sinful. Paul Tillich has said that sin is separation. Is not segregation an existential expression of man's tragic separation, his awful estrangement, his terrible sinfulness? Thus it is that I can urge men to obey the 1954 decision of the Supreme Court, for it is morally right; and I can urge them to disobey segregation ordinances, for they are morally wrong.

Let us consider a more concrete example of just and unjust laws. An unjust law is a code that a numerical or power majority group compels a minority group to obey but does not make binding on itself. This is *difference* made legal. By the same token, a just law is a code that a majority compels a minority to follow and that it is willing to follow itself. This is *sameness* made legal.

Let me give another explanation. A law is unjust if it is inflicted on a minority that, as a result of being denied the right to vote, had no part in enacting or devising the law. Who can say that the legislature of Alabama which set up that state's segregation laws was democratically elected? Throughout Alabama all sorts of devious methods are used to prevent Negroes from becoming registered voters, and there are some counties in which, even though Negroes constitute a majority of the population, not a single Negro is registered. Can any law enacted under such circumstances be considered democratically structured?

Sometimes a law is just on its face and unjust in its application. For instance, I have been arrested on a charge of parading without a permit. Now, there is nothing wrong in having an ordinance which requires a permit for a parade. But such an ordinance becomes unjust when it is used to maintain segregation and to deny citizens the First Amendment privilege of peaceful assembly and protest.

20   I hope you are able to see the distinction I am trying to point out. In no sense do I advocate evading or defying the law, as would the rabid segregationist. That would lead to anarchy. One who breaks an unjust law must do so openly, lovingly, and with a willingness to accept the penalty. I submit that an individual who breaks a law that conscience tells him is unjust and who

willingly accepts the penalty of imprisonment in order to arouse the conscience of the community over its injustice, is in reality expressing the highest respect for law.

Of course, there is nothing new about this kind of civil disobedience. It was evidenced sublimely in the refusal of Shadrach, Meshach and Abednego to obey the laws of Nebuchadnezzar, on the ground that a higher moral law was at stake. It was practiced superbly by the early Christians, who were willing to face hungry lions and the excruciating pain of chopping blocks rather than submit to certain unjust laws of the Roman Empire. To a degree, academic freedom is a reality today because Socrates practiced civil disobedience. In our own nation, the Boston Tea Party represented a massive act of civil disobedience.

We should never forget that everything Adolf Hitler did in Germany was "legal" and everything the Hungarian freedom fighters did in Hungary was "illegal." It was "illegal" to aid and comfort a Jew in Hitler's Germany. Even so, I am sure that, had I lived in Germany at the time, I would have aided and comforted my Jewish brothers. If today I lived in a Communist country where certain principles dear to the Christian faith are suppressed, I would openly advocate disobeying that country's antireligious laws.

I must make two honest confessions to you, my Christian and Jewish brothers. First, I must confess that over the past few years I have been gravely disappointed with the white moderate. I have almost reached the regrettable conclusion that the Negro's great stumbling block in his stride toward freedom is not the White Citizen's Counciler or the Ku Klux Klanner, but the white moderate, who is more devoted to "order" than to justice; who prefers a negative peace which is the absence of tension to a positive peace which is the presence of justice; who constantly says: "I agree with you in the goal you seek, but I cannot agree with your methods of direct action"; who paternalistically believes he can set the timetable for another man's freedom; who lives by a mythical concept of time and who constantly advises the Negro to wait for a "more convenient season." Shallow understanding from people of good will is more frustrating than absolute misunderstanding from people of ill will. Lukewarm acceptance is much more bewildering than outright rejection.

I had hoped that the white moderate would understand that law and order exist for the purpose of establishing justice and that when they fail in this purpose they become the dangerously structured dams that block the flow of social progress. I had hoped that the white moderate would understand that the present tension in the South is a necessary phase of the transition from an obnoxious negative peace, in which the Negro passively accepted his unjust plight, to a substantive and positive peace, in which all men will respect the dignity and worth of human personality. Actually, we who engage in nonviolent direct action are not the creators of tension. We merely bring to the surface the hidden tension that is already alive. We bring it out in the open, where it can be seen and dealt with. Like a boil that can never be cured so long as it is covered up but must be opened with all its ugliness to the natural medicines of air and light, injustice must be exposed, with all the tension its exposure creates, to the light of human conscience and the air of national opinion before it can be cured.

25   In your statement you assert that our actions, even though peaceful, must be condemned because they precipitate violence. But is this a logical assertion? Isn't this like condemning a robbed man because his possession of money precipitated the evil act of robbery? Isn't this like condemning Socrates because his unswerving commitment to truth and his philosophical inquiries precipitated the act by the misguided populace in which they made him drink hemlock? Isn't this like condemning Jesus because his unique God-consciousness and never-ceasing devotion to God's will precipitated the evil act of crucifixion? We must come to see that, as the federal courts have consistently affirmed, it is wrong to urge an individual to cease his efforts to gain his basic constitutional rights because the quest may precipitate violence. Society must protect the robbed and punish the robber.

I had also hoped that the white moderate would reject the myth concerning time in relation to the struggle for freedom. I have just received a letter from a white brother in Texas. He writes: "All Christians know that the colored people will receive equal rights eventually, but it is possible that you are in too great a religious hurry. It has taken Christianity almost two thousand years to accomplish what it has. The teachings of Christ take time to come to earth." Such an attitude stems from a tragic misconception of time, from the strangely rational notion that there is something in the very flow of time that will inevitably cure all ills. Actually, time itself is neutral; it can be used either destructively or constructively. More and more I feel that the people of ill will have used time much more effectively than have the people of good will. We will have to repent in this generation not merely for the hateful words and actions of the bad people but for the appalling silence of the good people. Human progress never rolls in on wheels of inevitability; it comes through the tireless efforts of men willing to be co-workers with God, and without this hard work, time itself becomes an ally of the forces of social stagnation. We must use time creatively, in the knowledge that the time is always ripe to do right. Now is the time to make real the promise of democracy and transform our pending national elegy into a creative psalm of brotherhood. Now is the time to lift our national policy from the quicksand of racial injustice to the solid rock of human dignity.

You speak of our activity in Birmingham as extreme. At first I was rather disappointed that fellow clergymen would see my nonviolent efforts as those of an extremist. I began thinking about the fact that I stand in the middle of two opposing forces in the Negro community. One is a force of complacency, made up in part of Negroes who, as a result of long years of oppression, are so drained of self-respect and a sense of "somebodiness" that they have adjusted to segregation; and in part of a few middle class Negroes who, because of a degree of academic and economic security and because in some ways they profit by segregation, have become insensitive to the problems of the masses. The other force is one of bitterness and hatred, and it comes perilously close to advocating violence. It is expressed in the various black nationalist groups that are springing up across the nation, the largest and best-known being Elijah Muhammad's Muslim movement. Nourished by the Negro's frustration over the continued existence of racial discrimination, this movement is made up of people who have lost faith in America, who have absolutely repudiated Christianity, and who have concluded that the white man is an incorrigible "devil."

I have tried to stand between these two forces, saying that we need emulate neither the "do-nothingism"

of the complacent nor the hatred and despair of the black nationalist. For there is the more excellent way of love and nonviolent protest. I am grateful to God that, through the influence of the Negro church, the way of nonviolence became an integral part of our struggle.

If this philosophy had not emerged, by now many streets of the South would, I am convinced, be flowing with blood. And I am further convinced that if our white brothers dismiss as "rabble-rousers" and "outside agitators" those of us who employ nonviolent direct action, and if they refuse to support our nonviolent efforts, millions of Negroes will, out of frustration and despair, seek solace and security in black-nationalist ideologies, a development that would inevitably lead to a frightening racial nightmare.

30 Oppressed people cannot remain oppressed forever. The yearning for freedom eventually manifests itself, and that is what has happened to the American Negro. Something within has reminded him of his birthright of freedom, and something without has reminded him that it can be gained. Consciously or unconsciously, he has been caught up by the Zeitgeist, and with his black brothers of Africa and his brown and yellow brothers of Asia, South America and the Caribbean, the United States Negro is moving with a sense of great urgency toward the promised land of racial justice. If one recognizes this vital urge that has engulfed the Negro community, one should readily understand why public demonstrations are taking place. The Negro has many pent-up resentments and latent frustrations, and he must release them. So let him march; let him make prayer pilgrimages to the city hall; let him go on freedom rides—and try to understand why he must do so. If his repressed emotions are not released in nonviolent ways, they will seek expression through violence; this is not a threat but a fact of history. So I have not said to my people: "Get rid of your discontent." Rather, I have tried to say that this normal and healthy discontent can be channeled into the creative outlet of nonviolent direct action. And now this approach is being termed extremist.

But though I was initially disappointed at being categorized as an extremist, as I continued to think about the matter I gradually gained a measure of satisfaction from the label. Was not Jesus an extremist for love: "Love your enemies, bless them that curse you, do good to them that hate you, and pray for them which despitefully use you, and persecute you." Was not Amos an extremist for justice: "Let justice roll down like waters and righteousness like an ever-flowing stream." Was not Paul an extremist for the Christian gospel: "I bear in my body the marks of the Lord Jesus." Was not Martin Luther an extremist: "Here I stand; I cannot do otherwise, so help me God." And John Bunyan: "I will stay in jail to the end of my days before I make a butchery of my conscience." And Abraham Lincoln: "This nation cannot survive half slave and half free." And Thomas Jefferson: "We hold these truths to be self-evident, that all men are created equal. . . ." So the question is not whether we will be extremists, but what kind of extremists we will be. We we be extremists for hate or for love? Will we be extremists for the preservation of injustice or for the extension of justice? In that dramatic scene on Calvary's hill three men were crucified. We must never forget that all three were crucified for the same crime—the crime of extremism. Two were extremists for immorality, and thus fell below their environment. The other, Jesus Christ, was an extremist for love, truth and goodness, and thereby rose above his environment. Perhaps the South, the nation, and the world are in dire need of creative extremists.

I had hoped that the white moderate would see this need. Perhaps I was too optimistic; perhaps I expected too much. I suppose I should have realized that few members of the oppressor race can understand the deep groans and passionate yearnings of the oppressed race, and still fewer have the vision to see that injustice must be rooted out by strong, persistent and determined action. I am thankful, however, that some of our white brothers in the South have grasped the meaning of this social revolution and committed themselves to it. They are still too few in quantity, but they are big in quality. Some—such as Ralph McGill, Lillian Smith, Harry Golden, James McBride Dabbs, Ann Braden and Sarah Patton Boyle—have written about our struggle in eloquent and prophetic terms. Others have marched with us down nameless streets of the South. They have languished in filthy, roach-infested jails, suffering the abuse and brutality of policemen who view them as "dirty nigger lovers." Unlike so many of their moderate brothers and sisters, they have recog-

nized the urgency of the moment and sensed the need for powerful "action" antidotes to combat the disease of segregation.

Let me take note of my other major disappointment. I have been so greatly disappointed with the white church and its leadership. Of course, there are some notable exceptions. I am not unmindful of the fact that each of you has taken some significant stands on this issue. I commend you, Reverend Stallings, for your Christian stand on this past Sunday, in welcoming Negroes to your worship service on a nonsegregated basis. I commend the Catholic leaders of this state for integrating Spring Hill College several years ago.

But despite these notable exceptions, I must honestly reiterate that I have been disappointed with the church. I do not say this as one of those negative critics who can always find something wrong with the church. I say this as a minister of the gospel, who loves the church; who was nurtured in its bosom; who has been sustained by its spiritual blessings and who will remain true to it as long as the cord of life shall lengthen.

35 When I was suddenly catapulted into the leadership of the bus protest in Montgomery, Alabama, a few years ago, I felt we would be supported by the white church, felt that the white ministers, priests, and rabbis of the South would be among our strongest allies. Instead, some have been outright opponents, refusing to understand the freedom movement and misrepresenting its leaders; all too many others have been more cautious than courageous and have remained silent behind the anesthetizing security of stained-glass windows.

In spite of my shattered dreams, I came to Birmingham with the hope that the white religious leadership of this community would see the justice of our cause and, with deep moral concern, would serve as the channel through which our just grievances could reach the power structure. I had hoped that each of you would understand. But again I have been disappointed.

I have heard numerous southern religious leaders admonish their worshipers to comply with a desegregation decision because it is the law, but I have longed to hear white ministers declare: "Follow this decree because integration is morally right and because the Negro is your brother." In the midst of blatant injustices inflicted upon the Negro, I have watched white churchmen stand on the sideline and mouth pious irrelevancies and sanctimonious trivialities. In the midst of a mighty struggle to rid our nation of racial and economic injustice, I have heard many ministers say: "Those are social issues, with which the gospel has no real concern." And I have watched many churches commit themselves to a completely other-worldly religion which makes a strange, un-Biblical distinction between body and soul, between the sacred and the secular.

I have traveled the length and breadth of Alabama, Mississippi and all the other southern states. On sweltering summer days and crisp autumn mornings I have looked at the South's beautiful churches with their lofty spires pointing heavenward. I have beheld the impressive outlines of her massive religious-education buildings. Over and over I have found myself asking: "What kind of people worship here? Who is their God? Where were their voices when the lips of Governor Barnett dripped with words of interposition and nullification? Where were they when Governor Wallace gave a clarion call for defiance and hatred? Where were their voices of support when bruised and weary Negro men and women decided to rise from the dark dungeons of complacency to the bright hills of creative protest?"

Yes, these questions are still in my mind. In deep disappointment I have wept over the laxity of the church. But be assured that my tears have been tears of love. There can be no deep disappointment where there is not deep love. Yes, I love the church. How could I do otherwise? l am in the rather unique position of being the son, the grandson and the great-grandson of preachers. Yes, I see the church as the body of Christ. But, oh! How we have blemished and scarred that body through social neglect and through fear of being nonconformists.

40   There was a time when the church was very powerful—in the time when the early Christians rejoiced at being deemed worthy to suffer for what they believed. In those days the church was not merely a thermometer that recorded the ideas and principles of popular opinion; it was a thermostat that transformed the mores of society. Whenever the early Christians entered a town, the people in power became disturbed and immediately sought to convict the Christians for being "disturbers of the peace" and "outside agitators." But the Christians pressed on, in the conviction that they were "a colony of heaven," called to obey God rather than man. Small in number, they were big in commitment. They were too God intoxicated to be "astronomically intimidated." By their effort and example they brought an end to such ancient evils as infanticide and gladiatorial contests.

Things are different now. So often the contemporary church is a weak, ineffectual voice with an uncertain sound. So often it is an archdefender of the status quo. Far from being disturbed by the presence of the church, the power structure of the average community is consoled by the church's silent and often even vocal sanction of things as they are.

But the judgment of God is upon the church as never before. If today's church does not recapture the sacrificial spirit of the early church, it will lose its authenticity, forfeit the loyalty of millions, and be dismissed as an irrelevant social club with no meaning for the twentieth century. Every day I meet young people whose disappointment with the church has turned into outright disgust.

Perhaps I have once again been too optimistic. Is organized religion too inextricably bound to the status quo to save our nation and the world? Perhaps I must turn my faith to the inner spiritual church, the church within the church, as the true ekklesia and the hope of the world. But again I am thankful to God that some noble souls from the ranks of organized religion have broken loose from the paralyzing chains of conformity and joined us as active partners in the struggle for freedom. They have left their secure congregations and walked the streets of Albany, Georgia, with us. They have gone down the highways of the South on tortuous rides for freedom. Yes, they have gone to jail with us. Some have been dismissed from their churches, have lost the support of their bishops and fellow ministers. But they have acted in the faith that right defeated is stronger than evil triumphant. Their witness has been the spiritual salt that has preserved the true meaning of the gospel in these troubled times. They have carved a tunnel of hope through the dark mountain of disappointment.

I hope the church as a whole will meet the challenge of this decisive hour. But even if the church does not come to the aid of justice, I have no despair about the future. I have no fear about the outcome of our struggle in Birmingham, even if our motives are at present misunderstood. We will reach the goal of freedom in Birmingham, and all over the nation, because the goal of America is freedom. Abused and scorned though we may be, our destiny is tied up with America's destiny. Before the pilgrims landed at Plymouth, we were here. Before the pen of Jefferson etched the majestic words of the Declaration of Independence across the pages of history, we were here. For more than two centuries our forebears labored in this country without wages; they made cotton king; they built the homes of their masters while suffering gross injustice and shameful humiliation—and yet out of a bottomless vitality they continued to thrive and develop. If the inexpressible cruelties of slavery could not stop us, the opposition we now face will surely fail. We will win our freedom because the sacred heritage of our nation and the eternal will of God are embodied in our echoing demands.

45   Before closing I feel impelled to mention one other point in your statement that has troubled me profoundly. You warmly commended the Birmingham police force for keeping "order" and "preventing violence." I doubt that you would have so warmly commended the police force if you had seen its dogs sinking their teeth into unarmed, nonviolent Negroes. I doubt that you would so quickly commend the policemen if you were to observe their ugly and inhumane treatment of Negroes here in the city jail; if you were to watch them push and curse old Negro women and young Negro girls; if you were to see them slap and kick old Negro men and young boys; if you were to observe them, as they did on two occasions, refuse to give us food because we wanted to sing our grace together. I cannot join you in your praise of the Birmingham police department.

It is true that the police have exercised a degree of discipline in handing the demonstrators. In this sense they have conducted themselves rather "nonviolently" in public. But for what purpose? To preserve the evil system of segregation. Over the past few years I have consistently preached that nonviolence demands that the means we use must be as pure as the ends we seek. I have tried to make clear that it is wrong to use immoral means to attain moral ends. But now I must affirm that it is just as wrong, or perhaps even more so, to use moral means to preserve immoral ends. Perhaps Mr. Connor and his policemen have been rather nonviolent in public, as was Chief Pritchett in Albany, Georgia, but they have used the moral means of nonviolence to maintain the immoral end of racial injustice. As T. S. Eliot has said: "The last temptation is the greatest treason: To do the right deed for the wrong reason."

I wish you had commended the Negro sit-inners and demonstrators of Birmingham for their sublime courage, their willingness to suffer and their amazing discipline in the midst of great provocation. One day the South will recognize its real heroes. They will be the James Merediths, with the noble sense of purpose that enables them to face jeering and hostile mobs, and with the agonizing loneliness that characterizes the life of the pioneer. They will be old, oppressed, battered Negro women, symbolized in a seventy-two-year-old woman in Montgomery, Alabama, who rose up with a sense of dignity and with her people decided not to ride segregated buses, and who responded with ungrammatical profundity to one who inquired about her weariness: "My feets is tired, but my soul is at rest." They will be the young high school and college students, the young ministers of the gospel and a host of their elders, courageously and nonviolently sitting in at lunch counters and willingly going to jail for conscience' sake. One day the South will know that when these disinherited children of God sat down at lunch counters, they were in reality standing up for what is best in the American dream and for the most sacred values in our Judaeo-Christian heritage, thereby bringing our nation back to those great wells of democracy which were dug deep by the founding fathers in their formulation of the Constitution and the Declaration of Independence.

Never before have I written so long a letter. I'm afraid it is much too long to take your precious time. I can assure you that it would have been much shorter if I had been writing from a comfortable desk, but what else can one do when he is alone in a narrow jail cell, other than write long letters, think long thoughts and pray long prayers?

If I have said anything in this letter that overstates the truth and indicates an unreasonable impatience, I beg you to forgive me. If I have said anything that understates the truth and indicates my having a patience that allows me to settle for anything less than brotherhood, I beg God to forgive me.

50 I hope this letter finds you strong in the faith. I also hope that circumstances will soon make it possible for me to meet each of you, not as an integrationist or a civil rights leader but as a fellow clergyman and a Christian brother. Let us all hope that the dark clouds of racial prejudice will soon pass away and the deep fog of misunderstanding will be lifted from our fear-drenched communities, and in some not too distant tomorrow the radiant stars of love and brotherhood will shine over our great nation with all their scintillating beauty.

Yours for the cause of
Peace and Brotherhood,

MARTIN LUTHER KING, JR.

Writing Strategies

1. King addresses eight fellow clergy members, but his letter is also written for a broader audience. How does the open letter format impact the arguments he offers?
2. Identify specific uses of counterargument and concession in King's letter. How do they affect King's argument?
3. King addresses a specific set of circumstances and laws in the 1960s, but he also makes several points about right and wrong, about patriotism, moderation, and law. What points extend beyond the situation of the 1960s? How does King's rhetoric help you to make a connection between then and now?
4. How does King use authorities as an effective support strategy for his argument? Which references to authorities are most effective, and why?
5. How does King use common ground to help the reader understand and accept his position? Identify at least one passage in his argument where he uses a shared assumption, value, or belief to connect his thinking and the opposition.

Exploring Ideas

1. With a group of peers, discuss how things have changed and/or remained the same since 1963: What passages from King's letter are most relevant today, and why?
2. King says, "We will reach the goal of freedom in Birmingham, and all over the nation, because the goal of America is freedom." (¶ 44) Is the goal of America freedom? What else might be America's goals? What evidence can you provide from everyday life to support your response?
3. By tracing the cause of the violence further back, beyond the protesters, King responds to the logic that his actions, though peaceful, "must be condemned because they precipitate vio-

lence." (¶ 25) First, summarize King's logic, and then apply the same logic to some other argument by tracing the cause of a problem further back than the original argument does.
4. King defines two types of laws: just and unjust. Provide an example from everyday life of a just law and of an unjust law. What law, if any, do you think should be broken because it is unjust? Would you be willing to break it?
5. King writes, "I submit that an individual who breaks a law that conscience tells him is unjust and who willingly accepts the penalty of imprisonment in order to arouse the conscience of the community over its injustice, is in reality expressing the highest respect for the law." (¶ 20) Provide a different example from history or current events that helps support King's idea. Then provide another example that complicates King's statement and encourages further exploration of its complexity.

For help inventing your own writing project, see the Point of Contact section on pp. 270–271.

⬛ ⬛ ⬛

Surrender Speech

Chief Joseph

MIP/Getty Images

In 1877, instead of moving to a reservation in Idaho as ordered, Chief Joseph and a band of Nez Perce retreated 1,400 miles across Idaho and Montana, pursued by General Oliver Otis Howard and the U.S. army. Along the way they fought several battles. The Nez Perce were finally stopped forty miles from Canada, and on October 5, 1877 at Bears Paw, Chief Joseph, known by his people as Hin-mah-too Yah-lat-kekt (Thunder Rolling in the Mountains), made this surrender speech.

Tell General Howard that I know his heart. What he told me before I have in my heart. I am tired of fighting. Our chiefs are killed. Looking Glass is dead, Tu-hul-hil-sote is dead. The old men are all dead. It is the young men who now say yes or no. He who led the young men [Joseph's brother Alikut] is dead. It is cold and we have no blankets. The little children are freezing to death. My people—some of them have run away to the hills and have no blankets and no food. No one knows where they are—perhaps freezing to death. I want to have time to look for my children and see how many of them I can find. Maybe I shall find them among the dead. Hear me, my chiefs, my heart is sick and sad. From where the sun now stands I will fight no more against the white man.

Research Chief Joseph and the Nez Perce trail. How does the context provided by additional background information, or knowledge, help develop your understanding of the speech?

■ ■ ■

A More Perfect Union

Barack Obama

Barack Obama delivered the following speech in Philadelphia, Pennyslvania, on March 18, 2008 during the primary campaign for U.S. President. The speech was a response to controversy about comments made by Obama's former pastor, Reverend Jeremiah Wright. When news programs played Wright's most controversial comments and critics connected them to Obama and his campaign, Obama responded by encouraging the nation to explore and grapple with the complexity of race in America.

"We the people, in order to form a more perfect union."

Two hundred and twenty one years ago, in a hall that still stands across the street, a group of men gathered and, with these simple words, launched America's improbable experiment in democracy. Farmers and scholars, statesmen and patriots who had traveled across an ocean to escape tyranny and persecution finally made real their declaration of independence at a Philadelphia convention that lasted through the spring of 1787.

The document they produced was eventually signed but ultimately unfinished. It was stained by this nation's original sin of slavery, a question that divided the colonies and brought the convention to a stalemate until the founders chose to allow the slave trade to continue for at least twenty more years, and to leave any final resolution to future generations.

Of course, the answer to the slavery question was already embedded within our Constitution—a Constitu-

tion that had at is very core the ideal of equal citizenship under the law; a Constitution that promised its people liberty, and justice, and a union that could be and should be perfected over time.

5   And yet words on a parchment would not be enough to deliver slaves from bondage, or provide men and women of every color and creed their full rights and obligations as citizens of the United States. What would be needed were Americans in successive generations who were willing to do their part—through protests and struggle, on the streets and in the courts, through a civil war and civil disobedience and always at great risk—to narrow that gap between the promise of our ideals and the reality of their time.

This was one of the tasks we set forth at the beginning of this campaign—to continue the long march of those who came before us, a march for a more just, more equal, more free, more caring, and more prosperous America. I chose to run for the presidency at this moment in history because I believe deeply that we cannot solve the challenges of our time unless we solve them together—unless we perfect our union by understanding that we may have different stories, but we hold common hopes; that we may not look the same and we may not have come from the same place, but we all want to move in the same direction—towards a better future for our children and our grandchildren.

This belief comes from my unyielding faith in the decency and generosity of the American people. But it also comes from my own American story.

I am the son of a black man from Kenya and a white woman from Kansas. I was raised with the help of a white grandfather who survived a Depression to serve in Patton's army during World War II and a white grandmother who worked on a bomber assembly line at Fort Leavenworth while he was overseas. I've gone to some of the best schools in America and lived in one of the world's poorest nations. I am married to a black American who carries within her the blood of slaves and slaveowners—an inheritance we pass on to our two precious daughters. I have brothers, sisters, nieces, nephews, uncles, and cousins, of every race and every hue, scattered across three continents, and for as long as I live, I will never forget that in no other country on Earth is my story even possible.

It's a story that hasn't made me the most conventional candidate. But it is a story that has seared into my genetic makeup the idea that this nation is more than the sum of its parts—that out of many, we are truly one.

10   Throughout the first year of this campaign, against all predictions to the contrary, we saw how hungry the American people were for this message of unity. Despite the temptation to view my candidacy through a purely racial lens, we won commanding victories in states with some of the whitest populations in the country. In South Carolina, where the Confederate flag still flies, we built a powerful coalition of African Americans and white Americans.

This is not to say that race has not been an issue in the campaign. At various stages in the campaign, some commentators have deemed me either "too black" or "not black enough." We saw racial tensions bubble to the surface during the week before the South Carolina primary. The press has scoured every exit poll for the latest evidence of racial polarization, not just in terms of white and black, but black and brown as well.

And yet, it has only been in the last couple of weeks that the discussion of race in this campaign has taken a particularly divisive turn.

On one end of the spectrum, we've heard the implication that my candidacy is somehow an exercise in affirmative action; that it's based solely on the desire of wide-eyed liberals to purchase racial reconciliation on the cheap. On the other end, we've heard my former pastor, Reverend Jeremiah Wright, use incendiary language to express views that have the potential not only to widen the racial divide, but views that denigrate both the greatness and the goodness of our nation; that rightly offend white and black alike.

I have already condemned, in unequivocal terms, the statements of Reverend Wright that have caused such controversy. For some, nagging questions remain. Did I know him to be an occasionally fierce critic of American domestic and foreign policy? Of course. Did I ever hear him make remarks that could be considered controversial while I sat in church? Yes. Did I strongly disagree with many of his political views? Absolutely— just as I'm sure many of you have heard remarks from your pastors, priests, or rabbis with which you strongly disagreed.

15   But the remarks that have caused this recent firestorm weren't simply controversial. They weren't simply a religious leader's effort to speak out against perceived injustice. Instead, they expressed a profoundly distorted view of this country— a view that sees white racism as endemic, and that elevates what is wrong with America above all that we know is right with America; a view that sees the conflicts in the Middle East as rooted primarily in the actions of stalwart allies like Israel, instead of emanating from the perverse and hateful ideologies of radical Islam.

As such, Reverend Wright's comments were not only wrong but divisive, divisive at a time when we need unity; racially charged at a time when we need to come together to solve a set of monumental problems—two wars, a terrorist threat, a falling economy, a chronic health care crisis, and potentially devastating climate change; problems that are neither black or white or Latino or Asian, but rather problems that confront us all.

Given my background, my politics, and my professed values and ideals, there will no doubt be those for whom my statements of condemnation are not enough. Why associate myself with Reverend Wright in the first place, they may ask? Why not join another church? And I confess that if all that I knew of Reverend Wright were the snippets of those sermons that have run in an endless loop on the television and YouTube, or if Trinity United Church of Christ conformed to the caricatures being peddled by some commentators, there is no doubt that I would react in much the same way

But the truth is, that isn't all that I know of the man. The man I met more than twenty years ago is a man who helped introduce me to my Christian faith, a man who spoke to me about our obligations to love one another; to care for the sick and lift up the poor. He is a man who served his country as a U.S. Marine; who has studied and lectured at some of the finest universities and seminaries in the country; and who for over thirty years led a church that serves the community by doing God's work here on Earth—by housing the homeless, ministering to the needy, providing day care services and scholarships and prison ministries, and reaching out to those suffering from HIV/AIDS.

In my first book, *Dreams From My Father,* I described the experience of my first service at Trinity:

People began to shout, to rise from their seats and clap and cry out, a forceful wind carrying the reverend's voice up into the rafters . . . . And in that single note—hope!—I heard something else; at the foot of that cross, inside the thousands of churches across the city, I imagined the stories of ordinary black people merging with the stories of David and Goliath, Moses and Pharaoh, the Christians in the lion's den, Ezekiel's field of dry bones. Those stories—of survival, and freedom, and hope—became our story, my story; the blood that had spilled was our blood, the tears our tears; until this black church, on this bright day, seemed once more a vessel carrying the story of a people into future generations and into a larger world. Our trials and triumphs became at once unique and universal, black and more than black; in chronicling our journey, the stories and songs gave us a means to reclaim memories that we didn't need to feel shame about . . . memories that all people might study and cherish—and with which we could start to rebuild.

20   That has been my experience at Trinity. Like other predominantly black churches across the country, Trinity embodies the black community in its entirety—the doctor and the welfare mom, the model student and the former gang-banger. Like other black churches, Trinity's services are full of raucous laughter and sometimes bawdy humor. They are full of dancing, clapping, screaming, and shouting that may seem jarring to the untrained ear. The church contains in full the kindness and cruelty, the fierce intelligence and the shocking ignorance, the struggles and successes, the love, and yes, the bitterness and bias that make up the black experience in America.

And this helps explain, perhaps, my relationship with Reverend Wright. As imperfect as he may be, he has been like family to me. He strengthened my faith, officiated my wedding, and baptized my children. Not once in my conversations with him have I heard him talk about any ethnic group in derogatory terms, or treat whites with whom he interacted with anything but courtesy and respect. He contains within him the con-

traditions—the good and the bad—of the community that he has served diligently for so many years.

I can no more disown him than I can disown the black community. I can no more disown him than I can my white grandmother—a woman who helped raise me, a woman who sacrificed again and again for me, a woman who loves me as much as she loves anything in this world, but a woman who once confessed her fear of black men who passed by her on the street, and who on more than one occasion has uttered racial or ethnic stereotypes that made me cringe.

These people are a part of me. And they are a part of America, this country that I love.

Some will see this as an attempt to justify or excuse comments that are simply inexcusable. I can assure you it is not. I suppose the politically safe thing would be to move on from this episode and just hope that it fades into the woodwork. We can dismiss Reverend Wright as a crank or a demagogue, just as some have dismissed Geraldine Ferraro, in the aftermath of her recent statements, as harboring some deep-seated racial bias.

25   But race is an issue that I believe this nation cannot afford to ignore right now. We would be making the same mistake that Reverend Wright made in his offending sermons about America—to simplify and stereotype and amplify the negative to the point that it distorts reality.

The fact is that the comments that have been made and the issues that have surfaced over the last few weeks reflect the complexities of race in this country that we've never really worked through—a part of our union that we have yet to perfect. And if we walk away now, if we simply retreat into our respective corners, we will never be able to come together and solve challenges like health care, or education, or the need to find good jobs for every American.

Understanding this reality requires a reminder of how we arrived at this point. As William Faulkner once wrote, "The past isn't dead and buried. In fact, it isn't even past." We do not need to recite here the history of racial injustice in this country. But we do need to remind ourselves that so many of the disparities that exist in the African-American community today can be directly traced to inequalities passed on from an earlier generation that suffered under the brutal legacy of slavery and Jim Crow.

Segregated schools were, and are, inferior schools; we still haven't fixed them, fifty years after *Brown v. Board of Education,* and the inferior education they provided, then and now, helps explain the pervasive achievement gap between today's black and white students.

Legalized discrimination—where blacks were prevented, often through violence, from owning property, or loans were not granted to African-American business owners, or black homeowners could not access FHA mortgages, or blacks were excluded from unions, or the police force, or fire departments—meant that black families could not amass any meaningful wealth to bequeath to future generations. That history helps explain the wealth and income gap between black and white, and the concentrated pockets of poverty that persists in so many of today's urban and rural communities.

30 A lack of economic opportunity among black men, and the shame and frustration that came from not being able to provide for one's family, contributed to the erosion of black families—a problem that welfare policies for many years may have worsened. And the lack of basic services in so many urban black neighborhoods—parks for kids to play in, police walking the beat, regular garbage pick-up, and building code enforcement—all helped create a cycle of violence, blight, and neglect that continue to haunt us.

This is the reality in which Reverend Wright and other African Americans of his generation grew up. They came of age in the late fifties and early sixties, a time when segregation was still the law of the land and opportunity was systematically constricted. What's remarkable is not how many failed in the face of discrimination, but rather how many men and women overcame the odds; how many were able to make a way out of no way for those like me who would come after them.

But for all those who scratched and clawed their way to get a piece of the American Dream, there were many who didn't make it—those who were ultimately defeated, in one way or another, by discrimination. That legacy of defeat was passed on to future generations—those young men and increasingly young women who

we see standing on street corners or languishing in our prisons, without hope or prospects for the future. Even for those blacks who did make it, questions of race, and racism, continue to define their worldview in fundamental ways. For the men and women of Reverend Wright's generation, the memories of humiliation and doubt and fear have not gone away; nor has the anger and the bitterness of those years. That anger may not get expressed in public, in front of white coworkers or white friends. But it does find voice in the barbershop or around the kitchen table. At times, that anger is exploited by politicians, to gin up votes along racial lines, or to make up for a politician's own failings.

And occasionally it finds voice in the church on Sunday morning, in the pulpit and in the pews. The fact that so many people are surprised to hear that anger in some of Reverend Wright's sermons simply reminds us of the old truism that the most segregated hour in American life occurs on Sunday morning. That anger is not always productive; indeed, all too often it distracts attention from solving real problems; it keeps us from squarely facing our own complicity in our condition, and prevents the African American community from forging the alliances it needs to bring about real change. But the anger is real; it is powerful; and to simply wish it away, to condemn it without understanding its roots, only serves to widen the chasm of misunderstanding that exists between the races.

In fact, a similar anger exists within segments of the white community. Most working- and middle-class white Americans don't feel that they have been particularly privileged by their race. Their experience is the immigrant experience—as far as they're concerned, no one's handed them anything, they've built it from scratch. They've worked hard all their lives, many times only to see their jobs shipped overseas or their pension dumped after a lifetime of labor. They are anxious about their futures, and feel their dreams slipping away; in an era of stagnant wages and global competition, opportunity comes to be seen as a zero sum game, in which your dreams come at my expense. So when they are told to bus their children to a school across town; when they hear that an African American is getting an advantage in landing a good job or a spot in a good college because of an injustice that they themselves never committed; when they're told that their fears about crime in urban neighborhoods are somehow prejudiced, resentment builds over time.

35   Like the anger within the black community, these resentments aren't always expressed in polite company. But they have helped shape the political landscape for at least a generation. Anger over welfare and affirmative action helped forge the Reagan coalition. Politicians routinely exploited fears of crime for their own electoral ends. Talk show hosts and conservative commentators built entire careers unmasking bogus claims of racism while dismissing legitimate discussions of racial injustice and inequality as mere political correctness or reverse racism.

Just as black anger often proved counterproductive, so have these white resentments distracted attention from the real culprits of the middle-class squeeze—a corporate culture rife with inside dealing, questionable accounting practices, and short-term greed; a Washington dominated by lobbyists and special interests; economic policies that favor the few over the many. And yet, to wish away the resentments of white Americans, to label them as misguided or even racist, without recognizing they are grounded in legitimate concerns—this too widens the racial divide, and blocks the path to understanding.

This is where we are right now. It's a racial stalemate we've been stuck in for years. Contrary to the claims of some of my critics, black and white, I have never been so naïve as to believe that we can get beyond our racial divisions in a single election cycle, or with a single candidacy—particularly a candidacy as imperfect as my own.

But I have asserted a firm conviction—a conviction rooted in my faith in God and my faith in the American people—that working together we can move beyond some of our old racial wounds, and that in fact we have no choice if we are to continue on the path of a more perfect union.

For the African American community, that path means embracing the burdens of our past without becoming victims of our past. It means continuing to insist on a full measure of justice in every aspect of American life.

But it also means binding our particular grievances—for better health care, and better schools, and better jobs—to the larger aspirations of all Americans—the white woman struggling to break the glass ceiling, the white man whose been laid off, the immigrant trying to feed his family. And it means taking full responsibility for own lives—by demanding more from our fathers, and spending more time with our children, and reading to them, and teaching them that while they may face challenges and discrimination in their own lives, they must never succumb to despair or cynicism; they must always believe that they can write their own destiny.

40   Ironically, this quintessentially American—and yes, conservative—notion of self-help found frequent expression in Reverend Wright's sermons. But what my former pastor too often failed to understand is that embarking on a program of self-help also requires a belief that society can change.

The profound mistake of Reverend Wright's sermons is not that he spoke about racism in our society. It's that he spoke as if our society was static; as if no progress has been made; as if this country—a country that has made it possible for one of his own members to run for the highest office in the land and build a coalition of white and black, Latino and Asian, rich and poor, young and old—is still irrevocably bound to a tragic past. But what we know—what we have seen—is that America can change. That is true genius of this nation. What we have already achieved gives us hope—the audacity to hope—for what we can and must achieve tomorrow.

In the white community, the path to a more perfect union means acknowledging that what ails the African American community does not just exist in the minds of black people; that the legacy of discrimination—and current incidents of discrimination, while less overt than in the past—are real and must be addressed. Not just with words, but with deeds—by investing in our schools and our communities; by enforcing our civil rights laws and ensuring fairness in our criminal justice system; by providing this generation with ladders of opportunity that were unavailable for previous generations. It requires all Americans to realize that your dreams do not have to come at the expense of my dreams; that investing in the health, welfare, and education of black and brown and white children will ultimately help all of America prosper.

In the end, then, what is called for is nothing more, and nothing less, than what all the world's great religions demand—that we do unto others as we would have them do unto us. Let us be our brother's keeper, Scripture tells us. Let us be our sister's keeper. Let us find that common stake we all have in one another, and let our politics reflect that spirit as well.

For we have a choice in this country. We can accept a politics that breeds division, and conflict, and cynicism. We can tackle race only as spectacle—as we did in the OJ trial—or in the wake of tragedy, as we did in the aftermath of Katrina—or as fodder for the nightly news. We can play Reverend Wright's sermons on every channel, every day, and talk about them from now until the election, and make the only question in this campaign whether or not the American people think that I somehow believe or sympathize with his most offensive words. We can pounce on some gaffe by a Hillary supporter as evidence that she's playing the race card, or we can speculate on whether white men will all flock to John McCain in the general election regardless of his policies.

45 We can do that.

But if we do, I can tell you that in the next election, we'll be talking about some other distraction. And then another one. And then another one. And nothing will change.

That is one option. Or, at this moment, in this election, we can come together and say, "Not this time." This time we want to talk about the crumbling schools that are stealing the future of black children and white children and Asian children and Hispanic children and Native American children. This time we want to reject the cynicism that tells us that these kids can't learn; that those kids who don't look like us are somebody else's problem. The children of America are not those kids, they are our kids, and we will not let them fall behind in a 21st century economy. Not this time.

This time we want to talk about how the lines in the emergency room are filled with whites and blacks and Hispanics who do not have health care; who don't have the power on their own to overcome the special interests in Washington, but who can take them on if we do it together.

This time we want to talk about the shuttered mills that once provided a decent life for men and women of every race, and the homes for sale that once belonged to Americans from every religion, every region, every walk of life. This time we want to talk about the fact that the real problem is not that someone who doesn't look like you might take your job; it's that the corporation you work for will ship it overseas for nothing more than a profit.

50 This time we want to talk about the men and women of every color and creed who serve together, and fight together, and bleed together under the same proud flag. We want to talk about how to bring them home from a war that never should've been authorized and never should've been waged, and we want to talk about how we'll show our patriotism by caring for them, and their families, and giving them the benefits they have earned.

I would not be running for President if I didn't believe with all my heart that this is what the vast majority of Americans want for this country. This union may never be perfect, but generation after generation has shown that it can always be perfected. And today, whenever I find myself feeling doubtful or cynical about this possibility, what gives me the most hope is the next generation—the young people whose attitudes and beliefs and openness to change have already made history in this election.

There is one story in particularly that I'd like to leave you with today—a story I told when I had the great honor of speaking on Dr. King's birthday at his home church, Ebenezer Baptist, in Atlanta.

There is a young, twenty-three-year-old white woman named Ashley Baia who organized for our campaign in Florence, South Carolina. She had been working to organize a mostly African American community since the beginning of this campaign, and one day she was at a roundtable discussion where everyone went around telling their story and why they were there.

And Ashley said that when she was nine years old, her mother got cancer. And because she had to miss days of work, she was let go and lost her health care.

They had to file for bankruptcy, and that's when Ashley decided that she had to do something to help her mom.

55　She knew that food was one of their most expensive costs, and so Ashley convinced her mother that what she really liked and really wanted to eat more than anything else was mustard and relish sandwiches. Because that was the cheapest way to eat.

She did this for a year until her mom got better, and she told everyone at the roundtable that the reason she joined our campaign was so that she could help the millions of other children in the country who want and need to help their parents too.

Now, Ashley might have made a different choice. Perhaps somebody told her along the way that the source of her mother's problems were blacks who were on welfare and too lazy to work, or Hispanics who were coming into the country illegally. But she didn't. She sought out allies in her fight against injustice.

Anyway, Ashley finishes her story and then goes around the room and asks everyone else why they're supporting the campaign. They all have different stories and reasons. Many bring up a specific issue. And finally they come to this elderly black man who's been sitting there quietly the entire time. And Ashley asks him why he's there. And he does not bring up a specific issue. He does not say health care or the economy. He does not say education or the war. He does not say that he was there because of Barack Obama. He simply says to everyone in the room, "I am here because of Ashley."

"I'm here because of Ashley." By itself, that single moment of recognition between that young white girl and that old black man is not enough. It is not enough to give health care to the sick, or jobs to the jobless, or education to our children.

But it is where we start. It is where our union grows stronger. And as so many generations have come to realize over the course of the two hundred and twenty one years since a band of patriots signed that document in Philadelphia, that is where the perfection begins.

Writing Strategies

1. What is Obama's main idea? What support strategies does he use to help the reader understand and accept it?
2. How does Obama use the concept of "a more perfect union" as a unifying device throughout his essay?
3. Explain how two passages from Obama's speech illustrate a Rogerian approach to argument.
4. How does Obama's concluding anecdote about Ashley help the reader understand and accept his argument?
5. Describe the "racial stalemate" to which Obama refers. (¶ 37) How does Obama suggest we approach the stalemate?

Exploring Ideas

1. Why does Obama think the U.S. Constitution was "signed but ultimately unfinished"? Summarize his argument about this point, then imagine how others might respond. Write down one argument that supports Obama's position and one that refutes it.
2. With a group of peers, discuss your responses to #1 above. Which group members think the constitution was, and is, ultimately unfinished, and why? Which group members disagree, and why?
3. According to Obama, Reverend Wright "contains within him the contradictions—the good and the bad—of the community that he served diligently for so many years." (¶ 21) What contradictions—good and bad—of your community do you contain?
4. Obama writes, "The fact is that the comments that have been made and the issues that have surfaced over the last few weeks reflect the complexities of race in this country that we've never really worked through—a part of our union we have yet to perfect." (¶ 26) Why haven't we worked through these issues?

For help inventing your own writing project, see the Point of Contact section on pp. 270–271.

Evaluating
No Country for Old Men

Roger Ebert

Movie reviewers such as Roger Ebert write evaluation essays about films. Ebert's review of *No Country for Old Men* (2007) argues the overall worth, or value, of the film, using both details about the film and details outside the film (such as alluding to *Fargo*) to support the essay's main evaluative claims. Ebert's reviews appear in the *Chicago Sun-Times* and online at rogerebert.com. The film *No Country for Old Men* was written and directed by Joel and Ethan Coen, and is based on the novel by Cormac McCarthy.

The movie opens with the flat, confiding voice of Tommy Lee Jones. He describes a teenage killer he once sent to the chair. The boy had killed his 14-year-old girlfriend. The papers described it as a crime of passion, "but he tolt me there weren't nothin' passionate about it. Said he'd been fixin' to kill someone for as long as he could remember. Said if I let him out of there, he'd kill somebody again. Said he was goin' to hell. Reckoned he'd be there in about 15 minutes."

These words sounded verbatim to me from *No Country for Old Men,* the novel by Cormac McCarthy, but I find they are not quite. And their impact has been improved upon in the delivery. When I get the DVD of this film, I will listen to that stretch of narration several times; Jones delivers it with a vocal precision and contained emotion that is extraordinary, and it sets up the entire film, which regards a completely evil man with wonderment, as if astonished that that such a merciless creature could exist.

The man is named Anton Chigurh. No, I don't know how his last name is pronounced. Like many of the words McCarthy uses, particularly in his masterpiece *Suttree,* I think it is employed like an architectural detail: The point is not how it sounds or what it means, but the brushstroke it adds to the sentence. Chigurh (Javier Bardem) is a tall, slouching man with lank, black hair and a terrifying smile, who travels through Texas carrying a tank of compressed air and killing people with a cattle stungun. It propels a cylinder into their heads and whips it back again.

Chigurh is one strand in the twisted plot. Ed Tom Bell, the sheriff played by Jones, is another. The third major player is Llewelyn Moss (Josh Brolin), a poor man who lives with his wife in a house trailer, and one day, while hunting, comes across a drug deal gone wrong in the desert. Vehicles range in a circle like an old wagon train. Almost everyone on the scene is dead. They even shot the dog. In the back of one pickup are neatly stacked bags of drugs. Llewelyn realizes one thing is missing: the money. He finds it in a briefcase next to a man who made it as far as a shade tree before dying.

The plot will involve Moss attempting to make this $2 million his own, Chigurh trying to take it away from him, and Sheriff Bell trying to interrupt Chigurh's ruthless murder trail. We will also meet Moss' child-like wife, Carla Jean (Kelly Macdonald); a cocky bounty hunter named Carson Wells (Woody Harrelson); the businessman (Stephen Root) who hires Carson to track the money after investing in the drug deal; and a series of hotel and store clerks who are unlucky enough to meet Chigurh.

No Country for Old Men is as good a film as the Coen brothers, Joel and Ethan, have ever made, and they made *Fargo*. It involves elements of the thriller and the chase but is essentially a character study, an examination of how its people meet and deal with a man so bad, cruel, and unfeeling that there is simply no comprehending him. Chigurh is so evil, he is almost funny sometimes. "He has his principles," says the bounty hunter, who has knowledge of him.

Consider another scene in which the dialogue is as good as any you will hear this year. Chigurh enters a rundown gas station in the middle of wilderness and begins to play a word game with the old man (Gene Jones) behind the cash register, who becomes very nervous. It is clear they are talking about whether Chigurh will kill him. Chigurh has by no means made up his mind. Without explaining why, he asks the man to call the flip of a coin. Listen to what they say, how they say it, how they imply the stakes. Listen to their timing. You want to applaud the writing, which comes from the Coen brothers, out of McCarthy.

The $2 million turns out to be easier to obtain than to keep. Moss tries hiding in obscure hotels. Scenes are meticulously constructed in which each man knows the other is nearby. Moss can run but he can't hide. Chigurh always tracks him down. He shadows him like his doom, never hurrying, always moving at the same measured pace, like a pursuer in a nightmare.

This movie is a masterful evocation of time, place, character, moral choices, immoral certainties, human nature, and fate. It is also, in the photography by Roger Deakins, the editing by the Coens, and the music by Carter Burwell, startlingly beautiful, stark and lonely. As McCarthy does with the Judge, the hairless exterminator in his *Blood Meridian* (Ridley Scott's next film), and as in his *Suttree,* especially in the scene where the riverbank caves in, the movie demonstrates how pitiful ordinary human feelings are in the face of implacable injustice. The movie also loves some of its characters, and pities them, and has an ear for dialogue not as it is spoken but as it is dreamed.

Many of the scenes in *No Country for Old Men* are so flawlessly constructed that you want them to simply continue, and yet they create an emotional suction drawing you to the next scene. Another movie that made me feel that way was *Fargo.* To make one such film is a miracle. Here is another.

Writing Strategies

1. What is Ebert's main evaluative claim about the movie?
2. Describe Ebert's support strategy. What details about the subject help the reader understand and accept his main evaluative claim? What details outside the subject help the reader understand and accept his main evaluative claim?
3. Describe Ebert's voice as a writer. Use two passages from this essay to support your description.
4. Does Ebert's review seem credible? Why or why not?
5. What criteria, or standards of judgment, does Ebert use?

Exploring Ideas

1. What passages from Ebert's review make you want to see the movie, and why?
2. Choose two films that should be evaluated based on different criteria for each one. List the criteria for each film, and explain

why they should be used. What common criteria can be used for both films?
3. What writing decisions does Ebert make because he is writing for a movie-literate audience? Refer to two passages that Ebert would have to alter if he assumed that his readers weren't avid moviegoers.

For help inventing your own writing project, see the Point of Contact section on pp. 270–271.

■ ■ ■

Revealing the Ugly Cartoonish Truth: *The Simpsons*

Simon Benlow

Evaluating entertainment can be dangerous, because writers might be tempted to give a list of likes and dislikes. Based on this essay, we can assume that Simon Benlow "likes" *The Simpsons,* but the essay does more than share Benlow's approval of the show. It argues about the purpose of mainstream entertainment—what it should or could do for American audiences. While celebrating *The Simpsons* and analyzing its specific qualities, Benlow reveals the shortcomings of mainstream American entertainment, and even pokes fun at the institutions of everyday life.

It's not often that a television sitcom does more than tickle our most simplistic pleasures. The vast majority of sitcoms, past and present, fill twenty-two minutes (or is it nineteen?) with cliché moralism, empty characters, and adolescent dialog. Every fall we can look forward to a new parade of bad jokes and simpleton plots—created primarily to allow American viewers to gawk at the latest celebrity hairstyles and tight shirts.

However, amidst an exhausting list of here-and-then-gone "real-life" sitcoms, *The Simpsons* has managed to create a new class of television. It has stretched what can (and should) be expected in prime-time entertainment. It goes where most sitcoms, most American entertainment, will not. It satirizes everything (and nearly anything) mainstream America cherishes. From SUVs to friendly fast-food chains, the familiar elements of everyday life are revealed as ridiculous creations of a culture blind to its own vices. Certainly, it takes shots at big targets: nuclear power, organized labor, corporate fraud, slick politicians, organized religion, hyperconsumerism, hyper-consumption, and even television programming (often slamming its own network, FOX). But these are more than easy targets; these are the entities that seem to run amuck consistently, the institutions that maintain their status despite repeated failings, the bullies of our culture that always seem in need of a punch to their maniacal eye sockets.

In "Homer's Odyssey," an episode from the first season, the show does its usual deconstruction of everyday life. The episode reveals some ugly truth: Beneath the daily façade, there lurks an entire set of systems barely working, hardly accomplishing anything beyond their own survival. In the first scene, in front of Springfield Elementary, the children wait for the tardy, pot-smoking bus driver, Otto (who loves to "get blotto"). Once they get settled, they drive in circles through town. They pass by the toxic waste dump where happy workers casually pour mysterious fluid into the river; they pass the prison where they are greeted by hosts of prisoners (who were set free during the children's last field trip). They pass the Springfield tire yard (which becomes the Springfield tire fire in later episodes), and finally arrive at the nuclear power plant. At the gate, several signs announce "employees only," but the guard is sucking on a beverage and watching Krusty the Clown on television, so the children pass on through unnoticed.

In the power plant, we see the gross fumblings and even grosser cover-ups of an unchecked system. While Joe Fission, a cartoon icon, feeds the children pro-nuclear propaganda, Homer flummoxes his job and wreaks havoc in the plant. Homer is the poster boy of incompetence—yet he's granted a typical place in the ill-defined bureaucracy of power: Is he the "supervising technician" or the "technical supervisor"? No one knows. Through the episode, Homer is fired and then, for no good reason, hired back. The status quo prevails; three-eyed fish swim happily in the lake and the town continues to live on the brink of nuclear disaster.

5   In the animated town of Springfield, nothing is worthy of the praise it wants. Schools are not great institutions of learning; they are poorly funded bureaucracies run by flawed and desperate individuals. Government is not "of the people"; it is a mob of self-perpetuating boozers and womanizers. Business is not ethical or productive; it is a race to monopolize and swindle everyone in sight. These are the hard truths that *The Simpsons* offers us. Of course, we get these truths thrown at us in sanctimonious movies and bad morning talk shows, but *The Simpsons* manages to reveal these ideas without romanticizing its own characters or actors.

The Simpsons throws at us what we all might be thinking had we not been programmed to dismiss it. We all might briefly consider the lies the nuclear power industry feeds us, the laziness and self-righteousness of city governments, or the emptiness and humiliation of most jobs, but we've been trained out of being appalled. We've become distracted by our own lives, and the constant barrage of material goodness, so we allow our own institutions to bully us, to humiliate us, to dismiss our general welfare entirely. But *The Simpsons* reminds us of the slip-shod work and flagrant thievery going on just outside our own television sets.

Some may argue that *The Simpsons* is just a show; it can't possibly have that much meaning. However, one thing we've learned in America is that our entertainment has more significance than history, literature, philosophy, and politics. Mainstream society gets its values, its slogans, its hairstyles, even its dialects from entertainment. We are, as the world knows, an over-entertained nation. The average American citizen reads very little (maybe a few books per year), but fills thousands of hours being massaged by the television. As the last thirty years proves undoubtedly, Americans can change their minds at the drop of a hat (about almost anything) if the television set prompts us to do so. When television maintains such influence, it is significant and meaningful when the television itself plays with, pokes at, and parodies that influence.

In a swirling array of giddy and capricious entertainment, *The Simpsons* is far more real than any "real-life" sitcom hopes to be (or wants to be). In its relentless pursuit to overturn our romantic notions of ourselves and our lovely creations, it is probably more real than the audience it attracts (and certainly more real than those whom it doesn't). In fact, if we take the show as seriously as it deserves, we might even see the broad strokes of its irony: that *we* are the cartoons, drawn and colored by the ridiculous institutions that constitute our society. However, as soon as we go that far, Homer belches, Bart moons a head of state, and Grandpa soils himself; *The Simpsons* won't allow anything, including itself, to be taken seriously.

Writing Strategies

1. What purpose or goal of *The Simpsons* does Benlow focus on?
2. In your own words, what is Benlow's main idea?
3. What details from Benlow's essay are most helpful in developing his main idea?
4. Identify one counterargument Benlow makes, and explain how it is important to his essay.

Exploring Ideas

1. Why does Benlow think *The Simpsons* is important?
2. Watch several episodes of *The Simpsons,* finding support for Benlow's argument.
3. After exploring the following statement with others, explain what Benlow means when he says we are "drawn and colored by the ridiculous institutions that constitute our society":

   In fact, if we take the show as seriously as it deserves, we might even see the broad strokes of its irony: that we are the cartoons, drawn and colored by the ridiculous institutions that constitute our society. (¶ 8)

For help inventing your own writing project, see the Point of Contact section on pp. 314–315.

■ ■ ■

Hip-Hop: A Roadblock or Pathway to Black Empowerment?

Geoffrey Bennett

Throughout American history, popular art forms and entertainment have pushed against mainstream tastes and mores: slam poetry, jazz, vaudeville, swing, rock and roll, punk, heavy metal, rap, hip-hop. Each of these shocked the sensibilities of the mainstream culture. And when they gained popularity, writers, politicians, church groups, sociologists, and thinkers of all stripes asked questions about the state of the civilization. In the past twenty years, hip-hop music has been the source (and target) of such commentary. In this essay, Geoffrey Bennett (former editor-in-chief of the *Maroon Tiger* college newspaper at Morehouse College)

explores the relationship between hip-hop and the black community. The essay originally appeared in the *Black Collegian Online* (2001).

In the early 1980s, a highly percussive, cadenced, and repetitive musical form seeped from the inner city streets of the South Bronx to a virtually exclusive African-American audience. Harbingered by originators such as Run DMC, the Sugar Hill Gang, Public Enemy, Afrika Bambaata, and others, the medium was a simple reflection of the daily lives of its creators with topics ranging from the trivial, such as the style of one's new Adidas sneakers, to the significant, like the infuriation spurred by police harassment.

Rap music, as it came to be known, lacked major commercial support in its early stages, and, as a result, it was authentic and unaffected; it was truly "CNN for the streets," as Chuck D once commented. Twenty years later, however, hip-hop culture has since flooded mainstream culture, and rap music is as prevalent in suburban homes as it once was in its native environment, moving from American subculture to the forefront of American attention. "Hip-hop is more powerful than any American cultural movement we've ever had," said rap music impresario Russell Simmons.

Hip-hop is one of the fastest-growing music genres in the United States, accounting for $1.84 billion in sales last year out of a $14.3 billion total for the U.S. recording industry, according to industry statistics. Interestingly, nearly 70 percent of those sales are to white suburban youth, a striking transformation considering rap music's beginnings. Most importantly, perhaps, rap music and its associated hip-hop culture have become a new component of the Black cultural aesthetic. With its rhythmical roots firmly planted in African tradition, hip-hop music is more than just musical expression. For some, it is a way of life, affecting their speech, style of dress, hairstyle, and overall disposition.

Like any other expressive art form, rappers have tested the boundaries of social responsibility, legality, free speech, and old-fashioned "good taste." Labeled as misogynistic, reckless, and even criminal, rappers endured years of public scrutiny with African Americans among some of their most relentless critics. After years of incessant scrutiny, hip-hop mogul Russell Simmons organized a three-day hip-hop music summit for 200 rappers, industry executives, and African-American politicians, the first event of its kind. Sean Combs, LL Cool J, Queen Latifah, Wyclef Jean, Wu-Tang Clan, Chuck D, Jermaine Dupri, KRS-1, Luther Campbell, Ja Rule, and Talib Kweli were just a few of the influential hip-hop artists in attendance at the conference held last June in New York City.

5   Stars joined forces with some of Black America's intellectual and political elite, including NAACP president Kweisi Mfume; Urban League president Hugh Price; Nation of Islam minister Louis Farrakhan; Martin Luther King, III, leader of the Southern Christian Leadership Council; Georgia Democratic congressional representative Cynthia McKinney; and authors Cornel West and Michael Eric Dyson. The summit ended with musicians and industry executives agreeing to follow voluntary guidelines to advise parents of music's lyrical content while vowing to protect rap artists' freedom of speech by fighting Congressional efforts to censor the music. Minister Louis Farrakhan of the Nation of Islam, one of the political activists who attended the summit, told rappers, "You've now got to accept the responsibility you've never accepted. You are the leaders of the youth of the world."

Today's African-American college students, many of whom as youth were the original fans during rap music's formative years, still remain avid rap music connoisseurs. Rap music, however, has taken a decidedly different direction in recent years. Since rap music is clearly a profitable commercial commodity, rappers consequently perpetuate images and stereotypes that will sell their products, ranging from the excessively violent to the extravagantly wealthy. "Many rappers do not live the type of lives they claim. Those that claim to be affluent often are not, and those that claim to be poor gang-bangers are often millionaires. Fortunately, most college students have the ability to decipher between rap's glamorous image and the realities of life. A problem arises for the younger, impressionable audience, many of whom buy into rap's surface image," said Morehouse College Student Government Association president Christopher J. Graves.

As role models, accepting of the designation or not, rappers have a unique responsibility to be cognizant of their message and their intended audience. Since American pop culture reveres stardom, rappers often garner more attention and respect than they deserve. Consequently, rap music and hip-hop culture have the power to either adversely or positively affect African Americans in specific, and the larger culture in general. While a summit on rap music cannot adequately address all of its dilemmas, a dialogue between interested parties must continue in order to preserve the distinctive art form, while protecting the rich heritage of the African-American cultural aesthetic.

Writing Strategies

1. Describe how Bennett's introduction functions. What is he attempting to do? How does it assist the reader in understanding the rest of the essay? What, if anything, else do you think...?
2. Describe Bennett's voice and evaluate its appropriateness for this subject matter. Provide several passages to support your evaluation.
3. How does Bennett get his main idea across to the reader? Does he state his main idea or imply it? What type of background information and evidence does he provide?
4. Evaluate the effectiveness of Bennett's sources. How do they help the reader to understand his argument or to accept his claims?

Exploring Ideas

1. How does Bennett encourage the reader to look at hip-hop?
2. How does Bennett's idea fit into a larger discussion? That is, how can what he says be applied not just to hip-hop but to other art forms?
3. Observe the relationship between different art forms (hip-hop, country music, film, painting, etc.) and people in your community. How does art seem to influence their thoughts and behavior? How do they seem to influence the art form?
4. In addition to art, what influences people? Go out and observe how people in your community choose to live—how they move around, shop, eat, work, play. What are the major influences on what they wear, what they eat, how they get around, what they do for a living, what they do in their spare time?

For help inventing your own writing project, see the Point of Contact section on pp. 314–315.

their children, when they were sure of a settlement for life to the poor babes, provided in some sort by the publick, to their annual profit instead of expence. We should soon see an honest emulation among the married women, which of them could bring the fattest child to the market. Men would become as fond of their wives, during the time of their pregnancy, as they are now of their mares in foal, their cows in calf, or sow when they are ready to farrow; nor offer to beat or kick them (as is too frequent a practice) for fear of a miscarriage.

25 Many other advantages might be enumerated. For instance, the addition of some thousand carcasses in our exportation of barrel'd beef: the propagation of swine's flesh, and improvement in the art of making good bacon, so much wanted among us by the great destruction of pigs, too frequent at our tables; which are no way comparable in taste or magnificence to a well grown, fat yearly child, which roasted whole will make a considerable figure at a Lord Mayor's feast, or any other publick entertainment. But this, and many others, I omit, being studious of brevity.

Supposing that one thousand families in this city, would be constant customers for infants flesh, besides others who might have it at merry meetings, particularly at weddings and christenings, I compute that Dublin would take off annually about twenty thousand carcasses; and the rest of the kingdom (where probably they will be sold somewhat cheaper) the remaining eighty thousand.

I can think of no one objection, that will possibly be raised against this proposal, unless it should be urged, that the number of people will be thereby much lessened in the kingdom. This I freely own, and 'twas indeed one principal design in offering it to the world. I desire the reader will observe, that I calculate my remedy for this one individual Kingdom of Ireland, and for no other that ever was, is, or, I think, ever can be upon Earth. Therefore let no man talk to me of other expedients: Of taxing our absentees at five shillings a pound: Of using neither cloaths, nor houshold furniture, except what is of our own growth and manufacture: Of utterly rejecting the materials and instruments that promote foreign luxury: Of curing the expensiveness of pride, vanity, idleness, and gaming in our women: Of introducing a vein of parsimony, prudence, and temperance: Of learning to love our country, wherein we differ even from Lap-

landers, and the inhabitants of Topinamboo: Of quitting our animosities and factions, nor acting any longer likethe Jews, who were murdering one another at the very moment their city was taken: Of being a little cautious not to sell our country and consciences for nothing: Of teaching landlords to have at least one degree of mercy towards their tenants. Lastly, of putting a spirit of honesty, industry, and skill into our shop-keepers, who, if a resolution could now be taken to buy onlyour native goods, would immediately unite to cheat and exact upon us in the price, the measure, and the goodness, nor could ever yet be brought to make one fair proposal of just dealing, though often and earnestly invited to it.

Therefore I repeat, let no man talk to me of these and the like expedients, 'till he hath at least some glympse of hope, that there will ever be some hearty and sincere attempt to put them into practice.

But, as to my self, having been wearied out for many years with offering vain, idle, visionary thoughts, and at length utterly despairing of success, I fortunately fell upon this proposal, which, as it is wholly new, so it hath something solid and real, of no expence and little trouble, full in our own power, and whereby we can incur no danger in disobliging England. For this kind of commodity will not bear exportation, and flesh being of too tender a consistence, to admit a long continuance in salt, although perhaps I could name a country, which would be glad to eat up our whole nation without it.

30 After all, I am not so violently bent upon my own opinion, as to reject any offer, proposed by wise men, which shall be found equally innocent, cheap, easy, and effectual. But before something of that kind shall be advanced in contradiction to my scheme, and offering a better, I desire the author or authors will be pleased maturely to consider two points. First, As things now stand, how they will be able to find food and raiment for a hundred thousand useless mouths and backs. And secondly, There being a round million of creatures in humane figure throughout this kingdom, whose whole subsistence put into a common stock, would leave them in debt two million of pounds sterling, adding those who are beggars by profession, to the bulk of farmers, cottagers, and labourers, with their wives and children, who are beggars in effect; I desire those politicians who dislike my overture, and may perhaps be so bold to

attempt an answer, that they will first ask the parents of these mortals, whether they would not at this day think it a great happiness to have been sold for food at a year old, in the manner I prescribe, and thereby have avoided such a perpetual scene of misfortunes, as they have since gone through, by the oppression of landlords, the impossibility of paying rent without money or trade, the want of common sustenance, with neither house nor cloaths to cover them from the inclemencies of the weather, and the most inevitable prospect of intailing the like, or greater miseries, upon their breed for ever.

I profess, in the sincerity of my heart, that I have not the least personal interest in endeavouring to promote this necessary work, having no other motive than the publick good of my country, by advancing our trade, providing for infants, relieving the poor, and giving some pleasure to the rich. I have no children, by which I can propose to get a single penny; the youngest being nine years old, and my wife past child-bearing.

Writing Strategies

1. What problem is Swift's essay a response to?
2. Beyond Swift's satiric proposal (to eat children), what does he seem to be proposing?

3. When using irony, writers must decide if they will give clues (or wink at) the reader. What clues does Swift give the reader that he is using irony?
4. What point is Swift making when he writes, "I grant this food will be somewhat dear, and therefore very proper for land-lords, who, as they have already devoured most of the parents, seem to have the best title to the children"? (¶ 10)
5. Aside from irony, what support strategies does Swift employ?

Exploring Ideas

1. Why can irony be an effective rhetorical strategy?
2. More subtle or quiet forms of irony may be difficult to pick up on. In small groups, generate a list of ironic statements from writing, movies, everyday life, and so on. Then discuss why some statements are more likely to be interpreted literally.
3. With a group of peers, come up with examples of irony from everyday life (movies, comics, friends, and so on). Who uses irony (politicans, professors, police, etc.), and who tends to avoid it? How does the audience help determine whether or not to use irony? How does the situation help determine whether or not to use irony?
4. Read Michael Moore's essay "Why Doesn't GM Sell Crack?" and identify at least two ironic statements.

For help inventing your own writing project, see the Point of Contact section on pp. 390–391.

Thinking Radically

Farming and the Global Economy

Wendell Berry

The first entry under "radical" in *The American Heritage College Dictionary* says: "1. Arising from or going to a root or source; basic." In this essay (as in other essays in this section and throughout the book), the writer thinks radically because he or she is getting at a root, or a source. This may sound like an easy thing to do, but because we are immersed in the ideology that surrounds us, we are often unable to see or imagine the root. In this essay, Wendell Berry, a novelist, farmer, and essayist, points out some root principles of food, energy, and consumption and argues that abandoning those principles comes with significant consequences.

We have been repeatedly warned that we cannot know where we wish to go if we do not know where we have been. And so let us start by remembering a little history.

As late as World War II, our farms were predominantly solar powered. That is, the work was accomplished principally by human beings and horses and mules. These creatures were empowered by solar energy, which was collected, for the most part, on the farms where they worked and so was pretty cheaply available to the farmer.

However, American farms had not become as self-sufficient in fertility as they should have been—or many of them had not. They were still drawing, without sufficient repayment, against an account of natural fertility accumulated over thousands of years beneath the native forest trees and prairie grasses.

The agriculture we had at the time of World War II was nevertheless often pretty good, and it was promising. In many parts of our country we had begun to have established agricultural communities, each with its own local knowledge, memory, and tradition. Some of our farming practices had become well adapted to local conditions. The best traditional practices of the Midwest, for example, are still used by the Amish with considerable success in terms of both economy and ecology.

5   Now that the issue of sustainability has arisen so urgently, and in fact so transformingly, we can see that the correct agricultural agenda following World War II would have been to continue and refine the already established connection between our farms and the sun and to correct, where necessary, the fertility deficit. There can be no question, now, that that is what we should have done.

It was, notoriously, not what we did. Instead, the adopted agenda called for a shift from the cheap, clean, and, for all practical purposes, limitless energy of the sun to the expensive, filthy, and limited energy of the fossil fuels. It called for the massive use of chemical fertilizers to offset the destruction of topsoil and the depletion of natural fertility. It called also for the displacement of nearly the entire farming population and the replacement of their labor and good farming practices by machines and toxic chemicals. This agenda has succeeded in its aims, but to the benefit of no one and nothing except the corporations that have supplied the necessary machines, fuels, and chemicals—and the corporations that have bought cheap and sold high the products that, as a result of this agenda, have been increasingly expensive for farmers to produce.

The farmers have not benefited—not, at least, as a class—for as a result of this agenda they have become one of the smallest and most threatened of all our minorities. Many farmers, sad to say, have subscribed to this agenda and its economic assumptions, believing that they would not be its victims. But millions, in fact, have been its victims—not farmers alone but also their supporters and dependents in our rural communities.

The people who benefit from this state of affairs have been at pains to convince us that the agricultural practices and policies that have almost annihilated the farming population have greatly benefited the population of food consumers. But more and more consumers are now becoming aware that our supposed abundance of cheap and healthful food is to a considerable extent illusory. They are beginning to see that the social, ecological, and even the economic costs of such "cheap food" are, in fact, great. They are beginning to see that a system of food production that is dependent on massive applications of drugs and chemicals cannot, by definition, produce "pure food." And they are beginning to see that a kind of agriculture that involves unprecedented erosion and depletion of soil, unprecedented waste of water, and unprecedented destruction of the farm population cannot by any accommodation of sense or fantasy be called "sustainable."

From the point of view, then, of the farmer, the ecologist, and the consumer, the need to reform our ways of farming is now both obvious and imperative. We need to adapt our farming much more sensitively to the nature of the places where the farming is done. We need to make our farming practices and our food economy subject to standards set not by the industrial system but by the health of ecosystems and of human communities.

10   The immediate difficulty in even thinking about agricultural reform is that we are rapidly running out of farmers. The tragedy of this decline is not just in its numbers; it is also in the fact that these farming people, assuming we will ever recognize our need to replace them, cannot be replaced anything like as quickly or easily as they have been dispensed with. Contrary to popular assumption, good farmers are not in any simple way part of the "labor force." Good farmers, like good musicians, must be raised to the trade.

The severe reduction of our farming population may signify nothing to our national government, but the members of country communities feel the significance of it—and the threat of it—every day. Eventually urban consumers will feel these things, too. Every day farmers feel the oppression of their long-standing problems: overproduction, low prices, and high costs. Farmers sell on a market that because of overproduction is characteristically depressed, and they buy their supplies on a market that is characteristically inflated—which is necessarily a recipe for failure, because farmers do not control either market. If they will not control production and if they will not reduce their dependence on purchased supplies, then they will keep on failing.

The survival of farmers, then, requires two complementary efforts. The first is entirely up to the farmers, who must learn—or learn again—to farm in ways that minimize their dependence on industrial supplies. They must diversify, using both plants and animals. They must produce, on their farms, as much of the required fertility and energy as they can. So far as they can, they must replace purchased goods and services with natural health and diversity and with their own intelligence. To increase production by increasing costs, as farmers have been doing for the last half century, is not only unintelligent; it is crazy. If farmers do not wish to cooperate any longer in their own destruction, then they will have to reduce their dependence on those global economic forces that intend and approve and profit from the destruction of farmers, and they will have to increase their dependence on local nature and local intelligence.

The second effort involves cooperation between local farmers and local consumers. If farmers hope to exercise any control over their markets, in a time when a global economy and global transportation make it possible for the products of any region to be undersold by the products of any other region, then they will have to look to local markets. The long-broken connections between towns and cities and their surrounding landscapes will have to be restored. There is much promise and much hope in such a restoration. But farmers must understand that this requires an economics of cooperation rather than competition. They must understand also that such an economy sooner or later will require some rational means of production control.

If communities of farmers and consumers wish to promote a sustainable, safe, reasonably inexpensive supply of good food, then they must see that the best, the safest, and most dependable source of food for a city is not the global economy, with its extreme vulnerabilities and extravagant transportation costs, but its own surrounding countryside. It is, in every way, in the best interest of urban consumers to be surrounded by productive land, well farmed and well maintained by thriving farm families in thriving farm communities.

15   If a safe, sustainable local food economy appeals to some of us as a goal that we would like to work for,

then we must be careful to recognize not only the great power of the interests arrayed against us but also our own weakness. The hope for such a food economy as we desire is represented by no political party and is spoken for by no national public officials of any consequence. Our national political leaders do not know what we are talking about, and they are without the local affections and allegiances that would permit them to learn what we are talking about.

But we should also understand that our predicament is not without precedent; it is approximately the same as that of the proponents of American independence at the time of the Stamp Act—and with one difference in our favor: In order to do the work that we must do, we do not need a national organization. What we must do is simple: We must shorten the distance that our food is transported so that we are eating more and more from local supplies, more and more to the benefit of local farmers, and more and more to the satisfaction of local consumers. This can be done by cooperation among small organizations: conservation groups, churches, neighborhood associations, consumer co-ops, local merchants, local independent banks, and organizations of small farmers. It also can be done by cooperation between individual producers and consumers. We should not be discouraged to find that local food economies can grow only gradually; it is better that they should grow gradually. But as they grow they will bring about a significant return of power, wealth, and health to the people.

One last thing at least should be obvious to us all: The whole human population of the world cannot live on imported food. Some people somewhere are going to have to grow the food. And wherever food is grown the growing of it will raise the same two questions: How do you preserve the land in use? And how do you preserve the people who use the land?

The farther the food is transported, the harder it will be to answer those questions correctly. The correct answers will not come as the inevitable by-products of the aims, policies, and procedures of international trade, free or unfree. They cannot be legislated or imposed by international or national or state agencies. They can only be supplied locally, by skilled and highly motivated local farmers meeting as directly as possible the needs of informed local consumers.

Writing Strategies

1. Describe Berry's opening strategy. How does his introduction lead the reader into the body of his essay?
2. Make an outline of Berry's essay, dividing it into several major sections. Describe Berry's organizational strategy.
3. Describe Berry's voice as a writer and identify several passages to support your description.
4. How does Berry express the public resonance of his ideas? That is, how does he relate his ideas to the reader?
5. How is Berry's essay an example of radical thinking?

Exploring Ideas

1. Based on this essay, what is Berry concerned about?
2. How is the way that you see farming different from the way that Berry sees it?
3. What does your response to the reading tell you about the way that you view the world?
4. How might you benefit by reconsidering your views of farming?
5. Based on interviews and observations, how do you think others view farming? What do they think is important, and how are their views similar to or different from Berry's and your own?

For help inventing your own writing project, see the Point of Contact section on pp. 424–425.

◼ ◼ ◼

Group Minds

Doris Lessing

Radical thinkers go beyond conventional wisdom, and sometimes they speak directly to it. They call out common thinking, name it, poke at it, and explain its harm. In this short essay, Doris Lessing, a novelist and essayist, critiques the way European and American societies ("the West") characterize identity. Although the essay deals with an abstract notion (a critique of identity), Lessing makes the idea concrete, makes it appear realistic, graspable, and vital. At the end of the essay, she even invites us to imagine her critique of identity being applied to education.

People living in the West, in societies that we describe as Western, or as the free world, may be educated in many different ways, but they will all emerge with an idea about themselves that goes something like this: I am a citizen of a free society, and that means I am an individual, making individual choices. My mind is my own, my opinions are chosen by me, I am free to do as I will, and at the worst the pressures on me are economic, that is, I may be too poor to do as I want.

This set of ideas may sound something like a caricature, but it is not so far off from how we see ourselves. It is a portrait that may not have been acquired consciously, but is part of a general atmosphere or set of assumptions that influence our ideas about ourselves.

People in the West therefore may go through their entire lives never thinking to analyze this very flattering picture, and as a result are helpless against all kinds of pressures on them to conform in many kinds of ways.

The fact is that we all live our lives in groups—the family, work groups, social, religious, and political groups. Very few people indeed are happy as solitaries, and they tend to be seen by their neighbors as peculiar or selfish or worse. Most people cannot stand being alone for long. They are always seeking groups to belong to, and if one group dissolves, they look for another. We are group animals still, and there is nothing wrong with that. But what is dangerous is not the belonging to a group, or groups, but not understanding the social laws that govern groups and govern us.

5 When we're in a group, we tend to think as that group does: We may even have joined the group to find "like-minded" people. But we also find our thinking changing because we belong to a group. It is the hardest thing in the world to maintain an individual dissident opinion, as a member of a group.

It seems to me that this is something we have all experienced—something we take for granted, may never have thought about it. But a great deal of experimentation has gone on among psychologists and sociologists on this very theme. If I describe an experiment or two, then anyone listening who may be a sociologist or psychologist will groan, oh God not again—for they will have heard of these classic experiments far too often. My guess is that the rest of the people will never have heard of these experiments, never have had these ideas presented to them. If my guess is true, then it aptly illustrates my general thesis, and the general idea behind these talks, that we (the human race) are now in possession of a great deal of hard information about ourselves, but we do not use it to improve our institutions and therefore our lives.

A typical test, or experiment, on this theme goes like this. A group of people are taken into the researcher's confidence. A minority of one or two are left in the dark. Some situation demanding measurement or assessment is chosen. For instance, comparing lengths of wood that differ only a little from each other, but enough to be perceptible, or shapes that are almost the same size. The majority in the group—according to instruction—will assert stubbornly that these two shapes or lengths are the same length, or size, while the solitary individual, or the couple, who have not been so instructed will assert that pieces of wood or whatever are different. But the majority will continue to insist—speaking metaphorically—that black is white, and after a period of exasperation, irritation, even anger, certainly incomprehension, the minority will fall into line. Not always, but nearly always. There are indeed glorious individuals who stubbornly insist on telling the truth as they see it, but most give in to the majority opinion, obey the atmosphere.

When put as badly, as unflatteringly, as this, reactions tend to be incredulous: "I certainly wouldn't give in, I speak my mind . . ." But would you?

People who have experienced a lot of groups, who perhaps have observed their own behavior, may agree that the hardest thing in the world is to stand out against one's groups, a group of one's peers. Many agree that among our most shameful memories is this: how often we said black was white because other people were saying it.

10   In other words, we know that this is true of human behavior, but how do we know it? It is one thing to admit it, in a vague uncomfortable sort of way (which probably includes the hope that one will never again be in such a testing situation) but quite another to make that cool step into a kind of objectivity, where one may say, "Right, if that's what human beings are like, myself included, then let's admit it, examine and organize our attitudes accordingly."

This mechanism, of obedience to the group, does not only mean obedience or submission to a small group, or one that is sharply determined, like a religious or political party. It means, too, conforming to those large, vague, ill-defined collections of people who may never think of themselves as having a collective mind because they are aware of differences of opinion—but

which, to people from outside, from another culture, seem very minor. The underlying assumptions and assertions that govern the group are never discussed, never challenged, probably never noticed, the main one being precisely this: That it is a group mind, intensely resistant to change, equipped with sacred assumptions about which there can be no discussion.

But suppose this kind of thing were taught in schools?

Let us just suppose it, for a moment. . . . But at once the nub of the problem is laid bare.

Imagine us saying to children, "In the last fifty or so years, the human race has become aware of a great deal of information about its mechanisms; how it behaves, how it must behave under certain circumstances. If this is to be useful, you must learn to contemplate these rules calmly, dispassionately, disinterestedly, without emotion. It is information that will set people free from blind loyalties, obedience to slogans, rhetoric, leaders, group emotions." Well, there it is.

Writing Strategies

1. How does Lessing's opening paragraph set up the rest of her essay?
2. What does Lessing conclude should be taught in schools but isn't?
3. What type of support does Lessing rely upon most?
4. What additional type of support might Lessing have used, and why?
5. How does Lessing interact with the reader? Identify several specific instances that illustrate Lessing's particular treatment of the reader.
6. Identify an important counterargument, qualifier, or concession in Lessing's argument. Or, suggest one that she does not make, but that would have strengthened her argument.

Exploring Ideas

1. In her opening paragraph, Lessing says most Westerners have the following idea of themselves: "I am a citizen of a free society, and that means I am an individual, making individual choices. My mind is my own, my opinions are chosen by me, I am free to do as I will, and at the worst the pressures on me are economic; that is, I may be too poor to do as I want." What does Lessing think is wrong with this self-image?
2. How has joining and conforming to a particular group changed your thinking?
3. Summarize Lessing's main idea about what should be, but isn't, taught in schools. Then ask others why they agree or disagree with Lessing. What reasons do others give for their agreeing or disagreeing?

4. Lessing states: "This mechanism, of obedience to the group, does not only mean obedience or submission to a small group, or one that is sharply determined, like a religious or political party. It means, too, conforming to those large, vague, ill-defined collections of people who may never think of themselves as having a collective mind because they are aware of differences of opinion—but which, to people from outside, from another culture, seem very minor." (¶ 11) In a small group, come up with several examples that support Lessing's point.

For help inventing your own writing project, see the Point of Contact section on pp. 424–425.

■ ■ ■

Not Homeschooling? What's Your Excuse?

Tricia Smith Vaughan

Is school boring? Is school harmful? In the following essay, published on NewsWithViews.com, Tricia Smith Vaughan puts forth a radical argument about why public, or government, schooling should be avoided.

My favorite excuse is "but the schools here are so wonderful!" The parent will go on and on about how little Johnny or JoEllen is learning the clarinet or Chinese or times tables in their local public kindergarten, something that Johnny or JoEllen's mommy and daddy claim not to be smart enough to teach. If you think that I'm being demeaning to the mommy or daddy, I am merely repeating what he or she has told me.

I've had moms of four-year-olds tell me how much their child is learning, things that the mom says that she couldn't possibly teach. When I pry with a question or two, I find that what I'm teaching my child at home is at least as good as what Johnny or JoEllen is learning at preschool or kindergarten. And if we need to find a clarinet teacher, we will.

My just-turned-five-year-old has not spent a day in a government institution of learning and yet, he talks with ease to adults, knows his alphabet, writes words correctly with an adult's spelling help, and works hard at learning to read. From all accounts, he's just as smart as the heavily schooled.

What's placed the idea in our heads that the government can educate our children better than we can

is none other than our public school system, the government darling of our unconstitutional Department of Education. Most of us grew up with the government's feeding us lunch, teaching us knowledge and values, and suggesting what careers we should have, all under the guise of educating us. Is it any wonder that we allow this seemingly benevolent entity to provide an education to our children?

5   As parents, we have grown to believe something that our ancestors of one hundred years ago would be shocked to see happening. The millennia-old concept of self-sufficient parents who educated their children at home has given way to a system in which parents believe that we are not smart enough to teach our children the alphabet and basic math.

We over-educated post-feminist moms allow the joyful opportunity to educate our children at home pass; we send our child to a government school that teaches not only the alphabet and numbers, but a little socialist school-to-work agenda along with it. Things have changed in the government schools, even in the past five years. Some call it progress; others call it a few steps closer to socialism.

One thing that hasn't changed, however, is that little Johnny and JoEllen will learn their place in a government school. Maybe they'll do well in group activities and the teacher will deem them fine to work in the new planned world order. But maybe not. A little deviation from the supposed norm and the little tykes can be diagnosed and sent to special education classes, something that John Taylor Gatto claims places them at a much lower level of the "reproductive sweepstakes."

According to Gatto, government schools encourage these sweepstakes by ranking children in groups and assigning those deemed not worthy to reproduce to special education classes. Let us not forget that these days, children deemed special by government change agents will be drugged, at least if President Bush and Congress continue to have their way via the Orwellian-named New Freedom Commission on Mental Health. Ah, the land of the free!

How else can I describe a country that requires its children to sit in a classroom all day? I must admit that I had never thought much about this strange paradox of freedom and confinement until I read John Taylor

Gatto's *The Underground History of American Education*. It's available free online at his website, www.johntaylorgatto.com; no one I've ever told this to, to my knowledge, has ever read the book. And yet moms continue to tell me how wonderfully their children are thriving in the government schools, never knowing the true history behind those schools.

10 According to Gatto, our public schools were set up to dumb us down so that we can be happy to be a cog in the planned economy. We have to understand that government schools in the U.S. were created to dull children's potential. Yes, read that part again—government schools were never about truly educating your child; they were and are about creating happy workers and taxpayers, people afraid to challenge the status quo and unable to read and think for themselves.

I used to teach students who'd been educated in government schools; I've seen the products of this lovely system. And as a product myself, I can tell you that the students I taught at a major research university in the 1990s were less able to read, write, and think for themselves, as a whole, than were the people whom I graduated with at my public high school in the 1980s.

Most of us can give examples of crappy experiences we had in public schools—my husband remembers a teacher's berating a girl who'd wet her pants in first grade; the teacher forced the class to laugh at the little girl. And this wonderful government school moment occurred in the 1970s.

If you think that kind of thing would never happen in your child's wonderful government school today, don't talk with the parents in Elizabeth, Pennsylvania. A principal there recently resigned because parents were outraged when they found out that she paraded a third-grader from class to class, calling the young child a "liar and thief." The principal didn't bother to investigate the accuser's story; the young accuser later "recanted the story."

Have you ever thought about the crappy overall experience you had in a government school? Even if you graduated at the top of your class? Even if you loved it at the time? Have you ever wondered what things you might have accomplished had you not been forced to attend high school? If schooling is such a wonderful thing, why don't we have the freedom to choose it for ourselves, instead of having it chosen for us? Personally, I can remember wanting to attend college when I was 13. No such luck—I was stuck in high school prison.

15 Take some time to understand why Our Government Masters developed the system that they did for dumbing us down. Learn how even the best of teachers must work in an atmosphere every day that does not allow the freedom to worship God as one wishes. If you don't believe me, try saying a softly spoken prayer before a meal or studying the Bible as God's sacred word at a government school, things we are able to do rather easily in a private restaurant or even in a public library.

Learn how your children are being tested for their values instead of their knowledge. And please, stop complaining about sex education classes that preach homosexuality or about recitation of the Pledge of Allegiance in the classroom that doesn't say "under God." Parents in San Francisco who complained recently that a sex survey was given to their children, some of whom were in first grade—yes, first grade!—were told by the court system that they had no rights. If you're surprised at this decision, do some reading on the true history of education.

Expecting the government schools to acquiesce to your demands is useless. Occasionally, the parents will win, as they did when they insisted that the Pennsylvania principal resign, but most of the time, parents lose. Do yourself a favor and stop trying to win. Take your children out of those schools.

The government schools are not going to teach your child Judeo-Christian values; they are going to teach him or her how to survive in a group, good practice for a future as a soldier of the United Nations. Your child, in a subtle or blatant way, will learn how to outbully and outsmart his or her classmates and vie for the teacher's attention in a classroom of twenty or so other children the same age. The experts will tell you that this socialization is wonderful for a child, but even in college, I have never encountered such a blatantly homogeneous group of people as I did in public school classrooms. My children are learning manners, which will allow them to be kind and polite to people of all ages, ethnicities, and religions; I am thankful that they are not having to fight for a teacher's attention in order to be properly socialized, whatever that vague term means.

It's tempting to blame the public school's state on politicians. It becomes easy to cite Bush, or Clinton, or any other politician, for doing or not doing something to help education. And then there's the other little blame darling: funding; public schools seem always to blame things on lack of funding. As long as you do this blaming thing and don't understand the full picture, you will consider the public schools a good thing. You will try to obtain your money's worth as a taxpayer and you may try to change the system: You will fail.

20   Only when you understand what the government's biggest propaganda campaign and cash cow is doing to your children, and has done to you, will you take your child away from the governmental change agents that our public schools contain. And only then will you refuse government money, even for a public charter school that allows you to teach your child at home.

On the other hand, if you've read John Taylor Gatto, Charlotte Iserbyt, and Beverly Eakman, and you're still okay with the U.S. government schools, keep your children in them. If you're okay with the links to the two largest U.S. teacher's unions, the NEA and the AFT, on the Communist Party USA's website, don't bother either to homeschool or to send your child to a private school with no financial ties to the federal government. If having the government interfere in your life and the life of your family, often without your consent, is okay with you, then leave your children exactly where they are.

But if you are interested in teaching your child about the true freedom of the individual that this country was founded upon, take your child as far from the government schools as possible. I know that in a few cases, it's difficult to homeschool. But for the most part, if you're literate, you can teach your child! Some single parents even homeschool. Don't let the government have control of your children's most precious asset: their mind. Take control yourself and thrive in the responsibility that God has given you. Take true responsibility for your child and for his or her education. And do it today!

Writing Strategies

1. What is Vaughan's main claim?
2. What support strategies does Vaughan use to help the reader understand and accept her position?

3. According to Vaughan, what is the relationship between drugs and government schools?
4. Vaughan writes, "As long as you do this blaming thing and don't understand the full picture, you will consider the public schools a good thing." (¶ 19) What is the full picture, according to Vaughan?
5. How does Vaughan's argument go beyond the basic argument for homeschooling? Or, if you think it doesn't go beyond it, how does it fit in with the other arguments you have heard for homeschooling?

Exploring Ideas

1. Vaughan states, "What's placed the idea in our heads that the government can educate our children better than we can is none other than the public school system. . . ." (¶ 4) What evidence does Vaughan provide to support this assertion? What additional evidence can you provide to support it? What evidence might refute it?
2. How is government education like a school-to-work agenda? What, if anything, about government education challenges a school-to-work agenda?
3. Vaughan questions an educational system "that requires its children to sit in a classroom all day?" (¶ 9) Why is or isn't a system like this effective? Is Vaughan's description accurate? (Do children sit in a classroom pretty much all day? Did you?)
4. Interview a variety of Americans of different ages and backgrounds to find out if they think "our public schools were set up to dumb us down so that we can be happy to be a cog in the planned economy" (¶ 10). How many people you interviewed seem open to the possibility? How many reject it immediately?

For help inventing your own writing project, see the Point of Contact section on pp. 424–425.

◼ ◼ ◼

Was I a Good American in the Time of George Bush?

Rebecca Solnit

Am I a good American? While the answer may be simple for a conventional thinker, radical thinkers grapple with such a question because they move beyond the conformity of mainstream thought and common sense; they challenge their own ideas and try to understand and accept the ideas of others, which complicates their thinking. History shows us over and over that radical thinkers, those who challenged the status quo, are often right. The following essay by Rebecca Solnit (1961–) was originally published in the *Guardian,* the British newspaper on March 14, 2007.

Was I a good American? How good an American was I? Did I do what I could to resist the takeover of my country and the brutalization of my fellow human beings? How much further could I have gone? Were the crimes of the Bush administration those that demand you give up your life and everyday commitments to throw yourself into maximum resistance? If not, then what were we waiting for? The questions have troubled me regularly these last five years, because I was one of the millions of American citizens who did not shut down Guantánamo Bay and stop the other atrocities of the administration.

I wrote. I gave money, sometimes in large chunks. I went to anti-war marches. I demonstrated. I also planted a garden, cooked dinners, played with children, wandered around aimlessly, and did lots of other things you do when the world is not crashing down around you. And maybe when it is. Was it? It was for the men in our gulag. And the boys there. And the rule of law in my native land.

Before the current administration, it had always been easy to condemn the "good Germans" who did nothing while Jews, Gypsies, and others were rounded up for extermination. One likes to believe that one will be different, will harbor Anne Frank in one's secret annex, smuggle people across the border, defy the authorities who do evil. Those we scornfully call good Germans merely did little while the mouth of hell opened up.

I now know the way that everyday life can be so absorbing, survival so demanding, that it seems impossible to do more on top of it or to drop the routine altogether and begin a totally different life. There is the garden to be watered, the aged parent in crisis, the deadline looming; but there are also the crimes against humanity waiting to be stopped. Ordinary obligations tug one way even when extraordinary ones tug the other way. The Bush administration is by no means the Third Reich, but it produced an extraordinary time that made extraordinary demands on U.S. citizens, demands that some of us rose to—and too many did not.

5   Periodically, I would speculate on what was the most extreme and radical thing I could do to stop the illegal prison camp at Guantánamo; picture chaining myself to the gates of the Senate, becoming one of those activists who takes up residence outside the White House or takes over a TV station to get a message out. I wanted to do something so epic that it would turn the tide, stop the crime. Then I would consider that the best approaches were probably already being taken, by the heroic lawyers at the Center for Constitutional Rights and other human rights organizations, and I would write another check and some more letters and feel a little futile and a little corrupt.

These days Americans seem to be waking up one at a time, groggy and embittered, from the hypnotic nightmare that was the Bush administration's one great success—spreading a miasma of fear and patriotic submissiveness that made it possible to mount an illegal and immoral war, piss on the bill of rights, burn the constitution, and violate international charters on human rights and prisoners of war with widespread torture. None of the sleepers seems to remember that they were part of the legions who obeyed the orders to fear and hate—but we welcome the latecomers into our ranks anyway.

What took them so long? How could people believe that a fairly defanged country, one we had been bombing since the first Gulf war, was an apocalyptic menace in a world where most nations were well-equipped for mass civilian murder? A year ago, the turning point was marked by the comedian Stephen Colbert's volley of (accurate) insults delivered to Bush's face, in the guise of giving the keynote address at the Washington press corps' annual dinner. He was just aggressively ignored by the mainstream media. Perhaps Katrina turned the tide: the indifference, incompetence, and obliviousness of the federal government was so gross that its pedestal melted.

And there were others who were in resistance all along. I remember with admiration the Japanese-Americans who came out in the months after 9/11 to testify that they had been incarcerated en masse during the Second World War, not for what they did but for who they were, and they were not going to remain silent as the same treatment was meted out to Arabs and Muslims. I remember the way that 20,000 of us in San Francisco came out to shut down the business district the day the war broke out, and the huge marches before and after. I remember the few congresspeople—mostly African American—who dared to stand in opposition early on. I went to Camp Casey outside Bush's vacation home in Texas and spent a day with Cindy Sheehan, who gave her life over to stopping the war after it took her soldier son. Others did as she did. Some of them are my friends.

There is resistance. But if it were enough, the crimes would have stopped, the war would have ended. When it does and they do, some will have been heroes. Some will have been honorable but moderate, in times that did not call for moderation. And some will have consented, through inaction, to crimes against humanity.

Writing Strategies

1. What main issue does Solnik explore? What passages from her essay help to complicate the issue?
2. Who is Solnik's intended audience? That is, who does she seem to be writing for? Who isn't she writing for? What infor- mation does Solnik provide or leave out that helped you deter- mine who her intended audience is?
3. How might Solnik's introduction connect with and engage the reader?
4. According to Solnik, why haven't more people taken stronger action?

Exploring Ideas

1. What is a hero? How can someone who opposed the war in Iraq be heroic?
2. What action is appropriate, based on Solnik's description of the "crimes of the Bush administration?" (¶ 1)
3. Solnik concludes that when the crimes have stopped and the war has ended, "Some will have been honorable but mod- erate, in times that did not call for moderation." (¶ 9) Read Martin Luther King, Jr's "Letter from Birmingham Jail" (pages 000–000) in which he discusses the role of the white mod- erate. How is Solnik's moderate similar to or different from the one King talks about?

For help inventing your own writing project, see the Point of Contact section on pp. 424–425.

RHETORICAL HANDBOOK

Chapter Contents

CHAPTER 15

Where to Find It

ORGANIZATION

Every essay has a structure, or organization. Like word choice, content, voice, and so on, organization is determined by considering one's purpose in writing, the reader, and the overall writing situation.

Controlling Idea An essay (like any piece of writing) is organized around a main (or controlling) idea. The main idea of an essay is also referred to as a thesis. Shorter pieces, such as the ones often written in college writing courses, benefit from having a narrow focus. Since those pieces are relatively short, there isn't enough time or space to deal with a broad topic. Longer writings may have a broader main idea, though even they benefit from a narrow focus. Whether the thesis is stated or implied, the support for the main idea (the rest of the essay) is carefully arranged to help the reader accept the main idea.

Beginning, Middle, and End An essay (letter, report, etc.) has a beginning, middle, and end. The beginning (or introduction) leads the reader into the meat of the essay. The bulk of an essay supports the main idea. (The essays in this text illustrate the various strategies that can be used.) The ending (or conclusion) of the essay brings it to a close in one of various ways. While a conclusion could just summarize the main points, this summary is often unnecessary. Instead, a strong conclusion might suggest or emphasize the public resonance of the essay, create a strong and lasting image, call the reader to action, and so on (see pages 692–693). Conclusions lead the reader out of the essay and back to the larger world. They try to answer the reader's main question: "So what? What is the point of this essay?" They (often subtly) encourage the reader to think or act differently. Finally, introductions and conclusions are not necessarily one paragraph each. They can bleed into several paragraphs—blurring the boundaries between beginning, middle, and end.

Remember, you should not feel that you must figure out the right organization, but instead that you must figure out an organization that engages readers, directs them through your ideas, and leaves them reflective in the end.

Controlling idea, main idea, and thesis all mean the same thing.

Activity

Study the organization of several essays in this text. What is each paragraph about, and how does it function in the overall scheme of the essay? How do the introduction and conclusion lead the reader into and out of the essay?

Beyond the Five-Paragraph Essay

One typical organization, often helpful but ultimately limiting, is the five-paragraph essay. It includes a brief introduction, three supporting paragraphs, and a conclusion.

Notice in the example below how each supporting paragraph will develop or support a clearly stated main idea. Notice also how key terms from the controlling idea are repeated, word for word or with synonyms, in the topic sentences (or main ideas for the supporting paragraphs):

Controlling Idea: Myrtle Beach is a great place to go on vacation.

Supporting Paragraph #1: Myrtle Beach has a lot of nice golf courses.
Supporting Paragraph #2: Myrtle Beach has a beautiful long beach.
Supporting Paragraph #3: Myrtle Beach has plenty of good nightlife.

Concluding Paragraph

There is a lot of potential for going beyond the five-paragraph essay in the above example. By narrowing the essay's focus, dealing with counterarguments and concessions, or establishing a purpose beyond merely describing some positive aspects of Myrtle Beach, the writer would naturally require a more complex (and less limiting) essay organization.

Instead of explaining three nice things about Myrtle Beach, a writer might show why Myrtle Beach is preferable to Daytona Beach, Panama City, Acapulco, or the New Jersey shore. This approach would likely include making counterarguments and concessions. Or the writer might narrow his or her focus to *just the beach*. Such an approach might deal briefly with the region's golf courses, night life, and other matters in the introduction or elsewhere, then focus more specifically on the virtues of the beach. Going beyond the five-paragraph approach requires more analysis and will produce a more engaging essay.

Caution: The five-paragraph essay can have more than five paragraphs—and still be limiting. The problem is not with the number of points or paragraphs, but with the lack of exploration and discovery. Often, the writer using the five-paragraph strategy avoids asking hard questions, dissecting points, analyzing assumptions—all the strategies that create an engaging essay.

Activities

1. To make sure you understand your own essay's organization, summarize each paragraph: (1) State the paragraph's main idea and (2) explain how the paragraph functions. This involves not just stating its main idea, but also explaining the paragraph's main idea in relationship to the overall piece—not just describing a spark plug, but explaining its role in the running of the automobile.

2. Make two lists, one naming the advantages of the five-paragraph essay structure, and one naming the disadvantages. Then, consider your relationship as a writer to the five-paragraph essay. When does it suit your needs? When doesn't it? Can you benefit at this point in your career from learning the five-paragraph approach, from using aspects of it, or from avoiding it altogether?

PARAGRAPHS

When revising, working toward a more unified, developed, and coherent essay will help create more readable writing.

Paragraphs serve different purposes. Some introduce the main idea of an essay; others support that idea; and others bring the essay to a satisfying conclusion. In longer writings, an introduction or conclusion may take several paragraphs, and one supporting point may require more than just one paragraph.

Three important qualities of paragraphs (and essays) are unity, development, and coherence.

Unity means that each paragraph is about one thing; that is, it has a purpose and it goes about achieving that purpose without significant digression.

Development means that each paragraph is sufficiently thorough. This can only be determined by considering each paragraph's purpose and what must be done to achieve that purpose.

Coherence means that the relationship between ideas is clear to the reader—that the writing flows. The writer assists the reader by arranging ideas in an appropriate order and by providing transitions, repeating key terms, and following conventions of grammar.

Supporting Paragraphs

Writers think about (1) how each paragraph functions within the overall essay and (2) how each paragraph is organized within itself. Read through several essays in this book, and notice how their paragraphs function and are organized. Paragraphs are often organized deductively—stating the main idea first, then supporting it. They also can be organized inductively—giving support first, then the main idea. Some paragraphs (called "turnabout paragraphs" in this text) begin with a point and then pivot, or move, the reader to a related point. Other paragraphs serve as transitions between the preceding and following paragraphs or sections of text.

Deductive If information is organized deductively, the main idea is presented first and the support for that idea follows. Stating the main idea first often helps the reader to understand the point of the paragraph more readily.

Sadly, the gap between these two groups grows even wider. The motivated student with good study skills (the one who has had at least an adequate high school education) attends class, takes notes, understands reading assignments, follows instructions, develops even better habits of mind, gains even more knowledge, and learns ways of making that knowledge work for her and his fellow humans. But in a system where B's are average and C's might indicate that although a student "tried" she did not demonstrate understanding or skill, the poorer students continue to advance through the system while remaining trapped at the bottom. Their level of thinking does not change much, while that of their better-prepared peers does.

The opening sentence of the preceding paragraph expresses a main idea: The gap between two groups of students grows wider. The rest of the paragraph explains *why*.

Inductive If information is organized inductively, the main idea is presented following the support. The deductive paragraph above can be reorganized by placing the main idea last.

> The motivated student with good study skills (the one who has had at least an adequate high school education) attends class, takes notes, understands reading assignments, follows instructions, develops even better habits of mind, gains even more knowledge, and learns ways of making that knowledge work for her and his fellow humans. But in a system where B's are average and C's might indicate that although a student "tried" she did not demonstrate understanding or skill, the poorer students continue to advance through the system while remaining trapped at the bottom. Their level of thinking does not change much, while that of their better-prepared peers does. Sadly, the gap between these two groups grows even wider.

Turnabout Writers often find it helpful to pivot from one idea to another within the same paragraph—the second idea being a major point that plays off of the first idea. The pivot, or turnabout, is usually signaled by a transition word or expression such as *but, however, on the other hand, still, yet,* and so on.

> In his book *Generation X Goes to College,* Peter Sacks describes, among other things, the sense of entitlement that some students in today's consumerist culture have toward a college education. One entire chapter explores this issue alone, providing examples of this "sense" and looking into its "humble beginnings." Sacks shows how consumerism has invaded education, leading some students to expect good grades for little effort. But he fails, it seems, to emphasize enough a most harmful effect of this sense of entitlement. The biggest problem, as I see it, is that although students are able to graduate from high school (and even some colleges) with minimal effort, those students may find themselves cheated in the long run.

Notice how the above paragraph turns on the word *But,* thus building on the previous point and moving in a different, yet appropriate, direction. The first part of the paragraph tells what Peter Sacks describes; the second part turns on *but* and tells what he *doesn't* do.

Transition Some paragraphs, especially in longer pieces, function as transitions that take the reader from one idea (usually a section of an essay) to another idea (another section of the essay).

> True enough, these are all ways that students who are allowed to just slide by end up getting cheated. But another way (and one less talked about) strikes me as being far more offensive. This reason hinges on the fact that many students are not just sliding by.

The above paragraph moves the reader from the previously mentioned ways that students are cheated to a far more offensive way that students are cheated. Then the rest of the essay develops this point.

Opening and Closing Paragraphs

Shorter essays often have an opening paragraph, several supporting paragraphs, and a closing paragraph. Opening paragraphs bring the reader into the essay, introducing the subject and setting the tone. Closing paragraphs take the reader out of the essay, back to the outside world. The ways of beginning and ending essays are unlimited. But readers respond well to introductions that open a door to a new way of thinking and conclusions that emphasize the most important idea in the essay.

STRATEGIES FOR INTRODUCTIONS

Test the approach: Will the introduction invite the reader into a new way of thinking?

1. Begin with a statistic, quotation, or anecdote.
2. Ask a question.
3. Create a strong visual image.
4. Provide necessary background.
5. Make a comparison.
6. Briefly explain what the essay is responding to.
7. Allude to the public resonance of the essay.
8. Create a tone for the essay.

Opening paragraphs bring the reader into the essay, introducing the subject and setting the tone.

STRATEGIES FOR CONCLUSIONS

1. Suggest or emphasize the public resonance.
2. State and explain the main idea.
3. Create a strong image.
4. Ask an important question.
5. Relate back to a point from the introduction.
6. Call the reader to thought or action.
7. Make a recommendation.
8. Suggest a consequence.

> Test the approach: Will the conclusion reinforce a new way of thinking . . . or just repeat what the reader might have already considered?

Activities

1. Read one essay in this book, and study its paragraphs. Note each paragraph's organization (deductive, inductive, turnabout) and function (transition, support). Do you think each paragraph is unified, developed, and coherent? Explain why or why not.

2. Revise one of your essays by writing out a main idea for each paragraph. Try moving the main idea to different places.

3. Read just the introductions of several essays in this book. How do they work? Do they fit into one of the strategies listed here, or do they use a different strategy? How does each introduction introduce the main idea and engage the reader?

4. Read just the conclusions of several essays. (Keep in mind that some may be more than one paragraph long.) How do they work? Do they leave the reader with something to ponder?

5. Analyze one introduction and one conclusion, either from an essay in this book or elsewhere. How did the introduction attempt to engage the reader? How did it introduce the topic? Was it successful? How did the conclusion emphasize the main point of the essay? Why was or wasn't it successful?

6. Rewrite your introduction with an eye towards getting into the essay more quickly. Cut anything that unnecessarily delays getting to main points or that takes away from the essay's forward momentum.

WRITING STYLE

Style is a term that characterizes the words and phrases that a writer decides to use in communicating with readers. Many different styles can be considered good writing. But an effective style in one situation may not work as well in another (for example, writing a letter to a friend vs. writing a college essay; writing an initial response to a movie vs. writing a research paper; writing a thank-you note vs. writing a letter to the college newspaper). Consider Daniel Bruno's writing style in "Entitlement Education." He writes:

> In our competitive world, the sad truth is that even some of the very good students, though their college dreams were to be doctors and lawyers and pharmacists and engineers, will be waiting tables.

In an e-mail to a friend—a less formal writing situation—Bruno might have written:

> Wake up! It's a dog-eat-dog world. Even a lot of good students won't get the job they're after.

Writing style is influenced by a variety of factors, including word choice, sentence structure, paragraph length, punctuation, figurative expressions, and writing purpose. For example, deciding to elevate one's vocabulary, use fewer commas, or make the reader laugh will affect a writer's style.

Problems with Style

Appropriate writing style helps a writer communicate with the reader. Inappropriate styles can interfere with the communication of ideas. For example, some writers stretching to sound educated or professional dress up simple ideas in unnecessarily complex or fancy language. This can make reading more difficult. Writing style should be focused on clearly expressing the ideas of the writer without drawing much attention to the writing style itself. Style that does not call attention to itself (but that instead focuses on the ideas being expressed) is usually the most effective. Consider the following passage from Daniel Bruno's essay "Entitlement Education."

> The problem, of course, is that the two students have entered college on different academic levels and the one on the higher level has graduated on an *even higher* level while the one on the lower level has remained pretty much the same.

Style is the way a writer treats his or her readers.

Bruno could have expressed the same idea in various ways, some of which might sound too elevated or too chatty to his audience, as the examples on the next page demonstrate. If the style of a college textbook or scholarly article sounds elevated, it could be that the subject matter is complex and requires a more technical vocabulary and complex sentence structure. Or it could be that the style is unnecessarily elevated.

Elevated

Upon careful study it appears that the problem, per se, is at the time of matriculation two collegians embarked upon higher education at dissimilar academic levels and the first such student ultimately graduated on a higher academic level of learning whereas the second such student continually resided upon the lower of the two academic levels.

Too Chatty

Well, the problem is two students go off to college and one is already better off school-wise than the other. And the better-off one graduates even better off, and the other one doesn't do so hot.

Not Thoughtful

Simply put, smart students learn a lot and dumb ones don't.

Wishy-Washy

It seems to me that perhaps the problem might be that two students could have entered college on different academic levels and, in my opinion, the one on the higher level might graduate on an even higher level while the one on the lower level might possibly not have learned as much.

Pig-Headed

Wake up! The problem is so simple I can't imagine why no one has done anything about it. Obviously, two students have entered college on different academic levels and the one on the higher level is bound to graduate on an even higher level. The one on the lower level gets what he deserves. Got it?

Formulaic

The problem is two students have entered college on different academic levels. The one on the higher level has graduated on an even higher level. The lower one has remained the same.

> If the style of a college textbook or scholarly article sounds elevated, it could be that the subject matter is complex and requires a more technical vocabulary and complex sentence structure. Or it could be that the style is unnecessarily elevated.

The Circle of Good Writing

The shared nature of language requires that a writer's style will fall within a certain area in most writing situations. We can call this area the Circle of Good Writing. Your writing need not be the same as your instructor's or anyone else's. In fact, it couldn't be exactly the same. But it should not vary significantly from the usual conventions that others—such as professors, employers, and clients— employ in their writing.

Circle of Good Writing

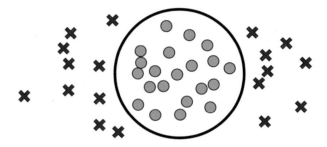

Because language is shared and because our purpose in writing is to offer ideas and new perspectives to others, we can judge writing by the degree to which it achieves its purpose.

Activities

1. Create or find three examples of different writing styles. Explain why each does or does not fall within the Circle of Good Writing. Explain in what situation each might or might not be appropriate.

2. Describe your own writing style. It may help to read through old essays, letters, e-mails, and so on. How does your writing style vary from one situation to another? How would you describe the writing style you use for college essays, and why do you use that style?

Communicate information from one person to another.

SENTENCE VITALITY

Vitality is liveliness. It is not a matter of right and wrong, correct and incorrect, but a matter of degree. Good writers persistently work at increasing the liveliness of their sentences. Whether sentences are short, long, or very long, they can often be livelier. Consider the following sentences. Which ones seem more alive—and why?

> The Gods, they say, give breath, and they take it away. But the same could be said—could it not?—of the humble comma. (Pico Iyer)

> Once he stamped so hard on my head that my neck was nearly broken. (Jane Goodall)

> Still, the city creeps closer, day by day. (Edward Abbey)

> Sadly, the gap between these two groups grows even wider. (Daniel Bruno)

> So here's what I don't understand: if profit is supreme, why doesn't a company like General Motors sell crack? (Michael Moore)

> I imagine that you are breathing the exhaust fumes of our disregard. (Simon Benlow)

> Situated on a lake, the Sea World I visited featured a water show with ski jumps and corny skits. (Jayme Stayer)

Sentence vitality is not about checking grammar, creating over-dramatic phrases, or puffing up language. Instead, it involves a range of strategies for making sentences more focused, cleaner, and more concentrated.

1. RELY ON ACTIVE (NOT PASSIVE) SENTENCES

While both active and passive sentences are useful, active sentences tend to express ideas more directly and thus contribute to sentence vitality. In an active sentence, the grammatical subject does the action; in a passive sentence, the grammatical subject is acted upon. Consider how these two sentences both express the same idea:

The farmer milked the cow.

The cow was milked by the farmer.

Vitality is the peculiarity distinguishing the living from the nonliving.

The first sentence is active because the grammatical subject—*the farmer*—is doing the action. The second sentence is passive because the grammatical subject—*the cow*—is being acted upon. To recognize passive sentences, look for the following: (1) the grammatical subject is being acted upon, (2) the verb requires a helping word (*was milked,* for example, instead of *milked*), (3) the noun doing the action is expressed in a prepositional phrase beginning with *by*, and (4) this *by* phrase could be eliminated from the sentence. Consider two more sentences (one active and one passive). Each could be used to express the same idea.

> The CEO made millions while employees lost their life savings.

> Millions were made by the CEO while their life savings was lost by the employees.

The first sentence consists of two clauses: (1) *The CEO* (subject) *made* (verb) and (2) *while* (subordinating conjunction) *employees* (subject) *lost* (verb). Both clauses are active because the grammatical subject is doing the action. The second sentence expresses the same idea but with a passive construction. The *by* phrases and the verb forms make the second sentence more wordy and cumbersome.

When to Use the Passive Voice Both active and passive sentences are important in writing. If focusing on the cow, the passive construction—*The cow was milked by the farmer*—may be more appropriate than the active sentence that features the farmer. Similarly, the newspaper headline *Kennedy Shot* is passive, yet more appropriate than an active expression of the same idea: *Oswald Shoots.* And in certain situations, it may be appropriate to avoid placing blame (or seeking praise) by saying *Millions were made* or *The cow was milked.*

2. ELIMINATE WORDINESS

Early drafts tend to contain unnecessary words that slow the pace of the reading and distract the reader. Writers weed sentences of unnecessary words the way a gardener removes unwanted plants from a flower garden, thus featuring the flowers. Notice the following concise and lively sentences and the fabricated wordier versions a writer might find in a rough draft.

> Concise: Still, the city creeps closer, day by day. (Edward Abbey)
> Wordy: In the final analysis, the city is still creeping a little bit closer each and every day.

> Concise: Sadly, the gap between these two groups grows even wider. (Daniel Bruno)
> Wordy: It is sad that the gap between the first group of students and the second group of students continues to grow wider and wider.

<u>Concise:</u> So here's what I don't understand: if profit is supreme, why doesn't a company like General Motors sell crack? (Michael Moore)
<u>Wordy:</u> I'm a little puzzled about something. If profit is really what is supreme, why wouldn't General Motors decide to sell something like crack instead of selling cars, trucks, SUVs, etc.?

3. AVOID UNNECESSARY EXPLETIVES

Expletives, phrases such as *there are* or *it is,* slow down sentences. They often take over as the main subject and verb of a sentence. They function like subjects and verbs—but contain no content. While expletives are sometimes helpful and even necessary, eliminating some expletives can add to sentence vitality. Consider the following two ways of expressing the same idea:

Idea expressed using an expletive:
There are laws that we can enact that will prevent companies from doing anything to hurt us.

Michael Moore's actual statement without the expletive:
We can enact laws to prevent companies from doing anything to hurt us.

In the first sentence above, the expletive construction is unnecessary and requires the sentence to be wordy. The writer could (1) simply eliminate the expletive, (2) eliminate the word *that,* and then (3) make a few adjustments to the rest of the sentence. The result is that the subject *(we)* and the verb *(can enact)* have been moved to the front of the sentence, and a few unhelpful words have been deleted. Similar revision could be done in the following sentence:

It was Joe who paid for the tickets.

Eliminating the expletive *(it was)* allows the writer to eliminate the relative pronoun *who* and create a more concise sentence:

Joe paid for the tickets.

Not all expletives are so easy to avoid, and not all expletives should be avoided. In many cases, instead of rewriting a single sentence, the writer will be able to combine several sentences, thus being even more concise.

4. EXPLORE THE STRATEGIES IN THE VITALITY SECTIONS IN CHAPTERS 2–12

Chapter 2
- Combine Sentences
- Repeat Structures
- Intensify Verbs

Chapter 3
- Avoid *Be* Verbs When Possible
- Turn Clauses to Phrases
- Turn Phrases to Words

Chapter 4
- Experiment with Length
- Experiment with Brevity
- Change Out Vague Nouns

Chapter 5
- Avoid Clichés
- Avoid Stilted Language

Chapter 6
- Avoid Blueprinting
- Subordinate Less Important Ideas
- Avoid Vague Pronouns

Chapter 7
- Avoid Unnecessary Attention to *I*
- Avoid Unnecessary Attention to *You*
- Vitalize with Verbs

Chapter 8
- Avoid Over-Embedding
- Break Bad Habits
- Clean Up Attributive Phrases
- Try Absolutes!

Chapter 9
- Avoid Unnecessary Interruption
- Repeat Clause or Phrase Patterns
- Condense Wordy Phrases

Chapter 10
- Avoid Strings of Phrases
- Intensify with a Series
- Avoid Expletives

Chapter 11
- Avoid the Obvious Content
- Get Rid of Obvious Padding
- Call a Fool a Fool

Chapter 12
- Try the Stylistic Fragment
- Deliberately Break Some Other Rule
- Give Your Essay an Engaging Title
- Sharpen Your Opening Sentence

COHERENCE AND CONCISENESS

Sentences, paragraphs, and essays (as well as letters, reports, and other writing) should be coherent and concise. **Coherence** involves connecting ideas in a systematic and logical way. If a piece of writing is coherent, it is logically or aesthetically arranged to help make its ideas clear and understandable. **Conciseness** involves expressing an idea without unnecessary words, sentences, or paragraphs. Concise writing is free of ornamentation and superfluous details. It makes its point economically, with little waste. A variety of concerns, ranging from purpose in writing to in-text documentation, contribute to coherence and conciseness. Notice how the following strategies combine to create coherence and conciseness in the essay "Entitlement Education":

- A title that expresses the focus of the essay
- Purposeful writing
- A purposeful introduction that moves steadily toward a main point
- Accurate word choice
- Sentence vitality (eliminating expletives, wordiness, etc.)
- Explicit statements (including statements of main ideas and statements of support)
- Summary of appropriate information
- Consistent verb tense
- Conventional punctuation (commas, colons, quotation marks, etc.)
- Transitional words, expressions, sentences, and paragraphs
- Pronouns
- Pronoun/antecedent agreement
- Subject/verb agreement
- Parallelism
- Parenthetical information
- Subordination/coordination
- Relevant use of sources
- Integration of borrowed material
- In-text documentation and a corresponding Works Cited page

Daniel Bruno
Composition I
Dr. Fritz Strisky
November 5, 2007

Entitlement Education

In his book <u>Generation X Goes to College</u>, Peter Sacks describes, among other things, the sense of entitlement that some students in today's consumerist culture have toward a college education. One entire chapter explores this issue alone, providing examples of this "sense" and looking into its "humble beginnings." Sacks shows how consumerism has invaded education, leading some students to expect good grades for little effort. But he fails, it seems, to emphasize enough a most harmful effect of this sense of entitlement. The biggest problem, as I see it, is that although students are able to graduate from high school (and even some colleges) with minimal effort, those students may find themselves cheated in the long run.

How might they be cheated? One might argue that students get cheated because entitlement doesn't go on forever. At some point it stops. For example, a college graduate with a marketing degree, but especially weak thinking or writing skills, may find himself disadvantaged on the job. It is not that his boss puts her foot down; instead, the job does. Our student finds himself not well prepared for it. He gets cheated because he is disadvantaged at his job—a job that he paid money to learn how to do. Of course the point isn't about marketing majors. The same is true of students in any field. (Marketing is just what came to mind.)

One might also claim that students will be cheated because their lives will somehow *be less.* This argument claims that a person's intelligence contributes to his quality of life. Here we must remember that "intelligence" is not just "knowledge." Instead, it is being able to use knowledge, to make connections and figure things out, to see causes and solve problems. A person may have much knowledge—that is, he may have accumulated a lot of facts—but not have much intelligence . . . or so the argument goes. As one goes from first grade to twelfth, from twelfth grade to college, and from freshman to senior, education shifts focus from mere accumulation of information (knowledge) to application of information (intelligence). And while we may accumulate more knowledge as a senior in college than we did as a senior in high school, the focus in college has (or should have) shifted from mere knowledge to intelligence—that is, to the ability to make good use of one's knowledge.

Other standard arguments claim other ways students might be cheated. For example, we might feel sorry for someone who doesn't get a joke—or a reference. Allusions to literature, history, philosophy and so on allow us to say much in few words. But does the listener understand? If a person is unaware of common references—the Battle of the Bulge, Normandy, Existentialism, T. S. Eliot, World War I, Rasputin, John the Baptist, Gandhi, apartheid, Jonas Salk, Johnny Appleseed, Lewis and Clark, the Trail of Tears, slavery, the

Donner Party, and so on—he misses out on conversations, on meaning, on *connecting with his fellow inmates*. Of course, here one might counter that you don't need to know all of these things. And, I agree, you don't. People tend to hang out with people who have similar interests and tastes.

5   One more argument claims that because we live in a democracy, we must be well-educated. Since all the citizens are responsible for the government, our forefathers promoted public education so that all citizens—not just the wealthy and elite—would know how to read and write. Thomas Jefferson wrote,

> I know no safe depository of the ultimate powers of society but the people themselves; and if we think them not enlightened enough to exercise their control with a wholesome discretion, the remedy is not to take it from them, but to inform their discretion by education. This is the true corrective of abuses of constitutional power. (278)

In what ways can educated citizens correct abuses in a democracy? A person's way of life, his purchases and activities—not just a person's vote or protest march—is part of the responsibility. Thus, consumers and neighbors and co-workers and so on should behave responsibly and think intelligently. It is our responsibility as citizens of a democracy.

True enough, these are all ways that students who are allowed to just slide by end up getting cheated. But another way (and one less talked about) strikes me as being far more offensive. This reason hinges on the fact that many students are not just sliding by. In Generation X Goes to College, Peter Sacks illustrates that all of today's college students cannot just be thrown in the same big barrel. In describing the modern/post-modern clash in education, he spends the majority of his time talking about those students who are underprepared, who lack the basic study skills required in academic work, and who demonstrate little real commitment to their own education. Yet, he does not discuss this problem in isolation. He also mentions another type of student. For example, he introduces the reader to Marissa and Carol: "As very good students, [their views] were virtually excluded by The College in order to accommodate the whiners and complainers" (61). And he says they "suffered not only educationally" (63). In addition to discussing specific good students, an entire chapter presents survey results about students' attitudes toward education. While he makes claims such as "nearly a quarter of the students . . . harbored a disproportionate sense of entitlement," this very statement tells the reader that a full three-quarters (that is, three out of four) students *do not* "harbor a disproportionate sense of entitlement" (54–59). He wraps up the book by focusing on another student, Andie, who he describes as "a good student, constantly picking [his] brain for information and feedback on her work" (186–87). His final paragraph, before the Epilogue, says, "Let's create a system that encourages people like Andie at least as much as the ones who don't give a damn" (187). Thus, Sacks shows that today's students are a more diverse group—in skill level, background, and attitude toward education—than has ever before been gathered together in the college classroom.

Items in a series (on conversations, on meaning, on connecting) expressed in parallel grammatical form contribute to coherence.

Explicit statements of main ideas, followed with support for that idea, contribute to coherence.

Smoothly integrating appropriate outside information and documenting correctly contribute to coherence.

The quoted material is discussed.

This entire paragraph provides coherence between two sections by taking the reader from the previous ideas to "another way."

Main ideas at the beginning of paragraphs provide coherence by letting the reader know the reason for the information that follows.

A properly used colon—to introduce a quote with words that could be punctuated as a sentence—provides coherence. The reader knows immediately the relationship of the words on the left and right of the colon. Quotation marks provide coherence by making clear that the words inside them are from a source.

In-text documentation that corresponds to a Works Cited page provides coherence by being inobtrusive while at the same time providing important information.

Works Cited

Jefferson, Thomas. <u>The Writings of Thomas Jefferson</u>. Ed. Andrew Adgate Lipscomb
    and Albert Ellery Bergh. Vol. 15. Washington, DC: Thomas Jefferson Memorial
    Assn., 1903-04.
Sacks, Peter. <u>Generation X Goes to College</u>. Open Court: Chicago, 1996.

Activity

1. Check your own essay for coherence and conciseness by referring to the strategies in Bruno's essay. For example, how does the title help focus the reader on the main idea, or how does your purpose in writing help to make the essay coherent and concise?

2. Weed your writing of unnecessary words. Then, if your essay fails to meet a length requirement for the assignment, return to the appropriate invention section in the text and explore your topic further, developing interesting ideas worth discussing in your essay.

3. Examine the table of contents of this book. What strategies do authors seem to use when titling their essays? Which titles are most intriguing, and why? Which essays do you want to read based on just the title? Describe how a few successful titles help to focus the reader on the writer's purpose in writing.

COMPLETE SENTENCES

Writers and readers share ideas about what constitutes a sentence or a part of a sentence. In academic and professional written English, sentences generally contain at least one **independent clause** (a group of related words with a subject and verb). Sometimes they contain more than one independent clause. Consider the following sentence basics:

- A group of words without an independent clause is a **sentence fragment.**
- A group of words made up of two independent clauses not connected by either a coordinating conjunction *(and, or, nor, for, yet, but, so)* or a semicolon is a **run-on sentence.**
- There are two kinds of run-on sentences: a **fused sentence** and a **comma splice.**

Sentence Fragment

A sentence fragment, since it contains no independent clause, can be a single word, a phrase, a dependent clause, or any combination of the three *without an independent clause.* Writers sometimes use fragments purposely, for effect. Such as here. This strategy is acceptable and can be effective if used sparingly, although fragments should not creep into one's writing by accident.

Phrases are not complete sentences.

> Falling off his horse and getting right back on it.

> The neighbor's new Siamese kitten, Lorenzo.

Dependent clauses are not complete sentences.

> When Joe passed his algebra test.

> As long as you and Susie are going to the game.

Combinations of phrases and dependent clauses are not complete sentences.

> Running to catch the bus so I won't be late for class.

> George Washington who was the first president of the United States and general of the Continental Army.

Run-On Sentence

In a run-on sentence, the two independent clauses are "run together," either with a comma (a comma splice) or with no punctuation at all (a fused sentence).

Comma splice

I went home, she stayed at the party.

I am tired of reading, I am going to bed now.

Joe flew the 767, he had never landed a plane before.

There is a mouse in the closet, we need a better mousetrap.

Fused sentence

I went home she stayed at the party.

I am tired of reading I am going to bed now.

Joe flew the 767 he had never landed a plane before.

There is a mouse in the closet we need a better mousetrap.

Activity

Which of the following are sentence fragments? Which are run-on sentences?

1. Even when the radio is turned up loud.

2. Fall is in the air, it feels like marching bands and football.

3. Miles Davis was a trumpeter, his magnum opus is Kind of Blue.

4. As darkness fell and the temperature dropped, making us wonder whether or not we should have worn heavier jackets.

5. The day after the game when everybody was still talking about the upset.

HOW TO IDENTIFY SENTENCE FRAGMENTS AND RUN-ON SENTENCES

To identify sentence fragments and run-on sentences in your writing, you must take a grammatical approach. Vague, non-grammatical approaches can be unhelpful. For example, fragments are not just incomplete thoughts. Run-on sentences are not just long sentences or sentences with a lot of ideas in them. And comma splices are not just the misuse of a comma. For example, all sentences are somewhat incomplete when it comes to meaning. *He was there* doesn't say who he is or where he is. Thus, its meaning is not complete, even though it is a grammatically complete sentence. *I went she stayed* is a run-on sentence even though it is short and contains only a few ideas. (And a much longer sentence—even one hundred words—can be a complete sentence, not a run-on sentence.) *I, went, and, she, stayed* is not a comma splice, even though commas are misused in the sentence. Feeling like a sentence might be a fragment or run-on is a starting place, but to be certain, you must take the following grammatical approach to the problem:

1. Identify the independent clauses in your sentence.
   - If there are no independent clauses, the sentence is a fragment.
   - If there is only one independent clause, the sentence is a complete sentence.
   - If there are two or more independent clauses, go to step 2.

2. If you found two or more independent clauses, how are they connected?
   - If with a coordinating conjunction (*and, or, nor, for, yet, but, so*), you have a complete sentence.

- If with a semicolon, you have a complete sentence.
- If with a comma, you have a comma splice.
- If with no punctuation, you have a fused sentence.

3. If you have a fragment, comma splice, or a fused sentence, you may revise your sentence in several ways.

HOW TO REVISE FRAGMENTS

Some writers use fragments sparingly to achieve a desired effect. But fragments should not occur by accident. Most sentence fragments should be identified and revised to read as complete sentences. While this can be done in various ways, the objective is always to either (1) attach the fragment to an independent clause, (2) add an independent clause to the fragment, or (3) restructure the sentence to create an independent clause.

Revising fragments that are phrases

(A **phrase** is a group of related words without a subject and a verb.)

> Falling off his horse and getting right back on it.
>
> a fragment because it is a phrase and has no independent clause

> Joe fell off his horse and got right back on it.
>
> a complete sentence because an independent clause—*Joe* (subject) *fell* and *got* (verb)—has been added

> Falling off his horse and getting right back on it, Joe joined the posse and captured the bandits.
>
> a complete sentence because the phrase has been connected to an independent clause—*Joe* (subject) *joined* and *captured* (verb)

Revising fragments that are dependent clauses

(A **dependent clause** is a clause preceded by a subordinating conjunction.)

> When Joe passed his algebra test.
>
> a fragment because it is a dependent clause and has no independent clause

> Joe passed his algebra test.
>
> a complete sentence because the subordinating conjunction—*when*—has been eliminated, thus creating an independent clause

> When Joe passed his algebra test, he let out a sigh of relief.
>
> a complete sentence because the dependent clause has been attached to an independent clause

AGREEMENT

Agreement—the grammatical relationship between a subject and a verb or between a pronoun and its antecedent—contributes to coherence, or the way a piece of writing flows smoothly from one idea to another. For example, a writer will decide to write in a particular tense—such as past or present—and then stick to that tense until there is a good reason to change. Unnecessary shifts in tense can be confusing and distracting. In the sentence below, the verbs do not agree in tense. The sentence shifts from present tense *(contributes)* to past tense *(was)*. The shift is unnecessary and distracting:

> One thing that contributes to coherence—or the way a piece of writing flows smoothly from one idea to another—was agreement.

Verb Tense Agreement

For more about verbs, see pages 700–707.

A piece of writing generally has one controlling tense—in other words, most of the verb tenses are the same. However, verb tense may shift to indicate a change in time:

> Liz **left** the football game early and **went** to a movie. She **is** not a big fan of the game. I **doubt** that she **will** ever **enjoy** football.

The first sentence above uses past-tense verbs *(left* and *went)*. But the follow-up sentence is written in present tense because Liz still *is* not a fan of the game. The third sentence uses a present tense verb *(doubt)* and a future tense verb *(will enjoy)*. These shifts in tense accurately express the time relationship among several ideas; thus, there is a good reason to change tense. Some shifts, however, are less purposeful and are confusing or distracting:

> Liz **left** the football game early and **goes** to a movie.

This shift is unnecessary. It is hard to imagine why the writer shifts from past tense *(left)* to present tense *(goes)*. While the meaning still seems clear, the shift is distracting. If further unnecessary shifts were to occur or if the passage were to deal with a more complex concept, the reader would eventually become confused.

Unnecessary tense shifts sometimes occur when the writer changes unexpectedly to the present tense after beginning in the past tense. This often occurs when narrating. Consider the following example:

> When I first **got** off the plane in Belgrade, I **noticed** how cool and crisp the air felt. I **see** the mountains in the distance and **want** to drive out to them and begin climbing.

The verb *see* in the second sentence marks an unnecessary shift from past tense to present. Because the verb tense is not consistent and because the change does not express an actual change in time, the shift is likely to distract the reader.

Shifts in Person

The passage below shifts not only from past tense to present, but also from first person to second—from *I* to *you*. An unnecessary shift in person may distract or confuse the reader.

> When **I** first got off the plane in Belgrade, **I** noticed how cool and crisp the air felt. **You** see the mountains in the distance and want to drive out to them and begin climbing.

Pronouns can be first, second, or third person. First-person pronouns refer to the person speaking *(I, me, mine; we, our, ours)*; second-person pronouns refer to the person being spoken to *(you, your, yours)*; and third-person pronouns refer to the person or thing being talked about *(he, him, his; she, her, hers; it, its; they, them, theirs)*. In the example above, the writer refers to himself in the first person *(I)*, then shifts unnecessarily to the second person *(you)*. The passage below is consistent in tense (past) and person (first).

For more about pronouns, see pages 698–699.

> When **I** first **got** off the plane in Belgrade, **I noticed** how cool and crisp the air felt. **I saw** the mountains in the distance and **wanted** to drive out to them and begin climbing.

Pronoun/Antecedent Agreement

Pronouns take the place of (or refer back to) nouns; the nouns they replace (or refer back to) are called their antecedents. For example, in the sentence below, *her* takes the place of *the little girl*—that is, it allows the writer to not repeat *the little girl*. Since *girl* is (1) singular, (2) feminine, and (3) in the third person, so is the pronoun that replaces it.

The little **girl** enjoyed **her** ride on the giant Ferris wheel.

      ↑   ↑

  antecedent   pronoun

Pronoun/antecedent agreement can be tricky in sentences more complex than the one above. When several sentences work together to form a paragraph or several paragraphs, more vigilance is required to make sure pronouns and antecedents agree. In the following example, Daniel Bruno consistently uses the third-person plural pronoun *they* because the passage begins with the plural noun *students:*

> Students would do well to look around **them,** at the room full of fellow classmates. **They** should imagine that many of those students will be graduating one day. And **they** should imagine the students in the classroom next door and across the hall and in all the other buildings on campus. **They** will be graduating, too.

Third-person singular Pronouns and antecedents require special attention when it comes to the third-person singular. In the example below, Bruno decides to use the feminine pronoun *she* to refer to both men and women.

> The injustice, then, has been done to the students (as Sacks says, the students are the victims). **While the student** has happily skipped (or unhappily slogged) along through sixteen years of formal education, **she** is allowed, if **she** wants, to come away with very little in terms of education. **She** is allowed, unfortunately, to escape practically unscathed by learning.

The use of a feminine pronoun to refer to both men and women might be considered unusual. In the past, *he* was commonly used this way. Although the singular pronoun (*he* or *she*) may be correct in number (matching the antecedent), it does not accurately represent the reality beyond grammar—the real men and women who are students. (For more discussion, see Gender Bias and Sensitivity in Language, page 684.) Generally, third-person singular situations such as this one provide the writer with a difficult decision. Writers can avoid the pronoun problem by changing singular antecedents (such as *student*) to the plural *(students)* and using *they* as the pronoun.

Subject/Verb Agreement

In addition to indicating tense (past, present, future), verbs indicate number—they can be singular or plural. Nouns, too, indicate number (*dog* is singular; *dogs* is plural). Singular nouns take singular verbs; and plural nouns take plural verbs.

> My **sister takes** the train to work.
> My **sisters take** the train to work.

A singular noun *(sister)* with a plural verb *(take)* conveys the same meaning as when the subject and verb agree. But in academic and professional written English, subjects and verbs agree in number. Consider the following questions:

- How important is it that subjects and verbs agree?
- In what situations would you consider *My sister take the train to work* to be acceptable? Unacceptable?
- How might an employer, colleague, classmate, teacher, English teacher, client, boyfriend, or girlfriend react to sentences in which subjects and verbs do not agree?
- How might an English teacher react in different situations, such as in the classroom, at the supermarket, at home?

OTHER SUBJECT/VERB AGREEMENT ISSUES

Phrases or clauses that act as subjects take singular verbs.

Having a kennel full of hungry puppies and no dog food is Marcia's biggest fear.

In academic and professional written English, collective nouns take singular verbs.

The government is taxing the citizens more now than in previous years.

(Other collective nouns to look for include *team, class, congress, orchestra,* and *administration.*)

Compound subjects joined by *and* take a plural verb; some other compound subjects take plural or singular verbs, depending upon the meaning.

Bob and Sue share a common interest in painting. (share is plural—two people share)

Bob shares a common interest with Sue. (shares is singular—one person shares)

Either Bob or Sue shares a common interest with Sally. (shares is singular—one or the other shares)

Neither Bob nor Sue shares a common interest with Sally. (shares is singular—not one or the other shares)

Indefinite pronouns, such as *everyone, everybody, all,* and *anybody,* usually take a singular verb and singular pronoun.

Everyone in our family goes to the annual ice cream social at the volunteer fire department.

Activities

1. Write a paragraph that changes verb tense to indicate different times. What is the controlling tense of your paragraph? Did you use any tenses besides simple past, present, and future? That is, did you use a perfect or progressive tense?

2. Write a paragraph with a controlling tense. Then try to distract and confuse the reader by shifting verb tenses unnecessarily.

3. Before turning in your next essay, check your pronoun/antecedent agreement. First, circle every *they, their,* and *them.* Then identify the word to which the pronoun refers (draw a line from the circled word to the word it replaces). Since *they, their,* and *them* are plural, the antecedent must also be plural. If it is not, revise the sentence accordingly.

PARALLELISM

Parallel items are related in two ways:

1. grammatical form

2. meaning

Parallelism (like agreement) contributes to the coherence of a piece of writing, or to how it flows. Parallel structure means using the same grammatical form (noun, verb, participial phrase, etc.) to help indicate that ideas are related. In the following, the first sentence is parallel; the second is not:

> Herbert **ate** a big dinner, **sat down** in his favorite chair, and **put on** his slippers.
>
> We see that Herbert did three things. Each is expressed by the same grammatical form—a verb phrase.

> Herbert **ate** a big dinner, **sat down** in his favorite chair, and **putting on** his slippers.
>
> Here, the third thing, *putting on his slippers*, is expressed in a different grammatical form—a participial phrase instead of a verb.

COORDINATING CONJUNCTIONS

For more about conjunctions, see page 708.

One way to ensure better parallelism is to identify all coordinating conjunctions *(and, or, nor, for, yet, but, so)* and then to make sure the sentence parts they connect are grammatically equal. For example, since *and* connects parallel (or coordinate) sentence parts, the words, phrases, or clauses connected by *and* should take the same grammatical form. This helps the reader to pick up on the relationship between the ideas more easily.

> Bob <u>went</u> fishing **and** <u>fell</u> into the lake.
>
> *And* connects two verbs—*went* and *fell.*

> The <u>man</u> in the green hat **and** the <u>woman</u> with the umbrella are old friends.
>
> *And* connects two *nouns—man* and *woman.*

> I went <u>to the market</u> **and** <u>to the bookstore</u> before it rained.
>
> *And* connects two prepositional phrases—*to the market* and *to the bookstore.*

> <u>The doctor was two hours behind schedule,</u> **and** <u>all the patients had to wait.</u>
>
> *And* connects two independent clauses—*The doctor was . . .* and *all the patients had. . . .*

It was raining, **yet** everyone had fun.

Yet connects two independent clauses—*It was raining* and *everyone had fun.*

We finished cleaning the garage, **but** not the basement.

But connects two nouns—*the garage* and *the basement.*

SEMICOLONS

Semicolons express a coordinate relationship, just as coordinating conjunctions do. The sentence parts connected by a semicolon should be grammatically equal because that's what a semicolon does: It connects sentence parts that are grammatically equal. In the sentence below, the semicolons connect independent clauses: (1) *Engineers will build defective bridges;* (2) *doctors will botch their operations;* (3) *marketers will have no clue how to market.*

> For example, one might argue that students find themselves cheated because upon graduation they will not be prepared to do their jobs: Engineers will build defective bridges; doctors will botch their operations; and marketers will have no clue how to market.

COMPARISONS/CONTRASTS

The parallel grammatical structure of comparison/contrast helps the reader to more easily notice the relationship between the ideas. A comparison/contrast relationship is indicated through parallelism: *the one on the higher level* and *the one on the lower level.*

> The problem, of course, is that the two students have entered college on different academic levels and **the one on the higher level** has graduated on an *even higher* level while **the one on the lower level** has remained pretty much the same.

LISTS

A grocery list provides a good example of how meaning and grammatical form work together. When meaning is parallel or equal (all things we can pick up at a grocery store) then form tends also to be parallel or equal (all nouns).

> eggs, cheese, butter, bagels, cookies, sauce, milk, bread, beans, soap, light bulbs

Notice that the listed items below are all nouns and are expressed in parallel terms:

> We bought eggs, cheese, butter, and milk.

The items in the following list are verb phrases:

> They have at least three options: (1) take advantage of the easy system and learn a little along the way; (2) motivate themselves, working harder (and learning more) than the system requires them to; and (3) attend a more academically rigorous school (of course, such schools still exist, though they are likely to cost more to attend).

HEADINGS

Notice the parallel structure of the headings in Paul Roberts's essay, "How to Say Nothing in 500 Words." They are all imperative statements:

> Avoid the Obvious Content
> Take the Less Usual Side
> Slip Out of Abstraction
> Get Rid of Obvious Padding

But headings need not be imperative statements. Any grammatical form can be used, though some will work better than others depending upon the situation. For example,

> Avoiding the Obvious Content
> Taking the Less Usual Side
> Slipping Out of Abstraction
> Getting Rid of Obvious Padding
>
> How to Avoid the Obvious Content
> How to Take the Less Usual Side
> How to Slip OUt of Abstraction
> How to Get Rid of Obvious Padding

Activities

1. Before turning in an essay, check for parallel structure.
   a. Identify all coordinating conjunctions *(and, or, nor, for, yet, but, so)* and make sure that the words or group of words they connect are the same grammatical form. This includes items in a series, such as *bread, cheese, butter, **and** milk.* (Note: The word *for* most often functions as a prepositional phrase and not a coordinating conjunction.)
   b. Find semicolons, and make sure that the words or group of words they connect have the same grammatical form.
2. Exchange essays with a classmate and check for parallel structure.

WORD CHOICE

The right word will be accurate and appropriate for the audience. To choose the right word, writers consider their purpose in writing, the reader, and the overall writing situation.

Accurate

Accuracy in word choice begins with understanding language as something that is shared. For example, people generally agree on what a cat is, and on what to call it. Thus, the word *cat* accurately expresses the idea *cat* (which corresponds to the material reality of a cat). This simple example illustrates how we share language. What I call a cat, you, too, call a cat. And we not only share the word *cat*—we also share the concept *cat*. Other, more abstract concepts—such as *patriotism, honesty, love, service,* and so on—can vary more in meaning from one person to another. As humans, we share not only words but categories of thoughts. We group various animals into *cats, dogs, rabbits,* or various people into *holy, heathen, pagan,* or *successful, struggling, washed up.* When we refer to a category of thought *(cat, love, rest, white, struggling),* we try to choose a word that will accurately express our thought to others—and thus allow us to be heard by them.

When choosing words, consider the following questions:

- Am I using this word in the way that it is usually understood?
- If I am using this word in an unusual sense, will my reader understand it? Should I define the word and/or illustrate it with an example?
- Could I replace this word with one that more accurately expresses my meaning?
- Have I used unusual words in an attempt to impress my reader with my vocabulary? If so, should I replace these words with plain, straightforward language?
- Am I comfortable with my word choice? How does it make me sound?

Appropriate

If writers are not attentive to their readers, the language can be accurate but not appropriate. For example, word choice might be too casual or too formal for a particular writing situation; it might be gender-biased, overly technical, insensitive, or archaic. Writers determine whether or not words are appropriate by sizing up each writing situation and considering how their word choice is likely to influence the reader. (See the Writer's Voice sections in Chapters 2–12 as you develop your writing.)

> The difference between the almost right word & the right word is really a large matter—it's the difference between the lightning bug and the lightning.
>
> —Mark Twain

Level of Formality Formality in word choice varies, depending upon the writing situation. An e-mail to a friend would probably be casual, a scientific report formal. As Chapter 4 explains, the expected level of formality varies in different essay writing situations. For more information about level of formality, refer to the discussion on pages 126–127.

- Slang can be used effectively in an essay; but slang used indiscriminately often indicates a lack of serious thought or a lack of sensitivity for the reader.

- Archaic (old and outdated) language strikes some modern readers as insincere, and thus should be used cautiously, if at all.

- Flowery writing draws attention to itself, not to the ideas being expressed. This type of writing can make for slow and difficult reading.

Gender Bias and Sensitivity in Language Writers must be aware of the consequences of gender-biased language. A job ad that states "the candidate must own his own tools" appears to be excluding female candidates. Thus, third-person singular pronouns (such as *he, she, he/she, s/he,* etc.) should be chosen carefully. Words once common, such as *congressman, policeman, chairman,* have been replaced with gender-neutral terms, such as *representative, police officer, chair.* Nurses are not assumed to be women, and CEOs are not assumed to be men. Showing awareness and sensitivity through one's choice of words invites the reader to listen—whereas showing insensitivity gives the reader a reason for tuning out. Also see Third-Person Singular (page 678).

Jargon The technical language of a field (jargon) must be used carefully with an audience that is not expert in that field. Technical language should be replaced with more common terms or defined. Experts use jargon to talk shop, but non-experts do not share the same language. Some readers will become suspicious of technical vocabulary, wondering why the writer cannot explain the idea more simply and directly. Using technical jargon is a matter of audience awareness. Will your audience understand the jargon or not? Good communicators are able to explain complex ideas in plain language.

General and Specific Language When choosing the right word, the writer must decide upon the appropriate level of abstraction. Some words are specific, or concrete, while other words are general, or abstract—that is, they express general qualities but do not provide specific detail about those qualities.

Every time a writer moves to a more specific term, possibilities of meaning are eliminated. For example, *farm animals* includes cows, pigs, mules, goats, sheep, ducks, chickens, and geese. But *fowl* eliminates cows, pigs, mules, and goats. *Fowl* can mean ducks, chickens, or geese—but *rooster* eliminates ducks and geese. Jim, our rooster, is specific. He is one particular rooster—though we can refer to "Jim" either *generally* over the course of his life or more *specifically,* such as "Jim when he was a chick," "Jim the day we got him," or "Jim the day he died."

Levels of Abstraction

life	*general*	transportation	*general*
animal life		public transportation	
farm animals		bus	
fowl		school bus	
rooster		bus #8	
Jim, our rooster	*specific*	bus #8, yesterday	*specific*

Writers must consider what level of abstraction to use. When we refer to examples and statistics and colors, we are being specific. But specifics are not always desirable; the reader can get bogged down in too much detail or side-tracked by irrelevant detail. A more specific word choice can be more accurate, but at times you will want to speak more generally. It is good to keep in mind two tips about using abstraction:

- Move back and forth between general and specific information
- Consider replacing general language with more specific language

Notice how the following paragraph from Pico Iyer's "In Praise of the Humble Comma" provides the reader with an appropriate balance of general and specific information.

> Punctuation thus becomes the signature of cultures. The hot-blooded Spaniard seems to be revealed in the passion and urgency of his doubled exclamation points and question marks ("¡Caramba! ¿Quién sabe?"), while the impassive Chinese traditionally added to his so-called inscrutability by omitting all directions from his ideograms. The anarchy and commotion of the sixties were given voice in the exploding exclamation marks, riotous capital letters, and Day-Glo italics of Tom Wolfe's spray-paint prose; and in Communist societies, where the State is absolute, the dignity—and divinity—of capital letters is reserved for Ministries, Subcommittees, and Secretariats.

This paragraph states a general idea first, and then develops that idea with specific information. Iyer supports his general claim that "punctuation thus becomes the signature of cultures" by providing specific examples (Spanish and Chinese punctuation, Tom Wolfe's "spray-paint prose," and capitalization in Communist societies). Notice how other writers throughout this text move back and forth from general ideas to specific support.

Activities

1. Read through some of your own writing, and identify words that may be inaccurate. How might a different word choice allow the reader a better chance of understanding what you meant?

2. Read through some of your own writing, and identify words that may be accurate yet inappropriate. Explain why the word choice might be inappropriate and how a different word choice might be better.

3. Take one paragraph from your own writing, and rewrite it two different ways: (1) using more formal diction and (2) using less formal diction. Do not make your changes too drastic—instead, experiment with fine adjustments in your writer's voice.

4. Find three paragraphs in this book that include both general and specific information. How many levels of abstraction can you identify? How does the writer move from one level to another?

5. Study one essay in this book to see how it presents general and abstract information. Consider highlighting general statements with one color and specific information with another color. Describe how the writer moves back and forth throughout the essay from general to specific.

PUNCTUATION

Understanding punctuation allows you to more clearly and concisely communicate your ideas. For example, notice how the basic end punctuation marks affect the following three sentences:

> Have a seat, George.
>
> Have a seat, George!
>
> Have a seat, George?

Because of punctuation, each sentence speaks to you differently. The same point could be illustrated by looking at how commas, dashes, and parentheses can be used to set off a sentence part.

> Notice how, because of punctuation, each sentence speaks to you differently.
>
> Notice how—because of punctuation—each sentence speaks to you differently.
>
> Notice how (because of punctuation) each sentence speaks to you differently.

Each of these sentences speaks to you differently, perhaps with a very slight difference, because of their punctuation. Setting off a sentence part with dashes (—) means something different than setting off a sentence part with parentheses ( ). Just as knowing what words mean (or what words suggest) allows you to communicate with others more effectively, knowing what different forms of punctuation mean (or suggest) does the same. Many readers know that when a writer places ideas within dashes, he or she means to emphasize those ideas and that ideas placed within parentheses are thought to be less important. Understanding these subtleties, which can be learned through reading about punctuation rules as well as by being attentive to how others punctuate, can help you as both a writer and a reader.

Commas

Commas separate parts of a sentence, and by doing so help to indicate the relationship between the parts.

> While I was talking on the phone, I was watering my plants.

The comma above separates the two main parts of the sentence: *While I was talking on the phone* (a dependent clause) and *I was watering my plants* (an independent clause).

> Mike Easler, left-handed power hitter for the Pirates, slugged one out of the park.

The two commas in this example, like bookends, stand at the beginning and ending of a sentence part *(left-handed power hitter for the Pirates)*. That sentence part interrupts the main part of the sentence *(Mike Easler slugged one out of the park)*. The interrupting part, an appositive, restates the noun that it follows (Mike Easler = left-handed power hitter for the Pirates). Commas separate ideas for the reader, who quickly makes sense of the relationship.

Quick Guide to Commas

1. Commas come after introductory clauses or phrases:

   After the party at Jake's house, we sang Calypso songs for days.
   Although they were tired from hunting, the hounds chased the children around the backyard.

2. Commas are generally used to separate items in a series:

   Alice gave Ralph a necktie, a bottle of cologne, and some chocolates.
   We ate good food, drank some tasty apple cider, and sang songs around the campfire.
   The Big Reds were moving the ball down the field, scoring touchdowns, and taking all the fun out of the game for the Spartans.

3. Commas are generally used between coordinate modifiers:

   Suzette is a lovely, intelligent girl.
   Some large, purple birds swooped down from above.

4. Commas are generally used to set off an interrupting element:

   The rest of our group, for example, is going home tomorrow.
   The parking on campus, though it doesn't bother me, has become a hot topic.
   Ella Fitzgerald, the famous jazz singer, was born in Newport News, Virginia.

5. Commas are also used in dates, addresses, place names, and long numbers:

   We drove through Whitley City, Kentucky, on August 16, 1972.
   John's truck has 124,618 miles on it.
   Please mail my refund to 35 Flarton Place, Burton, Maine 00178.

6. Commas are also used when a quotation follows a speaking verb:

   She said, "Are you coming?"
   After it rained for three days straight, Mrs. Merriweather asked, "Who wants to mop up all this water?"

Commas are often used in the following ways:

Before independent (or main) clauses

Whenever an introductory phrase, word, or clause begins a sentence, a comma comes directly after it. The comma helps separate the introductory material from the main part of the sentence:

Going down the road, the truck stopped to pick up the hitch-hiker.

introductory phrase

While I was talking on the phone, I was watering my plants.

introductory clause

Sadly, the Comets came out flat for the second half.

introductory word

Before coordinating conjunctions when they join two independent clauses

Commas usually appear before coordinating conjunctions connecting two independent clauses. But when coordinating conjunctions connect two dependent clauses, phrases, or words, commas are not used.

The fire was burning brightly, and the rain was still falling gently.

and connects two independent clauses

The Rangers were sitting around and talking.

and connects two participles—
sitting around and *talking*

Herbert felt awful after the firefighters' cookout and called his sister for advice.

and connects two verbs—*felt* and *called*

Not before dependent (or subordinate) clauses

For a list of subordinating conjunctions, see page 708.

Commas don't usually precede subordinating conjunctions (*because, since, although,* etc.) the way they do coordinating conjunctions (*and, or, nor, for, yet, but, so*). The sentence parts (an independent clause and a dependent clause) are distinct because of the subordinating conjunction and thus don't require a comma. At times, however, a comma may be used to build an even stronger distinction between the two clauses. For example, S. I. Hayakawa writes, "All new ideas sound foolish at first, because they are new." Writers size up the situation and decide whether or not inserting a comma before a dependent clause will help the reader to better see the intended relationship between ideas.

To set off interrupting elements

Some sentence parts interrupt. For example, *The dog, as you know, barked at the biker* can be viewed as having two parts: the main clause *(The dog barked at the biker)* and an interrupting element *(as you know)*. Interrupting elements can be one word, a phrase, or a clause.

> French fries, although I haven't had any for a while, sure do taste good.
>
> French fries, an American classic, are sold all around the world.
>
> French fries, yum, are my favorite kind of potatoes.

Notice how the interrupting elements are punctuated in the following sentences:

> A sadder truth, I am afraid, is that because of skills and attitudes developed in high school, for some students the reality of genuine learning (as opposed to just getting by) might already be too late. (Daniel Bruno)
>
> Soon, I predict, they and other companies will not be able to sell us out. (Michael Moore)
>
> I crouched low to avoid destroying a jewelled spider's web that stretched, exquisite and fragile, across the trail. (Jane Goodall)

Interrupting elements can also be set off with parentheses or dashes. In general, parentheses suggest that the inserted information is somehow less important compared to the main point being made. Yet, because this information is included, it is still important and interesting. Dashes—unlike parentheses— draw attention to the interrupting bit of information. Dashes and parentheses are stronger separators than the comma. Read more about dashes and parentheses on pages 692 and 693.

To separate items in a series

Placing a comma between each item in a series helps the reader know where one item stops and another begins. Thus, we punctuate the following sentence this way: *As individuals in a society, we conform to laws, clothing styles, hairstyles, and even culinary tastes (most Americans like French fries but not raw oysters).* Not punctuating the list *laws clothing styles hairstyles and even culinary tastes* would have been, at the least, distracting to the reader.

> Just go to any pet store and look at the vast array of foods, toys, beds, and treats, not to mention the shampoos and skin treatments. (David Hawes)
>
> If a person is unaware of common references—the Battle of the Bulge, Normandy, Existentialism, T. S. Eliot, World War I, Rasputin, John the Baptist, Gandhi, apartheid, Jonas Salk, Johnny Appleseed, Lewis and Clark, the Trail of Tears, slavery, the Donner Party, and so on—he misses out on conversations, on meaning, on connecting with his fellow inmates. (Daniel Bruno)

To separate coordinate modifiers

When side-by-side modifiers modify the same word independently of each other, the modifiers are usually separated with a comma.

the big, black dog

Each modifier (*big* and *black*) modifies the dog independently of the other. The dog is big. And the dog is black. Notice the use of coordinate modifiers *(black, brown, white carpet)* in the following passage:

> What happened was that I took a bite of honey and then I joined my sister and brother, two and ten years younger, watching Saturday morning cartoons together on the black, brown, white carpet, patterned in such a wild way that it was quickly making my head ache.

Another type of modifier, the compound modifier, is punctuated with a hyphen. See Hyphens on page 692.

Activities

1. Scan the essays in this book, noticing how commas are used. Find at least three examples of the following: (1) a comma before a main clause (or setting off an introductory element), (2) two commas setting off an interrupting element, (3) a comma between items in a series, (4) a comma between coordinate modifiers.

2. Scan your own writing—an essay, letter, e-mail—and notice how commas are used. Find at least three examples of the following: (1) a comma before a main clause (or setting off an introductory element), (2) two commas setting off an interrupting element, (3) a comma between items in a series, (4) a comma between coordinate modifiers.

Colons

Colons are useful for connecting a list, explanation, or quotation to the statement introducing it. Properly used colons can save time while connecting ideas clearly.

> So here's what I don't understand: if profit is supreme, why doesn't a company like General Motors sell crack? (Michael Moore)

> Punctuation, one is taught, has a point: to keep up law and order. (Pico Iyer)

Semicolons

Semicolons are stronger than commas and weaker than periods. They are used to connect sentence parts that are equal grammatically, such as two independent clauses, two dependent clauses, two phrases, or two words. They are not used to connect sentence parts that aren't grammatically equal, such as a clause and a phrase or an independent clause and a dependent clause.

> They burned the forest and changed the rainfall; they swept the buffalo from the plains, blasted the streams, set fire to the grass, and ran a reckless scythe through the virgin and noble timber. (John Steinbeck)

> The sky is clear and blue; however, the game has been postponed.

> Last summer I drove through Bangor, Maine; Hanover, New Hampshire; and Halifax, Nova Scotia.

In the first two examples above, the semicolon is used to connect two independent clauses. Notice that in the second example, the conjunctive adverb *however* is also used. Semicolons precede conjunctive adverbs when they connect two independent clauses. In the third example, the semicolons are used to connect (or separate) locations: Bangor, Maine; Hanover, New Hampshire; and Halifax, Nova Scotia. Semicolons are used because the sentence already contains commas between the cities and states.

Activities

Commas

1. Create a comma quiz for your peers by removing the commas from one page of your recent writing. Allow your peers ten minutes to punctuate the text, and then discuss how their punctuation compares to the original.

2. Find or create at least one example of the following: (1) a sentence that is clearer to the reader because it is punctuated one way instead of another, (2) a sentence that is clear but distracting to the reader because it is punctuated one way instead of another.

Colons, Semicolons, and Dashes

3. Scan the essays in this book, noticing how colons and semicolons are used. Carefully study several examples of each. How is the colon or semicolon used? What two sentence parts are being connected?

Hyphens

Hyphens are used to connect compound modifiers. A compound modifier is two or more words combined to function as one modifier.

We had thirty-five minutes to write an in-class essay.

The words *in* and *class* combine to modify *essay*. Each word alone is unable to modify *essay*. It is not an *in* essay or a *class* essay. It is an *in-class* essay. Thus, *in-class* is hyphenated. Notice also that numbers from twenty-one through ninety-nine are hyphenated. Consider these additional examples of compound modifiers: *give-it-to-me-now race for more, water-covered land:*

Although we probably would not have relented in our give-it-to-me-now race for more, we would have taken a solemn moment to raise a toast and drink to your hardship. (Simon Benlow)

One of the largest land-holding families in California took its richest holdings by a trick: By law a man could take up all the swamp or water-covered land he wanted. (John Steinbeck)

Coordinate modifiers (page 690) are punctuated with a comma—not a hyphen.

Dashes

Dashes—like this—are used to set off interrupting elements. As discussed on page 689, interrupting elements can be set off with commas, parentheses, or dashes. In general, dashes draw attention to the interrupting information, while parentheses suggest that the information is somehow less important compared to the main point being made.

So, a need or desire—to stay cool, to be entertained, to keep up with what's going on—is replaced not by a different need or desire but instead by a new way of meeting it. (Chester McCovey)

The Gods, they say, give breath, and they take it away. But the same could be said—could it not?—of the humble comma. (Pico Iyer)

Parentheses

Parentheses (like this) are used to set off interrupting elements. As discussed on page 689, interrupting elements can be set off with commas, parentheses, or dashes. Parentheses suggest that the information is somehow less important compared to the main point being made. Yet, because this information is still included it is somehow important and interesting.

> After my mother's never-subtle hints that if I'd just lose 20 pounds boys would like me and I might even win a beauty contest, it was my friend Bridget who wanted us to enter the Ottumwa (pronounced Uh-TUM-wuh) Junior Miss Pageant together. (Cindy Bosley)

> Doubtless, my sense of education at that time (as well as my sense of what constituted good writing) was more than mildly seasoned by huge doses of the Beats—Allen Ginsburg, Gregory Corso, William Burroughs, Kenneth Patchen, LeRoi Jones, and, of course, Jack Kerouac. (Leonard Kress)

> Wrought in stainless steel and plastic, this bit of industrial-designer paraphenalia (it holds my drug of choice) is every cup holder's dream. (Jim Crockett)

Activities

1. Explain the difference between a dash and a hyphen.

2. Write a paragraph in which you set off interrupting elements, one with commas, one with parentheses, and one with dashes. Use the forms of punctuation rhetorically, making sure the idea you set off with parentheses is less important and that you mean to emphasize the idea within dashes.

3. Explain the difference between a semicolon, a colon, and a comma.

4. Make your draft more lively and concise by using colons to connect a list, explanation, or quotation to the words introducing it.

What is grammar? Why is it important?

HOW SENTENCES WORK: A LOOK AT BASIC GRAMMAR

Every sentence is made up of words that cluster into related groups. If a group has a subject and a verb, it is called a *clause*. (If it doesn't, it is called a *phrase*.) When a noun (such as *dog*) and a verb (such as *sleeps* or *eats* or *barks* or *bites*) group together, a sort of reaction occurs. Other words group together around *dog* and *sleeps* to fill in the story. Some words describe the dog *(big, black, furry, stray),* while others describe the sleeping *(soundly, restlessly, peacefully).* Still other words connect, explaining the relationship between one word or word group and another. And, as you know, words change their forms to express number and time, so that instead of "one dog sleeps" we can say "two dogs slept" or "two big dogs slept soundly" and so on. The brief explanation of words, phrases, and clauses that follows is basically how that reaction works.

How Sentences Work (in Brief)

WORDS—PARTS OF SPEECH

1. **Noun**—A noun names a person, place, or thing.
2. **Pronoun**—A pronoun takes the place of a noun.
3. **Verb**—A verb expresses an action or a state of being.
4. **Adjective**—An adjective modifies a noun or pronoun.
5. **Adverb**—An adverb modifies a verb, adjective, or adverb.
6. **Conjunction**—A conjunction connects words, phrases, and clauses and shows a relationship.
7. **Preposition**—A preposition, placed before a noun and its modifiers, creates a modifying phrase.
8. **Interjection**—An interjection expresses surprise or strong emotion.

Words (parts of speech) are combined into phrases and clauses to create sentences (see next page).

PHRASES

1. **Prepositional**—Consisting of a preposition, modifiers, and a noun, the prepositional phrase functions most often as an adjective or adverb.

2. **Participial**—Consisting of a participle, modifiers, and a noun, the participial phrase functions as an adjective.

3. **Gerund**—Consisting of a gerund, modifiers, and a noun, the gerund phrase functions as a noun.

4. **Infinitive**—Consisting of an infinitive, modifiers, and a noun, the infinitive phrase functions as a noun, adjective, or adverb.

5. **Appositive**—An appositive (which may also be a single noun) describes or restates a noun.

6. **Absolute**—Consisting of a noun, modifiers, and often a participle, the absolute phrase modifies an entire clause.

CLAUSES

1. **Independent**—An independent clause (main clause) contains a subject and a verb, and is not preceded by a subordinating conjunction.

2. **Dependent**—A dependent clause (subordinate clause) contains a subject and a verb and is preceded by a subordinating conjunction or a relative pronoun.
   - **Noun clause**—Noun clauses function as subjects, objects, or complements.
   - **Adjective clause**—Adjective clauses modify nouns or pronouns.
   - **Adverb clause**—Adverb clauses modify verbs, adjectives, or adverbs.

SENTENCES—CLASSIFIED BY STRUCTURE

1. **Simple**—A simple sentence contains one independent clause.

2. **Compound**—A compound sentence contains two independent clauses.

3. **Complex**—A complex sentence contains one independent and one dependent clause.

4. **Compound-complex**—A compound-complex sentence contains at least two independent clauses and at least one dependent clause.

HOW PARTS OF SPEECH FUNCTION IN A SENTENCE

Words may function in different ways in a sentence. For example, *fish* can be a noun or a verb. *(Fish are fun to watch. I fish at my grandma's lake.)* Parts of speech may also function in different ways in a sentence. For example, a noun—such as *fish*—may be the subject of a sentence or the object of a sentence. *(Fish are fun to watch. I saw a fish.)*

1. **Subject**—The subject of a sentence is a noun (or noun phrase, noun clause, or pronoun). It normally precedes the verb (predicate), and it names who or what the sentence is about.

2. **Verb (Predicate)**—The predicate of a sentence (a verb and the words that complete its meaning) usually follows the subject and expresses what the subject does or what has been done to it.

3. **Object**—Objects are nouns (or noun phrases, noun clauses, or pronouns). They usually follow the verb and can be direct objects or indirect objects.

4. **Complement**—Complements are nouns (or noun phrases, noun clauses, or pronouns) but can also be adjectives (or adjective phrases). They usually follow a subject, verb, and any objects, and they can be subject complements, object complements, predicate nouns, or predicate adjectives.

5. **Adverbials**—Adverbials are adverbs (or adverb phrases or adverb clauses) that refer to the verb.

SENTENCES—CLASSIFIED BY PURPOSE

1. **Declarative**—A sentence that makes a statement and ends with a period.

2. **Imperative**—A sentence that expresses a command.

3. **Interrogative**—A sentence that asks a question.

4. **Exclamatory**—A sentence that expresses an emphatic statement and ends with an exclamation mark.

NINE WAYS OF COMBINING SIMPLE SENTENCES (INDEPENDENT CLAUSES)

1. Subject + verb. Subject + verb.

2. Subject + verb; subject + verb.

3. Subject + verb, coordinating conjunction + subject + verb.

4. Subject + verb; conjunctive adverb, subject + verb.

5. Subject + verb subordinating conjunction subject + verb.

6. Subordinating conjunction subject + verb, subject + verb.

7. Subject + relative clause (relative pronoun + verb) + verb.

8. Subject + verb + verb.

9. Phrase, subject + verb.

How Sentences Work (Expanded)

WORDS—PARTS OF SPEECH

Noun

A noun names a person, place, thing, idea, quantity, or condition. Nouns can be proper, common, collective, abstract, or concrete.

Proper nouns name specific people, places, and things. They are always capitalized.

Jane	Zaire
Eatonton, Georgia	the Red Cross
John Kenneth Galbraith	Mexican American
Gutenberg College	English
Star Wars	the Middle East

Common nouns name people, places, and things by general type. They are not capitalized.

woman	nation
town	organization
economist	nationality
college	language
movie	region

Collective nouns name groups of people or things and are treated as singular, not plural.

jury	band
congress	public
committee	

Abstract nouns name ideas, qualities, and conditions.

patriotism	despair
hatred	freedom
love	perfection
integrity	respect
joy	

Activity

What type of noun (proper, common, collective, abstract, concrete (see next page) is each of the following?

hope
rainbow
dog
choir
secret
fence
London
paint
loyalty
Main Street
main street

(Depending upon the context, some nouns may fit into different categories.)

Concrete nouns name things or qualities that are perceptible by the senses.

reporter	book
ball	hot dog
cricket	flower
letter	bed
check	

Pronoun

A pronoun takes the place of a noun. Pronouns can be personal, possessive, reflexive, interrogative, demonstrative, indefinite, or relative.

Personal pronouns refer to specific persons or things.

	Subject Form		**Object Form**	
	Singular	*Plural*	*Singular*	*Plural*
first person	I	we	me	us
second person	you	you	you	you
third person	he		him	
	she	they	her	them
	it		it	

Possessive pronouns indicate ownership.

	Singular	*Plural*
first person	my, mine	our, ours
second person	your, yours	your, yours
third person	his, his	
	her, hers	their, theirs
	its, its	

Reflexive pronouns show that someone or something is acting for or on itself.

	Singular	*Plural*
first person	myself	ourselves
second person	yourself	yourselves
third person	himself	
	herself	themselves
	itself	

Interrogative pronouns are used to ask questions.

Subject	*Object*	*Other*
who / whoever	whom / whomever	what / which / whose

Demonstrative pronouns point out particular persons or things.

Singular	*Plural*
this / that	these / those

Indefinite pronouns serve as general subjects or objects in a sentence.

Singular	*Plural*
another / any* / anybody / anyone / anything	all* / both / few
each / either / everybody / everyone / everything	many / several
neither / nobody / no one / nothing / one	some*
somebody / someone / something	

Some indefinite pronouns can be either singular or plural: singular if they refer to a unit or quantity and plural if they refer to individuals. For example, "Some of my friends **are** leaving" (plural); "Some of the money **is** gone" (singular).

Relative pronouns connect adjective clauses to nouns or pronouns.

Refer to People	*Refer to Things*	*Refer to People or Things*
who / whom whoever / whomever	that / what / whatever which / whichever	that / whose

Activity

Read through one of your essays and then one of the essays in CEL and identify as many types of pronouns as you can: personal, possessive, reflexive, interrogative, demonstrative, indefinite, relative.

Verb

A verb expresses an action or a state of being. The three types of verbs are *action, linking,* and *auxiliary.* Verbs can take other forms and become *verbals*—words formed from verbs that do not function as verbs. (See Verbals at the end of this section.)

Action verbs express action, either physical or mental. Action verbs are either transitive or intransitive.

Transitive verbs require direct objects to complete their meaning.

Joe sold . . .

subject   verb

Joe sold the boat.

The direct object names whom or what is directly acted upon.

Joe finally sold Tom the old sailboat in the backyard.

An indirect object names who or what was indirectly affected by the action of the verb. *Finally* modifies *sold. Old* modifies *sailboat,* as does the prepositional phrase *in the backyard.*

I love . . .

subject   verb

I love baseball.

The direct object names whom or what is directly acted upon.

I still love baseball after all these years.

Other words fill out the sentence. *Still* modifies *love,* as does the prepositional phrase *after all these years.*

Intransitive verbs do not require direct objects to complete their meaning.

The ship sank.

Chelsea skipped.

Scott flipped.

Other words—such as modifiers—can be added to the sentences, but as long as no object is required, the verb is considered to be intransitive.

The ship sank off the coast of South America.

Off the coast of South America is two prepositional phrases.

Chelsea, the little girl next door, skipped down the sidewalk.

The little girl next door is an appositive that describes *Chelsea; down the sidewalk* is a prepositional phrase.

Scott flipped. (intransitive)

Scott flipped a pancake. (transitive)

If Scott did a flip, then *flipped* requires no object and is intransitive. But if Scott flipped a pancake, then *flipped* has a direct object, *a pancake,* and the verb is therefore transitive. Thus, the same verb can be intransitive or transitive, depending upon whether or not an object is required to complete its meaning.

Linking verbs express a state of being or a condition, not an action.

The consumer is king. (Juliet Schor)

We were a young culture with no parents. (Simon Benlow)

The biggest problem as I see it is that although students are able to graduate from high school (and even some colleges) with minimal effort, those students may find themselves cheated in the long run. (Daniel Bruno)

Common Linking Verbs—Forms of *to be*

is	am	are	was
were	be	being	been

Common Linking Verbs—Other Forms

appear	feel	grow	look	become
make	seem	smell	taste	sound

Auxiliary verbs (also called helping verbs) work with other verbs to create verb tenses or form questions.

My mug <u>is insulated</u> so it delivers hot, delicious, organically shade-grown, fair trade coffee for a couple of hours at a time, and in so doing, helps me directly support the small coffee growers and their cooperatives around the world.
(Jim Crockett)

The verb of the main clause consists of two words: *is* (a helping verb) and *insulated* (a past participle).

Modern society <u>has adopted</u> the historically recent perspective that the purpose of education is training for the workplace.

The verb of the main clause consists of two words: *has* (a helping verb) and *adopted* (a past participle).

Common Linking Verbs—Forms of *to be*

is	am	are	was
were	be	being	been

Common Linking Verbs—Other Forms

appear	feel	grow	look	become
make	seem	smell	taste	sound

Verb forms

Verbs take different forms that can be categorized as infinitive, third-person singular present, past, present participle, and past participle.

Infinitive: The base form of a verb, often used with the word *to,* the infinitive (the form one would look up in the dictionary) indicates action that occurs in the present, occurs habitually, or is generally true.

Third-person singular present: Frequently ending in *-s* or *-es*, the third-person singular indicates action that occurs in the present, occurs habitually, or is generally true.

Past: Ending in *-d* or *-ed* (except in irregular verbs), the past tense indicates that something happened before now.

Present participle: Ending in *-ing,* the present participle with an auxiliary forms a verb; without an auxiliary verb, it functions as an adjective or a noun.

Activity

Which of the underlined words function as linking verbs and which function as auxiliary verbs?

1. Pittsburgh <u>is</u> the second largest city in Pennsylvania.

2. Rusty <u>is</u> going to call me later this evening.

3. I <u>was</u> reading an interesting article when the phone rang.

4. The Cowlicks <u>are</u> playing at the Dance Hall tonight.

5. They <u>are</u> the best band ever.

Past participle: Usually ending in *-d* or *-ed* (except in irregular verbs), the past participle with an auxiliary forms a verb; without an auxiliary, it functions as an adjective.

infinitive	(I, you, we) walk	say, sing, care
third-person singular present	(he, she, it) walks	says, sings, cares
past	(I, she, they) walked	said, sang, cared
present participle	(am, was) walking	saying, singing, caring
past participle	(have, has, was) walked	said, sung, cared

Many common English verbs are irregular and form their past tense and participle forms in unpredictable ways. Below is a partial list.

	Infinitive	*Past Tense*	*Past Participle*
Regular Verbs (most verbs in English are regular verbs)	walk	walked	walked
	jump	jumped	jumped
	follow	followed	followed
Irregular Verbs (many verbs in English are irregular verbs)	be	was/were	been
	begin	began	begun
	bite	bit	bitten
	blow	blew	blown
	break	broke	broken
	come	came	come
	cost	cost	cost
	do	did	done
	draw	drew	drawn
	drink	drank	drunk
	drive	drove	driven
	eat	ate	eaten
	fly	flew	flown
	freeze	froze	frozen
	give	gave	given
	go	went	gone
	read	read	read
	ring	rang	rung
	see	saw	seen

Verb Talk

- **Action verbs** express action, either physical or mental.
- **Intransitive verbs** show action that is limited to the subject.
- **Transitive verbs** transfer the action from an actor to a direct object.
- **Linking verbs** allow the word or words following them to complete the meaning of the subject.
- **Auxiliary,** or **helping, verbs** combine with the base or a participle form of another verb to create tense, mood, and voice (active or passive).
- **Verbals** are formed from verbs and act as adjectives, adverbs, and nouns.
- **Verb tense** indicates when an action or state of being occurs.
- **Verb mood** expresses whether the speaker considers a thing to be a fact, a command, or an unreal or hypothetical condition contrary to fact.
- **Voice** can be active or passive, depending upon whether the grammatical subject is doing the action or is being acted upon.

(continued)	*Infinitive*	*Past Tense*	*Past Participle*
	shoot	shot	shot
	spring	sprang	sprung
	swear	swore	sworn
	swim	swam	swum
	take	took	taken
	tear	tore	torn
	throw	threw	thrown
	wear	wore	worn
	write	wrote	written

Verbals

Verbals are formed from verbs but do not function as verbs. There are three types: *participles* (verbals that function as modifiers or as part of the verb), *gerunds* (verbals that function as nouns), and *infinitives* (verbals that function as nouns or modifiers). For example, a verb such as *fish* can be used as a participle, gerund, or infinitive.

> I fish with cousin Dan.
>
> *Fish* is a verb in this sentence. We might have used any other action verb: *swim, work, play, argue, eat,* etc.

Participles look like verbs and are formed from verbs but cannot function as verbs in a sentence. Participles can be present or past (present participles end in *-ing,* and past participles end in *-ed* or an irregular past tense form). Participles are used (1) in participial phrases that modify other sentence parts, (2) as modifying words, or (3) with a helping word or words to create a verb.

Participial phrase

> Fishing with cousin Dan, I lost my wallet.
> While fishing with cousin Dan, I lost my wallet.
> I lost my wallet fishing with cousin Dan.

Participle as modifier

> Cousin Dan is my fishing guru.
> I am cousin Dan's favorite fishing partner.
> Cousin Dan and I both enjoy the fishing life.

Activity

In the following sentences, how does each of the underlined verbals function: participial phrase, participle as modifier, participle as part of a verb, gerund, infinitive?

1. Everyone had a <u>jumping</u> good time at the shindig last night.

2. <u>Jumping</u> on a trampoline isn't much fun for me now.

3. <u>To jump</u> out of second story window is frightening.

4. Everybody was <u>jumping</u> around and singing.

5. While <u>jumping</u> over the moon, the cow saw a laughing dog.

Participle as part of a verb

> I go fishing with cousin Dan.
> I am fishing with cousin Dan.
> I have never been fishing with cousin Dan.

Gerunds are verbals that act as nouns.

> Fishing is fun.
> No one likes fishing like I do.
> You can watch TV shows about cooking, painting, hunting, and fishing.

Infinitives, like gerunds, can act as nouns.

> To fish is fun.
> No one likes to fish like I do.

Verb tense

Tense indicates time. Verbs have three simple tenses (present, past, and future) along with three perfect tenses (present perfect, past perfect, and future perfect) and six progressive tenses, one corresponding to each simple and perfect tense.

present	I dance. She sings.
past	I danced. She sang.
future	I will dance. She will sing.
present perfect	I have danced. She has sung.
past perfect	I had danced. She had sung.
future perfect	I will have danced. She will have sung.
present progressive	I am dancing. She is singing.
past progressive	I was dancing. She was singing.
future progressive	I will be dancing. She will be singing.
present perfect progressive	I have been dancing. She has been singing.
past perfect progressive	I had been dancing. She had been singing.
future perfect progressive	I will have been dancing. She will have been singing.

Tenses are indicated by the form of the main verb (*dance* and *sing* in the examples above) and the auxiliary verbs. Notice that *dance* is a regular verb: *dance, danced, danced.* And *sing* is an irregular verb: *sing, sang, sung.*

Name the verb mood in the following sentences:

1. Workers of the world, unite!

2. My parents built a house in the country.

3. Everyone should sit down.

4. If I were you, I'd take the train instead.

5. Remember to set your clocks one hour ahead tonight.

Verb mood

Mood reflects a writer's attitude towards a statement.

Indicative mood expresses a declarative statement or question.

> A weasel is wild. (Annie Dillard)
>
> I crouched low to avoid destroying a jewelled spider's web that stretched, exquisite and fragile, across the trail. (Jane Goodall)

Imperative mood expresses a command or a direct request.

> Vote.
> Help yourself to another burger.
> Take the less usual side. (Paul Roberts)

Subjunctive mood expresses a conditional situation, a hypothetical, a wish, or some statement contrary to fact.

> If I were the president, I would make some changes around here.
> I wish I were the president.

Adjective

An adjective modifies a noun or pronoun. The three articles—*a, an,* and *the*—mark, or precede, certain nouns and, therefore, function as a special type of adjective. An adjective answers one of the following questions:

What kind?	How many?
Which one?	Whose?

Adjectives modifying nouns

red balloon	Orwellian partyspeak
big river	skulking rhetoric
little women	bright, doomed city
recent layoffs	endless, obsessive preoccupation
practical goal	pure elation
blatant manipulation	everyday lives
amusing instance	simple euphemism

Adverb

An adverb modifies a verb, adjective, or adverb. Adverbs frequently end in *-ly* and answer the following questions:

How?	How often?
When?	To what extent?
Where?	

Adverbs modifying verbs

clearly said   reluctantly explained
jump quickly   suddenly stopped
constantly sang   replied sheepishly
will happily move   land smoothly
willingly applauded   dropped instantly

Interjection

An interjection expresses surprise or strong emotion.

Hey!   Wow! This cheesecake is delicious.
Oh!   Hey! Let's go to the coffeehouse and
Okay!   get a bagel.
Wow!

Good and Well

In casual, everyday speech, people often use the adjective *good* instead of the adverb *well*. For example:

"I did good at bowling last night." OR "I bowled good."

Or, if asked, "How did you bowl?" someone might respond,

"I did good."

Or someone might just say,

"Good."

Yet *good* is an adjective, and *well* is an adverb; adjectives modify nouns and pronouns while adverbs modify verbs, adjectives, and adverbs.

1. Do you consider *good* to be incorrect in the sentences above? Why or why not?

2. Why should, or shouldn't, you avoid using *good* as an adverb?

3. Interview several classmates and others outside of class to get their views on using *good* and *well* correctly.

4. Consider the following sentences. Would you say *good* or *well,* and why?

   Lisa does _____ at whatever she does.

   She hasn't felt _____ about New England since she left.
   Lorenzo is _____ at playing the spoons.
   Diamonds don't look _____ in that ring.
   I don't feel _____.

5. *Bad* and *badly* pose a similar problem. Which word would you use in the sentences below, and why?

   Martha golfed _____.
   I have never done so _____ on a math test.
   The _____ thing about it is the grinding sound.
   Dan is _____ at being on time.
   I feel _____ when it rains.

6. What word would you use below? Did you use an adjective or adverb? Why?

   Jefferson _____ explained his reason for leaving early.
   Georgia told a _____ story that helped me to understand.
   Next month we are _____ driving to Detroit.
   My head was _____ spinning after my second time on the Tilt-a-Whirl.
   Did you hear about the _____ strike at the refinery?

Conjunction

A conjunction connects words, phrases, and clauses and shows a relationship. Conjunctions may be coordinating, subordinating, or correlative.

Coordinating conjunctions link sentence parts of equal grammatical rank. There are only seven coordinating conjunctions.

> I went, <u>and</u> she stayed.
>
> She <u>and</u> I went to dinner <u>and</u> a movie.
>
> We went to a movie <u>but</u> not to dinner.

and   or   nor   for   yet   but   so

Subordinating conjunctions link clauses, making one clause dependent on, or subordinate to, the other. Many words act as subordinating conjunctions.

> Because I went, she stayed.
>
> I went although she stayed.
>
> Even though I went and she stayed, we still had fun.

after	however	that
although	if	though
as	in case	till
as if	in order that	unless
as far as	in that	until
as soon as	no matter how	when
as though	now that	whenever
because	once	where
before	since	wherever
even if	so that	whether
even though	supposing that	while
how	than	why

Correlative conjunctions work in pairs to link sentence parts.

> <u>Whether</u> it rains <u>or</u> not, I am washing my pickup truck tomorrow.
>
> I could go for <u>either</u> a bath <u>or</u> a shower right now.

both . . . and	either . . . or	whether . . . or
neither . . . nor	not only . . . but also	

Preposition

A preposition placed before a noun and its modifiers creates a prepositional phrase. Prepositional phrases function as either adverbs or adjectives.

> Paul left his umbrella <u>by the door</u>.

> The woman <u>at the counter</u> said the bus leaves <u>at noon</u>.

> Who said the majority <u>of customers in the carryout</u> were buying emergency supplies?

Common One-Word Prepositions

about	by	outside
above	concerning	over
across	despite	past
after	down	since
against	during	through
along	except	throughout
among	for	till
around	from	to
at	in	toward
before	inside	under
behind	into	underneath
below	like	until
beneath	near	up
beside	of	upon
besides	off	with
between	on	within
beyond	onto	without
but	out	

Common Multiple-Word Prepositions

according to	by way of	instead of
ahead of	due to	on account of
along with	except for	out of
apart from	in addition to	up to
as for	in case of	with regard to
as to	in front of	with respect to
as well as	in spite of	with the exception of
because of	inside of	

Activity

Some words can function as conjunctions or prepositions. Identify the underlined word as either a subordinating conjunction or a preposition:

1. Nobody can leave <u>until</u> you tell us a story.

2. Larry drove Raquel home <u>after</u> the Raspberry Festival.

3. Ace has to be home <u>before</u> midnight or he can't go out tomorrow.

4. I haven't seen Mike <u>since</u> he moved to Alabama.

Activity

Identify each of the underlined phrases: prepositional, participial, gerund, infinitive, appositive, absolute:

1. <u>Coming around the bend,</u> Jackie saw a moose.
2. The city council voted to close the school <u>at the end of the year.</u>
3. The fiddle contest, <u>a big event in these parts,</u> has been cancelled.
4. <u>His bike with a flat tire,</u> Bill decided to walk instead.
5. For some people, <u>going with the flow</u> isn't all that easy.
6. <u>To call Doug fantastic</u> is an understatement.

PHRASES

A phrase is a group of related words without a subject and a verb. Phrases can be categorized as prepositional, participial, gerund, infinitive, appositive, or absolute.

Prepositional: Consisting of a preposition, modifiers, and a noun, the prepositional phrase functions most often as an adjective or adverb.

Barney chased a rabbit <u>under the porch.</u>

The top executives met <u>in the conference room for about two hours.</u>

Participial: Consisting of a participle, modifiers, and a noun, the participial phrase functions as an adjective.

<u>Running after the rabbit,</u> Barney disappeared under the porch.

<u>While meeting in the conference room,</u> the executives voted to study the issue further.

Gerund: Consisting of a gerund, modifiers, and a noun, the gerund phrase functions as a noun.

<u>Running after a rabbit</u> is hard work for a small dog.

<u>Meeting in the conference room</u> is convenient for everyone except Mary.

Infinitive: Consisting of an infinitive, modifiers, and a noun, the infinitive phrase functions as a noun, adjective, or adverb.

<u>To run after a rabbit all day</u> is good exercise.

The most convenient place <u>to meet the new employee</u> is the conference room.

Appositive: An appositive (which may also be a single noun) describes or restates a noun.

Barney, <u>a short-haired terrier,</u> chased a wild rabbit under the porch.

Mary, <u>the only executive with an office across the street,</u> didn't mind meeting in the conference room.

Absolute: Consisting of a noun, modifiers, and often a participle, the absolute phrase modifies an entire clause.

<u>The rabbit hiding under the porch,</u> Barney barked frantically at the stairs.

Mary arrived at the meeting late, <u>her office being across town.</u>

CLAUSES

A clause is a group of words with a subject and a verb (or predicate). The two types of clauses are *independent* (or main) and *dependent* (or subordinate).

Independent: An independent (main) clause contains a subject and a verb not preceded by a subordinating conjunction.

Joe passed his math test.

Independent clause: subject *(Joe)* + verb *(passed)*

Gutenberg College is a great books college. (David Crabtree)

Independent clause: subject *(Gutenberg College)* + verb *(is)*

Dependent: A dependent (subordinate) clause contains a subject and a verb and is preceded by a subordinating conjunction or a relative pronoun. Dependent clauses can function as nouns, adjectives, or adverbs.

Because Joe passed his math test, he ordered a pizza with all the toppings.

Dependent clause: subordinating conjunction *(because)* + subject *(Joe)* + verb *(passed)*
Independent clause: subject *(he)* + verb *(ordered)*

As soon as he had the paper, he thumbed through it, looking for jobs he could feasibly apply to.

Dependent clause: subordinating conjunction *(As soon as)* + subject *(he)* + verb *(had)*
Independent clause: subject *(he)* + verb *(thumbed)*

Anyone who owns a computer and tries to keep up with the develpments in hardware, software, and the accompaying incompatiblities is all too aware of the speed of change. (David Crabtree)

The relative clause *who owns a computer and tries to keep up with the developments in hardware, software, and the accompanying incompatibilities* modifies the noun *anyone*. A relative clause modifies the noun that comes before it. Other relative pronouns include *that* and *which*. Relative pronouns are either followed by a subject and a verb or just a verb. In this example, the relative pronoun *who* is followed by a compound verb, *owns* and *tries*.

Activity

Identify the underlined clauses as either dependent or independent. Which, if any, is a relative clause?

1. Jane was going to the acupuncturist <u>when she heard the news.</u>
2. After his first semester, <u>Tim decided to get organized.</u>
3. We missed our turn <u>even though the road sign was large and in plain view.</u>
4. When he got back from the seminar, <u>Gary was, somehow, full of misinformation.</u>
5. The house <u>that has been empty for two years</u> is now for sale.

Examples of Relative Clauses

the lion that roared at Dorothy . . .

the band that the club owner hired . . .

the woman who won the marathon . . .

SENTENCES—CLASSIFIED BY STRUCTURE

Simple: A simple sentence contains one independent clause.

Bobby played the banjo on the back step.

Independent clause: subject *(Bobby)* + verb *(played)*

My daughter doesn't ask for $72 pants from the Gap or $58 shirts from Abercrombie & Fitch.

Independent clause: subject *(daughter)* + verb *(doesn't ask)*

Compound: A compound sentence contains two independent clauses.

Bobby played the banjo on the back step, and he made a musical dent in the night.

Independent clause: subject *(Bobby)* + verb *(played)*
Independent clause: subject *(he)* + verb *(made)*
Because *and* is a coordinating **(not a subordinating)** conjunction, the second clause is independent **(not dependent).**

For women, as for girls, intimacy is the fabric of relationships, and talk is the thread from which it is woven. (Deborah Tannen)

Independent clause: subject *(intimacy)* + verb *(is)*
Independent clause: subject *(talk)* + verb *(is)*
The coordinating conjunction that connects the two clauses is *and*.

Complex: A complex sentence contains one independent and one dependent clause.

> When Bobby played the banjo on the back step, he made a musical dent in the night.
>
> Dependent clause: subordinating conjunction *(when)* + subject *(Bobby)* + verb *(played)*
> Independent clause: subject *(he)* + verb *(made)*

> If you want the reader to believe that college football is bad for the players, you have to do more than say so. (Paul Roberts)
>
> Dependent clause: subordinating conjunction *(If)* + subject *(you)* + verb *(want)*
> Independent clause: subject *(you)* + verb *(have)*

Compound-complex: A compound-complex sentence contains at least two independent clauses and at least one dependent clause.

> When Bobby played the banjo on the back step, he made a musical dent in the night, and the neighbors complained.
>
> Dependent clause: subordinating conjunction *(when)* + subject *(Bobby)* + verb *(played)*
> Independent clause: subject *(he)* + verb *(made)*
> Independent clause: subject *(neighbors)* + verb *(complained)*

> Now this is a way to go about reaching five hundred words, and if you are content with a "D" grade, it is as good a way as any. (Paul Roberts)
>
> Independent clause: subject *(this)* + verb *(is)*
> Dependent clause: subordinating conjunction *(if)* + subject *(you)* + verb *(are)*
> Independent clause: subject *(it)* + verb *(is)*

HOW PARTS OF SPEECH FUNCTION IN A SENTENCE

Remember, words may function in different ways in a sentence. For example, *fish* can be a noun or a verb. *(Fish are fun to watch. I fish with cousin Dan at Carpenter Lake.)* Parts of speech may also function in different ways in a sentence. For example, a noun—such as *fish*—may be the subject of a sentence or the object of a sentence. *(Fish are fun to watch. I saw a fish.)*

Activity

Identify the parts of speech, particularly subjects and verbs, in the following sentences.

1. As health care professionals, we must regard this crisis with the utmost importance.

2. I like the story because it is put together so well.

3. As a concerned citizen and patient, I have become very alarmed at the growing addiction to prescription drugs in the United States.

4. At the same time, each fearless and self-sacrificing helper shows each victim a human face, stands for respect for that person's dignity, and is a source of hope for peace and reconciliation.

5. The President will address the nation tonight, upon his return to the White House.

1. **Subject**—The subject of a sentence is a noun (or noun phrase, noun clause, or pronoun). It normally precedes the verb (predicate), and it names who or what the sentence is about.

2. **Verb (Predicate)**—The predicate of a sentence (a verb and the words that complete its meaning) usually follows the subject and expresses what the subject does, what it is, or what has been done to it.

3. **Objects**—Objects are nouns (or noun phrases, noun clauses, or pronouns), usually follow the verb, and can be direct objects or indirect objects.

4. **Complements**—Complements are nouns (or noun phrases, noun clauses, or pronouns) but can also be adjectives (or adjective phrases). They usually follow a subject, verb, and any objects, and can be subject complements, object complements, predicate nouns, or predicate adjectives.

5. **Adverbials**—Adverbials are adverbs (or adverb phrases or adverb clauses) that refer to the verb.

SENTENCES—CLASSIFIED BY PURPOSE

Declarative: A sentence that makes a statement and ends with a period.

> Up in the trees the other chimpanzees of the group were moving about, getting ready for the new day. (Jane Goodall)

> We ourselves may never see this cottonwood reach maturity, probably will never take pleasure in its shade or birds or witness the pale gold of its autumn leaves. (Edward Abbey)

Imperative: A sentence that expresses a command.

> Avoid the Obvious Content. (Paul Roberts)

> Know that it causes real pain and real suffering to real people. (Ward Churchill)

Interrogative: A sentence that asks a question.

> And what is it that Sea World doesn't want its customers to think about? (Jayme Stayer)

> Does he feel like something is missing from his life, but he's not sure what it is? And worst of all, does he blame me for what is missing? (David Hawes)

Exclamatory: A sentence that expresses an emphatic statement and ends with an exclamation mark.

> She was no good! Why did she win? What were those judges thinking! (Cindy Bosley)

> If there was a crack house in your neighborhood, what would you do? You would try to get rid of it! (Michael Moore)

Activity

Identify each of the following sentences as either declarative, imperative, interrogative, or exclamatory:

1. Imagine all the possibilities.

2. The best solutions are often dismissed without serious consideration.

3. Why do we accept these bad ideas?

4. It's time for a change!

NINE WAYS OF COMBINING SIMPLE SENTENCES (INDEPENDENT CLAUSES)

1. **Subject + verb. Subject + verb. (two simple sentences)**

   Mary was relaxing in the meadow. Mary saw a dragonfly.

   Larry had never flown a plane before. He landed the 747 safely.

   A nickel isn't worth much anymore. George gave Susie a dime.

2. **Subject + verb; subject + verb. (one compound sentence)**

   Mary was relaxing in the meadow; Mary saw a dragonfly.

   Larry had never flown a plane before; he landed the 747 safely.

   A nickel isn't worth much anymore; George gave Susie a dime.

3. **Subject + verb, coordinating conjunction + subject + verb. (one compound sentence)**

   Mary was relaxing in the meadow, and she saw a dragonfly.

   Larry had never flown a plane before, yet he landed the 747 safely.

   A nickel isn't worth much anymore, so George gave Susie a dime.

4. **Subject + verb; conjunctive adverb, subject + verb. (one compound sentence)**

   Mary was relaxing in the meadow; therefore, she saw a dragonfly.

   Larry had never flown a plane before; nevertheless, he landed the 747 safely.

   A nickel isn't worth much anymore; hence, George gave Susie a dime.

5. **Subject + verb + subordinating conjunction + subject + verb. (one complex sentence)**

   Mary was relaxing in the meadow when she saw a dragonfly.

   Larry had never flown a plane before until he landed the 747 safely.

   A nickel isn't worth much anymore though George gave Susie a dime.

Combining sentences sometimes helps the reader see the relationship between ideas. For example, "I went. She stayed." can mean "I went because she stayed" or "I went although she stayed." Combining the sentences with a subordinating conjunction clarifies the relationship. The strategies on this page can be helpful for combining sentences, and for eliminating fused sentences and comma splices. For example, the comma splice "I went, she stayed." can be rewritten using strategies 1, 2, 3, 4, 5, or 6.

6. **Subordinating conjunction subject + verb, subject + verb. (one complex sentence)**

   Because Mary was relaxing in the meadow, she saw a dragonfly.

   Although Larry had never flown a plane before, he landed the 747 safely.

   Now that a nickel isn't worth much anymore, George gave Susie a dime.

7. **Subject + relative clause (relative pronoun + verb) + verb. (one complex sentence)**

   Mary, who was relaxing in the meadow, saw a dragonfly.

   Larry, who had never flown a plane before, landed the 747 safely.

   A nickel isn't worth much anymore. George gave Susie a dime.
   [A relative clause will not work.]

8. **Subject + verb + verb. (one simple sentence)**

   Mary was relaxing in the meadow and saw a dragonfly.

   Larry had never flown a plane before and landed the 747 safely.

   A nickel isn't worth much anymore. George gave Susie a dime.
   [A compound verb will not work.]

9. **Phrase, subject + verb. (one simple sentence)**

   Relaxing in the meadow, Mary saw a dragonfly.

   Never having flown a plane before, Larry landed the 747 safely.

   A nickel not being worth much anymore, George gave Susie a dime.

Activity

Combine the following simple sentences in each of the nine ways:

Samantha and Steve went to the Kentucky Derby. They'd never been to a horse race before.

CREDITS

This page constitutes an extension of the copyright page. We have made every effort to trace the ownership of all copyrighted materials to secure permission from the copyright holders. In the event of any question arising as to the use of any material, we will be pleased to make the necessary corrections in future printings. Thanks are due to the following authors, publishers, and agents for permission to use the material indicated.

Text Credits

Chapter 2: 30: From Steve Mockensturm. **33:** How I Lost the Junior Miss Pageant by Cindy Bosley. Reprinted with permission of author. **37:** The Thrill of Victory, The Agony of Parents by Jennifer Schwind-Pawlak. Reprinted with permission of author.

Chapter 3: 68: Source: Americans and the Land" from, AMERICA AND AMERICANS by John Steinbeck, copyright © 1996 by John Steinbeck, renewed © 1984 by Elaine Steinbeck and Thom Steinbeck. Used by permission of Viking Penguin, division of Penguin Group (USA) Inc. 72: Mugged by James Crockett. Reprinted with permission of author. **74:** Political Adaptation by Daniel P. Doezema. Reprinted with permission of the author.

Chapter 4: 102: "Living Like Weasels" from TEACHING A STONE TO TALK: EXPEDITIONS AND ENCOUNTERS by Annie Dillard. Copyright © 1982 by Annie Dillard. Reprinted by permission of HarperCollins Publishers. **109:** Corpse Colloguy by Justin Scott. Reprinted with permission of author.

Chapter 5: 137: From Nathan Shedroff, http://www.cybergeography.org/altas/conceptual. html. **138:** From S.I. Hayakawa, "What It Means to Be Creative," pp. 104–105 in THROUGH THE COMMUNICATION BARRIER: ON SPEAKING, LISTENING AND UNDERSTANDING, edited by Arthur Chandler. Copyright © 1979 New York: Harper & Row. Reprinted with permission. **143:** From Petra Pepellashi.

Chapter 6: 172: From Elizabeth Thoman, Rise of the Image Culture: Re-Imagining the American Dream, Media & Values, #57. Copyright © 1992 by Center for Media Literacy. Reprinted with permission by the Center for Media Literacy/www.medialit.org.

Chapter 7: 212: From David Crabtree, Why Great Books Education Is the Most Practical!, March 1996. Copyright © 1996 McKenzie Study Center, Gutenberg College, Eugene, Or. Reprinted by permission of David W. Crabtree, President, Gutenberg College. **216:** Cruelty, Civility, and Other Weighty Matters by Ann Marie Pau-

lin. Reprinted with permission of author. **222:** Elizabeth Bohnhorst, "Floppy Disk Fallacies." Reprinted by permission. **226:** From Jayme Stayer.

Chapter 8: 262: From What Orwell Didn't Know: Propaganda and the New American Politics, by Andras Szanto. Copyright © 2007. Reprinted with permission of Public Affairs, a member of Perseus Books, Group. **271:** Reality Check by Alison Hester. Reprinted with permission of author.

Chapter 9: 300: Copyright © 2005 Stephen Poole. Reproduced by permission of the author c/o Rogers, Coleridge & White Ltd., 20 Powis Mews, London W11 1JN. **308:** Star Trek by Jaren Provo. Reprinted with permission of author.

Chapter 10: 336: Sex, Lies and Conversation: Why Is It So Hard for Men and Women to Talk to Each Other?" by Deborah Tannen, The Washington Post, June 24, 1990, copyright Deborah Tannen, Reprinted by permission. This article is adapted in part from the author's book You Just Don't Understand (Quill, 1990) **340:** From Leonard Kress. Reprinted with permission of the author. **345:** From Jamie Bentley.

Chapter 11: 374: "How to Say Nothing in Five Hundred Words" from UNDERSTANDING ENGLISH by Paul Roberts. Copyright © 1958 by Paul Roberts. Reprinted by permission of Pearson Education, Inc. **380:** Deirdre Mahoney. **384:** Reverence for Food by Rachel Schofield. Reprinted with permission of author.

Chapter 12: 410: From DOWNSIZE THIS by Michael Moore, copyright 1996 by Michael Moore. Used by permission of Crown Publishers, a division of Random House, Inc. **419:** From Simon Wykoff.

Chapter 13: 498: Ben Wetherbee, "Branded." Reprinted by permission. **518:** Amanda Stremlow, "Vultures." Reprinted by permission.

Chapter 14: 530: From Leonard Kress. **532:** Samantha Tengelitsch, "The Greatest Gift." Reprinted by permission. **534:** From The New York Times, December 14, copyright © 2004. The New York Times. All rights reserved. **535:** From Cindy Bosley. **537:** From David Hawes. **539:** From Dean A. Meek. **541:** "Planting a Tree," from DOWN THE RIVER by Edward Abbey, Copyright © 1982 by Edward Abbey. Used by permission of Dutton, a division of Penguin Putnam, Inc. **542:** "Gombe," from THROUGH A WINDOW by Jane Goodall. Copyright © 1990 by Soko Publications, Ltd. Reprinted by Permission of Houghton Mifflin Harcourt Publishing Company. All rights reserved.

Photo and Illustration Credits

Chapter 1: 2: "Réunion des Musées Nationaux/Art Resource, Inc./ © 2008 Estate of Pablo Picasso/Artists Rights Society (ARS), New York"; **9:** Colin Dixon/Arcaid/CORBIS; **11:** Used by permission of the authors; **13:** Jeff Venuga/CORBIS

Chapter 2: 26: Stuart Whitmore/MorgueFile; **31:** Used by permission of the authors; **41:** Julie Elliot/StockXchng; **45:** *background:* Anita Patterson/MorgueFile; *insets top to bottom:* Kenn Kiser/MorgueFile; McRastrillo/MorgueFile; Malinda Welte/MorgueFile

Chapter 3: 64: Valeria Obregon/StockXchng; **73:** Used by permission of the authors; **81:** *background:* Norbert Machinke/StockXchng; *insets clockwise from left:* Hal Wilson/StockXchng; Dawn M. Turner/MorgueFile; Cengage Learning; Jonas Jordan, USACE/U.S. Army

Chapter 4: 98: Used by permission of the authors; **110:** Used by permission of the authors; **115:** Wanda aka Beata Laki/StockXchng

Chapter 5: 134: Nathan Shedroff, Experience Strategist, nathan.com; **145:** Used by permission of the authors; **151:** *background:* Phestus/MorgueFile; *insets clockwise from top:* Caio Cassoli/StockXchng; Library of Congress; Laura Kennedy/StockXchng; Cengage Learning

Chapter 6: 168: Bill Watterson/Universal Press Syndicate; **171:** Used by permission of the authors; **176:** Daimler-Chrysler Maybach; **181:** Autism Speaks; **186:** *top:* The Advertising Archives; *bottom:* The Advertising Archives; **187:** *clockwise from top right:* Used with permission; © 2005 Chin Music Press. Used with permission; Ron English/Popaganda; Bill Aron/PhotoEdit; U.S. Army; The Everett Collection; **189:** Dawn M. Turner/MorgueFile; **190:** *clockwise from top right:* Library of Congress; StockXchng; MorgueFile; Quentin Houyoux/StockXchng; Nate Powell/StockXchng; Nick Cowie/StockXchng; **192:** *bottom:* Holy Cross Family Ministries; *top:* National Fluid Milk Processor Promotion Board; **193:** Häagen Daz. Used by permission; **194:** *clockwise from top right:* Jeff Greenberg/PhotoEdit; Zane Williams/Getty Images; Beiot Tessier/Maxppp/Landov Media; Lydie/EPA/Landov Media

Chapter 7: 208: Big Pictures Media Corporation/The Kobal Collection/Picture Desk; **235:** *background:* NASA; *insets from top left:* George Zimzores/MorgueFile; Napster logo and marks reprinted with the permission of Napster, LLC.; Francie Manning/Index Stock Imagery/PhotoLibrary; **242:** Cengage Learning

Chapter 8: 258: Keith Syvinski/StockXchng; **270:** Cengage Learning; **277:** *background, top:* brookeb/StockXchng; *background, bottom:* Kevin Connors/MorgueFile; *insets clockwise from right:* Kenn Kiser/MorgueFile; StockXchng; Petra Giner/StockXchng

Chapter 9: 296: Wilfried Heider/StockXchng; **300:** Dwayne J. Perry; **301:** Courtesy of Steven Poole; **307:** CBS/Landov Media; **315:** Used by permission of the authors

Chapter 10: 332: Tim Dalek/MorgueFile; **349:** Used by permission of the authors; **353:** *background:* Milca Mulders/StockXchng; *insets from top to bottom:* Christopher Scott/MorgueFile; Adam Ciesielski/StockXchng; Image After; Tatiana Tsokolova/MorgueFile; **369:** *all four images:* Used by permission of the authors

Chapter 11: 370: Xian Studio, LLC/MorgueFile; **382:** Used by permission of the authors; **391:** *background:* Rich Stern/StockXchng; *foreground:* Ronnie Bergeron/MorgueFile; **405:** Used by permission of the authors

Chapter 12: 406: Michelin Tweel™ lets the air out of tire performance. Copyright © 2005 Michelin North America, Inc.; **418:** Used by permission of the authors; **421:** Used by permission of the authors; **425:** Carlos Paes/MorgueFile; **441:** *background:* Ray Sterner/John Hopkins University; *insets clockwise from top left:* Cengage Learning; Cengage Learning; Carl Dwyer/StockXchng; Lynsey Addario/CORBIS; Cengage Learning; Lars Sundström/StockXchng

Chapter 13: 458: Northwestern Michigan College, Mark and Helen Osterlin Library; **460:** Northwestern Michigan College, Mark and Helen Osterlin Library

Chapter 14: 528: The nthdegree. Used with permission; **545:** Bettman/CORBIS; **549:** Chuck Pefley/Alamy Limited; **555:** Adam Clark/StockXchng; **567:** Robert Crumb/The Everett Collection; **575:** Library of Congress; **599:** MIP/Getty Images; **630:** Bettmann/CORBIS; **631:** Used by permission of the authors; **651:** Used by permission of the authors

INDEX

biology, 67
computers, 67
deeper layer, 82
delivery, 97
interior design, 67
metaphor, 89
organizational strategies, 90–91
peer review, 96
point of contact, 80
public resonance, 85
readings, 78
revision, 87
rhetorical tools, 88–89
sentence length, 92
significance, 85
simile, 89
thesis, 86–87
vitality, 94–95
writer's voice, 92–93
Expletives, 367, 667
Explicit thesis, 51, 90, 120

F

Facts, 243, 433
False analogy, 249
"The Farm on the Hill" (Proudfoot),
    550–551
"Farming and the Global Economy"
    (Berry), 641–644
Faulty cause/effect, 248, 249, 397
Fear
    commitment, 359
    ongoing invention, 359
Federal Communications Commission,
    173
Field notes, 448–449
Figurative language, 432–433
    peer review, 96, 130
    rhetorical tools, 89
    writer's voice, 56, 162
First person, 200, 290–291. *See also* "I"
    Making Arguments, 254
    shift, 677
Five-paragraph essay, 657

"The Flag Code," 631
Flat statements, 20
Fliers, 10
"Floppy Disk Fallacies" (Bohnhorst),
    222–224
Flores, Royce ("Onward, Gamers,
    Onward!"), 548–549
Focus
    Analyzing Images, 188
    blurry, 321
    nouns, 87
    paragraphs, 294, 330
    thesis, 320, 358
    title, 669
Formality, 684
    documentation, 447
    essays, 127
    memos, 126
    reports, 126
    Thinking Radically, 437
    writer's voice, 126–127
Formulaic style, 663
Framing, 91, 204, 262–263
    Analyzing Images, 188
Freedom, 6–7
    concept of, 155
"Friend or Foe?" (Meek), 539–540
"The Front Porch" (McCovey), 105–107
Fused sentences, 674

G

Gabriel, Peter ("Digging in the Dirt"), 43
Gandhi, Mahatma, 409
    quotation, 175
Gender bias, 684
Gerunds, 695, 710
God, Analyzing Concepts of, 136
"Gombe" (Goodall), 542–548
Good, 707
Goodall, Jane, 98
    "Gombe," 542–548
"Goodbye, Cruel Word: A Personal
    History of Electronic Writing"
    (Poole), 300–302

Gore, Al *(An Inconvenient Truth)*, 264
"Got Milk?", 192
Government, 390
    documents, 461
Government Printing Office (GPO), 461
GPO. *See* Government Printing Office
Grammar, 694–717
    breaking rules, 438–439
Grammatical errors
    peer review, 166
    quotation, 478
"The Greatest Gift" (Tengelitsch),
    532–533
Grounds, 28, 280
Group inclusion, 401
"Group Minds" (Lessing), 644–645

H

Hacker, Andrew, 336
Harsh description, 253
    logical fallacies, 326
    peer review, 330
Hasty generalization, 249
"'Have It Your Way': Consumerism
    Invades Education" (Benlow),
    140–141
    public resonance, 155
Hawes, David ("Dog-Tied"), 537–538
Hayakawa, S. I. ("What It Means to Be
    Creative"), 138–139
Headings, 682
    organizational strategies, 200
Hester, Allison ("Reality Check"), 271–
    272
"Hip-Hop: A Roadblock or Pathway to
    Black Empowerment?" (Bennett),
    610–611
Hollingsworth, Rebecca ("An Imperfect
    Reality"), 181–182
"The Holy Land" (Reszka), 551–553
Home, 234
    Analyzing Concepts, 150
Horton, Susan R. (quotation), 136
"How I Lost the Junior Miss Pageant"
    (Bosley), 33–35, 47–48